KEY TREATIES
for the
GREAT POWERS
1814-1914

Volume 1   1814-1870

KEY TREATIES
for the
GREAT POWERS
1814-1914

Volume 1   1814-1870

(pages 1-458)

Selected and Edited by

MICHAEL HURST MA, FRSA, FR Hist S
Fellow in Modern History & Politics
St John's College, Oxford

DAVID & CHARLES : NEWTON ABBOT

ISBN 0 7153 5444 2

Set in Imprint & Times by C. E. Dawkins (Typesetters) Limited,
London SE1
and printed in Great Britain by
Redwood Press Limited, Trowbridge, Wiltshire
for David & Charles (Publishers) Limited
South Devon House Newton Abbot Devon

To

Roger Howell, Jnr

CONTENTS
VOLUME 1

VOLUME 2

xvi

INTRODUCTION

THIS collection is aimed at providing the student of international relations during the period 1814-1914 with the data he or she requires for finding out the precise terms of agreements vital to the course of events. The title has been carefully worded, for the items included were crucial for one or more of the Great Powers, whether they had signed it or not. All the texts included here have been published elsewhere in some form or other, but never together in a comparatively compact volume. From now on anyone eager to supplement ordinary secondary source reading in this field with material facilitating the development of an independent judgement can have a good ammunition magazine right at his elbow. Atlases avoid the trouble of having to chase hither and thither for single maps; now boring donkey work can be avoided with these treaties.

Older history books often reproduced generous extracts from documents, and treaties sometimes cropped up as part of this process. Today less raw material finds its way into print—even maps are not always given a sufficiently prominent role. Checking an author's own words has become more difficult. A mistake can become endlessly perpetuated. Indeed it was a misleading statement to be found in a highly esteemed piece of work relating to parts of this period which prompted the launching of this project: in his *European Alliances and Alignments*, 1871-1890 W. L. Langer states (pp. 127, 129 and 161) that Roumania ceded Bessarabia to Russia under the terms of the Treaty of Berlin of 1878, but there is nothing in the book, not even a map, to suggest that only a small portion of the province was transferred. By way of contrast A. J. P. Taylor covered the matter splendidly in *The Struggle for Mastery in Europe*, 1848-1918. Yet many read only Langer and others read both; ignorance or confusion or extra work are, therefore, likely to result. By using this treaty collection such ignorance can be ended, such confusion confounded and such extra work minimised. No scholar, teacher or student worthy of the name could pooh-pooh points like the Bessarabian cession; not only was the difference between the whole and part of Bessarabia vital to an understanding of the distribution of power at the Berlin Congress between the different participants, it makes a considerable difference to how one views the situations immediately preceding and succeeding that gathering. A number of instances like this can add up to quite a strong distortion in the history of a century.

Many attempts to provide primary sources just consist of excerpts drawn from a variety of backgrounds put together and entitled 'Readings' in this or that. Admittedly the practice is better than nothing, but picking and choosing of that degree is not calculated to do much more than whet the appetite of the enterprising reader. Here one has a selection, indeed, yet one giving a clear picture of development for the major spheres of international activity from the decline and fall of Napoleon I to the eve of World War I. The Congress of Vienna was the basis of power politics for the next decades. Subsequent agreements recorded consolidations, modifications and destructions of its work. One sees some sectors close down peacefully as they pass beyond dispute, others persisting as putrid trouble spots, yet others springing up as new complicators of life for the Chancelleries and General Staffs. Many have decried the use of treaties, for as instruments of diplomacy they are far from perfect. Nevertheless, for the historian they are of immense use as records of the actual state of play, as indicators of the real distribution of power at the time of signature. Taking each Great Power in turn, one can learn greatly by tracing through its role in the agreements of importance made during this most uneasy century of strike and counter-strike. From the texts leaps forth the sheer extent of the changes. So too does the interlocking of superficially dispersed problems. The global view is nurtured in the reader; once nurtured it can be indulged by recourse to products like Westermann's *Atlas zur Weltgeschichte* and the *New Cambridge Modern History Atlas*. Documents, globes and maps can illumine the secondary work. Used alongside it, they require little supplementary data. Hence no potted versions of the state of affairs at the signing of these treaties have been placed at the beginning of each document; all are complete and must be used in conjunction with something like, A. J. P. Taylor's *The Struggle for Mastery in Europe*, 1848-1918, R. Albrecht-Carrie's *A Diplomatic History of Europe Since the Congress of Vienna*, the various works of W. L. Langer and my forth-coming *Europe's Power Frontiers*, 1815-1939. Some may think insufficient attention has been given to Africa and to Latin America, but between 1814 and 1914 small pieces of Europe almost invariably enjoyed a vastly greater overall significance than whole tracts of these continents. There was, moreover, great vagueness and ignorance about such areas as the Congo and Niger basins even at the end of the nineteenth century and a British-backed Monroe Doctrine shielded the bulk of the western hemisphere from numerous or sustained incursions by other European Powers for most of the period. Thereafter, once the USA had itself become a Great Power the process was continued to even greater effect. No abortive schemes have been included. All the arrangements were duly ratified. Seen in the context created for the student of history by good secondary works, they speak for themselves. The index has obviated the need for cross-reference notes.

MICHAEL HURST,

Brunswick, Maine.   December 1970

1 TREATY OF PARIS

DEFINITIVE TREATY of Peace between Great Britain, &c. (Austria, Portugal, Prussia, Russia, Spain, Sweden), and France. Signed at Paris, 30th May, 1814. Ratification exchanged at London, 17th June, 1814.

In the Name of the Most Holy and Undivided Trinity.

His Majesty, the King of the United Kingdom of Great Britain and Ireland, and his Allies on the one part, and His Majesty the King of France and Navarre on the other part, animated by an equal desire to terminate the long agitations of Europe, and the sufferings of Mankind, by a permanent Peace, founded upon a just repartition of force between its States, and containing in its Stipulations the pledge of its durability; and His Britannic Majesty, together with his Allies, being unwilling to require of France, now that, replaced under the paternal Government of Her Kings, she offers the assurance of security and stability to Europe, the conditions and guarantees which they had with regret demanded from her former Government, Their said Majesties have named Plenipotentiaries to discuss, settle, and sign a Treaty of Peace and Amity; namely,

His Majesty the King of the United Kingdom of Great Britain and Ireland, the Right Honourable Robert Stewart, Viscount Castlereagh, one of His said Majesty's Most Honourable Privy Council, Member of Parliament, Colonel of the Londonderry Regiment of Militia, and his Principal Secretary of State for Foreign Affairs, &c., &c., &c.; the Right Honourable George Gordon, Earl of Aberdeen, Viscount Formartine, Lord Haddo, Methlic, Tarvis, and Kellie, &c., one of the Sixteen Peers representing the Peerage of Scotland in the House of Lords, Knight of His Majesty's Most Ancient and Most Noble Order of the Thistle, his Ambassador Extraordinary and Plenipotentiary to His Imperial and Royal Apostolic Majesty; the Right Honourable William Shaw Cathcart, Viscount Cathcart, Baron Cathcart and Greenock, one of His Majesty's Most Honourable Privy Council, Knight of his Order of the Thistle, and of the Orders of Russia, General in His Majesty's Army, and his Ambassador Extraordinary and Plenipotentiary to His Majesty the Emperor of all the Russias; and the Honourable Sir Charles William Stewart, Knight of His Majesty's Most Honourable Order of the Bath, Member of Parliament, Lieutenant-General in His Majesty's Army, Knight of the Prussian Orders of the Black and Red Eagle, and of several others, and his Envoy Extraordinary and Minister Plenipotentiary to His Majesty the King of Prussia;

And His Majesty the King of France and Navarre, Charles Maurice de Talleyrand Perigord, Prince of Benevent, Great Eagle of the Legion of Honour, Knight of the Black and Red Eagle of Prussia, Grand Cross of the Order of Leopold of Austria, Knight of the Russian Order of St. Andrew, and His said Majesty's Minister and Secretary of State for Foreign Affairs;

Who having exchanged their Full Powers, found in good and due form, have agreed upon the following Articles:

Peace and Friendship.

ART. I. There shall be from this day forward perpetual Peace and Friendship between His Britannic Majesty and his Allies on the one part, and His Majesty the King of France and Navarre on the other, their Heirs and Successors, their Dominions and Subjects, respectively.

The High Contracting Parties shall devote their best attention to maintain, not only between themselves, but, inasmuch as depends upon them, between all the States of Europe, that harmony and good understanding which are so necessary for their tranquillity.

Limits of France, as in 1792.

ART. II. The Kingdom of France retains its limits entire, as they existed on the 1st of January, 1792. It shall further receive the increase of Territory comprised within the line established by the following Article:

Increase of French Territory on side of Belgium, Germany, and Italy.

ART. III. On the side of Belgium, Germany, and Italy, the Ancient Frontiers shall be re-established as they existed the 1st of January, 1792, extending from the North Sea, between Dunkirk and Nieuport, to the Mediterranean between Cagnes and Nice, with the following modifications:

1. In the Department of Jemappes, the Cantons of Dour, Merbes-le-Chateau, Beaumont, and Chimay, shall belong to France; where the line of demarcation comes in contact with the Canton of Dour, it shall pass between that Canton and those of Boussu and Paturage, and likewise further on it shall pass between the Canton of Merbes-le-Chateau and those of Binch and Thuin.

2. In the Department of Sambre and Meuse, the Cantons of Walcourt, Florennes, Beauraing, and Gedinne, shall belong to France; where the demarcation reaches that Department it shall follow the line which separates the said Cantons from the Department of Jemappes, and from the remaining Cantons of the Department of Sambre and Meuse.

3. In the Department of the Moselle, the new demarcation, at the

point where it diverges from the old line of Frontier, shall be formed by a line to be drawn from Perle to Fremersdorff, and by the limit which separates the Canton of Tholey from the remaining Cantons of the said Department of the Moselle.

4. In the Department of La Sarre, the Cantons of Saarbruck and Arneval shall continue to belong to France, as likewise the portion of the Canton of Lebach which is situated to the south of a line drawn along the confines of the Villages of Herchenbach, Ueberhofen, Hilsbach, and Hall (leaving these different places out of the French Frontier), to the point where, in the neighbourhood of Querselle (which place belongs to France), the line which separates the Cantons of Arneval and Ottweiler reaches that which separates the Cantons of Arneval and Lebach. The Frontier on this side shall be formed by the line above described, and afterwards by that which separates the Canton of Arneval from that of Bliescastel.

Fortress of Landau to be retained by France.

5. The Fortress of Landau having, before the year 1792, formed an insulated point in Germany, France retains beyond her Frontiers a portion of the Departments of Mount Tonnerre and of the Lower Rhine, for the purpose of uniting the said Fortress and its radius to the rest of the Kingdom. The new demarcation from the point in the neighbourhood of Obersteinbach (which place is left out of the limits of France) where the Boundary between the Department of the Moselle and that of Mount Tonnerre reaches the Department of the Lower Rhine, shall follow the line which separates the Cantons of Wissenbourg and Bergzabern (on the side of France) from the Cantons of Permasens, Dahn, and Answeiler (on the side of Germany), as far as the point near the Village of Vollmersheim, where that line touches the ancient radius of the Fortress of Landau. From this radius, which remains as it was in 1792, the new Frontier shall follow the arm of the River de la Queich, which on leaving the said radius of Queichheim (that place remaining to France) flows near the Villages of Merlenheim, Knittelsheim, and Belheim (these places also belonging to France) to the Rhine, which from thence shall continue to form the boundary of France and Germany.

This Fortress was restored to Germany by Art. I of the Definitive Treaty of 20th November, 1815. By Art. II of the Treaty between Austria and Bavaria of 16th April, 1816, Landau was given to Bavaria. By Art. II of the Treaty between the 4 Allied Powers of 20th July, 1819, Bavaria was confirmed in the possession of Landau; and by Art. III of the same Treaty, the Fortress of Landau was declared to be one of the Fortresses of the Germanic Confederation. On the 6th July, 1869, a Protocol was signed between North Germany, Bavaria, &c., respecting the Joint Property of the Movable Materiel of War in the Federal Fortresses of Landau, &c.

Frontier of the Rhine.

The main stream (*Thalweg*) of the Rhine shall constitute the Frontier; provided, however, that the changes which may hereafter take place in the course of that river shall not affect the property of the Islands. The right of possession in these Islands shall be re-established as it existed at the signature of the Treaty of Luneville.

6. In the Department of the Doubs, the Frontier shall be so regulated as to commence above the Rançonnière near Locle, and follow the Crest of the Jura between the Cerneux-Pequignot and the Village of Fontenelles, as far as the peak of that mountain, situated about 7,000 or 8,000 feet to the north-west of the Village of La Brevine, where it shall again fall in with the ancient Boundary of France.

Geneva.

7. In the Department of the Leman, the Frontiers between the French Territory, the Pays de Vaud, and the different portions of the Territory of the Republic of Geneva (which is to form part of Switzerland) remain as they were before the incorporation of Geneva with France. But the Cantons of Frangy and of St. Julien (with the exception of the districts situated to the north of a line drawn from the point where the River of La Laire enters the Territory of Geneva near Chancy, following the confines of Sesequin, Laconex, and Seseneuve, which shall remain out of the limits of France), the Canton of Reignier (with the exception of the portion to the east of a line which follows the confines of the Muraz, Bussy, Pers, and Cornier, which shall be out of the French limits), and the Canton of La Roche (with the exception of the places called La Roche and Armanoy, with their districts) shall remain to France. The Frontier shall follow the limits of these different Cantons, and the line which separates the Districts continuing to belong to France, from those which she does not retain.

8. In the Department of Mont-Blanc, France acquires the Sub-Prefecture of Chambery (with the exception of the Cantons of L'Hôpital, St. Pierre d'Albigny, La Rocette, and Montmelian), and the Sub-Prefecture of Annecy (with the exception of the portion of the Canton of Faverges, situated to the east of a line passing between Ourechaise and Marlens on the side of France, and Marthod and Ugine on the opposite side, and which afterwards follows the crest of the mountains as far as the Frontier of the Canton of Thones); this line, together with the limit of the Cantons before mentioned, shall on this side form the new Frontier.

On the side of the Pyrenees, the Frontiers between the two Kingdoms of France and Spain remain such as they were on the 1st of January, 1792, and a Joint Commission shall be named on the part of the two Crowns for the purpose of finally determining the line.

Monaco.

France on her part renounces all rights of Sovereignty, *Suzeraineté*, and of possession, over all the Countries, Districts, Towns, and places situated beyond the Frontier above described, the Principality of Monaco being replaced on the same footing on which it stood before the 1st of January, 1792.

Avignon. Comitat Venaissin. Comté de Montbéliard.

The Allied Powers assure to France the possession of the Principality of Avignon, of the Comitat Venaissin, of the Comté of Montbéliard, together with the several insulated Territories which formerly belonged to Germany, comprehended within the Frontier above described, whether they have been incorporated with France before or after the 1st of January, 1792.

Fortifications. Private Property on the Frontiers.

The Powers reserve to themselves, reciprocally, the complete right to fortify any point in their respective States which they may judge necessary for their security.

To prevent all injury to Private Property, and protect, according to the most liberal principles, the property of Individuals domiciliated on the Frontiers, there shall be named, by each of the States bordering on France, Commissioners who shall proceed, conjointly with French Commissioners, to the delineation of the respective Boundaries.

Boundary Commissions. Maps.

As soon as the Commissioners shall have performed their task, Maps shall be drawn, signed by the respective Commissioners, and posts shall be placed to point out the reciprocal Boundaries.

Communications with Geneva. Versoy Road.

ART. IV. To secure the communications of the Town of Geneva with other parts of the Swiss Territory situate on the Lake, France consents that the Road by Versoy shall be common to the two Countries. The respective Governments shall amicably arrange the means for preventing smuggling, regulating the posts, and maintaining the said Road.

Navigation of the Rhine; and of other Rivers.

ART. V. The Navigation of the Rhine, from the point where it becomes navigable unto the sea, and *vice versâ*, shall be free, so that it can be interdicted to no one:—and at the future Congress attention shall be paid to the establishment of the principles according to which the duties to be raised by the States bordering on the Rhine may be regulated, in the mode the most impartial and the most favourable to the commerce of all Nations.

The future Congress, with a view to facilitate the communication between Nations, and continually to render them less strangers to each other, shall likewise examine and determine in what manner the above provisions can be extended to other Rivers which, in their navigable course, separate or traverse different States.

Territory and Sovereignty of Holland.

ART. VI. Holland, placed under the Sovereignty of the House of Orange, shall receive an increase of Territory. The title and exercise of that Sovereignty shall not in any case belong to a Prince wearing, or destined to wear, a Foreign Crown.

Federation of Germany.

The States of Germany shall be independent, and united by a Federative Bond.

Independence of Switzerland.

Switzerland, Independent, shall continue to govern herself.

Sovereign States of Italy.

Italy, beyond the limits of the countries which are to revert to Austria, shall be composed of Sovereign States.

Sovereignty of Malta.

ART. VII. The Island of Malta and its Dependencies shall belong in full right and Sovereignty to His Britannic Majesty.

Restoration by Great Britain of French Colonies, Fisheries, Factories, and Establishments. Cession of Tobago, St. Lucia, Isle of France (Mauritius) Rodrigues and Les Séchelles to Great Britain; and of part of St. Domingo to Spain.

ART. VIII. His Britannic Majesty, stipulating for himself and his Allies, engages to restore to His Most Christian Majesty, within the term which shall be hereafter fixed, the Colonies, Fisheries, Factories, and Establishments of every kind which were possessed by France on the 1st of January, 1792, in the Seas and on the Continents of America,

Africa, and Asia; with the exception, however, of the Islands of Tobago and St. Lucia, and of the Isle of France and its Dependencies, especially Rodrigues and Les Séchelles, which several Colonies and Possessions His Most Christian Majesty cedes in full right and Sovereignty to His Britannic Majesty, and also the portion of St. Domingo ceded to France by the Treaty of Basle, and which His Most Christian Majesty restores in full right and Sovereignty to His Catholic Majesty.

Restoration by Sweden of Guadaloupe to France.

Art. IX. His Majesty the King of Sweden and Norway, in virtue of the arrangements stipulated with the Allies, and in execution of the preceding Article, consents that the Island of Guadaloupe be restored to His Most Christian Majesty, and gives up all the rights he may have acquired over that Island.

Restoration by Portugal of French Guiana to France.

Art. X. Her Most Faithful Majesty, in virtue of the arrangements stipulated with her Allies, and in execution of the VIIIth Article, engages to restore French Guiana as it existed on the 1st of January, 1792, to His Most Christian Majesty, within the term hereafter fixed.

Mediation of Great Britain; Boundaries of French Guiana.

The renewal of the dispute which existed at that period on the subject of the Frontier, being the effect of this Stipulation, it is agreed that the dispute shall be terminated by a friendly arrangement between the two Courts, under the Mediation of His Britannic Majesty.

Fortresses, &c., in Colonies restored to France.

Art. XI. The Places and Forts in those Colonies and Settlements, which, by virtue of the VIIIth, IXth, and Xth Articles, are to be restored to His Most Christian Majesty, shall be given up in the state in which they may be at the moment of the signature of the present Treaty.

Commerce, &c., of France in British India.

Art. XII. His Britannic Majesty guarantees to the subjects of His Most Christian Majesty the same facilities, privileges, and protection, with respect to Commerce, and the security of their Persons and Property within the limits of the British Sovereignty on the Continent of India, as are now, or shall be granted to the most favoured Nations.

French Fortifications and Garrisons in India.

His Most Christian Majesty, on his part, having nothing more at heart than the perpetual duration of Peace between the two Crowns of England

and of France, and wishing to do his utmost to avoid anything which might affect their mutual good understanding, engages not to erect any Fortifications in the establishments which are to be restored to him within the limits of the British Sovereignty upon the Continent of India, and only to place in those establishments the number of Troops necessary for the maintenance of the Police.

French right of Fishery at Newfoundland and Gulf of St. Lawrence.

ART. XIII. The French right of Fishery upon the Great Bank of Newfoundland, upon the Coasts of the Island of that name, and of the adjacent Islands in the Gulf of St. Lawrence, shall be replaced upon the footing on which it stood in 1792.

Periods of Restoration of French Colonies, &c.

ART. XIV. Those Colonies, Factories, and Establishments, which are to be restored to His Most Christian Majesty by His Britannic Majesty or his Allies in the Northern Seas, or in the Seas on the Continents of America and Africa, shall be given up within the three months, and those which are beyond the Cape of Good Hope within the six months which follow the Ratification of the present Treaty.

Division of Ships of War, Arsenals, &c., between France and the Allies.

ART. XV. The High Contracting Parties having, by the IVth Article of the Convention of the 23rd of April last, reserved to themselves the right of disposing, in the present Definitive Treaty of Peace, of the Arsenals and Ships of War, armed and unarmed, which may be found in the Maritime Places restored by the IInd Article of the said Convention, it is agreed, that the said Vessels and Ships of War, armed and unarmed, together with the Naval Ordnance and Naval Stores, and all materials for building and equipment, shall be divided between France and the Countries where the said Places are situated, in the proportion of two-thirds for France, and one-third for the Power to whom the said Places shall belong. The Ships and Vessels on the stocks, which shall not be launched within six weeks after the signature of the present Treaty shall be considered as materials, and after being broken up shall be, as such, divided in the same proportions.

Return of Workmen, Seamen, &c., to France

Commissioners shall be named on both sides, to settle the division, and draw up a statement of the same, and Passports or Safe Conducts shall be granted by the Allied Powers for the purpose of securing the return into France of the Workmen, Seamen, and others in the employment of France.

Dutch Fleet in the Texel excepted.

The Vessels and Arsenals existing in the Maritime Places which were already in the power of the Allies before the 23rd April, and the Vessels and Arsenals which belonged to Holland, and especially the Fleet in the Texel, are not comprised in the above Stipulations.

The French Government engages to withdraw, or to cause to be sold, everything which shall belong to it by the above Stipulations, within the space of three months after the division shall have been carried into effect.

Port of Antwerp.

Antwerp shall for the future be solely a Commercial Port.

Persons and Property in Countries restored, and Debts of Private Individuals.

ART. XVI. The High Contracting Parties desirous to bury in entire oblivion the dissensions which have agitated Europe, declare and promise that no Individual, of whatever rank or condition he may be, in the Countries restored and ceded by the present Treaty, shall be prosecuted, disturbed, or molested, in his Person or Property, under any pretext whatsoever, either on account of his conduct or political opinions, his attachment either to any of the Contracting Parties, or to any Government which has ceased to exist, or for any other reason, except for Debts contracted towards individuals, or acts posterior to the date of the present Treaty.

Right of Emigration.

ART. XVII. The native Inhabitants and Aliens of whatever Nation and condition they may be, in those Countries which are to change Sovereigns, as well in virtue of the present Treaty as of the subsequent arrangements to which it may give rise, shall be allowed a period of six years, reckoning from the exchange of the Ratifications, for the purpose of disposing of their property, if they think fit, whether it be acquired before or during the present War, and retiring to whatever Country they may choose.

Renunciation of Government Claims for Contracts, &c.

ART. XVIII. The Allied Powers desiring to offer His Most Christian Majesty a new proof of their anxiety to arrest, as far as in them lies, the bad consequences of the disastrous epoch fortunately terminated by the present Peace, renounce all the sums which their Governments claim from France, whether on account of Contracts, Supplies, or any other advances whatsoever to the French Government, during the different Wars which have taken place since 1792.

His Most Christian Majesty, on his part, renounces every claim which he might bring forward against the Allied Powers on the same grounds. In execution of this Article, the High Contracting Parties engage reciprocally to deliver up all titles, obligations, and documents, which relate to the Debts they may have mutually cancelled.

Liquidation of Private Claims by France.

ART. XIX. The French Government engages to liquidate and pay all Debts it may be found to owe in Countries beyond its own Territory, on account of Contracts, or other formal engagements between Individuals, or Private Establishments, and the French Authorities, as well for Supplies, as in satisfaction of legal engagements.

Commissioners of Claims.

ART. XX. The High Contracting Parties, immediately after the exchange of the Ratifications of the present Treaty, shall name Commissioners to direct and superintend the execution of the whole of the Stipulations contained in the XVIIIth and XIXth Articles. These Commissioners shall undertake the examination of the Claims referred to in the preceding Article, the liquidation of the Sums claimed, and the consideration of the manner in which the French Government may propose to pay them. They shall also be charged with the delivery of the Titles, Bonds, and the Documents relating to the Debts which the High Contracting Parties mutually cancel, so that the approval of the result of their labours shall complete that reciprocal renunciation.

Debts in Countries no longer belonging to France.

ART. XXI. The Debts which in their origin were specially mortgaged upon the Countries no longer belonging to France, or were contracted for the support of their internal administration, shall remain at the charge of the said Countries. Such of those Debts as have been converted into Inscriptions in the Great Book of the Public Debt of France, shall accordingly be accounted for with the French Government after the 22nd of December, 1813.

The Deeds of all those Debts which have been prepared for inscription, and have not yet been entered, shall be delivered to the Governments of the respective Countries. The statement of all these Debts shall be drawn up and settled by a Joint Commission.

Pensions, &c., of Persons no longer French Subjects.

ART. XXII. The French Government shall remain charged with the reimbursement of all sums paid by the subjects of the said Countries into the French Coffers, whether under the denomination of Surety, Deposit, or Consignment.

In like manner all French Subjects, employed in the service of the said Countries, who have paid sums under the denomination of Surety, Deposit, or Consignment, into their respective Territories, shall be faithfully reimbursed.

Securities.

ART. XXIII. The Functionaries holding situations requiring Securities, who are not charged with the expenditure of public money, shall be reimbursed at Paris, with the interest by fifths and by the year, dating from the signature of the present Treaty.

With respect to those who are accountable, this reimbursement shall commence, at the latest, six months after the presentation of their Accounts, except only in cases of malversation. A Copy of the last Account shall be transmitted to the Government of their Countries, to serve for their information and guidance.

Caisse d'Amortissement.

ART. XXIV. The Judicial Deposits and Consignments upon the "Caisse d'Amortissement," in the execution of the Law of 28 Nivose, year 13 (18th January, 1805), and which belong to the Inhabitants of the Countries France ceases to possess, shall, within the space of one year from the exchange of the Ratifications of the present Treaty, be placed in the hands of the Authorities of the said Countries, with the exception of those Deposits and Consignments interesting French subjects, which last will remain in the " Caisse d'Amortissement," and will only be given up on the production of the vouchers resulting from the decisions of competent Authorities.

Caisse de Service, Caisse d'Amortissement, &c.

ART. XXV. The Funds deposited by the Corporations and Public Establishments in the " Caisse de Service " and in the " Caisse d'Amortissement," or other " Caisses," of the French Government, shall be reimbursed by fifths, payable from year to year, to commence from the date of the present Treaty; deducting the advances which have taken place, and subject to such regular charges as may have been brought forward against these Funds by the Creditors of the said Corporations and the said Public Establishments.

Termination of Pensions

ART. XXVI. From the first day of January, 1814, the French Government shall cease to be charged with the payment of Pensions,

Civil, Military, and Ecclesiastical, pensions for retirement, and allowances for reduction, to any Individual who shall cease to be a French Subject.

Guarantee of Purchasers of National Domains.

ART. XXVII. National Domains acquired for valuable considerations by French Subjects in the late Departments of Belgium, and of the left bank of the Rhine and the Alps, beyond the ancient limits of France, and which now cease to belong to her, shall be guaranteed to the purchasers.

Abolition of Droits d'Aubaine, de Détraction, &c., in Countries lately Incorporated with France.

ART. XXVIII. The abolition of the " Droits d'Aubaine," " de Détraction," and other duties of the same nature, in the Countries which have been formerly incorporated, or which have reciprocally made that stipulation with France, shall be expressly maintained.

Restitution by France of Foreign Bonds and Deeds.

ART. XXIX. The French Government engages to restore all Bonds, and other Deeds which may have been seized in the Provinces occupied by the French Armies or Administrations; and in cases where such restitution cannot be effected, these Bonds and Deeds become and continue void.

Sums Due for Public Works in Departments detached from France.

ART. XXX. The Sums which shall be due for all Works of public utility not yet finished, or finished after the 31st of December, 1812, whether on the Rhine or in the Departments detached from France by the present Treaty, shall be placed to the account of the future Possessors of the Territory, and shall be paid by the Commission charged with the liquidation of the Debts of that Country.

Archives, Maps, &c., of ceded Countries.

ART. XXXI. All Archives, Maps, Plans, and Documents whatever, belonging to the ceded Countries, or respecting their Administration, shall be faithfully given up at the same time with the said Countries; or if that should be impossible, within a period not exceeding six months after the cession of the Countries themselves.

This stipulation applies to the Archives, Maps, and Plates, which may have been carried away from the Countries during their temporary occupation by the different Armies.

Plenipotentiaries to meet in General Congress at Vienna.

ART. XXXII. All the Powers engaged on either side in the present War, shall, within the space of two months, send Plenipotentiaries to Vienna, for the purpose of regulating, in General Congress, the Arrangements which are to complete the provisions of the present Treaty.

Ratifications.

ART. XXXIII. The present Treaty shall be ratified, and the Ratifications shall be exchanged within the period of 15 days, or sooner if possible.

In witness whereof, the respective Plenipotentiaries have signed and affixed to it the Seals of their Arms.

Done at Paris, the 30th of May, in the year of Our Lord, 1814.

(L.S.)	CASTLEREAGH,	⎫
(L.S.)	ABERDEEN,	⎪ for Great
(L.S.)	CATHCART,	⎬ Britain.
(L.S.)	CHARLES STEWART, Lieut.-General,	⎭
(L.S.)	LE PRINCE DE BENEVENT,	for France.

(L.S.)	LE PRINCE DE METTERNICH,	⎫ for Austria.
(L.S.)	LE COMTE DE STADION,	⎭
(L.S.)	COMTE DE FUNCHAL,	for Portugal.
(L.S.)	BARON DE HARDENBURG,	⎫ for Prussia.
(L.S.)	BARON DE HUMBOLDT,	⎭
(L.S.)	COMTE DE RASOUMOFFSKI,	⎫ for Russia.
(L.S.)	COMTE DE NESSELRODE,	⎭
(L.S.)	M. DOMINGOS,	⎫
(L.S.)	ANTONIO DE SOUZA CON-TINHO,	⎬ for Spain.
(L.S.)	COMTE C. DE STEDINGK,	⎫ for Sweden.
(L.S.)	BR. G. DE WETTERSTEDT,	⎭

ADDITIONAL, SEPARATE, AND SECRET ARTICLES TO THE TREATY OF 30TH MAY, 1814.

SEPARATE AND SECRET ARTICLES. *Great Britain (Austria, Prussia, and Russia), and France. Paris, 30th May, 1814.*

Separate and Secret Articles. Great Britain, Austria, Prussia, Russia, and France.

Balance of Power in Europe.

ART. I. The disposal of the Territories given up by His Most Christian Majesty, under the IIIrd Article of the Public Treaty, and the relations from whence a system of real and permanent Balance of Power in Europe is to be derived, shall be regulated at the Congress upon the principles determined upon by the Allied Powers among themselves, and according to the general provisions contained in the following Articles.

Austrian and Sardinian Territories in Italy.

ART. II. The Possessions of His Imperial and Royal Apostolic Majesty in Italy, shall be bounded by the Po, the Tessino, and the Lago Maggiore. The King of Sardinia shall return to the possession of his ancient Dominions, with the exception of that part of Savoy secured to France by the IIIrd Article of the present Treaty. His Majesty shall receive an increase of Territory from the State of Genoa.

Port of Genoa.

The Port of Genoa shall continue to be a Free Port; the Powers reserving to themselves the right of making arrangements upon this point with the King of Sardinia.

Guarantee of Switzerland.

France shall acknowledge and guarantee, conjointly with the Allied Powers, and on the same footing, the political organization which Switzerland shall adopt under the auspices of the said Allied Powers, and according to the basis already agreed upon with them.

Territory of Holland. Dutch Frontiers.

ART. III. The establishment of a just Balance of Power in Europe requiring that Holland should be so constituted as to be enabled to support her Independence through her own resources, the Countries comprised between the Sea, the Frontiers of France, such as they are defined by the present Treaty, and the Meuse, shall be given up for ever to Holland.

The Frontiers upon the right bank of the Meuse shall be regulated according to the military convenience of Holland, and her neighbours.

Navigation of the Scheldt.

The freedom of the Navigation of the Scheldt shall be established upon the same principle which has regulated the Navigation of the Rhine, in the Vth Article of the present Treaty.

Territory of Prussia, Holland, &c.

ART. IV. The German Territories upon the left bank of the Rhine, which have been united to France since 1792, shall contribute to the aggrandizement of Holland, and shall be further applied to compensate Prussia, and other German States.

Renunciation by France of Claims for Endowments, Donations, Revenues of the Legion of Honour, &c.

ART. V. The Renunciation of the French Government contained in the XVIIIth Article extends especially to all Claims which might be brought forward against the Allied Powers, under the head of Endowments and Donations, Revenues of the Legion of Honour, Senatorships, Pensions, and other charges of the like kind.

Bank of Hamburgh.

ART. VI. The French Government having offered by the Secret Article of the Convention of the 23rd April [1814], to make search after, and to make every effort to recover the Funds of the Bank of Hamburgh, engages to set on foot the most severe scrutiny to discover the said Funds, and to pursue those who may be found to have detained them.

The present Separate and Secret Articles shall have the same force and validity as if they were inserted, word for word, in the Treaty Patent of this day.

They shall be ratified, and the Ratifications shall be exchanged at the same time.

In witness whereof, the respective Plenipotentiaries have signed and affixed to them the Seals of their Arms.

Done at Paris, the 30th day of May, in the year of Our Lord 1814.

        (L.S.)   CASTLEREAGH.
        (L.S.)   ABERDEEN.
        (L.S.)   CATHCART.
        (L.S.)   CHARLES STEWART, Lieut.-General.
(L.S.) LE PRINCE DE BENEVENT.

ADDITIONAL ARTICLES. *Great Britain and France. Paris, 30th May, 1814. Ratification exchanged at London, 17th June, 1814.*

Additional Articles. Great Britain and France.

Abolition of French Slave Trade. Colonial Slave Trade.

ART. I. His Most Christian Majesty, concurring without reserve in the sentiments of His Britannic Majesty, with respect to a description of Traffic repugnant to the principles of natural justice and of the enlightened age in which we live, engages to unite all his efforts to those of His Britannic Majesty, at the approaching Congress, to induce all the Powers of Christendom to decree the abolition of the Slave Trade, so that the said Trade shall cease universally, as it shall cease definitively, under any circumstances, on the part of the French Government, in the course of five years; and that, during the said period, no Slave Merchant shall import or sell Slaves, except in the Colonies of the State of which he is a subject.

Expenses of Prisoners of War.

Art. II. The British and French Governments shall name, without delay, Commissioners to liquidate the accounts of their respective expenses for the maintenance of Prisoners of War, in order to determine the manner of paying the balance which shall appear in favour of the one or the other of the two Powers.

Art. III. The respective Prisoners of War, before their departure from the place of their detention, shall be obliged to discharge the Private Debts they may have contracted, or shall at least give sufficient security for the amount.

Removal of Sequestrations.

Art. IV. Immediately after the Ratification of the present Treaty of Peace, the Sequesters, which since the year 1792 may have been laid on the Funds, Revenues, Debts, or any other effects of the High Contracting Parties or their Subjects shall be taken off.

Claims of British Subjects.

The Commissioners mentioned in the IInd Article shall undertake the examination of the Claims of His Britannic Majesty's Subjects upon the French Government, for the value of the Property, moveable or immoveable, illegally Confiscated by the French Authorities, as also for the total or partial loss of their Debts or other Property, illegally detained under Sequester since the year 1792.

France engages to act towards British Subjects in this respect, in the same spirit of justice which the French Subjects have experienced in Great Britain; and His Britannic Majesty, desiring to concur in the new pledge which the Allied Powers have given to His Christian Majesty, of their desire to obliterate every trace of that disastrous epoch so happily terminated by the present Peace, engages on his part, when complete justice shall be rendered to his Subjects, to renounce the whole amount of the balance which shall appear in his favour for support of the Prisoners of War, so that the Ratification of the Report of the above Commissioners and the discharge of the sums due to British Subjects,

as well as the restitution of the effects which shall be proved to belong
to them, shall complete the renunciation.

Commercial Relations.

ART. V. The two High Contracting Parties, desiring to establish the
most friendly relations between their respective Subjects, reserve to
themselves, and promise to come to a mutual understanding and
arrangement, as soon as possible, upon their Commercial interests, with
the view of encouraging and increasing the prosperity of their respective
States.

The present Additional Articles shall have the same force and
validity as if they were inserted word for word in the Treaty Patent of
this day. They shall be ratified, and the Ratifications shall be exchanged
at the same time.

In witness whereof, the respective Plenipotentiaries have signed and
affixed to them the Seals of their Arms.

Done at Paris, the 30th day of May, in the year of Our Lord, 1814.

      (L.S.)   CASTLEREAGH.
      (L.S.)   ABERDEEN.
      (L.S.)   CATHCART.
      (L.S.)   CHARLES STEWART, Lieut.-General.
(L.S.)   LE PRINCE DE BENEVENT.

ADDITIONAL ARTICLE. *Austria and France. Paris, 30th May, 1814.*

Annulment of effect of Treaties of 1805 and 1809, and of Decrees against French Subjects in the service of Austria.

THE High Contracting Parties, being desirous to obliterate every
trace of the unhappy events which have weighed upon their Countries,
have agreed explicity to annul the effects of the Treaties of 1805 and 1809,
in so much as they are not already annulled, in fact, by the present Treaty.
In consequence of this determination, His Most Christian Majesty
promises that the Decrees issued against French Subjects, or reputed
French, being, or having been, in the service of His Imperial and Royal
Apostolic Majesty, shall remain without effect, as well as the judgments
which may have been given in execution of those Decrees.

The present Additional Article shall have the same force and validity
as if it were inserted word for word in the Treaty Patent of this day.
It shall be ratified, and the Ratifications shall be exchanged at the same
time.

In witness whereof the respective Plenipotentiaries have signed the
same, and affixed to it the Seal of their Arms.

Done at Paris, the 30th of May, in the year of our Lord, 1814.
>   (L.S.)   LE PRINCE DE METTERNICH.
>   (L.S.)   LE COMTE DE STADION.
(L.S.)   LE PRINCE DE BENEVENT.

ADDITIONAL AND SECRET ARTICLES. *Austria and France.*

Payment of Lorraine Rente.

ART I. From the date of the signature of the present Treaty, the payment of the revenue (*rente*) called Lorraine, shall continue the same as up to 1791.

Delivery of all Acts relating to German Empire, Belgium, &c.

ART. II. The Court of France engages to deliver to the Commissioners, who shall be appointed for that purpose by the Court of Vienna, all the Acts bearing upon the Ancient Empire of Germany, Belgium, and other provinces which have formed part of the Austrian Monarchy, and which have been taken from the Archives of Vienna.

The present Additional and Secret Articles shall have the same force and validity as if they were inserted word for word in the Treaty of this day. They shall be ratified, and the Ratifications thereof shall be exchanged at the same time.

In witness whereof, the respective Plenipotentiaries have signed and affixed to them the Seals of their Arms.
>   (L.S.) LE PRINCE DE BENEVENT.
>   (L.S.) LE PRINCE DE METTERNICH.
>   (L.S.) LE COMTE DE STADION.

ADDITIONAL SECRET ARTICLES.   *France and Portugal.*
Paris, 30th May, 1814.

Restoration of French Guiana.

ART. I. His Royal Highness the Prince Regent of Portugal and of the Algarves, engages and binds himself that those clauses of the Capitulation of French Guiana which shall not have been executed, shall receive at the time of the restitution of that Colony to France, their full and entire fulfilment.

Claims.

ART. II. With reference to the claims which the subjects of one of the Contracting Parties may make on the other, there shall be perfect reciprocity, so that, for every kind of Claim, what has been done by one of the two Governments shall be the rule of the other.

Annulment of Treaties of Badajoz and Madrid of 1801, and of Convention of Lisbon of 1804.

ART. III. Although the Treaties, Conventions, and Acts concluded between the two Contracting Powers before the war, are annulled by the fact of the war, the High Contracting Parties have nevertheless considered it advisable again expressly to declare that the said Treaties, Conventions, and Acts, namely, the Treaties signed at Badajoz and at Madrid in 1801, and the Convention signed at Lisbon in 1804, are null and void so far as they concern France and Portugal, and that they mutually give up all right, and discharge themselves from every obligation which might arise out of them.

The present Additional Articles shall have the same force and validity as if they were word for word inserted in the Treaty Patent of this day. They shall be ratified, and the Ratifications shall be exchanged at the same time.

In witness whereof the respective Plenipotentiaries have signed the same, and have affixed thereto the Seal of their Arms.

Done at Paris, the 30th May, 1814.

   (L.S.) LE PRINCE DE BENEVENT.
   (L.S.) LE COMTE DE FUNCHAL.

ADDITIONAL ARTICLE. *France and Prussia. Paris, 30th May, 1814.*

Annulment of Treaties since 1795, and of Decrees against French Subjects in the service of Prussia.

ALTHOUGH the Treaty of Peace concluded at Bâle, the 5th April, 1795, that of Tilsit of the 9th July, 1807, the Convention of Paris of 20th September, 1808, as well as all the Conventions and Acts whatsoever concluded since the Peace of Bâle between Prussia and France, are already annulled in fact by the present Treaty, the High Contracting Parties have nevertheless considered it advisable again expressly to declare that the said Treaties cease to be binding in all their Articles, as well patent as secret, and that they mutually give up all right, and disengage themselves from every obligation which might arise out of them.

His Most Christian Majesty promises that the Decrees issued against French Subjects, or reputed French, being or having been in the service of his Prussian Majesty, shall remain without effect, as well as the judgments which may have been given in execution of those Decrees.

The present Additional Article shall have the same force and validity as if it were inserted word for word in the Treaty Patent of this day. It shall be ratified, and the Ratifications shall be exchanged at the same time.

In witness whereof the respective Plenipotentiaries have signed the same, and affixed to it the Seal of their Arms.

Done at Paris, the 30th of May, in the year of Our Lord, 1814.

(L.S.)   CHARLES AUGUSTE BARON DE HARDENBERG.
(L.S.)   CHARLES GUILLAUME BARON DE HUMBOLDT.
(L.S.)   LE PRINCE DE BENEVENT.

ADDITIONAL ARTICLE.   *France and Russia.   Paris, 30th May,* 1814.

Pecuniary Claims in the Duchy of Warsaw.

THE Duchy of Warsaw being under the administration of a Provisional Council, established by Russia, ever since that Country has been occupied by her arms, the two High Contracting Parties have agreed immediately to appoint a Special Commission, composed, on both sides, of an equal number of Commissioners, which shall be charged with the examination, liquidation, and all arrangements relative to their reciprocal pretentions.

The present Additional Article shall have the same force and validity as if it were inserted word for word in the Treaty Patent of this day. It shall be ratified, and the Ratifications shall be exchanged at the same time.

In witness whereof the respective Plenipotentiaries have signed the same, and affixed to it the Seal of their Arms.

Done at Paris, the 30th of May, in the year of Our Lord, 1814.

(L.S.)   ANDRE COMTE DE RASOUMOFFSKY.
(L.S.)   CHARLES ROBERT COMTE DE NESSELRODE.
(L.S.)   LE PRINCE DE BENEVENT.

ADDITIONAL AND SECRET ARTICLE.   *France and Sweden.* *Paris, 30th May,* 1814.

Union of Norway to Sweden.

HIS Most Christian Majesty recognises the Union of the Kingdom of Norway to the Kingdom of Sweden by virtue of its cession to His

Swedish Majesty by the Treaty of Kiel.

The present Additional Article shall have the same force and validity as if it were inserted word for word in the Treaty Patent of this day. It shall be ratified, and the Ratifications shall be exchanged at the same time.

In witness whereof the respective Plenipotentiaries have signed the same and have affixed to it the Seal of their Arms.

Done at Paris, the 30th May, in the year of Our Lord, 1814.

  (L.S.) LE PRINCE DE BENEVENT.
  (L.S.) C. STEDINGK.
  (L.S.) G. BARON DE WETTARSTEDT.

The Additional Article for the abrogation of the Treaties from 1805 to 1809, as well as the Separate and Secret Articles, are the same as those on pages oo.

Extracts from Treaty between Great Britain and Denmark.
Signed at Kiel, 14th January, 1814.

ART. III. His Majesty the King of the United Kingdom of Great Britain and Ireland consents to restore to His Danish Majesty all the Possessions and Colonies which have been conquered by the British Arms in this present War, except the Island of Heligoland, which His Britannic Majesty reserves to himself with full and unlimited Sovereignty.

ART. X. Whereas His Danish Majesty, in virtue of the Treaty of Peace this day concluded with His Majesty the King of Sweden, has ceded the Kingdom of Norway to His said Majesty for a certain indemnity provided by Sweden, His Britannic Majesty, who has thus seen his engagements contracted with Sweden in this respect fulfilled, promises, in concert with the King of Sweden, to employ his good offices with the Allied Powers, at the General Peace, to obtain for Denmark a proper indemnity for the cession of Norway.

2 TREATY OF GHENT

TREATY OF PEACE and Amity between Great Britain and the United States of America. Signed at Ghent, 24th December, 1814.

Preamble.

His Britannic Majesty and the United States of America, desirous of terminating the War which has unhappily subsisted between the two Countries, and of restoring, upon principles of perfect reciprocity,

Peace, Friendship, and good understanding between them, have for that purpose appointed their respective Plenipotentiaries, that is to say: His Britannic Majesty, on His part, has appointed The Right Honourable James Lord Gambier, late Admiral of the White, now Admiral of the Red Squadron of His Majesty's Fleet; Henry Goulburn, Esq., a Member of the Imperial Parliament, and Under Secretary of State; and William Adams, Esq., Doctor of Civil Laws:

And the President of the United States, by and with the advice and consent of the Senate thereof, has appointed John Quincey Adams, James A. Bayard, Henry Clay, Jonathan Russell, and Albert Gallatin, Citizens of the United States, who, after a reciprocal communication of their respective Full Powers, have agreed upon the following Articles:—

Peace and Amity. Restoration of Peace, Friendship, and good understanding upon principles of perfect reciprocity between Territories and Peoples respectively. Cessation of Hostilities after Ratification of Treaty. Restoration of Territory, Places, and Possessions captured during the War (excepting Islands near Boundary Line). Non-destruction nor removal of Artillery or other Public Property in Forts or Places, nor Slaves or other Private Property. Restoration of Archives, Records, &c.

ART. I. There shall be a firm and universal Peace between His Britannic Majesty and the United States, and between their respective countries, territories, cities, towns and people, of every degree, without exception of places or persons. All hostilities both by sea and land shall cease, as soon as this Treaty shall have been ratified by both Parties, as hereinafter mentioned. All territory, places, and possessions whatsoever, taken by either party from the other during the War, or which may be taken after the signing of this Treaty, excepting only the Islands hereinafter mentioned, shall be restored without delay, and without causing any destruction, or carrying away any of the artillery, or other Public Property, originally captured in the said Forts or Places, and which shall remain therein upon the exchange of the Ratifications of this Treaty, or any Slaves or other Private Property. And all Archives, Records, Deeds, and Papers, either of a public nature, or belonging to private persons, which, in the course of the War, may have fallen into the hands of the officers of either party, shall be, as far as may be practicable, forthwith restored, and delivered to the proper authorities and Persons to whom they respectively belong.

Temporary retention of Islands of the Bay of Passamaquoddy.
Such of the Islands in the Bay of Passamaquoddy as are claimed by

both parties, shall remain in the possession of the party in whose occupation they may be at the time of the exchange of the Ratifications of this Treaty, until the decision respecting the title to the said Islands shall have been made, in conformity with Article IV of this Treaty.

No disposition made by this Treaty, as to such possession of the Islands and Territories claimed by both parties, shall in any manner whatever be construed to affect the right of either.

Prizes taken after Ratification of Treaty. Periods for Cessation of Hostilities in different Latitudes at Sea.

ART. II. Immediately after the Ratifications of this Treaty by both parties, as herein after-mentioned, orders shall be sent to the armies, squadrons, officers, subjects and citizens of the two powers, to cease from all hostilities. And to prevent all causes of complaint, which might arise on account of the Prizes which may be taken at Sea after the said Ratifications of this Treaty, it is reciprocally agreed, that all Vessels and effects which may be taken after the space of 12 days from the said Ratifications upon all parts of the Coast of North America, from the latitude of 23 deg. North, to the latitude of 50 deg. North, and as far Eastward in the Atlantic Ocean as the 36th deg. of West longitude from the meridian of Greenwich, shall be restored on each side; that the time shall be 30 days in all other parts of the Atlantic Ocean North of the equinoctial line or Equator, and the same time for the British and Irish Channels, for the Gulf of Mexico, and all parts of the West Indies; 40 days for the North Seas, for the Baltic, and for all parts of the Mediterranean; 60 days for the Atlantic Ocean South of the Equator, as far as the latitude of the Cape of Good Hope; 90 days for every other part of the world south of the Equator; and 120 days for all other parts of the world without exception.

Restoration of Prisoners of War on their payment of their Debts. Repayment of Advances for Subsistence of Prisoners.

ART. III. All prisoners of war taken on either side, as well by land as by sea, shall be restored as soon as practicable after the Ratifications of this Treaty, as hereinafter mentioned, on their paying the Debts which they may have contracted during their captivity. The two Contracting Parties respectively engage to discharge in specie the advances which may have been made by the other for the sustenance and maintenance of such prisoners.

Boundary: Islands in the Bay of Passamaquoddy (part of Bay of Fundy) and Island of Grand Menan. Appointment of Commissioners to decide Claims thereto. Oath, and Place of Meeting. Decision by Declaration or Report, final and conclusive.

ART. IV. Whereas it was stipulated, by the IInd Article in the Treaty of Peace of 1783, between His Britannic Majesty and The United States of America, that the Boundary of the United States should comprehend " All Islands within twenty leagues of any part of the shores of the United States, and lying between lines to be drawn due East from the points where the aforesaid boundaries, between Nova Scotia on the one part, and East Florida on the other, shall respectively touch the Bay of Fundy and the Atlantic Ocean, excepting such Islands as now are, or heretofore have been, within the limits of Nova Scotia:" And whereas the several Islands in the Bay of Passamaquoddy, which is part of the Bay of Fundy, and the Island of Grand Menan, in the said Bay of Fundy, are claimed by the United States as being comprehended within their aforesaid Boundaries, which said Islands are claimed as belonging to His Britannic Majesty, as having been, at the time of and previous to the aforesaid Treaty of 1783, within the limits of the Province of Nova Scotia; in order, therefore, finally to decide upon these Claims, it is agreed that they shall be referred to two Commissioners, to be appointed in the following manner, viz.:—One Commissioner shall be appointed by His Britannic Majesty, and one by the President of the United States, by and with the advice and consent of the Senate thereof; and the said two Commissioners so appointed, shall be sworn impartially to examine and decide upon the said Claims, according to such evidence as shall be laid before them on the part of His Britannic Majesty and of the United States respectively. The said Commissioners shall meet at St. Andrew's, in the Province of New Brunswick, and shall have power to adjourn to such other place or places as they shall think fit. The said Commissioners shall, by a Declaration or Report, under their hands and seals, decide to which of the two Contracting Parties the several Islands aforesaid do respectively belong, in conformity, with the true intent of the said Treaty of Peace of 1783; and if the said Commissioners shall agree in their Decision, both Parties shall consider such Decision as final and conclusive.

Arbitration in case of Difference.

It is further agreed, that in the event of the two Commissioners differing upon all or any of the matters so referred to them, or in the event of both or either of the said Commissioners refusing or declining, or wilfully omitting to act as such, they shall make, jointly or separately, Report or Reports, as well to the Government of His Britannic Majesty as to that of the United States, stating in detail the points on which they differ, and the grounds upon which their respective opinions have been formed, or the grounds upon which they, or either of them, have so refused, declined, or omitted to act. And His Britannic Majesty and the

Government of the United States, hereby agree, to refer the Report or Reports of the said Commissioners to some Friendly Sovereign or State, to be then named for that purpose, and who shall be requested to decide on the differences which may be stated in the said Report or Reports, or upon the Report of one Commissioner, together with the grounds upon which the other Commissioner shall have refused, declined, or omitted to act, as the case may be. And if the Commissioner so refusing, declining, or omitting to act, shall also wilfully omit to state the grounds upon which he has so done, in such manner that the said statement may be referred to such friendly Sovereign or State, together with the Report of such other Commissioner, then such Sovereign or State shall decide, ex parte, upon the said Report alone, and His Britannic Majesty and the Government of the United States engaged to consider the Decision of such friendly Sovereign or State, to be final and conclusive on all the matters so referred.

Boundary: Determination of Point of Highlands North of River St. Croix, or North-West Angle of Nova Scotia, and North-Westernmost Head of Connecticut River. Survey of Line from River St. Croix to Nova Scotia along Highlands to Connecticut River, down River to 45th Degree, and Line West to River Iroquois, or Cataraguy (St. Lawrence).
ART. V. Whereas neither that point of the Highlands lying due North from the source of the River St. Croix, designated in the former Treaty of Peace between the two Powers, as the north-west angle of Nova Scotia, nor the north-westernmost head of Connecticut River have yet been ascertained; and whereas that part of the Boundary line between the dominions of the two Powers, which extends from the source of the River St. Croix, directly North to the above-mentioned north-west angle of Nova Scotia, thence along the said Highlands which divide those Rivers that empty themselves into the River St. Lawrence from those which fall into the Atlantic Ocean to the north-westernmost head of Connecticut River, thence down along the middle of that River to the 45th degree of north latitude, thence by a line due West on said latitude until it strikes the River Iroquois, or Cataraguy, has not yet been surveyed, it is agreed that for these several purposes two Commissioners shall be appointed, sworn, and authorised, to act exactly in the manner directed with respect to those mentioned in the next preceding Article, unless otherwise specified in the present Article.

Appointment of Commissioners, Oath, and Place of Meeting.
The said Commissioners shall meet at St. Andrew's, in the province of New Brunswick, and shall have power to adjourn to such other place or places as they shall think fit. The said Commissioners shall have

power to ascertain and determine the points above mentioned, in conformity with the provisions of the said Treaty of Peace of 1783; and shall cause the Boundary aforesaid, from the source of the River St. Croix to the River Iroquois, or Cataraguy, to be surveyed and marked according to the said provisions; the said Commissioners shall make a Map of the said boundary, and annex to it a Declaration under their hands and seals, certifying it to be the true Map of the said Boundary, and particularising the latitude and longitude of the north-west angle of Nova Scotia, of the north-westernmost head of Connecticut River, and of such other points of the said Boundary as they may deem proper.

Map and Declaration, Final and Conclusive.

And both parties agree to consider such Map and Declaration as finally and conclusively fixing the said Boundary.

Arbitration in case of Difference.

And in the event of the said two Commissioners differing, or both, or either of them, refusing, declining, or wilfully omitting to act, such reports, declarations or statements shall be made by them, or either of them, and such reference to a friendly Sovereign or State shall be made in all respects, as in the latter part of the IVth Article is contained, and in as full a manner as if the same was herein repeated.

Boundary: Water Line through River Iroquois (St. Lawrence), through Lakes Ontario, Erie, and Huron, to Lake Superior. Doubts as to Middle of Lakes and Islands therein.

ART. VI. Whereas by the former Treaty of Peace that portion of the Boundary of the United States from the point where the 45th degree of north latitude strikes the River Iroquois, or Cataraguy, to the Lake Superior, was declared to be " along the middle of said River into Lake Ontario, through the middle of said Lake, until it strikes the communication by water between that Lake and Lake Erie, thence along the middle of said communication into Lake Erie, through the middle of said Lake until it arrives at the water communication into the Lake Huron, thence through the middle of said Lake to the water communication between that Lake and Lake Superior;" and whereas doubts have arisen what was the middle of the said River, Lakes, and water communications, and whether certain Islands lying in the same were within the dominions of His Britannic Majesty or of the United States.

Appointment of Commissioners. Oath, and Place of Meeting.

In order, therefore, finally to decide these doubts, they shall be referred to two Commissioners, to be appointed, sworn, and authorised, to act exactly in the manner directed with respect to those mentioned in the next preceding Article, unless otherwise specified in this present Article. The said Commissioners shall meet, in the first instance, at Albany, in the State of New York, and shall have power to adjourn to such other place or places as they shall think fit.

Report or Declaration, Final and Conclusive.

The said Commissioners shall, by a Report or Declaration, under their hands and seals, designate the Boundary through the said Rivers, Lakes, and water communications, and decide to which of the two Contracting Parties the several Islands lying within the said Rivers, Lakes, and water communications, do respectively belong, in conformity with the true intent of the said Treaty of 1783. And both parties agree to consider such designation and Decision as final and conclusive.

Arbitration in case of Difference.

And in the event of the said two Commissioners differing, or both, or either of them refusing, declining, or wilfully omitting to act, such Reports, Declarations, or Statements, shall be made by them, or either of them, and such reference to a friendly Sovereign or State shall be made in all respects, as in the latter part of the IVth Article is contained, and in as full a manner as if the same was herein repeated.

Boundary: Determination, by Last Commissioners, of Water Line from Lake Huron and Lake Superior to the Lake of the Woods, and of Islands therein, and Latitude and Longitude of North-West Point of Lake of the Woods.

ART. VII. It is further agreed, that the said two last-mentioned Commissioners, after they shall have executed the duties assigned to them in the preceding Article, shall be, and they are hereby authorised, upon their oaths, impartially to fix and determine, according to the true intent of the said Treaty of Peace of 1783, that part of the boundary between the dominions of the two Powers, which extends from the water communication between Lake Huron and Lake Superior, to the most North-Western Point of the Lake of the Woods; to decide to which of the two Parties the several Islands lying in the Lakes, water communications, and Rivers, forming the said Boundary, do respectively belong, in conformity with the true intent of the said Treaty of Peace of 1783, and to cause such parts of said Boundary as require it, to be surveyed and marked.

Report and Declaration, Final and Conclusive.

The said Commissioners shall, by a Report or Declaration, under their hands and seals, designate the Boundary aforesaid, state their decision on the points thus referred to them, and particularise the latitude and longitude of the most North-Western Point of the Lake of the Woods, and of such other parts of the said Boundary as they may deem proper, and both Parties agree to consider such designation and Decision as final and conclusive.

Arbitration in case of Difference.

And in the event of the said two Commissioners differing, or both or either of them refusing, declining, or wilfully omitting to act, such Reports, Declarations, or Statements shall be made by them, or either of them, and such reference to a friendly Sovereign or State shall be made in all respects as in the latter part of Article IV is contained, and in as full a manner as if the same was herein repeated.

Boundary: Appointment of Secretary, Surveyor, and last Commissioners. Duplicates of Reports, Declarations, Statements, Decisions, Accounts, and Journals of Proceedings. Payments of Salaries and Expenses. Supply of Vacancies.

ART. VIII. The several Boards of two Commissioners, mentioned in the four preceding Articles, shall respectively have power to appoint a Secretary, and to employ such Surveyors or other persons as they shall judge necessary. Duplicates of all their respective Reports, Declarations, Statements, and Decisions, and of their Accounts, and of the Journal of their Proceedings, shall be delivered by them to the Agents of His Britannic Majesty, and to the Agents of the United States, who may be respectively appointed and authorised to manage the business on behalf of their respective Governments. The said Commissioners shall be respectively paid in such manner as shall be agreed between the two Contracting Parties, such agreement being to be settled at the time of the exchange of the Ratifications of this Treaty. And all other expenses attending the said Commissioners shall be defrayed equally by the Two Parties. And in case of death, sickness, resignation, or necessary absence, the place of every such Commissioner respectively shall be supplied in the same manner as such Commissioner was first appointed, and the new Commissioner shall take the same oath or affirmation, and do the same duties.

Validity of Grants of Land in Islands in question made by Power in possession before the War.

It is further agreed between the two Contracting Parties, that in case any of the Islands mentioned in any of the preceding Articles, which were in the possession of one of the parties prior to the commencement of the present War between the two Countries, should, by the decision of any of the Boards of Commissioners aforesaid, or of the Sovereign or State so referred to, as in the four next preceding Articles contained, fall within the dominions of the other party, all Grants of Land made previous to the commencement of the War by the party having had such possession, shall be as valid as if such Island or Islands had, by such decision or decisions, been adjudged to be within the dominions of the party having had such possession.

Cessation of Hostilities with all the Tribes or Nations of Indians. Restoration of their Possessions. Rights and Privileges as in 1811, previous to the War.

ART. IX. The United States of America engage to put an end, immediately after the Ratification of the present Treaty, to hostilities with all the Tribes or Nations of Indians with whom they may be at war at the time of such Ratification, and forthwith to restore to such Tribes or Nations respectively, all the possessions, rights, and privileges which they may have enjoyed or been entitled to in 1811, previous to such hostilities. Provided always, that such Tribes or Nations shall agree to desist from all hostilities against the United States of America, their citizens and subjects, upon the ratification of the present Treaty being notified to such Tribes or Nations, and shall so desist accordingly.

And His Britannic Majesty engages, on his part, to put an end, immediately after the ratification of the present Treaty, to hostilities with all the Tribes or Nations of Indians with whom he may be at war at the time of such ratification, and forthwith to restore to such Tribes or Nations respectively, all the possessions, rights, and privileges which they may have enjoyed or been entitled to in 1811, previous to such hostilities. Provided always, that such tribes or nations shall agree to desist from all hostilities against His Britannic Majesty and his subjects, upon the ratification of the present Treaty being notified to such Tribes or Nations, and shall so desist accordingly.

Continuance of efforts to promote entire extinction of the Slave Trade.

ART. X. Whereas the Traffic in Slaves is irreconcilable with the principles of humanity and justice, and whereas both His Majesty and the United States are desirous of continuing their efforts to promote its entire abolition, it is hereby agreed that both the Contracting Parties shall use their best endeavours to accomplish so desirable an object.

Ratifications without Alteration.

ART. XI. This Treaty, when the same shall have been ratified on both sides, without alteration by either of the Contracting Parties, and the Ratifications Mutually exchanged, shall be binding on both parties, and the Ratifications shall be exchanged at Washington, in the space of four months from this day, or sooner, if practicable.

In faith whereof, we, the respective Plenipotentiaries, have signed this Treaty, and have thereunto affixed our seals.

Done, in triplicate, at Ghent, the 24th day of December, 1814.

(L.S.)   GAMBIER.
(L.S.)   H. GOULBURN.
(L.S.)   WM. ADAMS.

(L.S.)   JOHN QUINCEY ADAMS.
(L.S.)   J. A. BAYARD.
(L.S.)   H. CLAY.
(L.S.)   JON. RUSSELL.
(L.S.)   ALBERT GALLATIN.

3   DECLARATION OF VIENNA

DECLARATION of the 8 Powers, on the Affairs of the Helvetic Confederacy. Signed at Vienna, 20th March, 1815.

This Declaration formed Annex XIA to the Vienna Congress Treaty of 9th June, 1815

Preamble.

THE Powers called upon to mediate in the arrangement of the affairs of Switzerland, in order to carry into effect Article VI of the Treaty of Paris of the 30th May, 1814, having acknowledged that the general interest demands that the Helvetic States should enjoy the benefit of a perpetual Neutrality; and wishing, by territorial restitutions and cessions, to enable it to secure its Independence and maintain its Neutrality;

After having obtained every information relative to the interests of the different Cantons, and taken into consideration the claims submitted to them by the Helvetic Legation;

Perpetual Neutrality.

Declare,

That as soon as the Helvetic Diet shall have duly and formally acceded to the stipulations contained in the present Instrument, an

Act shall be prepared, containing the acknowledgment and the guarantee, on the part of all the Powers, of the perpetual Neutrality of Switzerland, in her new frontiers; which Act shall form part of that which, in the execution of Article XXXII of the Treaty of Paris of the 30th May, was to complete the arrangements contained in that Treaty.

Integrity of the 19 *Cantons of Switzerland.*
ART I. (Embodied in Vienna Congress Treaty as Art. LXXIV.)

Switzerland.   Union of Three new Cantons (The Valais, Geneva, Neufchatel).   Vallée des Dappes.
ART. II. (Embodied in Vienna Congress Treaty as Art. LXXV.)

Switzerland.   Union of Bishopric of Basle, and Town and Territory of Bienne, with Canton of Berne.
ART. III. (Embodied in Vienna Congress Treaty as Art. LXXVI.)

Switzerland.   Rights of Inhabitants of Countries united with Canton of Berne.
ART. IV. (1, 2, 3, Embodied in Vienna Congress Treaty as Art. LXXVII.)

Collection of Ordinary Revenues.
4. The ordinary revenues of the country shall be collected on account of the present Administration, until the date of the accession of the Diet to the present transaction. The arrears of the said revenues shall be collected in like manner, but the extraordinary taxes, which have not yet been paid into the public chest, shall not be demanded.

Indemnity to the Prince Bishop of Basle.
5. No indemnity having been received by the Prince Bishop of Basle, for the quota of the revenues accruing to him from the Bishopric which hitherto formed a part of Switzerland, and a stipulation having been made in the *Récès* of the German Empire of 1803, in favour of those countries only which have become an integral part of the said Empire, the cantons of Berne and Basle are to pay to him, in addition to the said annuity, the sum of 12,000 florins of the Empire, dating from the union of the Bishopric of Basle to the Cantons of Berne and Basle; the fifth part of this sum shall be applied to, and remain as a provision for, the support of the canons of the ancient catheral of Basle, in order to make up the annuity which has been settled by the *Récès* of the German Empire.

Retention of Bishopric of Basle.

The Helvetic Diet shall determine whether it be expedient to retain a Bishopric in this part of Switzerland, or whether this diocese may not be united to that which, pursuant to the new arrangements, shall be formed out of the Swiss territory which belonged to the diocese of Constance.

Proportion to be paid by Canton of Berne to Bishopric of Basle.

In case the Bishopric of Basle should be continued, the Canton of Berne shall furnish, in the same proportion as the other countries which shall in future be placed under the spiritual administration of the Bishop, such a sum as may be necessary for the support of this prelate, of his chapter, and of his seminary.

Switzerland. Commercial and Military Communications between Town of Geneva and Canton of Vaud. Passage of Troops. Versoy Road.
ART. V. (Embodied in Vienna Congress Treaty as Art. LXXIX.)

Free Communication between the Town of Geneva and the Jurisdiction of Peney.

In the Additional Regulations to be made on this subject, the execution of the Treaties relative to the free Communication between the Town of Geneva and the Jurisdiction of Peney, shall be guaranteed in a manner most suitable to the interests of the inhabitants of Geneva. His Most Christian Majesty consents likewise, that the gendarmerie and militia of Geneva, after having communicated on the subject with the nearest military post of the French gendarmerie, shall pass on the high road of Meyrin, in the said jurisdiction, to and from the town of Geneva.

Accession of Territory for the Town of Geneva.

The Contracting Powers shall, moreover, interpose their good offices for the purpose of obtaining for the Town of Geneva a suitable accession of territory on the side of Savoy.

Switzerland. Mutual Compensations by Cantons of Argovia, Vaud, Tessin, and St. Gall to Cantons of Schweitz, Unterwald, Uri, Glaris, Zug, and Appenzell.
ART. VI. (Embodied in Vienna Congress Treaty as Art. LXXXI.)

A Commission appointed by the Diet shall superintend the execution of the preceding arrangements.

Switzerland. Disposal of Funds placed in England by Cantons of Zurich and Berne.
ART. VII. (Embodied in Vienna Congress Treaty as Art. LXXXII.)

Switzerland. Indemnity to Proprietors of " Lauds."
ART. VIII. (Embodied in Vienna Congress Treaty as Art. LXXXIII.)

Pensions to Prince Abbot of St. Gall and others.

ART. IX. The Mediating Powers, acknowledging the justice of securing to the Prince Abbot of St. Gall an honourable and independent existence, direct, that the Canton of St. Gall shall pay to him an annuity of 6,000 florins of the Empire, and to those under him, an annuity of 2,000. These pensions shall be paid by instalments (commencing from the 1st of January, 1815) into the hands of the directing canton, every three months, which shall place them at the disposal of the Prince Abbot of St. Gall, and of those under him respectively.

The Powers mediating in the affairs of Switzerland, by the above Declaration, afford a manifest proof of their desire to secure the internal tranquillity of the Confederation. They also feel it a duty to omit nothing which may accelerate its accomplishment.

Accession to Federal Union.

They expect, therefore, that the Cantons, laying aside, for the public good, every secondary consideration, will no longer delay their Accession to the Federal Union, freely consented to by a great majority of the Swiss States; the common interest imperiously demanding that every part of Switzerland should unite, as soon as possible, under the same Federative Constitution.

The Convention of the 16th August, 1814, annexed to the Act of the Federal Union, can no longer be an obstacle to their union. Its end being already attained by the Declaration of the Powers, it is in fact annulled.

Amnesty.

To insure still further the repose of Switzerland, the Powers desire that a general Amnesty be granted to all individuals who, led astray at a period of uncertainty and irritation, might have acted in some respect or other contrary to the present order of things. Far from weakening the legitimate authority of Governments, this act of clemency will afford them a new claim to exercise that salutary severity against whoever shall attempt in future to excite disturbance in the country.

Finally, the mediating Powers trust, that the patriotism and the good sense of the Swiss people will point out to them the propriety, as well as the necessity, of mutually obliterating the remembrance of those differences which have divided them, and of consolidating the work of their reorganisation by endeavouring to perfect it, in a spirit conducive to the public good, without any recollection of the past.

The present Declaration has been inserted in the Protocol of the Congress assembled at Vienna, at its sitting of the 19th March, 1815.

Done and certified by the Plenipotentiaries of the Eight Powers who signed the Treaty of Paris.

Vienna, 20th March, 1815.

AUSTRIA.	(L.S.) LE PRINCE DE METTERNICH.
	(L.S.) LE BARON DE WESSENBERG.
SPAIN (ESPAGNE).	(L.S.) P. GOMEZ LABRADOR.
FRANCE.	(L.S.) LE PRINCE DE TALLEYRAND.
	(L.S.) LE DUC DE D'ALBERG.
	(L.S.) LATOUR DUPIN.
	(L.S.) LE COMTE ALEXIS DE NOAILLES.
GREAT BRITAIN.	(L.S.) WELLINGTON.
	(L.S.) CLANCARTY.
	(L.S.) CATHCART.
	(L.S.) STEWART.
PORTUGAL.	(L.S.) LE COMTE DE PALMELLA.
	(L.S.) SALDANHA.
	(L.S.) LOBO.
PRUSSIA.	(L.S.) LE PRINCE DE HARDENBERG.
	(L.S.) LE BARON DE HUMBOLDT.
RUSSIA.	(L.S.) LE COMTE DE RASOUMOFFSKY.
	(L.S.) LE COMTE DE STACKELBERG.
	(L.S.) NESSELRODE.
SWEDEN.	(L.S.) LOWENHIELM.

The act of Accession of the Swiss Confederation to the above Declaration, signed at Zurich on the 27th May, 1815, formed Annex XIB to the Vienna Congress Treaty of 9th June, 1815.

An Act was also signed by the Protecting Powers (Great Britain, Austria, France, Prussia, and Russia), for the acknowledgment of the perpetual Neutrality of Switzerland, at Paris, on the 20th November, 1815, and the Inviolability of its Territory.

4

Federative Constitution of Germany. Vienna, 8th June, 1815.

[This Constitution formed Annex IX to the Vienna Congress Treaty of 9th June, 1815.]

Germanic Confederation.
ART. I. (Embodied in Vienna Congress Treaty as Art. LIII.)

Object of the Confederation.
ART. II. (Embodied in Vienna Congress Treaty as Art. LIV.)

Equality of the Members.
ART. III. (Embodied in Vienna Congress Treaty as Art. LV.)

Federative Diet.
ART. IV. (Embodied in Vienna Congress Treaty as Art. LVI.)

Presidency of Austria at Diet.
ART. V. (Embodied in Vienna Congress Treaty as Art. LVII.)

Composition of the General Assembly.
ART. VI. (Embodied in Vienna Congress Treaty as Art. LVIII.)

Arrangements relating to the Diet.
ART. VII. (Embodied in Vienna Congress Treaty as Art. LIX.)

Order of Voting in Diet.
ART. VIII. (Embodied in Vienna Congress Treaty as Art. LX.)

Diet to assemble at Frankfort.
ART. IX. (Embodied in Vienna Congress Treaty as Art. LXI.)

The Framing of Fundamental Laws.
ART. X. (Embodied in Vienna Congress Treaty as Art. LXII.)

*Maintenance of Peace in Germany.   Disputes to be settled through
Mediation of the Diet, or by an Austregal Court.*
ART. XI. 1. (Embodied in Vienna Congress Treaty as Art. LXIII.)

Particular Arrangements.
ART. XI. 2. Besides the points settled in the preceding Articles,
relative to the establishment of the Confederation, the Confederated
States have agreed to the arrangements contained in the following
Articles, with regard to the subjects hereafter mentioned, which
Articles shall have the same force and validity as the preceding ones.

Formation of Supreme Tribunals.
ART. XII. Those members of the Confederation whose possessions

do not contain a population to the number of 300,000 souls, shall unite themselves to the reigning Houses of the same line, or to others of the Confederated States whose population added to theirs will amount to the number here specified, for the purpose of jointly forming a Supreme Tribunal.

In those States, however, of a smaller population, where similar tribunals of the *Third Instance* already exist, they shall be continued on their present footing, provided the population of the State to which they belong be not less than 150,000 souls.

The Four Free Cities shall have the right of uniting together in the formation of a common and supreme Tribunal.

Each party appearing before these joint and supreme Tribunals shall be authorised to demand a reference of the proceedings to the Faculty of Law belonging to a foreign University, or to a Court of Reference (*siège d'échevin*) to whom the final sentence shall be submitted.

Separate Assemblies of States.

ART. XIII. There shall be Assemblies of the States in all the countries belonging to the Confederation.

Rights of Mediatised Princes.

ART. XIV. In order to secure to the ancient States of the Empire, mediatised in 1806, and in the subsequent years, the enjoyment of equal rights in all countries belonging to the Confederation, and conformable to the relations at present existing between them, the Confederated States establish the following principles :

A. The Houses of the Mediatised Princes and Counts are nevertheless to rank equally with the high Nobility of Germany, and are to retain the same privileges of birthright with the Sovereign Houses (*Ebenbürtigkeit*) as they have hitherto enjoyed.

B. The heads of these Houses are to form the principal class of the States in the countries to which they belong: they, as well as their families, are to be included in the number of the most privileged persons, particularly in respect to taxes.

C. With regard to themselves, their families and property, they are generally to retain all the rights and privileges attached to their possessions, and which do not belong to the Supreme Authority, or to the attributes of Government.

Among the rights which are secured to them by this Article, are specially included:—

1. The perfect liberty of residing in any State belonging to the Confederation, or at peace with it.

2. The maintenance of family compacts, conformably to the ancient

Constitution of Germany; and the right of connecting their estates and the members of their families by obligatory arrangements, which, however, ought to be made known to the Sovereign, and to the public authorities.

The laws by which this right has been hitherto restricted, shall not be applicable to future cases.

3. The privilege of being amendable only to superior tribunals, and of being exempt from all military conscription for themselves and families.

4. The exercise of civil and criminal jurisdiction, in the *First Instance*, and, if the possessions are sufficiently extensive, in the *Second Instance*, the exercise of the forest jurisdiction, of the local police, and of the inspection of churches, schools, and charitable institutions, the whole conformably to the laws of the country to which they remain subject, as well as to the military regulations and supreme authority reserved to the Governments, respecting objects of the above-mentioned prerogatives, for the better determining them, and, in general, for the adjusting and consolidating the rights of Mediatised Princes, Counts, and Lords, in a manner uniform to all the States of the German Confederation. The Ordinance issued upon this subject by His Majesty the King of Bavaria, in 1807, shall be adopted as a general rule.

Rights of the Ancient Nobility of the Empire.

The ancient and immediate Nobility of the Empire (*l'Ancienne Noblesse immédiate de l'Empire*) shall enjoy the rights specified in Sections 1 and 2, namely, of sitting in the Assembly of the States, of exercising the patrimonial and forest jurisdiction, of the local police, of presentations to Church benefices, as well as of not being amenable to the ordinary tribunals.

These rights shall, however, be exercised according to the regulations established by the laws of the country in which the members of this Nobility have possessions.

In the provinces detached from Germany by the Peace of Lunéville of the 9th of February, 1801, and which are at present reunited thereto, the principles above specified, relative to the ancient and immediate Nobility of the Empire, shall, in their application, be subject to such modifications as may be rendered necessary by the relations which exist in these provinces.

Guarantee by the Confederation of the Rents assigned upon the Navigation Duties of the Rhine, and of the Pensions to the Clergy or Laity.

ART. XV. The continuation of the direct and subsidiary Rents assigned upon the Duties of the Navigation of the Rhine, as well as the arrangements of the *Récès* of the Deputation of the Empire, dated the 25th of February, 1803, relative to the payment of Debts and Pensions granted to individuals of the Clergy or Laity, are guaranteed by the Confederation.

The members of the late chapters of the cathedral churches, as well as those of the free chapters of the Empire, shall have the benefit of the pensions secured to them by the said *Récès*, in every country at peace with the Germanic Confederation.

Pensions to Members of the Teutonic Order.

The members of the Teutonic Order, who have not yet obtained adequate pensions, shall obtain them according to the principles established for the chapters of cathedral churches by the *Récès* of the Deputation of the Empire of the year 1803; and the Princes who have acquired possessions formerly belonging to the Teutonic Order, shall pay these pensions, according to their proportion of the property of the Teutonic Order.

Fund for support of Bishops and Clergy on Left Bank of the Rhine.

The Diet of the Confederation shall deliberate upon the measures to be adopted for establishing a fund for the support and pensioning of Bishops and other members of the Clergy belonging to the countries on the left bank of the Rhine, the payment of which pensions shall be transferred to the Powers actually possessing the said countries. This matter shall be settled within a year, and until that time the pensions shall be paid as heretofore.

Equality of Civil and Political Rights to Christian Sects.

Art. XVI. The different Christian sects in the countries and territories of the Germanic Confederation shall not experience any difference in the enjoyment of civil and political rights.

Civil Rights of Jews.

The Diet shall consider of the means of effecting, in the most uniform manner, an amelioration in the civil state of those who profess the Jewish religion in Germany, and shall pay particular attention to the measures by which the enjoyment of civil rights shall be secured and guaranteed to them in the Confederated States, upon condition, however, of their submitting to all the obligations imposed upon other citizens. In the mean time, the privileges already granted to this sect by any particular State shall be secured to them.

Postal Revenues to be retained by Tour and Taxis.

ART. XVII. The family of the Princes of Tour and Taxis shall retain the revenues arising from the Post in the Confederated States, under the same Regulations as were granted by the *Récès* of the Deputation of the Empire of the 25th February, 1803, or by subsequent Conventions, in so far as they shall not have been altered by new Conventions freely acceded to on both sides.

In all cases the rights and pretensions of this House, whether with regard to retaining the Post, or to a fair indemnity for the same, such as the above *Récès* has settled, shall be maintained.

This Regulation also applies to the case where the former administration of the Post may have been abolished since 1803, in contravention of the *Récès* of the Deputation of the Empire, unless, however, an indemnity shall have been absolutely settled by a particular Convention.

Rights of Subjects of Confederated States.

ART. XVIII. The Princes and the Free Towns of Germany have agreed to secure to the subjects of the Confederated States, the following rights:

A. That of acquiring and possessing funded property beyond the limits of the State in which they are settled, without being liable to pay to the foreign Power any higher tax or duty than those paid by its own subjects.

B. 1. That of emigrating from one Confederated State to another, provided it be proved that the State in which they settle receive them as subjects.

2. That of entering into the civil or military service of any of the Confederated States, it being, however, understood, that the exercise of either of these rights does not release them from being liable to military service in their own country. And in order that the difference of the laws with regard to their liability to military service may not be attended with any partial advantages or injurious consequences to any particular State, the Diet of the Confederation shall consider of the means of establishing regulations upon this subject, as impartial as possible.

C. The exemption from all export duty, drawback, or other impost of that description, in case they remove their property from one Confederated State to another, unless it should be otherwise stipulated by particular Conventions concluded between them.

D. Upon its first meeting, the Diet shall frame laws for the liberty of the press in general, and shall adopt such measures as may secure authors and editors against the piracy of their works.

Commerce and Navigation from one State to another.

ART. XIX. The Confederated States reserve to themselves the right of deliberating, at the first meeting of the Diet at Frankfort, upon the manner of regulating the commerce and navigation from one State to another, according to the principles adopted by the Congress of Vienna.

Ratifications.

ART. XX. The present Act shall be ratified by all the Contracting Parties, and the ratifications shall, in six weeks, or sooner, if possible, be addressed to the Royal and State Chancery of His Majesty the Emperor of Austria at Vienna, and deposited in the Archives of the Confederation on the opening of the Diet.

In faith of which all the Plenipotentiaries have signed the present instrument, and have affixed thereunto the Seal of their Arms.

Done at Vienna, the 8th June, 1815.

(L.S.) PRINCE METTERNICH.

(L.S.) BARON WESSENBERG.

(L.S.) CHARLES PRINCE HARDENBERG.

(L.S.) WILLIAM BARON HUMBOLDT.

(L.S.) CH. COUNT BERNSTORFF.

(L.S.) J. COUNT BERNSTORFF.

(L.S.) A. COUNT RECHBERG AND ROTHEN-LOWEN.

(L.S.) H. A. BARON GLOBIG.

(L.S.) F. C. BARON GAGERN.

(L.S.) E. COUNT MUNSTER.

(L.S.) E. COUNT HARDENBERG.

(L.S.) COUNT KELLER, acting at the same time for Brunswick.

(L.S.) G. F. BARON LEPEL.

(L.S.) J. BARON TURCKHEIM.

(L.S.) BARON MINCKWITZ, in the place of M. de Gersdorff, Plenipotentiary of the Grand Duke of Weimar, and of the Dukes of Saxe-Gotha and of Saxe-Meiningen.

(L.S.) C. L. F. BARON BAUMBACH.

(L.S.) BARON FISCHLER VON TREUBERG.

(L.S.) BARON MALTZAHN.

(L.S.) LEOPOLD BARON PLESSEN.

(L.S.) BARON OERTZEN.

(L.S.) DE WOLFRAMSDORF.

(L.S.)   BARON FRANCK.
(L.S.)   FRANCIS ALOYSIUS KIRCHBAUER.
(L.S.)   F. MARSCHALL VON BIEBERSTEIN.
(L.S.)   D. GEORG WIESE, Plenipotentiary of the
         Princes Liechtenstein and Reuss.
(L.S.)   DE WEISE.
(L.S.)   BARON KETTELHOLDT.
(L.S.)   DE BERG, acting for Waldeck and Schaum-
         burg-Lippe.
(L.S.)   HELLWING.
(L.S.)   J. F. HACH.
(L.S.)   DANZ.
(L.S.)   SMIDT.
(L.S.)   GRIES.

5   VIENNA CONGRESS TREATY

GENERAL TREATY between Great Britain, Austria, France, Portugal, Prussia, Russia, Spain, and Sweden. —Signed at Vienna, 9th June, 1815, and ratified on the same date.

In the Name of the Most Holy and Undivided Trinity.

THE Powers who signed the Treaty concluded at Paris on the 30th of May, 1814, having assembled at Vienna, in pursuance of Article XXXII of that Act, with the Princes and States their Allies, to complete the provisions of the said Treaty, and to add to them the arrangements rendered necessary by the state in which Europe was left at the termination of the last war; being now desirous to embrace, in one common transaction, the various results of their negotiations, for the purpose of confirming them by their reciprocal Ratifications, have authorised their Plenipotentiaries to unite, in a general Instrument, the regulations of superior and permanent interest, and to join to that Act, as integral parts of the arrangements of Congress, the Treaties, Conventions, Declarations, Regulations, and other particular Acts, as cited in the present Treaty. And the above-mentioned Powers having appointed Plenipotentiaries to the Congress, that is to say:—

His Majesty the Emperor of Austria, King of Hungary and
Bohemia:

The Sieur Clement-Venceslas-Lothaire, Prince de Metternich-Winnebourg-Ochsenhausen, Knight of the Golden Fleece, Grand Cross of the Royal Order of St. Stephen, Knight of the Orders of St. Andrew, of St. Alexander-Newsky, and of St. Anne of the First Class, Grand Cordon of the Legion of Honour, Knight of the Order of the Elephant, of the Supreme Order of the Annunciation, of the Black Eagle and the Red Eagle, of the Seraphim, of St. Joseph of Tuscany, of St. Hubert, of the Golden Eagle of Wurtemberg, of Fidelity of Baden, of St. John of Jerusalem, and of several others; Chancellor of the Military Order of Maria-Theresa, a Trustee of the Academy of the Fine Arts, Chamberlain, Privy Councillor of His Majesty the Emperor of Austria, King of Hungary and Bohemia, his Minister of State, of Conferences, and of Foreign Affairs;

And the Sieur John-Philip, Baron de Wessenberg, Knight Grand Cross of the Military and Religious Order of St. Maurice and St. Lazarus, Grand Cross of the Order of the Red Eagle of Prussia, and of the Crown of Bavaria, Chamberlain, and Privy Councillor of His Imperial and Royal Apostolic Majesty:—

His Majesty the King of Spain, and the Indies:

Don Peter Gomes Labrador, Knight of the Royal and distinguished Order of Charles III; his Councillor of State:—

His Majesty the King of France and Navarre:

The Sieur Charles-Maurice de Talleyrand-Perigord, Prince of Talleyrand, Peer of France, Minister, Secretary of State in the Department of Foreign Affairs, Grand Cordon of the Legion of Honour, Knight of the Order of the Golden Fleece, Grand Cross of the Order of St. Stephen of Hungary, of the Order of St. Andrew, of the Orders of the Black Eagle and the Red Eagle, of the Order of the Elephant, of the Order of St. Hubert, of the Crown of Saxony, of the Order of St. Joseph, of the Order of the Sun of Persia, &c.;

The Sieur Duke D'Alberg, Minister of State to His Majesty the King of France and Navarre, Grand Cordon of the Legion of Honour, of that of Fidelity of Baden, and Knight of the Order of St. John of Jerusalem;

The Sieur Count Gouvernet de Latour du Pin, Knight of the Royal and Military Order of St. Louis, and of the Legion of Honour, Envoy Extraordinary and Minister Plenipotentiary of His said Majesty to His Majesty the King of the Netherlands;

And the Sieur Alexis Count de Noailles, Knight of the Royal and Military Order of St. Louis, Grand Cross of the Royal and Military Order of St. Maurice and St. Lazarus, Knight of the Order of St. John of Jerusalem, of Leopold, of St. Wolodimir, of Merit of Prussia, and Colonel in the service of France:—

His Majesty the King of the United Kingdom of Great Britain and Ireland:

The Right Honourable Robert Stewart, Viscount Castlereagh, Privy Councillor of His said Majesty, Member of Parliament, Colonel of the Londonderry Regiment of Militia, his Principal Secretary of State for Foreign Affairs, and Knight of the Most Noble Order of the Garter, &c.;

The Most Excellent and Most Illustrious Lord Arthur Wellesley, Duke, Marquess, and Earl of Wellington, Marquess of Douro, Viscount Wellington of Talavera and of Wellington, and Baron Douro of Wellesley, Privy Councillor of His said Majesty, Marshal of his Armies, Colonel of the Royal Regiment of Horse Guards, Knight of the Most Noble Order of the Garter, and Knight Grand Cross of the Most Honourable Military Order of the Bath; Duke of Ciudad Rodrigo, and Grandee of Spain of the First Class, Duke of Vittoria, Marquis of Torres Vedras, Conde de Vimeira in Portugal; Knight of the Most Illustrious Order of the Golden Fleece, of the Military Order of St. Ferdinand of Spain, Knight Grand Cross of the Imperial and Military Order of Maria-Theresa, Knight Grand Cross of the Military Order of St. George of Russia of the First Class; Knight Grand Cross of the Royal and Military Order of the Tower and Sword of Portugal; Knight Grand Cross of the Royal and Military Order of the Sword of Sweden, &c.;

The Right Honourable Richard Le Poer Trench, Earl of Clancarty, Viscount Dunlo, Baron Kilconnel, Privy Councillor of His said Majesty, President of the Committee of Council for the Affairs of Trade and Colonies, Postmaster-General, Colonel of the Galway Regiment of Militia, and Knight Grand Cross of the Most Honourable Order of the Bath;

The Right Honourable William Shaw, Earl Cathcart, Viscount Cathcart, Baron Cathcart and Greenock, Peer of Parliament, Privy Councillor of His said Majesty, Knight of the Most Ancient and Most Honourable Order of the Thistle, and of the Orders of Russia, General of his Armies, Vice-Admiral of Scotland, Colonel of the Second Regiment of Life Guards, his Ambassador Extraordinary and Plenipotentiary to His Majesty the Emperor of all the Russias, &c.;

And the Right Honourable Charles William Stewart, Lord Stewart, a Lord of His Majesty's Bedchamber, Privy Councillor of His said Majesty, Lieutenant-General of his Armies, Colonel of the 25th Regiment of Light Dragoons, Governor of Fort Charles in Jamaica, Knight Grand Cross of the Most Honourable Military Order of the Bath, Knight Grand Cross of the Orders of the Black and Red Eagle of Prussia, Knight Grand Cross of the Order of the Tower and Sword of Portugal, and Knight of the Order of St. George of Russia:—

His Royal Highness the Prince Regent of the Kingdoms of Portugal and the Brazils:

The Sieur Don Peter de Sousa-Holstein, Count of Palmella, a Member of his Council, Commander of the Order of Christ, Captain of the German Company of Body Guards, Grand Cross of the Royal and Distinguished Order of Charles III of Spain;

The Sieur Antonio de Saldanha da Gama, a Member of his Council and of the Finances, his Envoy Extraordinary and Minister Plenipotentiary to His Majesty the Emperor of all the Russias, Commander of the Military Order of St. Benedict of Avez, First Equerry to Her Royal Highness the Princess of Brazil;

And the Sieur Don Joachim Lobo da Silveira, a Member of his Council, Commander of the Order of Christ:—

His Majesty the King of Prussia:

The Prince of Hardenberg, his Chancellor of State, Knight of the Grand Orders of the Black Eagle and the Red Eagle of St. John of Jerusalem, and of the Iron Cross of Prussia, of the Orders of St. Andrew, of St. Alexander Newsky, and of St. Anne of the First Class of Russia, Grand Cross of the Royal Order of St. Stephen of Hungary, Grand Cordon of the Legion of Honour, Grand Cross of the Order of Charles III of Spain, of St. Hubert of Bavaria, of the Supreme Order of the Annunciation of Sardinia, Knight of the Order of the Seraphim of Sweden, of the Elephant of Denmark, of the Golden Eagle of Wurtemberg, and of several others;

And the Sieur Charles-William, Baron de Humboldt, his Minister of State, Chamberlain, Envoy Extraordinary and Minister Plenipotentiary to His Imperial and Royal Apostolic Majesty, Knight of the Grand Order of the Red Eagle, and of the Iron Cross of Prussia of the First Class, Grand Cross of the Order of St. Anne of Russia, of the Order of Leopold of Austria, and of the Crown of Bavaria:—

His Majesty the Emperor of all the Russias:

The Sieur Andrew, Prince de Rasoumoffsky, his Privy Councillor, Senator, Knight of the Orders of St. Andrew, of St. Wolodimir, of St. Alexander Newsky, and of St. Anne of the First Class, Grand Cross of the Royal Order of St. Stephen, and of those of the Black Eagle and the Red Eagle of Prussia;

The Sieur Gustavus, Count de Stackelberg, his Privy Councillor, Envoy Extraordinary and Minister Plenipotentiary to His Imperial and Royal Apostolic Majesty, Chamberlain, Knight of the Order of St. Alexander Newsky, Grand Cross of the Order of St. Wolodimir and of St. Anne of the First Class, Grand Cross of the Order of St. Stephen, of the Black Eagle and the Red Eagle of Prussia;

And the Sieur Charles, Count de Nesselrode, his Privy Councillor, Chamberlain, Secretary of State for Foreign Affairs, Knight of the Order of St. Alexander Newsky, Grand Cross of the Order of St. Wolodimir of the Second Class, of St. Stephen of Hungary, of the Red Eagle of Prussia, of the Polar Star of Sweden, and of the Golden Eagle of Wurtemberg:—

His Majesty the King of Sweden and Norway:

The Sieur Charles-Axel, Count de Lœwenhielm, Major-General of his Armies, Colonel of a Regiment of Infantry, Chamberlain, his Envoy Extraordinary and Minister Plenipotentiary to His Majesty the Emperor of all the Russias, Vice-Chancellor of his Orders, Commander of his Order of the Polar Star, and Knight of the Order of the Sword; Knight of the Orders of Russia, of St. Anne of the First Class, and of St. George of the Fourth Class; Knight of the Prussian Order of the Red Eagle of the First Class, and Commander of the Order of St. John of Jerusalem.

Such of the above Plenipotentiaries as have assisted at the close of the negotiations, after having produced their full powers, found in good and due form, have agreed to place in the said general Instrument the following Articles, and to affix to them their signatures:—

Part of Duchy of Warsaw to be united to Russia.   Title of King of Poland to be borne by the Czar.

ART. I. The Duchy of Warsaw, with the exception of the provinces and districts which are otherwise disposed of by the following Articles, is united to the Russian Empire. It shall be irrevocably attached to it by its Constitution, and be possessed by His Majesty the Emperor of all the Russias, his heirs and successors in perpetuity. His Imperial Majesty reserves to himself to give to this State, enjoying a distinct administration, the interior improvement which he shall judge proper. He shall assume with his other titles that of Czar, King of Poland, agreeably to the form established for the titles attached to his other possessions.

Poles to receive Representative and National Institutions.

The Poles, who are respective subjects of Russia, Austria, and Prussia, shall obtain a Representation and National Institutions, regulated according to the degree of political consideration, that each of the Governments to which they belong shall judge expedient and proper to grant them.

Part of Duchy of Warsaw to be possessed by Prussia as Grand Duchy of Posen.

ART. II. The part of the Duchy of Warsaw which His Majesty the King of Prussia shall possess in full sovereignty and property, for himself, his heirs, and successors, under the title of the Grand Duchy of Posen, shall be comprised within the following line:—

Proceeding from the frontier of Eastern Prussia to the village of Neuhoff, the new limit shall follow the frontier of Western Prussia, such as it subsisted from 1772 to the Peace of Tilsit [1807], to the village of Leibitsch, which shall belong to the Duchy of Warsaw; from thence shall be drawn a line, which, leaving Kompania, Grabowiec, and Szczytno to Prussia, passes the Vistula, near the last-mentioned place, from the other side of the river, which falls into the Vistula opposite Szczytno, to the ancient limit of the district of the Netze, near Gross-Opoczko, so that Sluzewo shall belong to the Duchy, and Przybranowa, Holláender, and Maciejevo, to Prussia. From Gross-Opoczko it shall pass by Chlewiska, which shall remain to Prussia, to the village of Przybyslaw, and from thence by the villages of Piaski, Chelmce, Witowiczki, Kobylinka, Woyczyn, Orchowo, to the town of Powidz.

From Powidz it shall continue by the town of Slupce to the point of confluence of the rivers Wartha and Prosna.

From this point it shall reascend the course of the river Prosna to the village of Koscielnawies, to within one league of the town of Kalisch.

Then leaving to that town (on the side of the left bank of the Prosna), a semi-circular territory measured be the distance from Koscielnawies to Kalisch, the line shall return to the course of the Prosna, and shall continue to follow it, reascending by the towns of Grabow, Wieruszow, Boleslawiec, so as to terminate near the village of Gola, upon the frontier of Silesia, opposite Pitschin.

Wieliczka Salt Mines and Territory to be possessed by Austria.

ART. III. His Imperial and Royal Apostolic Majesty shall possess, in full property and sovereignty, the salt-mines of Wieliczka, and the territory thereto belonging.

Frontier between Galicia and Russia.

ART. IV. The way or bed (*Thalweg*) of the Vistula shall separate Galicia from the territory of the Free Town of Cracow. It shall serve at the same time as the frontier between Galicia and that part of the ancient Duchy of Warsaw united to the States of His Majesty the Emperor of all the Russias, as far as the vicinity of the town of Zavichost.

From Zavichost to the Bug, the dry frontiers shall be determined by the line drawn in the Treaty of Vienna of 1809, excepting such modifications as by common consent may be thought necessary to be introduced.

The frontier from the Bug shall be re-established on this side (*de ce côté*) between the two Empires, such as it was before the said Treaty.

Restitution by Russia to Austria of Districts separated from Eastern Galicia.

ART. V. His Majesty the Emperor of all the Russias cedes to His Imperial and Royal Apostolic Majesty the districts which have been separated from Eastern Galicia, in consequence of the Treaty of Vienna of 1809, from the Circles of Zloczow, Brzezan, Tarnopol, and Zalesczyk, and the frontiers on this side (*de ce coté*) shall be re-established, such as they were before the date of the said Treaty.

Cracow declared to be a Free, Neutral, and Independent Town, under the Protection of Austria, Russia, and Prussia.

ART. VI. The Town of Cracow, with its Territory, is declared to be for ever a Free, Independent, and strictly Neutral City, under the protection of Austria, Russia, and Prussia.

Boundaries of the Territory of Cracow.

ART. VII. The territory of the Free Town of Cracow shall have for its frontier upon the left bank of the Vistula a line, which, beginning at the spot near the village of Woliça, where a stream falls into the Vistula, shall ascend this stream by Clo, and Koscielniki as far as Czulice, so that these villages may be included in the district of the Free Town of Cracow; from thence passing along the frontiers of these villages the line shall continue by Dzickanovice, Garlice, Tomaszow, Karniowice, which shall also remain in the territory of Cracow, to the point where the limit begins which separates the district of Krzeszovice from that of Olkusz; from thence it shall follow this limit between the two said provinces, till it reaches the frontiers of Silesian Prussia.

Cracow.　Privileges granted to Podgorze.

ART. VIII. His Majesty the Emperor of Austria, wishing particularly to facilitate as much as possible on his part, the commercial relations, and good neighbourhood between Galicia and the Free Town of Cracow, grants for ever to the town of Podgorze, the privileges of a Free Commercial Town, such as are enjoyed by the town of Brody. This liberty of commerce shall extend to a distance of 500 toises from the barrier of the suburbs of the town of Podgorze.

Cracow.　Austrian Right of Sovereignty over Podgorze.
Neutrality of Cracow.

In consequence of this perpetual concession, which nevertheless shall not affect the rights of sovereignty of His Imperial and Royal Apostolic Majesty, the Austrian custom-houses shall be established only in places situated beyond that limit. No military establishment shall be formed that can menace the Neutrality of Cracow, or obstruct the liberty of commerce which His Imperial and Royal Apostolic Majesty grants to the town and district of Podgorze.

Cracow.   Neutrality to be respected by Austria, Prussia, and Russia.

ART. IX. The Courts of Russia, Austria, and Prussia engage to respect, and to cause to be always respected, the Neutrality of the Free Town of Cracow and its Territory. No armed force shall be introduced upon any pretence whatever.

Cracow.   Surrender of Fugitive Deserters from Austria, Prussia, or Russia.

On the other hand it is understood and expressly stipulated that no asylum shall be afforded in the free town and territory of Cracow to fugitives, deserters, and persons under prosecution, belonging to the country of either of the High Powers aforesaid; and in the event of the demand of their surrender by the competent authorities, such individuals shall be arrested and given up without delay, and conveyed, under a proper escort, to the guard appointed to receive them at the frontier.

Constitution, Academy, and Bishopric of Cracow.

ART. X. The dispositions of the Constitution of the Free Town of Cracow, concerning the Academy, the Bishopric, and Chapter of that town, such as they are specified in Articles VII, XV, XVI, and XVII of the Additional Treaty relative to Cracow which is annexed to the present General Treaty, shall have the same force and validity as if they were textually inserted in this Act.

Poland.   General Amnesty.

ART. XI. A full, general, and special Amnesty shall be granted in favour of all individuals, of whatever rank, sex, or condition they may be.

Poland.   Sequestrations to be removed.   Prosecutions to be annulled.

ART. XII. In consequence of the preceding Article, no person in future shall be prosecuted or disturbed, in any manner, by reason of any participation, direct or indirect, at any time, in the political, civil, or military events in Poland. All proceedings, suits, or prosecutions are considered as null, the sequestrations and provisional confiscations shall be taken off, and every Act promulgated on this ground shall be of no effect.

Poland. Exceptions to preceding Article respecting Confiscation.

ART. XIII. From these general regulations on the subject of confiscation are excepted all those cases in which edicts or sentences, finally pronounced, have already been fully executed, and have not been annulled by subsequent events.

Free Navigation of the Rivers in Poland.

ART. XIV. The principles established for the free navigation of Rivers and Canals, in the whole extent of ancient Poland, as well as for the trade to the ports, for the circulation of articles the growth and produce of the different Polish provinces, and for the commerce, relative to goods in transitu, such as they are specified in Articles XXIV, XXV, XXVI, XXVIII, and XXIX of the Treaty between Austria and Russia, and in Articles XXII, XXIII, XXIV, XXV, XXVIII, and XXIX of the Treaty between Russia and Prussia, shall be invariably maintained.

Cessions from Saxony to Prussia.

ART. XV. His Majesty the King of Saxony renounces in perpetuity for himself, and all his descendants and successors, in favour of His Majesty the King of Prussia, all his right and title to the provinces, districts, and territories, or parts of territories, of the Kingdom of Saxony, hereafter named; and His Majesty the King of Prussia shall possess those countries in complete sovereignty and property, and shall unite them to his Monarchy. The districts and territories thus ceded shall be separated from the rest of the Kingdom of Saxony by a line, which henceforth shall form the frontier between the Prussian and Saxon territories, so that all that is comprised in the limit formed by this line, shall be restored to His Majesty the King of Saxony; but His Majesty renounces all those districts and territories that are situated beyond that line, and which belonged to him before the war.

The line shall begin from the frontiers of Bohemia, near Wiese, in the neighbourhood of Seidenberg, following the stream of the River Wittich, until its junction with the Neisse.

From the Neisse it shall pass to the Circle of Eigen, between Tauchritz, which shall belong to Prussia, and Bertschoff, which shall remain to Saxony; then it shall follow the northern frontier of the Circle of Eigen, to the angle between Paulsdorf and Ober-Sohland; thence it shall be continued to the limits that separate the Circle of Görlitz from that of Bautzen, in such a manner that Ober-Mittel and Nieder-Sohland, Olisch, and Radewitz remain in the possession of Saxony.

The great post road between Görlitz and Bautzen shall belong to Prussia, as far as the limits of the said Circles. Then the line shall follow the frontier of the Circle to Dubrauke; it shall then extend upon the heights to the right of the Löbauer-Wasser, so that this rivulet, with its two banks, and the places upon them, as far as Neudorf, shall remain, with this village, to Saxony.

The line shall then fall again upon the Spree, and the Schwarzwasser; Liska, Hermsdorf, Ketten and Solchdorf are assigned to Prussia.

From the Schwarz-Elster, near Solchdorf, a right line shall be drawn to the frontier of the Lordship of Königsbruck, near Gross-graebchen. This lordship remains to Saxony, and the line shall follow its northern boundary as far as the Bailiwick of Grossenhayn, in the neighbourhood of Ortrand. Ortrand, and the road from that place by Merzdorf, Stolzenhayn, Gröbeln, and Mühlberg (with the villages on that road, so that no part of it remain beyond the Prussian territory) shall be under the Government of Prussia. The frontier from Gröbeln shall be traced to the Elbe near Fichtenberg, and then shall follow the Bailiwick of Mühlberg. Fichtenberg shall be the property of Prussia.

From the Elbe to the frontier of the country of Merseburg, it shall be so regulated that the Bailiwicks of Torgau, Eilenburg, and Delitsch shall pass to Prussia, while those of Oschatz, Wurzen, and Leipsic, shall remain to Saxony. The line shall follow the frontier of these bailiwicks, dividing some inclosures and demi-inclosures. The road from Mühlberg to Eilenburg shall be wholly within the Prussian territory.

From Podelwitz (belonging to the Bailiwick of Leipsic, and remaining to Saxony) as far as Eytra, which also remains to her, the line shall divide the country of Merseburg in such a manner that Breitenfeld, Haenichen, Gross and Klein-Dolzig, Mark-Ranstädt and Knaut-Nauendorf, remain to Saxony; and Modelwitz, Skerditz, Klein-Liebenau, Alt-Ranstädt, Schkoehlen, and Zietschen, pass to Prussia.

From thence the line shall divide the Bailiwick of Pegau between the Floss-graben and the Weisse-Elster; the former, from the point where it separates itself above the town of Crossen (which forms part of the Bailiwick of Haynsburg) from the Weisse-Elster to the point where it joins the Saale, below the town of Merseburg, shall belong, in its whole course between those two towns, with both its banks, to the Prussian territory.

From thence, where the frontier touches upon that of the country of Zeitz, the line shall follow it as far as the boundary of the country of Altenburg, near Luckau.

The frontiers of the Circle of Neustadt, which wholly falls under the dominion of Prussia, remain untouched.

The inclosures of Voigtland, in the district of Reuss, that is to say

Gefäll, Blintendorf, Sparenberg, and Blankenberg, are comprised in the share of Prussia.

Duchy of Saxony.   Titles to be borne by the Kings of Prussia and Saxony.

ART. XVI. The provinces and districts of the Kingdom of Saxony, which are transferred to the dominion of His Majesty the King of Prussia, shall be distinguished by the name of the Duchy of Saxony, and His Majesty shall add to his Titles those of Duke of Saxony, Landgrave of Thuringia, Margrave of the two Lusatias, and Count of Henneberg.

His Majesty the King of Saxony shall continue to bear the title of Margrave of Upper Lusatia.

His Majesty shall also continue, with relation to, and in virtue of his right of eventual succession to the possessions of the Ernestine branch, to bear the title of Landgrave of Thuringia and Count of Henneberg.

Prussia and Saxony.   Guarantee by Great Britain, Austria, France, and Russia of Countries ceded by Saxony to Prussia.

ART. XVII. Austria, Russia, Great Britain, and France guarantee to His Majesty the King of Prussia, his descendants and successors, the possession of the countries marked out in Article XV, in full property and sovereignty.

Prussia and Saxony.   Renunciation by the Emperor of Austria of Rights of Sovereignty over Lusatia.

ART. XVIII. His Imperial and Royal Apostolic Majesty, wishing to give to the King of Prussia a fresh proof of his desire to remove every object of future discussion between their two Courts, renounces for himself and his successors his rights of Sovereignty over the Margraviates of Upper and Lower Lusatia, which belonged to him as King of Bohemia, as far as these rights concern the portion of these provinces placed under the dominion of His Majesty the King of Prussia by virtue of the Treaty with His Majesty the King of Saxony, concluded at Vienna on the 18th May, 1815.

As to the right of reversion of His Imperial and Royal Apostolic Majesty to the said portion of the Lusatias united to Prussia, it is transferred to the House of Brandenburg now reigning in Prussia, His Imperial and Royal Apostolic Majesty reserving to himself and his successors, the power of resuming that right in the event of the extinction of the said reigning House.

His Imperial and Royal Apostolic Majesty renounces also in favour of His Prussian Majesty, the districts of Bohemia inclosed within the part of Upper Lusatia ceded by the Treaty of the 18th May, 1815, to His

Prussian Majesty, which districts comprehend the places of Güntersdorf, Taubentraenke, Neukretschen, Nieder-Gerlachsheim, Winkel, and Ginkel, with their territories.

Prussia and Saxony.   Reciprocal Renunciation of Feudal Rights.

ART. XIX. His Majesty the King of Prussia and His Majesty the King of Saxony, wishing particularly to remove every object of future contest or dispute, renounce, each on his own part, and reciprocally in favour of one another, all feudal rights or pretensions which they might exercise or might have exercised beyond the frontiers fixed by the present Treaty.

Prussia and Saxony.   Reciprocal Freedom of Emigration.

ART. XX. His Majesty the King of Prussia promises to direct that proper care be taken relative to whatever may affect the property and interests of the respective subjects, upon the most liberal principles.

The present Article shall be observed, particularly with regard to the concerns of those individuals who possess property both under the Prussian and Saxon Governments, to the commerce of Leipsic, and to all other objects of the same nature; and in order that the individual liberty of the inhabitants, both of the ceded and other provinces, may not be infringed, they shall be allowed to emigrate from one territory to the other, without being exempted, however, from military service, and after fulfilling the formalities required by the laws. They may also remove their property without being subject to any fine or drawback (*Abzugsgeld*).

Prussia and Saxony.   Property of Religious Establishments.

ART. XXI. The communities, corporations, and religious establishments, and those for public instruction in the provinces ceded by His Majesty the King of Saxony to Prussia, or in the provinces and districts remaining to His Saxon Majesty, shall preserve their property, whatever changes they may undergo, as well as the rents becoming due to them, according to the act of their foundation, or which they have acquired by a legal title since that period under the Prussian and Saxon Governments; and neither party shall interfere in the administration and in the collection of the revenues, provided that they be conducted in a manner conformable to the laws, and that the charges be defrayed, to which all property or rents of the like nature are subjected, in the territory in which they occur.

Prussia and Saxony.   General Amnesty in Saxony.

ART. XXII. No individual domiciliated in the provinces which are under the dominion of His Majesty the King of Saxony, any more than an individual domiciliated in those which by the present Treaty pass under the dominion of the King of Prussia, shall be molested in his person, his property, rents, pensions, or revenues of any kind, in his rank or dignities, nor be prosecuted or called to account in any manner for any part which he, either in a civil or military capacity, may have taken in the events that have occurred since the commencement of the war, terminated by the Peace concluded at Paris on the 30th of May, 1814.

This Article equally extends to those who, not being domiciliated in either part of Saxony, may possess in it landed property, rents, pensions or revenues of any kind.

Designation of the Provinces of which Prussia resumes Possession.

ART. XXIII. His Majesty the King of Prussia having in consequence of the last war, reassumed the possession of the provinces and territories which had been ceded by the Peace of Tilsit [1807], it is acknowledged and declared by the present Article that His Majesty, his heirs and successors, shall possess anew, as formerly, in full property and Sovereignty, the following countries, that is to say;

Those of his ancient provinces of Poland specified in Article II;

The City of Dantzig and its territory, as the latter was determined by the Treaty of Tilsit [1807];

The Circle of Cottbus;

The Old March;

The part of the Circle of Magdeburg situated on the left bank of the Elbe, together with the Circle of the Saale;

The Principality of Halberstadt, with the Lordships of Derenburg, and of Hassenrode;

The Town and Territory of Quedlinburg (save and except the rights of Her Royal Highness the Princess Sophia Albertine of Sweden, Abbess of Quedlinburg, conformably to the arrangements made in 1803);

The Prussian part of the County of Mansfield;

The Prussian part of the County of Hohenstein;

The Eichsfeld;

The Town of Nordhausen with its territory;

The Town of Mühlhausen with its territory;

The Prussian part of the district of Trefourt with Dorla;

The Town and Territory of Erfurth, with the exception of Klein-Brembach and Berlstedt, inclosed in the Principality of Weimar, ceded to the Grand Duke of Saxe-Weimar by Article XXXIX;

The Bailiwick of Wandersleben, belonging to the County of Untergleichen;

The Principality of Paderborn, with the Prussian part of the Bailiwicks of Schwallenberg, Oldenburg, and Stoppelberg, and the jurisdictions (*Gerichte*) of Hagendorn and Odenhausen, situated in the territory of Lippe;

The County of Mark, with the part of Lipstadt belonging to it;

The County of Werden;

The County of Essen;

The part of the Duchy of Cleves on the right bank of the Rhine, with the town and fortress of Wesel; the part of the Duchy, situated on the left bank, specified in Article XXV;

The secularised Chapter of Elten;

The Principality of Munster, that is to say, the Prussian part of the former Bishopric of Munster, with the exception of that part which has been ceded to His Britannic Majesty, King of Hanover, in virtue of Article XXVII;

The secularised Provostship of Cappenburg;

The County of Tecklenburg;

The County of Lingen, with the exception of that part ceded to the kingdom of Hanover by Article XXVII;

The Principality of Minden;

The County of Ravensburg;

The secularised Chapter of Herford;

The Principality of Neufchatel, with the County of Valengin, such as their Frontiers are regulated by the Treaty of Paris, and by Article LXXVI of this General Treaty.

The same disposition extends to the rights of Sovereignty and *suzeraineté* over the County of Wernigerode, to that of high protection over the County of Hohen-Limbourg, and to all the other rights or pretensions whatsoever which His Prussian Majesty possessed and exercised, before the Peace of Tilsit [1807], and which he has not renounced by other Treaties, Acts, or Conventions.

Prussian Possessions on this side (en deça) *of the Rhine.*

ART. XXIV. His Majesty the King of Prussia shall unite to his Monarchy in Germany, on this side of the Rhine, to be possessed by him and his successors in full property and Sovereignty, the following countries:

The provinces of Saxony designated in Article XV, with the exception of the places and territories ceded, in virtue of Article XXXIX, to His Highness the Grand Duke of Saxe-Weimar;

The territories ceded to Prussia by His Britannic Majesty, King of Hanover, by Article XXIX;

Part of the Department of Fulda, and such of the territories comprehended therein as are specified in Article XL;

The Town and Territory of Wetzlar, according to Article XLII;

The Grand Duchy of Berg with the Lordships of Hardenberg, Broik, Styrum, Schöller and Odenthal, formerly belonging to the said Duchy under the Palatine Government;

The districts of the ancient Archbishopric of Cologne, lately belonging to the Grand Duchy of Berg;

The Duchy of Westphalia, as lately possessed by His Royal Highness the Grand Duke of Hesse;

The County of Dortmund;

The Principality of Corbey;

The Mediatised Districts specified in Article XLIII.

The ancient possessions of the House of Nassau-Dietz, having been ceded to Prussia by His Majesty the King of the Netherlands, and a part of these possessions having been exchanged for the districts belonging to their Serene Highnesses the Duke and Prince of Nassau, the King of Prussia shall possess them, in sovereignty and property, and unite them to his monarchy;

1. The Principality of Siegen with the Bailiwicks of Burbach and Neunkirchen, with the exception of a part containing 12,000 inhabitants, to belong to the Duke and Prince of Nassau;

Ehrenbreitstein, &c.

2. The Bailiwicks of Hohen-Solms, Greifenstein, Braunfels, Frensberg, Friedewald, Schönstein, Schönberg, Altenkirchen, Altenwied, Dierdorf, Neuerburg, Linz, Hammerstein, with Engers and Heddesdorf; the town and territory (*Banlieue Gemarkung*) of Neuwied; the parish of Ham, belonging to the Bailiwick of Hackenberg; the parish of Horhausen, constituting part of the Bailiwick of Hersbach, and the parts of the Bailiwicks of Vallendar and Ehrenbreitstein, on the right bank of the Rhine, designated in the Convention concluded between His Majesty the King of Prussia and their Serene Highnesses the Duke and Prince of Nassau, annexed to the present Treaty.

Prussian Possessions on the left bank of the Rhine.

ART. XXV. His Majesty the King of Prussia shall also possess in full property and sovereignty, the countries on the left bank of the Rhine, included in the frontier hereinafter designated:

This frontier shall commence on the Rhine at Bingen; it shall thence ascend the course of the Nahe to the junction of this river with the Glan, and along the Glan to the village of Medart, below Lauterecken; the towns of Kreutznach and Meisenheim, with their territories, to belong entirely to Prussia; but Lauterecken and its territory to remain beyond the Prussian frontier. From the Glan the frontier shall pass by Medart, Merzweiler, Langweiler, Nieder and Ober-Feckenbach, Ellenbach, Creunchenborn, Answeiler, Cronweiler, Nieder-brambach, Burbach, Boschweiler, Heubweiler, Hambach, and Rintzenberg, to the limits of the Canton of Hermeskeil; the above places shall be included within the Prussian frontiers, and shall, together with their territories, belong to Prussia.

From Rintzenberg to the Sarre the line of demarcation shall follow the cantonal limits, so that the Cantons of Hermeskeil and Conz (in which latter, however, are excepted the places on the left bank of the Sarre) shall remain wholly to Prussia, while the Cantons of Wadern, Merzig, and Sarreburg are to be beyond the Prussian frontier.

From the point where the limit of the Canton of Conz, below Gomlingen, traverses the Sarre, the line shall descend the Sarre till it falls into the Moselle; thence it shall re-ascend the Moselle to its junction with the Sarre, from the latter river to the mouth of the Our, and along the Our to the limits of the ancient Department of the Ourthe. The places traversed by these rivers shall not at all be divided, but shall belong, with their territories, to the Power in whose State the greater part of these places shall be situated; the Rivers themselves, in so far as they form the frontier, shall belong in common to the two Powers bordering on them.

In the old Department of the Ourthe, the five Cantons of Saint-Vith, Malmedy, Cronenburg, Schleiden, and Eupen, with the advanced point of the Canton of Aubel, to the south of Aix-la-Chapelle, shall belong to Prussia, and the frontier shall follow that of these cantons, so that a line, drawn from north to south, may cut the said point of the Canton of Aubel, and be prolonged as far as the point of contact of the three old Departments of the Ourthe, the Lower Meuse, and the Roer; leaving that point, the frontier shall follow the line which separates these two last departments till it reaches the river Worm, which falls into the Roer, and shall go along this river to the point where it again touches the limits of these two departments; when it shall pursue that limit to the south of Hillensberg, shall ascend from thence towards the north, and leaving Hillensberg to Prussia, and cutting the Canton of Sittard in two parts, nearly equal, so that Sittard and Susteren remain on the left, shall reach the old Dutch territory; then following the old frontier of that territory, to the point where it touched the old Austrian Principality of Guelders, on the side of Ruremonde, and directing itself towards the most eastern point of the Dutch territory, to the north of Swalmen, it shall continue to inclose this territory.

Then, setting out from the most eastern point, it joins that other part of the Dutch territory in which Venloo is situated, without including the latter town and its district; thence to the old Dutch frontier near Mook, situated below Genep, it shall follow the course of the Meuse, at such a distance from the right bank that all the places situated within a thousand Rhenish yards (*Rheinlandische Ruthen*) of this bank, shall, with their territories, belong to the kingdom of the Netherlands; it being well understood, however, in regard to the reciprocity of this principle, that no point of the bank of the Meuse shall constitute a portion of the Prussian territory, unless such point approach to within 800 Rhenish yards of it.

From the point where the line just described joins the old Dutch frontier, as far as the Rhine, this frontier shall remain essentially as it was in 1795, between Cleves and the United Provinces. It shall be examined by the Commission which shall be appointed without delay by the two Governments to proceed to the exact determination of the limits, both of the kingdom of the Netherlands, and the Grand Duchy of Luxemburg, designated in Articles LXVI and LXVIII, and this Commission shall regulate, with the aid of experienced persons, whatever concerns the hydro-technical constructions, and other analogous points, in the most equitable manner, and conformably to the mutual interests of the Prussian States and of those of the Netherlands. This same disposition extends to the regulation of the limits in the Districts of Kyfwaerd, Lobith, and all the territory to Kekerdom.

The places (*enclaves*) named Huissen, Malburg, Lymers, with the town of Sevenaer, and the Lordship of Weel, shall form a part of the kingdom of the Netherlands, and His Prussian Majesty renounces them in perpetuity for himself, his heirs and successors.

His Majesty the King of Prussia, in uniting to his States the provinces and districts designated in the present Article, enters into all the rights and takes upon himself all the charges and engagements stipulated with respect to the countries dismembered from France by the Treaty of Paris of the 30th May, 1814.

Grand Duchy of the Lower Rhine. Cologne.

The Prussian provinces upon the two banks of the Rhine, as far as above the town of Cologne, which shall also be comprised within this district, shall bear the name of Grand Duchy of the Lower Rhine, and His Majesty shall assume the title of it.

Kingdom of Hanover. Late Electorate of Brunswick-Luneburg.

ART. XXVI. His Majesty the King of the United Kingdom of Great Britain and Ireland, having substituted to his ancient title of Elector of the Holy Roman Empire, that of King of Hanover, and this title having been acknowledged by all the Powers of Europe, and by the Princes and

Free Towns of Germany, the countries which have till now composed
the Electorate of Brunswick-Luneburg, according as their limits have
been recognised and fixed for the future, by the following Articles, shall
henceforth form the Kingdom of Hanover.

Cessions made by Prussia to Hanover.

ART. XXVII. His Majesty the King of Prussia cedes to His Majesty
the King of the United Kingdom of Great Britain and Ireland, King of
Hanover, to be possessed by His Majesty and his successors, in full
property and Sovereignty:

1. The Principality of Hildesheim, which shall pass under the
Government of His Majesty, with all the rights and all the charges with
which the said Principality was transferred to the Prussian Government;

2. The Town and Territory of Goslar;

3. The Principality of East Frieseland (Ost Friese), including the
country called Harlingerland, under the conditions reciprocally stipulated in Article XXX for the navigation of the Ems and the commerce
of the port of Embden. The States of the Principality shall preserve
their rights and privileges;

4. The Lower County (*Nieder Grafschaft*) of Lingen, and the part of
the Principality of Prussian Munster which is situated between this
county and the part of Rheina-Wolbeck occupied by the Hanoverian
Government; but as it has been agreed that the kingdom of Hanover
shall obtain by this cession an accession of territory, comprising a
population of 22,000 souls, and as the Lower County of Lingen and the
part of the Principality of Munster here mentioned, might not come up
to this condition, His Majesty the King of Prussia engages to cause the
line of demarcation to be extended into the Principality of Munster, as
far as may be necessary to contain that population. The Commission,
which the Prussian and Hanoverian Governments shall name without
delay, to proceed to the exact regulation of the limits, shall be particularly
charged with the execution of this provision.

His Prussian Majesty renounces in perpetuity, for himself, his
descendants, and successors, the Provinces and Territories mentioned
in the present Article, as well as all the rights which have any relation
to them.

Hanover.   Renunciation by Prussia of the Chapter of St. Peter, in the Borough of Noerten.

ART. XXVIII. His Majesty the King of Prussia renounces in perpetuity, for himself, his descendants, and successors, all right and claim
whatever that His Majesty, in his quality of Sovereign of Eichsfeld,
might advance to the Chapter of St. Peter, in the borough of Noerten,
or to its dependencies, situated in the Hanoverian territory.

Cessions made by Hanover to Prussia.

ART. XXIX. His Majesty the King of the United Kingdom of Great Britain and Ireland, King of Hanover, cedes to His Majesty the King of Prussia, to be possessed by him and his successors, in full property and sovereignty:

1. That part of the Duchy of Lauenburg situated upon the right bank of the Elbe, with the villages of Luneburg, situated on the same bank. The part of the duchy upon the left bank remains to the kingdom of Hanover. The States of that part of the duchy which passes under the Prussian Government shall preserve their rights and privileges; especially those founded upon the provincial *Récès* of the 15th September, 1702, and confirmed by the King of Great Britain, now reigning, under date of 21st June, 1765;

2. The Bailiwick of Klötze;

3. The Bailiwick of Elbingerode;

4. The Villages of Rudigershagen and Gaenseteich;

5. The Bailiwick of Reckeberg.

His Britannic Majesty, King of Hanover, renounces for himself, his descendants and successors for ever, the Provinces and Districts specified in the present Article, and all the rights which have reference to them.

Navigation and Commerce between Hanover and Prussia, the Ems, and Port of Embden.

ART. XXX. His Majesty the King of Prussia, and His Britannic Majesty, King of Hanover, animated with the desire of entirely equalising the advantages of the commerce of the Ems and of the Port of Embden, and of rendering them common to their respective subjects, have agreed on this head to what follows:—

1. The Hanoverian Government engages to cause to be executed, at its expense, in the years 1815 and 1816, the works which a Commission, composed partly of artists, and to be immediately appointed by Prussia and Hanover, shall deem necessary to render navigable that part of the river Ems which extends from the Prussian frontier to its mouth, and to keep it, after the execution of such works, always in the same state in which those works shall have placed it for the benefit of navigation.

2. The Prussian subjects shall be allowed to import and export, by the port of Embden, all kinds of provisions, productions, and goods, whether natural or artificial, and to keep in the town of Embden, warehouses wherein to place the said goods for two years, dating from their arrival in the towns, without their being subject to any other inspection than that to which those of the Hanoverian subjects are liable.

3. The Prussian vessels and merchants of the same nation shall not pay for navigation, for exportation or importation of merchandise, or for

warehousing, any other tolls or duties than those charged upon the Hanoverian subjects. These tolls and duties shall be regulated by agreement between Prussia and Hanover, and no alteration shall be introduced into the tarif hereafter but by mutual consent. The privileges and liberties just specified extend equally to those Hanoverian subjects who navigate that part of the river Ems which remains to the King of Prussia.

4. Prussian subjects shall not be compellable to employ the merchants of Embden for the trade they carry on with that port; they shall be at liberty to dispose of their commodities either to the inhabitants of the town or to foreigners, without paying any other duties than those to which the Hanoverian subjects are subjected, and which cannot be raised but by mutual consent.

His Majesty the King of Prussia, on his part, engages to grant to Hanoverian subjects the free navigation of the canal of the Stecknitz, so as not to exact from them any other duties than those which shall be paid by the inhabitants of the Duchy of Lauenburg. His Prussian Majesty engages, besides, to insure these advantages to Hanoverian subjects, should he hereafter cede the Duchy of Lauenburg to another Sovereign.

Hanover and Prussia. Military Routes.

ART. XXXI. His Majesty the King of Prussia and His Majesty the King of the United Kingdom of Great Britain and Ireland, King of Hanover, mutually agree to three military roads through their respective dominions.

1st. One from Halberstadt, through the country of Hildesheim, to Minden.

2nd. A second from the Old March, through Gifhorn and Neustadt, to Minden.

3rd. A third from Osnabruck, through Ippenbüren and Rheina to Bentheim.

The two first in favour of Prussia, and the third in favour of Hanover.

The two Governments shall appoint, without delay, a Commission to prepare, by common consent, the necessary regulations for the establishment of the said roads.

Relations of the Duke de Looz-Corswaren and of the Count of Bentheim with the Kingdom of Hanover.

ART. XXXII. The Bailiwick of Meppen, belonging to the Duke of Aremberg, as well as the part of Rheina-Wolbeck, belonging to the Duke of Looz-Corswaren, which at this moment are provisionally occupied by the Hanoverian Government, shall be placed in such relations with the Kingdom of Hanover, as the Federative Constitution of Germany shall regulate for the mediatised territories.

The Prussian and Hanoverian Governments having nevertheless reserved to themselves to agree hereafter, if necessary, to the fixing of another line of frontier with regard to the county belonging to the Duke of Looz-Corswaren, the said Governments shall charge the Commission they may name for fixing the limits of the part of the County of Lingen ceded to Hanover, to deliberate thereupon, and to adjust definitively the frontiers of that part of the county belonging to the Duke of Looz-Corswaren, which, as aforesaid, is to be possessed by the Hanoverian Government.

The relations between the Hanoverian Government and the County of Bentheim shall remain as regulated by the Treaties of Mortgage existing between His Britannic Majesty and the Count of Bentheim; and when the rights derived from this Treaty shall have expired, the relations of the County of Bentheim towards the Kingdom of Hanover shall be such as the Federative Constitution of Germany shall regulate for the Mediatised territories.

Cession to be made by Hanover to Oldenburg.

ART. XXXIII. His Britannic Majesty, King of Hanover, in order to meet the wishes of His Prussian Majesty to procure a suitable arrondissement of territory for His Serene Highness the Duke of Oldenburg, promises to cede to him a district containing a population of 5,000 inhabitants.

Title of Grand Duke of Oldenburg.

ART. XXXIV. His Serene Highness the Duke of Holstein-Oldenburg shall assume the title of Grand Duke of Oldenburg.

Title of Grand Dukes of Mecklenburg-Schwerin and Strelitz.

ART. XXXV. Their Serene Highnesses the Dukes of Mecklenburg-Schwerin and Mecklenburg-Strelitz, shall assume the titles of Grand Dukes of Mecklenburg-Schwerin and Strelitz.

Title of Grand Duke of Saxe-Weimar.

ART. XXXVI. His Highness the Duke of Saxe-Weimar shall assume the title of Grand Duke of Saxe-Weimar.

Cessions to be made by Prussia to Saxe-Weimar.   Fulda.

ART. XXXVII. His Majesty the King of Prussia shall cede from the mass of his States, as they have been fixed and recognised by the present Treaty, to His Royal Highness the Grand Duke of Saxe-Weimar, districts containing a population of 50,000 inhabitants, contiguous to, or bordering upon, the Principality of Weimar.

His Prussian Majesty engages also to cede to His Royal Highness out of that part of the Principality of Fulda which has been given up to him in virtue of the same stipulations, districts containing a population of 27,000 inhabitants.

His Royal Highness the Grand Duke of Weimar shall possess the above districts in full property and Sovereignty, and shall unite them in perpetuity to his present States.

Prussia and Saxe-Weimar.   Ulterior Arrangements regarding these Cessions.

ART. XXXVIII. The districts and territories which are to be ceded to His Royal Highness the Grand Duke of Saxe-Weimar, in virtue of the preceding Article, shall be determined by a particular Convention; and His Majesty the King of Prussia engages to conclude this Convention, and to cause the above districts and territories to be given up to His Royal Highness, within two months from the date of the exchange of the ratifications of the Treaty concluded at Vienna, 1st June, 1815, between His Prussian Majesty and His Royal Highness the Grand Duke.

Prussia and Saxe-Weimar.   Territory to be given up immediately to the Grand Duke of Weimar.

ART. XXXIX. His Majesty the King of Prussia, however, cedes immediately, and promises to give up to His Royal Highness, in the space of a fortnight, reckoning from the signature of the above-mentioned Treaty, the following districts and territories; viz.,

The Lordship of Blankenhayn, with the reservation of the Bailiwick of Wandersleben, belonging to Unter-Gleichen, which is not to be comprised in this cession;

The Lower Lordship (Niedere-Herschaft) of Kranichfeld, the Commanderies of the Teutonic order of Zwaetzen, Lehesten, and Liebstädt, with their demesnial revenues, which, constituting a part of the Bailiwick of Eckartsberga, are inclosed in the territory of Saxe-Weimar, as well as all the other territories inclosed within the Principality of Weimar, and belonging to the said bailiwick; the Bailiwick of Tautenburg, with the exception of Droizen, Görschen, Wethalung, Wetterscheid, and Möllschütz, which shall remain to Prussia;

The Village of Remssla, as well as the Villages of Klein-Brembach and Berlstedt, inclosed within the Principality of Weimar, and belonging to the territory of Erfurth;

The property of the Villages of Bischoffsroda and Probsteizella, inclosed within the territory of Eisenach, the Sovereignty of which already belongs to His Royal Highness the Grand Duke.

The population of these different districts is understood to form part of that of 50,000 souls, secured to His Royal Highness the Grand Duke of Saxe-Weimar, by Article XXXVII, and shall be deducted from it.

Cession of a Portion of the former Department of Fulda to Prussia.

ART. XL. The Department of Fulda, together with the territories of the ancient Nobility (*l'Ancienne Noblesse immédiate de l'Empire*) comprised, at this moment, under the provisional administration of this department, viz.: Mansbach, Buchenau, Werda, Lengsfeld;—excepting, however, the following bailiwicks and territories, viz.; the Bailiwicks of Hammelburg, with Thulba and Saleck, Bruckenau with Motten, Saalmunster, with Urzel and Sonnerz; also the part of the Bailiwick of Biberstein, which contains the villages of Batten, Brand, Dietges, Findlos, Liebharts, Melperz, Ober-Bernhardt, Saifferts, and Thaiden, as well as the domain of Holzkirchen, inclosed in the Grand Duchy of Wurtzburg;—is ceded to His Majesty the King of Prussia, and he shall be put in possession of it within three weeks from and after the 1st June of this year.

His Prussian Majesty engages to take upon himself, in proportion to that part of the territory which he obtains by the present Article, his share of the obligations which all the new possessors of the heretofore Grand Duchy of Frankfort will have to fulfil, and to transfer such engagements to the Princes with whom His Majesty may hereafter make exchanges or cessions of these districts and territories of the Department of Fulda.

Arrangements relative to the Purchasers of Domains in the Principality of Fulda and the County of Hanau.

ART. XLI. The domains of the Principality of Fulda and of the County of Hanau having been sold to purchasers, who have not as yet made good all their instalments, a Commission shall be named by the Princes to whom the said domains are transferred, to regulate, in an uniform manner, whatever has any reference to this transaction, and to do justice to the claims of the purchasers of the said domains. This Commission shall pay particular attention to the Treaty concluded at Frankfort, on the 2nd December, 1813, between the Allied Powers and His Royal Highness the Elector of Hesse; and it is laid down as a principle, that in case the sale of these domains should not be considered as binding, the purchasers shall receive back the sums already discharged, and they shall not be obliged to quit before such restitution shall have had its full and entire effect.

Cession of Town and Territory of Wetzlar to King of Prussia.

ART. XLII. The Town and Territory of Wetzlar passes, in all property and Sovereignty, to His Majesty the King of Prussia.

Relations of the Mediatised Districts of the Old Circle of Westphalia with the Prussian Monarchy.

ART. XLIII. The following Mediatised districts, viz.; the possessions which the Princes of Salm-Salm, and Salm-Kyrburg, the Counts called the *Rhein- und Wildgrafen*, and the Duke of Croy, obtained by the principal *Récès* of the extraordinary Deputation of the Empire, of the 25th February, 1803, in the old Circle of Westphalia, as well as the Lordships of Anholt and Gehmen, the possessions of the Duke of Looz-Corswaren, which are in the same situation (in so far as they are not placed under the Hanoverian Government), the County of Steinfurt, belonging to the Count of Bentheim-Bentheim, the County of Recklingshausen, belonging to the Duke of Aremberg, the Lordships of Rheda, Gutersloh, and Gronau, belonging to the Count of Bentheim-Tecklenburg, the County of Rittberg, belonging to the Prince of Kaunitz, the Lordships of Neustadt and Gimborn, belonging to the Count of Walmoden, and the Lordship of Homburg, belonging to the Princes of Sayn-Wittgenstein-Berleburg, shall be placed in such relations with the Prussian Monarchy as the Federative Constitution of Germany shall regulate for the Mediatised territories.

The possessions of the ancient Nobility (*l'Ancienne Noblesse immédiate de l'Empire*) within the Prussian territory, and particularly the Lordship of Wildenberg, in the Grand Duchy of Berg, and the Barony of Schauen, in the Principality of Halberstadt, shall belong to the Prussian Monarchy.

Cession of the Grand Duchy of Wurtzburg, and of the Principality of Aschaffenburg to the King of Bavaria.

ART. XLIV. His Majesty the King of Bavaria shall possess, for himself, his heirs and successors, in full property and Sovereignty, the Grand Duchy of Wurtzburg, as it was held by His Imperial Highness the Archduke Ferdinand of Austria, and the Principality of Aschaffenburg, such as it constituted part of the Grand Duchy of Frankfort, under the denomination of Department of Aschaffenburg.

Maintenance of the Prince Primate.

ART. XLV. With respect to the rights and prerogatives, and the maintenance of the Prince Primate as an ancient ecclesiastical Prince, it is determined;

1st. That he shall be treated in a manner analogous to the Articles of the *Récès*, which, in 1803, regulated the situation of the secularised Princes, and to the practice observed with regard to them.

2ndly. He shall receive for this purpose, dating from the 1st of June, 1814, the sum of 100,000 florins, by payments of three months, in good specie, at the rate of 24 florins to the mark, as an annuity.

This annuity shall be paid by the Sovereigns under whose Governments the provinces or districts of the Grand Duchy of Frankfort pass, in proportion to the part which each of them shall possess.

3dly. The advances made by the Prince Primate, from his private purse, to the general chest of the Principality of Fulda, such as they have been liquidated and proved, shall be refunded to him, his heirs, or executors.

This expenditure shall be defrayed in proportions by the Sovereigns who shall possess the provinces and districts composing the Principality of Fulda.

4thly. The furniture and other objects which may be proved to belong to the private property of the Prince Primate, shall be restored to him.

5thly. The officers of the Grand Duchy of Frankfort, as well civil and ecclesiastical as military and diplomatic, shall be treated conformably to the principles of Article LIX of the *Récès* of the Empire, dated the 25th February, 1803, and from the 1st of June the pensions shall be proportionably paid by the Sovereigns who enter on the possession of the States which formed the said Grand Duchy since the 1st of June, 1814.

6thly. A Commission shall be established without delay, composed of members appointed by the said Sovereigns, to regulate whatever relates to the execution of the dispositions comprised in this Article.

7thly. It is understood, that in virtue of this arrangement, any claim that might be advanced against the Prince Primate, in his character of Grand Duke of Frankfort, shall be annulled, and that he shall not be molested on account of any reclamation of this nature.

The Free Town of Frankfort.

ART. XLVI. The City of Frankfort, with its territory, such as it was in 1803, is declared Free, and shall constitute a part of the Germanic League. Its institutions shall be founded upon the principle of a perfect equality of rights for the different sects of the Christian religion. This equality of rights shall extend to all civil and political rights, and shall be observed in all matters of government and administration. The disputes which may arise, whether in regard to the establishment of the Constitution, or in regard to its maintenance, shall be referred to the Germanic Diet, and can only be decided by the same.

Indemnities to the Grand Duke of Hesse.

ART. XLVII. His Royal Highness the Grand Duke of Hesse, in

exchange for the Duchy of Westphalia, ceded to His Majesty the King of Prussia, obtains a territory on the left bank of the Rhine, in the ancient Department of Mont-Tonnerre, comprising a population of 140,000 inhabitants. His Royal Highness shall possess this territory in full Sovereignty and property. He shall likewise obtain the property of that part of the Salt Mines of Kreutznach which is situated on the left bank of the Nahe, but the Sovereignty of them shall remain to Prussia.

Reinstatement of the Landgrave of Hesse-Homburg.

ART. XLVIII. The Landgrave of Hesse-Homburg is reinstated in his possessions, revenues, rights, and political relations, of which he was deprived in consequence of the Confederation of the Rhine.

Cession of Territory to Oldenburg, Saxe-Coburg, Mecklenburg-Strelitz, Hesse-Homburg, and the Count of Pappenheim.

ART. XLIX. In the ci-devant Department of the Sarre, on the Frontiers of the States of His Majesty the King of Prussia, there is reserved a district, containing a population of 69,000 souls, to be disposed of in the following manner:—The Duke of Saxe-Coburg and the Duke of Oldenburg shall obtain each a territory comprising 20,000 inhabitants. The Duke of Mecklenburg-Strelitz and the Landgrave of Hesse-Homburg, each a Territory comprising 10,000 inhabitants; and the Count of Pappenheim a Territory comprising 9,000 inhabitants.

The territory of the Count of Pappenheim shall be under the Sovereignty of His Prussian Majesty.

Future Arrangements relative to these Territories.

ART. L. The acquisitions assigned by the preceding Article to the Dukes of Saxe-Coburg, Oldenburg, Mecklenburg-Strelitz, and the Landgrave of Hesse-Homburg, not being contiguous to their respective States, their Majesties the Emperor of Austria, the Emperor of all the Russias, and the Kings of Great Britain and Prussia, promise to employ their good offices, at the close of the present war, or as soon as circumstances shall permit, in order to procure for the said Princes, either by exchanges or any other arrangements, the advantages that they are disposed to insure to them; and that the administration of the said districts may be rendered less complicated, it is agreed that they shall be provisionally under the Prussian administration for the benefit of the new proprietors.

Territory and Possessions on the Banks of the Rhine ceded to Austria.

ART. LI. All the territories and possessions, as well on the left bank of the Rhine, in the old Departments of the Sarre and Mont-Tonnerre, as in the former Departments of Fulda and Frankfort, or inclosed in the adjacent countries, placed at the disposal of the Allied Powers by the Treaty of Paris of 30th May, 1814, and not disposed of by other Articles of the present Treaty, shall pass in full Sovereignty and property, under the Government of His Majesty the Emperor of Austria.

Principality of Isenburg given to Austria.

ART. LII. The Principality of Isenburg is placed under the Sovereignty of His Imperial and Royal Apostolic Majesty, and shall belong to him, under such limitations as the Federative Constitution of Germany shall regulate for the Mediatised States.

Germanic Confederation.

ART. LIII. The Sovereign Princes and Free Towns of Germany, under which denomination, for the present purpose, are comprehended their Majesties the Emperor of Austria, the Kings of Prussia, of Denmark, and of the Netherlands; that is to say:—

The Emperor of Austria and the King of Prussia, for all their possessions which anciently belonged to the German Empire;

The King of Denmark, for the Duchy of Holstein;

And the King of the Netherlands, for the Grand Duchy of Luxemburg;

establish among themselves a perpetual Confederation, which shall be called " The Germanic Confederation."

Germanic Confederation. Object of the Confederation.

ART. LIV. The object of this Confederation is the maintenance of the external and internal safety of Germany, and of the Independence and Inviolability of the Confederated States.

Germanic Confederation. Equality of the Members.

ART. LV. The Members of the Confederation, as such, are equal with regard to their rights; and they all equally engage to maintain the Act which constitutes their union.

Germanic Confederation. Federative Diet.

ART. LVI. The affairs of the Confederation shall be confined to a Federative Diet, in which all the Members shall vote by their Plenipotentiaries, either individually or collectively, in the following manner, without prejudice to their rank:—

1. Austria	..	..	..	..	..	1 Vote.
2. Prussia	..	..	..	..	..	1 ,,
3. Bavaria	..	..	..	..	..	1 ,,

4. Saxony	..	..	1 Vote.
5. Hanover ..	..	..	1 ,,
6. Wurtemberg	..	..	1 ,,
7. Baden	..	..	1 ,,
8. Electoral Hesse [Hesse-Cassel] ..		..	1 ,,
9. Grand Duchy of Hesse [Hesse-Darmstadt] ..	..	..	1 ,,
10. Denmark, for Holstein ..	..	..	1 ,,
11. The Netherlands, for Luxemburg	..	1 ,,
12. Grand-Ducal and Ducal Houses of Saxony ..	..	..	1 ,,
13. Brunswick and Nassau ..	..	..	1 ,,
14. Mecklenburg-Schwerin and Strelitz	..	1 ,,
15. Holstein-Oldenburg, Anhalt and Schwartzburg ..	..	..	1 ,,
16. Hohenzollern, Liechtenstein, Reuss, Schaumburg-Lippe, Lippe and Waldeck	..	..	1 ,,
17. The Free Towns of Lubeck, Frankfort, Bremen, and Hamburgh	..	1 ,,

Total ..   .. 17 Votes.

Germanic Confederation. Presidency of Austria at Diet.

ART. LVII. Austria shall preside at the Federative Diet. Each State of the Confederation has the right of making propositions, and the presiding State shall bring them under deliberation within a definite time.

Germanic Confederation. Composition of the General Assembly.

ART. LVIII. Whenever fundamental laws are to be enacted, changes made in the fundamental laws of the Confederation, measures adopted relative to the Federative Act itself, and organic institutions or other arrangements made for the common interest, the Diet shall form itself into a General Assembly, and, in that case, the distribution of votes shall be as follows, calculated according to the respective extent of the individual States:—

Austria shall have	..	..	..	4 Votes.
Prussia	..	..	..	4 ,,
Saxony	..	..	..	4 ,,
Bavaria	..	..	..	4 ,,
Hanover	..	..	..	4 ,,
Wurtemberg ..	..	..	..	4 ,,

Baden..	3 Votes.
Electoral Hesse [Hesse-Cassel]	3 ,,
Grand Duchy of Hesse [Hesse-Darmstadt]	3 ,,
Holstein	3 ,,
Luxemburg	3 ,,
Brunswick	2 ,,
Mecklenburg-Schwerin	2 ,,
Nassau	2 ,,
Saxe-Weimar	1 Vote.
Saxe-Gotha	1 ,,
Saxe-Coburg..	1 ,,
Saxe-Meiningen	1 ,,
Saxe-Hildburghausen	1 ,,
Mecklenburg-Strelitz	1 ,,
Holstein-Oldenburg..	1 ,,
Anhalt-Dessau	1 ,,
Anhalt-Bernburg	1 ,,
Anhalt-Köthen	1 ,,
Schwartzburg-Sondershausen	1 ,,
Schwartzburg-Rudolstadt	1 ,,
Hohenzollern-Heckingen	1 ,,
Liechtenstein	1 ,,
Hohenzollern-Sigmaringen..	1 ,,
Waldeck	1 ,,
Reuss (Elder Branch) [Reuss Greitz] ..	1 ,,
Reuss (Younger Branch) [Reuss Schleitz]..	1 ,,
Schaumburg-Lippe	1 ,,
Lippe..	1 ,,
The Free Town of Lubeck..	1 ,,
,, ,, Frankfort	1 ,,
,, ,, Bremen	1 ,,
,, ,, Hamburgh	1 ,,

Total ..   .. 69 Votes.

The Diet in deliberating on the organic laws of the Confederation, shall consider whether any collective votes ought to be granted to the ancient Mediatised States of the Empire.

Germanic Confederation.   Arrangements relating to the Diet.

ART. LIX. The question, whether a subject is to be discussed by the General Assembly, conformably to the principles above established, shall be decided in the Ordinary Assembly by a majority of votes. The same Assembly shall prepare the drafts of resolutions which are to be proposed to the General Assembly, and shall furnish the latter with all the necessary information, either for adopting or rejecting them.

The plurality of votes shall regulate the decisions, both in the Ordinary and General Assemblies, with this difference, however, that in the Ordinary Assembly, an absolute majority shall be deemed sufficient, while, in the other, two-thirds of the votes shall be necessary to form the majority.

When the votes are even in the Ordinary Assembly, the President shall have the casting vote; but when the Assembly is to deliberate on the acceptance or change of any of the fundamental laws, upon organic institutions, upon individual rights, or upon affairs of religion, the plurality of votes shall not be deemed sufficient, either in the Ordinary or in the General Assembly.

The Diet is permanent: it may, however, when the subjects submitted to its deliberation are disposed of, adjourn for a fixed period, which shall not exceed four months.

All ulterior arrangements relative to the postponement or the dispatch of urgent business which may arise during the recess shall be reserved for the Diet, which will consider them when engaged in preparing the organic laws.

Germanic Confederation.   Order of Voting in Diet.

ART. LX. With respect to the order in which the members of the Confederation shall vote, it is agreed, that while the Diet shall be occupied in framing organic laws, there shall be no fixed regulation; and whatever may be the order observed on such an occasion, it shall neither prejudice any of the members, nor establish a precedent for the future. After framing the organic laws, the Diet will deliberate upon the manner of arranging this matter by a permanent regulation, for which purpose it will depart as little as possible from those which have been observed in the ancient Diet, and more particularly according to the *Récés* of the Deputation of the Empire in 1803. The order to be adopted shall in no way affect the rank and precedence of the members of the Confederation except in as far as they concern the Diet.

Germanic Confederation.   Diet to assemble at Frankfort.

ART. LXI. The Diet shall assemble at Frankfort on the Maine. Its first meeting is fixed for the 1st of September, 1815.

Germanic Confederation.   The Framing of Fundamental Laws.

ART. LXII. The first object to be considered by the Diet after its opening shall be the framing of the fundamental laws of the Confederation, and of its organic institutions, with respect to its exterior, military, and interior relations.

Germanic Confederation. Maintenance of Peace in Germany. Disputes
  to be settled through Mediation of the Diet, or by an Austregal Court.

ART. LXIII. The States of the Confederation engage to defend not
only the whole of Germany, but each individual State of the Union,
in case it should be attacked, and they mutually guarantee to each other
such of their possessions as are comprised in this Union.

When war shall be declared by the Confederation, no member can
open a separate negotiation with the enemy, nor make peace, nor
conclude an armistice, without the consent of the other members.

The Confederated States engage, in the same manner, not to make
war against each other, on any pretext, nor to pursue their differences
by force of arms, but to submit them to the Diet, which will attempt a
mediation by means of a Commission. If this should not succeed, and
a juridical sentence becomes necessary, recourse shall be had to a well
organized *Austregal* Court (*Austrägalinstanz*), to the decision of which
the contending parties are to submit without appeal.

Germanic Confederation. Particular Arrangements.

ART. LXIV. The Articles comprised under the title of *Particular
Arrangements*, in the Act of the Germanic Confederation, as annexed
to the present General Treaty, both in original and in a French translation, shall have the same force and validity as if they were textually
inserted herein.

Territories forming the Kingdom of the Netherlands. Recognition
  by Austria of Royal Dignity in House of Orange-Nassau.

ART. LXV. The ancient United Provinces of the Netherlands and the
late Belgic Provinces, both within the limits fixed by the following
Article, shall form,—together with the countries and territories designated in the same Article, under the Sovereignty of His Royal Highness
the Prince of Orange-Nassau, Sovereign Prince of the United Provinces,
—the Kingdom of the Netherlands, hereditary in the order of succession
already established by the Act of the Constitution of the said United
Provinces. The title and the prerogatives of the Royal dignity are
recognised by all the Powers in the House of Orange-Nassau.

Boundaries of the Kingdom of the Netherlands.

ART. LXVI. The line comprising the territories which compose the
Kingdom of the Netherlands is determined in the following manner:—

It leaves the sea, and extends along the frontiers of France on the
side of the Netherlands, as rectified and fixed by Article III of the Treaty
of Paris of the 30th May, 1814, to the Meuse; thence along the same
frontiers to the old limits of the Duchy of Luxemburg. From this point

it follows the direction of the limits between that Duchy and the ancient
Bishopric of Liège, till it meets (to the south of Deiffelt) the western
limits of that canton, and of that of Malmédy, to the point where the
latter reaches the limits between the old Departments of the Ourthe
and the Roer; it then follows these limits to where they touch those of
the former French Canton of Eupen, in the Duchy of Limburg, and
following the western limit of that canton, in a northerly direction,
leaving to the right a small part of the former French Canton of Aubel,
joins the point of contact of the three old Departments of the Ourthe,
the Lower Meuse, and the Roer; parting again from this point, this line
follows that which divides the two latter departments, until it reaches
the Worm (a river falling into the Roer), and goes along this river to the
point where it again reaches the limit of these two departments, pursues
this limit to the south of Hillensberg (the old Department of the Roer),
from whence it reascends to the north, and leaving Hillensberg to the
right and dividing the Canton of Sittard into two nearly equal parts, so
that Sittard and Susteren remain on the left, it reaches the old Dutch
territory, from whence, leaving this territory to the left, it goes on
following its eastern frontier to the point where it touches the old
Austrian Principality of Guelders, on the south side of Ruremonde, and
directing itself towards the most eastern point of the Dutch territory,
to the north of Swalmen, continues to inclose this territory.

Lastly, setting out from the most eastern point it joins that part of
the Dutch territory in which Venloo is situated; that town and its territory
being included within it. From thence to the old Dutch frontier near
Mook, situated above Genep, the line follows the course of the Meuse
at such a distance from the right bank that all the places within 1,000
Rhenish yards (*Rheinländische Ruthen*) from it shall belong, with their
territories, to the Kingdom of the Netherlands; it being understood,
however, as to the reciprocity of this principle, that the Prussian territory
shall not at any point touch the Meuse, or approach it within the
distance of 1,000 Rhenish yards.

Frontier between Cleves and United Provinces.

From the point where the line just described reaches the ancient
Dutch frontier, as far as the Rhine, this frontier shall remain essentially
the same as it was in 1795, between Cleves and the United Provinces.

Mixed Commission between Prussia and the Netherlands.

This line shall be examined by a Commission, which the Governments
of Prussia and the Netherlands shall name without delay, for the purpose
of proceeding to the exact determination of the limits, as well of the
Kingdom of the Netherlands, as of the Grand Duchy of Luxemburg,

specified in Article LXVIII; and this Commission, aided by professional persons, shall regulate everything concerning the hydrotechnical constructions, and other similar points, in the most equitable manner, and the most conformable to the mutual interests of the Prussian States, and of those of the Netherlands. This same arrangement refers to the fixing of limits in the Districts of Kyfwaerd, Lobith, and in the whole territory as far as Kekerdom.

Prussian Renunciation of Huissen, Malburg, Lymers, Sevenaer, and Weel.

The *enclaves* of Huissen, Malburg, Lymers, with the town of Sevenaer and Lordship of Weel, shall form a part of the Kingdom of the Netherlands; and His Prussian Majesty renounces them in perpetuity, for himself, his heirs and successors.

Grand Duchy of Luxemburg.   Sovereignty of the King of the Netherlands.   Succession.

ART. LXVII. That part of the old Duchy of Luxemburg which is comprised in the limits specified in the following Article, is likewise ceded to the Sovereign Prince of the United Provinces, now King of the Netherlands, to be possessed in perpetuity by him and his successors, in full property and Sovereignty. The Sovereign of the Netherlands shall add to his titles that of Grand Duke of Luxemburg, His Majesty reserving to himself the privilege of making such family arrangement between the Princes his sons, relative to the succession to the Grand Duchy, as he shall think conformable to the interests of his monarchy and to his paternal intentions.

Grand Duchy of Luxemburg a State of the Germanic Confederation.

The Grand Duchy of Luxemburg, serving as a compensation for the Principalities of Nassau-Dillenburg, Siegen, Hadamar and Dietz, shall form one of the States of the Germanic Confederation; and the Prince, King of the Netherlands, shall enter into the system of this Confederation as Grand Duke of Luxemburg, with all the prerogatives and privileges enjoyed by the other German Princes.

Luxemburg a Fortress of the Germanic Confederation.   Right of King of Netherlands to appoint Governor and Military Commandant.

The Town of Luxemburg, in a military point of view, shall be considered as a Fortress of the Confederation; the Grand Duke shall, however, retain the right of appointing the Governor and military Commandant of this Fortress, subject to the approbation of the executive power of the Confederation, and under such other conditions as it may be judged necessary to establish, in conformity with the future Constitution of the said Confederation.

Boundaries of the Grand Duchy of Luxemburg.

ART. LXVIII. The Grand Duchy of Luxemburg shall consist of all the territory situated between the Kingdom of the Netherlands, as it has been designated by Article LXVI, France, the Moselle, as far as the mouth of the Sure, the course of the Sure, as far as the junction of the Our, and the course of this last river, as far as the limits of the former French Canton of St. Vith, which shall not belong to the Grand Duchy of Luxemburg.

Luxemburg. Arrangements respecting the Duchy of Bouillon.
Disputes to be settled by Arbitration.

ART. LXIX. His Majesty the King of the Netherlands, Grand Duke of Luxemburg, shall possess in perpetuity, for himself and his successors, the full and entire Sovereignty of that part of the Duchy of Bouillon, which is not ceded to France by the Treaty of Paris; and which, therefore, shall be united to the Grand Duchy of Luxemburg.

Disputes having arisen with respect to the said Duchy of Bouillon, the competitor who shall legally establish his right, in the manner hereafter specified, shall possess, in full property, the said part of the Duchy, as it was enjoyed by the last Duke, under the Sovereignty of His Majesty the King of the Netherlands, Grand Duke of Luxemburg.

This decision shall be made by Arbitration, and be without appeal. For this purpose there shall be appointed a certain number of arbitrators, one by each of the two competitors, and others, to the number of three, by the Courts of Austria, Prussia, and Sardinia. They shall assemble at Aix-la-Chapelle, as soon as the state of the war and other circumstances may admit of it, and their determination shall be made known within six months from their first meeting.

In the interim, His Majesty the King of the Netherlands, Grand Duke of Luxemburg, shall hold in trust the property of the said part of the Duchy of Bouillon, in order that he may restore it, together with the revenues of the provisional administration, to the competitor in whose favour the arbitrators shall decide; and His said Majesty shall indemnify him for the loss of the revenues arising from the rights of Sovereignty, by means of some equitable arrangement. Should the restitution fall to Prince Charles of Rohan, this property, when in his possession, shall be regulated by the laws of the substitution which constitutes his title thereto.

Cession to Prussia of the German Possessions of the House of Nassau-Orange.

ART. LXX. His Majesty the King of the Netherlands renounces, in perpetuity for himself, his heirs, and successors, in favour of His Majesty the King of Prussia, the sovereign possessions which the House of Nassau-Orange held in Germany, namely, the Principalities of Dillenburg, Dietz, Siegen, and Hadamar, with the Lordships of Beilstein, such as those possessions have been definitively arranged between the two branches of the House of Nassau, by the Treaty concluded at the Hague on the 14th July, 1814.

Principality of Fulda.

His Majesty also renounces the Principality of Fulda, and the other districts and territories which were secured to him by Article XII of the Principal *Récès* of the Extraordinary Deputation of the Empire of the 25th of February, 1803.

Family Pact of the Princes of Nassau.   Succession.

ART. LXXI. The right and order of Succession, established between the two branches of the House of Nassau, by the Act of 1783, called *Nassauischer Erbverein*, is confirmed, and transferred from the four Principalities of Orange-Nassau to the Grand Duchy of Luxemburg.

Charges and Engagements relating to the Provinces detached from France.

ART. LXXII. His Majesty the King of the Netherlands, in uniting under his Sovereignty the Countries designated in Articles LXVI and LXVIII, enters into all the rights, and takes upon himself all the charges and all the stipulated engagements, relative to the Provinces and Districts detached from France by the Treaty of Peace concluded at Paris the 30th May, 1814.

Basis of the Union of the Belgic Provinces.

ART. LXXIII. His Majesty the King of the Netherlands, having recognised and sanctioned, under date of the 21st July, 1814, as the Basis of the Union of the Belgic Provinces with the United Provinces, the 8 Articles contained in the document annexed to the present Treaty, the said Articles shall have the same force and validity as if they were inserted, word for word, in the present Instrument.

Integrity of the 19 Cantons of Switzerland.

ART. LXXIV. The integrity of the Nineteen Cantons, as they existed in a political body, from the signature of the Convention of the 29th December, 1813, is recognised as the basis of the Helvetic system.

Switzerland. Union of Three new Cantons. The Valais, Geneva, and Neufchatel.

ART. LXXV. The Valais, the territory of Geneva, and the Principality of Neufchatel, are united to Switzerland, and shall form Three new Cantons.

La Vallée des Dappes.

La Vallée des Dappes, having formed part of the Canton of Vaud, is restored to it.

Switzerland. Union of Bishopric of Basle, and Town and Territory of Bienne, with Canton of Berne.

ART. LXXVI. The Bishopric of Basle, and the city and territory of Bienne, shall be united to the Helvetic Confederation, and shall form part of the Canton of Berne.

The following districts, however, are excepted from this last arrangement:

1. A District of about three square leagues in extent, including the Communes of Altschweiler, Schönbuch, Oberweiler, Terweiler, Ettingen, Fürstentein, Plotten, Pfeffingen, Aesch, Bruck, Reinach, Arlesheim; which District shall be united to the Canton of Basle.

An Enclave given to Neufchatel.

2. A small *Enclave*, situated near the Neufchatel village of Lignières, which is at present, with respect to civil jurisdiction, dependant upon the Canton of Neufchatel, and with respect to criminal jurisdiction upon that of the Bishopric of Basle, shall belong in full Sovereignty to the Principality of Neufchatel.

Switzerland. Rights of Inhabitants of Countries united with Canton of Berne.

ART. LXXVII. The inhabitants of the Bishopric of Basle, and those of Bienne, united to the Cantons of Berne and Basle, shall enjoy, in every respect, without any distinction of Religion (which shall be maintained in its present state) the same political and civil rights which are enjoyed, or may be enjoyed, by the inhabitants of the ancient parts of the said cantons; they shall, therefore, be equally competent to become candidates for the places of Representatives, and for all other appointments, according to the constitution of the cantons. Such municipal privileges as are compatible with the constitution and the general regulations of the Canton of Berne, shall be preserved to the town of Bienne, and to the villages that formed part of its jurisdiction.

The sale of the national domains shall be confirmed, and the feudal rights and tithes cannot be re-established.

The respective Acts of the union shall be framed, conformably to the principles above declared, by Commissions, composed of an equal number of deputies from each of the directing parties concerned. Those from the Bishopric of Basle shall be chosen by the canton from amongst the most eminent citizens of the country. The said Acts shall be guaranteed by the Swiss Confederation. All points upon which the parties cannot agree, shall be decided by a court of Arbitration, to be named by the Diet.

Switzerland. Restoration of the Lordship of Razüns to the Canton of Grisons.

ART. LXXVIII. The cession, made by Article III of the Treaty of Vienna, of the 14th October, 1809, of the Lordship of Razüns, inclosed in the country of the Grisons, having expired; and His Majesty the Emperor of Austria, being restored to all the rights attached to the said possession, confirms the disposition which he made of it, by a Declaration, dated the 20th March, 1815, in favour of the Canton of the Grisons.

Switzerland. Commercial and Military Communications between Town of Geneva and Canton of Vaud. Versoy Road.

ART. LXXIX. In order to ensure the commercial and military communications of the Town of Geneva with the Canton of Vaud, and the rest of Switzerland; and with a view to fulfil, in that respect, Article IV of the Treaty of Paris of the 30th May, 1814, His Most Christian Majesty consents so to place the line of custom-houses, that the road which leads from Geneva into Switzerland by Versoy, shall at all times be free, and that neither the post nor travellers, nor the transport of merchandize, shall be interrupted by any examination of the officers of the Customs, nor subjected to any duty.

Switzerland. Passage of Troops. Versoy Road.

It is equally understood that the passage of Swiss troops on this road shall not, in any manner, be obstructed.

In the additional regulations to be made on this subject, the execution of the Treaties relative to the free communication between the town of Geneva and the jurisdiction of Peney, shall be assured in the manner most convenient to the inhabitants of Geneva. His Most Christian Majesty also consents that the gendarmerie and militia of Geneva, after having communicated on the subject with the nearest military post of the French gendarmerie, shall pass on the high road of Meyrin, to and from the said jurisdiction and the town of Geneva.

Switzerland. Cession by the King of Sardinia to the Canton of Geneva. Savoy. Simplon Road.

ART. LXXX. His Majesty the King of Sardinia cedes that part of Savoy which is situated between the river Arve, the Rhone, the limits of that part of Savoy ceded to France, and the mountain of Salève, as far as Veiry inclusive, together with that part which lies between the high road called that of the Simplon, the Lake of Geneva, and the present territory of the canton of Geneva, from Venezas to the point where the river Hermance crosses the said road; and from thence, following the course of that river to where it enters the Lake of Geneva, to the east of the village of Hermance (the whole of the road of the Simplon continuing to be possessed by His Majesty the King of Sardinia) in order that these countries shall be united (*réunis*) to the canton of Geneva; with the reservation, however, of determining more precisely, by Commissioners respectively, their limits, particularly that part which relates to the demarcation above Veiry and on the mountain of Salève; His said Majesty renouncing for himself and his successors, in perpetuity, without exception or reservation, all rights of Sovereignty, or other rights which may belong to him in the places and territories comprised within this demarcation.

Switzerland. Simplon Road. Passage of Troops.

His Majesty the King of Sardinia also agrees, that the communication between the canton of Geneva and the Valais, by the road of the Simplon, shall be established, in the same manner as it has been agreed to by France, between Geneva and the canton of Vaud, by the route of Versoy. A free communication shall also be at all times granted for the Genevese troops, between the territory of Geneva and the jurisdiction of Jussy, and such facilities shall be allowed as may be necessary for proceeding by the lake to the road of the Simplon.

Switzerland. Exemption from Transit Dues.

On the other hand, an exemption from all duties of transit shall be granted for all merchandise and goods which, coming from the States of His Majesty the King of Sardinia and the Free Port of Genoa, shall traverse the road called the Simplon in its whole extent, through the Valais and the State of Geneva. This exemption shall, however, be confined to the transit, and shall extend neither to the tolls established for the maintenance of the road, nor to duties levied on merchandise or goods intended to be sold or consumed in the interior. The same reservation shall apply to the communication granted to the Swiss between the Valais and the canton of Geneva; and the different Governments shall for this purpose take such measures as, by common agreement, they shall judge necessary, either for taxation or for preventing contraband trade in their territories, respectively.

Switzerland. Compensations by Cantons of Argovia, Vaud, Tessin, and St. Gall, to Cantons of Schweitz, Unterwald, Uri, Glaris, Zug, and Appenzell.

ART. LXXXI. With a view to the establishing of reciprocal compensations, the Cantons of Argovia, Vaud, Tessin, and St. Gall, shall furnish to the ancient Cantons of Schweitz, Unterwald, Uri, Glaris, Zug and Appenzell (*Rhode Intérieure*) a sum of money to be applied to purposes of public instruction, and to the expenses of general administration, but principally to the former object, in the said cantons.

The quota, manner of payment, and division of this pecuniary compensation, are fixed as follows:—

The Cantons of Argovia, Vaud, and St. Gall shall furnish to the Cantons of Schweitz, Unterwald, Uri, Zug, Glaris, and Appenzell (*Rhode Intérieure*), a fund of 500,000 Swiss livres.

Each of the former cantons shall pay the interest of its quota, at the rate of 5 per cent. per annum, or have the option of discharging the principal, either in money or funded property.

The division, either of the payment or receipt of these funds, shall be made according to the scale of contributions laid down for providing the federal expenses.

The Canton of Tessin shall pay every year to the Canton of Uri, a moiety of the produce of the tolls in the Levantine Valley.

Switzerland. Disposal of Funds placed in England by Cantons of Zurich and Berne.

ART. LXXXII. To put an end to the discussions which have arisen, with respect to the funds placed in England by the Cantons of Zurich and Berne, it is determined:

1. That the Cantons of Berne and Zurich shall preserve the property of the funded capital as it existed in 1803, at the period of the dissolution of the Helvetic Government, and shall receive the interest thereof, from the 1st January, 1815;

2. That the accumulated interest due since the year 1798, up to the year 1814, inclusive, shall be applied to the payment of the remaining capital of the national debt, known under the denomination of the Helvetic debt;

3. That the surplus of the Helvetic debt shall remain at the charge of the other cantons, those of Berne and Zurich being exonerated by the above arrangement. The quota of each of the cantons which remain charged with this surplus, shall be calculated and paid according to

the proportion fixed for the contributions destined to defray federal expenses. The countries incorporated with Switzerland since 1813 shall not be assessed on account of the old Helvetic debt.

If it shall happen that an overplus remains after discharging the above debt, that overplus shall be divided between the Cantons of Berne and Zurich, in the proportion of their respective capitals.

The same regulations shall be observed with regard to those other debts, the documents concerning which are deposited in the custody of the President of the Diet.

Switzerland.   Indemnity to Proprietors of "Lauds."

ART. LXXXIII. To conciliate disputes respecting *Lauds* abolished without indemnification, an indemnity shall be given to persons who are owners of such *Lauds;* and for the purpose of avoiding all further differences on this subject between the Cantons of Berne and Vaud, the latter shall pay to the Government of Berne the sum of 300,000 Swiss livres, which shall be shared between the Bernese claimants, proprietors of *Lauds.* The payments shall be made at the rate of a fifth part each year, commencing from the 1st January, 1816.

Switzerland.   Confirmation of the Declaration of 20th March, 1815.

ART. LXXXIV. The Declaration of the 20th March, addressed by the Allied Powers who signed the Treaty of Paris, to the Diet of the Swiss Confederation, and accepted by the Diet through the Act of Adhesion of the 27th May, is confirmed in the whole of its tenor; and the principles established, as also the arrangements agreed upon, in the said Declaration, shall be invariably maintained.

Frontiers of the States of the King of Sardinia.

ART. LXXXV. The frontiers of the States of His Majesty the King of Sardinia shall be:—

On the side of France, such as they were on the 1st of January, 1792, with the exception of the changes effected by the Treaty of Paris of the 30th May, 1814;

On the side of the Helvetic Confederation, such as they existed on the 1st of January, 1792, with the exception of the change produced by the cession in favour of the Canton of Geneva, as specified by Article LXXX of the present Act;

On the side of the States of His Majesty the Emperor of Austria, such as they existed on the 1st of January, 1792; and the Convention concluded between their Majesties the Empress Maria Theresa and the King of Sardinia, on the 4th October, 1751, shall be reciprocally confirmed in all its stipulations;

On the side of the States of Parma and Placentia, the frontier as far as it concerns the ancient States of the King of Sardinia, shall continue to be the same as they were on the 1st of January, 1792.

The borders of the former States of Genoa, and of the countries called Imperial Fiefs, united to the States of His Majesty the King of Sardinia, according to the following Articles, shall be the same as those which, on the 1st of January, 1792, separated those countries from the States of Parma and Placentia, and from those of Tuscany and Massa.

Island of Capraja.

The island of Capraja, having belonged to the ancient republic of Genoa, is included in the cession of the States of Genoa, to His Majesty the King of Sardinia.

Union of the States of Genoa with the States of the King of Sardinia.

Art. LXXXVI. The States which constituted the former republic of Genoa, are united in perpetuity to those of His Majesty the King of Sardinia, to be, like the latter, possessed by him in full Sovereignty and hereditary property; and to descend, in the male line, in the order of primogeniture, to the two branches of his house, viz.: the royal branch, and the branch of Savoy-Carignan.

Title of King of Sardinia; Duke of Genoa.

Art. LXXXVII. The King of Sardinia shall add to his present titles, that of Duke of Genoa.

Sardinia.   Rights of Privileges of the Genoese.

Art. LXXXVIII. The Genoese shall enjoy all the rights and prileges, specified in this Act, intituled "Conditions which are to serve as the basis of the Union of the Genoese States to those of His Sardinian Majesty," and the said Act, such as it is annexed to this General Treaty, and shall be considered as an integral part thereof, and shall have the same force and validity as if it were textually inserted in the present Article.

Sardinia.   Union of the " Imperial Fiefs " of late Ligurian Republic.

Art. LXXXIX. The countries called Imperial Fiefs, formerly united to the ancient Ligurian Republic, are definitely united to the States of His Majesty the King of Sardinia, in the same manner as the rest of the Genoese States; and the inhabitants of these countries shall enjoy the same rights and privileges as those of the States of Genoa, specified in the preceding Article.

Sardinia.   Right of Fortifying.

ART. XC. The right that the Powers who signed the Treaty of Paris of the 30th May, 1814, reserved to themselves by Article III of that Treaty, of fortifying such points of their States as they might judge proper for their safety, is equally reserved, without restriction, to His Majesty the King of Sardinia.

Savoy.   Cession by the King of Sardinia to the Canton of Geneva.

ART. XCI. His Majesty the King of Sardinia cedes to the Canton of Geneva the districts of Savoy, designated in Article LXXX above recited, according to the conditions specified in the Act, intituled " Cession made by His Majesty the King of Sardinia to the Canton of Geneva." This Act shall be considered as an integral part of this General Treaty, to which it is annexed, and shall have the same force and validity as if it were textually inserted in the present Article.

Switzerland and Sardinia.   Neutrality of Chablais, Faucigny, and part of Savoy.

ART. XCII. The Provinces of Chablais and Faucigny, and the whole of the territory of Savoy to the north of Ugine, belonging to His Majesty the King of Sardinia, shall form a part of the Neutrality of Switzerland, as it is recognised and guaranteed by the Powers.

Passage of Troops.

Whenever, therefore, the neighbouring Powers to Switzerland are in a state of open or impending hostility, the troops of His Majesty the King of Sardinia which may be in those provinces, shall retire, and may for that purpose pass through the Valais, if necessary. No other armed troops of any other Power shall have the privilege of passing through or remaining in the said territories and provinces, excepting those which the Swiss Confederation shall think proper to place there; it being well understood that this state of things shall not in any manner interrupt the administration of these countries, in which the civil agents of His Majesty the King of Sardinia may likewise employ the municipal guard, for the preservation of good order.

Description of the Territories, &c., of which the Emperor of Austria takes possession on the side of Italy.   Istria, Dalmatia, Mouths of the Cattaro, Venice, Tyrol, Vorarlberg, &c.

ART. XCIII. In pursuance of the Renunciations agreed upon by the Treaty of Paris of the 30th May, 1814, the Powers who sign the present Treaty, recognise His Majesty the Emperor of Austria, his heirs and successors, as legitimate Sovereign of the Provinces and Territories which had been ceded, either wholly or in part, by the Treaties of

Campo-Formio of 1797, of Lunéville of 1801, of Presburg of 1805, by the additional Convention of Fontainebleau of 1807, and by the Treaty of Vienna of 1809; the possession of which provinces and territories His Imperial and Royal Apostolic Majesty obtained in consequence of the last war; such as, Istria, Austrian as well as heretofore Venetian, Dalmatia, the ancient Venetian Isles of the Adriatic, the Mouths of the Cattaro, the City of Venice, with its waters, as well as all the other provinces and districts of the formerly Venetian States of the Terra Firma upon the left bank of the Adige, the Duchies of Milan and Mantua, the Principalities of Brixen and Trente, the County of Tyrol, the Vorarlberg, the Austrian Frioul, the ancient Venetian Frioul, the territory of Montefalcone, the Government and Town of Trieste, Carniola, Upper Carinthia, Croatia on the right of the Saye, Fiume and the Hungarian *Littorale*, and the District of Castua.

Territories united to the Austrian Monarchy. The Valteline, Bormio, Chiavenna, Ragusa, &c.

ART. XCIV. His Imperial and Royal Apostolic Majesty shall unite to his monarchy, to be possessed by him and his successors in full property and Sovereignty:—

1. Besides the portions of the Terra Firma in the Venetian States mentioned in the preceding Article, the other parts of those States, as well as all other territories situated between the Tessino, the Po, and the Adriatic Sea.

2. The Vallies of the Valteline, of Bormio, and of Chiavenna.

3. The teritories which formerly composed the Republic of Ragusa.

Austrian Frontiers in Italy.

ART. XCV. In consequence of the stipulations agreed upon in the preceding Articles, the frontiers of the States of His Imperial and Apostolic Majesty, in Italy, shall be:—

1. On the side of the States of His Majesty the King of Sardinia, such as they were on the 1st of January, 1792;

2. On the side of the States of Parma, Placentia, and Guastalla, the course of the Po, the line of demarcation following the *Thalweg* of the River;

3. On the side of the States of Modena, such as they were on 1st of January, 1792;

4. On the side of the Papal States, the course of the Po, as far as the mouth of the Goro;

5. On the side of Switzerland, the ancient frontier of Lombardy, and that which separates the Vallies of the Valteline, of Bormio, and Chiavenna, from the Cantons of the Grisons and the Tessino.

Islands in the Po.

In those places where the *Thalweg* of the Po forms the frontier, it is agreed, that the changes which the course of the river may undergo shall not, in future, in any way affect the property of the Islands therein contained.

Navigation of the Po.

ART. XCVI. The general principles, adopted by the Congress at Vienna, for the Navigation of Rivers, shall be applicable to that of the Po.

Commissioners shall be named by the States bordering on rivers, within three months at latest after the termination of the Congress, to regulate all that concerns the execution of the present Article.

Arrangements respecting the " Mont-Napoleon " at Milan.

ART. XCVII. As it is indispensable to preserve, to the establishment known by the name of the Mont-Napoleon at Milan, the means of fulfilling its engagements towards its creditors; it is agreed, that the landed and other immovable property of this establishment, in countries which formed part of the ancient Kingdom of Italy, and have since passed under the government of different Princes of Italy, as well as the capital belonging to the said establishment placed out at interest in these different countries, shall be appropriated to the same object.

The unfunded and unliquidated debts of the Mont-Napoleon, such as those arising from the arrears of its charges, or from any other increase of the outgoings of this establishment, shall be divided between the territories which composed the late Kingdom of Italy; and this division shall be regulated according to the joint bases of their population and revenue.

The Sovereigns of the said countries shall appoint Commissioners, within the space of three months, dating from the termination of the Congress, to arrange with Austrian Commissioners whatever relates to this object. This Commission shall assemble at Milan.

Duchies of Modena, Reggio, and Mirandola; Duchy of Massa; Principality of Carrara, and Imperial Fiefs in La Lunigiana.

ART. XCVIII. His Royal Highness the Archduke Francis d'Este, his heirs and successors, shall possess, in full Sovereignty, the Duchies of Modena, Reggio, and Mirandola, such as they existed at the signature of the Treaty at Campo Formio (1797).

The Archduchess Maria Beatrice d'Este, her heirs and successors, shall possess, in full Sovereignty and property, the Duchy of Massa and the Principality of Carrara, as well as the Imperial Fiefs in La Lunigiana.

The latter may be applied to the purpose of exchanges, or other arrangements made by common consent, and according to mutual convenience, with His Imperial Highness the Grand Duke of Tuscany.

The rights of Succession and Reversion, established in the branches of the Archducal Houses of Austria, relative to the Duchies of Modena, Reggio, and Mirandola, and the Principalities of Massa and Carrara, are preserved.

Duchies of Parma, Placentia, and Guastalla.

ART. XCIX. Her Majesty the Empress Maria Louisa shall possess, in full property and Sovereignty, the Duchies of Parma, Placentia, and Guastalla, with the exception of the districts lying within the States of His Imperial and Royal Apostolic Majesty on the left bank of the Po.

The Reversion of these countries shall be regulated by common consent, with the Courts of Austria, Russia, France, Spain, England and Prussia; due regard being had to the rights of Reversion of the House of Austria, and of His Majesty the King of Sardinia, to the said countries.

Possessions of the Grand Duke of Tuscany.   The Presidii, Elba, Piombino, Imperial Fiefs, &c.

ART. C. His Imperial Highness the Archduke Ferdinand of Austria is re-established, himself, his heirs and successors, in all the rights of Sovereignty and property, in the Grand Duchy of Tuscany and its dependencies, which he possessed previous to the Treaty of Luneville (1801).

The stipulations of the second Article of the Treaty of Vienna, of the 3rd October, 1735, between the Emperor Charles VI and the King of France, to which the other Powers acceded, are fully renewed in favour of His Imperial Highness and his descendants, as well as the guarantees resulting from those stipulations.

There shall be likewise united to the said Grand Duchy, to be possessed in full property and Sovereignty by the Grand Duke Ferdinand, his heirs, and descendants:—

1. The State of the Presidii.

2. That part of the Island of Elba, and its appurtenances, which were under the *Suzeraineté* of His Majesty the King of the Two Sicilies before the year 1801.

3. The *Suzeraineté* and Sovereignty of the Principality of Piombino and its dependencies.

Prince Ludovisi Buoncompagni shall retain, for himself and his legitimate successors, all the property which his family possessed in the Principality of Piombino, and in the Island of Elba and its dependencies, previously to the occupation of those countries by the French troops in 1799, together with the mines, foundries, and salt-mines.

The Prince Ludovisi shall likewise preserve his right of Fishery, and enjoy an entire exemption from duties, as well for the exportation of the produce of his Mines, foundries, salt mines, and domains, as for the importation of Wood and other articles necessary for working the mines: he shall also be indemnified by His Imperial Highness the Grand Duke of Tuscany, for all the revenues the family of the latter derived from the crown duties before the year 1801. In case any difficulties should arise in the valuation of this indemnity, the parties concerned shall refer the decision to the Courts of Vienna and Sardinia.

4. The late Imperial Fiefs of Vernio, Montanto, and Monte Santa Maria, lying within the Tuscan States.

Duchy of Lucca.

ART. CI. The Principality of Lucca shall be possessed in full Sovereignty by Her Majesty the Infanta Maria Louisa, and her descendants, in the direct male line.

The Principality is erected into a Duchy, and shall have a form of government founded upon the principles of that which it received in 1805.

An Annuity of 500,000 francs shall be added to the revenue of the Principality of Lucca, which His Majesty the Emperor of Austria, and His Imperial Highness the Grand Duke of Tuscany, engage to pay regularly, as long as circumstances do not admit of procuring another establishment for Her Majesty the Infanta Maria Louisa, her son, and his descendants. This annuity shall be specially mortgaged upon the Lordships in Bohemia, known by the name of Bavaro Palatines; which, in case of the Duchy of Lucca reverting to the Grand Duke of Tuscany, shall be freed from this charge, and shall again form a part of the private domain of His Imperial and Royal Apostolic Majesty.

Reversion of the Duchy of Lucca. Fivizano, &c.

ART. CII. The Duchy of Lucca shall revert to the Grand Duke of Tuscany; either in case of its becoming vacant by the death of Her Majesty the Infanta Maria Louisa, or of her son Don Carlos, and of their direct male descendants; or in case the Infanta Maria Louisa or her direct heirs should obtain any other establishment, or succeed to another branch of their dynasty.

The Grand Duke of Tuscany, however, engages, should the said Reversion fall to him, to cede to the Duke of Modena, as soon as he shall have entered into possession of the Principality of Lucca, the following territories:—

1. The Tuscan districts of Fivizano, Pietra Santa, and Barga.
2. The Lucca districts of Castiglione and Gallicano, lying within the

States of Modena, as well as those of Minucciano and Monte-Ignose, contiguous to the country of Massa.

Restoration of the Marches, Benevento, and Ponte-Corvo, to the Holy See.

ART. CIII. The Marches, with Camerino, and their dependencies, as well as the Duchy of Benevento and the Principality of Ponte-Corvo, are restored to the Holy See.

Restoration of the Legations of Ravenna, Bologna, and Ferrara, to the Holy See.

The Holy See shall resume possession of the Legations of Ravenna, Bologna, and Ferrara, with the exception of that part of Ferrara which is situate on the left bank of the Po.

Austrian Right to Garrison Ferrara and Commachio.

His Imperial and Royal Apostolic Majesty and his successors shall have the right of placing Garrisons at Ferrara and Commachio.

Rights of Inhabitants returning under Government of Holy See.

The inhabitants of the countries who return under the Government of the Holy See, in consequence of the stipulations of Congress, shall enjoy the benefit of Article XVI of the Treaty of Paris of the 30th May, 1814.

Acquisitions of Individuals. Public Debt. Pensions.

All acquisitions made by individuals, in virtue of a title acknowledged as legal by the existing laws, are to be considered as good, and the arrangements necessary for the guarantee of the public debt and the payment of pensions, shall be settled by a particular Convention between the Courts of Rome and Vienna.

Restoration of King Ferdinand IV to Naples as King of the Two Sicilies.

ART. CIV. His Majesty King Ferdinand IV, his heirs, and successors, is restored to the throne of Naples, and His Majesty is acknowledged by the Powers as King of the Two Sicilies.

Affairs of Portugal. Restitution of the Town of Olivença.

ART. CV. The Powers, recognising the justice of the claims of His Royal Highness the Prince Regent of Portugal and the Brazils, upon the Town of Olivença, and the other territories ceded to Spain by the Treaty of Badajos of 1801, and viewing the restitution of the same as a measure necessary to insure that perfect and constant harmony between the Two Kingdoms of the Peninsula, the preservation of which in all parts of Europe, has been the constant object of their arrangements, formally engage to use their utmost endeavours, by amicable means, to procure the retrocession of the said territories in favour of Portugal. And the Powers declare, as far as depends upon them, that this arrangement shall take place as soon as possible.

Relations between France and Portugal.   French Guiana.

ART. CVI. In order to remove the difficulties which opposed the Ratification on the part of His Royal Highness the Prince Regent of the Kingdoms of Portugal and the Brazils, of the Treaty signed on the 30th of May, 1814, between Portugal and France; it is determined that the stipulations contained in Article X of that Treaty, and all those which relate to it, shall be of no effect, and that with the consent of all the Powers the provisions contained in the following Article shall be substituted for them, and which shall alone be considered as valid: with this exception, all the other clauses of the above Treaty of Paris shall be maintained, and regarded as mutually binding on the Two Courts.

France and Portugal.   Restitution of French Guiana.

ART. CVII. His Royal Highness the Prince Regent of the Kingdoms of Portugal and the Brazils, wishing to give an unequivocal proof of his high consideration for His Most Christian Majesty, engages to restore French Guiana to His said Majesty, as far as the river Oyapock, the mouth of which is situated between the fourth and fifth degree of north latitude, and which has always been considered by Portugal as the Limit appointed by the Treaty of Utrecht.

The period for giving up this Colony shall be determined, as soon as circumstances shall permit, by a Particular Convention between the two Courts; and they shall enter into an amicable arrangement, as soon as possible, with regard to the definitive demarcation of the limits of Portuguese and French Guiana, conformably to the precise meaning of Article VIII of the Treaty of Utrecht.

Navigation of Rivers traversing different States.

ART. CVIII. The Powers whose States are separated or crossed by the same navigable River engage to regulate, by common consent, all that regards its navigation. For this purpose they will name Commissioners, who shall assemble, at latest, within 6 months after the termination of the Congress, and who shall adopt, as the bases of their proceedings, the Principles established by the following Articles.

Rivers: Freedom of Navigation.

ART. CIX. The navigation of the Rivers, along their whole course, referred to in the preceding Article, from the point where each of them becomes navigable, to its mouth, shall be entirely free, and shall not, in respect to Commerce, be prohibited to any one; it being understood that the Regulations established with regard to the Police of this navigation shall be respected, as they will be framed alike for all, and as favourable as possible to the Commerce of all nations.

Rivers: Uniformity of System for Collection of Dues.

ART. CX. The system that shall be established both for the collection of the Duties and for the maintenance of the Police, shall be, as nearly as possible, the same along the whole course of the River; and shall also extend, unless particular circumstances prevent it, to those of its Branches and Junctions, which, in their navigable course, separate or traverse different States.

Rivers: Regulation of Tariff.

ART. CXI. The Duties on navigation shall be regulated in an uniform and settled manner, and with as little reference as possible to the different quality of the merchandize, in order that a minute examination of the cargo may be rendered unnecessary, except with a view to prevent fraud and evasion. The amount of the Duties, which shall in no case exceed those now paid, shall be determined by local circumstances, which scarcely allow of a general rule in this respect. The Tariff shall, however, be prepared in such a manner as to encourage commerce by facilitating navigation; for which purpose the Duties established upon the Rhine, and now in force on that River, may serve as an approximating rule for its construction.

The Tariff once settled, no increase shall take place therein, except by the common consent of the States bordering on the Rivers; nor shall the navigation be burdened with any other Duties than those fixed in the Regulation.

Rivers: Offices for Collection of Dues.

ART. CXII. The Offices for the collection of Duties, the number of which shall be reduced as much as possible, shall be determined upon in the above Regulation, and no change shall afterwards be made, but by common consent, unless any of the States bordering on the Rivers should wish to diminish the number of those which exclusively belong to the same.

Rivers: Towing Paths.

ART. CXIII. Each State bordering on the Rivers is to be at the expense of keeping in good repair the Towing Paths which pass through its territory, and of maintaining the necessary works through the same extent in the channels of the river, in order that no obstacle may be experienced to the navigation.

Rivers: Duties of Riverain States.

The intended Regulation shall determine the manner in which the States bordering on the Rivers are to participate in these latter works, where the opposite banks belong to different Governments.

Rivers: Port and Harbour Duties.

ART. CXIV. There shall nowhere be established Store-house, Port, or Forced Harbour Duties (*Droits d'étape, d'échelle et de relâche forcée*). Those already existing shall be preserved for such time only, as the States bordering on Rivers (without regard to the local interest of the place or the country where they are established) shall find them necessary or useful to navigation and commerce in general.

Rivers: Custom-Houses.

ART. CXV. The Custom-Houses belonging to the States bordering on Rivers shall not interfere in the duties of navigation. Regulations shall be established to prevent officers of the Customs, in the exercise of their functions, throwing obstacles in the way of the navigation; but care shall be taken, by means of a strict Police on the bank, to preclude every attempt of the inhabitants to smuggle goods, through the medium of boatmen.

Rivers: Regulations to be settled by a General Arrangement.

ART. CXVI. Everything expressed in the preceding Articles shall be settled by a general arrangement, in which there shall also be comprised whatever may need an ulterior determination.

The arrangement once settled, shall not be changed, but by and with the consent of all the States bordering on Rivers, and they shall take care to provide for its execution with due regard to circumstances and locality.

Rivers: Confirmation of the Particular Regulations relative to the Navigation of the Rhine, Neckar, Maine, Moselle, Meuse, and Scheldt.

ART. CXVII. The Particular Regulations relative to the navigation of the Rhine, the Neckar, the Maine, the Moselle, the Meuse, and the Scheldt, such as they are annexed to the present Act, shall have the same force and validity as if they were textually inserted herein.

Confirmation of Treaties and Particular Acts annexed to the General Treaty.

ART. CXVIII. The Treaties, Conventions, Declarations, Regulations, and other particular Acts which are annexed to the present Act, viz.;—

1. The Treaty between Russia and Austria, relative to Poland, of the 21st April/3rd May, 1815;
2. The Treaty between Russia and Prussia, relative to Poland, of the 21st April/3rd May, 1815;
3. The Additional Treaty, relative to Cracow, between Austria, Prussia, and Russia, of the 21st April/3rd May, 1815;
4. The Treaty between Prussia (Austria and Russia) and Saxony of the 18th May, 1815;
5. The Declaration of the King of Saxony respecting the rights of the House of Schœnburg, of the 18th May, 1815;
6. The Treaty between Prussia and Hanover, of the 29th May, 1815;
7. The Convention between Prussia and the Grand Duke of Saxe-Weimar, of the 1st June, 1815;
8. The Convention between Prussia and the Duke and Prince of Nassau, of the 31st May, 1815;
9. The Act concerning the Federative Constitution of Germany, of the 8th June, 1815;
10. The Treaty between the King of the Netherlands, and Prussia, England, Austria, and Russia, of the 31st May, 1815;
11. The Declaration of the (8) Powers on the Affairs of the Helvetic Confederation of the 20th March; and the Act of Accession of the Diet of the 27th May, 1815;
12. The Protocol of the 29th March, 1815, on the Cessions made by the King of Sardinia to the Canton of Geneva;
13. The Treaty between the King of Sardinia, Austria, England, Russia, Prussia, and France, of the 20th May, 1815;
14. The Act entitled " Conditions which are to serve as the Basis of the Union of the States of Genoa with those of His Sardinian Majesty;"
15. The Declaration of the 8 Powers on the Aboltion of the Slave Trade, of the 8th February, 1815;
16. The Regulations respecting the Free Navigation of Rivers;
17. The Regulation concerning the Precedence of Diplomatic Agents;

Shall be considered as integral parts of the Arrangements of the Congress, and shall have, throughout, the same force and validity as if they were inserted, word for word, in the General Treaty.

Invitation to Accede to the General Treaty addressed to the Powers assembled in Congress.

Art. CXIX. All the Powers assembled in Congress, as well as the Princes and Free Towns, who have concurred in the arrangements specified, and in the Acts confirmed, in this General Treaty, are invited to accede to it.

Reservations as to the use of the French Language in the drawing up of this Act.

Art. CXX. The French Language having been exclusively employed in all the copies of the present Treaty, it is declared, by the Powers who have concurred in this Act, that the use made of that Language shall not be construed into a Precedent for the future; every Power, therefore, reserves to itself the adoption in future Negociations and Conventions, of the Language it has heretofore employed in its diplomatic relations; and this Treaty shall not be cited as a Precedent contrary to the established practice.

Ratification of the Treaty and Deposition of the Original in the Archives of the Court and State of Vienna.

Art. CXXI. The present Treaty shall be ratified, and the Ratifications exchanged in six months, and by the Court of Portugal in a year, or sooner, if possible.

A copy of this General Treaty shall be deposited in the Archives of the Court and State of His Imperial and Royal Apostolic Majesty, at Vienna, in case any of the Courts of Europe shall think proper to consult the original text of this Instrument.

In faith of which the respective Plenipotentiaries have signed this Act, and have affixed thereunto the Seals of their Arms.

Done at Vienna, the 9th of June, in the year of Our Lord, 1815.

(The Signatures follow in the Alphabetical Order of the Courts.)

Austria,

(L.S.)   LE PRINCE DE METTERNICH.
(L.S.)   LE BARON DE WESSENBERG.

Spain.

France,

(L.S.)   LE PRINCE DE TALLEYRAND.
(L.S.)   LE DUKE D'ALBERG.
(L.S.)   LE COMTE ALEXIS DE NOAILLES.

GREAT BRITAIN,

(L.S.) CLANCARTY.
(L.S.) CATHCART.
(L.S.) STEWART, L. G.

PORTUGAL,

(L.S.) LE COMTE DE PALMELLA.
(L.S.) ANTONIO DE SALDANHA DA GAMA.
(L.S.) D. JOAQUIM LOBO DA SILVERIA.

PRUSSIA,

(L.S.) LE PRINCE DE HARDENBERG.
(L.S.) LE BARON DE HUMBOLDT.

RUSSIA,

(L.S.) LE PRINCE DE RASOUMOFFSKY.
(L.S.) LE COMTE DE STACKELBERG.
(L.S.) LE COMTE DE NESSELRODE.

SWEDEN,

(L.S.) LE COMTE CHARLES-AXEL DE LOWENHIELM.
(Save and except the reservation made to the Articles
CI, CII, and CIV of the Treaty.)

ANNEXES TO THE VIENNA CONGRESS TREATY OF
9TH JUNE, 1815.

VIII. Convention (Territorial). *Prussia* and the
Duke and Prince of *Nassau* .... 31 May,

IX. Act, concerning the Federative Constitution
of *Germany* .... 8 June,

X. Treaty. *Netherlands* and *Austria* (*Prussia*,
England, and *Russia*) relating to the King-
dom of the *Netherlands* .... 31 May,
(Annex) Act for the Acceptance of the Sove-
reignty of the Provinces of *Belgium* by the
Sovereign Prince. The Hague, 21 July, 1814........

XIA. Delcaration of the 8 Powers on the affairs of
the *Helvetic Confederation* .... 20 March,

XIB. Act of Accession of the *Swiss Diet* to the said
Declaration .... 27 May,

XII. Protocol of Conference (8 Powers) on the
Cessions made by *Sardinia* to the Canton of
Geneva .... 29 March,

XIII. Treaty (Territorial). *Sardinia* and *Austria*
(*England*, *France*, *Prussia*, and *Russia*).... 20 May,
(Annex) Cession made by *Sardinia* to the
Canton of *Geneva* ....

XIV. Act entitled " Conditions which are to serve
as the Basis for the Union of the States of
Genoa to those of his *Sardinian* Majesty "........

XV. Declaration of the 8 Powers on the Abolition
of the *Slave Trade* .... 8 February,

XVI. Regulations for the Free Navigation of
Rivers:—
Articles concerning the Navigation of Rivers
which, in their course of Navigation, sepa-
rate or traverse different States......... March,
Articles concerning the Navigation of the
Rhine .... March,
Articles concerning the Navigation of the
Neckar, the *Main*, the *Moselle*, the *Meuse*,
and the *Scheldt*...................... March,

XVII. Regulation on the *Rank* and *Precedence of
Diplomatic Agents* .... 19 March,

*ACTS OF RATIFICATION of the General Treaty of Congress of
Vienna, of 9th June, 1815.*

Memorandum.—The Acts of Ratification of the present Treaty of the

Congress of Vienna and its Annexes, by the Emperor of Austria, the King of France, the King of Great Britain, the Prince Regent of Portugal, the King of Prussia, the Emperor of Russia, and the King of Sweden, were executed by those Sovereigns respectively, in the following Form, subject to the requisite variations of Title, Country, &c.

GEORGE THE THIRD, by the Grace of God, King of the United Kingdom of Great Britain and Ireland, Defender of the Faith, King of Hanover, Duke of Brunswick and Luneburg, &c., &c., &c. To all and singular to whom these presents shall come, greeting.

Whereas the Powers who signed the Treaty of Paris of the 30th of May, 1814, met at Vienna conformably to Article XXXII of that instrument, together with the Princes and States, their Allies, in order to complete the measures which therein originated: And whereas there was concluded and signed at Vienna, on the 9th June, this present year 1815, between His Britannic Majesty; His Majesty the Emperor of Austria, King of Hungary and Bohemia; His Majesty the King of France and Navarre; His Royal Highness the Prince Regent of the Kingdoms of Portugal and The Brazils; His Majesty the King of Prussia; His Majesty the Emperor of all the Russias; and His Majesty the King of Sweden and Norway; one general and common Treaty, in Eight original Acts, each of them word for word the same, and throughout conformable one to the other, of which 8 Acts one is in the possession of each of the 7 signing Powers, and the 8th is deposited, in execution of Article CXXI of the said Instrument, among the Public Archives at Vienna, to serve as a document common as well to the parties who signed the same, as above mentioned, as to the other Powers and States acceding thereto: And whereas the said General Treaty received on the 9th June, 1815, amongst other signatures, those of His Britannic Majesty's Plenipotentiaries, and those of the Plenipotentiaries of His Imperial and Royal Apostolic Majesty.

We, having read and examined, as well the General Treaty of the 9th June, 1815, as the Treaties, Conventions, Declarations, Regulations, and other Instruments, recited in Article CXVIII thereof, and making part of the same, all of which are to be regarded as if they were here inserted, word for word, have found them altogether conformable to our will and pleasure; in consequence whereof, we have approved, confirmed, and ratified them, as by these presents we approve, confirm, and ratify them; promising, as well for His Majesty, as for his heirs and successors, faithfully to fulfil what is therein contained.

In faith whereof We have signed and caused to be affixed the Great Seal of the United Kingdom of Great Britain and Ireland to these Acts of Ratification, in seven corresponding Instruments, one of which shall be annexed to the original copy of the Treaty, deposited as above, in the

Imperial Archives at Vienna, to serve as a Document to all; and the 6 others shall be exchanged with the 6 Signing Powers, and this present Instrument shall be exchanged against the Act of Ratification of His Imperial and Royal Apostolic Majesty.

Done in Duplicate, in order that one copy of the Ratification of His Imperial and Royal Apostolic Majesty may be deposited in the Public Archives of Vienna, together with the General Treaty, and the other in the Office of His Majesty's Principal Secretary of State for Foreign Affairs.

Given at the Palace of Carlton House, the   day of   in the year of Our Lord, 1815, and in the 56th year of His Majesty's reign.

In the name and on behalf of His Majesty.

GEORGE, P.R.

6   THE HOLY ALLIANCE

TREATY between Austria, Prussia, and Russia. Signed at Paris, 18/26th September, 1815.

In the name of the Most Holy and Indivisible Trinity.

Holy Alliance of Sovereigns of Austria, Prussia, and Russia.

THEIR Majesties the Emperor of Austria, the King of Prussia, and the Emperor of Russia, having, in consequence of the great events which have marked the course of the three last years in Europe, and especially of the blessings which it has pleased Divine Providence to shower down upon those States which place their confidence and their hope on it alone, acquired the intimate conviction of the necessity of settling the steps to be observed by the Powers, in their reciprocal relations, upon the sublime truths which the Holy Religion of our Saviour teaches;

Government and Political Relations.

They solemnly declare that the present Act has no other object than to publish, in the face of the whole world, their fixed resolution, both in the administration if their respective States, and in their political relations with every other Government, to take for their sole guide the precepts of that Holy Religion, namely, the precepts of Justice, Christian Charity, and Peace, which, far from being applicable only to private concerns, must have an immediate influence on the councils of Princes, and guide all their steps, as being the only means of consolidating human institutions and remedying their imperfections. In consequence, their Majesties have agreed on the following Articles:—

Principles of the Christian Religion.

ART. I. Conformably to the words of the Holy Scriptures, which command all men to consider each other as brethren, the Three contracting Monarchs will remain united by the bonds of a true and indissoluble fraternity, and considering each other as fellow countrymen, they will, on all occasions and in all places, lend each other aid and assistance; and, regarding themselves towards their subjects and armies as fathers of families, they will lead them, in the same spirit of fraternity with which they are animated, to protect Religion, Peace, and Justice.

Fraternity and Affection.

ART. II. In consequence, the sole principle of force, whether between the said Governments or between their Subjects, shall be that of doing each other reciprocal service, and of testifying by unalterable good will the mutual affection with which they ought to be animated, to consider themselves all as members of one and the same Christian nation; the three allied Princes looking on themselves as merely delegated by Providence to govern three branches of the One family, namely, Austria, Prussia, and Russia, thus confessing that the Christian world, of which they and their people form a part, has in reality no other Sovereign than Him to whom alone power really belongs, because in Him alone are found all the treasures of love, science, and infinite wisdom, that is to say, God, our Divine Saviour, the Word of the Most High, the Word of Life. Their Majesties consequently recommend to their people, with the most tender solicitude, as the sole means of enjoying that Peace which arises from a good conscience, and which alone is durable, to strengthen themselves every day more and more in the principles and exercise of the duties which the Divine Saviour has taught to mankind.

Accession of Foreign Powers.

ART. III. All the Powers who shall choose solemnly to avow the sacred principles which have dictated the present Act, and shall acknowledge how important it is for the happiness of nations, too long agitated, that these truths should henceforth exercise over the destinies of mankind all the influence which belongs to them, will be received with equal ardour and affection into this Holy Alliance.

Done in triplicate, and signed at Paris, the year of Grace 1815, 14/26th September.

(L.S.)   FRANCIS.
(L.S.)   FREDERICK WILLIAM.
(L.S.)   ALEXANDER.

(The greater part of the Christian Powers acceded to this Treaty. France acceded to it in 1815; the Netherlands and Wurtemberg did so in

1816; and Saxony, Switzerland, and the Hanse Towns in 1817. But neither the Pope nor the Sultan were invited to accede.)

The following is a copy of the Invitation sent to the Prince Regent of Great Britain to accede; and of His Royal Highness's reply.

(1.)—*The Sovereigns of Austria, Prussia, and Russia to the Prince Regent of Great Britain.*

(Translation.)   *Paris, 26th September, 1815.*

SIR OUR BROTHER AND COUSIN,

THE events which have afflicted the world for more than 20 years have convinced us that the only means of putting an end to them is to be found in the most free and most intimate Union between the Sovereigns whom Divine Providence has placed over the heads of the Peoples of Europe.

The history of the three memorable years which are about to pass away, bear witness to the beneficial effects of which this union has been for the good of mankind; but in order to assure to this bond the solidity which the grandeur and the purity of the aim to which it tends imperiously demands, we have thought it should be founded on the sacred principles of the Christian Religion.

Deeply convinced of this important truth, we have concluded and signed the Act which we now submit to the consideration of your Royal Highness. Your Royal Highness may be assured that its object is to strengthen the relations which unite us, in forming of all the nations of Christendom one single Family, and assuring them by this, under the protection of the Almighty, happiness, security, the benefits of peace, and the bonds of fraternity for ever indissoluble. We deeply regretted that your Royal Highness was not united with us at the important moment when we concluded this transaction. We invite you, as our first and most intimate Ally, to agree with it, and complete a work singularly consecrated to the good of mankind, and which we ought to consider the best reward for our efforts.

FRANCIS.
FREDERICK WILLIAM.
ALEXANDER.

Our Brother and Cousin,
The Prince Regent of Great Britain.

(2.)—*The Prince Regent of Great Britain to the Sovereigns of Austria, Prussia, and Russia, respectively.*

Carlton House, 6th October, 1815.

SIR MY BROTHER AND COUSIN,

I HAVE had the honour of receiving your Imperial Majesty's letter, together with the copy of the Treaty signed by your Majesty and your august Allies, at Paris, on the 26th of September.

As the forms of the British Constitution, which I am called upon to administer in the name and on behalf of the King, my father, preclude me from acceding formally to this Treaty, in the shape in which it has been presented to me, I adopt this course of conveying to the august Sovereigns who have signed it, my entire concurrence in the principles they have laid down, and in the declaration which they have set forth, of making the Divine Precepts of the Christian Religion the invariable rule of their conduct, in all their relations, social and political, and of cementing the union which ought ever to subsist between all Christian Nations; and it will be always my earnest endeavour to regulate my conduct, in the station in which Divine Providence has vouchsafed to place me, by these sacred maxims, and to co-operate with my august Allies in all measures which may be likely to contribute to the peace and happiness of mankind.

With the most invariable sentiments of friendship and affection,

I am,

Sir, my Brother and Cousin,

Your Imperial Majesty's

good Brother and Cousin,

GEORGE, P.R.

His Imperial Majesty
   The Emperor of Austria.
(*Prussia and Russia respectively.*)

This Alliance was referred to in the Circular addressed by Austria, Prussia, and Russia to Foreign Courts, dated Troppau, 8th December, 1820.

7

PROTOCOL of Conference between Great Britain, Austria, Prussia, and Russia, respecting the Territorial Arrangements, and Defensive System of the Germanic Confederation. Paris, 3rd November, 1815.

THE Ministers of the Imperial and Royal Courts of Austria, of Russia, of Great Britain, and of Prussia, having taken into consideration the measures become necessary by those arrangements with France which are to terminate the present War, have agreed to lay down, in the present Protocol;—

1. The dispositions relative to the territorial cessions to be made by France, and to the contributions destined for strengthening the line of defence of the bordering States.

2. Provisions relating to certain changes of Territory in Germany.

3. Those which relate to the system of Defence of the Germanic Confederation.

A. *Provisions respecting the Cession to be made by France.* Kingdom of the Low Countries (Netherlands). Philippeville, Marienburg, &c.

ART. I. Considering that His Majesty the King of the Low Countries ought to participate in a just proportion in the advantages resulting from the present arrangement with France, and considering that state of his Frontiers on the side of that country, it is agreed, that the Districts which formed part of the Belgic Provinces, of the Bishopric of Liège, and of the Duchy of Bouillon, as well as the towns of Philippeville and Marienburg, with their Territories, which France is to cede to the Allies, shall be assigned to His Majesty the King of the Low Countries, to be united to his dominions.

Pecuniary Indemnity towards Defence of the Low Countries.

His Majesty the King of the Low Countries shall receive, moreover, out of that part of the French contribution which is destined towards strengthening the line of Defence of the States bordering upon France, the sum of 60,000,000 of Francs, which shall be laid out in fortifying the Frontiers of the Low Countries, in conformity with the plans and regulations which the Powers shall settle in this respect.

Pecuniary Indemnities towards Austria and Prussia.

It is besides agreed, that in consideration of the advantages which His Majesty the King of the Low Countries will derive from these dispositions, both in the increase of, and in the means for defending his territory, that that proportion of the Pecuniary Indemnity payable by France to which His said Majesty might lay claim shall serve towards putting the Indemnities of Austria and Prussia on the level of a just proportion.

Acquisitions of Prussia. Fortress of Sarre-Louis, &c.

ART. II. The districts which, by the new Treaty with France, will be detached from the French territory in the department of the Sarre and the Moselle, including the Fortress of Sarre-Louis, shall be united to the dominions of the King of Prussia.

Acquisitions of Austria. Town and Fortress of Landau.

ART. III. The territories which France is to cede in the department of the Lower Rhine, including the Town and Fortress of Landau, shall be united to those possessions on the left bank of the Rhine which devolve to His Imperial and Royal Apostolic Majesty by the Final Act of the Congress of Vienna. His Majesty may dispose of his possessions on the left bank of the Rhine, in the territorial arrangements with Bavaria, and other States of the Germanic Confederation.

Helvetic Confederation.   Versoy and part of the Pays de Gex to be added to Geneva.

ART. IV. Versoy, with that part of the Pays de Gex, which is to be ceded by France, shall be united to Switzerland, and form part of the Canton of Geneva.

Neutrality of Switzerland to include Territory from Upper Savoy: Ugina to Lake of Bourget.

The Neutrality of Switzerland shall be extended to that territory, which is placed north of a line to be drawn from Ugina (including that Town) to the south of the Lake of Annecy, and from thence to the Lake of Bourget, as far as the Rhone, in the same manner as it has been extended to the Provinces of Chablais and Faucigny by Article XCII of the Final Act of the Congress of Vienna.

Sardinia.   Part of Savoy to be given to Sardinia and part to Geneva.

ART. V. In order that His Majesty the King of Sardinia may participate, in a just proportion, in the advantages resulting from the present arrangement with France, it is agreed, that the portion of Savoy which remained to France in virtue of the Treaty of Paris of the 30th May, 1814, shall be united (*réunis*) to the dominions of His said Majesty, with the exception of the Commune of St. Julian, which shall be given up to the Canton of Geneva.

Proposed Cessions to Geneva.

The Cabinets of the Allied Courts will use their good offices for inducing His Sardinian Majesty to cede to the Canton of Geneva the Communes of Chesne, Thonex, and some others necessary for disengaging the Swiss territory of Jussy from the effects of the retrocession, by the Canton of Geneva, of that territory situated between the road of Euron and the Lake, which had been ceded by His Sardinian Majesty, by the Act of the 29th March, 1815.

Custom Houses.

The French Government having consented to withdraw its lines of custom and excise from the frontiers of Switzerland, on the side of the Jura, the Cabinets of the Allied Powers will employ their good offices for inducing His Sardinian Majesty to withdraw in like manner, his lines of custom and excise, on the side of Savoy, at least upwards of a league from the Swiss frontiers, and on the outside of the great road of Saleve, and of the mountains of Sion and Waache.

Pecuniary Indemnity to Sardinia.

His Majesty the King of Sardinia shall receive, moreover, out of that part of the French contribution which is destined for the strengthening of the line of Defence of the States bordering upon France, the sum of 10,000,000 of Francs, which is to be laid out in fortifying his frontiers, in conformity with the plans and regulations which the Powers shall settle in this respect.

Pecuniary Indemnities to Austria and Prussia.

It is likewise agreed, that, in consideration of the advantages which His Sardinian Majesty will derive from these dispositions, both in the extension and in the means for defending his territory, that part of the pecuniary Indemnity payable by France, to which His said Majesty might lay claim, shall serve towards putting the indemnities of Austria and Prussia on the level of a just proportion.

B. Provisions respecting the Territorial Arrangements in Germany, Austria, and Prussia.

Cessions by Austria to Prussia in Department of La Sarre.

ART. VI. His Imperial and Royal Apostolic Majesty shall cede to His Majesty the King of Prussia, in the department of La Sarre, the districts shown in the annexed Schedule. His Majesty the King of Prussia engages on his part to satisfy the Grand Dukes of Mecklenburg-Strelitz and Oldenburg, the Duke of Coburg, the Landgrave of Hesse-Homburg, and the Count of Papenheim, conformably with Article LIV of the Final Act of the Congress of Vienna.

Arrangements relating to Bavaria.

ART. VII. His Majesty the Emperor of all the Russias, His Majesty the King of Great Britain, and His Majesty the King of Prussia engage to use every means to obtain for His Imperial and Royal Apostolic Majesty from His Majesty the King of Bavaria the reconveyance of the territories and the objects designated in the annexed Schedule (2), in exchange for the indemnity designated in the same Schedule. They undertake at the same time with the Court of Bavaria to exchange with His Royal Highness the Elector of Hesse, the districts of Aufenau, Wört, and Hochst, and the road from Saalmünster to Gelnhausen for a sufficient part of the bailiwick of Lohrhaupten.

In consideration of the arrangements above specified the Four Powers insure to His Majesty the King of Bavaria the following advantages:—

a. An amount proportional to the part of the French contributions intended to reinforce the defensive line of the frontier States, which amount shall be employed according to the plans and regulations which shall be generally fixed in this matter.

b. The Reversion of the part of the Palatinate belonging to the House of Baden, after the extinction of the direct line of the reigning Grand Duke.

c. A military road from Würzburg to Frankenthal.

Landau to be a Fortress of the Germanic Confederation. Bavaria to have Right to Garrison.

d. The right of garrison in the fortified Town of Landau, which will be one of the Fortresses of the Germanic Confederation.

These Articles will be regarded as fully obligatory as soon as the Court of Bavaria shall have declared its adhesion to the arrangements specified above.

The Countries devolved to His Imperial and Royal Apostolic Majesty under Article LI of the Final Act of the Congress of Vienna, and of which His Majesty can dispose by exchange with the other Princes of the Germanic Confederation, being still found, in spite of the representations on this subject made by the Imperial Court of Austria, partly occupied by the Bavarian authorities, there will be made by the Four Cabinets a simultaneous action against the Bavarian Government, in order that the said countries may be placed without delay at the free disposal of His Imperial and Royal Apostolic Majesty.

Austrian Cessions to Grand Duke of Hesse.

ART. VIII. Austria shall cede to the Grand Duke of Hesse, as an indemnity for the Duchy of Westphalia, a territory on the left bank of the Rhine, comprising a population of 140,000 inhabitants, conformably to the Treaty between Austria, Prussia, and the Grand Duke, of 10th June, 1815. The arrangements with the Grand Duke of Hesse shall be made according to the annexed Schedule (3), drawn up on the basis of the exchange of territory between Austria and Bavaria, such as may be found indicated in the preceding Article.

Austrian Cession to Bavaria.

ART. IX. The Reversion of the part of the Palatinate belonging to the Grand Duke of Baden having been assured to Austria by the Protocol of 10th June, 1815, of the Conferences of the Congress of Vienna, His Imperial and Royal Apostolic Majesty is ready to renounce this

Reversion in favour of His Majesty the King of Bavaria, in order to facilitate the arrangements indicated by Article VII of the present Protocol. The Reversion of Brisgau, which has also been assured to Austria by the said Protocol of 10th June, will be carried out.

C. Defensive System of the Germanic Confederation.
Mayence, Luxemburg, and Landau to be Fortresses of the Germanic Confederation.

ART. X. The Fortresses of Mayence, Luxemburg, and Landau are declared Fortresses of the Germanic Confederation, with the exception of the territorial Sovereignty of the Fortresses.

Fortress of Mayence.   Right of Garrisoning Fortress.

The Plenipotentiaries of Austria and Prussia, not being authorised, considering the Acts formerly existing, and the absence of their Sovereigns, to renounce the right of garrisoning the Fortress of Mayence to one or other of their respective Courts, it is agreed that the military service and the administration shall continue to subsist in that Fortress according to the actual arrangement in force, until the Allied Courts shall come to some definitive arrangement on this point.

Fortress of Luxemburg.   Right of Garrisoning, and of Nominating Governor.

Their Majesties, the Emperor of Austria, the Emperor of all the Russias, and His Majesty the King of Great Britain, will employ their best offices in order to obtain for His Majesty the King of Prussia the right of garrisoning the Fortress of Luxemburg, conjointly with His Majesty the King of the Netherlands, as well as the right of nominating the Governor of that Fortress.

Fortress of Landau.   Right of Garrisoning.

The garrison of Landau shall be, until the time of its exchange, entirely composed of Austrian troops, and in like manner after the transfer it shall be in time of peace entirely composed of Bavarian troops. Nevertheless, in the case of war, the Grand Duke of Baden shall furnish a third of the garrison necessary for the defence of the Fortress.

Distribution of Sums of Money to be devoted to the Defensive System of Germany.

The Powers having agreed to devote to the defensive system of Germany the sum of 60,000,000 francs, to be taken from a part of the French contribution destined to strengthen the line of Defence of the frontier States, the said sum shall be distributed as follows:—

His Majesty the King of Prussia shall receive 20,000,000 Francs of it for the fortification of the Lower Rhine; 20,000,000 shall be reserved for the construction of a fourth Federal Fortress on the Upper Rhine; His Majesty the King of Bavaria, or some other Sovereign of the countries bordering upon France between the Rhine and the Prussian States, shall have 15,000,000; and 5,000,000 shall be employed to complete the works at Mayence. These different sums shall be disposed of, conformably to the plans and regulations which shall be settled with reference to them.

Protocol to have same force as a Convention.

Art. XI. The present Protocol shall have the force of a Convention between the four Powers, until the arrangements to which they refer may be definitively completed.

Done and signed at Paris, 3rd November, 1815.

WELLINGTON.   RASOUMOFFSKY.
METTERNICH.   CAPO D'ISTRIAS.
HARDENBERG.   HUMBOLDT.
CASTLEREAGH.   WESSENBERG.

(*Annex* 1).—*Austrian Cessions to Prussia.*

Austria shall cede to Prussia on the left bank of the Rhine:—

a. Saarburg, with the remainder of Conz, according to the limits of the Peace of 1814, and exclusively of Parcelles, on the right bank of the Moselle, which formerly belonged to Luxemburg.

b. Moertzig.

c. Wadern.

d. Tholey.

e. Part of Lebach according to the conditions of 1814.

f. Ottweiler.

g. St. Wendel.

h. The remainder of Birkenfeld and Hermeskeil.

i. The remainder of Baumholder and Grumbach.

(*Annex* 2).—*Arrangement with Bavaria.*
Cessions demanded from Bavaria.

	Population.
1. The Hausruckviertel	92,396
2. The Innviertel	125,671
3. The Principality of Salzburg, with the exception of the Bailiwicks of Waging, Tettmanning, Seisendorf, and Laufen; the three last, so far as they are situated on left bank of the Salzbach and the Saal	168,000
4. The Tyrolese Bailiwick of Vils	946
Total. . . .	387,013

His Majesty the King of Bavaria would grant freedom of transit on the road which leads from the Tyrol to Bregenz by the Bavarian States, for a quantity of salt and corn, to be agreed upon.

Indemnities.

A. *On the Left Bank of the Rhine.*

	Population.
1. *In the Department of Mont-Tonnerre.*	
a. The district of Deux-Ponts..................	93,596
b. The district of Kaiserslautern	73,022
c. The district of Spire, excepting the cantons of Worms and Pfeddersheim...................	144,042
d. In the district of Alzey, the canton of Kercheim-Poland......................................	12,066
2. *In the Department of the Sarre.*	
a. The canton of Waldmohr	10,795
b. The canton of Bliecastel.....................	14,636
c. The canton of Coussel, excepting certain places on the road from St. Wendel to Baumholder—approximately	8,698
3. *In the Department of the Lower Rhine.*	
The canton of Landau, with the territory on the left bank of the Lauter...........................	53,887
B. *On the Right Bank of the Rhine.*	
a. The bailiwicks of Fuldois....................	26,304
b. The bailiwick of Radewitz	3,000
c. Of Darmstadt—the bailiwicks of Mittenberg, Amorbach, Heubach, and Alzenau................	24,661
d. Of Bade—part of the bailiwick of Wertheim......	4,927
Total....	469,634

(*Annex* 3).—*Territorial Transfers by the Grand Duke of Darmstadt.*

Darmstadt would cede:

A. *To Prussia.*   Subjects.

The Duchy of Westphalia.......................... 140,000

B. *To Bavaria.*
The bailiwicks of Mittenberg	8,094	*Subjects.*
Amorbach	7,092	
Heubach	3,505	
Alzenau	5,970	
	24,661	

C. *To Hesse-Cassel.*
The bailiwick of Hanau, conformably to the Conventions
of Frankfort 14,018

D. *To the Landgrave of Hesse-Homburg.*
The Sovereignty over............................. 6,366

Total.... 185,045

The Grand Duke of Darmstadt would make himself liable for one-half of the private debts of the Prince of Ysemburg.

The overplus of the above-named Indemnities will be employed to obtain for His Prussian Majesty the Sovereignty of the possessions of Wittgenstein and Berleburg.

The best endeavours will be made to use the part of the country of Ysemburg, situated on the left bank of the Maine, in the exchanges which the Grand Duke of Hesse is to make with the Elector of Hesse for the bailiwicks above mentioned, sub Lit. C., and to obtain from the Elector of Hesse the whole of the road from Saalmünster to Haynau.

Darmstadt would obtain:

A. *On the Left Bank of the Rhine:*   *Subjects.*
The Town of Mayence	26,400
Nieder-Olm	12,113
Ober-Ingelheim	13,523
Bingen	8,191
Wöllstein	10,806
Wörstädt	15,403
Oppenheim	14,606
Bechtheim	15,834
Alzey	15,961
Pfeddersheim	14,573
Worms	5,718

B. *On the Right Bank of the Rhine:*
The villages of Nieder-Ursel and Ober-Erlenbach	1,164
The Principality of Ysemburg	47,454
Total....	201,646

C. The ownership of the Salt Mines of Kreutznach.

8

CONVENTION between Great Britain, Austria, Prussia, and Russia, and France, relative to the Occupation of a Military Line in France by an Allied Army. Signed at Paris, 20th November, 1815.

[This Convention was annexed to the Definitive Treaty of the same date. See Art. II].

Convention between Great Britain and France, concluded in conformity to Article V of the Principal Treaty, relative to the Occupation of a Military Line in France, by an Allied Army.

Composition of Army of Occupation.

ART. I. The composition of the Army of 150,000 men, which, in virtue of Article V of the Treaty of this day, is to occupy a Military Line along the Frontiers of France, the force and nature of the contingents to be furnished by each Power, as well as the choice of the Generals who are to command those troops, shall be determined by the Allied Sovereigns.

Maintenance of Army of Occupation by French Government.

ART. II. This Army shall be maintained by the French Government, in the manner following:—

The lodging, the fuel, and lighting, the provisions and forage, are to be furnished in kind.

Daily Rations.

It is agreed that the total amount of Daily Rations shall never exceed 200,000 for men, and 50,000 for horses, and that they shall be issued according to the tariff annexed to the present Convention.

Pay, Equipment, Clothing, &c.

With respect to the pay, the Equipment, the Clothing, and other incidental matters, the French Government will provide for such expense, by the payment of a sum of 50,000,000 of francs per annum, payable in specie from month to month, from the 1st of December of the year 1815, into the hands of the Allied Commissioners.

Amount to be paid by French Government.

But the Allied Powers, in order to concur as much as possible in every thing which can satisfy His Majesty the King of France, and relieve his subjects, consent that only 30,000,000 of francs, on account of pay, shall be paid in the first year, on condition of the difference being made up in the subsequent years of the Occupation.

Maintenance of Fortresses by French Government.

Art. III. France engages equally to provide for the keeping up of the Fortifications, and of the buildings of the military and civil administrations, as well as for the arming and provisioning the Fortresses which, in virtue of Article V of the Treaty of this day, are to remain as a deposit in the hands of the Allied Troops.

Services required by Commander-in-Chief of Allied Troops to be executed by French Government.

These respective services, which are to be regulated upon the principles adopted by the French administration of the War Department, shall be executed upon a demand, addressed to the French Government by the Commander-in-Chief of the Allied Troops, with whom some plan shall be agreed upon for ascertaining what may be needful, and concerting the measures necessary to remove all difficulties which may arise, and for accomplishing the object of this Stipulation, in a manner equally satisfactory to the interests of the respective Parties.

French Government to secure accomplishment of Services required.

The French Government will take such measures as it shall judge to be the most effectual, for securing the accomplishment of the different services stated in this and in the preceding Article; and will concert to that effect with the Commander-in-Chief of the Allied Troops.

Military Line to be occupied by Allied Troops.

Art. IV. In conformity with Article V of the Principal Treaty, the Military Line to be occupied by the Allied Troops, shall extend along the frontiers which separate the Departments of the Pas de Calais, of the North, of the Ardennes, of the Meuse, of the Moselle, of the Lower Rhine, and of the Upper Rhine, from the interior of France.

Territories not to be occupied by Allied or French Troops.

It is further agreed, that neither the Allied Troops nor the French troops shall occupy (except it be for particular reasons, and by common consent) the territories and districts hereafter named: *id est:*—

In the Department of the Somme, all the country north of that river, from Ham to where it falls into the sea.

In the Department of the Aisne, the districts of St. Quentin, Vervins, and Laôn.

In the Department of the Marne, those of Rheims, St. Ménéhould, and Vitry;

In the Department of the Upper Marne, those of St. Dizier and Joinville.

In the Department of the Meurthe, those of Toul, Dieuze, Sarrebourg, and Blamont.

In the Department of the Vosges, those of St. Diez, Brugères, and Remiremont.

The District of Lure, in the Department of the Upper Saône, and that of St. Hyppolite, in the Department of the Doubs.

Towns to be Garrisoned by French Troops.

Notwithstanding the occupation by the Allies of the portion of Territory fixed by the Principal Treaty, and by the present Convention, His Most Christian Majesty may, in the Towns situated within the territory occupied, maintain garrisons, the number of which, however, shall not exceed what is laid down in the following enumeration:—

	Men.
At Calais	1,000
„ Gravelines	500
„ Bergues	500
„ St. Omer	1,500
„ Bethune	500
„ Montreuil	500
„ Hesdin	250
„ Ardres	150
„ Aire	500
„ Arras	1,000
„ Boulogne	300
„ St. Venant	300
„ Lille	3,000
„ Dunkirk and its Forts	1,000
„ Douay and Fort de Scarpe	1,000
„ Verdun	500
„ Metz	3,000
„ Lauterburg	200
„ Weissenburg	150
„ Lichtenberg	150
„ Petite Pierre	100
„ Phalsburg	600

				Men.
At Strasburg	..	..	..	3,000
„ Schlestadt	..	..	..	1,000
„ Neuf Brisach and Fort Mortier				1,000
„ Belfort	..	..	..	..	1,000

Matériel not belonging to Fortresses to be removed by French Government.

It is, however, well understood, that the *Matériel* belonging to the Engineer and Artillery Departments, as well as such articles of military equipment as do not properly belong to those Fortresses, shall be withdrawn from them, and shall be transported to such places as the French Government shall think fit, provided those places are situated without the line occupied by the Allied Troops, and without the districts in which it is agreed not to leave any troops, either Allied or French.

Infraction of Stipulations to be Redressed by French Government.

If any infraction of the above stipulations should come to the knowledge of the Commander-in-Chief of the Allied Armies, he shall make his representations on the subject to the French Government, which engages to do what is right thereupon.

Garrisoning of Fortresses by French Troops.

The Fortresses abovementioned being at this moment unprovided with garrisons, the French Government can place therein, as soon as it shall think fit, the number of troops fixed as above; apprizing always before hand the Commander-in-Chief of the Allied Troops, in order to avoid any difficulty and delay which the French troops might experience in their march.

Military Command by General-in-Chief of Allied Troops.

ART. V. The Military Command in the whole extent of the Departments which shall remain occupied by the Allied Troops, shall belong to the General-in-Chief of those troops; it is, however, distinctly understood, that it shall not extend to the Fortresses which the French troops are to occupy, in virtue of Article IV of the present Convention nor to a rayon of 1,000 toises around each of those places.

Civil Administration, &c., to remain in hands of French Government.

ART. VI. The Civil Administration, the Administration of Justice, and the collection of taxes and contributions of all sorts, shall remain in the hands of the agents of His Majesty the King of France.

Customs to remain in hands of French Government.

The same shall be the case with respect to the Customs. They shall remain in their present state, and the Commanders of the Allied Troops shall throw no obstacle in the way of the measures to be taken by the officers employed in that service, to prevent frauds; they shall even give them in case of need, succour and assistance.

Prevention of Abuses of Customs Regulations.

ART. VII. To prevent all abuses which might affect the regulations of the Customs, the clothing, and equipments, and other necessary articles destined for the Allied Troops, shall not be allowed to enter, except they be furnished with a certificate of origin, and in pursuance of a communication to be made by the commanding officers of the different corps, to the General-in-Chief of the Allied Army, who will, on his part, cause information to be given thereof to the French Government, who will, in consequence thereof, issue the proper orders to their officers employed in the administration of the Customs.

Services of the Gendarmerie.

ART. VIII. The service of the *Gendarmerie* being acknowledged as necessary to the maintenance of order and public tranquillity, shall continue, as hitherto, in the countries occupied by the Allied Troops.

Evacuation by Allied Troops.

ART. IX. The Allied Troops, with the exception of those that are to form the Army of Occupation, shall evacuate the Territory of France in 21 days, after the signature of the Principal Treaty.

Delivery of Territories and Fortresses to Allies.

The Territories which, according to that Treaty, are to be ceded to the Allies, as well as the Fortresses of Landau and Sarre-Louis, shall be delivered up by the French authorities and troops, in 10 days from the date of the signature of the Treaty.

Those places shall be given up in the state in which they were on the 20th of September last.

Commissioners to ascertain State of Places delivered to Allies.

Commissioners shall be named on both sides, to ascertain and declare that state, and to deliver and receive respectively the artillery, the military stores, plans, models, and archives, belonging as well to the said places as to the different districts ceded by France, according to the Treaty of this day.

Commissioners to ascertain State of Places occupied by French Troops.

Commissioners shall also be named, to examine and ascertain the state of those places still occupied by the French Troops, and which, according to Article V of the Principal Treaty, are to be held in deposit, for a certain time, by the Allies.

Places occupied by French Troops to be delivered up to Allies.

These places shall also be delivered up to the Allied Troops in 10 days, from the date of the signature of the Treaty.

Commissioners to ascertain State of Fortresses and Military Stores, &c., contained therein.

Commissioners shall also be named by the French Government, on the one part, and by the General Commanding-in-Chief the Allied Troops destined to remain in France, on the other; also by the General Commanding the Allied Troops which are at present in possession of the Fortresses of Avesnes, Landrecies, Maubeuge, Rocroy, Givet, Montmédy, Longwy, Mezières, and Sedan, to ascertain and declare the state of those places, and of the military stores, maps, plans, models, &c., which they shall contain, at the moment which shall be considered as that of the occupation in virtue of the Treaty.

Restoration at Expiration of Temporary Occupation.

The Allied Powers engage to restore, at the expiration of the temporary Occupation, all the places named in Article V of the Principal Treaty, in the state in which they shall have been found at the time of that occupation, save and except the damages which may have been caused by time, and which the French Government should not have provided against by the necessary repairs.

Done at Paris, this 20th day of November, in the year of Our Lord, 1815.

(L.S.)   CASTLEREAGH.

(L.S.)   RICHELIEU.   (L.S.)   WELLINGTON.

ADDITIONAL ARTICLE.   DESERTERS.   *Paris, 20th November, 1815.*

Mutual Delivery of Military Deserters.

The High Contracting Parties having agreed, by Article V of the Treaty of this day, to occupy for a certain period with an Allied Army, military positions in France; and being desirous of anticipating all that might hazard the order and discipline which it is so important to maintain in that Army, it is determined upon by the present Additional

Article, that every Deserter who, from either of the corps of the said Army, should go over to the French side, shall immediately be arrested by the French authorities, and delivered up to the nearest Commander of the Allied Troops, in like manner as all Deserters from the French troops, who might come over towards the Allied Army, shall be immediately delivered up to the nearest French Commandant.

Delivery of Deserters previous to Signature of Treaty.

The tenor of this Article is to apply equally to such Deserters from either side, who may have forsaken their colours previously to the signature of the Treaty; the same to be without delay restored and delivered up to the respective corps to which they may belong.

The present Additional Article shall have the same force and validity, as if it were inserted, word for word, in the Military Convention of this day.

In faith whereof, the respective Plenipotentiaries have signed it, and have affixed thereunto the Seal of their Arms.

Done at Paris, the 20th November, in the year of Our Lord, 1815.

(L.S.)   CASTLEREAGH.
(L.S.)   WELLINGTON.
(L.S.)   RICHELIEU.

(Annex.)—Tariff annexed to the Convention relative to the Occupation of a Military Line in France by an Allied Army.
I. Provisions, Forage, Quarters, and Fuel.
Ordinary Portion of the Soldier.

Two pounds (*poids de marc*) of meslin bread, or $1\frac{2}{3}$ of a pound of flour, or $1\frac{1}{6}$ of a pound of biscuit.

Quarter of a pound of oatmeal or grits, or $\frac{3}{16}$ of a pound of rice, or $\frac{1}{2}$ of a pound of fine wheaten flour, peas, or lentils, or $\frac{1}{2}$ of a pound of potatoes, carrots, turnips, or other fresh vegetables.

Half a pound of fresh meat, or $\frac{3}{4}$ of a pound of bacon.

One-tenth of a litre of spirits, or $\frac{1}{2}$ of a litre of wine, or 1 litre of beer.

One-thirtieth of a pound of salt.

1. In case the troops should be quartered on the inhabitants, they shall enjoy the use of fire and candle; in barracks, wood for the rooms and kitchens; and lights for the rooms and corridors shall be allowed, according to circumstances, in exact proportion to what is strictly necessary. The same shall be observed with respect to the Guard.

2. Substitutes for the usual articles of the ration are not to be given at the discretion of the troops, but according to circumstances.

The articles of provision shall, where practicable, be varied according to the season, giving generally a preference to farinaceous vegetables.

Bacon may be given where the troops are willing to receive it.

3. Flour, for bread, shall not be given in lieu of bread, excepting with the consent of the troops; and in that case, wood, and the necessary conveniences for baking, must be granted; biscuit shall be given only in case of a movement, or of necessity, or to complete the ten days' supply in reserve, with which the troops should be provided in their flying hospitals.

This store shall be furnished in addition to the daily supply; moreover in order to ensure a regular supply, it is to be understood that, within the space of two months, the magazines are to be so provisioned, that there be always a supply of provisions and forage (meat excepted) in store for a fortnight in advance, under the inspection of the French Storekeepers.

The Commissaries of the several Corps d'Armée shall be authorised to inspect this store in reserve when they may think proper.

4. The meat shall be delivered slaughtered, without including the head, feet, lights, liver, and other internal parts. If, with the consent of the troops, live cattle be delivered, the weight shall be fixed by an exact computation, including the head, the fat, and whatever is eatable.

The hides shall, in this case, belong to the troops.

5. On a march, and on other occasions where the soldier shall be fed *par étape*, the same tariff shall be in force; the soldier shall then receive his portion, or an adequate equivalent, prepared and divided into two meals, and in the morning a portion of bread and spirits.

6. Receipts shall be granted by regiments, companies, and detachments, for the number of rations and portions received; which receipt shall be revised and confirmed in each corps, by a Mixed Commission, whose official expenses shall be regulated and paid by the French Government.

7. As several of the troops are accustomed to tobacco for smoking and as the soldier will not be able to purchase this article at the very high price that exists in France, it is stipulated, that regiments, companies, or detachments, shall be entitled to demand half a kilogramme of tobacco, per month, for each man present, on paying 60 centimes for each half kilogramme of the most inferior quality sold in the shops, but fresh. In order to prevent any contraband practices arising therefrom, upon the issues to be distributed amongst the regiments, there shall be specified the quantities of tobacco delivered.

Officer's Portion.

Two pounds of white bread.
Quarter of a pound of fine grits, or substitutes.
Two pounds of meat.

A portion of liquor of good quality.

Two tallow candles, eight to the pound.

To prevent inconvenience, it were to be wished, that this part of the portion should be estimated at a certain sum per diem, for all the Corps d'Armée, and should always be given in money.

Moreover, $\frac{1}{15}$ of a *stère* of hard firewood, or, according to circumstances, soft wood, coal, or turf, in the proportion established in the French Service.

This part of the portion shall be always given in kind, except during a march. The summer ration shall be one-half that of the winter, and there shall be reckoned six months to the winter.

In those provinces where coal is generally burnt, the commutation between wood and coal shall be made, as well for the Officer as for the soldier, according to the tariff of commutation of the same articles in use in the French Army.

Likewise the quarters, with beds and bedding.

The portions and the quarters shall be given to the Officers according to the following table:—

Rank.	Number of portions of provisions.	Number of rations of fuel.	Number of suitable apartments.	Number of places for Servants.	Observations.
Subalterns	1	1	1	1 to 2	
Captains of Cavalry, of Infantry, and en second	2	2	2	3	
Majors	3	3	3	3	Commanding a Regiment, one additional ration of provision and fuel, one room, one servant's room more.
Lieutenant-Colonels . . .	4	3	3	4	
Colonels	5	3	3	4	
Major-Generals	7	4	4	5	Commanding a Division or attached to the Staff, one portion more of each article.
Lieutenant-Generals . .	9	5	5	7	
*Generals of Cavalry, of Infantry, or commanding a Corps d'Armée	12	..	..	..	* They shall be lodged in suitable hotels, properly supplied with fuel.

1. The servant shall likewise receive the portion of the soldier, but only when borne as effective on the muster-roll, and not beyond the number allowed in each Army.

2. The Civil and Medical Departments shall be assimilated with the Military, in every thing, according to their respective ranks.

3. In case of necessity, more particularly on a march, a smaller number of apartments shall suffice. In barracks the quarters shall be regulated according to circumstances, and conjointly with the Commandants.

Forage.—Light Ration.

Oats, $\frac{2}{3}$ of a bushel.
Hay, 10 pounds.
Straw, 3 pounds.

Heavy Ration.

Oats, 1 bushel (Paris measure).
Hay, 10 pounds.
Straw, 3 pounds.

1. The heavy ration shall be given for the saddle horses of Officers, for horses of regular cavalry, light and heavy, for artillery horses that draw the guns and caissons.

All other horses, including cossack horses, shall receive only the light ration, except by the rules of the service of each Army there should be other draft horses entitled to the heavy ration.

On a march which may continue for more than four days, all the horses on the march shall receive the heavy ration.

2. The forage may be varied in case of necessity, by reckoning six rations of barley, and, in extreme scarcity, as many of rye, for eight rations of oats; and half a light ration of oats for five pounds of hay. The latter substitute may be demanded as a matter of right, by those troops whose ration of hay is generally under ten pounds, and that of oats more liberal.

3. Straw shall be furnished from the magazines for the stables of the barracks, and the dung shall belong to the troops who are to remove it themselves.

When quartered on the inhabitant, he shall supply straw according to the tariff, and shall have the advantage of the dung.

4. Stabling shall be granted to regiments and companies for the effective number of horses, also light and accommodation for the guard, and place for the baggage and forage.

5. Forage for the horses of the Officers of different ranks shall be given to each Army, according to the regulations in force with them

respectively, previous to the date of the present tariff. It shall be delivered according to such Returns, without any deduction.

Officers shall claim stable-room for the actual number of their horses, and room for their baggage and forage, but not candlelight. For each horse there shall be allotted a space of 8 feet long and 4 feet broad.

General Remarks.

Beyond the present tariff, the troops shall not be entitled to claim anything, and shall be obliged to purchase at their own expense the articles not comprehended in it, such as soap, butter, chalk, pipe-clay, &c.

With respect to guard-houses and sentry-boxes, the towns will provide for them at their own expense.

II. Hospitals.

The administration of the Hospitals shall in general be in the hands of the French authorities, according to the established order; but in the subsistence of the sick, respect shall be had to the Regulation published by each Army on its entrance into France. Everything necessary, medicines included, shall be provided at the expense of the French Government. On the other hand, nothing shall be granted for Regimental Hospitals, beyond the usual portions and quarters, which shall be claimed by regiments for their sick, as well as for their effective. Each Corps d'Armée shall send to the Hospital destined for its sick, the necessary medical or other assistance, to secure proper treatment. All soldiers sent to the Hospitals shall be received, and the Hospitals shall be established at convenient distances.

III. Transport.

When the troops are on a march, carriages shall be furnished by the French Government, on the demand of the Commander-in-Chief. The same rule shall be observed for the transport of the sick. The necessary relays for the communication between different parts of a Corps d'Armée shall also be granted; but the greatest moderation shall be observed on this subject. With respect to the conveyance of military effects to the Army from beyond the French frontier, such conveyances shall be made by relays of the country, only till the 1st of February, 1816, and merely for moderate quantities.

IV. Posts, Dispatches, Couriers, &c.

All Dispatches connected with the interior service of the different corps, and correspondence with the French authorities, bearing an

Official Seal, shall be received and forwarded, without payment, at the usual posts. Estafettes and private letters of the Military shall be paid for at the usual prices. Couriers and travellers, military or otherwise, shall pay punctually for post-horses.

V. *Douanes.*

Articles for the clothing of the troops shall enter free from duty, on Certificates well authenticated. Military persons joining the Armies, or leaving France, shall be exempt from payment of all duties, on whatever is for their own use, or that of the troops.

Agreed upon, and signed at Paris, the 20th of November, in the year of Our Lord, 1815.

(L.S.) CASTLEREAGH.

(L.S.) RICHELIEU.   (L.S.) WELLINGTON.

9

ACT, signed by the Protecting Powers, Austria, France, Great Britain, Prussia and Russia, for the acknowledgment and Guarantee of the Perpetual Neutrality of Switzerland, and the Inviolability of its Territory. Paris, 20th November, 1815.

THE Accession of Switzerland to the Declaration published at Vienna the 20th March, 1815, by the Powers who signed the Treaty of Paris, having been duly notified to the Ministers of the Imperial and Royal Courts, by the Act of the Helvetic Diet on the 27th of the month of May following, there remained nothing to prevent the Act of Acknowledgment and Guarantee of the perpetual Neutrality of Switzerland from being made conformably to the above-mentioned Declaration. But the Powers deemed it expedient to suspend till this day the signature of that Act, in consequence of the changes which the events of the war, and the arrangements which might result from it might possibly occasion in the limits of Switzerland, and in respect also to the modifications resulting therefrom, in the arrangements relative to the federated territory, for the benefit of the Helvetic Body.

These changes being fixed by the stipulations of the Treaty of Paris signed this day, the Powers who signed the Declaration of Vienna of the 20th March declare, by this present Act, their formal and authentic Acknowledgment of the perpetual Neutrality of Switzerland; and they Guarantee to that country the Integrity and Inviolability of its Territory in its new limits, such as they are fixed, as well by the Act of the Congress of Vienna as by the Treaty of Paris of this day, and such as they will be hereafter; *conformably to the Arrangement of the Protocol of the 3rd November, extract of which is hereto annexed, which stipulates in favour of the Helvetic Body a new increase of Territory, to be taken from Savoy, in order to disengage from Enclaves, and complete the circle of the Canton of Geneva.*

The Powers acknowledge likewise and guarantee the Neutrality of those parts of Savoy designated by the Act of the Congress of Vienna of the 20th May, 1815, and by the Treaty of Paris signed this day, the same being entitled to participate in the Neutrality of Switzerland, equally as if they belonged to that country.

The Powers who signed the Declaration of the 20th of March acknowledge, in the most formal manner, by the present Act, that the Neutrality and Inviolability of Switzerland, and her Independence of all foreign influence, enter into the true interests of the policy of the whole of Europe.

They declare that no consequence unfavourable to the rights of Switzerland with respect to its Neutrality and the Inviolability of its Territory can or ought to be drawn from the events which led to the passage of the Allied Troops across a part of the Helvetic States. This passage, freely consented to by the Cantons in the Convention of the 20th May, was the necessary result of the free adherence of Switzerland to the principles manifested by the Powers who signed the Treaty of Alliance of the 25th March.

The Powers acknowledged with satisfaction that the conduct of Switzerland under these trying circumstances has shown that she knew how to make great sacrifices to the general good, and to the support of a cause which all the Powers of Europe defended, and that, in fine, Switzerland has deserved the advantages which have been secured to her, whether by the Arrangements of the Congress of Vienna, by the Treaty of Paris of this day, or by the present Act, to which all the Powers in Europe are invited to accede.

In faith of which the present Declaration has been concluded and signed at Paris the 20th November, 1815.

The Signatures follow in the Alphabetical Order of the Courts.

AUSTRIA.	(L.S.)	LE PRINCE DE METTERNICH.
	(L.S.)	LE BARON DE WESSENBERG.
FRANCE.	(L.S.)	RICHELIEU.
GREAT BRITAIN.	(L.S.)	CASTLEREAGH.
	(L.S.)	WELLINGTON.
PRUSSIA.	(L.S.)	LE PRINCE DE HARDENBERG.
	(L.S.)	LE BARON DE HUMBOLDT.
RUSSIA.	(L.S.)	LE PRINCE DE RASOUMOFFSKI.
	(L.S.)	LE COMTE CAPO D'ISTRIA.

10

TREATY of Alliance and Friendship between Great Britain, Austria (Prussia, and Russia). Signed at Paris, 20th November, 1815.

In the Name of the Most Holy and Undivided Trinity.

THE purpose of the Alliance concluded at Vienna the 25th day of March, 1815, having been happily attained by the re-establishment in France of the order of things which the last criminal attempt of Napoleon Bonaparte had momentarily subverted; Their Majesties the King of the United Kingdom of Great Britain and Ireland, the Emperor of Austria, King of Hungary and Bohemia, the Emperor of all the Russias, and the King of Prussia, considering that the repose of Europe is essentially interwoven with the confirmation of the order of things founded on the maintenance of the Royal Authority and of the Constitutional Charter, and wishing to employ all their means to prevent the general Tranquillity (the object of the wishes of mankind and the constant end of their efforts), from being again disturbed; desirous moreover to draw closer the ties which unite them for the common interests of their people, have resolved to give to the principles solemnly laid down in the Treaties of Chaumont of the 1st March, 1814, and of Vienna of the 25th of March, 1815, the application the most analogous to the present state of affairs, and to fix beforehand by a solemn Treaty the principles which they propose to follow, in order to guarantee Europe from dangers by which she may still be menaced; for which purpose the High Contracting Parties have named to discuss, settle and sign the conditions of this Treaty, namely;

His Majesty the King of the United Kingdom of Great Britain and Ireland, the Right Honourable Robert Stewart Viscount Castlereagh, &c., &c., &c., and the Most Illustrious and Most Noble Lord Arthur, Duke, Marquis and Earl of Wellington, Marquis of Douro, Viscount Wellington of Talavera and of Wellington, and Baron Douro, of Wellesley, &c., &c., &c.,

And His Majesty the Emperor of Austria, King of Hungary and Bohemia, the Sieur Clement Wenceslas Lothaire, Prince of Metternich-Winnebourg-Ochsenhausen, &c., &c., and the Sieur John Philip Baron of Wessenberg, &c., &c., who, after having exchanged their full powers, found to be in good and due form, have agreed upon the following Articles:

Execution of Treaties of Peace, &c., with France, of 20th November, 1815.

Art. I. The High Contracting Parties reciprocally promise to maintain, in its force and vigour, the Treaty signed this day with His Most Christian Majesty, and to see that the stipulations of the said Treaty, as well as those of the Particular Conventions which have reference thereto, shall be strictly and faithfully executed in their fullest extent.

Confirmation of Arrangements of 1814 and 1815. Exclusion of Bonaparte Family from Supreme Power in France. Measures of General Security.

Art. II. The High Contracting Parties, having engaged in the War which has just terminated, for the purpose of maintaining inviolably the Arrangements settled at Paris last year, for the safety and interest of Europe, have judged it advisable to renew the said Engagements by the present Act, and to confirm them as mutually obligatory, subject to the modifications contained in the Treaty signed this day with the Plenipotentiaries of His Most Christian Majesty, and particularly those by which Napoleon Bonaparte and his family, in pursuance of the Treaty of the 11th of April, 1814, have been for ever excluded from Supreme Power in France, which exclusion the Contracting Powers bind themselves, by the present Act, to maintain in full vigour, and, should it be necessary, with the whole of their forces. And as the same Revolutionary Principles which upheld the last criminal usurpation, might again, under other forms, convulse France, and thereby endanger the repose of other States; under these circumstances, the High Contracting Parties solemnly admitting it to be their duty to redouble their watchfulness for the tranquillity and interests of their people, engage, in case so unfortunate an event should again occur, to concert amongst themselves, and with His Most Christian Majesty, the measures which they may judge necessary to be pursued for the safety of their respective States, and for the general Tranquillity of Europe.

Military Line in France. Renewal of Alliance of Chaumont.

Art. III. The High Contracting Parties, in agreeing with His Most Christian Majesty that a Line of Military Positions in France should be occupied by a corps of Allied Troops during a certain number of years, had in view to secure, as far as lay in their power, the effect of the stipulations contained in Articles I and II of the present Treaty, and, uniformly disposed to adopt every salutary measure calculated to secure the Tranquillity of Europe by maintaining the order of things re-established in France, they engage, in case the said body of troops should be attacked or menaced with an attack on the part of France, that the said Powers should be again obliged to place themselves on a war establishment against that Power, in order to maintain either of the said stipulations, or to secure and support the great interests to which they relate, each of the High Contracting Parties shall furnish, without delay, according to the stipulations of the Treaty of Chaumont, and especially in pursuance of Articles VII and VIII of this Treaty, its full contingent of 60,000 men, in addition to the forces left in France, or such part of the said contingent as the exigency of the case may require, should be put in motion.

Additional Forces in the event of War. Conditions of Peace.

Art. IV. If, unfortunately, the forces stipulated in the preceding Article should be found insufficient, the High Contracting Parties will concert together, without loss of time, as to the additional number of troops to be furnished by each for the support of the common cause; and they engage to employ, in case of need, the whole of their forces, in order to bring the War to a speedy and successful termination, reserving to themselves the right to prescribe, by common consent, such conditions of Peace as shall hold out to Europe a sufficient guarantee against the recurrence of a similar calamity.

Duration of Engagements.

Art. V. The High Contracting Parties having agreed to the dispositions laid down in the preceding Articles, for the purpose of securing the effect of their engagements during the period of the temporary occupation, declare, moreover, that even after the expiration of this measure, the said engagements shall still remain in full force and vigour, for the purpose of carrying into effect such measures as may be deemed necessary for the maintenance of the stipulations contained in Articles I and II of the present Act.

Renewal of Meetings of the Allies for Maintenance of Peace of Europe.

Art. VI. To facilitate and to secure the execution of the present Treaty, and to consolidate the connections which at the present moment so closely unite the Four Sovereigns for the happiness of the world, the High Contracting Parties have agreed to renew their Meetings at fixed periods, either under the immediate auspices of the Sovereigns themselves, or by their respective Ministers, for the purpose of consulting upon their common interests, and for the consideration of the measures which at each of those periods shall be considered the most salutary for the repose and prosperity of Nations, and for the maintenance of the Peace of Europe.

Ratifications.

ART. VII. The present Treaty shall be ratified, and the Ratifications shall be exchanged within two months, or sooner, if possible.

In faith of which the respective Plenipotentiaries have signed it, and affixed thereto the Seal of their Arms.

Done at Paris, the 20th of November, in the year of Our Lord. 1815.

(L.S.)   CASTLEREAGH.   (L.S.)   METTERNICH.
(L.S.)   WELLINGTON.   (L.S.)   WESSENBERG.

[NOTE.—Separate Treaties were signed on the same day by the Plenipotentiaries of Great Britain, Russia, and Prussia, respectively.]

11

CONVENTION between Great Britain (Austria, Prussia, and Russia) and France, relative to the Pecuniary Indemnity to be paid by France to the Allied Powers. Signed at Paris, 20th November, 1815.

[This Convention was annexed to the Definitive Treaty of the same date, see Art. IV.]

Convention between Great Britain and France, concluded in conformity with Article IV of the Principal Treaty, relative to the Payment of the Pecuniary Indemnity to be furnished by France to the Allied Powers.

THE payment to which France has bound herself to the Allied Powers, as an Indemnity, by Article IV of the Treaty of this day, shall take place in the form and at the periods prescribed by the following Articles:—

Payment of Indemnity in Five Years.

ART. I. The sum of 700,000,000 of francs, being the amount of the Indemnity, shall be discharged, day by day, in equal portions, in the space of 5 years, by means of *Bons au Porteur* on the Royal Treasury of France, in the manner that shall be now set forth.

Mode of Paying Indemnity.

ART. II. The Treasury shall give over, immediately, to the Allied Powers, 15 Engagements for 46,000,000 and two-thirds each, forming together the sum of 700,000,000; the first Engagement payable on the 31st March, 1816, the second on the 31st of July of the same year, and so on in every fourth month during the five successive years.

Engagements to be exchanged for Bons au Porteur.

ART. III. These Engagements shall not be negotiable, but they shall be periodically exchanged against *Bons au Porteur*, negotiable, drawn in the form used in the ordinary service of the Royal Treasury.

Time at which Engagements are to be exchanged for Bons au Porteur.

ART. IV. In the month which shall precede the four, in the course of which an Engagement is to be paid, that Engagement shall be divided by the Treasury of France, into *Bons au Porteur* payable in Paris, in equal portions, from the first to the last day of the four months.

Thus the Engagement of 46,000,000 and two-thirds, falling due the 31st of March, 1816, shall be exchanged in the month of November, 1815, against *Bons au Porteur*, payable in equal portions from the 1st of December, 1815, to the 31st of March, 1816.

The Engagement of 46,000,000 and two-thirds, which will fall due the 31st of July, 1816, shall be exchanged in the month of March of the same year, against *Bons au Porteur*, payable in equal portions from the 1st of April, 1816, to the 31st of July of the same year, and so on every four months.

Issue of Bons au Porteur in Coupures or Bills.

ART. V. No single *Bon au Porteur* shall be delivered for the sum due each day, but the sum so due shall be divided into several *Coupures* or Bills, of 1,000, 2,000, 5,000, 10,000 and 20,000 francs, the which sums added together, will amount to the sum total of the payment due for each day.

Limit to amount of Bons au Porteur.

ART. VI. The Allied Powers, convinced that it is as much their interest as that of France, that too considerable a sum of *Bons au Porteur* should not be issued at once, agree that there never shall be in circulation *Bons* for more than 50,000,000 of francs at a time.

Non-payment of Interest.

ART. VII. No Interest shall be paid by France for the delay of 5 years, which the Allied Powers allow to her for the payment of the 700,000,000 of francs.

Guarantee to be made over by France to Allied Powers.

ART. VIII. On the 1st of January, 1816, there shall be made over by France to the Allied Powers, as a Guarantee for the regularity of the payments, a Fund of Interest inscribed in the *Grand Livre* of the Public

Debt of France, of 7,000,000 of francs, on a capital of 140,000,000. This Fund of Interest shall be used to make good, if there should be need of it, the deficiencies in the *Acceptances* of the French Government, and to render the payments equal, at the end of every six months, to the *Bons au Porteur* which shall have fallen due, as shall be hereafter detailed.

Persons in whose Name the Fund of Interest is to be Inscribed.

ART. IX. This Fund of Interest shall be inscribed in the name of such persons as the Allied Powers shall point out; but these persons cannot be the holders of the Inscriptions, except in the case provided for in Article XI ensuing.

Right of Allies to transfer Inscriptions in other Names.

The Allied Powers further reserve to themselves the right to transfer the Inscriptions to other names, as often as they shall judge necessary.

Deposit of Inscriptions.

ART. X. The deposit of these Inscriptions shall be confined to one Treasurer named by the Allied Powers, and to another named by the French Government.

Appointment of Mixed Commission.

ART. XI. There shall be a Mixed Commission, composed of an equal number on both sides, of Allied and French Commissioners, who shall examine every six months the state of the payments, and shall regulate the balance.

Payments. Arrears.

The *Bons* of the Treasury paid shall constitute the Payments; those which shall not yet have been presented to the Treasury of France, shall enter into the account of the subsequent balance; those also which shall have fallen due, been presented, and not paid, shall constitute the arrear, and the sum of Inscriptions to be applied, at the market price of the day, to cover the deficit.

Bons unpaid to be given up to French Commissioners and paid over to Allied Commissioners.

As soon as that operation shall have taken place, the *Bons* unpaid shall be given up to the French Commissioners, and the Mixed Commission shall order the Treasurers to pay over the sum so determined upon, and the Treasurers shall be authorised and obliged to pay it over to the Commissioners of the Allied Powers, who shall dispose of it as they shall think proper.

Full amount of Inscriptions to be always in hands of Treasurers.

ART. XII. France engages to replace immediately in the hands of the Treasurers, an amount of Inscriptions equal to that which may have been made use of, according to the foregoing Article, in order that the Fund stipulated in Article VIII may be always kept at its full amount.

Interest on Bons au Porteur not Paid when Presented.

ART. XIII. France shall pay an interest of 5 per cent. per annum, from the date of the *Bons au Porteur* falling due, upon all such *Bons* the payment of which may have been delayed by the act of France.

Facilities for Payment of last 100,000,000 Francs Indemnity.

ART. XIV. When the first 600,000,000 of Francs shall have been paid, the Allies in order to accelerate the entire liberation of France, will accept, should it be agreeable to the French Government, the Fund mentioned in Article VIII, at the market price of that day, to such an amount as will be equal to the remainder due of the 700,000,000. France will only have to furnish the difference, should any exist.

Facilities for Payment of last 100,000,000 Francs Indemnity.

ART. XV. Should this plan not be convenient to France, the 100,000,000 of francs which would remain due, may be discharged in the manner pointed out in Articles II, III, IV, and V; and, after the complete payment of the 700,000,000, the Inscriptions stipulated for in Article VIII shall be returned to France.

Fulfilment by France of Engagements relative to Clothing and Equipment of Allied Armies.

ART. XVI. The French Government engages to execute, independently of the Pecuniary Indemnity stipulated by the present Convention, all the Engagements stipulated for in the Special Conventions concluded with the different Powers and their Co-Allies, relative to the clothing and equipment of their Armies; and engages for the exact deliverance and payment of the *Bons* and *Mandats* arising from the said Conventions, in as far as they shall not have been already discharged, at the time of the signature of the Principal Treaty, and of the present Convention.

Done at Paris, this 20th day of November, in the year of Our Lord, 1815.

(L.S.)   CASTLEREAGH.
(L.S.)   WELLINGTON.
(L.S.)   RICHELIEU.

12 TREATY OF PARIS

DEFINITIVE TREATY of Peace between Great Britain, Austria, Prussia, and Russia, and France. Signed at Paris, 20th November, 1815.

[See special references to this Treaty, and the Conventions annexed thereto, in the Treaty of Alliance concluded between the 4 Powers, on the same day.]

In the Name of the Most Holy and Undivided Treaty.

THE Allied Powers having by their united efforts, and by the success of their arms, preserved France and Europe from the convulsions with which they were menaced by the late enterprise of Napoleon Bonaparte, and by the revolutionary system reproduced in France, to promote its success; participating at present with His Most Christian Majesty in the desire to consolidate, by maintaining inviolate the Royal authority, and by restoring the operation of the Constitutional Charter, the order of things which had been happily re-established in France, as also in the object of restoring between France and her neighbours those relations of reciprocal confidence and goodwill which the fatal effects of the Revolution and of the system of Conquest had for so long a time disturbed: persuaded, at the same time, that this last object can only be obtained by an arrangement framed to secure to the Allies proper indemnities for the past and solid guarantees for the future, they have, in concert with His Majesty the King of France, taken into consideration the means of giving effect to this arrangement; and being satisfied that the Indemnity due to the Allied Powers cannot be either entirely Territorial or entirely Pecuniary, without prejudice to France in the one or other of her essential interests, and that it would be more fit to combine both the modes, in order to avoid the inconvenience which would result, were either resorted to separately, their Imperial and Royal Majesties have adopted this basis for their present transactions; and agreeing alike as to the necessity of retaining for a fixed time in the Frontier Provinces of France, a certain number of allied troops, they have determined to combine their different arrangements, founded upon these bases, in a Definitive Treaty. For this purpose, and to this effect, His Majesty the King of the United Kingdom of Great Britain and Ireland, for himself and his Allies on the one part, and His Majesty the King of France and Navarre on the other part, have named their Plenipotentiaries to discuss, settle and sign the said Definitive Treaty; namely, His Majesty the King of the United Kingdom of Great Britain and Ireland, the Right Honourable Robert Stewart Viscount Castlereagh, Knight of the Most Noble Order of the Garter, His said Majesty's Principal Secretary of State for Foreign Affairs, &c.; and the Most Illustrious and Most Noble Lord Arthur, Duke, Marquess, and Earl of Wellington, Marquess of Douro, Viscount Wellington, of Talavera and of Wellington, and Baron Douro of Wellesley, a Member of His said Majesty's Most Honourable Privy Council, a Field Marshal of his Armies, Colonel of the Royal Regiment of Horse Guards, Knight of the Most Noble Order of the Garter, &c.;

And His Majesty the King of France and of Navarre, the Sieur Armand Emanuel du Plessis Richelieu, Duke of Richelieu, Peer of France, First Gentleman of the Chamber of His Most Christian Majesty, his Minister and Secretary of State for Foreign Affairs, and President of the Council of his Ministers, &c.

Who having exchanged their Full Powers, found to be in good and due form, have signed the following Articles:—

Frontiers of France: as in 1790.

ART. I. The Frontiers of France shall be the same as they were in the year 1790, save and accept the modifications on one side and on the other, which are detailed in the present Article.

Fortress of Philippeville and Marienburg, &c.

1st, on the Northern Frontiers the line of demarcation shall remain as it was fixed by the Treaty of Paris, as far as opposite to Quiévrain, from thence it shall follow the ancient limits of the Belgian Provinces, of the late Bishopric of Liège, and of the Duchy of Bouillon, as they existed in the year 1790, leaving the Territories included within that line (enclavés), of Philippeville and Marienburg, with the Fortresses so called, together with the whole of the Duchy of Bouillon without the Frontiers of France. From Villers, near Orval, upon the confines of the Department Des Ardennes, and of the Grand Duchy of Luxemburg, as far as Perle, upon the great road leading from Thionville to Treves, the line shall remain as it was laid down by the Treaty of Paris. From Perle it shall pass by Lauensdorff, Walwich, Schardorff Niederveiling, Pellweiler (all these places with their Banlieues or dependencies remaining to France) to Houvre; and shall follow from thence the old limits of the District (Pays) of Sarrebruck, leaving Sarrelouis and the course of the Sarre, together with the places situated to the right of the line above-described, and their Banlieues or dependencies without the limits of France. From the limits of the district of Sarrebruck the line of demarcation shall be the same which at present separates from Germany, the departments of the Moselle and of the Lower Rhine, as far as to the Lauter, which River shall from thence serve as the Frontier until it falls into the Rhine.

Fortress of Landau, &c.

All the territory on the left bank of the Lauter, including the Fortress of Landau, shall form part of Germany. The Town of Weissenburg, however, through which the River runs, shall remain entirely to France, with a rayon on the left bank, not exceeding 1,000 toises, and which shall be more particularly determined by the Commissioners who shall be charged with the approaching designation of the Boundaries.

2ndly, leaving the mouth of the Lauter, and continuing along the departments of the Lower Rhine, the Upper Rhine, the Doubs, and the Jura to the Canton de Vaud, the Frontiers shall remain as fixed by the Treaty of Paris. The *Thalweg* of the Rhine shall form the Boundary between France and the States of Germany, but the property of the Islands shall remain in perpetuity, as it shall be fixed by a new survey of the course of that river, and continue unchanged whatever variation that course may undergo in the lapse of time. Commissioners shall be named on both sides, by the High Contracting Parties, within the space of three months, to proceed upon the said survey. One half of the bridge between Strasbourg and Kehl shall belong to France, and the other half to the Grand Duchy of Baden.

3rdly, in order to establish a direct communication between the Canton of Geneva and Switzerland, that part of the Pays de Gex, bounded on the east by the Lake Léman; on the south, by the territory of the Canton of Geneva; on the north, by that of the Canton de Vaud; on the west, by the course of the Versoix, and by a line which comprehends the Communes of Collex-Bossy, and Meyrin, leaving the Commune of Ferney to France, shall be ceded to the Helvetic Confederacy, in order to be united to the Canton of Geneva. The line of the French Custom-houses shall be placed to the west of the Jura, so that the whole of the Pays de Gex shall be without that line.

4thly, from the frontiers of the Canton of Geneva, as far as the Mediterranean, the line of demarcation shall be that which in the year 1790 separated France from Savoy and from the County of Nice.

Monaco, &c.

The Relations which the Treaty of Paris of 1814 had re-established between France and the Principality of Monaco shall cease for ever, and the same Relations shall exist between that Principality and His Majesty the King of Sardinia.

5thly, all the Territories and Districts included within the Boundary of the French territory (*enclavés*), as determined by the present Article, shall remain united to France.

6thly, the High Contracting Parties shall name within 3 months after the signature of the present Treaty, Commissioners to regulate everything relating to the designation of the Boundaries of the respective Countries, and as soon as the labours of the Commissioners shall have terminated, Maps shall be drawn and landmarks shall be erected, which shall point out the respective limits.

Fortresses, &c., to be placed at disposal of Allied Powers.
ART. II. The Fortresses, Places, and Districts, which, according to the preceding Article are no longer to form part of the French territory, shall be placed at the disposal of the Allied Powers, at the periods fixed by Article IX of the Military Convention annexed to the present Treaty; and His Majesty the King of France renounces for himself, His heirs, and successors for ever, the rights of Sovereignty and property which he has hitherto exercised over the said Fortresses, Places, and Districts.

Fortifications of Huninguen to be destroyed.
ART. III. The Fortifications of Huninguen having been constantly an object of uneasiness to the town of Bâle, the High Contracting Parties, in order to give to the Helvetic Confederacy a new proof of their good will and of their solicitude for its welfare, have agreed among themselves to demolish the fortifications of Huninguen, and the French Government engages from the same motive not to re-establish them at any time, and not to replace them by other Fortifications at a distance of less than that of 3 leagues from the town of Bâle.

Extension of Neutrality of Switzerland to part of Savoy.
The Neutrality of Switzerland shall be extended to the territory situated to the north of a line to be drawn from Ugine, that Town being included, to the south of the Lake of Annecy, by Faverge, as far as Lecheraine, and from thence by the Lake of Bourget, as far as the Rhone, in like manner as it was extended to the Provinces of Chablais and of Faucigny, by Article XCII of the Final Act of the Congress of Vienna.

Indemnity to be Paid by France.
ART. IV. The pecuniary part of the Indemnity to be furnished by France to the Allied Powers is fixed at the sum of 700,000,000 of Francs. The modes, the periods, and the guarantees for the payment of this sum shall be regulated by a Special Convention, which shall have the same force and effect as if it were inserted, word for word, in the present Treaty.

Military Occupation by Allies along the Frontiers of France.
ART. V. The state of uneasiness and of fermentation, which after so

many violent convulsions, and particularly after the last catastrophe, France must still experience, notwithstanding the paternal intentions of her King, and the advantages secured to every class of his subjects by the Constitutional Charter, requiring, for the security of the neighbouring States, certain measures of precaution and of temporary guarantee, it has been judged indispensable to occupy, during a fixed time, by a corps of Allied Troops certain military positions along the frontiers of France, under the express reserve, that such occupation shall in no way prejudice the Sovereignty of His Most Christian Majesty, nor the state of possession, such as it is recognized and confirmed by the present Treaty. The number of these troops shall not exceed 150,000 men. The Commander-in-Chief of this army shall be nominated by the Allied Powers. This army shall occupy the Fortresses of Condé, Valenciennes, Bouchain, Cambray, Le Quesnoy, Maubeuge, Landrecies, Avesnes, Rocroy, Givet with Charlemont, Mezières, Sedan, Montmédy, Thionville, Longwy, Bitsch, and the Tête-de-Pont of Fort Louis. As the maintenance of the army destined for this service is to be provided by France, a Special Convention shall regulate everything which may relate to that object. This Convention, which shall have the same force and effect as if it were inserted word for word in the present Treaty, shall also regulate the relations of the Army of Occupation with the civil and military authorities of the country. The utmost extent of the duration of this military occupation is fixed at 5 years. It may terminate before that period if, at the end of 3 years, the Allied Sovereigns, after having, in concert with His Majesty the King of France, maturely examined their reciprocal situation and interests, and the progress which shall have been made in France in the re-establishment of order and tranquillity, shall agree to acknowledge that the motives which led them to that measure have ceased to exist. But whatever may be the result of this deliberation, all the Fortresses and Positions occupied by the Allied troops shall, at the expiration of 5 years, be evacuated without further delay, and given up to His Most Christian Majesty, or to his heirs and successors.

Evacuation of French Territory.

ART. VI. The Foreign Troops, not forming part of the Army of Occupation, shall evacuate the French Territory within the term fixed by Article IX of the Military Convention annexed to the present Treaty.

Period fixed for Emigration and Disposal of Property in ceded Territories.

ART. VII. In all Countries which shall change Sovereigns, as well in virtue of the present Treaty as of the arrangements which are to be made in consequence thereof, a period of 6 years from the date of the exchange of the Ratifications shall be allowed to the inhabitants, natives or foreigners, of whatever condition and nation they may be, to dispose of their Property, if they should think fit so to do, and to retire to whatever country they may choose.

Ceded Countries. Application of Treaty of 30th May, 1814, to present Treaty.

ART. VIII. All the dispositions of the Treaty of Paris of the 30th of May, 1814, relative to the Countries ceded by the Treaty, shall equally apply to the several territories and districts ceded by the present Treaty.

Conventions of Claims.

ART. IX. The High Contracting Parties having caused representation to be made of the different Claims arising out of the non-execution of Articles XIX and following of the Treaty of the 30th of May, 1814, as well as of the Additional Articles of that Treaty signed between Great Britain and France, desiring to render more efficacious the stipulations made thereby, and having determined, by two Separate Conventions, the line to be pursued on each side for that purpose, the said two Conventions, as annexed to the present Treaty, shall, in order to secure the complete execution of the above-mentioned Articles, have the same force and effect as if the same were inserted, word for word, herein.

Restoration of Prisoners.

ART. X. All Prisoners taken during the hostilities, as well as all hostages which may have been carried off or given, shall be restored in the shortest time possible. The same shall be the case with respect to the prisoners taken previously to the Treaty of the 30th of May, 1814, and who shall not already have been restored.

Maintenance of Treaty of 30th May, 1814, and of Final Act of Vienna Congress of 9th June, 1815.

ART. XI. The Treaty of Paris of the 30th of May, 1814 and the Final Act of the Congress of Vienna of the 9th of June 1815, are confirmed, and shall be maintained in all such of their enactments which shall not have been modified by the Articles of the present Treaty.

Ratifications.

ART. XII. The present Treaty, with the Conventions annexed thereto, shall be ratified in one Act, and the Ratifications thereof shall be exchanged in the space of two months, or sooner, if possible.

In witness whereof the respective Plenipotentiaries have signed the same, and have affixed thereunto the Seals of their Arms.

Done at Paris, this 20th day of November, in the year of Our Lord, 1815.

(L.S.) CASTLEREAGH.   (L.S.) RICHELIEU.
(L.S.) WELLINGTON.

ADDITIONAL ARTICLE.   *Abolition of the Slave Trade.*
Paris, 20th November, 1815.

The High Contracting Powers, sincerely desiring to give effect to the measures on which they deliberated at the Congress of Vienna relative to the complete and universal abolition of the Slave Trade, and having, each in their respective dominions, prohibited, without restriction, their Colonies and Subjects from taking any part whatever in this traffic, engage to renew conjointly their efforts, with the view of securing final success to their principles which they proclaimed in the Declaration of the 4th (8th) of February, 1815, and of concerting, without loss of time, through their Ministers at the Courts of London and of Paris, the most effectual measures for the entire and definitive abolition of a Commerce so odious, and so strongly condemned by the laws of Religion and of Nature.

The present Additional Articles shall have the same force and effect as if it were inserted, word for word, in the Treaty signed this day. It shall be included in the Ratification of the said Treaty.

In witness whereof the respective Plenipotentiaries have signed the same, and have affixed thereunto the Seals of their Arms.

Done at Paris, this 20th day of November, 1815.

(L.S.) CASTLEREAGH.   (L.S.) RICHELIEU.
(L.S.) WELLINGTON.

13

PROTOCOL of Conference between Great Britain, Austria, Prussia, and Russia, respecting the Fortification of the Netherlands, Germany, and Savoy. Vienna, 21st November, 1815.

[Referred to in Art. II of the Treaty between Prussia and Netherlands of 8th November 1816.]

Disposal of Contributions payable by France.

THE Ministers of the Four Courts have taken into consideration the rules to be laid down for the employment of that part of the Contributions payable by France, which, according to their general determinations contained in the *Procès-verbal* of the 6th of November, 1815, are to be wholly appropriated to the strengthening of the Defensive Line of the States bordering on France; their Excellencies have recognized, in the adoption of this essentially European system, that the general safety and interests of all, and not the private advantage of any one State, is the object in view, and consequently that all the Powers who have concurred therein, should have an equal right reciprocally to watch over its execution, and from time to time to take cognizance of the application of the funds destined for an object of such high importance.

They have further resolved, that, in order to execute this measure in concert, and by regularly combined operations, it will be expedient to confide to such of the Great Powers as may be most conveniently situated for that purpose, the care of arranging with the Sovereigns directly interested in the several works, the plan to be pursued and the most convenient means of carrying it into effect.

Sums to be applied towards Fortifications in the Netherlands.

1. For this purpose the Undersigned Ministers have agreed, that the British Government shall, conjointly with that of the Netherlands, determine upon the special employment of the Sums destined for fortifying the latter Country.

New Defensive Works for Germany.

2. That with respect to the Defensive System of Germany, the Courts of Austria and of Prussia shall arrange, as well with each other as with those Sovereigns in whose territories new defensive works are to be constructed, the plans that are to be adopted and the measures that are to be pursued respecting them.

Fortification of Savoy.

3. That the Austrian Government shall enter into Relations with the King of Sardinia, relative to the Fortification of Savoy, exactly similar to those in which Great Britain is placed with respect to those of the Netherlands.

That the Powers reserve the right of coming to an understanding with Spain, conformably to the principles herein established, and as their Excellencies have conceived it indispensable, that the operations which are about to be projected and executed, should form one general System, and be as closely connected as possible, it is further agreed that frequent communications shall take place between the Cabinets, for the purpose of respectively informing themselves of the different measures which may have been adopted, for the most advantageous employment of the Sums appropriated to ensuring the success of the said operations.

The present *Procès-verbal* is solely intended to testify the unanimity of the subscribing Ministers on the principle of the question of which it treats, and to form the basis of the instructions which shall be given with regard to it to the Ministers at the different Courts.

CASTLEREAGH.
METTERNICH.
CAPO D'ISTRIA.
HARDENBERG.
RASOUMOFFSKY.

14

TREATY between Great Britain and the Netherlands respecting Luxemburg, &c. Signed at Frankfort, 16th November, 1816.

[This Treaty formed Annex V. to the General Treaty of Frankfort of 20th July, 1819.]
In the Name of the Most Holy and Undivided Trinity.

Preamble. Reference to Treaty of 20th November, 1815.

His Majesty the King of the United Kingdom of Great Britain and Ireland, and His Majesty the King of the Netherlands, Grand Duke of Luxemburg, desiring, in common with their Majesties the Emperor of Austria, the Emperor of all the Russias, and the King of Prussia, to give effect, by a Particular Treaty, to the Articles and Stipulations of the Treaty of Peace, concluded at Paris the 20th day of November, 1815, as well those relating to the Kingdom of the Netherlands as those which concern the Grand Duchy of Luxemburg, and to consolidate the Arrangements therefrom arising, have nominated for the above purpose the following Plenipotentiaries, viz.:

His Majesty the King of the United Kingdom of Great Britain and Ireland, The Right Honourable Richard Le Poer Trench, Earl of Clancarty, Viscount Dunlo, Baron Kilconnel, Baron Trench of Garbally in the United Kingdom of Great Britain and Ireland, Member of the Most Honourable Privy Council of Great Britain, and also of that of Ireland, President of the Committee of the former for the Affairs of Trade and Plantations, Colonel of the County of Galway Regiment of Militia, Ambassador Extraordinary and Plenipotentiary to His Majesty the King of the Netherlands, &c.;

And His Majesty the King of the Netherlands, Grand Duke of Luxemburg, the Sieur Hans Christopher Ernest Baron de Gagern, His Envoy Extraordinary and Minister Plenipotentiary to the German Diet, and to the Free Town of Frankfort, &c.

Who, after having exchanged their Full Powers, found in good and due form, have agreed upon, concluded, and signed the following Articles:—

Sovereignty of the Netherlands over Belgic Provinces of the Bishopric of Liège and the Duchy of Bouillon. Fortresses of Philippeville and Marienburg.

ART. I. His Majesty the King of the Netherlands, Grand Duke of Luxemburg, shall possess for Himself, His Descendants and Successors in full Property and Sovereignty, all the districts which, having made part of the Belgic Provinces of the Bishopric of Liège, and of the Duchy of Bouillon, in 1790, were ceded by France to the Allied Powers by the Treaty concluded at Paris the 20th day of November, 1815, as well as the territories enclosed (*enclavés*) with the Fortresses of Philippeville and Marienburg ceded by the same Treaty.

Boundaries.

In consequence of this determination, the Boundaries of the States of His Majesty the King of the Netherlands, Grand Duke of Luxemburg, and those of France, beginning from the North Sea, shall remain as they were fixed by the Treaty of Paris of the 30th day of May, 1814, as far as opposite Quiévrain.

From Quiévrain the Line of Demarcation shall follow the ancient external Boundaries of Belgium, of the former Bishopric of Liège, and of the Duchy of Bouillon, as far as Villers, near Orval, as they were in 1790, taking in the whole of those Countries, and especially the Fortresses and Territories of Philippeville and Marienburg, in conformity with the Stipulations of Article I. of the said Treaty of the 20th day of November, 1815, and without otherwise changing the Boundaries of the Kingdom of the Netherlands, and of the Grand Duchy of Luxemburg, which shall remain the same as they were fixed by the Treaty of Vienna of the 31st day of May, 1815, which Treaty is in all other respects fully confirmed.

French Pecuniary Indemnity.

ART. II. A part of the Pecuniary Indemnifications which His Most Christian Majesty has agreed to pay, by Article IV. of the Treaty of Paris of the 20th of November, 1815, being in virtue of the Arrangement agreed upon at Paris, between the Allied Powers, intended to defray the expense of strengthening the Line of Defence of the States bordering on France, His Majesty the King of the Netherlands, Grand Duke of Luxemburg, shall receive for this purpose the sum of 60,000,000 francs.

Part of Indemnity to be employed for Defence of Frontiers.

His Majesty the King of the Netherlands, Grand Duke of Luxemburg, engages to employ that sum on the works necessary for the Defence of the Frontiers of His States, in conformity with the system adopted, and according to the concert agreed upon on this subject between the Allied Powers, by the Protocol of the Conference of their Ministers of the 21st day of November, 1815, hereunto annexed, and which shall have the same force and validity as if it were inserted word for word in the present Treaty.

Relinquishment of Claim to Indemnification under Treaty of 20th November, 1815.

ART. III. His Majesty the King of the Netherlands, Grand Duke of Luxemburg, justly appreciating the advantages which result from the preceding arrangements, as well in respect to the extension of His territory, as to its means of defence, gives up, in reference to the sums stipulated in Article IV. of the Treaty of Paris of the 20th November, 1815, the share which His Majesty might claim under the head of Indemnifications, and which was fixed by the Protocol of the Conference of the 21st of November, 1815, at the sum of 21,264,832 fr. 22½c.

Indemnity to be divided between Austria and Prussia.

His Majesty agrees that this share shall serve to complete the Indemnifications to Austria and Prussia, and be divided in equal proportions between those Powers.

Fortress of Luxemburg to be a Fortress of the Germanic Confederation.

ART. IV. Article III. of the Treaty concluded at Vienna the 31st May, 1815, and Article LXVII. of the Act of the Congress of Vienna, having stipulated that the Fortress of Luxemburg should be considered as a Fortress of the Germanic Confederation, this arrangement is maintained and expressly confirmed by the present Convention.

Prussia to appoint Governor and Commandant of Fortress of Luxemburg. Composition of Garrison.

ART. V. His Majesty the King of the Netherlands, Grand Duke of Luxemburg, concedes to His Majesty the King of Prussia the right of naming the Governor and the Commandant of that Fortress, and agrees that the Garrison in general, as well as each particular description of force, shall be composed of three-fourths Prussian troops and one-fourth Belgic troops (*Troupes des Pays-Bas*); thus relinquishing the right of appointment which Article LXVII. of the Act of the Congress of Vienna secured to His Majesty; but in such wise that this arrangement, made solely upon military grounds, shall in no respect affect the rights of Sovereignty of His Majesty the King of the Netherlands, Grand Duke of Luxemburg, over the Town and Fortress of Luxemburg.

Civil Government over City and Fortress of Luxemburg vested in King of Netherlands.

ART. VI. The right of Sovereignty belonging in all its plenitude to His Majesty the King of the Netherlands, Grand Duke of Luxemburg, over the City and Fortress of Luxemburg, as well as throughout the whole of the Grand Duchy, the administration of Justice, the collection of Duties and Taxes of every description, as well as every other branch of the Civil Adminstration, shall remain exclusively in the hands of those employed by His Majesty.

Confirmation of Treaties of 1815.

ART. VII. The Treaty concluded with His Majesty the King of the Netherlands, Grand Duke of Luxemburg, at Vienna, the 31st day of May, 1815, as well as all the Articles of the Act of the Congress of Vienna of the 9th of June, 1815, which concern His Majesty's interests, or which have been stipulated with Him are confirmed in all the points and arrangements which are not expressly changed by the present Convention, or by that concluded between His Majesty the King of Prussia and His said Majesty the King of the Netherlands, Grand Duke of Luxemburg, the 8th day of November, 1816.

Ratifications.

ART. VIII. The present Convention shall be ratified, and the Acts of Ratification shall be exchanged within the space of 3 months, or sooner if practicable.

In testimony whereof, the respective Plenipotentiaries have signed it, and have thereunto affixed the Seal of their Arms.

Done at Frankfort on the Mayne, this 16th day of November, in the Year of our Lord, 1816.

(L.S.)   CLANCARTY.
(L.S.)   LE BARON DE GAGERN.

ANNEX.—Protocol of Conference of 21st November, 1815.

15

CONVENTION between Great Britain (Austria, Prussia, Russia), and France, for the Evacuation of the French Territory by the Allied Troops. Signed at Aix-la-Chapelle, 9th October, 1818.

In the Name of the Most Holy and Undivided Trinity.

Preamble. Reference to Treaty of 20th November, 1815. Evacuation of France at end of 3rd year of Occupation.

THEIR Majesties the Emperor of Austria, the King of Prussia, and the Emperor of all the Russias, having repaired to Aix-la-Chapelle; and their Majesties the King of the United Kingdom of Great Britain and Ireland, and the King of France and Navarre, having sent thither their Plenipotentiaries; the Ministers of the 5 Courts have assembled in Conference together; and the Plenipotentiary of France having intimated, that in consequence of the state of France, and the faithful execution of the Treaty of 20th November, 1815, His Most Christian Majesty was desirous that the Military Occupation stipulated by Article V. of the said Treaty, should cease as soon as possible; the Ministers of the Courts of Austria, Great Britain, Prussia, and Russia, after having, in concert with the said Plenipotentiary of France, maturely examined every thing that could have an influence on such an important decision, have declared, that their Sovereigns would admit the principle of the Evacuation of the French Territory at the end of the 3rd year of the Occupation; and wishing to confirm this resolution by a formal Convention, and to secure, at the same time, the definitive execution of the said Treaty of 20th November, 1815,—His Majesty the King of the United Kingdom of Great Britain and Ireland, on the one part, and His Majesty the King of France and Navarre, on the other part, have, for this purpose, named as their Plenipotentiaries, viz.:—

His Majesty the King of the United Kingdom of Great Britain and Ireland, the Right Honourable Robert Stewart, Viscount Castlereagh, Knight of the Most Noble and Illustrious Order of the Garter, His Principal Secretary of State for Foreign Affairs, &c.

And the Most Excellent and Most Illustrious Lord, Arthur, Duke, Marquis, and Earl of Wellington, Marquis Douro, Viscount Wellington of Talavera and of Wellington, and Baron Douro of Wellesley; a Member of His Britannic Majesty's Most Honourable Privy Council, a Field-Marshal of his Forces, &c.

And His Majesty the King of France and Navarre, the Sieur Armand Emanuel du Plessis Richelieu, Duke of Richelieu, Peer of France, His Minister and Secretary of State for Foreign Affairs, and President of the Council of His Ministers, &c.:

Who, after having mutually communicated to each other their respective Full Powers, found to be in good and due form, have agreed upon the following Articles:—

Withdrawal of Army of Occupation from France.

ART. I. The Troops composing the Army of Occupation shall be withdrawn from the Territory of France by the 30th of November next, or sooner, if possible.

Strong Places and Fortresses to be given up to France.

ART. II. The strong Places and Fortresses which the said Troops occupy, shall be given up to Commissioners named for that purpose by His Most Christian Majesty, in the state in which they were at the time of their occupation, conformably to Article IX. of the Convention concluded in execution of Article V. of the Treaty of 20th November, 1815.

Pay, Equipment, and Clothing of Troops of Army of Occupation.

ART. III. The sum destined to provide for the pay, the equipment, and the clothing of the Troops of the Army of Occupation, shall be paid, in all cases, up to the 30th of November next, on the same footing on which it has existed since the 1st of December, 1817.

Pecuniary Indemnity to be paid by France to Allied Powers.

ART. IV. All the accounts between France and the Allied Powers having been regulated and settled, the Sum to be paid by France, to complete the execution of the IVth Article of the Treaty of 20th November, 1815, is definitively fixed at 265,000,000 of francs.

Payment in Inscriptions of Rentes.

ART. V. Of this sum the amount of 100,000,000, effective value, shall be paid by Inscriptions of Rentes on the Great Book of the Public Debt of France, bearing interest from the 22nd of September 1818. The said Inscriptions shall be received at the rate of the Funds on Monday the 5th of October, 1818.

Payments by Monthly Instalments.

ART. VI. The remaining 165,000,000 shall be paid by 9 monthly instalments, commencing on the 6th of January next, by Bills on the

Houses of Hope and Co. and Baring, Brothers and Co., which, as well as the Inscriptions of *Rentes*, mentioned in the above Article, shall be delivered to Commissioners of the Courts of Austria, Great Britain, Prussia, and Russia, by the Royal Treasury of France, at the time of the complete and definitive evacuation of the French Territory.

Bonds to be delivered by Commissioners of Allied Powers to Royal Treasury of France.

ART. VII. At the same period, the Commissioners of the said Courts shall deliver to the Royal Treasury of France, the 6 Bonds not yet discharged, which shall remain in their hands, of the 15 Bonds delivered conformably to Article II. of the Convention concluded for the execution of Article IV. of the Treaty of 20th November, 1815. The said Commissioners shall, at the same time, deliver the Inscription of 7,000,000 of *Rentes*, created in virtue of Article VIII. of the said Convention.

Ratifications.

ART. VIII. The present Convention shall be ratified, and the Ratifications thereof exchanged at Aix-la-Chapelle in the space of a fortnight, or sooner if possible.

In witness whereof, the respective Plenipotentiaries have signed the same, and have thereunto affixed the Seal of their Arms.

Done at Aix-la-Chapelle, the 9th day of October, in the Year of our Lord 1818.

(L.S.)   CASTLEREAGH.
(L.S.)   WELLINGTON.
(L.S.)   RICHELIEU.

NOTE.—Similar Conventions were concluded at Aix-la-Chapelle, on the same day, between France and Austria, Prussia, and Russia, respectively.

16

NOTE addressed by the Plenipotentiaries of Great Britain, Austria, Prussia, and Russia to the Duke of Richelieu. Aix-la-Chapelle, 4th November, 1818.

[This Note formed Annex A to the Protocol of 15th November, 1818.]

Reference to Treaty of 20th November, 1815.

THE Undersigned Ministers of the Cabinets of Austria, Great Britain, Prussia, and Russia, have received orders from their august masters to address to His Excellency the Duke of Richelieu the following communication:—

Called by Article V. of the Treaty of 20th November, 1815, to examine, in concert with His Majesty the King of France, whether the military occupation of a part of the French territory, stipulated by the said Treaty, might cease at the end of the third year, or ought to be prolonged to the end of the fifth, their Majesties the Emperor of Austria, the King of Prussia, and the Emperor of all the Russias, have repaired to Aix-la-Chapelle, and have charged their Ministers to assemble there, in conference with the Plenipotentiaries of their Majesties the King of France and the King of Great Britain, in order to proceed to the examination of this important question.

In this examination the attention of the Ministers and Plenipotentiaries had for its particular object the internal situation of France; it was said to be directed to the execution of the engagements contracted by the French Government, towards the co-subscribing Powers to the Treaty of the 20th November, 1815.

The internal state of France having long been the subject of serious deliberations in the Cabinets, and the Plenipotentiaries assembled at Aix-la-Chapelle having mutually communicated the opinions which they had formed in that respect, the august Sovereigns, after having weighed these opinions in their wisdom, have recognised with satisfaction, that the order of things happily established in France, by the restoration of the legitimate and constitutional Monarchy, and the success which has hitherto crowned the paternal care of His Most Christian Majesty, fully justify the hope of a progressive consolidation of that order of things so essential to the repose and prosperity of France, and so strictly connected with the great interests of Europe.

With regard to the execution of the engagements, the communications which, since the opening of the Conferences, the Plenipotentiary of His Most Christian Majesty has addressed to the Ministers of the other Powers have left no doubt on this question, as they prove that the French Government has fulfilled, with the most scrupulous and honourable punctuality, all the clauses of the Treaties and Conventions of the 20th November; and propose, with respect to those clauses, the fulfilment of which was reserved for more remote periods, arrangements which are satisfactory to all the contracting parties.

Such being the results of the examination of these grave questions, their Imperial and Royal Majesties congratulated themselves, that they have only to listen to those sentiments and those personal wishes which induced them to put an end to a measure which disastrous circumstances, and the necessity of providing for their own security, and that of Europe, could alone have dictated to them.

From that moment the august Sovereigns resolved to cause the Military Occupation of the French Territory to be discontinued; and the Convention of the 9th October sanctioned this resolution. They regard this solemn act as the final completion of the General Peace.

Considering now, as the first of their duties, that of preserving to their people the benefits which that Peace assures to them, and to maintain in their integrity the transactions which have established and consolidated it, their Imperial and Royal Majesties flatter themselves that His Most Christian Majesty, animated by the same sentiments, will receive with the interest which he attaches to everything tending to the welfare of mankind, and to the glory and prosperity of his country, the proposition which their Imperial and Royal Majesties address to him, to unite henceforth his councils and his efforts to those which they will not cease to devote to so salutary a work.

The undersigned, charged to request the Duke of Richelieu to convey the wish of their august Sovereigns to the knowledge of the King his master, at the same time invite his Excellency to take part in their present and future deliberations, consecrated to the maintenance of the peace, the treaties on which it is founded, the rights and mutual relations established or confirmed by these treaties, and recognised by all the European Powers.

In transmitting to the Duke of Richelieu this solemn proof of the confidence which their august Sovereigns have placed in the wisdom of the King of France, and in the loyalty of the French nation, the undersigned are ordered to add the expression of the unalterable attachment which their Imperial and Royal Majesties profess towards the person of His Most Christian Majesty and his family, and of the sincere interest which they never cease to take in the tranquillity and happiness of his kingdom.

They have the honour, at the same time, to offer to the Duke of Richelieu the assurance of their very particular consideration.

Aix-la-Chapelle, 4th November, 1818.

METTERNICH.	HARDENBERG.
CASTLEREAGH.	BERNSTORFF.
WELLINGTON.	NESSELRODE.
	CAPO D'ISTRIA.

17

NOTE addressed by the Duke of Richelieu to the Plenipotentiaries of Austria, Great Britain, Prussia, and Russia, in reply to their Note of the 4th November, 1818. Aix-la-Chapelle, 12th November, 1818.

[This Note formed Annex B to the Protocol of 15th November, 1818.]

TABLE.

Acceptance by *France* of Invitation to take part in the deliberations of the Allied Powers for Maintenance of Peace, and the execution of the Treaties upon which it was founded.

THE Undersigned Minister and Secretary of State to His Most Christian Majesty, has received the communication which their Excellencies the Ministers of the Cabinets of Austria, of Great Britain, of Prussia, and of Russia, did him the honour of addressing to him on the 4th of this month, by order of their august Sovereigns. He hastened to make it known to the King his Master. His Majesty has received with real satisfaction, this new proof of the confidence and friendship of the Sovereigns who have taken part in the deliberations at Aix-la-Chapelle. The justice which they render to his constant cares for the happiness of France, and above all to the loyalty of his people, has deeply touched his heart. Looking back to the past, and observing that at no other period, no other nation has been able to fulfil with a more scrupulous fidelity, engagements such as France had contracted, the King has felt that it was indebted, for this new kind of glory, to the influence of the institutions which govern it; and he sees with joy, that the consolidation of these institutions is considered by his august Allies to be no less advantageous to the repose of Europe, than essential to the prosperity of France. Considering that the first of his duties is to endeavour to perpetuate and augment, by all the means in his power, the benefits which the complete re-establishment of general Peace promises to all nations; persuaded that the intimate union of governments is the surest pledge of its duration; and that France, which could not remain a stranger to a system, the whole force of which must spring from a perfect unanimity of principle and action, will join the association with her characteristic frankness; and that her concurrence must add strength to the well-founded hope of the happy results which such an alliance must produce for the benefit of mankind, His Most Christian Majesty most readily accepts the proposal made to him of uniting his councils and his efforts with those of their Majesties, for the purpose of accomplishing the salutary work which they have in view. He has, therefore, authorized the undersigned to take part in all the deliberations of their Ministers and Plenipotentiaries, for the object of consolidating the peace, of securing the maintenance of the Treaties on which it rests, and of guaranteeing the mutual rights and relations established by these same Treaties, and recognized by all the States of Europe.

The undersigned, while he begs their Excellencies to have the goodness to transmit to their august Sovereigns, the expression of the intentions and sentiments of the King his master, has the honour of offering them the assurance of his highest consideration.

RICHELIEU.

18

PROTOCOL of Conference, between the Plenipotentiaries of Austria, France, Great Britain, Prussia, and Russia. Signed at Aix-la-Chapelle, 15th November, 1818.

Reference to Treaty of 30th May, 1814; to Vienna Congress Treaty of 9th June, 1815; to Treaty of 20th November, 1815; and to Convention of 9th October, 1818.

THE Ministers of Austria, France, Great Britain, Prussia, and Russia, in pursuance of the exchange of the Ratifications of the Convention signed on the 9th of October, 1818, relative to the Evacuation of the French Territory by the Foreign Troops, and after having addressed to each other the Notes, of which copies are annexed, have assembled in conference, to take into consideration the Relations which ought to be established, in the actual state of affairs, between France and the co-subscribing Powers of the Treaty of Peace of the 20th of November, 1815—Relations which, by assuring to France the place that belongs to her in the European system, will bind her more closely to the pacific and benevolent views in which all the Sovereigns participate, and will thus consolidate the general tranquillity

After having maturely investigated the conservative principles of the great interests which constitute the order of things established in Europe, under the auspices of Divine Providence, by the Treaty of Paris of the 30th of May, 1814, the *Récès* of Vienna (9th June, 1815), and the Treaty of Peace of the year 1815 (20th November), the Courts subscribing the present Act, do, accordingly, unanimously acknowledge and declare:—

1. That they are firmly resolved never to depart, neither in their mutual Relations, nor in those which bind them to other States, from the principle of intimate Union which has hitherto presided over all their common relations and interests—a Union rendered more strong and indissoluble by the bonds of Christian fraternity which the Sovereigns have formed among themselves.

2. That this Union, which is the more real and durable, inasmuch as it depends on no separate interest or temporary combination, can only have for its object the Maintenance of general Peace, founded on a religious respect for the engagements contained in the Treaties, and for the whole of the rights resulting therefrom.

3. That France, associated with other Powers by the restoration of the legitimate Monarchial and Constitutional Power, engages henceforth to concur in the maintenance and consolidation of a System which has given Peace to Europe, and which can alone insure its duration.

4. That if, for the better attaining the above declared object, the Powers which have concurred in the present Act, should judge it necessary to establish particular meetings, either of the Sovereigns themselves, or of their respective Ministers and Plenipotentiaries, there to treat in common of their own interests, in so far as they have reference to the object of their present deliberations, the time and place of these meetings shall, on each occasion, be previously fixed by means of diplomatic communications; and that in the case of these meetings having for their object affairs specially connected with the interests of the other States of Europe, they shall only take place in pursuance of a formal invitation on the part of such of those States as the said affairs may concern, and under the express reservation of their right of direct participation therein, either directly or by their Plenipotentiaries.

5. That the resolutions contained in the present Act shall be made known to all the Courts of Europe, by the annexed Declaration, which shall be considered as sanctioned by the Protocol, and forming part thereof.

Done in quintuple, and reciprocally exchanged in the original, by the subscribing Cabinets.

Aix-la-Chapelle, 15th November, 1818.

METTERNICH.	HARDENBERG.
RICHELIEU.	BERNSTORFF.
CASTLEREAGH.	NESSELRODE.
WELLINGTON.	CAPO D'ISTRIA.

19

DECLARATION of the Five Cabinets (Great Britain, Austria, France, Prussia, and Russia). Signed at Aix-la-Chapelle, 15th November, 1818.

[This Declaration formed Annex C to the Protocol of 15th November, 1818.]

AT the period of completing the Pacification of Europe by the resolution of withdrawing the Foreign Troops from the French Territory; and when there is an end of those measures of precaution which unfortunate circumstances had rendered necessary, the Ministers and

Plenipotentiaries of their Majesties the Emperor of Austria, the King of France, the King of Great Britain, the King of Prussia, and the Emperor of all the Russias, have received orders from their Sovereigns, to make known to all the Courts of Europe, the results of their meeting at Aix-la-Chapelle, and with that view to publish the following Declaration:—

The Convention of the 9th October, 1818, which definitively regulated the execution of the engagements agreed to in the Treaty of Peace of 20th November, 1815, is considered by the Sovereigns who concurred therein, as the accomplishment of the work of Peace, and as the completion of the political System destined to ensure its solidity.

The intimate Union established among the Monarchs, who are joint parties to this System, by their own principles, no less than by the interests of their people, offers to Europe the most sacred pledge of its future tranquillity.

The object of this Union is as simple as it is great and salutary. It does not tend to any new political combination—to any change in the Relations sanctioned by existing Treaties. Calm and consistent in its proceedings, it has no other object than the maintenance of Peace, and the guarantee of those transactions on which the Peace was founded and consolidated.

The Sovereigns, in forming this august Union, have regarded as its fundamental basis their invariable resolution never to depart, either among themselves, or in their Relations with other States, from the strictest observation of the principles of the Right of Nations; principles, which, in their application to a state of permanent Peace, can alone effectually guarantee the Independence of each Government, and the stability of the general association.

Faithful to these principles, the Sovereigns will maintain them equally in those meetings at which they may be personally present, or in those which shall take place among their Ministers; whether they be for purpose of discussing in common their own interests, or whether they shall relate to questions in which other Governments shall formally claim their interference. The same spirit which will direct their councils, and reign in their diplomatic communications, will preside also at these meetings; and the repose of the world will be constantly their motive and their end.

It is with these sentiments that the Sovereigns have consummated the work to which they were called. They will not cease to labour for its confirmation and perfection. They solemnly acknowledge that their duties towards God and the people whom they govern make it peremptory on them to give to the world, as far as it is in their power, an example of justice, of concord, and of moderation; happy in the power of consecrating, from henceforth, all their efforts to protect the arts of peace, to increase the internal prosperity of their States, and to awaken those sentiments of religion and morality, whose influence has been but too much enfeebled by the misfortune of the times.

Aix-la-Chapelle, 15th November, 1818.

METTERNICH.	HARDENBERG.
RICHELIEU.	BERNSTORFF.
CASTLEREAGH.	NESSELRODE.
WELLINGTON.	CAPO D'ISTRIA.

20

FINAL ACT of the Ministerial Conferences held at Vienna to complete and consolidate the Organization of the Germanic Confederation. Signed at Vienna, 15th May, 1820.

Preamble.

THE Sovereign Princes and the Free Towns of Germany, mindful of the engagement which they undertook at the time of the formation of the Germanic Confederation, to strengthen and perfect their union, by developing the fundamental Regulations of the Federal Act, convinced, moreover, that in order to fasten indissolubly the bonds which unite the the whole of the States of Germany in peace and harmony, they ought no longer to delay the fulfilment of that engagement, and the satisfaction of a want generally felt, by entering upon deliberations in common, have appointed Plenipotentiaries for that purpose, namely:—

His Majesty the Emperor of Austria, King of Hungary and of Bohemia, the Sieur Clement Venceslas Lothaire, Prince of Metternich-Winnebourg Ochsenhausen, Duke of Portella, Chamberlain, actual intimate Councillor of His Imperial and Royal Apostolic Majesty, His Minister of State, of Conferences, and of Foreign Affairs, &c.;

His Majesty the King of Prussia, the Sieur Christian Günther, Count de Bernstorff, His Minister of State, of the Cabinet, and of Foreign Affairs, &c.;

The Sieur Frederic Guillaume Louis, Baron de Krusemarc, Lieutenant-General of His Armies, His Envoy Extraordinary and Minister Plenipotentiary to His Imperial and Royal Apostolic Majesty, &c.;

And the Sieur Jean Emanuel de Küster, His intimate Councillor of State, Envoy Extraordinary and Minister Plenipotentiary to His Majesty the King of Wirtemberg, and His Royal Highness the Grand Duke of Baden, &c.;

His Majesty the King of Bavaria, the Sieur Frederic, Baron de Zentner, His actual intimate Councillor, and Director-General of the Ministry of the Interior, Councillor of the Empire, &c.; and the Sieur

Gottlieb Edouard, Baron de Stainlein, His intimate Councillor and Minister Plenipotentiary to His Imperial and Royal Apostolic Majesty, &c.;

His Majesty the King of Saxony, the Sieur Detlev, Count de Einsiedel, His Minister and Secretary of State for the Department of the Interior, Chamberlain, &c.;

The Sieur Frederic Albert, Count de Schulenbourg-Closteroda, His intimate Councillor, Chamberlain, and Minister Plenipotentiary at the Imperial Austrian Court, &c.;

And the Sieur Jean Auguste Fürchtegott de Globig, His intimate Councillor, Chamberlain, &c.;

His Majesty the King of the United Kingdom of Great Britain and Ireland, King of Hanover, the Sieur Erneste Frederic Herbert, Count de Münster, Hereditary Grand Marshal of the Kingdom, His Minister of State and of the Cabinet, &c.;

And the Sieur Erneste Chrétien George Auguste, Count de Hardenberg, His Minister of State and of the Cabinet, Envoy Extraordinary and Minister Plenipotentiary to His Imperial and Royal Apostolic Majesty, &c.;

His Majesty the King of Wurtemberg, the Sieur Ulrick-Lebrecht, Count de Mandelsloh, His Minister of State, and Minister Plenipotentiary to His Imperial and Royal Apostolic Majesty, &c.;

His Royal Highness the Grand Duke of Baden, the Sieur Reinhart, Baron de Berstett, His actual intimate Councillor, Minister of State and of Foreign Affairs, &c.;

And the Sieur Frederic Charles, Baron de Tettenborn, Lieutenant-General and General Aide-de-Camp of the Grand Duke, Envoy Extraordinary and Minister Plenipotentiary to His Imperial and Royal Apostolic Majesty, &c.;

His Royal Highness the Elector of Hesse, Baron Munchausen, His intimate Councillor and Chamberlain, Envoy Extraordinary and Minister Plenipotentiary to His Imperial and Royal Apostolic Majesty, &c.;

His Royal Highness the Grand Duke of Hesse, the Sieur Charles du Bos, Baron du Thil, His actual intimate Councillor, &c.;

His Majesty the King of Denmark, Duke of Holstein and Lauenburg, the Sieur Joachim Frederic, Count de Bernstorff, His intimate Councillor of Conferences, Envoy Extraordinary and Minister Plenipotentiary to His Imperial and Royal Apostolic Majesty, &c.;

His Majesty the King of the Netherlands, Grand Duke of Luxemburg, the Sieur Antoine Reinhart de Falck, Minister of Public Instruction, of National Industry, and of the Colonies, &c.;

His Royal Highness the Grand Duke of Saxe-Weimar, and their Serene Highnesses the Dukes of Saxe-Gotha, Saxe-Coburg, Saxe-

Meiningen, and Saxe-Hildburghausen, the Sieur Charles Guillaume, Baron de Fritsch, actual intimate Councillor of the Grand Duke of Saxe-Weimar-Eisenach, Minister of State, &c.;

His Serene Highness the Duke of Brunswick Wolfenbüttel, the Count Munster, &c.; and the Count de Hardenberg, &c. (as above described);

His Serene Highness the Duke of Nassau, the Sieur Ernest Francis Louis Maréschal, Baron de Bieberstein, His directing Minister of State, &c.;

Their Royal Highnesses the Grand Dukes of Mecklenburg-Schwerin and Strelitz, the Sieur Leopold Hartwig, Baron de Plessen, Minister of State and of Cabinet of Mecklenburg-Schwerin, &c.;

Their Serene Highnesses the Dukes of Holstein-Oldenburg, Anhalt-Köthen, Anhalt-Dessau, and Anhalt-Bernburg, the Princes of Schwartz-burg-Sondershausen and Rudolstadt, the Sieur Günther Henri de Berg, President of the High Court of Cassation of Oldenburg, Envoy of the Duchy of Holstein-Oldenburg, of the Dukes of Anhalt, and of the Princes of Schwartzburg, to the German Confederation;

Their Serene Highnesses the Princes of Hohenzöllern-Hechingen and Hohenzöllern-Sigmaringen, Lichtenstein, Reuss (both branches), Schaumburg-Lippe, Lippe and Waldeck, the Baron de Bieberstein, &c. (as above described);

The Free Towns of Lubeck, Frankfort, Bremen, and Hamburg, the Sieur Jean Frederic Hach, Senator of Lubeck and Envoy;

Who, being assembled in Conference at Vienna, after the exchange of their Full Powers, found to be in good and due form, and after maturely considering and adjusting the various views, desires, and proposals of their Governments, have definitively agreed upon the following Articles:—

Federative Union of Sovereigns and Free Towns of Germany.

ART. I. The Germanic Confederation is a union according to international law of the Sovereign Princes and Free Towns of Germany, for the preservation of the independence and inviolability of the States comprised in it, and for maintaining the internal and external security of Germany.

Internal and Foreign Relations.

ART. II. As to its internal relations, this Union consists of a community of States independent of each other, with reciprocal and equal rights and obligations stipulated by Treaties. As to its external relations, it constitutes a collective Power, bound together in political unity.

Exercise of Powers of Confederation.

ART. III. The compass and the limitations which the Confederation has assigned for its operation are laid down in the Federal Act, which is the primitive compact, and the first fundamental law of this union. While it declares the object of the Confederation, that Act determines at the same time its rights and obligations.

Extension and Completion of Federal Act.

Art. IV. The right of developing and perfecting the Confederation Act, in so far as the object proposed therein renders this necessary, belongs to the whole of the Members of the Confederation. But the resolutions to be adopted for this purpose must not be in contradiction to the spirit of the Federal Act, nor depart from the primitive character of the Federation.

No Member can separate himself from the Confederation.

Art. V. The Confederation is established as an indissoluble Union, and therefore none of its Members can be at liberty to secede from it.

Admission of new Members. Consent of all the Members to Changes. Voluntary Cession of Rights of Sovereignty to a Member of Confederation only.

Art. VI. According to its original intent, the Confederation is limited to the States which now belong to it. The admission of a new Member can only take place if all the Members of the Confederation consider it compatible with the existing relations, and accordant with the interests of the whole. Changes in the present state of the possession of the Members of the Confederation cannot alter their rights and obligations in reference to the Confederation, without the express consent of all its Members. A voluntary cession of rights of sovereignty belonging to a territory of the Confederation, cannot take place without such consent, except in favour of one of the Confederate States.

Federal Diet the Constitutional Organ of the Federated States.

Art. VII. The Federative Diet, formed by the Plenipotentiaries of all the Members of the Confederation, represents the Confederation in its entirety; it is the constitutional and perpetual organ of its will and action.

Plenipotentiaries at Diet.

Art. VIII. The Plenipotentiaries at the Diet are individually dependent on those who delegate them, and responsible only to them for the faithful observance of their instructions, as well as for their proceedings in general.

Powers of Federative Diet.

ART. IX. The Federative Diet exercises its rights and fulfils its obligations only within the limits prescribed to it. Its action is determined by the provisions of the Federal Act, and by the Fundamental Laws passed or to be passed in conformity with that.Act; but where these are not sufficient, by the objects of the Confederation as defined in the Fundamental Act.

Resolutions of Diet to be binding.

ART. X. The collective will of the Confederation is declared by the Resolutions of the Diet constitutionally passed; and those Resolutions are constitutionally passed which, being within the competency of the Diet, have been voted freely after discussion, either in the ordinary Council or in the General Assembly ("Plenum"), according as the one or the other is prescribed by the Fundamental legal provisions.

Majority of Voices, in Resolutions of Diet on ordinary matters.

ART. XI. As a general rule, the Diet passes such Resolutions as are required for the management of the common affairs of the Confederation in the ordinary Council, and by an absolute majority of votes. This form of Resolution is adopted in all cases wherein the general principles already established are to be applied, or laws and arrangements already decided upon are to be put into execution; and in general in all matters of deliberations not positively excepted therefrom by the Federal Act or by subsequent Resolutions.

When Diet can form itself into a General Council.

ART. XII. The Diet forms itself into a General Assembly ("Plenum") only in cases expressly specified by the Federal Act, and also in the event of a Declaration of War, or of the Ratification of a Treaty of Peace on the part of the Confederation, or when the question of the admission of a new Member into the Confederation is to be decided. If in particular cases the question arises whether a subject belongs to the General Assembly, the Ordinary Council has to decide thereon. No discussion or deliberation takes place in the General Assembly. It decides only whether a Resolution prepared in the Ordinary Council is to be adopted or rejected. For a valid Resolution of the General Assembly, a majority of two-thirds of the votes is necessary.

Plurality of Voices not valid.

ART. XIII. No decision by plurality of votes can take place in the following instances:—

Adoption of New Laws, or Modifications.

1. In the adoption of new fundamental laws, or alteration of those already in force.

Organic Institutions.

2. In organic arrangements, that is to say, in those permanent regulations which form the means of accomplishing the declared objects of the Confederation.

New Members.

3. In the admission of new Members into the Confederation.

Religious Affairs.

4. In Religious affairs.

Opposition to Majority.

There can, however, be no definitive decision on matters of this nature until after due examination and discussion of the reasons which separate Members of the Confederation have to give in opposition, and the explanation of those reasons can in no case be refused.

Organic Institutions to be restored in General Assembly by unanimous Vote.

ART. XIV. With reference particularly to the organic institutions, not only must the preliminary question whether they are necessary under the existing circumstances, but also the scheme and design thereof in their general outlines and essential arrangements, be decided on by a unanimous vote of the General Assembly ("Plenum").

Details in Permanent Council by Plurality.

If the decision is favourable to the proposed institution all further proceedings in regard to the details belong to the Ordinary Assembly, which decides by a majority of votes upon other questions still arising thereon, and, if necessary, appoints a Commission from amongst its Members, in order to adjust the different opinions and propositions with the greatest possible indulgence and respect to the relations and wishes of each.

Individual Rights.

ART. XV. In cases where the Members of the Confederation appear, not in their pacted unity but as individual, self-existent, and independent States, and consequently *jura singulorum* prevail, or where there is required from individual Members of the Confederation a special performance or allowance towards the Confederation, that is not included in the common obligations of all, no resolution that is binding on them can be passed without the free consent of all that are interested.

Possessions of one of the Sovereign Houses passing to another by Right of Succession. Vote of such new Member.

ART. XVI. Whenever the possessions of a Sovereign German House pass by succession to another, it depends upon the whole Confederation whether and to what extent the votes attached to the said possessions in the General Assembly ("Plenum") shall be given to the new possessor, considering that no Member of the Confederation can have more than one vote in the ordinary Assembly.

Interpretation of Doubts.

ART. XVII. For the maintenance of the real meaning of the Federal Act, the Diet is called upon to explain the provisions contained therein in conformity with the object of the Confederation, should any doubt arise as to their interpretation, and to secure in all cases that occur the proper application of the directions of this document.

Maintenance of Peace.

ART. XVIII. As concord and peace are to be maintained undisturbed among the Members of the Confederation, if the internal tranquillity and security of the Confederation be in any way threatened or disturbed, the Diet has to take counsel upon the means of preserving or re-establishing them, and to pass the resolutions adapted thereto, under the guidance of the provisions contained in the following Articles.

Preliminary Measures.

ART. XIX. If acts of violence are to be feared or have actually occurred between Members of the Confederation, the Diet is called upon to take preliminary measures whereby all self-help may be prevented or stopped if already undertaken. For this purpose the Diet has above all to take care that the state of possession is maintained.

Assistance of Diet claimed by a Member to maintain Right of Possession.

ART. XX. If the help of the Diet be claimed by a Member of the Confederation for the protection of the state of possession, and the most recent state of possession is disputed, for this special case the Diet shall be authorized to invite a Member of the Confederation in the vicinity of the territory to be protected, and not interested in the matter, to have the case of the most recent possession and the intended disturbance thereof summarily examined without delay before its Supreme Court of

Justice, and a legal sentence passed thereon, the execution of which is to be accomplished by the Diet with the means assigned to it for the purpose, if the Confederate State against which it is directed does not on previous invitation voluntarily comply with it.

Differences submitted to Diet.   Arbitration (Austregal) Decision.

ART. XXI. In all differences between the Members of the Confederation submitted to the Diet by virtue of the Federal Act, the Diet shall first try the way of conciliation by means of a Committee. If the differences cannot be settled in this way the Diet has to procure the decision of it by an Arbitration Court (Austrägal-Instanz), observing therein, so long as no other convention shall have been made among the Members of the Confederation respecting arbitration tribunals, the regulations contained in the resolutions of the Diet of 16th June, 1817, as well as the special resolution to be passed in consequence of simultaneous instructions issued to the Envoys of the Diet.

Arbitration (Austregal) Court to decide matters in Dispute.

ART. XXII. If, according to the above-mentioned Resolution of the Diet, the Supreme Court of a Confederate State has been chosen as an Arbitration (Austrägal-Instanz) Court, to it alone belongs the direction of the proceedings and the decision of the affair in all its principal and accessory points unrestrictedly and without any further interference, either of the Diet or the Government of the country therein. Nevertheless, the latter, upon the motion of the Diet, or of the litigating parties, in case of delay on the part of the Court of Justice, will issue the necessary directions to accelerate the decision.

Principles upon which Arbitration (Austregal) Court is to decide.

ART. XXIII. Where there are no special rules for deciding, the Arbitration (Austregal) Tribunal is to have recourse to those legal sources subsidiarily observed by the tribunals of the Empire in legal cases of the same kind, in so far as they are still applicable to the actual relations of the Members of the Confederation.

Special Arbitration or Compromise.

ART. XXIV. The Members of the Confederation are free, moreover, to come to an agreement both with regard to individual disputes and to all future cases, by special arbitration or compromise, inasmuch as previously existing arbitration authorities settled by family compact, or by Treaty, are not abolished or altered by the institution of the Arbitration Court of the Confederation.

Maintenance of Order and Tranquillity.

ART. XXV. The maintenance of internal tranquillity and order in the Confederate States belongs to the respective Governments only. As an exception, however, with regard to the internal security of the whole Confederation, and in consequence of the obligation of its Members mutually to assist each other, the whole may co-operate for the preservation or restoration of tranquillity, in case of the resistance of subjects against their Government, in that of an open revolt, or dangerous movements in several States of the Confederation.

Demand of Assistance against Revolution to be complied with by Diet.

ART. XXVI. When the internal tranquillity of a Confederate State is immediately endangered by the resistance of subjects to the authorities, and the spreading of the seditious movements is to be feared, or when an actual revolt has broken out, and the Government of the country, after having exhausted all constitutional and legal means, calls for the assistance of the Confederation, the Diet is bound to cause the most prompt assistance to be given for the re-establishment of order. If, in the latter case, the Government of the country is notoriously unable to repress the revolt by its own forces, and is at the same time prevented by circumstances from claiming the assistance of the Confederation, the Diet is nevertheless bound, even without being called upon, to proceed to the restoration of order and security. In any case, however, the measures adopted must not continue any longer than the Government to which the aid of the Confederation has been afforded considers necessary.

The Government requiring assistance to explain reasons.

ART. XXVII. The Government which has received such assistance is bound to inform the Diet of the cause of the disturbances which have arisen, and to send in a satisfactory account of the measures taken for securing the re-established legal order.

Diet to adopt measures in cases of danger to Confederate States by Associations and dangerous machinations.

ART. XXVIII. If public tranquillity and legal order are threatened in several of the Confederated States by dangerous Associations and designs, and against which sufficient measures can only be taken by the co-operation of the whole, then the Diet is authorized and called upon to deliberate upon and to pass such measures, after having communicated with the Governments most immediately in danger.

Denial of Justice.   Interference in favour of Complainant.

ART. XXIX. If the case of a denial of justice occur in one of the

States of the Confederation, and effective aid cannot be obtained in a legal manner, the Diet is bound to entertain, when proved, the complaints of the denial or stoppage of justice, which must be judged according to the Constitution and the laws of each country, and thereupon to cause the Federal Government which has given cause for the complaints, to give the legal aid required.

Private Claims. Decision by Arbitration (Austregal) Judgment.

ART. XXX. If claims made by private persons cannot be adjusted on account of the obligation to satisfy them being doubtful or contested between several Members of the Confederation, the Diet, at the request of those interested, is first of all to try to effect an arrangement in a friendly way; if, however, that endeavour does not succeed, and the Members of the Confederation concerned do not agree to a compromise within a period to be fixed, it shall cause the preliminary question in dispute to be legally decided by an Arbitration Court.

Obligation of Diet to watch over Execution of Federal Act, &c.

ART. XXXI. The Diet has the right and is bound to watch over the execution of the Federal Act, and the other Fundamental Laws of the Confederation, the resolutions adopted in accordance with its competence, the awards pronounced by Arbitration Courts, the compromises guaranteed by the Confederation, and the arrangements effected by the mediation of the Diet, as well as the maintenance of the special guarantees undertaken by the Confederation; and for this purpose, after exhausting all other Federal Constitutional means, to have recourse to the requisite executionary measures, strictly observing the provisions and rules established for this purpose in the special execution regulations.

Each Government of the Confederation to see to Execution of the Common Laws. Exceptions.

ART. XXXII. Each Government of the Confederation being obliged to see to the execution of the Federal Resolutions, and the Diet not being authorized to interfere directly in the internal administration of the Confederated States, measures of execution can only as a rule be taken against the Government itself. Exceptions to this rule occur, however, when a Government, in default of insufficient means of its own, claims the assistance of the Confederation, or when the Diet, under the circumstances mentioned in Article XXVI. is obliged, without being called upon, to take measures for the re-establishment of order and general security. In the first case, however, it must always proceed according to the propositions of the Government to which the assistance is given; and in the second case also, so soon as the Government has recovered its authority.

Measures of Execution.   Military Forces.

ART. XXXIII. Measures of execution are decided on and accomplished in the name of the Confederation. For that purpose the Diet, in consideration of local circumstances and of particular relations, charges one or more Governments not interested in the matter with the execution of the measures decided on, and determines at the same time the strength of the troops to be employed, and the duration of their employment, which are to be regulated in accordance with the object of the execution in each case.

Government charged with execution obliged to do so.   Civil
Commissioner to be appointed under Instructions of the Diet.

ART. XXXIV. The Government on which the charge is laid, and which it is bound to undertake as a Federal duty, appoints a Civil Commissioner for the purpose, who has the immediate conduct of the execution proceedings, in conformity with the special instructions drawn up according to the directions of the Diet by the Government which has to carry them out. If the charge has been entrusted to several Governments, the Diet decides which of them is to appoint the Civil Commissioner. The Government charged with the execution shall, during the proceedings, keep the Diet informed of their progress, and shall acquaint it with the termination of the business so soon as the object shall have been fully accomplished.

Right of Confederation to declare War, make Peace, enter into
Alliances, and negotiate Treaties.

ART. XXXV. The Confederation has the right, as a Collective Power, to declare war, to make peace, to contract alliances, and to conclude other Treaties. According, however, to the object of the Confederation expressed in Article II. of the Federal Act, it only exercises this right for its own defence, for the maintenance of the self-existence and external security of Germany, as well as for the independence and inviolability of the individual States of the Confederation.

Defence of Confederation and of each separate State against
infringement by Foreign Powers.

ART. XXXVI. As all the Members of the Confederation have engaged by Article XI. of the Federal Act to defend the whole of Germany, as well as each individual State of the Confederation, against every attack, and reciprocally to guarantee the integrity of the whole of their Possessions comprised within the Union, no individual State of the Confederation can be injured by a foreign Power, without the injury affecting at the same time, and to an equal degree, the whole of the Confederation.

Provocation to Foreign Powers to be avoided. Reparation to be required by Diet.

On the other hand, the individual States of the Confederation are bound on their side not to give any cause for such injuries, and not to do any to foreign States. In case a foreign State should complain to the Diet of any injury inflicted on it by a Member of the Confederation, and this complaint should prove to be well founded, the Diet is bound to require the Member that has given cause for the complaint to make prompt and satisfactory reparation, and to unite with this requisition, according to the circumstances, such measures as may prevent in time any further consequences injurious to peace.

Examination of Differences between a Foreign Power and a State of the Confederation. Action of the Diet.

ART. XXXVII. If a State of the Confederation calls for the intervention of the Confederation in a difference between that State and a foreign Power, the Diet has to examine carefully into the origin of the difference and the real state of the case. Should the result of that examination be that right is not on the side of the Confederated State, the Diet is earnestly to dissuade it from continuing the contest, to refuse the desired intervention, and, in case of necessity, to take proper measures for the maintenance of peace. Should the result be to the contrary, the Diet is bound to employ its mediation and intercession in favour of the injured State in the most effectual manner, and to extend them as far as is necessary to obtain complete security and appropriate satisfaction for that State.

Measures of Defence in case of Danger to a State of the Confederation.

ART. XXXVIII. When from the notification of a Member of the Confederation, or other authentic information, there is reason to believe that an individual State of the Confederation, or the whole Confederation, is threatened with a hostile attack, the Diet must immediately take into consideration the question whether there is any real danger of such an attack, and decide thereon with the least possible delay. If the danger is recognized there must be passed simultaneously with the decision to that effect, a resolution relative to the measures of defence which are immediately to be taken in such a case. Both the decision and resolution above-mentioned proceed from the ordinary Assembly, which proceeds therein according to its standing rule of the absolute majority of votes.

Invasion of Territory of Confederation by a Foreign Power.

Art. XXXIX. If the territory of the Confederation is invaded by a foreign Power, the state of war commences immediately, and in this case whatever may be the ulterior decision of the Diet, the necessary measures of defence must be adopted without delay.

General Assembly to declare War.

Art. XL. If the Confederation finds itself under the necessity of formally declaring war, that declaration can only be decided on in the General Assembly, according to the established rule, by a majority of two-thirds of the votes.

All the Confederate States bound to assist in measures of Defence.

Art. XLI. The Resolution passed in the ordinary Assembly as to the reality of the danger of a hostile attack, binds all the States of the Confederation to take such measures of defence as are considered necessary by the Diet. In like manner, the Declaration of War pronounced by the General Assembly binds all the Confederated States to take an immediate part in the common war.

Minority may concert measures amongst themselves.

Art. XLII. If the preliminary question relative to the existence of danger is decided in the negative by a majority of votes, such of the Confederated States as are convinced of the reality of the danger are nevertheless at liberty to agree among themselves upon common measures of defence.

Mediation of Diet.

Art. XLIII. If in any case wherein the danger and defence concern individual States of the Confederation, one of the contending parties applies for the mediation of the Confederation, the Diet will undertake the mediation, with the previous consent of the other party, in so far as it may be considered compatible with the state of things and with its own position; nevertheless, there must be no hindrance therefrom in the resolutions respecting the measures of defence to be adopted for the security of the territory of the Confederation, nor any stoppage or postponement in the execution of those already decided on.

Any State may furnish a larger Contingent than required.

Art. XLIV. When war has broken out every State of the Confederation is at liberty to furnish, for the common defence, a larger force than its Federal contingent amounts to; but no claim can be made on the Confederation on this account.

Neutrality in Wars between Foreign Powers.

ART. XLV. If in a war between foreign Powers, or in other cases, circumstances arise which occasion the apprehension of an infraction of the neutrality of the Federal territory, the Diet is to decide in the ordinary Assembly without delay upon the requisite measures for the maintenance of that neutrality.

Confederation no Party to a War by a State having Possessions outside of Limits of Confederation.

ART. XLVI. If a Confederate State having possessions beyond the limits of the Confederation enters into a war in its position as an European Power, such a war, so long as it does not affect the relations and obligations of the Confederation, remains quite foreign to it.

Exceptions.

ART. XLVII. In cases wherein such a State is threatened or attacked in its possessions situated beyond the Confederation, the liability of the Confederation only extends to common measures of defence, or to participation and assistance only in so far as the Diet, after previous deliberation, has recognized by a majority of votes in the ordinary Assembly, the existence of danger for the Federal territory. In the latter case the provisions of the preceding Articles are equally applicable.

War being declared by the Confederation, no separate State can enter into negotiations of Peace.

ART. XLVIII. The stipulation of the Federal Act in virtue whereof, when once war is declared by the Confederation, no Member thereof can enter by itself upon negotiations with the enemy, nor by itself agree to an armistice, or conclude peace, is equally binding upon all the Confederated States, whether they have possessions out of the territories of the Confederation or not.

Powers for Negotiating Peace.

ART. XLIX. When negotiations are carried on, on the part of the Confederation, for the conclusion of peace, or of an armistice, the Diet has to appoint a Committee for the special direction of them; but for the actual business of the negotiations it has to nominate its own Plenipotentiaries, and to furnish them with appropriate instructions. The acceptation and confirmation of a Treaty of Peace can only take place in the General Assembly.

Obligations of Diet relative to Foreign Affairs.

ART. L. With reference to foreign affairs in general, it is the duty of the Diet:—

1. To watch, as organ of the whole Confederation, over the maintenance of peaceable and friendly relations with foreign States;

2. To receive the Envoys of foreign Powers accredited to the Confederation, and to appoint Envoys, if it should be found necessary, to represent the Confederation at foreign Courts;

3. To conduct negotiations and to conclude Treaties for the whole Confederation, when occasions require;

4. To employ the intercession of the Confederation with foreign Governments for individual Federal Governments upon their requisition, and, in like manner, to intervene with individual Members of the Confederation on the requisition of foreign States.

Military System of the Confederation. Defensive Establishments.

ART. LI. The Diet is moreover bound to decide upon the organic institutions relating to the military system of the Confederation, and upon the defensive arrangements required for the security of its territory.

Pecuniary Contributions.

ART. LII. As the attainment of the purpose and the administration of the affairs of the Confederation require pecuniary contributions from the Members, the Diet has,—

1. To fix the amount of the ordinary Constitutional expenses, so far as that can, in general, be done;

2. To determine, as occasions arise, the extraordinary expenses required for the execution of special resolutions adopted in reference to recognized purposes of the Confederation, and the necessary contributions to provide for the expenses thereof;

3. To fix the normal proportion according to which the Members of the Confederation are to contribute;

4. To arrange and superintend the collection, the application, and the accounts of the contributions.

Internal Administration and Organization of Confederate States.

ART. LIII. The independence guaranteed by the Federal Act to the individual States of the Confederation certainly excludes in general all interference of the Confederation in the internal organization and administration of those States. As, however, the Members of the Confederation have, in the second part of the Federal Act, agreed upon some special provisions, bearing partly on the guarantee of secured rights, partly on the settled relations of subjects, the Diet is bound to see to the fulfilment of these contracted engagements, if it shall appear by conclusive information from those interested that such has not been the case. Nevertheless, the application in particular cases of the general

Ordinances adopted in conformity with the said engagements is reserved to the Governments only.

Assemblies of States in the Countries of the Confederation.
ART. LIV. As, according to the meaning of Article XIII. of the Federal Act, and the subsequent declarations thereon, there are to be Constitutions of national estates in all the States of the Confederation, the Diet has to take care that this stipulation does not remain without effect in any Confederate State.

Sovereign Princes to regulate Assemblies of States.
ART. LV. It is left to the Sovereign Princes of the Confederate States to regulate this domestic affair with regard both to the heretofore legally existing rights of the estates, and the present prevailing relations.

Constitutions to be Constitutionally changed.
ART. LVI. The Constitutions of national estates now in recognized activity can only be altered again by Constitutional means.

Sovereign Powers to rest with the Supreme Chief of the Government.
ART. LVII. As the Germanic Confederation, with the exception of the Free Cities, consists of Sovereign Princes, so, according to the fundamental idea thereof hereby given, the whole power of the State must remain united in the Supreme Chief of the State, and the Sovereign cannot be bound by a Constitution of national estates to admit of the co-operation of the estates, except in the exercise of determined rights.

No Constitution can restrict the Duties imposed by the Federative Union.
ART. LVIII. The Sovereign Princes united in the Confederation cannot be impeded or restricted in the fulfilment of their Federal obligations by any Constitution of national estates.

Liberty of Opinion.
ART. LIX. Where the publicity of the proceedings of the national estates is allowed by the Constitution, care must be taken in the business regulations, that the legal limits of free expression be not overstepped either in the proceedings themselves, or in their publication by the press, in such a manner as to imperil the tranquillity of the individual State, or of the whole of Germany.

Guarantee of Constitution of Assemblies of States by the Diet.

ART. LX. If a Member of the Confederation solicits the guarantee of the Confederation for the Constitution of the national estates established in his country, the Diet is authorized to undertake it. It thereby acquires the right, on the application of those concerned, of maintaining the Constitution, and of arranging any differences that have arisen as to its interpretation or application, by friendly mediation or compromise, if no other method and way are legally prescribed.

Cases in which Diet cannot interfere in Affairs of Assemblies of States.

ART. LXI. Excepting in the case of having undertaken a special guarantee of a Constitution of national estates and of the maintenance of the stipulations respecting Article XIII. of the Federal Act here established, the Diet is not authorized to interfere in the affairs of national estates or in disputes between the Sovereigns and their estates, so long as they do not assume the character denoted in Article XXVI., in which case the provisions in this, as well as of Article XXVII., also become applicable. But Article XLVI. of the Act of the Congress of Vienna of the year 1815, relative to the Constitution of the Free City of Frankfort, is in no way altered hereby.

Limit to which Article XIII. of Federal Act is applicable to the Free Cities.

ART. LXII. The preceding stipulations in regard to Article XIII. of the Federal Act are applicable to the Free Cities, in so far as their special Constitutions and relations admit of it.

Mediatized Princes.

ART. LXIII. The Diet has to attend to the exact and perfect fulfilment of the stipulations contained in Article XIV. of the Federal Act relative to the former States of the Empire now mediatized, and to the former immediate nobility of the Empire. Those Members of the Confederation in whose territories the possessions of the same are incorporated, are bound towards the Confederation to the steadfast maintenance of the relations of public right created by those stipulations. And although the disputes arising upon the application of Ordinances issued, or of Conventions concluded in conformity with Article XIV. of the Federal Act, must be submitted to the decision of the competent authorities of the States in which the possessions of the mediatized Princes, Counts, and Lords are situated, they are free, nevertheless, in case legal and Constitutional relief is denied them, or a partial legislative declaration is made injurious to the rights secured to them by the Federal Act, to have recourse to the Diet, which, in such a case, is bound to see that satisfactory redress is given, if the complaint prove well founded.

Proposed measures for the good of the Confederate States.

ART. LXIV. If individual Members of the Confederation propose to the Diet measures of public benefit, the accomplishment of which can only be attained by the co-operating participation of all the Confederated States, and that the Diet recognizes the expediency and feasibility of the proposed measures in general, it has then to take into careful consideration the means of carrying them out, and use its persevering endeavours to obtain the necessary voluntary agreement among all the Members of the Confederation for the purpose.

Stipulations reserved for future deliberation.

ART. LXV. The matters submitted to the consideration of the Diet in the special stipulations of the Federal Act, Articles XVI., XVIII., and XIX. are reserved for its further deliberation, in order to effect by common consent arrangements as uniform as possible.

Act to be submitted to Diet to be converted into a Fundamental Law of the Confederation.

The present Act shall be submitted to the Diet by means of a presidential proposal, as the result of an unchangeble engagement among the Members of the Confederation, and thereafter declarations to the same effect by the Confederated Governments shall, by a formal resolution of the Diet, be enacted as a Fundamental Law of the Confederation, which shall have the same force and validity as the Federal Act itself, and shall serve the Diet as a rule of conduct not to be deviated from.

In witness whereof all the Plenipotentiaries here assembled have signed the present Act, and sealed it with their Arms.

Done at Vienna, on the 15th of May, 1820.

(L.S.)   FURSTEN VON METTERNICH.
(L.S.)   GRAFEN VON BERNSTORFF.
(L.S.)   FREIHERRN VON KRUSEMARCK.
(L.S.)   J. E. VON KUSTER.
(L.S.)   FREIHERRN VON ZENTNER.
(L.S.)   FREIHERRN VON STAINLEIN.
(L.S.)   GRAFEN VON EINSEDEL.
(L.S.)   GRAFEN VON SCHULENBURG.
(L.S.)   H. A. F. VON GLOBIG.
(L.S.)   E. F. N. GRAFEN VON MUNSTER.
(L.S.)   E. C. G. A. GRAFEN VON HARDENBERG.
(L.S.)   U. L. GRAFEN VON MANDELSLOH.

(L.S.)   FREIHERRN VON BERSTETT.
(L.S.)   FREIHERRN VON TETTENBORN.
(L.S.)   FREIHERRN VON MUNCHHAUSEN.
(L.S.)   K. DU BOS FREIHERRN DU THIL.
(L.S.)   J. F. GRAFEN VON BERNSTORFF.
(L.S.)   A. R. FALCK.
(L.S.)   C. W. FREIHERRN VON FRITSCH.
(L.S.)   E. F. L. M. FREIHERRN VON BIEBERSTEIN.
(L.S.)   L. H. FREIHERRN VON PLESSEN.
(L.S.)   G. H. VON BERG.
(L.S.)   J. F. HACH.

[The foregoing Final Act became the Fundamental Law of the Confederation by a Resolution of the General Assembly of the Germanic Diet, dated 8th June, 1820.]

21

PROTOCOL of Conference between the British and Russian Plenipotentiaries, relative to the Mediation of Great Britain between the Ottoman Porte and the Greeks. Signed at St. Petersburgh, 23rd March/4th April, 1826.

[This Protocol was referred to in the Russian Declaration of War against Turkey, of 26th April, 1828.]

His Britannic Majesty having been requested by the Greeks to interpose his good offices, in order to obtain their reconciliation with the Ottoman Porte,—having, in consequence, offered his mediation to that Power, and being desirous of concerting the measures of his Government, upon this subject, with His Majesty the Emperor of all the Russias; and His Imperial Majesty, on the other hand, being equally animated by the desire of putting an end to the contest of which Greece and the Archipelago are the theatre, by an Arrangement, which shall be consistent with the principles of religion, justice, and humanity:

The Undersigned have agreed:

Proposal to be made to the Porte.

I. That the Arrangement to be proposed to the Porte, if that Government should accept the proffered Mediation, should have for its object, to place the Greeks towards the Ottoman Porte, in the relation hereafter mentioned:

Greece to be a Dependency of Turkey, and to pay Tribute. Choice of Greek Authorities.

Greece should be a Dependency of that Empire, and the Greeks should pay to the Porte an annual Tribute, the amount of which should be permanently fixed by common consent. They should be exclusively governed by authorities to be chosen and named by themselves, but in the nomination of which authorities the Porte should have a certain influence.

Liberty of Conscience and Freedom of Commerce.

In this state, the Greeks should enjoy a complete liberty of Conscience, entire freedom of Commerce, and should, exclusively, conduct their own internal Government.

Property of Turks to be purchased by Greeks.

In order to effect a complete separation between individuals of the two nations, and to prevent the collisions which must be the necessary consequences of a contest of such duration, the Greeks should purchase the Property of Turks, whether situated on the Continent of Greece, or in the islands.

Russia to exert her Influence in favour of Mediation.

II. In case the principle of a Mediation between Turks and Greeks should have been admitted, in consequence of the steps taken, with that view, by His Britannic Majesty's Ambassador at Constantinople, His Imperial Majesty would exert, in every case, His influence to forward the object of that Mediation. The mode in which, and the time at which, His Imperial Majesty should take part in the ulterior negotiations with the Ottoman Porte, which may be the consequence of that Mediation, should be determined hereafter by the common consent of the Governments of His Britannic Majesty and His Imperial Majesty.

Basis of Mediation to be maintained in case of refusal of Turkey.

III. If the Mediation offered by His Britannic Majesty should not have been accepted by the Porte, and whatever may be the nature of the relations between His Imperial Majesty and the Turkish Government, His Britannic Majesty and His Imperial Majesty will still consider the terms of the Arrangement specified in Article I of this Protocol, as the basis of any reconciliation to be effected by their intervention, whether in concert or separately, between the Porte and the Greeks; and they will avail themselves of every favourable opportunity to exert their influence with both parties, in order to effect this reconciliation on the above-mentioned basis.

Great Britain and Russia to settle Details of Arrangement.

IV. That His Britannic Majesty and His Imperial Majesty should reserve to themselves to adopt, hereafter, the measures necessary for the settlement of the details of the Arrangement in question, as well as the limits of the Territory, and the names of the Islands of the Archipelago to which it shall be applicable, and which it shall be proposed to the Porte to comprise under the denomination of Greece.

Advantages conferred on Great Britain and Russia to be enjoyed by all other Nations.

V. That, moreover, His Britannic Majesty and His Imperial Majesty will not seek, in this Arrangement, any increase of Territory, nor any exclusive influence, nor advantage in commerce for their subjects, which shall not be equally attainable by all other nations.

Proposed Guarantee of Treaty to be concluded.

VI. That His Britannic Majesty and His Imperial Majesty, being desirous that their Allies should become parties to the definitive Arrangements of which this Protocol contains the outline, will communicate this Instrument, confidentially, to the Courts of Vienna, Paris, and Berlin, and will propose to them that they should, in concert with the Emperor of Russia, guarantee the Treaty by which the reconciliation of Turks and Greeks shall be effected, as His Britannic Majesty cannot guarantee such a Treaty.

Done at St. Petersburgh, the 23rd March/4th April, 1826.

(L.S.)   WELLINGTON.

(L.S.)   NESSELRODE.

(L.S.)   LIEVEN.

22   CONVENTION OF AKKERMAN

CONVENTION between Russia and Turkey, explanatory of the Treaty of Bucharest. Signed at Akkerman, 25th September/7th October, 1826.

THE Imperial Court of Russia and the Sublime Porte, animated by a sincere desire to put a stop to the discussions which have arisen between them since the conclusion of the Treaty of Bucharest, and wishing to consolidate the relations of the two Empires, by giving them as bases a perfect harmony and an entire reciprocal confidence, have agreed to open by means of an assembling of respective Plenipotentiaries, an amicable negotiation, with the sole intention of removing from their mutual relations every subject of ulterior differences, and to insure, for the future, the full execution of the Treaty of Bucharest, as well as the Treaties and Acts which it renews or confirms, and the observance of which can alone guarantee the maintenance and the durability of the Peace so happily established between the Imperial Court of Russia and the Sublime Ottoman Porte. His Majesty the Emperor and Padishah of all the Russias, and His Majesty the Emperor and Padishah of the Ottomans, have therefore appointed as their Plenipotentiaries, namely; His Majesty the Emperor and Padishah of All the Russias, the Sieurs Count Michel Woronzoff, General Aide-de-Camp, General of Infantry, Member of the Council of the Empire, Governor-General of New Russia, and Commissary Plenipotentiary of the Province of Bessarabia, &c.; and Alexander de Ribeaupierre, Private Councillor and Actual Chamberlain, Envoy Extraordinary and Minister Plenipotentiary to the Sublime Porte, &c.; and His Highness the Sieurs Seid-Mehmed-Hadi-Effendi, Comptroller-General of Anatolia, First Plenipoteniary, and Seid-Ibrahim-Iffet-Effendi, Provisional Cadi of Sophia, with the rank of Molla of Scutari, Second Plenipotentiary; who after having assembled in the town of Ackermann, and having exchanged the authentic copies of their Full Powers, found to be in good and due form, have agreed to, concluded, and signed the following Articles:

Confirmation of Treaty of Bucharest.

ART. I. All the clauses and stipulations of the Treaty of Peace concluded at Bucharest, the 16th May, 1812 (17th day of the moon of Djemaziul Ewel of the year of the Hejira, 1227), are confirmed in all their force and value by the present Convention, as if the Treaty of Bucharest were word for word inserted therein, the explanations which form the object of this Convention serving only to determine the precise sense and to corroborate the tenor of the Articles of the said Treaty.

Alteration in Limits of Islands of the Danube opposite Ismael, at Kili.

ART. II. Article IV of the Treaty of Bucharest having stipulated for the two great Islands of the Danube, situated opposite Ismael, at Kili, which, whilst they continue in the possession of the Ottoman Porte, are to remain partly deserted and inhabited, a method of demarcation, the execution of which has been recognised as impossible, considering the inconveniences arising from the frequent overflowing of the River, and experience having, besides, shown the necessity of establishing a fixed separation and sufficiently extended between the respective Riverains, to remove all point of contact, and thereby to put a stop to the continual differences and troubles resulting therefrom, the Sublime

Ottoman Porte wishing to give an unequivocal proof to the Imperial Court of Russia of her sincere desire to cement the relations of friendship and good neighbourhood between the two States, engages to execute and to maintain the arrangement agreed upon at Constantinople between the Russian Envoy and the Ministers of the Sublime Porte, in the Conference of the 21st August, 1817, in conformity with the dispositions consigned in the Protocol of that Conference. Therefore, the dispositions contained in that Protocol and relating to the object in question shall be considered as forming an integral part of the present Convention.

Privileges of Moldavia and Wallachia.

ART. III. The Treaties and Acts relative to the Privileges enjoyed by Moldavia and Wallachia, having been confirmed by an express clause of Article V of the Treaty of Bucharest, the Sublime Porte solemnly engages to observe the said Privileges, Treaties, and Acts, on all occasions, with the most scrupulous fidelity, and promises to renew, within the space of six months after the ratification of the present Convention, the Hatti-Sheriffs of 1802, which have specified and guaranteed those Privileges. Besides, considering the misfortunes which those provinces have sustained in consequence of the last events, considering the choice made of Wallachian and Moldavian Boyards as Hospodars of the two Principalities, and considering that the Imperial Court of Russia has given its consent to that measure, it has been recognised, as well by the Sublime Porte as by the Court of Russia, that the Hatti-Sheriffs above mentioned of the year 1802, were to be indispensably completed by means of the clauses recorded in the annexed Separate Act, which the respective Plenipotentiaries have agreed to, and which is and shall be considered as forming an integral part of the present Convention.

Asiatic Frontiers. Restoration of Fortresses, &c.

ART. IV. It has been stipulated by Article VI of the Treaty of Bucharest that, on the side of Asia, the frontier between the two Empires should be re-established as it existed before the war, and that the Imperial Court of Russia should restore to the Sublime Ottoman Porte the Fortresses and Castles situated in the interior of that Frontier and conquered by its arms. In accordance with this Stipulation, and considering that the Imperial Court of Russia has evacuated and restored immediately after the peace, such of those Fortresses as had been taken, only during the war, from the troops of the Ottoman Porte, it is agreed on both sides, that henceforth the Asiatic Frontiers between the two Empires shall remain such as they exist at present, and that a term of two years is fixed in order reciprocally to consider upon the best means of maintaining the tranquillity and security of the respective subjects.

Privileges of Servia.

ART. V. The Sublime Ottoman Porte, wishing to give to the Imperial Russian Court a striking testimony of her amicable disposition, and of her scrupulous attention to fulfil in their entirety the conditions of the Treaty of Bucharest, will immediately put into execution all the clauses of Article VIII of that Treaty, relative to the Servian Nation, which being *ab antiquo*, subject and tributary to the Ottoman Porte, must on all occasions experience the effects of its clemency and generosity. In accordance therewith the Sublime Porte shall settle with the Deputies of the Servian Nation the measures which shall be considered the most convenient to secure the Privileges stipulated in her favour, Privileges, the enjoyment of which shall at the same time be the just reward and the best pledge of the fidelity of which that Nation has given proofs to the Ottoman Empire. As a term of 18 months is considered necessary to proceed to the verifications necessary to its attainment, in conformity with the Separate Act hereto annexed, agreed upon between the respective Plenipotentaries, the said measures shall be regulated and agreed upon in concert with the Servian Deputation at Constantinople, and inserted in detail in a Supreme Firman invested by the Hatti-Sheriff, which shall be enforced with as little delay as possible, and at latest within the said term of 18 months, and shall also be communicated to the Imperial Court of Russia, and considered from that time as forming an integral part of the present Convention.

Appointment of Commissioners for the Liquidation of Claims, &c.

ART. VI. In accordance with the express stipulations of Article X of the Treaty of Bucharest all the affairs and Claims of the respective subjects, which had been suspended by the war, having to be renewed and terminated, also the debts due to the respective subjects, as well as on the exchequer, having to be examined and regulated in all justice, and promptly and entirely liquidated, it is agreed that all the affairs and Claims of Russian subjects on the occasion of losses sustained by them by the depredations of Moorish Pirates, the confiscations made at the time of the rupture between the two Courts in 1806, and other acts of a similar nature, including those which have occurred since the year 1821, shall give rise to an equitable liquidation and Indemnity. For that purpose, Commissioners shall be appointed, on either side, who shall verify the state of those losses, and shall fix the amount of the Indemnity. All the labours of those Commissioners shall be terminated, and the sum to which the Indemnity above mentioned shall amount, shall be given in a lump sum to the Imperial Russian Legation at Constantinople, within the term of 18 months, dating from the ratification of the present Convention. A similar reciprocity shall be observed towards the subjects of the Ottoman Porte.

Depredations of Barbary Pirates.

ART. VII. The redress of damages caused to subjects and merchants of the Imperial Court of Russia by the Pirates of the Regencies of Algiers, Tunis, and Tripoli, and the full execution of the stipulations of the Treaty of Commerce, and of Article VII of the Treaty of Jassy, being strictly binding on the Ottoman Porte, by virtue of the express clauses of Article XII of the Treaty of Bucharest, which, jointly with Article III, renews and confirms all former transactions, the Sublime Porte solemnly renews her promise to fulfil henceforth with the most scrupulous fidelity, all engagements to that effect. Consequently:

Indemnity for Losses by Pirates.

1. The Sublime Porte will take every care to prevent the Pirates of the Barbary Regencies, under any pretext whatever, from molesting Russian commerce or navigation, and in case of depredation on their part, as soon as she is informed thereof, she engages anew to enforce without delay the restitution of all Captures made by the said Pirates, to give compensation to the Russian subjects for the losses which they may have sustained, to address to that effect a severe Firman to the Barbary Regencies, in order that it may not be necessary to renew it a second time, and in case that Firman should not be executed, to pay the amount of the Indemnity, out of her Imperial Treasury, within the term of two months, specified in Article VII of the Treaty of Jassy, dating from the day on which the Claim shall have been presented to that effect by the Russian Minister, after having examined it.

Freedom of Commerce and Navigation to Russian Subjects and Vessels.

2. The Sublime Porte engages rigorously to observe all the conditions of the said Treaty of Commerce, to raise all the prohibitions which are contrary to the express tenor of its stipulations, to place no impediments to the free Navigation of merchant vessels under Russian colours, in all the seas and waters of the Ottoman Empire without any exception; in short, that all Russian merchants, captains, and subjects in general, shall enjoy the advantages and privileges, as well as entire liberty of Commerce, formally stipulated for by the Treaties existing between the two Empires.

Freedom of Navigation and Commerce in the Canal of Constantinople.

3. In conformity with Article I of the Treaty of Constantinople, which stipulates in favour of all Russian subjects in general, for liberty of Navigation and Commerce in all the States of the Sublime Porte, as well by land as by sea, and wherever Russian subjects may wish, and by virtue of the clauses of Articles XXXI and XXXV of the said Treaty, which ensure a free passage through the Canal of Constantinople to all Russian merchant vessels laden with provisions or other Russian merchandise and productions, or of other States not under the dominion of the Ottoman Empire, as well as the free disposal of those provisions, merchandise, and productions, the Sublime Porte promises to put no obstacle or impediment in the way of Russian vessels laden with corn and other provisions, on their arrival in the Canal of Constantinople, the case of necessity arising, transhipping their cargo on board other vessels, whether Russian or foreign, to be conveyed out of the States of the Sublime Porte.

Entrance into Black Sea of Vessels chartered for Russian Commerce.

4. The Sublime Porte will accept the good offices of the Imperial Russian Court in granting, in accordance with former precedents, the entrance of the Black Sea to vessels of Powers friendly to the Ottoman Government, which have not, as yet, obtained that privilege, so that the import trade of Russia, by means of these vessels, and the export of Russian produce on board of them, may not be subject to any impediment.

Ratifications.

ART. VIII. The present Convention, serving as an elucidation and complement to the Treaty of Bucharest, shall be ratified by His Majesty the Emperor and Padishah of All the Russias, and by the Emperor and Padishah of the Ottomans, by means of solemn Ratifications signed by them in the usual manner, which shall be exchanged by the respective Plenipotentiaries within the term of six weeks, or sooner, if possible, dating from the day of the signature of the present Convention.

Done at Ackermann, 25th September, 1826.

(L.S.)   COMTE M. WORONZOW.
(L.S.)   RIBEAUPIERRE.

(*Annex* 1.)   *SEPARATE ACT relative to the Principalities of Moldavia and Wallachia.* 7th October, 1826.

Election of Hospodars.

THE Hospodars of Moldavia and Wallachia, being chosen from

amongst the native Boyards, their election shall henceforth be made in each of those Provinces, with the consent and pleasure of the Sublime Porte, by the General Assembly of the Divan, in accordance with the ancient customs of the country.

Choice of a Hospodar from amongst the Boyards.

The Boyards of the Divan of each Province, as a Body of the Country, and with the general consent of the inhabitants, shall make choice for the dignity of Hospodar of one of the oldest Boyards, as the best able to fill the post, and they shall present to the Sublime Porte by petition (Arz. Mahzar) the candidate elect, who, should the Sublime Porte agree, shall be appointed Hospodar, and receive his investiture. Should the nomination of the candidate elect not be, on account of serious reasons, in accordance with the wishes of the Sublime Porte, in such case, after those serious reasons shall have been proved by the two Courts, it shall be permissible to recommend to the said Boyards to proceed to the election of another eligible person.

Hospodars to be Elected for Seven Years.

The continuance of the Administration of the Hospodars shall be fixed, as in former time, at 7 complete and entire years, dating from the day of their appointment, and they cannot be dismissed during that time. Should they commit any offence during the term of their administration, the Sublime Porte shall inform the Russian Minister thereof, and should it be proved that the Hospodar had actually been guilty of any offence, after re-examination thereof by either party, his dismissal shall be allowed in that case only.

Re-appointment of Hospodars.

The Hospodars who shall have completed their term of 7 years without having given, either to the two Courts or to the country, any cause of legitimate and grave complaint, shall be appointed for another 7 years, if the request is made to the Sublime Porte by the Divans of the Provinces, and if the general consent of the inhabitants is in their favour.

Abdication of Hospodar.

Should it so happen that a Hospodar abdicates before the completion of the term of 7 years, on account of old age, or from infirmity, or any other cause, the Sublime Porte shall inform the Court of Russia thereof, and the abdication may take effect with the previous consent of the two Courts.

Disqualifications of former Hospodars.

Every Hospodar who shall have been discharged after having finished his term, or who shall have abdicated, shall incur the loss of his title, and shall be allowed to return into the class of Boyards, on condition that he remains peaceable and quiet, without, however, being able to remain a member of the Divan, or to fulfil any public function, or to be re-elected Hospodar.

Qualification of Sons of Hospodars.

The sons of Hospodars who have been discharged, or who have abdicated, shall preserve their title as Boyards, shall be eligible to hold offices of State, and to be elected Hospodars.

Administration during Vacancy.

In case of dismissal, of abdication, or death of a Hospodar, and until a successor shall have been appointed, the administration of the vacant Principality shall be entrusted to Caimacans appointed by the Divans of the said Principalities.

Boyards of Divans to regulate the Taxes, &c.

The Hatti-Sheriff of 1802 having ordered the abolition of Taxes and Duties introduced since the year 1198 (1783), the Hospodars, with the Boyards of the respective Divans, shall settle and fix the taxes and annual charges of Moldavia and Wallachia, taking as a basis the regulations established by the Hatti-Sheriff of 1802. The Hospodars shall under no circumstances fail in the strict performance of this arrangement. They shall take into consideration the representations of the Minister of His Imperial Majesty, and to those which Russian Courts shall make by his orders, as well on this subject as on the maintenance of the privileges of the country, and especially on the observance of the clauses and articles inserted in the present Convention.

Appointment of Beschlis and Agas.

The Hospodars, together with the respective Divans, shall fix the number of Beschlis in accordance with the number which existed previous to the disturbances of 1821. That number, once fixed, cannot be increased under any pretext whatever, unless its urgent necessity is recognised on either side, and it is well understood that the Beschlis shall continue to be formed and organised as they were previous to the disturbances of 1821, that the Agas shall continue to be chosen and appointed in the same manner as previous to the said period, and, in short, that the Beschlis and their Agas shall never fill any other functions than those for which they have been originally appointed, not being able to interfere in the affairs of the country, or of taking upon themselves any other duties.

Restoration of Wallachian Territory.

The usurpations over Wallachian territory near Ibraila, Giurgevo, and Coulé, and beyond the Olta, shall be restored to the proprietors, and a term shall be fixed for their restitution, in the Firmans relating thereto, which shall be addressed to whom it may concern.

Boyards to return freely to their Country.

Those Moldavian and Wallachian Boyards who were obliged to leave their country solely on account of the late disturbances, shall be allowed to return freely, without being molested in any way, and be restored to the full and entire enjoyment of their rights, prerogatives, goods, and estates, as in time past.

Payment of Tribute and Dues.   Liberty of Commerce.

The Sublime Porte, taking into consideration the misfortunes which have weighed on the Principalities of Moldavia and Wallachia, from the late disturbances, will grant unto them 2 years' exemption from Tributes and Dues which they are bound to pay; at the expiration of the term of exemption above mentioned, the said tributes and dues shall be paid according to the rates fixed by the Hatti-Sheriffs of 1802, and shall not be increased under any circumstances whatever. The Sublime Porte will also grant to the inhabitants of the two Principalities liberty of Commerce in all productions of the soil and of their industry, which they shall be at liberty to dispose of as they like, save the exceptions required on the one side for the annual supplies due to the Sublime Porte, of which these Provinces are the granaries, on the other, for the victualling of the country. All the provisions of the Hatti-Sheriff of 1802, relative to those supplies, of their regular payment at the current prices, according to which they are to be settled, and the rating of which shall, in case of litigation, be settled by the respective Divans, shall be renewed and observed for the future with scrupulous punctuality.

Submission of Boyards to the Hospodars.

The Boyards shall be bound to execute the orders of the Hospodars and be in perfect submission to them. On their part, the Hospodars shall not act harshly against the Boyards, nor shall they make them undergo undeserved punishments and unless they shall have committed some proved fault, and the latter shall not undergo any punishment until they have been judged according to the laws and customs of the country.

Framing of General Regulations for the Internal Administration of
each Principality.

The disorders of the last few years in Moldavia and Wallachia, having caused the most severe injury to order in the different branches of Internal Administration, the Hospodars shall be bound with the least possible delay, together with the respective Divans, to take the necessary measures to improve the condition of the Principalities confided to their care, and those measures shall form the subject of a general regulation for each province, which shall be put into immediate execution.

Maintenance of Rights and Privileges.

All the other rights and privileges of the Principalities of Moldavia and Wallachia, and all the Hatti-Sheriffs relating thereto, shall be maintained and observed, in so far as they are not modified by the present Act.

Therefore we, the Undersigned, Plenipotentiaries of the Emperor and Padishah of All the Russias, furnished with sovereign Full Powers, jointly with the Plenipotentiaries of the Sublime Ottoman Porte, have concluded and determined, with reference to Moldavia and Wallachia, the above clauses, which are the result of Article III of the explanatory and confirmatory Convention of the Treaty of Bucharest, concluded in 8 Articles, at the Conference at Ackermann between us and the Ottoman Plenipotentiaries.

Accordingly, the present Separate Act has been drawn up, sealed, and signed by us, and delivered into the hands of the Plenipotentiaries of the Sublime Porte.

Done at Ackermann, 25th September/7th October, 1826.

(L.S.)   COMTE M. WORONZOW.
(L.S.)   RIBEAUPIERRE.

(Annex 2.)   SEPARATE ACT relating to Servia.
7th October, 1826.

Privileges to be granted to the Servian Nation.

THE Sublime Porte, with the sole intention of faithfully fulfilling the stipulations of Article VIII of the Treaty of Bucharest, having heretofore allowed the Servian Deputies at Constantinople to lay before her the demands of their nation upon the matters most suitable for the consolidation of the security and well-being of the country, those Deputies had heretofore set forth in their memorial the wish of the nation with respect to certain of those matters, such as freedom of Religious Worship, the choice of its Chiefs, the Independence of its Internal Administration, the re-annexation of the Districts detached from Servia, the consolidation of the various Taxes into a single sum, the making over to the Servians the administration of the Properties belonging to Mussulmans, subject to the payment of the proceeds thereof at the same time with the tribute, liberty of Commerce, permission for the Servian merchants to travel in the Ottoman dominions with their own Passports, the establishment of Hospitals, Schools, and Printing-houses; and, finally, the prohibition to Mussulmans, other than those belonging to the Garrisons, to establish themselves in Servia. Whilst the Articles above specified were being inquired into and settled, certain obstacles which occurred were the occasion of their being deferred. But the Sublime Porte, still persisting at the present time in the firm resolution of granting to the Servian nation the advantages stipulated in Article VIII of the Treaty of Bucharest, will settle, in concert with the Servian Deputies at Constantinople, the above-mentioned demands of that faithful and submissive nation, as well as all the other demands which may be laid before her by the Servian Deputation, and which may in no respect be contrary to the character of subjects of the Ottoman Empire.

Court of Russia to be informed of Privileges granted to Servia.

The Sublime Porte will acquaint the Imperial Court of Russia with the manner in which Article VIII of the Treaty of Bucharest shall have been executed, and will communicate to it the Firman decorated with the Hatti Sheriff, by which the above-mentioned advantages shall be granted.

Wherefore, we the Undersigned, Plenipotentiaries of His Majesty the Emperor and Padishah of All the Russias, furnished with sovereign Full Powers, in concert with the Plenipotentiaries of the Sublime Ottoman Porte, have agreed upon and settled, with respect to the Servians, the above points, which are the result of Article V of the Convention explanatory and confirmatory of the Treaty of Bucharest, concluded in 8 Articles in the conferences at Ackermann, between us and the Ottoman Plenipotentiaries.

Accordingly, the present Separate Act has been drawn up, sealed, and signed by us, and delivered to the Plenipotentiaries of the Sublime Porte.

Done at Ackermann, the 25th September/7th October, 1826.

(L.S.)   COMTE M. WORONZOW.

(L.S.)   RIBEAUPIERRE.

23   TREATY OF LONDON

TREATY between Great Britain, France, and Russia, for the Pacification of Greece. Signed at London, 6th July, 1827.

In the Name of the Most Holy and Undivided Trinity.

HIS Majesty the King of the United Kingdom of Great Britain and Ireland, His Majesty the King of France and Navarre, and His Majesty the Emperor of All the Russias, penetrated with the necessity of putting an end to the sanguinary struggle which, while it abandons the Greek Provinces and the Islands of the Archipelago to all the disorders of anarchy, daily causes fresh impediments to the commerce of the States of Europe, and gives opportunity for acts of Piracy which not only expose the subjects of the High Contracting Parties to grievous losses, but also render necessary measures which are burthensome for their observation and suppression;

His Majesty the King of the United Kingdom of Great Britain and Ireland, and His Majesty the King of France and Navarre, having moreover received from the Greeks an earnest invitation to interpose their Mediation with the Ottoman Porte; and, together with His Majesty the Emperor of All the Russias, being animated with the desire of putting a stop to the effusion of blood, and of preventing the evils of every kind which the continuance of such a state of affairs may produce;

They have resolved to combine their efforts, and to regulate the operation thereof, by a formal Treaty, for the object of re-establishing peace between the contending parties, by means of an arrangement called for, no less by sentiments of humanity, than by interests for the tranquillity of Europe.

For these purposes, they have named their Plenipotentiaries to discuss, conclude, and sign the said Treaty, that is to say:—

His Majesty the King of the United Kingdom of Great Britain and Ireland, the Right Honourable John William Viscount Dudley, a Peer of the United Kingdom of Great Britain and Ireland, a Member of His said Majesty's Most Honourable Privy Council, and his Principal Secretary of State for Foreign Affairs;

His Majesty the King of France and Navarre, the Prince Jules, Count de Polignac, a Peer of France, Knight of the Orders of His Most Christian Majesty, Maréchal-de-Camp of his Forces, Grand Cross of the Order of St. Maurice of Sardinia, &c., &c., and his Ambassador at London;

And His Majesty the Emperor of All the Russias, the Sieur Christopher Prince de Lieven, General of Infantry of His Imperial Majesty's Forces, his Aide-de-Camp General, his Ambassador Extraordinary and Plenipotentiary to His Britannic Majesty, &c.;

Who, after having communicated to each other their Full Powers, found to be in due and proper form, have agreed upon the following Articles:

Offer of Mediation.

ART. I. The Contracting Powers shall offer their Mediation to the Ottoman Porte, with the view of effecting a reconciliation between it and the Greeks.

This offer of Mediation shall be made to that Power immediately after the Ratification of the present Treaty, by means of a joint Declaration, signed by Plenipotentiaries of the Allied Courts at Constantinople; and, at the same time, a demand for an immediate Armistice shall be made to the Two Contending Parties, as a preliminary and indispensable condition to the opening of any negotiation.

Bases of Arrangement.

ART. II. The Arrangement to be proposed to the Ottoman Porte shall rest upon the following bases:

Greece to be a Dependency of Turkey and Pay Tribute. Appointment of Greek Authorities.

The Greeks shall hold under the Sultan as under a Lord paramount; and, in consequence thereof, they shall pay to the Ottoman Empire an annual Tribute, the amount of which shall be fixed, once for all, by common agreement. They shall be governed by authorities whom they shall choose and appoint themselves, but in the nomination of whom the Porte shall have a defined right.

Greeks to become Possessors of all Turkish Property on Payment of Indemnity.

In order to effect a complete separation between the individuals of the two nations, and to prevent the collisions which would be the inevitable consequence of so protracted a struggle, the Greeks shall become possessors of all Turkish Property situated either upon the Continent, or in the Islands of Greece, on condition of indemnifying the former proprietors, either by an annual sum to be added to the tribute which they shall pay to the Porte, or by some other arrangement of the same nature.

Details of Arrangement and Boundaries to be settled by Negotiation.
ART. III. The details of this Arrangement, as well as the Limits of the
Territory upon the Continent, and the designation of the Islands of the
Archipelago to which it shall be applicable, shall be settled by a negotia-
tion to be hereafter entered into between the High Powers and the Two
Contending Parties.

Pacification of Greece.
ART. IV. The Contracting Powers engage to pursue the salutary work
of the Pacification of Greece, upon the bases laid down in the preceding
Articles, and to furnish, without the least delay, their Representatives
at Constantinople with all the Instructions which are required for the
execution of the Treaty which they now sign.

Equal Advantages to be Conferred on all Nations.
ART. V. The Contracting Powers will not seek, in these Arrangements,
any augmentation of territory, any exclusive influence, or any commercial advantage for their subjects, which those of every other nation may
not equally obtain.

Guarantee of 3 Powers.
ART. VI. The arrangements for reconciliation and Peace which shall
be definitively agreed upon between the Contending Parties, shall be
guaranteed by those of the Signing Powers who may judge it expedient
or possible to contract that obligation. The operation and the effects
of such Guarantee shall become the subject of future stipulation between
the High Powers.

Ratifications.
ART. VII. The present Treaty shall be ratified, and the Ratifications
shall be exchanged in 2 months, or sooner if possible.

In witness whereof, the respective Plenipotentiaries have signed the
same, and have affixed thereto the Seals of their Arms.

Done at London, the 6th day of July, in the year of Our Lord,
1827.

(L.S.)   DUDLEY.
(L.S.)   LE PRINCE DE POLIGNAC.
(L.S.)   LIEVEN.

ADDITIONAL ARTICLE.

IN case the Ottoman Porte should not, within the space of one month,
accept the Mediation which is to be proposed to it, the High Contracting Parties agree upon the following measures:

Commercial Relations to be entered into with Greece in case of Turkish Refusal of Mediation.

I. It shall be declared to the Porte, by their Representatives at Constantinople, that the inconveniences and evils described in the patent Treaty as inseparable from the state of things which has, for six years, existed in the East, and the termination of which, by the means at the command of the Sublime Ottoman Porte, appears to be still distant, impose upon the High Contracting Parties the necessity of taking immediate measures for forming a connection with the Greeks.

It is understood that this shall be effected by establishing commercial relations with the Greeks, and by sending to and receiving from them, for this purpose, Consular Agents, provided there shall exist in Greece authorities capable of supporting such relations.

Measures to be adopted by Allied Powers in case of Non-observance of Armistice.

II. If, within the said term of one month, the Porte does not accept the Armistice proposed in Article I of the patent Treaty, or if the Greeks refuse to carry it into execution, the High Contracting Powers shall declare to either of the Contending Parties which may be disposed to continue hostilities, or to both of them, if necessary, that the said High Powers intend to exert all the means which circumstances may suggest to their prudence, for the purpose of obtaining the immediate effects of the Armistice of which they desire the execution, by preventing, as far as possible, all collision between the Contending Parties; and in consequence, immediately after the above-mentioned declaration, the High Powers will, jointly, exert all their efforts to accomplish the object of such Armistice, without, however, taking any part in the hostilities between the Two Contending Parties.

Immediately after the signature of the present Additional Article, the High Contracting Powers will, consequently, transmit to the Admirals commanding their respective squadrons in the Levant, conditional Instructions in conformity to the arrangements above declared.

Measures to be adopted in case of Refusal of Ottoman Porte.

III. Finally, if, contrary to all expectation, these measures do not prove sufficient to procure the adoption of the propositions of the High Contracting Parties by the Ottoman Porte; or, if, on the other hand, the Greeks decline the conditions stipulated in their favour, by the Treaty of this date, the High Contracting Powers will, nevertheless, continue to pursue the work of pacification, on the bases upon which they have agreed; and, in consequence, they authorise, from the present moment, their Representatives at London, to discuss and determine the future measures which it may become necessary to employ.

The present Additional Article shall have the same force and validity as if it were inserted, word for word, in the Treaty of this day. It shall be ratified, and the Ratifications shall be exchanged at the same time as those of the said Treaty.

In witness whereof the respective Plenipotentiaries have signed the same, and have affixed thereto the Seals of their Arms.

Done at London, the 6th day of July, in the year of Our Lord, 1827.

(L.S.)   DUDLEY.
(L.S.)   LE PRINCE DE POLIGNAC.
(L.S.)   LIEVEN.

[The Porte declared its Entire adhesion to the Stipulations of this Treaty, by a Declaration signed on the 9th September, 1829, and in Art. X of the Treaty of 14th September, 1829.]

24

CONVENTION BETWEEN GREAT BRITAIN AND THE USA for submitting the northeastern boundary dispute to arbitration. Concluded 29th September, 1827. Ratifications exchanged 2nd April, 1828.

Whereas it is provided by the fifth article of the treaty of Ghent, that, in case the Commissioners appointed under that article, for the settlement of the boundary line therein described, should not be able to agree upon such boundary line, the report or reports of those Commissioners, stating the points on which they had differed, should be submitted to some friendly Sovereign or State, and that the decision given by such Sovereign or State, on such points of difference, should be considered by the contracting parties as final and conclusive: That case having now arisen, and it having, therefore, become expedient to proceed to and regulate the reference as above described, the United States of America, and His Majesty the King of the United Kingdom of Great Britain and Ireland have, for that purpose, named their Plenipotentiaries, that is to say:

The President of the United States has appointed Albert Gallatin, their Envoy Extraordinary and Minister Plenipotentiary at the Court of His Britannic Majesty; and His said Majesty, on his part, has appointed the Right Honourable Charles Grant, a member of Parliament, a member of His said Majesty's Most Honourable Privy Council, and President of the Committee of the Privy Council for Affairs of Trade and Foreign Plantations, and Henry Unwin Addington, Esquire;

Who, after having exchanged their respective full powers, found to be in due and proper form, have agreed to and concluded the following articles:

ARTICLE I. It is agreed that the points of difference which have arisen in the settlement of the boundary between the American and British dominions, as described in the 5th article of the treaty of Ghent, shall be referred, as therein provided, to some friendly Sovereign or State, who shall be invited to investigate, and make a decision upon, such points of difference.

The two contracting Powers engage to proceed in concert, to the choice of such friendly Sovereign or State, as soon as the ratifications of this convention shall have been exchanged, and to use their best endeavours to obtain a decision, if practicable, within two years after the Arbiter shall have signified his consent to act as such.

ARTICLE II. The reports and documents, thereunto annexed, of the Commissioners appointed to carry into execution the 5th article of the treaty of Ghent, being so voluminous and complicated as to render it improbable that any Sovereign or State should be willing or able to undertake the office of investigating and arbitrating upon them, it is hereby agreed to substitute, for those reports, new and separate statements of the respective cases, severally drawn up by each of the contracting parties, in such form and terms as each may think fit.

The said statements, when prepared, shall be mutually communicated to each other by the contracting parties, that is to say, by the United States to His Britannick Majesty's Minister or Chargé d'Affaires at Washington, and by Great Britain to the Minister or Chargé d'Affaires of the United States at London, within fifteen months after the exchange of the ratifications of the present convention.

After such communication shall have taken place, each party shall have the power of drawing up a second and definitive statement, if it thinks fit so to do, in reply to the statement of the other party, so communicated, which definitive statements shall also be mutually communicated, in the same manner as aforesaid, to each other, by the contracting parties, within twenty-one months after the exchange of ratifications of the present convention.

ARTICLE III. Each of the contracting parties shall, within nine months after the exchange of ratifications of this convention, communicate to the other, in the same manner as aforesaid, all the evidence intended to be brought in support of its claim, beyond that which is contained in the reports of the Commissioners, or papers thereunto annexed, and other written documents laid before the Commission, under the 5th article of the treaty of Ghent.

Each of the contracting parties shall be bound, on the application of

the other party, made within six months after the exchange of the
ratifications of this convention, to give authentic copies of such individually specified acts of a public nature, relating to the territory in
question, intended to be laid as evidence before the Arbiter, as have
been issued under the authority, or are in the exclusive possession, of
each party.

No maps, surveys, or topographical evidence of any description, shall
be adduced by either party, beyond that which is hereinafter stipulated,
nor shall any fresh evidence of any description be adduced or adverted
to, by either party, other than that mutually communicated or applied
for as aforesaid.

Each party shall have full power to incorporate in, or annex to, either
its first or second statement, any portion of the reports of the Commissioners, or papers thereunto annexed, and other written documents
laid before the Commission under the 5th article of the treaty of Ghent,
or of the other evidence mutually communicated or applied for as above
provided, which it may think fit.

ARTICLE IV. The map called Mitchell's map, by which the farmers of
the treaty of 1783 are acknowledged to have regulated their joint and
official proceedings, and the map A, which has been agreed on by the
contracting parties, as a delineation of the water-courses, and of the
boundary lines in reference to the said water-courses, as contended for
by each party respectively, and which has accordingly been signed by the
above-named Plenipotentiaries, at the same time with this convention,
shall be annexed to the statements of the contracting parties, and be the
only maps that shall be considered as evidence, mutually acknowledged
by the contracting parties, of the topography of the country.

It shall, however, be lawful for either party to annex to its respective
first statement, for the purposes of general illustration, any of the maps,
surveys, or topographical delineations, which were filed by the Commissioners under the 5th article of the treaty of Ghent, any engraved
map heretofore published, and also a transcript of the above-mentioned
map A, or of a section thereof, in which transcript each party may lay
down the highlands, or other features of the country, as it shall think
fit; the water courses and the boundary lines, as claimed by each party,
remaining as laid down in the said map A.

But this transcript, as well as all the other maps, surveys, or topographical delineations, other than the map A, and Mitchell's map,
intended to be thus annexed, by either party, to the respective statements, shall be communicated to the other party, in the same manner
as aforesaid, within nine months after the exchange of the ratification of
this convention, and shall be subject to such objections and observations
as the other contracting party may deem it expedient to make thereto,

and shall annex to his first statement, either in the margin of such transcript, map or maps, or otherwise.

ARTICLE V. All the statements, papers, maps, and documents, above mentioned, and which shall have been mutually communicated as aforesaid, shall, without any addition, subtraction, or alteration, whatsoever, be jointly and simultaneously delivered in to the arbitrating Sovereign or State within two years after the exchange of ratifications of this convention, unless the Arbiter should not, within that time, have consented to act as such; in which case all the said statements, papers, maps, and documents shall be laid before him within six months after the time when he shall have consented so to act. No other statements, papers, maps, or documents shall ever be laid before the Arbiter, except as hereinafter provided.

ARTICLE VI. In order to facilitate the attainment of a just and sound decision on the part of the Arbiter, it is agreed that, in case the said Arbiter should desire further elucidation or evidence in regard to any specifick point contained in any of the said statements submitted to him, the requisition for such elucidation or evidence shall be simultaneously made to both parties, who shall thereupon be permitted to bring further evidence, if required, and to make, each, a written reply to the specific questions submitted by the said Arbiter, but no further; and such evidence and replies shall be immediately communicated by each party to the other.

And in case the Arbiter should find the topographical evidence, laid as aforesaid before him, insufficient for the purposes of a sound and just decision, he shall have the power of ordering additional surveys to be made of any portions of the disputed boundary line or territory, as he may think fit; which surveys shall be made at the joint expense of the contracting parties, and be considered as conclusive by them.

ARTICLE VII. The decision of the Arbiter, when given, shall be taken as final and conclusive; and it shall be carried, without reserve, into immediate effect, by Commissioners appointed for that purpose by the contracting parties.

ARTICLE VIII. This convention shall be ratified, and the ratifications shall be exchanged in nine months from the date hereof, or sooner if possible.

In witness whereof, we, the respective Plenipotentiaries, have signed the same, and have affixed thereto the seals of our arms.

Done at London the twenty-ninth day of September, in the year of our Lord one thousand eight hundred and twenty-seven.

ALBERT GALLATIN.
CHA. GRANT.
HENRY UNWIN ADDINGTON.

On January 10, 1831, the King of the Netherlands submitted an award which was not accepted by either Government. The boundary was finally determined by the convention of August 9, 1842.

25   TREATY OF ADRIANOPLE

TREATY of Peace between Russia and Turkey. Signed at Adrianople, 14th September, 1829.

In the name of Almighty God.

His Imperial Majesty the very high and very powerful Emperor and Autocrat of All the Russias, and His Highness the very high and very powerful Emperor of the Ottomans, animated by an equal desire of putting an end to the calamities of war and of re-establishing Peace, friendship, and good harmony between their Empires, upon solid and immutable bases, have resolved, by mutual consent, to confide this salutary work to the care and management of their respective Plenipotentiaries; that is to say: His Imperial Majesty of All the Russias to the most Illustrious and most Excellent Count de Diebitsch, &c., who, by virtue of the supreme Full Powers with which he is furnished, has delegated and nominated as Plenipotentiaries on the part of the Imperial Court of Russia the most Excellent and most Honourable Count Alexis Orloff, &c., and Count Frederick Pahlen, &c.; and His Majesty the Emperor of the Ottomans, the most Excellent and most Honourable Mehemmed Sadik Effendi, Acting Grand Defterdar of the Sublime Ottoman Porte, and Abdoul-Kadir-Bey, Cazi-Asker of Anatolia; who, having assembled in the city of Adrianople, after having exchanged their Full Powers, have agreed upon the following Articles:—

Cessation of Hostilities.

ART. I. All hostility and dissention which, up to the present time, have existed between the two Empires shall cease from the date hereof, as well by land as by sea, and there shall be perpetual Peace, amity, and good intelligence between His Majesty the Emperor and Padisha of All the Russias, and His Highness the Emperor and Padisha of the Ottomans, their heirs and successors to the Throne, as well as between their respective Empires. The two High Contracting Powers will employ a special attention for preventing all that may cause the renewal of any misunderstanding between their respective subjects. They will scrupulously fulfil all the conditions of the present Treaty of Peace, and will use all their vigilance to prevent its being contravened in any manner, either directly or indirectly.

Restoration of Moldavia, Wallachia, &c., to Turkey.

ART. II.. His Majesty the Emperor and Padisha of All the Russias, desirous of giving His Highness the Emperor and Padisha of the Ottomans a proof of the sincerity of his amicable disposition, restores to the Sublime Porte the Principality of Moldavia, with the same limits which that Principality had before the commencement of the War which has just been terminated by the present Treaty. His Imperial Majesty likewise restores the Principality of Wallachia, the Banat of Crajova, without any exception whatsoever, Bulgaria and the country of Dobridgia, from the Danube as far as to the sea, together with Silistria, Hirchova, Matchin, Issactchi, Toultcha, Baba-dagh, Bazardjik, Varna, Pravadi, and other cities, towns, and villages which it contains, the whole extent of the Balkan from Emineh-Bournou as far as Kazan, and all the country from the Balkans as far as to the sea, together with Selimno, Ianboli, Aïdos, Carnabat, Messembria, Ahioli, Bourgas, Sizeboli, Kirk-Klissa, the city of Adrianople, Lulé-Bourgas, and lastly, all the cities, towns, and villages, and, in general, all the places which the Russian troops have occupied in Roumelia.

Pruth to form Boundary of the two Empires. Navigation of the Danube by Merchant Vessels and Ships of War.

ART. III. The Pruth shall continue to form the Boundary of the two Empires, from the point where that River touches the Territory of Moldavia as far as its confluence with the Danube. From this place the frontier line shall follow the course of the Danube as far as the embouchure of St. George, so that while leaving all the Islands formed by the different branches of this River in the possession of Russia, the right bank will remain, as heretofore, in that of the Ottoman Porte. It is, nevertheless, agreed that this right bank, commencing from the point where the St. George branch separates from that of Souline, shall remain uninhabited, to the distance of two hours from the river, and that no establishment of any kind whatsoever shall be formed thereon, and that in like manner it shall not be permitted to make any establishment or construct any fortification upon the Islands which shall remain in the possession of the Court of Russia, excepting always the quarantines which shall be thereon established. The merchant-vessels of the two Powers shall be competent to navigate the Danube throughout its whole course, and those which bear the Ottoman flag may freely enter the Kili and Souline embouchures, that of St. George remaining common to the war and merchant flags of the two Contracting Powers. But the Russian Ships of War must not, in sailing up the Danube, go beyond the place of its junction with the Pruth.

Asiatic Boundary between Russia and Turkey.

ART. IV. Georgia, Imeritia, Mingrelia, Gouriel, and several other Provinces of the Caucasus, having been for a long time and in perpetuity annexed to the Empire of Russia, and this Empire having moreover acquired by the Treaty concluded with Persia at Tourkmantchaï, on the 10th/22nd of February, 1828, the Khanates of Erivan and Naktchivan, the two High Contracting Powers have been convinced of the necessity of establishing between their respective States, throughout the whole of this line, a well-defined frontier and such as shall prevent all future misunderstanding. They have likewise taken into consideration the necessary means for opposing insurmountable obstacles to the incursions and depredations which, up to the present time, have been practised by the frontier tribes, and which have so often compromised the relations of amity and good fellowship between the two Empires. In consequence whereof it has been agreed to recognize henceforth for the frontier between the States of the Imperial Court of Russia and those of the Sublime Ottoman Porte in Asia, the line which, following the present boundary of the Province of Gouriel, from the Black Sea, ascends to that of Imeritia, and thence in the most direct line to the point where the frontiers of the Pashalics of Akhaltzik and of Kars unite with those of Georgia, leaving, in this manner, to the north and within this line the city of Akhaltzik and the fort of Alkhalkhaliki, at a distance which must not be less than two hours. All the countries situated to the south and west of this line of demarcation towards the Pashalics of Kars and of Trebizond, together with the greater part of the Pashalic of Akhaltzik, shall remain in perpetuity under the domination of the Sublime Porte, whilst those which are situated to the north and east of the said line, towards Georgia, Imeritia, and Gouriel, as well as the whole of the coast of the Black Sea, from the mouth of the Kouban as far as the port of St. Nicholas inclusively, shall remain in perpetuity under the dominion of the Empire of Russia. In consequence of which the Imperial Court of Russia gives up and restores to the Sublime Porte the remaining portion of the Pashalic of Akhaltzik, the city and the Pashalic of Kars, the city and the Pashalic of Bayazid, the city and the Pashalic of Erzeroum, as well as all the places occupied by the Russian troops, and which are situated without the above-mentioned line.

Moldavia and Wallachia placed under Suzerainty of the Porte,
enjoying an Independent National Government.

ART. V. The Principalities of Moldavia and Wallachia having been in consequence of a Capitulation placed under the Suzerainty of the Sublime Porte, and Russia having guaranteed their prosperity, it is understood that they shall preserve all the privileges and immunities

which have been granted to them either by their Capitulations
Treaties concluded between the two Empires, or by the Ha
promulgated at different times. In consequence whereof, they sl
the free exercise of their Worship, perfect security, an ind
national Government, and full liberty of Commerce. The a........
clauses to the preceding stipulations, clauses which are judged to be
necessary in order to secure to these two Provinces the enjoyment of their
Rights, are consigned to the Separate Act hereunto annexed (1), which
is and shall be considered as forming an integral part of the present
Treaty.

Measures for Tranquillity of Servia.

ART. VI. The circumstances which have occurred since the conclusion
of the Convention of Ackermann, not having allowed the Sublime Porte
to occupy itself immediately with the carrying into execution the clauses
of the Separate Act relative to Servia, and annexed to Article V of the
said Convention; it undertakes in the most solemn manner to fulfil them
without the least delay, and with the most scrupulous exactitude, and to
proceed especially to the immediate restitution of the six districts
detached from Servia, so as to secure for ever the tranquillity and welfare
of that faithful and devoted nation. The Firman furnished with the
Hatti-Sherif commanding the execution of the said clauses shall be
delivered and officially communicated to the Imperial Court of Russia
within the term of one month, reckoning from the signature of the present
Treaty of Peace.

Freedom of Trade in Turkey.

ART. VII. Russian subjects shall enjoy, throughout the whole extent
of the Ottoman Empire, as well by land as by sea, the full and entire
freedom of trade secured to them by the Treaties concluded heretofore
between the two High Contracting Powers. This freedom of trade shall
not be molested in any way, nor shall it be fettered in any case, or under
any pretext, by any prohibition or restriction whatsoever, nor in consequence of any regulation or measure, whether of public government
or internal legislation. Russian subjects, ships, and merchandise, shall be
protected from all violence and imposition. The first shall remain under
the exclusive jurisdiction and control of the Russian Minister and
Consuls; Russian ships shall never be subjected to any search on the
part of the Ottoman authorities, neither out at sea nor in any of the ports
or roadsteads under the dominion of the Sublime Porte; and all merchandise or goods belonging to a Russian subject may, after payment of
the Custom-house dues imposed by the tariffs, be freely sold, deposited
on land in the warehouses of the owner or consignee, or transhipped on

board another vessel of any nation whatsoever, without the Russian subject being required, in this case, to give notice of the same to any of the local authorities, and much less to ask their permission so to do. It is expressly agreed that the different kinds of wheat coming from Russia shall partake of the same privileges, and that their free transit shall never, under any pretext, suffer the least difficulty or hindrance.

Free Passage to Russian Merchant Vessels in Straits of Constantinople and Bosphorus.

The Sublime Porte engages, moreover, to take especial care that the trade and navigation of the Black Sea, particularly, shall be impeded in no manner whatsoever. For this purpose it admits and declares the passage of the Strait of Constantinople and that of the Dardanelles to be entirely free and open to Russian vessels under the merchant flag, laden or in ballast, whether they come from the Black Sea for the purpose of entering the Mediterranean, or whether, coming from the Mediterranean, they wish to enter the Black Sea: such vessels, provided they be merchant ships, whatever their size and tonnage, shall be exposed to no hindrance or annoyance of any kind, as above provided. The two Courts shall agree upon the most fitting means for preventing all delay in issuing the necessary instructions. In virtue of the same principle the passage of the Strait of Constantinople and of that of the Dardanelles is declared free and open to all the merchant ships of Powers who are at Peace with the Sublime Porte, whether going into the Russian ports of the Black Sea or coming from them, laden or in ballast, upon the same conditions which are stipulated for vessels under the Russian flag.

Freedom of Trade and Navigation in the Black Sea.

Lastly, the Sublime Porte, recognizing in the Imperial Court of Russia the right of securing the necessary guarantees for this full freedom of trade and navigation in the Black Sea, declares solemnly, that on its part not the least obstacle shall ever, under any pretext whatsoever, be opposed to it. Above all, it promises never to allow itself henceforth to stop or detain vessels laden or in ballast, whether Russian or belonging to nations with whom the Ottoman Porte should not be in a state of declared war, which vessels shall be passing through the Strait of Constantinople and that of the Dardanelles, on their way from the Black Sea into the Mediterranean, or from the Mediterranean into the Russian ports of the Black Sea. And if, which God forbid, anyone of the stipulations contained in the present Article should be infringed, and the remonstrances of the Russian Minister thereupon should fail in obtaining a full and prompt redress, the Sublime Porte recognizes beforehand in the Imperial Court of Russia the right of considering such an infraction as an act of hostility, and of immediately having recourse to reprisals against the Ottoman Empire.

Indemnity due to Russia.

ART. VIII. The arrangements formerly stipulated by Article VI of the Convention of Ackermann, for the purpose of regulating and liquidating the claims of the respective subjects and merchants relatively to the indemnification for the losses incurred at various times since the War of 1806, not having been carried into execution, and the Russian trade having, since the conclusion of the aforesaid Convention of Ackermann, suffered fresh injury to a considerable extent, in consequence of the measures adopted with respect to the navigation of the Bosphorus, it is agreed and determined that the Sublime Porte, by way of reparation for these losses and injuries, shall pay to the Imperial Court of Russia, within the course of 18 months, at periods which shall hereafter be agreed upon, the sum of 1,500,000 ducats of Holland; so that the payment of this sum shall put an end to every reciprocal demand or claim of the two Contracting Powers, on the score of the circumstances above mentioned.

Cession of Territory to Russia to be agreed upon in Part Payment of Indemnity.

ART. IX. The prolongation of the War to which the present Treaty of Peace happily puts an end, having occasioned the Imperial Court considerable expenses, the Sublime Porte acknowledges the necessity of offering it a suitable indemnification. Therefore, independently of the cession of a small portion of territory in Asia, stipulated in Article IV, which the Court of Russia consents to receive in part of the said Indemnity, the Sublime Porte engages to pay it a sum of money, the amount of which shall be fixed by mutual agreement.

Adhesion of Turkey to Act of 22nd March, 1829, between Great Britain, France, and Russia.

ART. X. In declaring its entire adhesion to the stipulations of the Treaty concluded at London on the 24th June/6th July, 1827, between Russia, Great Britain, and France, the Sublime Porte equally accedes to the Act entered into on the 10th/22nd of March, 1829, with common consent, between those same Powers upon the bases of the said Treaty, and containing the arrangements of detail relating to its definitive execution. Immediately after the exchange of the Ratifications of the present Treaty of Peace, the Sublime Porte will appoint Plenipotentiaries for the purpose of agreeing with those of the Imperial Court of Russia, and of the Courts of England and of France, upon the carrying into execution the said stipulation and arrangements.

Evacuation of Ottoman Territory by Russia.

ART. XI. Immediately after the signing of the present Treaty of Peace between the two Empires, and the exchange of the Ratifications of the two Sovereigns, the Sublime Porte shall take the necessary measures for the prompt and scrupulous execution of the stipulations contained therein, and especially of the Articles III and IV, relative to the Boundaries which are to separate the two Empires, as well in Europe as in Asia, and of the Articles V and VI, concerning the Principalities of Moldavia and Wallachia, as well as Servia; and from the moment when these different Articles may be considered as having been executed, the Imperial Court of Russia will proceed to the evacuation of the territory of the Ottoman Empire, conformably to the principles established by a Separate Act (2), which forms an integral part of the present Treaty of Peace.

Until the complete Evacuation of the Countries occupied, the administration and order of things which are there now established under the influence of the Imperial Court of Russia, shall be maintained, nor can the Sublime Porte interfere therein in any manner whatsoever.

Cessation of Hostilities.

ART. XII. Immediately after the signature of the present Treaty of Peace, orders shall be issued to the Commanders of the respective forces, as well on land as on sea, to cease from all hostilities; such as shall have been committed after the signature of the present Treaty shall be considered as not having occurred, and shall produce no change in the stipulations therein contained. In like manner, whatever conquests which, during this interval, shall have been made by the troops of either of the High Contracting Powers, must be restored without the least delay.

Amnesty. Liberty of respective Subjects to dispose of their Landed Property.

ART. XIII. The High Contracting Powers, upon re-establishing between themselves the relations of a sincere friendship grant a general pardon and a full and complete Amnesty to all such of their subjects, of whatever condition they may be, who, during the continuance of the War now happily terminated, shall have taken part in the military operations, or have shown, either by their conduct or their opinions, their attachment to one or other of two Contracting Powers. In consequence whereof, none of these individuals shall be molested or prosecuted, either in person or property, on account of their past conduct, and each of them, recovering the landed property which he before possessed, shall have the peaceable enjoyment of the same, under the protection of the laws, or else shall be at liberty to dispose thereof within the space of 18 months, in order to transfer himself, together with his family and his movable property, into any country which he may select; and this without undergoing any molestation, or being opposed by any obstacle whatsoever.

Power of respective Subjects of Ceded Countries to dispose of their Landed Property and to Reside in either Country.

There shall, moreover, be granted to the respective subjects, established in the Countries restored to the Sublime Porte, or ceded to the Imperial Court of Russia, the same term of 18 months, to be reckoned from the exchange of the Ratifications of the present Treaty of Peace, for the purpose, should they think fit so to do, of disposing of their Landed Property, acquired either before or since the War; and of retiring with their assets and their movable Property from the States of one of the Contracting Powers into those of the others, and reciprocally.

Restoration of Prisoners. Exception in favour of Christians who have become Mahometans, and Mahometans who have become Christians.

ART. XIV. All the Prisoners of War, of whatsoever nation, condition, and sex they may be, who are in the two Empires, must, immediately after the exchange of the Ratifications of the present Treaty of Peace, be delivered up and restored without the least ransom or payment. Exception is made in favour of the Christians who, of their own free will, have embraced the Mahometan religion, in the States of the Sublime Porte, and of the Mahometans, who in like manner, of their own free will, have embraced the Christian religion in the States of the Empire of Russia.

Prisoners taken after conclusion of Peace to be Restored.

The same shall be observed with respect to the Russian subjects, who, after the signing of the present Treaty of Peace, may have, in any manner, fallen into captivity, and who are in the States of the Sublime Porte. The Imperial Court of Russia promises, on its part, to act in the same manner towards the subjects of the Sublime Porte.

Expenses of Prisoners of War not to be reimbursed.

No reimbursement of the sums which have been expended by the High Contracting Powers for the maintenance of the Prisoners of War, shall be required. Each of them shall provide all that is necessary for them during their journey to the frontier, where they will be exchanged by Commissioners appointed respectively.

Confirmation of Treaties.

ART. XV. All the Treaties, Conventions, and Stipulations, entered into and concluded at different epochs, between the Imperial Court of Russia and the Sublime Ottoman Porte, excepting the Articles which have been modified or changed by the present Treaty of Peace, are confirmed in all their force and integrity, and the two High Contracting Powers engage to observe them religiously and inviolably.

Ratifications.

ART. XVI. The present Treaty of Peace shall be ratified by the two High Contracting Powers, and the exchange of the Ratifications between the respective Plenipotentiaries shall be effected within the space of six weeks, or sooner if possible.

The present Document of Peace, containing 16 Articles, and which shall be completed by the exchange of the respective Ratifications, has been, in virtue of our Full Powers, signed and sealed by us, and exchanged against a similar one, signed by the undermentioned Plenipotentiaries of the Sublime Ottoman Porte, and sealed with their Seals.

Done at Adrianople, the 2nd/14th September, 1829.

> (L.S.)   SADIK EFFENDI.
> (L.S.)   ABDOUL KADIR BEY.
> (L.S.)   COUNT ALEXIS ORLOFF.
> (L.S.)   COUNT F. PAHLEN.

SEPARATE ACTS annexed to the Treaty signed at Adrianople, 14th September, 1829.

SEPARATE ACT (1) *relative to the Principalities of Moldavia and Wallachia.*

Hospodars to be Elected for Life.

In the Name of Almighty God.

THE two High Contracting Powers, at the same time that they confirm all that has been stipulated by the Separate Act of the Convention of Ackermann, relative to the mode of electing the Hospodars of Moldavia and Wallachia, have been convinced of the necessity of imparting to the Government of those Provinces a basis more stable and better adapted to the real interests of the two countries. For this purpose it has been definitively agreed upon and determined, that the duration of the government of the Hospodars should no longer be limited to 7 years, as heretofore, but that they should henceforth be invested with that dignity for life, excepting in cases of voluntary abdication, or of deprivation by reason of criminality, foreseen by the said Separate Act.

Powers of Hospodars.

The Hospodars shall have full liberty in the management of the internal affairs of their provinces, after consulting their respective Divans, without, however, the power of injuring in any degree the rights guaranteed to the two countries by Treaties or Hatti-sheriffs, and they shall not be disturbed in their internal administration by any order contrary to those rights.

Non-interference by Turkish Authorities in Adjoining Provinces to Interfere in Affairs of Moldavia and Wallachia.

The Sublime Porte promises and engages to take especial care that the privileges granted to Moldavia and Wallachia, be not in any manner infringed upon by its officers commanding in the adjoining provinces, and not to allow any interference on their part in the affairs of the two provinces, as well as to prevent all inroads of the inhabitants of the right bank of the Danube upon the Wallachian or Moldavian territory.

Boundary of Principalities.

All the Islands belonging to the left bank of the Danube shall be considered as forming an integral part of this territory, and the stream (Thalweg) of this River shall form the Boundary of the two Principalities, from its entrance into the Ottoman States as far as its confluence with the Pruth.

Porte not to retain any Fortified Point, or allow any Establishment by Mussulman Subjects on Left Bank of the Danube.

For the better securing the inviolability of the Moldavian and Wallachian territory, the Sublime Porte engages not to retain any Fortified Point, nor to allow any establishment whatsoever of its Mussulman subjects on the left bank of the Danube. In consequence whereof it is permanently ordained, that upon the whole of that bank in Great and Little Wallachia, as well as in Moldavia, no Mussulman can ever establish his residence, and that the only Mahometans who can be admitted therein are merchants provided with firmans, whose object in repairing thither is to purchase, on their own account in the Principalities, the goods necessary for the consumption of Constantinople, or other articles.

Turkish Towns on Left Bank of the Danube to be Restored to Wallachia. Mussulmans to Sell their Landed Estates.

The Turkish towns situated upon the left bank of the Danube shall, as well as their territories (Rayahs), be restored to Wallachia, in order to be henceforward united to that Principality, and the fortifications heretofore standing upon that bank can never be rebuilt. Such Mussulmans as possess landed estates not unjustly obtained from private individuals, whether situated in these same towns, or upon any other point of the left bank of the Danube shall be required to sell them to natives within the space of 18 months.

Quarantine Establishment. Militia for Security of Frontier, &c.

The Government of the two Principalities, possessing all the privileges of an independent internal administration, is at liberty to establish Sanitary cordons and Quarantines along the course of the Danube, and elsewhere in the country where they shall be needed, without the strangers who arrive there, as well Mussulmans as Christians, being allowed to exempt themselves from the exact observance of the Sanitary Regulations. For the Quarantine service, as well as for watching over the security of the Frontiers, for the maintenance of good order in the towns and country places, and for the execution of the laws and regulations, the Government of each Principality may keep in pay such a number of armed guards as shall be strictly necessary for these different duties. The number and maintenance of this Militia shall be regulated by the Hospodars, in concert with their respective Divans, the examples of former times forming the bases of these arrangements.

Principalities freed from furnishing Supplies for Constantinople, &c., or provide Workmen for erection of Fortresses, &c. Indemnity to Porte for relinquishing Rights. Sum to be paid on each Appointment of Hospodars.

The Sublime Porte, animated by the sincere desire of insuring to the two Principalities all the welfare of which they are susceptible, and being informed of the abuses and annoyances to which they were subjected on account of the supplies required for the consumption of Constantinople, the provisioning of the Fortresses situated upon the Danube, and the requisitions of the Arsenal, fully and entirely relinquishes in their favour its right in this respect. Wallachia and Moldavia shall, in consequence, be for ever dispensed from furnishing grains and other commodities, sheep, and building timber, all of which they were formerly required to supply. In like manner, these provinces shall never be compelled, under any circumstances, to provide Workmen for the erection of Fortresses, nor for any other Public Works of whatever kind. But in order to indemnify the Imperial Treasury for the losses which this total cession of its rights might cause it, independently of the annual Tribute which the two Principalities are bound to pay to the Sublime Porte, under the denominations of "haratch," "idige," and "kekiabiye" (according to the tenor of the Hatti-sheriffs of 1802), Moldavia and Wallachia shall each pay annually to the Sublime Porte, by way of compensation, a sum of money, the amount of which shall be determined hereafter by common consent. Besides which, at each reappointment of the Hospodars, whether in consequence of decease, abdication, or legal deprivation by the titularies, the Principality in which the circumstance shall have taken place shall be bound to pay to the Sublime Porte a sum equivalent to the annual Tribute of the province as fixed by the Hatti-sheriffs. With the exception of these sums, there shall never be exacted from the country, nor from the Hospodars, any other Tribute, contribution, or gift, under any pretext whatsoever.

Liberty of Trade to Inhabitants of Principalities, and Freedom of Navigation of the Danube.

By virtue of the abolishment of the supplies above mentioned, the inhabitants of the two Principalities shall enjoy the full liberty of Trade for all the productions of their soil and of their industry, stipulated by the Separate Act of the Convention of Ackermann, without any restrictions save those which the Hospodars, in concert with their respective Divans, may consider it expedient to establish, in order to insure the supply of provisions for the country. They may freely navigate the Danube with their own ships, provided with Passports from their Government, and carry on trade in the other towns or ports of the Sublime Porte, without being molested by the collectors of the "haratch," or being exposed to any other annoyance.

Exemption from Taxes for Two Years.

Moreover, the Sublime Porte, considering all the calamities which Moldavia and Wallachia have had to undergo, and moved by an especial sentiment of benevolence, consents to exempt the inhabitants of these provinces for the space of two years, reckoning from the day in which the Principalities shall have been entirely evacuated by the Russian troops, from the payment of the annual Taxes paid into its treasury.

Confirmation of Administrative Regulations by the Porte.

Lastly, the Sublime Porte, desirous of securing, by every means, the future prosperity of the two Principalities, solemnly promises to confirm the administrative regulations which, during the occupation of these two provinces by the armies of the Imperial Court, have been made in consequence of the wish expressed by the assemblies of the most influential inhabitants of the country, and which shall, in future, serve as bases for the internal government of the two provinces, with the full understanding, however, that the said regulations shall in no way compromise the rights of sovereignty of the Sublime Porte.

In consequence whereof we, the Undersigned, Plenipotentiaries of

His Majesty the Emperor and Padishah of All the Russias, in concert with the Plenipotentiaries of the Sublime Ottoman Porte, have agreed upon and determined with respect to Moldavia and Wallachia the above dispositions, which are the sequel of Article V of the Treaty of Peace concluded at Adrianople between ourselves and the Ottoman Plenipotentiaries. In pursuance of which the present Separate Act has been drawn up, subscribed by us, sealed with our seals, and delivered into the hands of the Plenipotentiaries of the Sublime Porte.

Done at Adrianople, the 2nd/14th September, 1829.

> (L.S.) COUNT ALEXIS ORLOFF.
> (L.S.) COUNT F. PAHLEN.
> (L.S.) SADIK EFFENDI.
> (L.S.) ABDOUL KADIR BEY.

SEPARATE ACT (2) *relative to Indemnifications for Losses in Trade, War Expenses, and Expenses attending the Evacuation.*

In the Name of Almighty God.

As the Peace so happily concluded between the Imperial Court of Russia and the Sublime Ottoman Porte must be maintained perpetually between the two High Empires, it has been judged necessary, for the purpose of preventing every possible subject of dispute in future, to regulate, by a Separate Act, all that relates to the Indemnification for Losses in Trade, to those for the War Expenses, and to the Evacuation, by means of the following Articles:—

Demolition of Fortress of Giurgevo.

ART. I. In one of the paragraphs of the Separate Act relative to the Principalities of Moldavia and Wallachia, and annexed to Article V of the Treaty of Peace, it is stipulated that "the Turkish towns situated upon the left bank of the Danube shall, as well as their territories (Rayahs), be restored to Wallachia, in order to be henceforward united to that Principality, and that the Fortifications heretofore standing upon that bank can never be rebuilt," &c.

In consequence of this stipulation, the Fortress of Giurgevo, which is still occupied by the troops of the Sublime Porte, must be evacuated and delivered up to the Russian troops, and its fortifications demolished. This evacuation shall be effected within the space of fifteen days after the signing of the Treaty of Peace. The Turkish troops shall retire to Rustchuk, taking with them all the artillery, ammunition, their property and effects. In like manner the Mussulman inhabitants shall be equally empowered to carry away with them their property and goods.

Indemnity due to Russia.

ART. II. By Article VIII of the Treaty of Peace, it is stipulated that "the Sublime Porte, by way of reparation for the losses and injuries suffered by Russian subjects and merchants at various times since the year 1806, shall pay to the Imperial Court of Russia, within the course of 18 months, at periods which shall be assigned further down, the sum of 1,500,000 ducats of Holland."

Periods of Payment of Indemnity.

In consequence of this stipulation it is agreed, that upon the exchange of the Ratifications of the Treaty of Peace, the Ottoman Porte shall pay 100,000 ducats; that within the term of six months after the exchange of the Ratifications, it shall pay 400,000 ducats; that in the six months following it shall pay 500,000 ducats; and lastly, that in the other six months it shall pay the remaining 500,000 ducats, which will complete the entire payment of the said sum of 1,500,000 ducats, within the term of 18 months.

Indemnity to be paid to Russia.

ART. III. It is stipulated in Article IX of the Treaty of Peace that "the Sublime Porte engages to pay to the Imperial Court of Russia, by way of Indemnification for the expenses of the War, a sum of money, the amount of which shall be fixed by mutual agreement."

In consequence of this stipulation, it is agreed and determined that the said Indemnity shall be fixed at 10,000,000 of ducats of Holland, and the Sublime Porte promises to pay the said sum of money according to the mode of payment which shall be determined by His Majesty the Emperor of All the Russias, relying, as the Sublime Porte does, upon his generosity and magnanimity.

Moreover, in order to alleviate, as much as possible, the onus of this payment in specie, and to allow every facility necessary for that purpose, it is agreed that the Imperial Court of Russia shall consent to receive on account of the sum above mentioned compensations in kind, in articles which shall, by mutual consent, be considered as receivable in part payment of the said Indemnity.

Russian Evacuation of Turkish Territory.

ART. IV. It is stipulated in Article XI of the Treaty of Peace that "the Imperial Court of Russia will proceed to the Evacuation of the territory of the Ottoman Empire, conformably to the principles established by a Separate Act which shall form an integral part of the Treaty of Peace."

In consequence of this stipulation it is agreed and determined, that as soon as the 100,000 ducats, in part payment of the stipulated indemnity for the losses of Russian subjects and merchants shall have been paid in the manner agreed upon above in Article II of the present Separate Act; that as soon as Article VI of the Treaty of Peace relative to Servia shall have been completely executed; and that the Evacuation and delivery up of Giurgevo to the Russian troops shall have been effected in the manner specified above in Article I of the present Act, then and within the term of one month after the exchange of the Ratifications of the Treaty of Peace, the Russian army shall evacuate the city of Adrianople, Kirk-Klissa, Lulé-Bougas, Midiah, and Iniada, and other places, which shall be immediately given up to the authorities empowered by the Ottoman Porte to receive them. Immediately after the payment of the 400,000 ducats of the said Indemnity for the losses of Russian subjects and merchants shall have been exactly effected, that is to say, six months after the exchange of the Ratifications, the Russian troops shall evacuate, within the space of one month, the whole extent of the country from the Balkan as far as the sea and the Gulf of Bourgas, so that all the cities, towns, and villages shall be delivered up to the authorities empowered by the Ottoman Porte to receive them, and the Russian troops shall retire and pass over on the other side of the Balkan into Bulgaria and the country of Dobridzia.

When the payment of the 500,000 ducats of the said Indemnity for the losses of Russian subjects and merchants shall have been effected in the manner above specified, in the space of the other six months, then the Russian troops shall entirely evacuate and deliver up to the authorities of the Porte the whole of Bulgaria and the country of Dobridzia, with all the cities, towns, and villages therein comprised, from the Danube as far as the Black Sea.

The other remaining 500,000 ducats ducats shall be paid within the term of other six months, that is to say, eighteen months after the exchange of the Ratifications. And as to the evacuation above mentioned, the town of Silistria and the provinces of Wallachia and Moldavia shall be exempted from it, and shall be kept as a security by the Imperial Court of Russia until the entire discharge of the sum which the Ottoman Porte has engaged itself to pay as an indemnification for the war expenses, as has been stipulated in Article III of the present Act; so that immediately upon the full payment of the above sum Moldavia, Wallachia, and the town of Silistria shall be evacuated within two months by the Russian troops, and be formally given up to the authorities of the Ottoman Porte.

With respect to the Evacuation by the Russian troops of the countries which, on the Asiatic side, are to be restored to the Ottoman Porte conformably to Article IV of the Treaty of Peace, it is agreed that this Evacuation shall commence three months after the exchange of the Ratifications, and this shall be done by virtue of a particular Convention, which the General-in-Chief, Count Paskewitch d'Erivan, shall conclude with the Commanders of the Ottoman Porte in those countries, in such manner, however, that the entire evacuation of the countries restored to the Ottoman Empire may be effected within the term of 8 months after the exchange of the Ratifications.

In consequence whereof the present Explanatory Act, consisting of 4 Articles, has been drawn up, signed by us, sealed with our seals, and delivered into the hands of the Plenipotentiaries of the Sublime Porte, and the Ratifications of the same shall be exchanged, together with those of the Treaty of Peace, of which it forms an integral part.

Done at Adrianople, the 2nd/14th September, 1829.

(L.S.) COUNT ALEXIS ORLOFF.
(L.S.) COUNT F. PAHLEN.
(L.S.) SADIK EFFENDI.
(L.S.) ABDOUL KADIR BEY.

By virtue of supreme Full Powers, I accept and confirm the conditions contained in the preceding Treaty and Separate Acts.

COUNT J. DIEBITSCH ZABALKANSKY.

26

TREATY between Great Britain, Austria, France, Prussia, and Russia, and Belgium, relative to the Separation of Belgium from Holland. Signed at London, 15th November, 1831.

THE Courts of Great Britain, Austria, France, Prussia, and Russia, taking into consideration the events which have occured in the United Kingdom of the Netherlands since the month of September of the year 1830, the obligation which they are under to prevent these events from disturbing the general Peace, and the necessity which arises from these events of making certain modifications in the transactions of the year 1815, by which the United Kingdom of the Netherlands was created and established; and His Majesty the present King of the Belgians participating in these intentions of the above-mentioned Courts, they have named for their Plenipotentiaries, viz.:—

His Majesty the King of the United Kingdom of Great Britain and Ireland, the Right Honourable Henry John, Viscount Palmerston, Baron Temple, a Peer of Ireland, a Member of His Britannic Majesty's

Most Honourable Privy Council, a Member of Parliament, and his Principal Secretary of State for Foreign Affairs;

His Majesty the Emperor of Austria, King of Hungary and Bohemia, the Prince Paul Esterhazy, Chamberlain, and Privy Councillor of His Imperial and Royal Apostolic Majesty, and his Ambassador Extraordinary and Plenipotentiary to His Britannic Majesty, &c.;—and the Sieur John Philip, Baron de Wessenberg, Chamberlain, Privy Councillor of His Imperial and Royal Apostolic Majesty, &c.;

His Majesty the King of the French, the Sieur Charles Maurice de Talleyrand-Périgord, Prince-Duke de Talleyrand, Peer of France; his said Majesty's Ambassador Extraordinary and Minister Plenipotentiary to His Britannic Majesty, &c.;

His Majesty the King of Prussia, the Sieur Henry William, Baron de Bülow, his Chamberlain, Privy Councillor of Legation, Envoy Extraordinary and Minister Plenipotentiary to His Britannic Majesty, &c.;

His Majesty the Emperor of All the Russias, the Sieur Christopher, Prince of Lieven, General of Infantry in his Armies, his Aide-de-Camp General, Ambassador Extraordinary and Plenipotentiary to His Britannic Majesty, &c.; and the Sieur Adam, Comte Matuszewic, Privy Councillor of his said Majesty, &c.;

And His Majesty the King of the Belgians, the Sieur Sylvain Van de Weyer, his Envoy Extraordinary and Minister Plenipotentiary to His Britannic Majesty;

Who, after having exchanged their Full Powers, found in good and due form, have agreed upon and signed the following Articles:

Composition of Belgian Territory.

Art. I. The Belgian territory shall be composed of the provinces of South Brabant, Liège, Namur, Hainhault, West Flanders, East Flanders, Antwerp, and Limburg, such as they formed part of the United Kingdom of the Netherlands constituted in 1815, with the exception of those districts of the province of Limbourg which are designated in Article IV.

The Belgian territory shall, moreover, comprise that part of the Grand Duchy of Luxemburg which is specified in Article II.

Belgian Limits of Luxemburg.

Art. II. In the Grand Duchy of Luxemburg, the limits of the Belgian territory shall be such as will be hereinafter described:

Commencing from the frontier of France, between Rodange, which shall remain to the Grand Duchy of Luxemburg, and Athus, which shall belong to Belgium, there shall be drawn, according to the annexed Map, a line which, leaving to Belgium the road from Arlon to Longwy, the town of Arlon with its district, and the road from Arlon to Bastogne, shall pass between Mesancy, which shall be on the Belgian territory, and Clemancy, which shall remain to the Grand Duchy of Luxemburg, terminating at Steinfort, which place shall also remain to the Grand Duchy.

From Steinfort this line shall be continued in the direction of Eischen, Hecbus, Guirsch, Ober-Pallen, Grende, Nothomb, Parette, and Perlé, as far as Martelange: Hecbus, Guirsch, Grende, Nothomb, and Parette, being to belong to Belgium, and Eischen, Ober-Pallen, Perlé, and Martelange, to the Grand Duchy.

From Martelange the said line shall follow the course of the Sure, the water-way (*thalweg*) of which River shall serve as the limit between the two States, as far as opposite to Tintange, from whence it shall be continued, as directly as possible, towards the present frontier of the arrondissement of Diekirch, and shall pass between Surret, Harlange, and Tarchamps, which places shall be left to the Grand Duchy of Luxemburg, and Honville, Livarchamp, and Loutremange, which places shall form part of the Belgian territory. Then having, in the vicinity of Doncols and Soulez, which shall remain to the Grand Duchy, reached the present boundary of the arrondissement of Diekirch, the line in question shall follow the said boundary to the frontier of the Prussian territory.

All the territories, towns, fortresses, and places situated to the west of this line, shall belong to Belgium; and all the territories, towns, fortresses, and places, situated to the east of the said line shall continue to belong to the Grand Duchy of Luxemburg.

It is understood, that, in making out this line, and in conforming as closely as possible to the description of it given above, as well as to the delineation of it on the map, which, for the sake of greater clearness, is annexed to the present Article, the Commissioners of Demarcation, mentioned in Article VI, shall pay due attention to the localities, as well as to the mutual necessity for accommodation which may result therefrom.

Territorial Indemnity to Netherlands in Limburg.

ART. III. In return for the cessions made in the preceding Article, there shall be assigned to His Majesty the King of the Netherlands, Grand Duke of Luxemburg, a Territorial Indemnity in the province of Limburg.

Cessions made to Holland on the Meuse.

ART. IV. In execution of that part of Article I, which relates to the province of Limburg, and in consequence of the cessions specified in Article II, there shall be assigned to His Majesty the King of the

Netherlands, either to be held by him in his character of Grand Duke of Luxemburg, or for the purpose of being united to Holland, those territories, the limits of which are hereinafter described:

1st. On the right bank of the Meuse: to the old Dutch enclaves upon the said bank in the province of Limburg, shall be united those districts of the said province upon the same bank, which did not belong to the States-General in 1790; in such wise that the whole of that part of the present province of Limburg, situated upon the right bank of the Meuse, and comprised between that River on the west, the frontier of the Prussian territory on the east, the present frontier of the province of Liège on the south, and Dutch Guelderland on the north, shall henceforth belong to His Majesty the King of the Netherlands, either to be held by him in his character of Grand Duke of Luxemburg, or in order to be united to Holland.

2nd. On the left bank of the Meuse: commencing from the southernmost point of the Dutch province of North Brabant, there shall be drawn, according to the annexed Map, a line which shall terminate on the Meuse below Wessem, between that place and Stevenswaardt, at the point where the frontiers of the present arrondissement of Ruremonde and Maestricht meet, on the left bank of the Meuse; in such manner that Bergerot, Stamproy, Neer Itteren, Ittervoord, and Thorne, with their districts, as well as all the other places situated to the north of this line, shall form part of the Dutch territory.

The old Dutch enclaves in the province of Limburg, upon the left bank of the Meuse, shall belong to Belgium, with the exception of the town of Maestricht, which, together with a radius of territory extending 1,200 toises from the outer glacis of the fortress on the said bank of this River, shall continue to be possessed in full sovereignty and property by His Majesty the King of the Netherlands.

Netherlands to agree with Germanic Confederation and Nassau, relative to Territorial Cessions.

ART. V. It shall be reserved to His Majesty the King of the Netherlands, Grand Duke of Luxemburg, to come to an agreement with the Germanic Confederation, and with the Agnates of the House of Nassau, as to the application of the stipulations contained in Articles III and IV, as well as upon all the arrangements which the said Articles may render necessary, either with the above-mentioned Agnates of the House of Nassau, or with the Germanic Confederation.

Renunciation to Territories, &c., by Netherlands and Belgium.

ART. VI. In consideration of the territorial arrangements above stated, each of the two Parties renounces reciprocally, and for ever, all pretention to the territories, towns, fortresses, and places, situated within the limits of the possessions of the other Party, such as those limits are described in Articles I, II, and IV.

Boundary Commissioners.

The said limits shall be marked out in conformity with those Articles, by Belgian and Dutch Commissioners of Demarcation, who shall meet as soon as possible in the town of Maestricht.

Belgium to form an Independent and Neutral State.

ART. VII. Belgium, within the limits specified in Articles I, II, and IV, shall form an independent and perpetually Neutral State. It shall be bound to observe such Neutrality towards all other States.

Drainage of Waters of the two Flanders.

ART. VIII. The drainage of the waters of the two Flanders shall be regulated between Holland and Belgium, according to the stipulations on this subject, contained in Article VI of the Definitive Treaty, concluded between His Majesty the Emperor of Germany and the States-General, on the 8th of November, 1785; and in conformity with the said Article, Commissioners, to be named on either side, shall make arrangements for the application of the provisions contained in it.

Free Navigation of Rivers.

ART. IX. The provisions of Articles CVIII to CXVII inclusive, of the General Act of the Congress of Vienna, relative to the Free Navigation of navigable Rivers, shall be applied to those navigable Rivers which separate the Belgian and the Dutch territories, or which traverse them both.

Navigation of the Scheldt.

So far as regards specially the Navigation of the Schedlt, it shall be agreed that the pilotage and the buoying of its channel, as well as the conservation of the channels of the Scheldt below Antwerp, shall be subject to a joint superintendence; that this joint superintendence shall be exercised by Commissioners, to be appointed on both sides for this purpose; that moderate pilotage dues shall be fixed by mutual agreement; and that such dues shall be the same for the Dutch as for the Belgian commerce.

Navigation of Intermediate Channels between the Scheldt and the Rhine.

It is also agreed that the Navigation of the Intermediate Channels between the Scheldt and the Rhine, in order to proceed from Antwerp to the Rhine, and *vice versâ*, shall continue reciprocally free, and that it shall be subject only to moderate tolls, which shall provisionally be the same for the commerce of the two countries.

Appointment of Commissioners. Amount of Tolls. Fishing.

Commissioners on both sides shall meet at Antwerp in the space of one month, as well to determine the definite and permanent amount of these Tolls, as to agree upon a general Regulation for the execution of the provisions of the present Article, and to include therein a provision for the exercise of the right of Fishing and of trading in fish, throughout the whole extent of the Scheldt, on a footing of perfect reciprocity in favour of the subjects of the two countries.

River Tariffs.

In the mean time, and until the said Regulations shall be prepared, the Navigation of the navigable Rivers above mentioned shall remain free to the commerce of the two countries, which shall adopt provisionally, in this respect, the Tariffs of the Convention signed at Mayence on the 31st March, 1831, for the free Navigation of the Rhine, as well as the other provisions of that Convention, so far as they may be applicable to those navigable Rivers which divide the Dutch and Belgian territories, or traverse both.

Free use of Canals.

ART. X. The use of the Canals which traverse both countries shall continue to be free and common to the inhabitants of both. It is understood that they shall enjoy the use of the same reciprocally, and on equal conditions, and that on either side moderate duties only shall be levied upon the navigation of these Canals.

Commercial Communication through Maestricht and Sittard.

ART. XI. The commercial communications through the town of Maestricht, and through Sittard, shall remain entirely free, and shall not be impeded under any pretext whatsoever.

Use of Roads leading to Frontiers of Germany.

The use of the Roads which, passing through these towns, lead to the frontiers of Germany, shall be subject only to the payment of moderate Turnpike Tolls, for the repair of the said roads, so that the transit commerce may not experience any obstacle thereby, and that, by means of the tolls above mentioned, these roads may be kept in good repair, and fit to afford facilities to that commerce.

Construction of new Road or Cutting a new Canal in Belgium, opposite Sittard, and from thence to Frontiers of Germany.

ART. XII. In the event of a new Road having been constructed, or a new Canal cut, in Belgium, terminating at the Meuse, opposite the Dutch canton of Sittard, in that case, Belgium shall be entitled to demand of Holland, who, on the other hand, shall not in such case refuse her consent, that the said Road, or the said Canal, shall be continued, according to the same plan, and entirely at the cost and charge of Belgium, through the canton of Sittard, to the frontiers of Germany. This road or canal, which shall be used only as a commercial communication, shall be constructed, at the option of Holland, either by engineers and workmen, whom Belgium shall obtain permission to employ for that purpose in the canton of Sittard, or by engineers and workmen to be furnished by Holland, and who shall execute the works agreed upon at the expense of Belgium; the whole without any charge whatsoever to Holland, and without prejudice to her exclusive rights of sovereignty over the territory which may be traversed by the Road or Canal in question.

Duties and Tolls to be levied on said Road or Canal.

The two Parties shall fix, by mutual agreement, the amount and the mode of collection of the Duties and Tolls which should be levied upon the said Road or Canal.

Division of Public Debt.

ART. XIII. 1. From and after the 1st of January, 1832, Belgium, with reference to the division of the Public Debt of the United Kingdom of the Netherlands, shall remain charged with the sum of 8,400,000 Netherland florins of annual interest, the capital of which shall be transferred from the debit of the Great Book at Amsterdam, or from the debit of the General Treasury of the United Kingdom of the Netherlands, to the debit of the Great Book of Belgium.

2. The capitals transferred, and the annuities inscribed upon the debit of the Great Book of Belgium, in consequence of the preceding paragraph, to the amount of the total sum of 8,400,000 Netherland florins of annual interest, shall be considered as forming part of the Belgic National Debt; and Belgium engages not to admit, either at present or in future, any distinction between this portion of her Public Debt, arising from her union with Holland, and any other Belgic National Debt already created, or which may be created hereafter.

3. The payment of the above-mentioned sum of 8,400,000 Netherland florins of annual interest shall take place regularly every six months, either at Brussels or at Antwerp, in ready money, without deduction of any kind whatsoever, either at present or in future.

4. In consideration of the creation of the said sum of 8,400,000 florins of annual interest, Belgium shall be released from all obligation towards Holland, on account of the division of the Public Debt of the United Kingdom of the Netherlands.

Appointment of Commissioners for the Division of the Public Debt.

5. Commissioners to be named on both sides, shall meet within the space of 15 days in the town of Utrecht, in order to proceed to a settlement of the accounts of the fund of the *Syndicat d'Amortissement*, and of the Bank of Brussels, charged with the service of the General Treasury of the United Kingdom of The Netherlands. No additional charge shall result to Belgium from this settlement; the sum of 8,400,000 florins of annuities comprehending the whole of the charge which she is to take upon herself. But if it should appear from such settlement, that there is a balance to be received, Belgium and Holland shall share the same in the proportion of the taxes paid by each of the two countries during their union, according to the Budgets voted by the States-General of the United Kingdom of the Netherlands.

6. In the settlement of the administration of the Sinking Fund, shall be comprised the credits secured on the public lands, called *Domein losrenten*. These are alluded to in the present Article only for the purpose of record.

7. The Dutch and Belgian Commissioners mentioned in 5 of the present Article, and who are to meet in the town of Utrecht, shall, in addition to the settlement with which they are charged, proceed to the transfer of the capitals and annual interest which, upon the division of the Public Debt of the United Kingdom of the Netherlands, are to fall to the charge of Belgium, up to the amount of 8,400,000 florins of annual interest.

Delivery of Archives, Maps, &c., to Belgium.

They shall also proceed to deliver up the Archives, Maps, Plans, and other Documents whatsoever, which belong to Belgium, or which relate to her administration.

Reimbursement by Belgium of Advances made by Holland.

ART. XIV. Holland having, since the 1st of November, 1830, exclusively made all the necessary Advances to meet the charge of the whole of the Public Debt of the Kingdom of the Netherlands, and having still to make those advances, for the half-year ending the 1st of January, 1832, it is agreed that the said advances, calculated from the 1st of November, 1830, to the 1st of January, 1832, for 14 months, at the rate of 8,400,000 Netherland florins per annum, with which Belgium remains charged, shall be reimbursed by thirds to the Dutch Treasury, by the Treasury of Belgium. The first third of this reimbursement shall be paid by the Belgian to the Dutch Treasury, on the 1st of January, 1832, the second on the 1st of April, and the third on the 1st of July, of the same year. On the two last thirds, interest at the rate of 5 per cent. per annum shall be paid to Holland, until they are completely discharged at the aforesaid periods.

Antwerp to be a Port of Commerce.

ART. XV. The Port of Antwerp, in conformity with the Stipulations of Article XV of the Treaty of Paris, of the 30th of May, 1814, shall continue to be solely a Port of Commerce.

Canals, Roads, &c., to belong to respective Countries.

ART. XVI. Works of public or private utility, such as Canals, Roads, or others of a similar nature, constructed wholly or in part at the expense of the United Kingdom of the Netherlands, shall belong, together with the advantages and charges thereunto attached, to the country in which they are situated.

Capitals borrowed for Construction of Roads, &c.

It is understood that the capitals borrowed for the construction of these Works, and specifically charged thereupon, shall be comprised in the aforesaid charges, in so far as they may not yet have been repaid, and without giving rise to any claim on account of repayments already made.

Removal of Sequestrations.

ART. XVII. The Sequestrations which may have been imposed in Belgium, during the troubles, for political causes, on any property or hereditary estates whatsoever, shall be taken off without delay, and the enjoyment of the property and estates above mentioned shall be immediately restored to the lawful owners thereof.

Right to transfer Residence, and Dispose of Property, &c.

ART. XVIII. In the two countries of which the separation takes place in consequence of the present Articles, the inhabitants and proprietors, if they wish to transfer their residence from one country to the other, shall, during two years, be at liberty to dispose of their Property, moveable or immoveable, of whatever nature the same may be, to sell it, and to carry away the produce of the sale, either in money or in any other shape, without hindrance, and without the payment of any duties other than those which are now in force in the two countries upon changes and transfers.

Droit d'Aubaine et de Détraction abandoned.

It is understood that the collection of the *Droit d'Aubaine et de Détraction* upon the persons and property of Dutch in Belgium, and of Belgians in Holland, is abandoned, both now and for the future.

Character of a Subject, with regard to Property.

ART. XIX. The character of a subject of the two Governments, with regard to Property, shall be acknowledged and maintained.

Rights of Persons holding Property in both Countries.

ART. XX. The Stipulations of Articles XI to XXI, inclusive, of the Treaty concluded between Austria and Russia, on the 3rd of May, 1815, which forms an integral part of the General Act of the Congress of Vienna, stipulations relative to persons who possess Property in both countries, to the election of residence which they are required to make, to the rights which they shall exercise as subjects of either State, and to the relations of neighbourhood in properties cut by the frontiers, shall be applied to such proprietors, as well to such properties, in Holland, in the Grand Duchy of Luxemburg, or in Belgium, as shall be found to come within the cases provided for by the aforesaid Stipulations of the Acts of Congress of Vienna. The *Droits d'Aubaine et de Détraction*, being henceforth abolished, as between Holland, the Grand Duchy of Luxemburg, and Belgium, it is understood that such of the above-mentioned stipulations as may relate to those duties, shall be considered null and void in the 3 countries.

Persons changing their Residence not to be molested.

ART. XXI. No person in the territories which change domination, shall be molested or disturbed in any manner whatever, on account of any part which he may have taken directly or indirectly, in political events.

Payment of Pensions and Allowances.

ART. XXII. The Pensions and Allowances of expectants, of persons unemployed or retired, shall in future be paid, on either side, to all those individuals entitled thereto, both civil and military, conformably to the laws in force previous to the 1st of November, 1830.

It is agreed that the above-mentioned Pensions and Allowances to persons born in the territories which now constitute Belgium, shall remain at the charge of the Belgian Treasury; and the Pensions and Allowances of persons born in the territories which now constitute Holland, shall be at the charge of the Dutch Treasury.

Claims of Belgians on Private Establishments.

ART. XXIII. All Claims of Belgian subjects upon any Private Establishments, such as the Widows' Fund, and the Fund known under the denomination of the *Fonds des Leges*, and of the Chest of Civil and Military Retired Allowances, shall be examined by the Mixed Commission of Liquidation mentioned in Article XIII, and shall be determined according to the tenor of the regulations by which these Funds or Chests are governed.

Restoration of Securities, &c.

The Securities furnished, as well as the payments made, by Belgian accountants, and the judicial deposits and consignments, shall equally be restored to the parties entitled thereto, on the presentation of their proofs.

Claims called French Liquidations.

If, under the head of what are called the *French Liquidations*, any Belgian subjects should still be able to bring forward claims to be inscribed, such claims shall also be examined and settled by the said Commission.

Evacuation of Territories, Towns, &c.

ART. XXIV. Immediately after the exchange of the Ratifications of the Treaty to be concluded between the two Parties, the necessary orders shall be transmitted to the Commanders of the respective troops for the Evacuation of the Territories, Towns, Fortresses, and places which change domination. The Civil Authorities thereof shall also at the same time receive the necessary orders for delivering over the said territories, towns, fortresses, and places, to the Commissioners who shall be appointed by both Parties for this purpose.

This evacuation and delivery shall be effected so as to be completed in the space of 15 days, or sooner if possible.

Guarantee of Execution of Treaty by 5 Powers.

ART. XXV. The Courts of Great Britain, Austria, France, Prussia, and Russia guarantee to His Majesty the King of the Belgians the execution of all the preceding Articles.

Peace between 5 Powers and Belgium.

ART. XXVI. In consequence of the stipulations of the present Treaty there shall be Peace and Friendship between their Majesties the King of the United Kingdom of Great Britain and Ireland, the Emperor of Austria, the King of the French, the King of Prussia, and the Emperor of All the Russias, on the one part, and His Majesty the King of the Belgians, on the other part, their heirs and successors, their respective States and subjects, for ever.

Ratifications.

ART. XXVII. The present Treaty shall be ratified, and the Ratifications shall be exchanged at London in the space of two months, or sooner if possible.

In witness whereof the respective Plenipotentiaries have signed the same, and have affixed thereto the Seal of their Arms.

Done at London the 15th day of November, in the year of Our Lord, 1831.

         (L.S.)   PALMERSTON.
         (L.S.)   ESTERHAZY.
         (L.S.)   WESSENBERG.
         (L.S.)   TALLEYRAND.
         (L.S.)   BULOW.
         (L.S.)   LIEVEN.
         (L.S.)   MATUSZEWIC.
         (L.S.)   S. VAN DE WEYER.

27

CONVENTION between Great Britain, Austria, Prussia, and Russia, and Belgium, relative to the Belgic Fortresses. Signed at London, 14th December, 1831.

Preamble.   Reference to Treaties of 1815.

THEIR Majesties the King of the United Kingdom of Great Britain and Ireland, the Emperor of Austria, King of Hungary and Bohemia, the King of Prussia, and the Emperor of All the Russias, on the one part, and His Majesty the King of the Belgians, on the other, having taken into consideration the present state of Belgium, and the changes effected in the relative position of that country, by its political Independence, as well as by the perpetual Neutrality which has been guaranteed to it; and being desirous of concerting the modifications which this new situation of Belgium renders necessary in the system of Military Defence which was therein adopted, in pursuance of the Treaties and Engagements of the year 1815, they have resolved to comprise in a special Convention a series of joint determinations on this subject.

With this view, their said Majesties have named as their Plenipotentiaries, viz.:—

His Majesty the King of the United Kingdom of Great Britain and Ireland, the Right Honourable Henry John Viscount Palmerston, his Principal Secretary of State for Foreign Affairs;

His Majesty the Emperor of Austria, King of Hungary and Bohemia, the Prince Paul Esterhazy, his Ambassador Extraordinary and Plenipotentiary to His Britannic Majesty, &c.;—And the Sieur John Philip Baron de Wessenberg, &c.;

His Majesty the King of Prussia, the Sieur Henry William Baron de Bülow, Envoy Extraordinary and Minister Plenipotentiary to His Britannic Majesty, &c.;

His Majesty the Emperor of All the Russias, the Sieur Christopher, Prince of Lieven, Ambassador Extraordinary and Plenipotentiary to His Britannic Majesty, &c.;—And the Sieur Adam, Count Matuszewic, &c.;

And His Majesty the King of the Belgians, the Sieur Albert Goblet, General of Brigade;

Who, after having exchanged their Full Powers, found to be in good and due form, have agreed upon and signed the following Articles:

Demolition of Belgian Fortresses.

ART. I. In consequence of the changes which the Independence and the Neutrality of Belgium have effected in the military situation of that country, as well as in its disposable means of defence, the High Contracting Parties agree to cause to be dismantled such of the Fortresses constructed, repaired, or enlarged in Belgium since the year 1815, either wholly or partly at the cost of the Courts of Great Britain, Austria, Prussia, and Russia, of which the maintenance would henceforward only become a useless charge.

Fortresses of Menin, Ath, Mons, Philippeville, and Marienburg to be demolished.

In conformity with this principle, all the fortified works of the Fortresses of Menin, Ath, Mons, Philippeville, and Marienburg, shall be demolished within the periods fixed by the following Articles.

Artillery Stores, &c., to be removed from Fortresses.

ART. II. The artillery, the stores, and all the articles which form part of the equipment of those Fortresses, of which the dismantling is determined upon by the preceding Article, shall be withdrawn from the said Fortresses within the space on one month from the ratification of the present Convention, or sooner if possible, and shall be transported into those Fortresses which are to be maintained.

Immediate partial Demolition of Fortresses.

ART. III. In each of the places destined to be dismantled steps shall immediately be taken for the demolition of two fronts, as well as of the works which are situated in advance of those fronts, and also of the means of inundation which might serve to cover them, in such wise that each of the said places shall be rendered open by such demolition, which shall be effected within the space of two months after the Ratification of the present Convention.

Period of entire Demolition.

With regard to the entire Demolition of the fortified works of the places above mentioned, it shall be completed by the 31st of December, 1833.

Maintenance of Belgian Fortresses.

ART. IV. The Fortresses of Belgium, which are not mentioned in Article I of the present Convention as destined to be dismantled, shall be maintained: His Majesty the King of the Belgians engages to keep them constantly in good order.

Residue of sums appropriated to Defence of Belgium to be made over to Belgium.

ART. V. If in consequence of a settlement of accounts which shall be made, the 4 Courts, or either of them, should find that they have at their disposal any residue of the sums originally appropriated to the system of Defence of Belgium, such residue shall be made over to His Majesty the King of the Belgians, in order to be employed for the purpose to which the said sums were destined.

Reservation of 4 Powers.

ART. VI. The Courts of Great Britain, Austria, Prussia, and Russia reserve to themselves to ascertain, according to the periods fixed in Articles II and III, that the said Articles have been carried into full and entire execution.

Ratifications.

ART. VII. The present Convention shall be ratified, and the Ratifications shall be exchanged at London within the space of two months, or sooner if possible.

In witness whereof the respective Plenipotentiaries have signed the same, and have affixed thereto the Seal of their Arms.

Done at London, the 14th day of December, in the year of Our Lord, 1831.

                            (L.S.) PALMERSTON.
                            (L.S.) ESTERHAZY.
                            (L.S.) WESSENBERG.
                            (L.S.) BULOW.
                            (L.S.) LIEVEN.
                            (L.S.) MATUSZEWIC.

(L.S.) A. GOBLET.

28

ARRANGEMENT between Great Britain, France, Russia, and Turkey, for the Definitive Settlement of the Continental Limits of Greece. Signed at Constantinople, 21st July, 1832.

THE Representatives of the 3 Powers, parties to the Treaty of London, of the 6th of July, 1827, namely, the Right Honourable Sir Stratford Canning, Ambassador Extraordinary and Plenipotentiary of His Britannic Majesty, on a special mission to the Ottoman Sublime Porte; the Sieur Appolinaire Bouteneff, Envoy Extraordinary and Minister Plenipotentiary of His Majesty the Emperor of All the Russias; and the Sieur Jacques Edouard, Baron Burignot de Varenne, Chargé d'Affaires of His Majesty the King of the French,—having made known to the Sublime Ottoman Porte the changes which it was necessary to make in the Frontier of Greece, and having communicated to it the object of the instructions, and of the powers with which they were furnished, to propose to it a Definite Boundary line, upon condition of compensating, by an equitable indemnity, the losses which might result therefrom:— the Sublime Porte, animated with the desire of consolidating the arrangements to which, out of consideration of the 3 Allied Courts, and relying on their sincere intentions, it had previously agreed, has consented to enter upon a negotiation for this purpose, and has charged therewith two of its Ministers, namely, His Excellency Mustapha Behdjet Effendi, Ex-Cazesker of Roumelia, at the present time First Physician of His Highness, and His Excellency Elhadj Mehemed Akif Effendi, present Reis Effendi.

The above-mentioned Plenipotentiaries, filled with the sentiments of their respective Governments, and having no other object in view than that of terminating the Greek Affair in a way that shall be durable, and calculated to prevent all further discussion on this question, have met several times for this salutary purpose; and the complete result of their conferences has been recorded in the present document, exchanged between the Parties as the instrument of their final transaction.

New Boundary.

It was agreed that:—

ART. I. With respect to Boundary:—On the eastern side, the extreme point of separation of the two States shall be fixed at the mouth of the little River which flows near the Village of Gradiza. The Frontier line shall ascend this River to its source, shall thence reach the chain of Mount Othryx, leaving to Greece the Passage of the Klomo, provided the crest of that chain be not passed: thence it shall follow, in a westerly direction, the crest of the same chain along the whole extent thereof, and especially the Peak of Varibovo, in order to attain the height which, under the denomination of Veluchi, forms the point of connection of the three great chains of mountains of the country. From this height the line shall continue, adapting itself as much as possible to the salient features of the country, across the Valley of the Aspropotamos to the Gulf of Arta, terminating at that Gulf between Coprina and Menidi, in such manner as that in any case the Bridge of Tartarina, the Defile and the Tower of Macrinoros shall be comprised within the Limits of Greece, and that the Bridge of Coracos and the Salt Springs of Coprina shall be left to the Ottoman Porte. Thus, the shore of the Gulf of Arta to the north and west of the point where the Boundary line meets its waters, will be retained by the Ottoman Empire; and the shore of this Gulf to the south and west of the line is assigned to the State of Greece, with the exception of the Fort of Punta, which will continue to belong to the Porte, with a radius of Territory which shall not be less than half-an-hour, nor more than an hour.

Nevertheless, as the Representatives, full of deference for the wish which has been expressed in the name of His Highness, relative to the portion of the district of Zeitoun, situate to the left of the Sperchius, have agreed that reference should be made on the subject to the Conference of London, upon the express condition that the decision and execution of the measures consequent thereupon should not be retarded thereby; it has become necessary to provide for the contingency of that portion of the Territory of Zeitoun remaining to the Ottoman Empire.

The Boundary line to the east will in that case commence at the mouth of the River Sperchius, and will run up its left Bank to the point of contact of the districts of Zeitoun and of Patradjik; thence it will reach the summit of the chain of the Othryx, following the common Boundary of those two districts, and the most direct line, in the event of that common Boundary not attaining the summit of the chain of the Othryx.

It will continue in the manner before mentioned, in order to terminate at the Gulf of Arta.

Indemnity to Turkey.

Art. II. With respect to the Indemnity, it remains fixed at the sum of 40,000,000 of Turkish piastres, provided the portions of the district of Zeitoun, situate to the left of the River Sperchius shall have been, in consequence of the decision of the Conference of London, definitively assigned to the Greek State.

If, on the other hand, in consequence of the decision of the Conference of London, those portions of the district of Zeitoun are to continue to belong to the Ottoman Empire, the indemnity which the Porte will receive remains fixed at the sum of 30,000,000 of Turkish piastres.

Appointment of Boundary Commissioners.

Art. III. The Commissioners of the 3 Courts shall immediately proceed to the marking out of the Boundary now settled. A Commissioner shall be appointed by the Sublime Porte to join in the labours of this Demarcation. It is clearly understood that no delay shall arise in this operation, whether from the absence of one or two of the Commissioners or from any other cause. A Commissioner appointed by the Greek Government may co-operate in the same labours, which should be completed in the space of 6 months, dating from this day. In case of difference of opinion between the Commissioners, the question shall be equitably resolved by a majority of voices.

Payment of Indemnity.

Art. IV. The Indemnity which is due to the Sublime Porte in virtue of the present Arrangement, shall be paid on the 31st of December of the present year, on which day, in conformity with the following Article, all the Territories, without exception, which are to constitute Greece shall be evacuated, if not sooner, by the troops and authorities of the Sublime Porte. This payment shall be effected at Constantinople on the 1st of December, 1832, at the rate of exchange of the day of the signing of this instrument, by drafts on London, Paris, Vienna, or Petersburgh; and the Porte shall be officially informed on this matter on the arrival of the formal confirmation of this transaction.

Turkish Evacuation of Greek Territories.

Art. V. On the 31st of December of the present year, or sooner if possible, the Territories which form the object of the present Arrangement shall be entirely evacuated by the Ottoman troops and Authorities. With respect to the Territories previously assigned to Greece, and which are still occupied by the Sublime Porte, they also shall be evacuated within the same period, so that on the day specified, the evacuation of all the Territories, without exception, which are to constitute Greece, shall have been in every instance completely effected.

Passage of Greek Vessels through the Gulf of Arta.

ART. VI. The Fort of Punta, as has been said above, being intended to remain to the Porte to complete the means of defence of Prevesa, and in order the better to secure the safety of its commerce, there shall only be permitted therein a garrison sufficient for the occupation of that post. It is understood that the Ottoman Authorities will not oppose any obstacle to the passage of Greek Vessels; and, excepting Customs dues and other imposts which would be due to the Sublime Porte in cases where Vessels may put into Punta, Prevesa, or other Turkish ports of the Gulf of Arta, the Authorities shall demand nothing for the passage.

Permission to Individuals to quit Ceded Territories and to sell their Estates.

ART. VII. A term of 18 months, dating from the day on which the labours of the Demarcation shall have been completed, is accorded to such individuals as may desire to quit the Territories which form the object of the present Arrangement, and to sell their estates. This term of 18 months may, in special cases, and under unforeseen circumstances, be prolonged some months, and a Commission of Arbitration shall determine on the validity of these cases for exception, and shall assist in causing the sales to be effected at a fair price.

Similar Privileges to Inhabitants of Eubea and Attica, and Proprietors of Thebes.

The same advantages are accorded to the inhabitants of the Island of Eubea and of Attica, and to the Proprietors of Thebes, who would at the present day be in the receipt of their rightful revenues if that district were occupied by the Ottoman troops at the date of the assent of the Porte to the preceding arrangements of the 3rd of February, 1830.

It is understood that these individuals will alike be allowed to dispose, and within the same period, of any beneficial interest which they may have, either as tenants, or as hereditary administrators, in the *Vacoufs*, the whole of which is transferred to the Greek State.

Appointment of Commercial Agents.

ART. VIII. In conformity with the preceding stipulations, the Government of the new King of Greece will have the power of entering into negotiation for the purpose of regulating its relations of commerce and navigation with the Sublime Porte on a principle of reciprocity; and

Agents duly accredited on either side shall be received in the Ports of Turkey and Greece, according to the usual forms, so that Ottoman subjects shall have an acknowledged right to traffic at their will in the State of Greece, and that, on their side, the Greeks shall cease to have recourse to foreign protection to frequent the Ports and Trading Towns of the Ottoman Empire.

Definitive Settlement of Greek Question.
The undersigned Plenipotentiaries of the 3 Courts, and those of the Sublime Porte, having brought to a close the Conferences which they have held for the purpose of effecting the Definitive Settlement of the Boundary of Greece, as above described, declare that, considering the arrangements recorded by common agreement in the present instrument, the object of the Treaty of London of the 6th July, 1827, and of the Protocol under different dates which relate thereto, is completely attained, that the prolonged negotiations to which those stipulations have given rise, are terminated in such a manner as never to be renewed; in fact, that the Greek Question is irrevocably settled.

Confirmation of Arrangement to have same force as a Ratification.
The final Confirmation of the present Final Arrangement by the 3 August Courts shall be transmitted to the Sublime Porte within the period of 4 months, dating from this day; and that Confirmation shall have, with respect to this Act, all the force of a Ratification.

Done at Constantinople, the 9th/21st July, 1832 (the 23rd of the month Safer, 1248 of the Hegira).

             (L.S.)   STRATFORD CANNING.
             (L.S.)   A. BOUTENEFF.
             (L.S.)   E. B. VARENNE.

[A Copy, corresponding with the Original, signed by the 3 Representatives, and exchanged for a Turkish Version, was also signed by the Ottoman Ministers.]

29

CONVENTION between Great Britain and France, relative to the Netherlands. Signed in London, 22nd October, 1832.

Reference to Treaty of 15th November, 1831.
His Majesty the King of the United Kingdom of Great Britain and Ireland, and His Majesty the King of the French, having been called upon by His Majesty the King of the Belgians to carry into execution

the stipulations of the Treaty relative to the Netherlands, concluded at London, on the 15th of November, 1831, the execution whereof, by the terms of Article XXV of the said Treaty, has been jointly guaranteed by their said Majesties, and by their Majesties the Emperor of Austria, the King of Prussia, and the Emperor of Russia;

Having besides perceived that all the efforts made in common by the 5 Powers, Parties to the said Treaty, to accomplish its execution by means of Negotiation, have been, up to the present time, ineffectual:

Being moreover convinced that any further delay in the execution of the same would seriously endanger the general Peace of Europe, their said Majesties, notwithstanding the regret which they experience at finding that their Majesties the Emperor of Austria, the King of Prussia, and the Emperor of Russia, are not, at present, prepared to concur in the active measures which are requisite for the execution of the said Treaty, have resolved to fulfil their own engagements in this respect without further delay; and it is with the view of arriving at that end; by immediately concerting the measures best calculated for that purpose, that their Majesties the King of the United Kingdom of Great Britain and Ireland, and the King of the French, have named as their Plenipotentiaries, viz.:

His Majesty the King of the United Kingdom of Great Britain and Ireland, the Right Honourable Henry John, Viscount Palmerston, Baron Temple, a Peer of Ireland, a Member of His said Majesty's Most Honourable Privy Council, a Member of Parliament, and his Principal Secretary of State for Foreign Affairs, &c.;

And His Majesty the King of the French, the Sieur Charles Maurice de Talleyrand-Périgord, Prince-Duke de Talleyrand, a Peer of France, His said Majesty's Ambassador Extraordinary and Plenipotentiary at the Court of His Britannic Majesty, &c.;

Who, after having communicated to each other their respective Full Powers, found to be in due and proper form, have agreed upon and concluded the following Articles:

Withdrawal of Netherlands Troops from Belgium, and of Belgian Troops from Netherlands Territory.

ART. I. His Majesty the King of the United Kingdom of Great Britain and Ireland, and His Majesty the King of the French, will notify to His Majesty the King of the Netherlands, and to His Majesty the King of the Belgians, respectively, that it is their intention to proceed forthwith to carry into execution the said Treaty of the 15th of November, 1831, in conformity with the engagements thereby contracted by them: and, as a first step towards the accomplishment of that purpose, their said Majesties will require His Majesty the King of the

Netherlands to enter, on or before the 2nd day of the next ensuing month of November, into an engagement to withdraw, on or before the 12th day of the same month of November, all his Troops from the Territories which, by Articles I and II of the said Treaty, are to form the Kingdom of Belgium, of which Kingdom the High Contracting Parties to that Treaty have guaranteed the Independence and Neutrality: and their said Majesties will also require His Majesty the King of the Belgians to enter, on or before the 2nd day of the ensuing month of November, into an engagement to withdraw, on or before the 12th day of the same month, all his Troops from the Territories of His Majesty the King of the Netherlands; so that after the 12th day of November next there shall be no Netherland Troops within the limits of the Kingdom of Belgium, and no Belgian Troops within the Territories of the King of the Netherlands; and their Majesties the King of the United Kingdom of Great Britain and Ireland, and the King of the French, will, at the same time, declare to the King of the Netherlands, and to the King of the Belgians respectively, that if this requisition shall not be complied with, their said Majesties will proceed, without further notice or delay, to take such measures as may appear to them necessary for enforcing the same.

Embargo on Dutch Vessels in case of refusal to Evacuate.

ART. II. If the King of the Netherlands shall refuse to enter into the engagement mentioned in the foregoing Article, their Majesties the King of the United Kingdom of Great Britain and Ireland, and the King of the French, will immediately cause an Embargo to be laid upon all Netherland Vessels within the ports of their respective dominions, and will order their respective cruizers to detain and send in all Netherland Vessels which they may meet with at sea; and a combined British and French squadron shall be stationed off the Coast of Holland, for the more effectual execution of this measure.

French Troops to compel Evacuation of Belgian Territory.

ART. III. If on the 15th of November next ensuing, the Netherland troops should still continue within the Belgian territory, a French force shall advance into Belgium for the purpose of compelling the Netherland troops to evacuate the said Territories, provided that the King of the Belgians shall have previously signified his wish for the entrance of such French force into his Dominions for the aforesaid purpose.

French Troops to retire on Evacuation of Belgian Territory by Dutch Troops.

ART. IV. If the measure contemplated in the preceding Article shall become necessary, its object shall be confined to the expulsion of the Netherland troops from the Citadel of Antwerp, and from the Forts and places dependent thereupon; and His Majesty the King of the French, in his lively solicitude for the Independence of Belgium, as well as for that of all established Governments, expressly engages that the French troops which may be employed in such service, shall not occupy any of the fortified places of the Kingdom of Belgium, that when the Citadel of Antwerp, and the Forts and places dependent thereupon, shall have surrendered, or shall have been taken, or shall have been evacuated by the Netherland troops, they shall be immediately delivered over to the Military Authorities of the King of the Belgians; and that the French troops shall thereupon forthwith retire within the French Territories.

Ratifications.

ART. V. The present Convention shall be ratified, and the Ratifications shall be exchanged at London, in the space of 8 days from the date hereof, or sooner of possible.

In witness whereof, the respective Plenipotentiaries have signed the same, and have affixed thereto the Seals of their Arms.

Done at London, the 22nd day of October, in the year of Our Lord, 1832.

(L.S.)   PALMERSTON.
(L.S.)   TALLEYRAND.

30

CONVENTION between Belgium and France, relative to the entrance of a French Army into Belgium. Signed at Brussels, 10th November, 1832.

Reference to Treaty of 15th November, 1831.

HIS Majesty the King of the French having determined, at the request of His Majesty the King of the Belgians, to send an Army into Belgium, with the view of bringing about the evacuation of the Citadel of Antwerp and of the Forts and Places belonging thereto, in conformity with the stipulations of the Treaty of the 15th November, 1831, whereof the 5 Powers represented at the Conference of London, guaranteed the execution, their Majesties recognising the necessity of regulating, by a Special Convention, everything connected therwith, have appointed as their Plenipotentiaries, namely:—

His Majesty the King of the French, the Sieur Armand Charles Septime, Count de la Tour Maubourg, his Envoy Extraordinary and

Minister Plenipotentiary to His Majesty the King of the Belgians, &c.;

And His Majesty the King of the Belgians, the Sieur Albert Goblet, his Minister of State, &c.;

Who, after having exchanged their Full Powers, found to be in good and due form, have agreed to and signed the following Articles:—

1. *French* Army not to occupy any of the strongholds of the Kingdom of *Belgium*.

2. *Belgian* Troops to give up to *French* Army all the Posts round the Citadel and Forts on both banks of the *Scheldt*.

3. *Belgian* garrison to occupy the Town of *Antwerp*, and not to take part in attack on Citadel and Forts occupied by the *Dutch*.

4. Position to be assigned to *Belgian* Army.

5. Fortress of *Antwerp* to be delivered over to *Belgian* Troops on *Dutch* evacuation.

6. *Belgian* Army to abstain from all aggression.

7. *Dutch* aggression on *Belgium* to be repelled by combined *French* and *Belgian* Armies.

8. Ratifications.

In testimony whereof the respective Plenipotentiaries have signed it, and have affixed thereto the Seal of their Arms.

Done at Brussels, 10th November, 1832.

(L.S.)   COUNT DE LA TOUR MAUBOURG.
(L.S.)   GOBLET.

[The Citadel of Antwerp capitulated on the 23rd December, 1832.]

31   TREATY OF UNKIAR SKELESSI

TREATY of Defensive Alliance between Russia and Turkey. Signed at Constantinople, 8th July, 1833.

In the name of Almighty God.

HIS Imperial Majesty, the Most High and Most Mighty Emperor and Autocrat of All the Russias, and His Highness the Most High and Most Mighty Emperor of the Ottomans, being equally animated with the sincere desire of maintaining the system of peace and good harmony happily established between the two Empires, have resolved to extend and strengthen the perfect friendship and confidence which reign between them by the conclusion of a Treaty of Defensive Alliance.

Their Majesties have accordingly chosen and named as their Plenipotentiaries; that is to say:

His Majesty the Emperor of All the Russias, the Most Excellent and Most Honourable Alexis, Count Orloff, his Extraordinary Ambassador at the Sublime Ottoman Porte, and the Most Excellent and Most Honourable Apollinaire Bouténeff, his Envoy Extraordinary and Minister Plenipotentiary at the Sublime Ottoman Porte, &c.;

And His Highness the Sultan of the Ottomans, the Most Illustrious and Most Excellent, the Most Anicent of his Viziers, Hosrew Mehemet Pasha, Seraskier, Commander-in-Chief of the Regular Troops of the Line, and Governor-General of Constantinople, &c., and the Most Excellent and Most Honourable Ferzi Akhmet Pasha, Mouchir and Commander of the Guard of His Highness, &c., and the Most Excellent and Most Honourable Hadgi Mehmet Akiff Reis Effendi, actual Reis Effendi, &c.;

Who, after having exchanged their Full Powers, found in good and due form, have agreed upon the following Articles:

Peace, Amity, and Alliance.

ART. I. There shall be for ever Peace, Amity, and Alliance between His Majesty the Emperor of All the Russias and His Majesty the Emperor of the Ottomans, their Empires and their Subjects, as well by land as by sea. This Alliance having solely for its object the common defence of their dominions against all attack, their Majesties engage to come to an unreserved understanding with each other upon all the matters which concern their respective tranquillity and safety, and to afford to each other mutually for this purpose substantial aid, and the most efficacious assistance.

Confirmation of Treaties.

ART. II. The Treaty of Peace concluded at Adrianople on the 2nd/14th September, 1829, as well as all the other Treaties comprised therein, as also the Convention signed at St. Petersburgh on the 14th/26th April, 1830[1] and the Arrangement relating to Greece, concluded at Constantinople on the 9th/21st July, 1832, are fully confirmed by the present Treaty of Defensive Alliance, in the same manner as if the said transactions had been inserted in it word for word.

Maintenance by Russia of Independence of Turkey.

ART. III. In consequence of the principle of conservation and mutual defence, which is the basis of the present Treaty of Alliance, and by reason of a most sincere desire of securing the permanence, maintenance, and entire Independence of the Sublime Porte, His Majesty the Emperor of All the Russias, in the event of circumstances occurring which should again determine the Sublime Porte to call for the naval and military assistance of Russia, although, if it please God, that case is

1. Reduction of War Indemnity.

by no means likely to happen, engages to furnish, by land and by sea, as many troops and forces as the two High Contracting Parties may deem necessary. It is accordingly agreed, that in this case the Land and Sea Forces, whose aid the Sublime Porte may call for, shall be held at its disposal.

Land and Sea Forces to be Maintained by the Power requesting Assistance.

ART. IV. In conformity with what is above stated, in the event of one of the two Powers requesting the assistance of the other, the expense only of provisioning the Land and the Sea Forces which may be furnished, shall fall to the charge of the Power who shall have applied for the aid.

Duration of Treaty.

ART. V. Although the two High Contracting Parties sincerely intend to maintain this engagement to the most distant period of time, yet, as it is possible that in process of time circumstances may require that some changes should be made in this Treaty, it has been agreed to fix its duration at 8 years from the day of the exchange of the Imperial Ratifications. The two parties, previously to the expiration of that term, will concert together, according to the state of affairs at that time, as to the renewal of the said Treaty.

Ratifications.

ART. VI. The present Treaty of Defensive Alliance shall be ratified by the two High Contracting Parties, and the Ratifications thereof shall be exchanged at Constantinople within the space of two months, or sooner if possible.

The present Instrument, consisting of 6 Articles, and to be finally completed by the exchange of the respective Ratifications, having been agreed upon between us, we have signed it, and sealed it with our Seals, in virtue of our Full Powers, and have delivered it to the Plenipotentiaries of the Sublime Ottoman Porte in exchange for a similar Instrument.

Done at Constantinople, the 26th June/8th July, 1833 (the 20th of the moon Safer, in the 1249th year of the Hegira).

(L.S.)   CTE. ALEXIS ORLOFF.
(L.S.)   A. BOUTENEFF.

SEPARATE ARTICLE.

Strait of the Dardanelles to be closed to Foreign Ships of War during War between Russia and any other Foreign Power.

IN virtue of one of the clauses of Article I of the Patent Treaty of Defensive Alliance concluded between the Imperial Court of Russia and the Sublime Porte, the two High Contracting Parties are bound to afford to each other mutually substantial aid, and the most efficacious assistance for the safety of their respective dominions. Nevertheless, His Majesty the Emperor of All the Russias, wishing to spare the Sublime Ottoman Porte the expense and inconvenience which might be occasioned to it by affording substantial aid, will not ask for that aid if circumstances should place the Sublime Porte under the obligation of furnishing it, the Sublime Ottoman Porte, in place of the aid which it is bound to furnish in case of need, according to the principle of reciprocity of the Patent Treaty, shall confine its action in favour of the Imperial Court of Russia to closing the Strait of the Dardanelles, that is to say, to not allowing any Foreign Vessels of War to enter therein under any pretext whatsoever.

The present Separate and Secret Article shall have the same force and value as if it was inserted word for word in the Treaty of Alliance of this day.

Done at Constantinople, the 26th June/8th July, 1833 (the 20th of the moon of Safer, in the 1249th year of the Hegira).

(L.S.) CTE. ALEXIS ORLOFF.
(L.S.) A. BOUTENEFF.

32

TREATY between Russia and Turkey respecting Moldavia and Wallachia. Signed at St. Petersburgh, 29th January, 1834.

Reference to Treaty of 14th September, 1829.

THE Most High and Most Powerful Ottoman Emperor, my benefactor and master, on the one part, and the Most High and Most Magnanimous Emperor of All the Russias, on the other, animated by the desire with which they are inspired by the sincere friendship, cordiality, and confidence that happily subsist between them, to arrange definitively certain points of the Treaty concluded between the two High Powers at Adrianople, which have not been hitherto carried into execution, have named for this purpose as their Plenipotentiaries, that is to say: His Majesty the Ottoman Emperor, his Excellency Mouchir Ahmed Pacha, Military Counsellor of the Seraglio, Ambassador Extraordinary of the Sublime Porte at the Imperial Court of Russia, &c.; and His Majesty the Emperor of Russia, their Excellencies the Count Nesselrode, Vice-Chancellor of the Empire, and the Count Alexis Orloff, General of Cavalry, Aide-de-camp of the Emperor, &c.; who, after having reciprocally exhibited their Full Powers, have agreed on the following Articles:

Map of Boundary.

ART. I. The two High Courts having deemed it necessary to establish, as has been stipulated in the Treaty of Adrianople, a Line of Demarcation between the two Empires in the East, such as may henceforth prevent every species of dispute and discussion, it has been agreed that a Line shall be traced that shall completely prevent the depredations which the neighbouring tribes have been in the habit of committing, and which have more than once compromised the relations of neighbourhood and friendship between the two Empires. Therefore, after the Commissioners on both sides have examined the localities, and obtained the necessary information for this purpose, the two Contracting Parties have resolved to proceed to the settlement of the Frontiers, in such manner that the object judicially proposed in the Treaty of Adrianople should be completely fulfilled; and with that view they have adopted, by common consent, the Line which may be seen traced in red on the Map which is annexed to the present Treaty.

Line of Boundary.

Conformably to Article IV of the Treaty of Adrianople, this Line departs from Port St. Nicholas on the coast of the Black Sea, follows the existing Frontiers of the Province of Gouriel, ascends up to the Limits of Juira, thence traverses the Province of Akhiskha [Akhaltzik], and terminates at the point where the Provinces of Akhiskha and of Kars join the Province of Georgia. Thus the greatest part of the Province of Akhiskha remains, together with the other Countries and Territories referred to in the said Treaty, under the dominion of the Sublime Porte, as may be seen by the Map, of which two copies have been made and compared by the Plenipotentiaries of the two Powers, and which, considered as forming part of the present Treaty, are to be annexed to it, as evidence of the manner in which the future Limits of the two Empires have been settled.

Commissioners to erect Posts defining Boundary.

After the exchange of the Ratifications of the present Treaty, and so soon as Posts shall have been erected by the Commissioners named on both parts, according to the Line traced on the Map, from one side to the other, the Russian troops shall evacuate the Territories situate beyond that line, and retire within the Limits which it prescribes. So also the Mussulmans who inhabit the inconsiderable Territories which are comprised within the line that passes in front of the district of

Ghroubhan and the extremities of the districts of Ponskron and of Djildir, and who may wish to establish themselves within the Territories of the Sublime Porte, shall be at liberty, within the term of 18 months, from the date of the exchange of the Ratifications of the Treaty, to settle the affairs which connected them with the country, and to remove to the Turkish States without molestation.

Recognition by Turkey of Constitution of Principalities of Wallachia and Moldavia.

Art. II. By the instrument executed separately at Adrianople relative to the Principalities of Wallachia and Moldavia, the Sublime Porte undertook to recognise formally the Regulations made, while the Russian troops occupied those Provinces, by the principal inhabitants for their internal administration; the Sublime Porte finding nothing in the Articles of that Constitution which can affect its Rights of Sovereignty, consents henceforth formally to recognise the said Constitution.

It engages to publish for that purpose a Firman, accompanied by a Hatti-sheriff, two months after the exchange of the Ratifications, and to give a copy of the same to the Russian Mission at Constantinople.

Appointment of Hospodars of Wallachia and Moldavia.

After the formal recognition of the Constitution, the Hospodars of Wallachia and Moldavia shall be named, but for this time only, and as a special case, in the manner which was agreed upon some time since between the two Contracting Powers, and they will proceed to govern the two Provinces conformably to the Constitution, which is a consequence of the Stipulations above mentioned.

Evacuation of Principalities by Russia. Tribute to be Paid to Turkey by Wallachia and Moldavia.

His Majesty the Emperor of Russia, wishing to afford a new proof of the esteem and consideration which he entertains towards His Highness, and to hasten the moment when the Sublime Porte shall exercise the rights which the Treaties secure to it over the two Provinces, will order his troops, so soon as the Princes shall have been named, to retire from the two Provinces. This measure shall be executed two months after the nomination of the Princes. And as compensation is justly due for the advantages which the Sublime Porte grants in favour of the Wallachians and Moldavians, it is agreed and ordained that the annual Tribute, which the two Provinces ought to pay according to the Treaties, shall be fixed henceforth at 6,000 purses (that is to say, at 3,000,000 Turkish piastres); and the Princes shall take care that this sum be annually paid, counting from the 1st of January, 1835.

*Number of Troops in Principalities to be Fixed by Turkey. Colours
to Garrisons and Flag to Moldo-Wallachian Merchant Vessels.*

It is agreed between the two Courts that the number of troops which
shall be employed as Garrisons in the interior of the two Provinces,
shall be fixed in an invariable manner and at the pleasure of the Porte,
which shall give Colours to the Garrisons and a Flag to the Valacho-
Moldavian merchant-vessels that navigate the Danube.

Turkish Engagements Modified.

ART. III. Agreeably to the desire manifested by His Highness to
execute scrupulously the engagements which he has undertaken by
Article III of the Explanatory and Separate Act, which is annexed to
the Treaty of Adrianople, and by the Treaty of St. Petersburgh, relative
thereunto, His Majesty the Emperor of All the Russias has been pleased
to afford to the Sublime Porte new facilities for the execution of the
engagements contracted by the Acts above mentioned; and it is accordingly agreed:

Payment of Indemnities to Russia.

1. That, although it has been stipulated by Article II of the Treaty
of St. Petersburgh that the Sublime Porte shall pay annually and
during eight years 1,000,000 Dutch ducats, it shall pay only 500,000
ducats per annum.

2. That the Sublime Porte shall no longer be obliged, as it has
hitherto been, to pay in the month of May of each year, and at one time,
the whole sum due for the year, and that it shall henceforth pay the
500,000 ducats by degrees; the entire sum being, however, paid within
the interval between the month of May of one year and the month of
May of the following year.

3. That His Imperial Majesty renounces his right to demand the
difference, which existed at the period of each payment of the portion
of the Indemnities for the expenses of the War and for Commerce,
between the price at which the Sublime Porte paid the ducat in Turkish
piastres and the real value of the ducats.

Reduction of Indemnity.

4. That His Imperial Majesty, moreover, taking into consideration
the embarrassments in which the Treasury of that Empire has been
lately involved, consents to the immediate reduction of 2,000,000
ducats, which is one-third of the amount of the Indemnities for the
expenses of the War.

Periods of Payment.

5. That considering the deduction above specified, and the other arrangements already mentioned, the sum total of the Indemnities amounts to 4,000,000 Dutch ducats, of which the first portion, to be paid in one year, as one instalment, consists of 500,000 ducats, and shall be paid between the 1st of May, 1834, and the 1st of May, 1835, and the corresponding portions in the following years in the same manner, until the whole debt be discharged; but upon condition that the securities, guarantees, and facilities stipulated in Articles IV, V, VI, VII, and IX of the Treaty of St. Petersburgh shall continue down to that period in all their force, as if they had been inserted word for word in the present Treaty.

Ratifications.

In virtue of the powers which have been given to me, I have concluded the present Treaty, which shall be ratified by the two Contracting Parties, and the Ratifications of which shall be exchanged at Constantinople, within the term of 6 weeks, or sooner if possible; I have affixed to it my Seal and Signature; and I have delivered it to their Excellencies the Plenipotentiaries of the Court of Russia at St. Petersburgh, in exchange for the instrument which they have delivered to me.

Done the 18th Ramazan, 1249.   [29th January, 1834.]

(L.S.)   NESSELRODE.

(L.S.)   ALEXIS ORLOFF.

(L.S.)   MOUCHIR AHMED PACHA.

33

TREATY between Great Britain, France, Portugal, and Spain, for the Pacification of the Peninsula. Signed at London, 22nd April, 1834.

HER Majesty the Queen Regent of Spain, during the minority of her daughter Donna Isabella the Second, Queen of Spain, and His Imperial Majesty the Duke of Braganza, Regent of the Kingdom of Portugal and of the Algarves, in the name of the Queen Donna Maria the Second, being impressed with the conviction that the interests of the two Crowns and the security of their respective dominions require the immediate and vigorous exertion of their joint efforts to put an end to Hostilities which, though directed in the first instance against the Throne of Her Most Faithful Majesty, now afford shelter and support to disaffected and rebellious subjects of the Crown of

Spain; and their Majesties being desirous at the same time to provide the necessary means for restoring to the subjects of each the blessings of internal Peace, and to confirm, by mutual good offices, the friendship which they are desirous of establishing and cementing between their respective States, they have come to the determination of uniting their forces in order to compel the Infant Don Carlos of Spain and the Infant Dom Miguel of Portugal to withdraw from the Portuguese Dominions.

In consequence of this Agreement, their Majesties the Regents have addressed themselves to their Majesties the King of the United Kingdom of Great Britain and Ireland, and the King of the French; and their said Majesties, considering the interest they must always take in the security of the Spanish Monarchy, and being further animated by the most anxious desire to assist in the establishment of Peace in the Peninsula, as well as in every other part of Europe; and His Britannic Majesty considering, moreover, the special obligations arising out of his ancient Alliance with Portugal, their Majesties have consented to become Parties to the proposed engagement.

Their Majesties have therefore named as their Plenipotentiaries, that is to say:

His Majesty the King of the United Kingdom of Great Britain and Ireland, the Right Honourable Henry John Viscount Palmerston, Baron Temple, a Peer of Ireland, a Member of His Britannic Majesty's Most Honourable Privy Council, and his Principal Secretary of State for Foreign Affairs, &c.;

Her Majesty the Queen Regent of Spain, during the minority of her daughter Donna Isabella the Second, Queen of Spain, Don Manuel Pando, Fernandez de Pinedo, Alava y Dabila, Marquis of Miraflores, Count of Villapaterna, and of Floridablanca, Lord of Villagarcia, a Grandee of Spain, Envoy Extraordinary and Minister Plenipotentiary to His Britannic Majesty, &c.;

His Majesty the King of the French, the Sieur Charles Maurice de Talleyrand-Perigord, Prince-Duke de Talleyrand, Peer of France, His said Majesty's Ambassador Extraordinary and Minister Plenipotentiary to His Britannic Majesty, &c.;

And His Imperial Majesty the Duke of Braganza, Regent of the Kingdom of Portugal and the Algarves in the name of the Queen Donna Maria the Second, the Sieur Christopher Peter de Moraes Sarmento, a Member of the Council of Her Most Faithful Majesty, Nobleman Knight of the Royal House, and Her Most Faithful Majesty's Envoy Extraordinary and Minister Plenipotentiary to His Britannic Majesty, &c.;

Who have agreed upon the following Articles:

Expulsion of Don Carlos from Portugal.

ART. I. His Imperial Majesty the Duke of Braganza, Regent of the Kingdom of Portugal and the Algarves in the name of the Queen Donna Maria the Second, engages to use all the means in his power to compel the Infant Don Carlos to withdraw from the Portuguese Dominions.

Co-operation of Spanish Troops to enforce withdrawal of Don Carlos and Dom Miguel from Portugul.

ART. II. Her Majesty the Queen Regent of Spain during the minority of her daughter Donna Isabella the Second, Queen of Spain, being hereby requested and invited thereto by His Imperial Majesty the Duke of Braganza, Regent, in the name of the Queen Donna Maria the Second; and having moreover received just and grave cause of complaint against the Infant Dom Miguel, by the countenance and support given by him to the Pretender to the Spanish Crown, engages to cause such a body of Spanish Troops as may hereafter be agreed upon between the two Parties, to enter the Portuguese territory, in order to co-operate with the troops of Her Most Faithful Majesty, for the purpose of compelling the Infants Don Carlos of Spain and Dom Miguel of Portugal to withdraw from the Portuguese Dominions. And Her Majesty the Queen Regent of Spain further engages that these troops shall be maintained at the expense of Spain, and without any charge to Portugal; the said Spanish Troops being nevertheless received and treated in all other respects in the same manner as the troops of Her Most Faithful Majesty; and Her Majesty the Queen Regent engages that her troops shall withdraw from the Portuguese territory as soon as the above-mentioned object of the expulsion of the Infants shall have been accomplished, and when the presence of those troops in Portugal shall no longer be required by His Imperial Majesty the Duke Regent in the name of the Queen Donna Maria the Second.

Naval Force to be supplied by Great Britain.

ART. III. His Majesty the King of the United Kingdom of Great Britain and Ireland engages to co-operate, by the employment of a Naval Force, in aid of the operations to be undertaken, in conformity with the engagements of this Treaty, by the troops of Spain and Portugal.

Co-operation of France.

ART. IV. If the co-operation of France should be deemed necessary by the High Contracting Parties, for the complete attainment of the object of this Treaty, His Majesty the King of the French engages to do, in this respect, whatever might be settled by common consent between himself and his 3 August Allies.

Amnesty.

ART. V. It is agreed between the High Contracting Parties, that in pursuance of the stipulations contained in the foregoing Articles, a declaration shall be immediately issued, announcing to the Portuguese Nation the principles and object of the engagements of this Treaty. And His Imperial Majesty the Duke Regent, in the name of the Queen Donna Maria the Second, animated by a sincere desire to obliterate all remembrance of the past, and to unite around the Throne of Her Most Faithful Majesty the whole of that Nation over which the will of Divine Providence has called her to reign, declares his intention to proclaim, at the same time, a complete and general amnesty in favour of all such of the subjects of Her Most Faithful Majesty as shall, within a time to be specified, return to their allegiance; and His Imperial Majesty the Duke Regent, in the name of the Queen Donna Maria the Second, also declares his intention to secure to the Infant Dom Miguel, on his retiring from the Spanish and Portuguese Dominions, a provision suitable to his birth and rank.

Provision to Infant Don Carlos.

ART. VI. Her Majesty the Queen Regent of Spain, during the minority of her daughter Donna Isabella the Second, Queen of Spain, hereby declares her intention to secure to the Infant Don Carlos, on his retiring from the Spanish and Portuguese Dominions, a provision suitable to his birth and rank.

Ratifications.

ART. VII. The present Treaty shall be ratified, and the Ratifications shall be exchanged at London in one month from this date, or sooner if possible.

In witness whereof the respective Plenipotentiaries have signed the same, and have affixed thereto the Seals of their Arms.

Done at London, the 22nd day of April, in the year of Our Lord, 1834.

(L.S.) MIRAFLORES.
(L.S.) TALLEYRAND.
(L.S.) C. P. DE MORAES SARMENTO.
(L.S.) PALMERSTON.

34

ADDITIONAL ARTICLES to the Treaty between Great Britain, France, Portugal, and Spain, of 22nd April, 1834. Signed at London, 18th August, 1834.

Reference to Treaty of 22nd April, 1834.

His Majesty the King of the United Kingdom of Great Britain and Ireland; Her Majesty the Queen Regent of Spain during the minority of her daughter Donna Isabella the Second, Queen of Spain; His Majesty the King of the French; and His Imperial Majesty the Duke of Braganza, Regent of the Kingdom of Portugal and the Algarves in the name of the Queen Donna Maria the Second, the High Contracting Parties to the Treaty of the 22nd April, 1834; having taken into their serious consideration the recent events which have occurred in the Peninsula, and being deeply impressed with the conviction that, in this new state of things, new measures have become necessary for the complete attainment of the objects which it was the purpose of the said Treaty to accomplish; the undersigned, Henry John Viscount Palmerston, Baron Temple, His Britannic Majesty's Principal Secretary of State for Foreign Affairs, &c., Don Manuel Pando, Fernandez de Pinedo, Alava y Davila, Marquis of Miraflores, Her Catholic Majesty's Envoy Extraordinary and Minister Plenipotentiary to His Britannic Majesty, &c.; Charles Maurice de Talleyrand-Perigord, Prince-Duke de Talleyrand, Ambassador Extraordinary and Minister Plenipotentiary from His Majesty the King of the French to His Britannic Majesty, &c.; and Christopher Peter de Moraes Sarmento, Her Most Faithful Majesty's Envoy Extraordinary and Minister Plenipotentiary to His Britannic Majesty, &c., being furnished with the authority of their respective Governments, have agreed upon the following additional Articles to the Treaty of the 22nd April, 1834:—

Prevention of Succours from French Territory.

Art. I. His Majesty the King of the French engages to take such measures in those parts of his Dominions which adjoin to Spain, as shall be best calculated to prevent any Succours of men, arms, or warlike stores, from being sent from the French Territory to the Insurgents in Spain.

Warlike Stores to be supplied by Great Britain to Spain, and Naval Force if necessary.

Art. II. His Majesty the King of the United Kingdom of Great Britain and Ireland engages to furnish to Her Catholic Majesty such supplies of Arms and Warlike Stores as Her Majesty may require, and further to assist Her Majesty, if necessary, with a Naval Force.

Co-operation of Portugal in Spain.

Art. III. His Imperial Majesty the Duke of Braganza, Regent of Portugal and the Algarves in the name of the Queen Donna Maria the

Second, fully sharing the sentiments of his August Allies, and desirous moreover to make a just return for the engagements contracted by Her Majesty the Queen Regent of Spain by Article II of the Treaty of the 22nd April, 1834, engages to co-operate, if necessity should arise, in aid of Her Catholic Majesty, with such means as may be in his power, and in such mode and manner as may hereafter be agreed upon between their said Majesties.

Ratifications.

ART. IV. The foregoing Articles shall have the same force and effect as if they were inserted, word for word, in the Treaty of the 22nd April, 1834, and shall be considered as forming a part of the same:—they shall be ratified, and the Ratifications thereof shall be exchanged at London within 40 days, or sooner if possible.

In witness whereof, the respective Plenipotentiaries have signed the same, and have affixed thereto the Seals of their Arms.

Done at London, the 18th day of August, 1834.

> (L.S.) MIRAFLORES.
> (L.S.) TALLEYRAND.
> (L.S.) C. P. DE MORAES SARMENTO.

(L.S.) PALMERSTON.

35 TREATY OF LONDON

TREATY between Great Britain, Austria, France, Prussia, and Russia, on the one part, and The Netherlands, on the other. Signed at London, 19th April, 1839.

Reference to Treaties of 14th October, 1831; and 15th November, 1831.

In the Name of the Most Holy and Indivisible Trinity.

HER Majesty the Queen of the United Kingdom of Great Britain and Ireland, His Majesty the Emperor of Austria, King of Hungary and Bohemia, His Majesty the King of the French, His Majesty the King of Prussia, and His Majesty the Emperor of All the Russias, having taken into consideration their Treaty concluded with His Majesty the King of the Belgians, on the 15th of November, 1831; and His Majesty the King of the Netherlands, Grand Duke of Luxemburg, being disposed to conclude a Definitive Arrangement on the basis of the 24 Articles agreed upon by the Plenipotentiaries of Great Britain, Austria, France, Prussia, and Russia, on the 14th of October, 1831; their said Majesties have named for their Plenipotentiaries, that is to say:

Her Majesty the Queen of the United Kingdom of Great Britain

and Ireland, the Right Honourable Henry John Viscount Palmerston, Baron Temple, a Peer of Ireland, a Member of Her Britannic Majesty's Most Honourable Privy Council, a Member of Parliament, and Her Britannic Majesty's Principal Secretary of State for Foreign Affairs, &c.;

His Majesty the Emperor of Austria, King of Hungary and Bohemia, the Sieur Frederic Christian Louis, Count de Senfft-Pilsach, Chamberlain and Privy Councillor of His Imperial and Royal Apostolic Majesty, and his Envoy Extraordinary and Minister Plenipotentiary to His Majesty the King of the Netherlands, &c.;

His Majesty the King of the French, the Sieur Horace Francis Bastien, Count Sebastiani-Porta, a Lieutenant-General in his armies, a Member of the Chamber of Deputies of France, his Ambassador Extraordinary and Minister Plenipotentiary to Her Britannic Majesty, &c.;

His Majesty the King of Prussia, the Sieur Henry William, Baron de Bülow, his Chamberlain, Privy Councillor of Legation, Envoy Extraordinary and Minister Plenipotentiary to Her Britannic Majesty, &c.;

His Majesty the Emperor of All the Russias, the Sieur Charles Andrew, Count Pozzo di Borgo, a General of Infantry in his Armies, his Aide-de-Camp General, Ambassador Extraordinary and Plenipotentiary to Her Britannic Majesty, &c.;

And His Majesty the King of the Netherlands, Grand Duke of Luxemburg, the Sieur Solomon Dedel, his Envoy Extraordinary and Minister Plenipotentiary to Her Britannic Majesty, &c.;

Who, after having communicated to each other their Full Powers, found in good and due form, have agreed upon the following Articles:—

Treaty to be entered into between Belgium and the Netherlands.

ART. I. His Majesty the King of the Netherlands, Grand Duke of Luxemburg, engages to cause to be immediately converted into a Treaty with His Majesty the King of the Belgians, the Articles annexed to the present Act, and agreed upon by common consent, under the auspices of the Courts of Great Britain, Austria, France, Prussia, and Russia.

Articles annexed to have same Force as Treaty.

ART. II. Her Majesty the Queen of the United Kingdom of Great Britain and Ireland, His Majesty the Emperor of Austria, King of Hungary and Bohemia, His Majesty the King of the French, His Majesty the King of Prussia, and His Majesty the Emperor of All the Russias, declare that the Articles mentioned in the preceding Article, are considered as having the same force and validity as if they were textually inserted in the present Act, and that they are thus placed under the guarantee of their said Majesties.

Union between Holland and Belgium dissolved.

ART. III. The Union which has existed between Holland and Belgium, in virtue of the Treaty of Vienna of the 31st of May, 1815, is acknowledged by His Majesty the King of the Netherlands, Grand Duke of Luxemburg, to be dissolved.

Ratifications.

ART. IV. The present Treaty shall be ratified, and the Ratifications shall be exchanged at London at the expiration of 6 weeks, or sooner, if possible. The exchange of these Ratifications shall take place at the same time as that of the Ratifications of the Treaty between Holland and Belgium.

In witness whereof, the respective Plenipotentiaries have signed the present Treaty, and have affixed thereto the Seal of their Arms.

Done at London, the 19th day of April, in the year of Our Lord, 1839.

(L.S.) PALMERSTON.   (L.S.) DEDEL.
(L.S.) SENFF.
(L.S.) H. SEBASTIANI.
(L.S.) BULOW.
(L.S.) POZZO DI BORGO.

ANNEX to the Treaty signed at London, on the 19th of April, 1839, between Great Britain, Austria, France, Prussia, and Russia, on the one part, and the Netherlands, on the other part.

Composition of Belgian Territory.

ART. I. The Belgian Territory shall be composed of the Provinces of—

South Brabant;
Liège;
Namur;
Hainault;
West Flanders;
East Flanders;
Antwerp; and
Limburg;

such as they formed part of the United Kingdom of the Netherlands constituted in 1815, with the exception of those Districts of the Province of Limburg which are designated in Article IV.

The Belgian Territory shall, moreover, comprise that part of the Grand Duchy of Luxemburg which is specified in Article II.

Limits of Belgian Territory in Grand Duchy of Luxembourg.

ART. II. In the Grand Duchy of Luxemburg, the limits of the

Belgian Territory shall be such as will be hereinafter described, viz.:—

Commencing from the Frontier of France between Rodange, which shall remain to the Grand Duchy of Luxemburg, and Athus, which shall belong to Belgium, there shall be drawn, according to the annexed Map, a line which, leaving to Belgium the road from Arlon to Longwy, the Town of Arlon with its district, and the road from Arlon to Bastogne, shall pass between Messancy, which shall be on the Belgian Territory, and Clemancy, which shall remain to the Grand Duchy of Luxemburg, terminating at Steinfort, which place shall also remain to the Grand Duchy. From Steinfort this line shall be continued in the direction of Eischen, Hecbus, Guirsch, Ober-Pallen, Grende, Nothomb, Parette, and Perlé, as far as Martelange: Hecbus, Guirsch, Grende, Nothomb, and Parette, being to belong to Belgium, and Eischen, Ober-Pallen, Perlé, and Martelange, to the Grand Duchy. From Martelange the said line shall follow the course of the Sure, the waterway (Thalweg) of which River shall serve as the limit between the two States, as far as opposite to Tintange, from whence it shall be continued, as directly as possible, towards the present Frontier of the Arrondissement of Diekirch, and shall pass between Surret, Harlange, and Tarchamps, which places shall be left to the Grand Duchy of Luxemburg, and Honville, Livarchamps, and Loutremange, which places shall form part of the Belgian Territory. Then having, in the vicinity of Doncols and Soulez, which shall remain to the Grand Duchy, reached the present Boundary of the Arrondissement of Diekirch, the line in question shall follow the said Boundary to the Frontier of the Prussian Territory. All the Territories, Towns, Fortresses, and places situated to the west of this line, shall belong to Belgium; and all the Territories, Towns, Fortresses, and places situated to the east of the said line, shall continue to belong to the Grand Duchy of Luxemburg.

It is understood, that in marking out this line, and in conforming as closely as possible to the description of it given above, as well as to the delineation of it on the Map, which, for the sake of greater clearness, is annexed to the present Article, the Commissioners of Demarcation, mentioned in Article V, shall pay due attention to the localities, as well as to the mutual necessity for accommodation which may result therefrom.

Territorial Indemnity to Holland in the Province of Limburg.

ART. III. In return for the cessions made in the preceding Article, there shall be assigned to His Majesty the King of the Netherlands, Grand Duke of Luxemburg, a Territorial Indemnity in the Province of Limburg.

Limits of Dutch Territory in Province of Limburg.

ART. IV. In execution of that part of Article I which relates to the Province of Limburg, and in consequence of the cessions which His Majesty the King of the Netherlands, Grand Duke of Luxemburg, makes in Article II, His said Majesty shall possess, either to be held by him in his character of Grand Duke of Luxemburg, or for the purpose of being united to Holland, those Territories, the limits of which are hereinafter described.

1st. On the right bank of the Meuse: to the old Dutch *enclaves* upon the said bank in the Province of Limburg, shall be united those districts of the said Province upon the same bank, which did not belong to the States General in 1790; in such wise that the whole of that part of the present Province of Limburg, situated upon the right bank of the Meuse, and comprised between that River on the west, the Frontier of the Prussian Territory on the east, the present Frontier of the province of Liège on the south, and Dutch Guelderland on the north, shall henceforth belong to His Majesty the King of the Netherlands, either to be held by him in his character of Grand Duke of Luxemburg, or in order to be united to Holland.

2nd. On the left bank of the Meuse: commencing from the southernmost point of the Dutch Province of North Brabant, there shall be drawn, according to the annexed Map, a line which shall terminate on the Meuse above Wessem, between that place and Stevenswaardt, at the point where the Frontiers of the present Arrondissements of Ruremonde and Maestricht meet, on the left bank of the Meuse; in such manner that Bergerot, Stamproy, Neer-Itteren, Ittervoordt, and Thorn, with their districts, as well as all the other places situated to the north of this line, shall form part of the Dutch Territory.

The old Dutch *enclaves* in the province of Limburg, upon the left bank of the Meuse, shall belong to Belgium, with the exception of the town of Maestricht, which, together with a radius of territory, extending 1,200 *toises* from the outer glacis of the fortress, on the said bank of this River, shall continue to be possessed, in full Sovereignty and Property, by His Majesty the King of the Netherlands.

King of the Netherlands to come to an Agreement with Germanic Confederation and Nassau.

ART. V. His Majesty the King of the Netherlands, Grand Duke of Luxemburg, shall come to an Agreement with the Germanic Confederation, and with the Agnates of the House of Nassau, as to the application of the stipulations contained in Articles III and IV, as well as upon all the arrangements which the said Articles may render necessary, either with the above-mentioned Agnates of the House of Nassau, or with the Germanic Confederation.

Reciprocal Renunciation of Territories.

Art. VI. In consideration of the territorial arrangements above stated, each of the two Parties renounces reciprocally and for ever, all pretension to the Territories, Towns, Fortresses, and Places situated within the limits of the possessions of the other Party, such as those limits are described in Articles I, II, and IV.

The said limits shall be marked out in conformity with those Articles, by Belgian and Dutch Commissioners of Demarcation, who shall meet as soon as possible in the town of Maestricht.

Belgium to form an Independent and Neutral State.

Art. VII. Belgium, within the limits specified in Articles I, II, and IV, shall form an Independent and perpetually Neutral State. It shall be bound to observe such Neutrality towards all other States.

Drainage of Waters of the Two Flanders.

Art. VIII. The drainage of the waters of the Two Flanders shall be regulated between Holland and Belgium, according to the stipulations on this subject contained in Article VI of the Definitive Treaty concluded between His Majesty the Emperor of Germany and the States-General, on the 8th of November, 1785, and in conformity with the said Article, Commissioners, to be named on either side, shall make arrangements for the application of the provisions contained in it.

Navigation of the Scheldt and the Meuse.

Art. IX. 1. The provisions of Articles CVIII to CXVII, inclusive, of the General Act of the Congress of Vienna, relative to the Free Navigation of navigable Rivers, shall be applied to those navigable Rivers which separate the Belgian and the Dutch territories, or which traverse them both.

2. So far as regards specially the Navigation of the Scheldt, and of its mouths, it is agreed, that the Pilotage and the Buoying of its channel, as well as the conservation of the channels of the Scheldt below Antwerp, shall be subject to a joint superintendence; and that this joint superintendence shall be exercised by Commissioners to be appointed for this purpose by the two Parties. Moderate Pilotage Dues shall be fixed by mutual agreement, and those dues shall be the same for the vessels of all nations.

In the meantime, and until these dues shall be fixed, no higher Pilotage Dues shall be levied than those which have been established by the Tariff of 1829, for the mouths of the Meuse from the High Sea to Helvoet, and from Helvoet to Rotterdam, in proportion to the distances. It shall be at the choice of every vessel proceeding from the High Sea to Belgium, or from Belgium to the High Sea, to take what pilot she pleases; and upon the same principle it shall be free for the two countries to establish along the whole course of the Scheldt and at its mouths, such Pilotage establishments as shall be deemed necessary for furnishing Pilots. Everything relating to these establishments shall be determined by the regulation to be concluded in conformity with 6 hereinafter following. These establishments shall be placed under the joint superintendence mentioned in the beginning of the present paragraph. The two Governments engage to preserve the navigable channels of the Scheldt, and of its mouths, and to place and maintain therein the necessary beacons and buoys, each for its own part of the River.

3. There shall be levied by the Government of the Netherlands, upon the navigation of the Scheldt and of its mouths, a single duty of 1fl. 50c. per ton, that is to say, 1fl. 12c. on vessels which, coming from the High Sea, shall ascend the Western Scheldt in order to proceed to Belgium by the Scheldt or by the Canal of Terneuze; and of 38c. per ton on vessels which, coming from Belgium by the Scheldt or by the Canal of Terneuze, shall descend the Western Scheldt in order to proceed to the High Sea. And in order that the said vessels may not be subject to any visit, nor to any delay or hindrance whatever within the Dutch waters, either in ascending the Scheldt from the High Sea, or in descending the Scheldt in order to reach the High Sea, it is agreed that the collection of the duty above mentioned shall take place by Dutch agents at Antwerp and at Terneuze. In the same manner, vessels arriving from the High Sea in order to proceed to Antwerp by the Western Scheldt, and coming from places suspected in regard to health, shall be at liberty to continue their course without hindrance or delay, accompanied by one health guard, and thus to proceed to the place of their destination. Vessels proceeding from Antwerp to Terneuze, and *vice versâ*, or carrying on in the River itself Coasting Trade or Fishery (in such manner as the exercise of the latter shall be regulated in pursuance of 6 hereinafter) shall not be subjected to any duty.

4. The branch of the Scheldt called the Eastern Scheldt not being in its present state available for the navigation from the High Sea to Antwerp and Terneuze, and *vice versâ*, but being used for the navigation between Antwerp and the Rhine, this eastern branch shall not be burthened, in any part of its course, with higher duties or tolls than those which are levied, according to the Tariffs of Mayence of the 31st of March, 1831 upon the navigation from Gorcum to the High Sea, in proportion to the distances.

5. It is also agreed that the navigation of the intermediate channels between the Scheldt and the Rhine, in order to proceed from Antwerp to the Rhine, and *vice versâ*, shall continue reciprocally free, and that it shall be subject only to moderate tolls, which shall be the same for the commerce of the two countries.

6. Commissioners on both sides shall meet at Antwerp in the space of one month, as well to determine the definitive and permanent amount of these tolls, as to agree upon a general regulation for the execution of the provisions of the present Article, and to include therein a provision for the exercise of the right of Fishing and of trading in fish, throughout the whole extent of the Scheldt, on a footing of perfect reciprocity and equality in favour of the subjects of the two countries.

7. In the mean time, and until the said regulations shall be prepared, the navigation of the Meuse and of its branches shall remain free to the commerce of the two countries, which shall adopt provisionally, in this respect, the Tariffs of the Convention signed at Mayence on the 31st March, 1831, for the Free Navigation of the Rhine, as well as the other provisions of that Convention, so far as they may be applicable to the said River.

8. If natural events or works of art should hereafter render impracticable the lines of navigation mentioned in the present Article, the Government of the Netherlands shall assign to Belgian navigation other lines equally safe, and equally good and commodious, instead of the said lines of navigation become impracticable.

Reciprocal use of Canals.

ART. X. The use of the Canals which traverse both countries shall continue to be free and common to the inhabitants of both. It is understood that they shall enjoy the use of the same reciprocally, and on equal conditions; and that on either side moderate duties only shall be levied upon the navigation of the said Canals.

Commercial communication through Maestricht and Sittardt.

ART. XI. The commercial communications through the town of Maestricht, and through Sittardt, shall remain entirely free, and shall not be impeded under any pretext whatsoever.

Turnpike Tolls on Roads.

The use of the roads which, passing through these towns, lead to the Frontiers of Germany, shall be subject only to the payment of moderate Turnpike Tolls, for the repair of the said roads, so that the transit commerce may not experience any obstacle thereby, and that by means of the Tolls above mentioned, these roads may be kept in good repair, and fit to afford facilities to that commerce.

Construction of New Road or New Canal by Belgium.

ART. XII. In the event of a new Road having been constructed, or a new Canal cut, in Belgium, terminating at the Meuse, opposite the Dutch canton of Sittardt, in that case Belgium shall be entitled to demand of Holland, who, on the other hand, shall not in such case refuse her consent, that the said Road, or the said Canal, shall be continued, according to the same plan, and entirely at the cost and charge of Belgium, through the canton of Sittardt, to the frontiers of Germany. This Road or Canal, which shall be used only as a commercial communication, shall be constructed, at the option of Holland, either by engineers and workmen whom Belgium shall obtain permission to employ for that purpose in the canton of Sittardt, or by engineers and workmen to be furnished by Holland, and who shall execute the works agreed upon at the expense of Belgium; the whole without any charge whatsoever to Holland, and without prejudice to her exclusive rights of Sovereignty over the Territory which may be traversed by the Road or Canal in question.

The two Parties shall fix, by mutual agreement, the amount and the mode of collection of the Duties and Tolls which should be levied upon the said Road or Canal.

Division of Public Debt.

ART. XIII. 1. From and after the 1st of January, 1839, Belgium, with reference to the division of the Public Debt of the Kingdom of the Netherlands, shall remain charged with the sum of 5,000,000 of Netherland florins of annual interest, the capital of which shall be transferred from the debit of the Great Book of Amsterdam, or from the debit of the General Treasury of the Kingdom of the Netherlands, to the debit of the Great Book of Belgium.

2. The capitals transferred, and the annuities inscribed upon the debit of the Great Book of Belgium, in consequence of the preceding paragraph, to the amount of the total sum of 5,000,000 Netherland florins of annual interest, shall be considered as forming part of the Belgian National Debt; and Belgium engages not to admit, either at present or in future, any distinction between this portion of her Public Debt arising from her union with Holland, and any other Belgian National Debt already created, or which may be created hereafter.

3. The payment of the above-mentioned sum of 5,000,000 Netherland florins of annual interest, shall take place regularly every 6 months, either at Brussels or at Antwerp, in ready money, without deduction of any kind whatsoever, either at present or in future.

4. In consideration of the creation of the said sum of 5,000,000 florins of annual interest, Belgium shall be released from all obligation

towards Holland, on account of the division of the Public Debt of the Kingdom of the Netherlands.

5. Commissioners to be named on both sides shall meet within the space of 15 days in the town of Utrecht, in order to proceed to the transfer of the capitals and annual interest which, upon the division of the Public Debt of the Kingdom of the Netherlands, are to pass to the charge of Belgium, up to the amount of 5,000,000 florins of annual interest.

They shall also proceed to deliver up the Archives, Maps, Plans, and other documents whatsoever which belong to Belgium, or which relate to her administration.

Port of Antwerp to be a Port of Commerce.

ART. XIV. The Port of Antwerp, in conformity with the stipulations of Article XV of the Treaty of Paris, of the 30th of May, 1814, shall continue to be solely a Port of Commerce.

Works of Public Utility to belong to Country in which they are situated.

ART. XV. Works of Public or Private utility, such as canals, roads, or others of a similar nature, constructed wholly or in part at the expense of the Kingdom of the Netherlands, shall belong, together with the advantages and charges thereunto attached, to the Country in which they are situated.

It is understood that the capitals borrowed for the construction of these works, and specifically charged thereupon, shall be comprised in the aforesaid charges, in so far as they may not yet have been repaid, and without giving rise to any claim on account of repayments already made.

Sequestrations in Belgium to be Removed.

ART. XVI. The Sequestrations which may have been imposed in Belgium, during the troubles, for political causes, on any Property or Hereditary Estates whatsoever, shall be taken off without delay, and the enjoyment of the Property and Estates above mentioned shall be immediately restored to the lawful owners thereof.

Liberty to Inhabitants and Proprietors to Transfer their Residences. Droit d'Aubaine et de Détraction abolished.

ART. XVII. In the two countries of which the separation takes place in consequence of the present Articles, inhabitants and proprietors, if they wish to transfer their residence from one country to the other, shall, during two years, be at liberty to dispose of their property, movable or immovable, of whatever nature the same may be, to sell it, and to carry away the produce of the sale, either in money or in any other shape, without hindrance, and without the payment of any duties other than those which are now in force in the two countries upon changes and transfers.

It is understaood that the collection of the *Droit d'Aubaine et de Détraction* upon the persons and property of Dutch in Belgium, and of Belgians in Holland, is abandoned, both now and for the future.

Character of a Subject with regard to Property.
ART. XVIII. The character of a subject of the two Governments, with regard to Property, shall be acknowledged and maintained.

Right of Persons holding Property in both Countries.
ART. XIX. The stipulations of Articles from XI to XXI, inclusive, of the Treaty concluded between Austria and Russia, on the 3rd of May, 1815, which forms an integral part of the General Act of the Congress of Vienna, stipulations relative to Persons who possess Property in both Countries, to the election of residence which they are required to make, to the rights which they shall exercise as subjects of either State, and to the relations of neighbourhood in Properties cut by the Frontiers, shall be applied to such Proprietors, as well as to such Properties, in Holland, in the Grand Duchy of Luxemburg, or in Belgium, as shall be found to come within the cases provided for by the aforesaid stipulations of the Acts of the Congress of Vienna. It is understood that mineral productions are comprised among the productions of the soil mentioned in Article XX of the Treaty of the 3rd of May, 1815, above referred to. The *Droits d'Aubaine et de Détraction*, being henceforth abolished, as between Holland, the Grand Duchy of Luxemburg, and Belgium, it is understood that such of the above-mentioned stipulations as may relate to those duties, shall be considered null and void in the 3 Countries.

Persons not to be molested on account of their Political Conduct.
ART. XX. No person in the territories which change domination shall be molested or disturbed in any manner whatever, on account of any part which he may have taken, directly or indirectly, in Political Events.

Payment of Pensions and Allowances.
ART. XXI. The Pensions and Allowances of expectants, of persons unemployed or retired, shall in future be paid, on either side, to all those individuals entitled thereto, both civil and military, conformably to the laws in force previous to the 1st November, 1830.

It is agreed that the above-mentioned Pensions and Allowances to persons born in the Territories which now constitute Belgium, shall remain at the charge of the Belgian Treasury; and the Pensions and Allowances of persons born in the Territories which now constitute the Kingdom of the Netherlands, shall be at the charge of the Netherland Treasury.

Claims of Belgians on Private Establishments.

ART. XXII. All Claims of Belgian subjects upon any Private Establishments, such as the Widows' Fund, and the fund known under the denomination of the *Fonds des Leges*, and of the chest of civil and military retired allowances, shall be examined by the Mixed Commission mentioned in Article XIII, and shall be determined according to the tenour of the regulations by which these funds or chests are governed.

Restoration of Securities.

The Securities furnished, as well as the payments made, by Belgian accountants, the judicial deposits and consignments, shall equally be restored to the parties entitled thereto, on the presentation of their proofs.

Claims called French Liquidations.

If, under the head of what are called *the French Liquidations*, any Belgian subjects should still be able to bring forward Claims to be inscribed, such Claims shall also be examined and settled by the said Commission.

Maintenance of Judgments, &c., in Limburg and Luxemburg.

ART. XXIII. All Judgments given in Civil and Commercial matters, all acts of the civil power, and all acts executed before a notary or other public officer under the Belgian administration, in those parts of Limburg and of the Grand Duchy of Luxemburg, of which His Majesty the King of the Netherlands, Grand Duke of Luxemburg, is to be replaced in possession, shall be maintained in full force and validity.

Evacuation of Territories, Towns, Fortresses, &c.

ART. XXIV. Immediately after the exchange of the Ratifications of the Treaty to be concluded between the two Parties, the necessary orders shall be transmitted to the Commanders of the respective Troops, for the evacuation of the Territories, Towns, Fortresses, and Places which change domination. The Civil Authorities thereof shall also, at the same time, receive the necessary orders for delivering over the said Territories, Towns, Fortresses, and Places, to the Commissioners who shall be appointed by both Parties for this purpose.

This evacuation and delivery shall be effected so as to be completed in the space of 15 days, or sooner if possible.

(L.S.) PALMERSTON.   (L.S.) DEDEL.
(L.S.) SENFFT.
(L.S.) II. SEBASTIANI.
(L.S.) BULOW.
(L.S.) POZZO DI BORGO.

[An Arreté of the Germanic Diet, accepting the incorporation of the Duchy of Limburg with the Territory of the Confederation, was signed on the 5th September, 1839.]

36

TREATY between Great Britain, Austria, France, Prussia, and Russia, on the one part, and Belgium on the other. Signed at London, 19th April, 1839.

Reference to Treaties of 15th November, 1831, and 19th April, 1839.

In the Name of the Most Holy and Indivisible Trinity.

HER Majesty the Queen of the United Kingdom of Great Britain and Ireland, His Majesty the Emperor of Austria, King of Hungary and Bohemia, His Majesty the King of the French, His Majesty the King of Prussia, and His Majesty the Emperor of All the Russias, taking into consideration, as well as His Majesty the King of the Belgians, their Treaty concluded at London on the 15th of November, 1831, as well as the Treaties signed this day, between their Majesties the Queen of the United Kingdom of Great Britain and Ireland, the Emperor of Austria, King of Hungary and Bohemia, the King of the French, the King of Prussia, and the Emperor of All the Russias, on the one part, and His Majesty the King of the Netherlands, Grand Duke of Luxemburg, on the other part, and between His Majesty the King of the Belgians and His said Majesty the King of the Netherlands, Grand Duke of Luxemburg, their said Majesties have named as their Plenipotentiaries, that is to say:—

Her Majesty the Queen of the United Kingdom of Great Britain and Ireland, the Right Honourable Henry John Viscount Palmerston, Baron Temple, a Peer of Ireland, a Member of Her Britannic Majesty's Most Honourable Privy Council, a Member of Parliament, and Her

Britannic Majesty's Principal Secretary of State for Foreign Affairs, &c.;

His Majesty the Emperor of Austria, King of Hungary and Bohemia, the Sieur Frederick Christian Louis, Count de Senfft-Pilsach, Chamberlain and Privy Councillor of His Imperial and Royal Apostolic Majesty, and his Envoy Extraordinary and Minister Plenipotentiary to His Majesty the King of the Netherlands, &c.;

His Majesty the King of the French, the Sieur Horace Francis Bastien, Count Sebastiani-Porta, a Lieutenant-General in his Armies, a Member of the Chamber of Deputies in France, his Ambassador Extraordinary and Minister Plenipotentiary to Her Britannic Majesty, &c.;

His Majesty the King of Prussia, the Sieur Henry William Baron de Bülow, his Chamberlain, Privy Councillor of Legation, Envoy Extraordinary and Minister Plenipotentiary to Her Britannic Majesty, &c.;

His Majesty the Emperor of All the Russias, the Sieur Charles Andrew, Count Pozzo di Borgo, a General of Infantry in his Armies, his Aide-de-Camp General, Ambassador Extraordinary and Minister Plenipotentiary to Her Britannic Majesty, &c.;

And His Majesty the King of the Belgians, the Sieur Sylvain Van de Weyer, his Envoy Extraordinary and Minister Plenipotentiary to Her Britannic Majesty, &c.;

Who, after having communicated to each other their Full Powers, found in good and due form, have agreed upon the following Articles:

Articles annexed to have same Force as the Treaty.   Guarantee of the 5 Powers.

ART. I. Her Majesty the Queen of the United Kingdom of Great Britain and Ireland, His Majesty the Emperor of Austria, King of Hungary and Bohemia, His Majesty the King of the French, His Majesty the King of Prussia, and His Majesty the Emperor of All the Russias, declare, that the Articles hereunto annexed, and forming the tenor of the Treaty concluded this day between His Majesty the King of the Belgians and His Majesty the King of the Netherlands, Grand Duke of Luxemburg, are considered as having the same force and validity as if they were textually inserted in the present Act, and that they are thus placed under the Guarantee of their said Majesties.

Treaty of 15th November, 1831, not obligatory upon High Contracting Parties.

ART. II. The Treaty of the 15th of November, 1831, between their Majesties the Queen of the United Kingdom of Great Britain and Ireland, the Emperor of Austria, King of Hungary and Bohemia, the King of the French, the King of Prussia, and the Emperor of All the

Russias, and His Majesty the King of the Belgians, is declared not be to obligatory upon the High Contracting Parties.

Ratifications.

ART. III. The present Treaty shall be ratified, and the Ratifications shall be exchanged at London at the expiration of 6 weeks, or sooner if possible. This exchange shall take place at the same time as that of the Ratifications of the Treaty between Belgium and Holland.

In witness whereof, the respective Plenipotentiaries have signed the present Treaty, and have affixed thereto the Seal of their Arms.

Done at London, the 19th day of April, in the year of Our Lord, 1839.

(L.S.) SYLVAIN VAN DE WEYER.

(L.S.) PALMERSTON.
(L.S.) SENFFT.
(L.S.) H. SEBASTIANI.
(L.S.) BULOW.
(L.S.) POZZO DI BORGO.

(ANNEX).—*The* 24 *Articles annexed were Word for Word the same as those Annexed to the Treaty between the* 5 *Powers and the King of the Netherlands.* (No. 35).

37

TREATY of Separation, between Belgium and the Netherlands. Signed at London, 19th April, 1839.

Reference to Treaties of 15th November, 1831; and 19th April, 1839.

In the Name of the Most Holy and Indivisible Trinity.

HIS Majesty the King of the Belgians, and His Majesty the King of the Netherlands, taking into consideration their Treaties concluded with the Courts of France, Great Britain, Prussia, and Russia, namely: by His Majesty the King of the Belgians, on the 15th November, 1831, and by His Majesty the King of the Netherlands, Grand Duke of Luxemburg, this day, their said Majesties have named as their Plenipotentiaries, that is to say:—

His Majesty the King of the Belgians, the Sieur Sylvain Van de Weyer, his Envoy Extraordinary and Minister Plenipotentiary to Her Britannic Majesty, &c.;

And His Majesty the King of the Netherlands, Grand Duke of Luxemburg, the Sieur Salomon Dedel, his Envoy Extraordinary and Minister Plenipotentiary to Her Britannic Majesty, &c.;

Who, after having communicated to each other their Full Powers, found in good and due form, have agreed upon the following Articles:—

ARTS. I to XXIV *were the same as those of the Treaty between Great Britain, &c., and the Netherlands, of 19th April, 1839 (No. 35).*

Peace and Friendship.

ART. XXV. After the Stipulations of the present Treaty, there shall be Peace and Friendship between His Majesty the King of the Belgians on the one part, and His Majesty the King of the Netherlands, Grand Duke of Luxemburg, on the other part, their heirs and successors, their respective States and Subjects.

Ratifications.

ART. XXVI. The present Treaty shall be ratified, and the Ratifications shall be exchanged at London, at the expiration of 6 weeks, or sooner if possible. This exchange shall take place at the same time as the Ratifications of the Treaty concluded this day between His Majesty the King of the Netherlands and their Majesties the Emperor of Austria, King of Hungary and Bohemia, the King of the French, the Queen of the United Kingdom of Great Britain and Ireland, the King of Prussia, and the Emperor of All the Russias.

In witness whereof, the respective Plenipotentiaries have signed the present Treaty, and have affixed thereto the Seal of their Arms.

Done at London, the 19th April, 1839.

(L.S.) DEDEL.

(L.S.) SYLVAIN VAN DER WEYER.

38

CONVENTION between Great Britain, Austria, Prussia and Russia, and Turkey, for the Pacification of the Levant. Signed at London, 15th July, 1840.

In the name of the Most Merciful God.

His Highness the Sultan having addressed himself to their Majesties the Queen of the United Kingdom of Great Britain and Ireland, the Emperor of Austria, King of Hungary and Bohemia, the King of Prussia, and the Emperor of All the Russias, to ask their support and assistance in the difficulties in which he finds himself placed by reason of the hostile proceedings of Mehemet Ali, Pasha of Egypt,—difficulties which threaten with danger the Integrity of the Ottoman Empire, and the Independence of the Sultan's Throne,—their said Majesties, moved by the sincere friendship which subsists between them and the Sultan; animated by the desire of maintaining the Integrity and Independence of the Ottoman Empire as a security for the Peace of Europe; faithful to the engagement which they contracted by the Collective Note presented to the Porte by their Representatives at Constantinople, on the 27th of July, 1839;[1] and desirous, moreover, to prevent the effusion of blood which would be occasioned by a continuance of the hostilities which have recently broken out in Syria between the authorities of the Pasha of Egypt and the subjects of the Sultan; their said Majesties and His Highness the Sultan have resolved, for the aforesaid purposes, to conclude together a Convention, and they have therefore named as their Plenipotentiaries, that is to say:

Her Majesty the Queen of the United Kingdom of Great Britain and Ireland, the Right Honourable Henry John, Viscount Palmerston, Baron Temple, a Peer of Ireland, a Member of Her Britannic Majesty's Most Honourable Privy Council, .Knight Grand Cross of the Most Honourable Order of the Bath, a Member of Parliament, and her Principal Secretary of State for Foreign Affairs;

His Majesty the Emperor of Austria, King of Hungary and Bohemia, the Sieur Philip, Baron de Neumann, his Aulick Councillor, and his Plenipotentiary to Her Britannic Majesty, &c.;

His Majesty the King of Prussia, the Sieur Henry William, Baron de Bülow, his Chamberlain, Actual Privy Councillor, Envoy Extraordinary and Minister Plenipotentiary to Her Britannic Majesty, &c.;

His Majesty the Emperor of All the Russias, the Sieur Philip, Baron de Brunnow, his Privy Councillor, Envoy Extraordinary and Minister Plenipotentiary to Her Britannic Majesty, &c.;

And His Majesty the Most Nobel, Most Powerful, and Most Magnificent Sultan Abdul-Medjid, Emperor of the Ottomans, Chekib Effendi, decorated with the Nichan Iftihar of the first class, Beylikdgi of the Imperial Divan, Honorary Councillor of the Department for Foreign Affairs, his Ambassador Extraordinary to Her Britannic Majesty;

---

[1] The Undersigned have this morning received instructions from their respective Governments, in virtue of which they have the honour to inform the Sublime Porte that the 5 Great Powers have come to an understanding on the Eastern Question, and to prevail upon her to suspend all definitive determination without their co-operation.

Constantinople, 27th July, 1839.

BARON DE STURMER.	BARON ROUSSIN.
PONSONBY.	COMTE DE KŒNIGSMARCK.
A. BOUTENEFF.	

Who, having reciprocally communicated to each other their Full Powers, found to be in good and due form, have agreed upon and signed the following Articles:

Arrangement in favour of Mehemet Ali.

ART. I. His Highness the Sultan having come to an agreement with their Majesties the Queen of the United Kingdom of Great Britain and Ireland, the Emperor of Austria, King of Hungary and Bohemia, the King of Prussia, and the Emperor of All the Russias, as to the conditions of the arrangement which it is the intention of His Highness to grant to Mehemet Ali, conditions which are specified in the Separate Act hereunto annexed; their Majesties engage to act in perfect accord, and to unite their efforts in order to determine Mehemet Ali to conform to that arrangement; each of the High Contracting Parties reserving to itself to co-operate for that purpose, according to the means of action which each may have at his disposal.

Measures to be adopted in case of refusal by Mehemet Ali.   Naval Assistance to Turkey by Great Britain and Austria.

ART. II. If the Pasha of Egypt should refuse to accept the above-mentioned arrangement, which will be communicated to him by the Sultan, with the concurrence of their aforesaid Majesties; their Majesties engage to take, at the request of the Sultan, measures concerted and settled between them, in order to carry that arrangement into effect. In the meanwhile, the Sultan having requested his said Allies to unite with him in order to assist him to cut off the communication by sea between Egypt and Syria, and to prevent the transport of troops, horses, arms, and warlike stores of all kinds, from the one province to the other; their Majesties the Queen of the United Kingdom of Great Britain and Ireland, and the Emperor of Austria, King of Hungary and Bohemia, engage to give immediately, to that effect, the necessary orders to their naval Commanders in the Mediterranean. Their said Majesties further engage that the naval Commanders of their squadrons shall, according to the means at their command, afford, in the name of the Alliance, all the support and assistance in their power to those subjects of the Sultan who may manifest their fidelity and allegiance to their Sovereign.

Defence of Constantinople by Allied Powers against Mehemet Ali.

ART. III. If Mehemet Ali, after having refused to submit to the conditions of the arrangements above mentioned, should direct his land or sea forces against Constantinople, the High Contracting Parties, upon the express demand of the Sultan, addressed to their Representatives at Constantinople, agree, in such case, to comply with the request of that

Sovereign, and to provide for the defence of his Throne by means of a co-operation agreed upon by mutual consent, for the purpose of placing the two Straits of the Bosphorus and Dardanelles, as well as the capital of the Ottoman Empire, in security against all aggression.

Allied Forces to withdraw at request of Sultan.

It is further agreed that the forces which, in virtue of such concert may be sent as aforesaid, shall there remain so employed as long as their presence shall be required by the Sultan; and when His Highness shall deem their presence no longer necessary, the said forces shall simultaneously withdraw, and shall return to the Black Sea and to the Mediterranean respectively.

Entrance of Straits of Dardanelles and Bosphorus for Defence of Constantinople exceptional. Rule prohibiting Foreign Ships of War to enter Dardanelles and Bosphorus to be maintained.

ART. IV. It is, however, expressly understood that the co-operation mentioned in the preceding Article, and destined to place the Straits of the Dardanelles and of the Bosphorus, and the Ottoman capital, under the temporary safeguard of the High Contracting Parties against all aggression of Mehemet Ali, shall be considered only as a measure of exception adopted at the express demand of the Sultan, and solely for his defence in the single case above mentioned; but it is agreed, that such measure shall not derogate in any degree from the ancient rule of the Ottoman Empire, in virtue of which it has in all times been prohibited for Ships of War of Foreign Powers to enter the Straits of the Dardanelles and of the Bosphorus. And the Sultan, on the one hand, hereby declares that excepting the contingency above mentioned, it is his firm resolution to maintain in future this principle invariably established as the ancient rule of his Empire, and as long as the Porte is at Peace, to admit no Foreign Ship of War into the Straits of the Bosphorus and of the Dardanelles; on the other hand, their Majesties the Queen of the United Kingdom of Great Britain and Ireland, the Emperor of Austria, King of Hungary and Bohemia, the King of Prussia, and the Emperor of All the Russias, engage to respect this determination of the Sultan, and to conform to the above-mentioned principle.

Ratifications.

The present Convention shall be ratified, and the Ratifications thereof shall be exchanged at London at the expiration of two months, or sooner if possible.

In witness whereof the respective Plenipotentiaries have signed the same, and have affixed thereto the Seals of their Arms.

Done at London, the 15th day of July, in the year of Our Lord, 1840.
(L.S.) PALMERSTON. (L.S.) CHEKIB.
(L.S.) NEUMANN.
(L.S.) BULOW.
(L.S.) BRUNNOW.

(ANNEX.)—*Separate Act to the Convention of 15th July,*
1840.

His Highness the Sultan intends to grant, and to cause to be notified to Mehemet Ali, the conditions of the Arrangement hereinafter detailed:

Grant of Pashalic of Egypt to Mehemet Ali and his descendants. Administration of Southern Syria by Mehemet Ali during his life. Title of Pasha of Acre.

1. His Highness promises to grant to Mehemet Ali, for himself and for his descendants in the direct line, the administration of the Pashalic of Egypt; and His Highness promises, moreover, to grant to Mehemet Ali, for his life, with the title of Pasha of Acre, and with the command of the Fortress of St. John of Acre, the administration of the southern part of Syria, the limits of which shall be determined by the following line of demarcation:

Limits of Southern Syria to be administered by Mehemet Ali.

This line, beginning at Cape Ras-el-Nakhora, on the coast of the Mediterranean, shall extend direct from thence as far as the mouth of the River Seizaban, at the northern extremity of the Lake of Tiberias; it shall pass along the western shore of that Lake; it shall follow the right bank of the River Jordan, and the western shore of the Dead Sea; from thence it shall extend straight to the Red Sea, which it shall strike at the northern point of the Gulf of Akaba; and from thence it shall follow the western shore of the Gulf of Akaba, and the eastern shore of the Gulf of Suez, as far as Suez.

Conditions imposed on Mehemet Ali. Withdrawal of Egyptian Troops from Arabia, Candia, &c.

The Sultan, however, in making these offers, attaches thereto the condition, that Mehemet Ali shall accept them within the space of 10 days after communication thereof shall have been made to him at Alexandria, by an agent of His Highness; and that Mehemet Ali shall, at the same time, place in the hands of that agent the necessary instructions to the Commanders of his sea and land forces, to withdraw immediately from Arabia, and from all the Holy Cities which are therein situated; from the Island of Candia; from the district of Adana; and from all other parts of the Ottoman Empire which are not comprised within the limits of Egypt, and within those of the Pashalic of Acre, as above defined.

Time within which Mehemet Ali is to accept Arrangement.

2. If within the space of 10 days, fixed as above, Mehemet Ali should not accept the above-mentioned arrangement, the Sultan will then withdraw the offer of the life administration of the Pashalic of Acre; but His Highness will still consent to grant to Mehemet Ali, for himself and for his descendants in the direct line, the administration of the Pashalic of Egypt, provided such offer be accepted within the space of the 10 days next following, that is to say, within a period of 20 days, to be reckoned from the day on which the communication shall have been made to him; and provided that in this case also, he places in the hands of the agent of the Sultan, the necessary instructions to his military and naval commanders to withdraw immediately within the limits, and into the ports of the Pashalic of Egypt.

Tribute to be paid to the Sultan.

3. The annual Tribute to be paid to the Sultan by Mehemet Ali, shall be proportioned to the greater or less amount of territory of which the latter may obtain the administration, according as he accepts the first or the second alternative.

Mehemet Ali to deliver up Turkish Fleet.

4. It is, moreover, expressly understood that, in the first as in the second alternative, Mehemet Ali (before the expiration of the specified period of 10 or of 20 days), shall be bound to deliver up the Turkish fleet, with the whole of its crews and equipments, into the hands of the Turkish agent who shall be charged to receive the same. The Commanders of the allied squadrons shall be present at such delivery.

Maintenance of Ottoman Fleet by Mehemet Ali.

It is understood, that in no case can Mehemet Ali carry to account, or deduct from the Tribute to be paid to the Sultan, the expenses which he has incurred in the maintenance of the Ottoman fleet, during any part of the time it shall have remained in the ports of Egypt.

Treaties and Laws of Ottoman Empire applicable to Egypt and Syria. Taxes and Imposts to be collected by Pasha of Egypt. Civil and Military Expenses to be defrayed by the Pasha.

5. All the Treaties, and all the Laws of the Ottoman Empire, shall be

applicable to Egypt, and to the Pashalic of Acre, such as it has been above defined, in the same manner as to every other part of the Ottoman Empire. But the Sultan consents, that on condition of the regular payment of the Tribute above mentioned, Mehemet Ali and his descendants shall collect, in the name of the Sultan, and as the delegate of His Highness, within the provinces the administration of which shall be confided to them, the taxes and imposts legally established. It is moreover understood that, in consideration of the receipt of the aforesaid taxes and imposts, Mehemet Ali and his descendants shall defray all the expenses of the civil and military administration of the said provinces.

Military and Naval Forces to be maintained for Service of the State.

6. The Military and Naval Forces which may be maintained by the Pasha of Egypt and Acre, forming part of the forces of the Ottoman Empire, shall always be considered as maintained for the service of the State.

Offers to be withdrawn if not accepted within 20 Days.

7. If, at the expiration of the period of 20 days after the communication shall have been made to him (according to the stipulation of 2), Mehemet Ali shall not accede to the proposed arrangement, and shall not accept the hereditary Pashalic of Egypt, the Sultan will consider himself at liberty to withdraw that offer, and to follow, in consequence, such ulterior course as his own interests and the counsels of his Allies may suggest to him.

Separate Act to form part of Convention of 15th July, 1840.

8. The present Separate Act shall have the same force and validity as if it were inserted, word for word, in the Convention of this date. It shall be ratified, and the Ratifications thereof shall be exchanged at London at the same time as those of the said Convention.

In witness whereof the respective Plenipotentiaries have signed the same, and have affixed thereto the Seals of their Arms.

Done at London, the 15th day of July, in the year of Our Lord, 1840.

(L.S.) PALMERSTON.   (L.S.) CHEKIB.

(L.S.) NEUMANN.

(L.S.) BULOW.

(L.S.) BRUNNOW.

39

CONVENTION between Great Britain, Austria, France, Prussia, Russia, and Turkey, respecting the Straits of the Dardanelles and of the Bosphorus. Signed at London, 13th July, 1841.

In the Name of the Most Merciful God.

THEIR Majesties the Queen of the United Kingdom of Great Britain and Ireland, the Emperor of Austria, King of Hungary and Bohemia, the King of the French, the King of Prussia, and the Emperor of All the Russias, being persuaded that their union and their agreement offer to Europe the most certain pledge for the preservation of the general Peace, the constant object of their solicitude; and their said Majesties being desirous of testifying this agreement, by giving to the Sultan a manifest proof of the respect which they entertain for the inviolability of his sovereign rights, as well as of their sincere desire to see consolidated the repose of his Empire; their said Majesties have resolved to comply with the invitation of His Highness the Sultan, in order to record in common, by a formal Act, their unanimous determination to conform to the ancient rule of the Ottoman Empire, according to which the passage of the Straits of the Dardanelles and of the Bosphorus is always to be closed to Foreign Ships of War, so long as the Porte is at peace.

Their said Majesties, on the one part, and His Highness the Sultan, on the other part, having resolved to conclude between them a Convention on this subject, have named for that purpose as their Plenipotentiaries, that is to say :—

Her Majesty the Queen of the United Kingdom of Great Britain and Ireland, the Right Honourable Henry John, Viscount Palmerston, Baron Temple, a Peer of Ireland, a Member of Her Britannic Majesty's Most Honourable Privy Council, a Member of the Parliament of the United Kingdom, and Her Britannic Majesty's Principal Secretary of State for Foreign Affairs, &c. ;

His Majesty the Emperor of Austria, King of Hungary and Bohemia, the Sieur Paul, Prince Esterhazy of Galantha, Count of Edelstett, Chamberlain, Actual Privy Councillor of His Majesty the Emperor of Austria, and his Ambassador Extraordinary and Plenipotentiary to Her Britannic Majesty, &c. ; and the Sieur Philip, Baron de Neumann, Aulick Councillor, and his Plenipotentiary to Her Britannic Majesty, &c. ;

His Majesty the King of the French, the Sieur Francis Adolphus,

Baron de Bourqueney, Master of Requests in his Council of State, his Chargé d'Affaires and Plenipotentiary at London, &c. ;

His Majesty the King of Prussia, the Sieur Henry William, Baron de Bülow, his Chamberlain, Actual Privy Councillor, Envoy Extraordinary and Minister Plenipotentiary to Her Britannic Majesty, &c. ;

His Majesty the Emperor of All the Russias, the Sieur Philip, Baron de Brunnow, his Privy Councillor, Envoy Extraordinary and Minister Plenipotentiary to Her Britannic Majesty, &c. ;

And His Majesty the Most Majestic, Most Powerful, and Most Magnificent Sultan Abdul Medjid, Emperor of the Ottomans, Chekib Effendi, Beylikdgi of the Imperial Divan, Honorary Councillor of the Department for Foreign Affairs, his Ambassador Extraordinary to Her Britannic Majesty, &c. ;

Who, having reciprocally communicated to each other their Full Powers, found to be in good and due form, have agreed upon and signed the following Articles :

Closing of Straits of Dardanelles and Bosphorus to Foreign Ships of War in time of Peace.

ART. I. His Highness the Sultan, on the one part, declares that he is firmly resolved to maintain for the future the principle invariably established as the ancient rule of his Empire, and in virtue of which it has at all times been prohibited for the Ships of War of Foreign Powers to enter the Straits of the Dardanelles and of the Bosphorus; and that, so long as the Porte is at Peace, His Highness will admit no Foreign Ship of War into the said Straits.

And their Majesties the Queen of the United Kingdom of Great Britain and Ireland, the Emperor of Austria, King of Hungary and Bohemia, the King of the French, the King of Prussia, and the Emperor of All the Russias, on the other part, engage to respect this determination of the Sultan, and to conform themselves to the principle above declared.

Firmans to be issued for Vessels under Flag of War used by Foreign Missions.

ART. II. It is understood that in recording the inviolability of the ancient rule of the Ottoman Empire mentioned in the preceding Article, the Sultan reserves to himself, as in past times, to deliver Firmans of passage for light Vessels under Flag of War, which shall be employed as is usual in the service of the Missions of Foreign Powers.

Invitation to Foreign Powers to accede to Convention.

ART. III. His Highness the Sultan reserves to himself to communicate the present Convention to all the Powers with whom the Sublime Porte is in relations of friendship, inviting them to accede thereto.

Ratifications.

ART. IV. The present Convention shall be ratified, and the Ratifications thereof shall be exchanged at London at the expiration of two months, or sooner if possible.

In witness whereof the respective Plenipotentiaries have signed the same, and have affixed thereto the Seals of their Arms.

Done at London, the 13th day of July, in the year of Our Lord, 1841.

(L.S.) PALMERSTON.   (L.S.) CHEKIB.
(L.S.) ESTERHAZY.
(L.S.) NEUMANN.
(L.S.) BOURQUENEY.
(L.S.) BULOW.
(L.S.) BRUNNOW.

40

CONVENTION BETWEEN GREAT BRITAIN AND THE USA as to boundaries, suppression of slave trade, and extradition. (Webster-Ashburton Treaty.) Concluded 9th August, 1842. Ratifications exchanged 13th October, 1842.

Whereas certain portions of the line of boundary between the United States of America and the British dominions of North America, described in the second article of the treaty of peace of 1783, have not yet been ascertained and determined, notwithstanding the repeated attempts which have been heretofore made for that purpose; and whereas it is now thought to be for the interest of both parties, that, avoiding further discussion of their respective rights, arising in this respect under the said treaty, they should agree on a conventional line in said portions of the said boundary, such as may be convenient to both parties, with such equivalents and compensations as are deemed just and reasonable; and whereas, by the treaty concluded at Ghent on the 24th day of December, 1814, between the United States and His Britannic Majesty, an article was agreed to and inserted of the following tenor, vizt: "Art. 10. Whereas the traffic in slaves is irreconcilable with the principles of humanity and justice; and whereas both His Majesty and the United

States are desirous of continuing their efforts to promote its entire abolition, it is hereby agreed that both the contracting parties shall use their best endeavours to accomplish so desirable an object;" and whereas, notwithstanding the laws which have at various times been passed by the two Governments, and the efforts made to suppress it, that criminal traffic is still prosecuted and carried on; and whereas the United States of America and Her Majesty the Queen of the United Kingdom of Great Britain and Ireland are determined that, so far as may be in their power, it shall be effectually abolished; and whereas it is found expedient, for the better administration of justice and the prevention of crime within the territories and jurisdiction of the two parties respectively, that persons committing the crimes hereinafter enumerated, and being fugitives from justice, should, under certain circumstances, be reciprocally delivered up: The United States of America and Her Britannic Majesty, having resolved to treat on these several subjects, have for that purpose appointed their respective Plenipotentiaries to negotiate and conclude a treaty, that is to say:

The President of the United States has, on his part, furnished with full powers Daniel Webster, Secretary of State of the United States, and Her Majesty the Queen of the United Kingdom of Great Britain and Ireland has, on her part, appointed the Right Honourable Alexander Lord Ashburton, a peer of the said United Kingdom, a member of Her Majesty's Most Honourable Privy Council, and Her Majesty's Minister Plenipotentiary on a special mission to the United States;

Who, after a reciprocal communication of their respective full powers, have agreed to and signed the following articles:

ART. I. It is hereby agreed and declared that the line of boundary shall be as follows: Beginning at the monument at the source of the river St. Croix as designated and agreed to by the Commissioners under the fifth article of the treaty of 1794, between the Governments of the United States and Great Britain; thence, north, following the exploring line run and marked by the surveyors of the two Governments in the years 1817 and 1818, under the fifth article of the treaty of Ghent, to its intersection with the river St. John, and to the middle of the channel thereof; thence, up the middle of the main channel of the said river St. John, to the mouth of the river St. Francis, thence, up the middle of the channel of the said river St. Francis, and of the lakes through which it flows, to the outlet of the Lake Pohenagamook; thence, southwesterly, in a straight line, to a point on the northwest branch of the river St. John, which point shall be ten miles distant from the main branch of the St. John, in a straight line, and in the nearest direction; but if the said point shall be found to be less than seven miles from the nearest point of the summit or crest of the highlands that divide those rivers which empty themselves into the river Saint Lawrence from those which fall into the river Saint John, then the said point shall be made to recede down the said northwest branch of the river St. John, to a point seven miles in a straight line from the said summit or crest; thence, in a straight line, in a course about south, eight degrees west, to the point where the parallel of latitude of 46° 25' north intersects the southwest branch of the St. John's; thence, southerly, by the said branch, to the source thereof in the highlands at the Metjarmette portage; thence, down along the said highlands which divide the waters which empty themselves into the river Saint Lawrence from those which fall into the Atlantic Ocean, to the head of Hall's Stream; thence, down the middle of said stream, till the line thus run intersects the old line of boundary surveyed and marked by Valentine and Collins, previously to the year 1774, as the 45th degree of north latitude, and which has been known and understood to be the line of actual division between the States of New York and Vermont on one side, and the British province of Canada on the other; and from said point of intersection, west, along the said dividing line, as heretofore known and understood, to the Iroquois or St. Lawrence River.

Art. II. It is moreover agreed, that from the place where the joint Commissioners terminated their labours under the sixth article of the treaty of Ghent, to wit, at a point in the Neebish Channel, near Muddy Lake, the line shall run into and along the ship-channel between Saint Joseph and St. Tammany Islands, to the division of the channel at or near the head of St. Joseph's Island; thence, turning eastwardly and northwardly around the lower end of St. George's or Sugar Island, and following the middle of the channel which divides St. George's from St. Joseph's Island; thence up the east Neebish Channel, nearest to St. George's Island, through the middle of Lake George; thence, west of Jonas' Island, into St. Mary's River, to a point in the middle of that river, about one mile above St. George's or Sugar Island, so as to appropriate and assign the said island to the United States; thence, adopting the line traced on the maps by the Commissioners, thro' the river St. Mary and Lake Superior, to a point north of Ile Royale, in said lake, one hundred yards to the north and east of Ile Chapeau, which last-mentioned island lies near the northeastern point of Ile Royale, where the line marked by the Commissioners terminates; and from the last-mentioned point, southwesterly, through the middle of the sound between Ile Royale and the northwestern main land, to the mouth of Pigeon River, and up the said river, to and through the north and south Fowl Lakes, to the lakes of the height of land between Lake Superior and the Lake of the Woods; thence, along the water communication to Lake Saisaginaga, and through that lake; thence, to and through

Cypress Lake, Lac du Bois Blanc, Lac la Croix, Little Vermillion Lake, and Lake Namecan and through the several smaller lakes, straits, or streams, connecting the lakes here mentioned, to that point in Lac la Pluie, or Rainy Lake, at the Chaudière Falls, from which the Commissioners traced the line to the most northwestern point of the Lake of the Woods; thence, along the said line, to the said most northwestern point, being in latitude 49° 23' 55" north, and in longitude 95° 14' 38" west from the observatory at Greenwich; thence, according to existing treaties, due south to its intersection with the 49th parallel of north latitude, and along that parallel to the Rocky Mountains. It being understood that all the water communications and all the usual portages along the line from Lake Superior to the Lake of the Woods, and also Grand Portage, from the shore of Lake Superior to the Pigeon River, as now actually used, shall be free and open to the use of the citizens and subjects of both countries.

ARTICLE III. In order to promote the interests and encourage the industry of all the inhabitants of the countries watered by the river St. John and its tributaries, whether living within the State of Maine or the province of New Brunswick, it is agreed that, where, by the provisions of the present treaty, the river St. John is declared to be the line of boundary, the navigation of the said river shall be free and open to both parties, and shall in no way be obstructed by either; that all the produce of the forest, in logs, lumber, timber, boards, staves, or shingles, or of agriculture, not being manufactured, grown on any of those parts of the State of Maine watered by the river St. John, or by its tributaries, of which fact reasonable evidence shall, if required, be produced, shall have free access into and through the said river and its said tributaries, having their source within the State of Maine, to and from the sea-port at the mouth of the said river St. John's, and to and round the falls of the said river, either by boats, rafts, or other conveyance; that when within the province of New Brunswick, the said produce shall be dealt with as if it were the produce of the said province; that, in like manner, the inhabitants of the territory of the upper St. John, determined by this treaty to belong to Her Britannic Majesty, shall have free access to and through the river, for their produce, in those parts where the said river runs wholly through the State of Maine; Provided, always, that this agreement shall give no right to either party to interfere with any regulations not inconsistent with the terms of this treaty which the governments, respectively, of Maine or of New Brunswick may make respecting the navigation of the said river, where both banks thereof shall belong to the same party.

ARTICLE IV. All grants of land heretofore made by either party, within the limits of the territory which by this treaty falls within the dominions of the other party, shall be held valid, ratified, and confirmed to the persons in possession under such grants, to the same extent as if such territory had by this treaty fallen within the dominions of the party by whom such grants were made; and all equitable possessory claims, arising from a possession and improvement of any lot or parcel of land by the person actually in possession, or by those under whom such person claims, for more than six years before the date of this treaty, shall, in like manner, be deemed valid, and be confirmed and quieted by a release to the person entitled thereto, of the title to such lot or parcel of land, so described as best to include the improvements made thereon; and in all other respects the two contracting parties agree to deal upon the most liberal principles of equity with the settlers actually dwelling upon the territory falling to them, respectively, which has heretofore been in dispute between them.

ARTICLE V. Whereas in the course of the controversy respecting the disputed territory on the northeastern boundary, some moneys have been received by the authorities of Her Britannic Majesty's province of New Brunswick, with the intention of preventing depredations on the forests of the said territory, which moneys were to be carried to a fund called the " disputed territory fund," the proceeds whereof it was agreed should be hereafter paid over to the parties interested, in the proportions to be determined by a final settlement of boundaries, it is hereby agreed that a correct account of all receipts and payments on the said fund shall be delivered to the Government of the United States within six months after the ratification of this treaty; and the proportion of the amount due thereon to the States of Maine and Massachusetts, and any bonds or securities appertaining thereto shall be paid and delivered over to the Government of the United States; and the Government of the United States agrees to receive for the use of, and pay over to, the States of Maine and Massachusetts, their respective portions of said fund, and further, to pay and satisfy said States, respectively, for all claims for expenses incurred by them in protecting the said heretofore disputed territory and making a survey thereof in 1838; the Government of the United States agreeing with the States of Maine and Massachusetts to pay them the further sum of three hundred thousand dollars, in equal moieties, on account of their assent to the line of boundary described in this treaty, and in consideration of the conditions and equivalents received therefor from the Government of Her Britannic Majesty.

ARTICLE VI. It is furthermore understood and agreed that, for the purpose of running and tracing those parts of the line between the source of the St. Croix and the St. Lawrence River which will require to be run and ascertained, and for marking the residue of said line by proper monuments on the land, two Commissioners shall be appointed, one by the President of the United States, by and with the advice and consent of the Senate thereof, and one by Her Britannic Majesty; and the said Commissioners shall meet at Bangor, in the State of Maine, on the first day of May next, or as soon thereafter as may be, and shall proceed to mark the line above described, from the source of the St. Croix to the river St. John; and shall trace on proper maps the dividing-line along said river and along the river St. Francis to the outlet of the Lake Pohenagamook; and from the outlet of the said lake they shall ascertain, fix, and mark, by proper and durable monuments on the land, the line described in the first article of this treaty; and the said Commissioners shall make to each of their respective Governments a joint report or declaration, under their hands and seals, designating such line of boundary, and shall accompany such report or declaration with maps, certified by them to be true maps of the new boundary.

ARTICLE VII. It is further agreed that the channels in the river St. Lawrence on both sides of the Long Sault Islands and of Barnhart Island, the channels in the river Detroit on both sides of the island Bois Blanc, and between that island and both the American and Canadian shores, and all the several channels and passages between the various islands lying near the junction of the river St. Clair with the lake of that name, shall be equally free and open to the ships, vessels, and boats of both parties.

ARTICLE VIII. The parties mutually stipulate that each shall prepare, equip, and maintain in service on the coast of Africa a sufficient and adequate squadron or naval force of vessels of suitable numbers and descriptions, to carry in all not less than eighty guns, to enforce, separately and respectively, the laws, rights, and obligations of each of the two countries for the suppression of the slave-trade, the said squadrons to be independent of each other, but the two Governments stipulating, nevertheless, to give such orders to the officers commanding their respective forces as shall enable them most effectively to act in concert and co-operation, upon mutual consultation, as exigencies may arise, for the attainment of the true object of this article, copies of all such orders to be communicated by each Government to the other, respectively.

ARTICLE IX. Whereas, notwithstanding all efforts which may be made on the coast of Africa for suppressing the slave-trade, the facilities for carrying on that traffic and avoiding the vigilance of cruisers, by the fraudulent use of flags and other means, are so great, and the temptations for pursuing it, while a market can be found for slaves, so strong, as that the desired result may be long delayed unless all markets be shut against the purchase of African negroes, the parties to this treaty agree that they will unite in all becoming representations and remonstrances with any and all Powers within whose dominions such markets are allowed to exist, and that they will urge upon all such Powers the propriety and duty of closing such markets effectually, at once and forever.

ARTICLE X. It is agreed that the United States and Her Britannic Majesty shall, upon mutual requisitions by them, or their Ministers, officers, or authorities, respectively made, deliver up to justice all persons who, being charged with the crime of murder, or assault with intent to commit murder, or piracy, or arson, or robbery, or forgery, or the utterance of forged paper, committed within the jurisdiction of either, shall seek an asylum or shall be found within the territories of the other: Provided, that this shall only be done upon such evidence of criminality as, according to the laws of the place where the fugitive or person so charged shall be found, would justify his apprehension and commitment for trial if the crime or offence had there been committed; and the respective judges and other magistrates of the two Governments shall have power, jurisdiction, and authority, upon complaint made under oath, to issue a warrant for the apprehension of the fugutive or person so charged, that he may be brought before such judges or other magistrates, respectively, to the end that the evidence of criminality may be heard and considered; and if, on such hearing, the evidence be deemed sufficient to sustain the charge, it shall be the duty of the examining judge or magistrate to certify the same to the proper executive authority, that a warrant may issue for the surrender of such fugitive. The expense of such apprehension and delivery shall be borne and defrayed by the party who makes the requisition and receives the fugitive.

ARTICLE XI. The eighth article of this treaty shall be in force for five years from the date of the exchange of the ratifications, and afterwards until one or the other party shall signify a wish to terminate it. The tenth article shall continue in force until one or the other of the parties shall signify its wish to terminate it, and no longer.

ARTICLE XII. The present treaty shall be duly ratified, and the mutual exchange of ratifications shall take place in London, within six months from the date hereof, or earlier if possible.

In faith whereof we, the respective Plenipotentiaries, have signed this treaty and have hereunto affixed our seals.

Done in duplicate at Washington, the ninth day of August, anno Domini one thousand eight hundred and forty-two.

DANL. WEBSTER.
ASHBURTON.

41   TREATY OF NANKING

TREATY of Peace, Friendship, Commerce, Indemnity, &c., between Great Britain and China. Signed at Nanking, 29th August, 1842. Ratifications exchanged at Hong Kong, 26th June, 1843.

HER Majesty the Queen of the United Kingdom of Great Britain and Ireland, and His Majesty the Emperor of China, being desirous of putting an end to the misunderstandings and consequent hostilities which have arisen between the two countries, have resolved to conclude a Treaty for that purpose, and have therefore named as their Plenipotentiaries, that is to say:—   o

Her Majesty the Queen of Great Britain and Ireland, Sir Henry Pottinger, Bart., a Major-General in the service of the East India Company, &c.;

And His Imperial Majesty the Emperor of China, the High Commissioners Keying, a Member of the Imperial House, a guardian of the Crown Prince, and General of the garrison of Canton; and Elepoo, of the Imperial Kindred, graciously permitted to wear the insignia of the first rank, and the distinction of a peacock's feather, lately Minister and Governor-General, &c., and now Lieutenant-General Commanding at Chapoo.

Who, after having communicated to each other their respective full powers, and found them to be in good and due form, have agreed upon and concluded the following Articles:—

Peace and Friendship. Protection of Persons and Property.
ARTICLE I. There shall henceforward be peace and friendship between Her Majesty the Queen of the United Kingdom of Great Britain and Ireland and His Majesty the Emperor of China, and between their respective subjects, who shall enjoy full security and protection for their persons and property within the dominions of the other.

Canton, Amoy, Foochow, Ningpo, and Shanghai opened to British Subjects and their Trade.
ARTICLE II. His Majesty the Emperor of China agrees, that British subjects, with their families and establishments, shall be allowed to reside, for the purpose of carrying on their mercantile pursuits, without molestation or restraint, at the cities and towns of Canton, Amoy, Foochowfoo, Ningpo, and Shanghai.

Appointment of British Superintendents or Consuls at those places; their Duties.

And Her Majesty the Queen of Great Britain, &c., will appoint Superintendents, or Consular Officers, to reside at each of the above named cities or towns, to be the medium of communication between the Chinese authorities and the said merchants, and to see that the just duties and other dues of the Chinese Government, as hereafter provided for, are duly discharged by Her Britannic Majesty's subjects.

Cession of Hong Kong to Great Britain.

ARTICLE III. It being obviously necessary and desirable that British subjects should have some port at which they may careen and refit their ships, when required, and keep stores for that purpose, His Majesty the Emperor of China cedes to Her Majesty the Queen of Great Britain, &c., the Island of Hong Kong, to be possessed in perpetuity by Her Britannic Majesty, her heirs and successors, and to be governed by such laws and regulations as Her Majesty the Queen of Great Britain, &c., shall see fit to direct.

Indemnity. Payment by China of 6,000,000 dollars for value of Opium delivered up as a Ransom for British Subjects.

ARTICLE IV. The Emperor of China agrees to pay the sum of 6,000,000 dollars, as the value of the Opium which was delivered up at Canton in the month of March, 1839, as a ransom for the lives of Her Britannic Majesty's Superintendent and subjects, who had been imprisoned and threatened with death by the Chinese High Officers.

Abolition of Privileges of Hong Merchants at Ports of residence of British Merchants. Payment by China of 3,000,000 dollars for Debts due to British Subjects by certain Hong Merchants.

ARTICLE V. The Government of China having compelled the British merchants trading at Canton to deal exclusively with certain Chinese merchants, called Hong merchants (or Co-Hong), who had been licenced by the Chinese Government for that purpose, the Emperor of China agrees to abolish that practice in future at all ports where British merchants may reside, and to permit them to carry on their mercantile transactions with whatever persons they please; and His Imperial Majesty further agrees to pay to the British Government the sum of 3,000,000 dollars, on account of debts due to British subjects by some of the Hong merchants or Co-Hong, who have become insolvent, and who owe very large sums of money to subjects of Her Britannic Majesty.

Indemnity. Payment by China of 12,000,000 dollars for Expenses of British Expedition to demand Redress. Deduction of ransom received by British Forces for Chinese towns.

ARTICLE VI. The Government of Her Britannic Majesty having been obliged to send out an expedition to demand and obtain redress for the violent and unjust proceedings of the Chinese High Authorities towards Her Britannic Majesty's Officers and subjects, the Emperor of China agrees to pay the sum of 12,000,000 dollars, on account of the expenses incurred; and Her Britannic Majesty's Plenipotentiary voluntarily agrees, on behalf of Her Majesty, to deduct from the said amount of 12,000,000 dollars, any sums which may have been received by Her Majesty's combined forces, as ransom for cities and towns in China, subsequent to the 1st day of August, 1841.

Periods for payment to be made by China of Indemnities of 21,000,000 dollars.

ARTICLE VII. It is agreed, that the total amount of 21,000,000 dollars, described in the 3 preceding Articles, shall be paid as follows:—
6,000,000 immediately.
6,000,000 in 1843; that is, 3,000,000 on or before the 30th of the month of June, and 3,000,000 on or before the 31st of December.
5,000,000 in 1844; that is, 2,500,000 on or before the 30th day of June, and 2,500,000 on or before the 31st of December.
4,000,000 in 1845; that is, 2,000,000 on or before the 30th of June, and 2,000,000 on or before the 31st of December.

Interest on Arrears.

And it is further stipulated, that interest, at the rate of 5 per cent. per annum, shall be paid by the Government of China on any portion of the above sums that are not punctually discharged at the periods fixed.

ARTICLE VIII. *All British Subjects (European and Indian) confined in China to be released.*

ARTICLE IX. *Amnesty. Release and Indemnity to Chinese formerly in British employ.*

Tariff to be issued of Import, Export, and Transit Duties.

ARTICLE X. His Majesty the Emperor of China agrees to establish at all the ports which are, by Article II of this Treaty, to be thrown open for the resort of British merchants, a fair and regular tariff of export and import customs and other dues, which tariff shall be publicly notified and promulgated for general information.

Transit Duties on British Goods conveyed by Chinese into the Interior.

And the Emperor further engages, that when British merchandise shall have once paid at any of the said ports the regulated customs and dues, agreeable to the tariff to be hereafter fixed, such merchandise may be conveyed by Chinese merchants to any province or city in the interior of the Empire of China, on paying a further amount as transit duties, which shall not exceed   per cent. on the tariff value of such goods.

Correspondence between British and Chinese Authorities.

ARTICLE XI. It is agreed that Her Britannic Majesty's Chief High Officer in China shall correspond with the Chinese High Officers, both at the capital and in the provinces, under the term "communication"

照會 ; the subordinate British Officers and Chinese High Officers in the provinces, under the terms " statement " 申陳 on the part of the former, and on the part of the latter, " declaration "

劄行 ; and the subordinates of both countries on a footing of perfect equality: merchants and others not holding official situations, and therefore not included in the above, on both sides, to use the term

" representation " 稟明 in all papers addressed to, or intended for the notice of, the respective Governments.

Evacuation of Nanking and Grand Canal by British Forces.—Kulangsu and Chusan to be held by British Forces until Settlement of Money Payments.

ARTICLE XII. On the assent of the Emperor of China to this Treaty being received, and the discharge of the first instalment of money, Her Britannic Majesty's forces will retire from Nanking and the Grand Canal, and will no longer molest or stop the trade of China. The military post at Chinhai will also be withdrawn; but the Islands of Kulangsu, and that of Chusan, will continue to be held by Her Majesty's forces until the money payments, and the arrangements for opening the ports to British merchants, be completed.

Ratifications. Provisions of Treaty to take effect in the meantime.

ARTICLE XIII. The ratification of this Treaty by Her Majesty the Queen of Great Britain, &c., and His Majesty the Emperor of China, shall be exchanged as soon as the great distance which separates England from China will admit; but, in the meantime, counterpart copies of it, signed and sealed by the Plenipotentiaries, on behalf of their respective Sovereigns, shall be mutually delivered, and all its provisions and arrangements shall take effect.

Done at Nanking, and signed and sealed by the Plenipotentiaries on board Her Britannic Majesty's ship " Cornwallis," this 20th day of August, 1842; corresponding with the Chinese date, 29th day of the 7th month, in the 22nd year of Taoukwang.

(L.S.) HENRY POTTINGER.

Her Majesty's Plenipotentiary.

42

TREATY BETWEEN GREAT BRITAIN AND THE USA establishing boundary west of the Rocky Mountains. Concluded 15th June, 1846. Ratifications exchanged 17th July, 1846.

The United States of America and Her Majesty the Queen of the United Kingdom of Great Britain and Ireland, deeming it to be desirable for the future welfare of both countries that the state of doubt and uncertainty which has hitherto prevailed respecting the sovereignty and government of the territory on the northwest coast of America, lying westward of the Rocky or Stony Mountains, should be finally terminated by an amicable compromise of the rights mutually asserted by the two parties over the said territory, have respectively named Plenipotentiaries to treat and agree concerning the terms of such settlement, that is to say:

The President of the United States of America has, on his part, furnished with full powers James Buchanan, Secretary of State of the United States, and Her Majesty the Queen of the United Kingdom of Great Britain and Ireland has, on her part, appointed the Right Honourable Richard Pakenham, a member of Her Majesty's Most Honourable Privy Council, and Her Majesty's Envoy Extraordinary and Minister Plenipotentiary to the United States;

Who, after having communicated to each other their respective full powers, found in good and due form, have agreed upon and concluded the following articles:

ART. I. From the point on the forty-ninth parallel of north latitude, where the boundary laid down in existing treaties and conventions between the United States and Great Britain terminates, the line of boundary between the territories of the United States and those of Her Britannic Majesty shall be continued westward along the said forty-ninth parallel of north latitiude to the middle of the channel which separates the continent from Vancouver's Island; and thence southerly through the middle of the said channel, and of Fuca's Straits, to the Pacific Ocean: Provided, however, that the navigation of the whole of the said channel and straits, south of the forty-ninth parallel of north latitude, remain free and open to both parties.

ART. II. From the point at which the forty-ninth parallel of north latitude shall be found to intersect the great northern branch of the Columbia River, the navigation of the said branch shall be free and open to the Hudson's Bay Company, and to all British subjects trading with the same, to the point where the said branch meets the main stream of the Columbia, and thence down the said main stream to the ocean, with free access into and through the said river or rivers, it being understood that all the usual portages along the line thus described shall, in like manner, be free and open. In navigating the said river or rivers, British subjects, with their goods and produce, shall be treated on the same footing as citizens of the United States; it being, however, always understood that nothing in this article shall be construed as preventing, or intended to prevent, the Government of the United States from making any regulations respecting the navigation of the said river or rivers not inconsistent with the present treaty.

ART. III. In the future appropriation of the territory south of the forty-ninth parallel of north latitude, as provided in the first article of this treaty, the possessory rights of the Hudson's Bay Company, and of all British subjects who may be already in the occupation of land or other property lawfully acquired within the said territory, shall be respected.

ART. IV. The farms, lands, and other property of every description belonging to the Puget's Sound Agricultural Company, on the north side of the Columbia River, shall be confirmed to the said company. In case, however, the situation of those farms and lands should be considered by the United States to be of public and political importance, and the United States Government should signify a desire to obtain possession of the whole, or of any part thereof, the property so required shall be transferred to the said Government, at a proper valuation, to be agreed upon between the parties.

ART. V. The present treaty shall be ratified by the President of the United States, by and with the advice and consent of the Senate thereof, and by Her Britannic Majesty; and the ratifications shall be exchanged at London, at the expiration of six months from the date thereof, or sooner if possible.

In witness whereof the respective Plenipotentiaries have signed the same, and have affixed thereto the seals of their arms.

Done at Washington the fifteenth day of June, in the year of our Lord one thousand eight hundred and forty-six.

JAMES BUCHANAN.

RICHARD PAKENHAM.

43

CONVENTION between Austria, Prussia, and Russia, uniting the Free City of Cracow to the Austrian Monarchy. Signed at Cracow, 6th November, 1846.

THE Lieutenant Field-Marshal Count Castiglione, President of the Provisional Government of the Free City of Cracow, in the name of the 3 Protecting Powers, Austria, Prussia, and Russia, causes it to be known, in the name and by the authority of those Powers, that they have concluded and signed at Vienna, the 6th of the present month, a Convention, of which the following is the tenor:—

The 3 Courts of Austria, Prussia, and Russia,

Considering, that the Conspiracy which in the month of February, 1846, produced the well-known events in the Grand Duchy of Posen, in Cracow, and in Gallicia, was organized in places at a distance from the Country in which it was supported by numerous accomplices;

Considering, that the criminal faction took up arms at the hour appointed, committed hostilities, and published proclamations exciting to general revolt;

Considering, that Cracow became the seat of a central authority calling itself the *Revolutionary Government*, and that the acts which emanated from that authority were intended to direct the insurrection;

Considering, that all these combined circumstances have constituted, on the part of the State of Cracow, a real State of War, which would have authorised the Courts of Austria, of Prussia, and of Russia, to avail themselves of all the rights given by War;

Considering, that on this ground alone they would have the right to dispose of a Territory which has taken an hostile attitude towards them;

Considering, that there is no question for the 3 Powers of causing the City of Cracow to submit to the Law of the Strongest, inasmuch as that law cannot be applicable where so great a disparity exists;

Considering, that there is, moreover, as little question of exercising towards Cracow an act of vengeance, or of inflicting a punishment; but that the High Protecting Powers desire only to restore order and peace to the Territory of Cracow, and that they have no other object but that of guarding their subjects against the recurrence of events which have so deeply compromised their tranquillity;

Considering, moreover, that by the Treaty concluded between them, the 21st April/3rd May, 1815, the City of Cracow, with its Territory, was declared a Free and Independent and strictly Neutral City under the Protection of the 3 High Contracting Parties;

Considering, that by this Stipulation the 3 Courts were desirous of giving effect to the Article relating to the City of Cracow, in their respective Treaties concluded the 21st April/3rd May, 1815, the one between His Majesty the Emperor of Austria and His Majesty the Emperor of All the Russias, the other concluded on the same date between His Majesty the Emperor of All the Russias and the King of Prussia;

Considering, that the existence of the Free City of Cracow, far from being in conformity with their intentions, has on the contrary been a source of disturbance and disorders, which during nearly 20 years not only compromised the peace and prosperity of this Free City, and the security of the adjoining Provinces, but, moreover, tended to overthrow the order of things established by the Treaties of 1815;

Considering, that numerous facts of this nature, the notoriety of which renders enumeration superfluous, have completely altered the nature of the existence of the Free City of Cracow; that by acts contrary to the tenor of Treaties, Cracow has on several occasions freed herself from the obligations which the condition of strict Neutrality imposed upon her; that these acts have on several occasions led to the Armed Intervention of the 3 Powers; that all the modifications introduced into the internal Constitution for the purpose of giving to its Government more power, have not sufficed to prevent the recurrence of these deplorable facts;

Considering, that the forbearance of the 3 Governments, shown by these benevolent arrangements, far from bearing fruit, have only served to promote the projects of the irreconcileable enemies of established order; that in becoming the centre of a new and vast conspiracy, the ramifications of which embrace all the Provinces formerly Polish, and in superadding to this culpable and disloyal project, an act of armed aggression, the Free City of Cracow has become the point of which the spirit of revolution availed itself in order to sap the internal tranquillity of adjoining States;

Considering, that the City of Cracow has proved that it was a political body evidently too weak to resist the unceasing machinations of the Polish Emigration, who held it morally subjected; that accordingly that City no longer presents any guarantee to the Powers against the recurrence of attempts already repeated at various times;

Considering, that attempts of this nature are a manifest infraction of the Treaty of 1815, as well as of Article II of the Constituent Statute of the Free City of Cracow of the 30th of May, 1833;

Considering, that the stipulations relative to Cracow resolved upon by the 3 Courts have only been repeated in Articles VI, VII, VIII, IX, and X of the General Act of the Congress of Vienna, of the 9th of June, 1815, for the purpose of including in that Act the several results of their individual negotiations;

Considering, that the 3 Courts, in now changing a state of things which had spontaneously been created by them in 1815, with regard to Cracow, only re-enter into the exercise of an incontestable right;

Considering all these reasons, and taking finally into mature consideration the care which the security of their States, so often compromised by the Free City of Cracow, so imperiously demands;

Have agreed upon the following resolutions:—

1. The 3 Courts of Austria, Prussia, and Russia, revoke the Articles relative to the City of Cracow, of the Treaties which they respectively concluded, the one between His Majesty the Emperor of Austria, and His Majesty the Emperor of All the Russias, and His Majesty the King of Prussia, signed by them the 21st April/3rd May, 1815, as well as the Additional Treaty between Austria, Prussia, and Russia of the same date.

2. In consequence of this resolution, the City of Cracow and its Territory shall be restored to the Court of Austria for the purpose of being re-united to the Austrian Monarchy, and of being possessed by His Imperial and Royal Apostolic Majesty in the same manner as he possessed them before the year 1809.

Cracow, 6th November, 1846.

4 4

PROTOCOL of Conference between Great Britain, France, Portugal and Spain, relative to Measures to be taken for the Pacification of Portugal. London, 21st May, 1847.

Present:
The Plenipotentiaries of Spain; of France; of Great Britain;
and of Portugal.

THE Plenipotentiaries of Spain, of France, of Great Britain, and of Portugal, having met in conference on the invitation of the Plenipotentiary of Portugal:

The Portuguese Plenipotentiary stated that he had learnt by advices which he had this day received from his Government, that the efforts made at Oporto by Colonel Wylde and the Marquis d'España, to put an end to the Civil War in Portugal, upon the conditions which those officers were authorised by the Queen of Portugal to make known to the Junta, had failed; and he added, that as the Queen of Portugal had offered those conditions in accordance with the advice of her Allies, he was now commanded by Her Most Faithful Majesty to renew the application which Her Most Faithful Majesty had previously made to those of Her Allies who had been parties to the Treaty of the 22nd April, 1834, for assistance to enable her to effect the Pacification of her Dominions.

The Baron Moncorvo further stated that the conditions which had thus been communicated to the Junta of Oporto by Her Most Faithful Majesty's authority, were:

1st. A full and general Amnesty for all political offences committed since the beginning of October last, and an immediate recall of all persons who, since that time, have been sent out of Portugal for political reasons.

2nd. An immediate revocation of all the Decrees which have been issued since the beginning of October last, and which infringe upon, or conflict with, the established Laws and Constitution of the Kingdom.

3rd. A convocation of the Cortes so soon as the elections, which are to take place without delay, shall have been completed.

4th. The immediate appointment of an Administration composed of men not belonging to the party of the Cabrals, nor being members of the Oporto Junta.

The British Plenipotentiary confirmed the statement of Baron de Moncorvo, and said that the British Government had also received this morning from Colonel Wylde, despatches reporting the failure of the mission upon which he and the Marquis d'España had been employed, and the refusal of the Junta either to put an end to the Civil War upon the terms proposed to them by Her Most Faithful Majesty, or to consent even to a temporary suspension of arms.

The Plenipotentiaries of Spain, France, and Great Britain, having taken these matters into their serious consideration, and bearing in mind the deep interest which their respective Governments take in the welfare of the Kingdom of Portugal, and the anxious desire which those Governments feel, that the Civil War which now desolates that country should be brought to an end, upon conditions which should, on the one hand, be founded upon a due regard to the Dignity and Constitutional Rights of the Crown, and should, on the other hand, afford a just security for the Liberties of the People; and being moreover of opinion that the arrangements proposed by Her Most Faithful Majesty were well calculated to attain those ends, agree that a case has now presented itself, in which their respective Governments may, in full accordance with the principles by which they are guided, comply with the application for assistance addressed to them by the Queen of Portugal.

The Plenipotentiary of Portugal, after expressing the satisfaction with which he received this declaration on the part of the Plenipotentiaries of the 3 Powers, impressed upon them the urgent necessity that immediate measures should be taken to carry those declarations into effect, and represented that in the present state of affairs in Portugal, delay must lead to a renewal of bloodshed and an aggravation of the calamities by which Portugal is now afflicted.

Adverting to these circumstances, and sensible of the urgency of the case, the Plenipotentiaries of the 3 Powers agreed to yield to the request of the Portuguese Plenipotentiary; and it was therefore determined by the Plenipotentiaries of the 4 Powers, that the assistance to be afforded to the Queen of Portugal should be given forthwith; and accordingly the Plenipotentiaries of Spain, France, and Great Britain engage that the Naval Forces of their respective Governments now stationed on the coast of Portugal shall immediately co-operate with the Naval Force of Her Most Faithful Majesty in any operations which the commanders of those combined forces may judge necessary or expedient for carrying into effect the objects of this Agreement; and the Plenipotentiary of Spain further engages that a body of Troops, the number of which shall be agreed upon between the Spanish and Portuguese Governments, shall enter Portugal for the purpose of co-operating with the Troops of Her Most Faithful Majesty; and that those Troops shall withdraw from the Portuguese Territory within two months after the time when they shall enter, or as soon as the objects for which they shall have entered shall have been accomplished.

The Plenipotentiaries of the 4 Powers undertake that orders, in conformity with the engagements of this Protocol, shall be sent forthwith to the Naval Officers of the respective Governments on the Coast of Portugal, and to the general officers commanding the Spanish troops on the Frontiers of Spain.

> XAVIER DE ISTURIZ.
> JARNAC.
> PALMERSTON.
> TORRE DE MONCORVO

45   ACT OF BALTA-LIMAN

ACT between Russia and Turkey, relative to Moldavia and Wallachia. Signed at Balta-Liman, 1st May, 1849.

His Imperial Majesty the Most High and Most Mighty Emperor and Autocrat of All the Russias, and His Imperial Majesty the Most High and Most Mighty Emperor and Padishah of the Ottomans, animated by an equal solicitude for the wellbeing of the Principalities of Moldavia and of Wallachia, and faithful to the antecedent Engagements which secure to the said Principalities the privilege of a distinct administration and certain other local immunities, have recognised that in consequence of the commotions by which those Provinces, and more particularly Wallachia, have been agitated, it becomes necessary to adopt by common Agreement extraordinary and effectual measures for the protection of those immunities and privileges, either against revolutionary and anarchical convulsions, or against the abuses of power which paralysed the execution of the laws therein, and deprived the peaceable inhabitants of the benefits of the administration which the two Principalities ought to enjoy in virtue of the solemn Treaties between Russia and the Sublime Porte.

For this purpose we, the Undersigned, by order and by the express authorisation of His Majesty the Emperor of All the Russias, and His Highness Reshid Pasha, Grand Vizier, and His Excellency Ali Pasha, Minister for Foreign Affairs of the Sublime Ottoman Porte, by order and by the express authorisation of His Majesty the Sultan, after having duly communicated and concerted together, have agreed upon and concluded the following Articles:

Election of Hospodars of Moldavia and Wallachia by the Sultan.

ART. I. Considering the exceptional circumstances brought on by the recent events, the two Imperial Courts have agreed, that instead of following the mode established by the Regulation of 1831 for the election of the Hospodars of Moldavia and Wallachia, those high functionaries shall be nominated by His Majesty the Sultan according to a mode especially agreed upon for this occasion between the two Courts, with the view of confiding the administration of those Provinces to the candidates most worthy, and enjoying the best reputation among their fellow-countrymen. For this occasion likewise, the two Hospodars shall only be nominated for 7 years, the two Courts reserving to themselves, a year before the expiration of the term fixed for the present Agreement, to take into consideration the internal state of the Principalities, and the services which may have been rendered by the two Hospodars, in order, by mutual agreement, to consider of the further determinations to be taken.

Alterations in Organic Statute of 1831.

ART. II. The Organic Statute granted to the Principalities in 1831 shall remain in force, saving the alterations and modifications of which the necessity shall have been proved by experience, specifically in regard to the Ordinary and Extraordinary Assemblies of the Boyards. These Assemblies, in the form in which they have heretofore been composed and elected, having more than once given rise to deplorable conflicts, and even to acts of open insubordination, their convocation shall continue to be suspended, and the two Courts reserve to themselves to come to an understanding on the subject of their re-establishment on bases settled with all requisite deliberation, at the time when they shall judge that that measure can be carried into effect without inconvenience as regards the maintenance of public tranquillity in the two Principalities. The deliberative functions shall be provisionally entrusted to Councils or Divans, *ad hoc*, composed of the Boyards who are the most notable and the most worthy of confidence, and of some members of the higher Clergy. The principal attributes of these Councils shall be the assessment of the Taxes, and the examination into the yearly Budget in the two Provinces.

Commissions of Revision of Organic Statute to be Established at Jassy and Bucharest.

ART. III. In order to proceed with all necessary deliberation to the organic improvements required by the actual state of the Principalities and the administrative abuses which have been introduced there, two Commissions of Revision shall be established, one at Jassy and the other at Bucharest, composed of the Boyards most commendable from their character and abilities, to whom shall be entrusted the task of revising the existing Regulations and of pointing out the modifications best calculated to confer upon the Administration of the Country the Regularity and Unity in which they have frequently been deficient.

Work of Commissioners to be sanctioned by Ottoman Government.

The work of these Commissioners shall be submitted with the shortest delay possible to the examination of the Ottoman Government, which, after having come to an understanding with the Court of Russia thereupon, and having thus proved their mutual approbation, shall grant to the said modifications its definitive sanction, which shall be published in the usual manner by a Hatti-sheriff of His Majesty the Sultan.

Occupation of the Country by Ottoman and Russian Troops.

ART. IV. The troubles which have so deeply disturbed the Principalities having demonstrated the necessity of affording to their Governments the support of a Military Force capable of promptly repressing every Insurrectional Movement, and of causing the established authorities to be respected, the two Imperial Courts have agreed to prolong the presence of a certain portion of the Russian and Ottoman Troops which at present occupy the country ; and specifically, in order to preserve the Frontiers of Wallachia and of Moldavia from casualties from abroad, it has been determined to leave therein, for the time, from 25,000 to 35,000 men of each of the two Parties. After the tranquillity of the said Frontiers shall be re-established, there shall remain in the two Countries about 10,000 men on each side, until the completion of the work of the Organic Improvement and the Consolidation of the Internal Tranquillity of the two Provinces. Thereupon the troops of the two Powers shall completely evacuate the Principalities, but they shall still remain at hand to re-enter immediately, in case the occurrence of serious events in the Principalities should require that measure to be again adopted. Independently of that, provision shall be made for completing without delay the reorganisation of the Native Militia, so that by its discipline and efficiency it may afford a sufficient guarantee for the maintenance of legal order.

Extraordinary Russian and Ottoman Commissioners to Reside in·
Principalities.
ART. V. Pending the duration of the Occupation the two Courts shall continue to cause an Extraordinary Russian Commissioner and an Extraordinary Ottoman Commissioner to reside in the Principalities. These Special Agents will be commissioned to watch over the progress of affairs, and to offer in common to the Hospodars their advice and counsel whensoever they shall observe any serious abuses or any measure prejudicial to the tranquillity of the Country. The said Extraordinary Commissioners shall be furnished with identic instructions agreed upon between the two Courts, which shall prescribe to them their duties and the degree of interference which they will have to exercise in the affairs of the Principalities. The two Commissioners will likewise have to agree together upon the choice of the members of the Commissions of Revision to be established in the Principalities, as has been stated in Article III. They will give an account to the respective Courts of the work of those Commissions, adding thereto their own observations.

Agreement to last 7 Years.
ART. VI. The duration of the present Arrangement is fixed at 7 years, at the expiration of which the two Courts reserve to themselves to take into consideration the situation in which the Principalities may then be, and to determine upon the ulterior measures which they may judge most suitable and proper to insure for a long time hereafter the well-being and the tranquillity of those Provinces.

Treaties, &c., respecting Principalities to remain in force.

ART. VII. It is understood that by the present Instrument, occasioned by exceptional circumstances, and concluded for a limited time, none of the stipulations existing between the two Courts in regard to the Principalities of Wallachia and Moldavia are set aside, and that all previous Treaties confirmed by the Separate Act of the Treaty of Adrianople retain their full force and effect.

The 7 preceding Articles having been agreed upon and concluded, our Signature and the Seal of our Arms have been affixed to the present Instrument, which is delivered to the Sublime Porte, in exchange for that delivered to us by His Highness the Grand Vizier and His Excellency the Minister for Foreign Affairs aforesaid.

Done at Balta-Liman, 10th April/1st May, 1849 (and of the Hegira, the 8th Djemasi-ul-Akhir, 1265).

(L.S.) RESHID PASHA.
(L.S.) AALI PASHA.

(L.S.) VLADIMIR TITOFF,
Envoy Extraordinary and Minister
Plenipotentiary of His Majesty
the Emperor of Russia at the
Sublime Ottoman Porte.

46

CONVENTION BETWEEN GREAT BRITAIN AND THE USA as to ship-canal connecting Atlantic and Pacific oceans. (Clayton-Bulwer Treaty.) Concluded 19th April, 1850. Ratifications exchanged 4th July, 1850.

The United States of America and Her Britannic Majesty, being desirous of consolidating the relations of amity which so happily subsist between them by setting forth and fixing in a convention their views and intentions with reference to any means of communication by ship-canal which may be constructed between the Atlantic and Pacific Oceans by the way of the river San Juan de Nicaragua, and either or both of the lakes of Nicaragua or Managua, to any port or place on the Pacific Ocean, the President of the United States has conferred full powers on John M. Clayton, Secretary of State of the United States, and Her Britannic Majesty on the Right Honourable Sir Henry Lytton Bulwer, a member of Her Majesty's Most Honourable Privy Council, Knight Commander of the Most Honourable Order of the Bath, and Envoy Extraordinary and Minister Plenipotentiary of Her Britannic Majesty to the United States, for the aforesaid purpose; and the said Plenipotentiaries, having exchanged their full powers, which were found to be in proper form, have agreed to the following articles:

ART. I. The Governments of the United States and Great Britain hereby declare that neither the one nor the other will ever obtain or maintain for itself any exclusive control over the said ship-canal; agreeing that neither will ever erect or maintain any fortifications commanding the same, or in the vicinity thereof, or occupy, or fortify, or colonize, ir assume or exercise any dominion over Nicaragua, Costa Rica, the Mosquito coast, or any part of Central America; nor will either make use of any protection which either affords or may afford, or any alliance which either has or may have to or with any State or people for the purpose of erecting or maintaining any such fortifications, or of occupying, fortifying, or colonizing Nicaragua, Costa Rica, the Mosquito coast, or any part of Central America, or of assuming or exercising dominion over the same; nor will the United States or Great Britain take advantage of any intimacy, or use any alliance, connection, or influence that either may possess, with any State or Government through whose territory the said canal may pass, for the purpose of acquiring or holding, directly or indirectly, for the citizens or subjects of the one any rights or advantages in regard to commerce or navigation through the said canal which shall not be offered on the same terms to the citizens or subjects of the other.

ART. II. Vessels of the United States or Great Britain traversing the said canal shall, in case of war between the contracting parties, be exempted from blockade, detention, or capture by either of the belligerents; and this provision shall extend to such a distance from the two ends of the said canal as may hereafter be found expedient to establish.

ART. III. In order to secure the construction of the said canal, the contracting parties engage that, if any such canal shall be undertaken upon fair and equitable terms by any parties having the authority of the local government or governments through whose territory the same may pass, then the persons employed in making the said canal, and their property used or to be used for that object, shall be protected, from the commencement of the said canal to its completion, by the Governments of the United States and Great Britain, from unjust detention, confiscation, seizure, or any violence whatsoever.

ART. IV. The contracting parties will use whatever influence they respectively exercise with any State, States, or Governments possessing, or claiming to possess, any jurisdiction or right over the territory which the said canal shall traverse, or which shall be near the waters applicable thereto, in order to induce such States or Governments to facilitate the construction of the said canal by every means in their power; and, furthermore, the United States and Great Britain agree to use their good offices, wherever or however it may be most expedient, in order to procure the establishment of two free ports, one at each end of the said canal.

ART. V. The contracting parties further engage that when the said canal shall have been completed they will protect it from interruption, seizure, or unjust confiscation, and that they will guarantee the neutrality thereof, so that the said canal may forever be open and free, and the capital invested therein secure. Nevertheless, the Governments of the United States and Great Britain, in according their protection to the construction of the said canal, and guaranteeing its neutrality and security when completed, always understand that this protection and guarantee are granted conditionally, and may be withdrawn by both Governments, or either Government, if both Governments or either Government should deem that the persons or company undertaking or managing the same adopt or establish such regulations concerning the traffic thereupon as are contrary to the spirit and intention of this convention, either by making unfair discriminations in favour of the commerce of one of the contracting parties over the commerce of the other, or by imposing oppressive exactions or unreasonable tolls upon passengers, vessels, goods, wares, merchandise, or other articles. Neither party, however, shall withdraw the aforesaid protection and guarantee without first giving six months' notice to the other.

ART. VI. The contracting parties in this convention engage to invite every State with which both or either have friendly intercourse to enter into stipulations with them similar to those which they have entered into with each other, to the end that all other States may share in the honour and advantage of having contributed to a work of such general interest and importance as the canal herein contemplated. And the contracting parties likewise agree that each shall enter into treaty stipulations with such of the Central American States as they may deem advisable for the purpose of more effectually carrying out the great design of this convention, namely, that of constructing and maintaining the said canal as a ship communication between the two oceans, for the benefit of mankind, on equal terms to all, and of protecting the same; and they also agree that the good offices of either shall be employed, when requested by the other, in aiding and assisting the negotiation of such treaty stipulations; and should any differences arise as to right or property over the territory through which the said canal shall pass, between the States or Governments of Central America, and such differences should in any way impede or obstruct the execution of the said canal, the Governments of the United States and Great Britain will use their good offices to settle such differences in the manner best suited to promote the interests of the said canal, and to strengthen the bonds of friendship and alliance which exist between the contracting parties.

ART. VII. It being desirable that no time should be unnecessarily lost in commencing and constructing the said canal, the Governments of the United States and Great Britain determine to give their support and encouragement to such persons or company as may first offer to commence the same, with the necessary capital, the consent of the local authorities, and on such principles as accord with the spirit and intention of this convention; and if any persons or company should already have, with any State through which the proposed ship-canal may pass, a contract for the construction of such a canal as that specified in this convention, to the stipulations of which contract neither of the contracting parties in this convention have any just cause to object, and the said persons or company shall, moreover, have made preparations and expended time, money, and trouble on the faith of such contract, it is hereby agreed that such persons or company shall have a priority of claim over every other person, persons, or company to the protection of the Governments of the United States and Great Britain, and be allowed a year from the date of the exchange of the ratifications of this convention for concluding their arrangements and presenting evidence of sufficient capital subscribed to accomplish the contemplated undertaking; it being understood that if, at the expiration of the aforesaid period, such persons or company be not able to commence and carry out the proposed enterprise, then the Governments of the United States and Great Britain shall be free to afford their protection to any other persons or company that shall be prepared to commence and proceed with the construction of the canal in question.

ART. VIII. The Governments of the United States and Great Britain having not only desired, in entering into this convention, to accomplish a particular object, but also to establish a general principle, they hereby agree to extend their protection, by treaty stipulations, to any other practicable communications, whether by canal or railway, across the isthmus which connects North and South America, and especially to the interoceanic communications, should the same prove to be practicable, whether by canal or railway, which are now proposed to be established by the way of Tehuantepec or Panama. In granting, however, their joint protection to any such canals or railways as are by this article specified, it is always understood by the United States and Great Britain that the parties constructing or owning the same shall impose no other charges or conditions of traffic thereupon than the aforesaid

Governments shall approve of as just and equitable; and that the same canals or railways, being open to the citizens and subjects of the United States and Great Britain on equal terms, shall also be open on like terms to the citizens and subjects of every other State which is willing to grant thereto such protection as the United States and Great Britain engage to afford.

ART. IX. The ratifications of this convention shall be exchanged at Washington within six months from this day, or sooner if possible.

In faith whereof we, the respective Plenipotentiaries, have signed this convention, and have hereunto affixed our seals.

Done at Washington the nineteenth day of April, anno Domini one thousand eight hundred and fifty.

JOHN M. CLAYTON.
HENRY LYTTON BULWER.

47   TREATY OF BERLIN

TREATY OF PEACE between the King of Prussia, in his own name and in the name of the Germanic Confederation, on the one part, and Denmark on the other part. Signed at Berlin, 2nd July, 1850.

HIS Majesty the King of Prussia, in his own name and in the name of the Germanic Confederation on the one part, and His Majesty the King of Denmark on the other part, animated by the desire to re-establish between the said Confederation and Denmark the peace and good understanding which was interrupted by the Differences relating to the Duchies of Schleswig and of Holstein, have for that purpose named and authorised as their Plenipotentiaries, that is to say:

His Majesty the King of Prussia, Charles George Louis Guido d'Usedom, his Envoy Extraordinary and Minister Plenipotentiary to the Holy See, and to the Courts of Tuscany, Parma, and Modena, &c.;

His Majesty the King of Denmark, Frederick Baron Pechlin, his Chamberlain and Privy Councillor, &c.;

Holger Christian de Reedtz, his Chamberlain, &c.;

And Anthony William de Scheel, Doctor in Law, Auditor-General of his Army, &c.;

The above-named Plenipotentiaries, with the concurrence of the Earl of Westmorland, a Peer of the United Kingdom of Great Britain and Ireland, Lieutenant-General in Her Britannic Majesty's Army, Colonel of the 56th Regiment of the Line, &c., one of Her Britannic Majesty's Privy Council, and her Envoy Extraordinary and Minister Plenipotentiary to His Majesty the King of Prussia, as Representative of the Mediating Power, after having exchanged their respective Full Powers, found to be in good form, have agreed upon the following Articles:—

Peace and Friendship.
ART. I. There shall be for the future Peace, Friendship, and good understanding between Denmark and the Germanic Confederation.

The greatest attention shall be devoted by both Parties to the maintenance of the harmony so happily re-established, and they will carefully avoid everything which may disturb it.

Renewal of Treaties.
ART. II. All the Treaties and Conventions concluded between Denmark and the Germanic Confederation are by the present Treaty re-established.

Reservation of Rights.
ART. III. The High Contracting Parties reserve to themselves all the Rights which reciprocally belonged to them before the War.

Exercise of Authority for the Pacification of Holstein.
ART. IV. After the conclusion of the present Treaty, His Majesty the King of Denmark, Duke of Holstein, in conformity with the Federal law, may claim [pourra réclamer] the Intervention of the Germanic Confederation, to re-establish the exercise of his Legitimate Authority in Holstein, communicating at the same time his intentions with respect to the Pacification of the Country. If upon this application the Confederation should not consider it to be its duty to interfere for the time, or if its Intervention should prove to be inefficacious, His Danish Majesty shall be at liberty to extend Military measures to Holstein, and to employ an armed force for that purpose.

Appointment of Boundary Commissioners.
ART. V. Within 6 months after the signature of the present Treaty, His Majesty the King of Denmark and the Germanic Confederation shall name Commissioners to determine, according to the documents and other proofs relative to the subject, the Boundary between those States of His Danish Majesty not comprised in the Germanic Confederation and those which belong thereto.

Ratifications.
ART. VI. The present Treaty shall be ratified, and the Ratifications shall be exchanged at Berlin within 3 weeks, or sooner, if possible.

In witness whereof the Minister of the Mediating Power and the respective Plenipotentiaries have signed the present Treaty, and have affixed thereto their Seals.

Done at Berlin, 2nd July, 1850.

	(L.S.)	WESTMORLAND.
	(L.S.)	F. PECHLIN.
	(L.S.)	H. C. REEDTZ.
(L.S.) USEDOM.	(L.S.)	A. W. SCHEEL.

SECRET ARTICLE.

Prussia to take part in Negotiations regulating the order of Succession in Denmark.

HIS Majesty the King of Prussia engages to take part in the Negotiations which His Majesty the King of Denmark will initiate for regulating the Order of Succession in the States united under the Sceptre of His Danish Majesty.

The present Secret Article shall be ratified at the same time as the Protocol of this day, and the Ratifications thereof shall be simultaneously exchanged.

Done at Berlin, 2nd July, 1850.

(L.S.) USEDOM.	(L.S.)	WESTMORLAND.
	(L.S.)	F. PECHLIN.
	(L.S.)	H. C. REEDTZ.
	(L.S.)	A. W. SCHEEL.

NOTE EXPLANATORY OF THE WORDS " POURRA RÉCLAMER " IN ARTICLE IV OF THE TREATY OF 2ND JULY, 1850.

The British Minister at Berlin to the Prussian Minister for Foreign Affairs.
(Private).

M. LE BARON,   *Berlin, 4th July*, 1850.

I HAVE received from Baron de Pechlin, in his name and in the name of his colleagues, the assurance that he has only considered the words " pourra réclamer " substituted for the words " réclamera," in Article IV of the Treaty of Peace between the German Confederation and Denmark, signed on the 2nd instant, as authorising the King of Denmark to endeavour by conciliatory means to re-establish peaceable relations with the Duchy of Holstein, without the Intervention of the Confederation.

If his efforts should be unsuccessful, Baron de Pechlin recognises the obligation of the King, contracted by the Treaty, to apply to the Confederation, before having recourse to any Military measures to restore the exercise of his authority in that Duchy.

It is only in case the Intervention so claimed was not acceded to, or should prove ineffective, that the King would be authorised to employ his Military means for that purpose.

I avail, &c.,

Baron Schleinitz.   WESTMORLAND.

48

AGREEMENT between the Austrian and Prussian Ministers, respecting the affairs of Holstein and Hesse-Cassel. Olmütz, 29th November, 1850.

AT the confidential Conference which took place yesterday and to-day between the Undersigned, the following propositions were set forth as possible points for the Settlement of existing Differences, and as means adapted for the prevention of conflicts ; and they will be submitted as speedily as possible for the final sanction of the High Governments concerned.

Electoral Hessian and Holstein affairs to be settled by German Governments.

1. The Governments of Austria and Prussia declare that it is their intention to bring about the Final and Definitive Settlement of the Electoral Hessian and Holstein affairs, by the common decision of all the German Governments.

Commissioners to be appointed by German Confederation, and by Prussia and her Allies.

2. In order to render the co-operation of the Governments represented at Frankfort and of the other German Governments possible, there shall be named, as soon as may be, on the part of the members of the Confederation represented at Frankfort, as well as on the part of Prussia and her Allies, a Commissioner for each, who will have to agree upon the measures to be taken in common.

Establishment of Legal state of things in Electoral Hesse and Holstein.

3. As it is, however, for the general interest that both in Electoral Hesse and in Holstein, there should be established a legal state of things conformable with the Fundamental Laws of the Confederation, and

rendering the fulfilment of the Federal duties possible ; as, moreover, Austria has given to the full, in her own name, and in that of the States allied with her, the guarantees for the security of the interests of Prussia required by the latter in regard to the occupation of the Electorate, the two Governments of Austria and Prussia agree, in order to proceed with the discussion of the questions, and without prejudice to the future decision, as follows :

Maintenance of Tranquility in Hesse-Cassel.

A. In Electoral Hesse, Prussia will oppose no impediment to the action of the Troops called in by the Elector, and, therefore, will issue the necessary orders to the Generals in command there, to allow a thoroughfare by the military roads occupied by Prussia. The two Governments of Austria and Prussia will, in concert with their Allies, call upon His Royal Highness the Elector to give his consent for one battalion of the Troops called in by the Electoral Government, and one Royal Prussian battalion to remain at Cassel, in order to Maintain Tranquillity and Order.

Austria and Prussia to send to Holstein Commissioners to demand Cessation of Hostilities.

B. After consultation with their Allies, Austria and Prussia will send to Holstein, and that as speedily as possible, joint Commissioners, who shall demand of the Stadtholdership, in the name of the Confederation, the Cessation of Hostilities, the withdrawal of the troops behind the Eyder, and the reduction of the Army to one-third of its now existing strength, threatening common execution in case of refusal. On the other hand, both Governments will endeavour to prevail on the Danish Government not to station in the Duchy of Schleswig more troops than are necessary for the preservation of Tranquillity and Order.

Conferences to be held at Dresden.

4. Ministerial Conferences will immediately take place at Dresden. The invitation to them will be issued by Austria and Prussia conjointly, and will be so arranged that the Conferences may be opened about the middle of December.

(L.S.)   SCHWARZENBERG.

(L.S.)   MANTEUFFEL.

49

PROTOCOL between Denmark and Russia, relative to the Danish Succession. Warsaw, 24th May/5th June, 1851.

HIS Majesty the Emperor of All the Russias, and His Majesty the King of Denmark, taking into consideration the engagements entered into between their august predecessors, in the years 1767 and 1773 ;

Considering that, as well for establishing the tranquillity of the North of Europe on a durable footing, as for removing all that could then, or for the future, give rise to misunderstandings or differences in the august House of Oldenburg, the Emperor Paul, of glorious memory, then Grand Duke of Russia, renounced for himself, as also for his heirs and descendants, in favour of His Majesty King Christian VII, of glorious memory, as also of the heirs of his Royal Crown, all his rights and pretensions to the Duchy of Schleswig in general, and to the heretofore princely portion of that Duchy in particular ;

That in the same manner, and from the same motives, His Majesty the Emperor Paul ceded for himself, as also for his descendants, heirs, and successors, all that he possessed in the Duchy of Holstein, whether in common with His Majesty the King of Denmark, or separately ;

Considering that this Act of Cession of the Duchy of Holstein has only been made expressly in favour of His Majesty King Christian VII, and of his male lineage, and also eventually in favour of the late Prince Frederick, the King's brother, and of the male lineage of that Prince, and that the eventualities which the terms themselves of this Act of Cession admitted, have already in part been realised by the extinction of the male lineage of King Christian VII, or may be realised at a period more or less near, without the said transactions having in any manner provided for them ;

Foreseeing the dangers which this silence in existing Treaties may cause to the Danish Monarchy, if, on the extinction of the male line actually on the throne of Denmark, the *lex regia* should receive its pure and simple application to one part of the Monarchy ;

Have acknowledged the obligation and the right, as successors of the august Contracting Parties, to the engagements of 1767 and 1773, to come to an understanding as to the ulterior arrangements most suited to the double objects which they have had in view.

In consequence, the Undersigned, after mature examination of all the questions connected with this affair, have agreed amongst themselves, under the express reservation of the high approbation of their respective Sovereigns, and have embodied in the present Protocol the points which follow :

1. The objects proposed in the interest of the Peace of the North, as well as that of the internal Peace of the august House of Oldenburg, namely, the maintenance of the Integrity of the Danish Monarchy, can only be realised by means of an arrangement summoning to the Succession of the whole of the States actually united under the sceptre of His Majesty the King of Denmark, the male lineage solely, to the exclusion of women.

2. The male lineage of Prince Christian of Schleswig-Holstein-Sonderbourg-Glücksbourg and of his consort the Princess Louise of Hesse, unites in itself the rights of inheritance, which, on the extinction of the male line actually reigning in Denmark, devolve upon it in virtue of the Renunciations of Her Royal Highness the Landgravine Charlotte of Hesse, of her son Prince Frederick of Hesse, and of her daughter the Princess Mary of Anhalt-Dessau.

3. Wishing on his part to complete the Titles resulting from these Renunciations, and thus to effect an arrangement which would be of such high importance and interest for the maintenance of the Danish Monarchy in its Integrity, His Majesty the Emperor of All the Russias, as chief of the elder branch of Holstein Gottorp, would be ready to renounce the eventual Rights which belong to him in favour of Prince Christian of Glücksbourg, and of his male lineage.

Nevertheless it is understood :

That the eventual Rights of the two Younger Branches of Holstein Gottorp should be expressly reserved ;

That those which the August Chief of the Elder Branch should abandon for himself and for his male lineage in favour of Prince Christian of Glücksbourg and of his male lineage, should be revived in the Imperial House of Russia whenever (which God forbid) the male lineage of that Prince should become extinct.

That inasmuch as the Renunciation of His Majesty the Emperor would principally have for its object to facilitate an arrangement called for by the first interests of the Monarchy, the offer of such a renunciation would cease to be obligatory if the arrangement itself should fail.

4. In consequence of the considerations which are above pointed out by the above 2 and 3, the Prince Christian of Glücksbourg, conjointly with the Princess, his consort, and in their default, the male lineage of their Highnesses, would have, more than any other branch, claims which qualify them to succeed, if the contingency should arrive, to the States actually united under the sceptre of His Danish Majesty.

Consequently the two Courts of Copenhagen and of St. Petersburgh have agreed ;

That His Majesty the King of Denmark shall designate the Prince and Princess of Glücksbourg conjointly as heirs presumptive of his

Crown, in case the male line of the dynasty actually reigning should become extinct ;

That His Majesty shall make known his high determination to the Powers in amity with Denmark ;

That if, to ensure the complete success of this arrangement, still further renunciations should be deemed useful and desirable, it would be for His Danish Majesty to make himself responsible for the indemnities to which just and equitable Claims should be established ;

Finally, that the negotiations necessary to give to the arrangements in virtue whereof the Prince and Princess of Glücksbourg shall be acknowledged as successors presumptive to the throne of Denmark, the character of an European transaction shall take place in London.

The Undersigned reserve to themselves to submit the present Protocol to their august Sovereigns, and to solicit their high approbation in favour of the provisions it contains.

Warsaw, 24th May/5th June, 1851.

> NESSELRODE.
> MEYENDORFF.
> REEDTZ.

50   TREATY OF LONDON

TREATY between Great Britain, Austria, France, Prussia, Russia, and Sweden and Norway, on the one part, and Denmark on the other part, relative to the Succession to the Crown of Denmark. Signed at London, 8th May, 1852.

In the name of the Most Holy and Indivisible Trinity.

Balance of Power in Europe.

HER Majesty the Queen of Great Britain and Ireland, His Majesty the Emperor of Austria, King of Hungary and Bohemia, the Prince President of the French Republic, His Majesty the King of Prussia, His Majesty the Emperor of All the Russias, and His Majesty the King of Norway and Sweden, taking into consideration that the maintenance of the Integrity of the Danish Monarchy, as connected with the general interests of the Balance of Power in Europe is of high importance to the preservation of Peace, and that an Arrangement by which the Succession to the whole of the Dominions now united under the sceptre of His Majesty the King of Denmark should devolve upon the male line, to the exclusion of females, would be the best means of securing the Integrity of that Monarchy, have resolved, at the invitation of His Danish

Majesty, to conclude a Treaty, in order to give to the arrangements relating to such order of Succession an additional pledge of stability by an act of European acknowledgment.

In consequence, the High Contracting Parties have named as their Plenipotentiaries, that is to say:

Her Majesty the Queen of the United Kingdom of Great Britain and Ireland, the Right Honourable James Howard, Earl of Malmesbury, Her Britannic Majesty's Principal Secretary of State for Foreign Affairs, &c.;

His Majesty the Emperor of Austria, King of Hungary and Bohemia, the Sieur Lewis Baron de Kübeck, Chargé d'Affaires of His Imperial and Royal Apostolic Majesty at the Court of Her Britannic Majesty, &c.;

The Prince President of the French Republic, the Sieur Alexander Colonna Count Walewski, Ambassador of the French Republic to Her Britannic Majesty, &c.;

His Majesty the King of Prussia, the Sieur Christian Charles Josiah Bunsen, Privy Councillor of His Majesty the King of Prussia, his Envoy Extraordinary and Minister Plenipotentiary to Her Britannic Majesty, &c.;

His Majesty the Emperor of All the Russias, the Sieur Philip Baron de Brunnow, his Privy Councillor, Envoy Extraordinary and Minister Plenipotentiary to Her Britannic Majesty, &c.;

His Majesty the King of Sweden and Norway, the Sieur John Gothard Baron de Rehausen, his Chamberlain, Envoy Extraordinary and Minister Plenipotentiary to Her Britannic Majesty, &c.; and

His Majesty the King of Denmark, the Sieur Christian de Bille, Envoy Extraordinary and Minister Plenipotentiary to Her Britannic Majesty, &c.;

Who, after having communicated to each other their respective Full Powers, found in good and due form, have agreed upon the following Articles:

Order of Succession by order of Primogeniture, from Male to Male.

ART. I. After having taken into serious consideration the interests of his Monarchy, His Majesty the King of Denmark, with the assent of His Royal Highness the Hereditary Prince, and of his nearest cognates, entitled to the Succession by the Royal Law of Denmark, as well as in concert with His Majesty the Emperor of All the Russias, Head of the elder Branch of the House of Holstein-Gottorp, having declared his wish to regulate the order of Succession in his dominions in such manner that, in default of issue male in a direct line from King Frederick III of

Denmark, his Crown should devolve upon His Highness the Prince Christian of Schleswig-Holstein-Sonderbourg-Glücksbourg, and upon the issue of the marriage of that Prince with Her Highness the Princess Louisa of Schleswig-Holstein-Sonderbourg-Glücksbourg, born a Princess of Hesse, by order of Primogeniture from Male to Male; the High Contracting Parties, appreciating the wisdom of the views which have determined the eventual adoption of that arrangement, engage by common consent, in case the contemplated contingency should be realized, to acknowledge in His Highness the Prince Christian of Schleswig-Holstein-Sonderbourg-Glücksbourg, and his issue male in the direct line by his marriage with the said Princess, the Right of Succeeding to the whole of the Dominions now united under the sceptre of His Majesty the King of Denmark.

Integrity of Danish Monarchy.

Art. II. The High Contracting Parties, acknowledging as permanent the principle of the Integrity of the Danish Monarchy, engage to take into consideration the further propositions which His Majesty the King of Denmark may deem it expedient to address to them in case (which God forbid) the extinction of the issue male, in the direct line, of His Highness the Prince Christian of Schleswig-Holstein-Sonderbourg-Glücksbourg, by his marriage with Her Highness the Princess Louisa of Schleswig-Holstein-Sonderbourg-Glücksbourg, born a Princess of Hesse, should become imminent.

Rights and Obligations of Denmark and of the Germanic Confederation concerning the Duchies of Holstein and Lauenburg.

Art. III. It is expressly understood that the reciprocal Rights and Obligations of His Majesty the King of Denmark, and of the Germanic Confederation, concerning the Duchies of Holstein and Lauenburg, Rights and Obligations established by the Federal Act of 1815, and by the existing Federal Right, shall not be affected by the present Treaty.

Invitation to other Powers to accede.

Art. IV. The High Contracting Parties reserve to themselves to bring the present Treaty to the knowledge of the other Powers, and to invite them to accede to it.

Ratifications.

Art. V. The present Treaty shall be ratified, and the Ratifications shall be exchanged at London at the expiration of 6 weeks, or sooner if possible.

In witness whereof, the respective Plenipotentiaries have signed the same, and have affixed thereto the Seal of their Arms.

Done at London, the 8th day of May, in the year of Our Lord, 1852.

(L.S.) BILLE.   (L.S.) MALMESBURY.
                                 (L.S.) KUBECK.
                                 (L.S.) A. WALEWSKI.
                                 (L.S.) BUNSEN.
                                 (L.S.) BRUNNOW.
                                 (L.S.) REHAUSEN.

In accordance with Article IV of this Treaty, the following Powers were invited to accede to it:—

Baden.   Netherlands.
Bavaria.   Oldenburg.
Belgium.   Portugal.
Greece.   Sardinia.
Hanover.   Saxe-Weimar.
Hesse-Cassel.   Saxony.
Hesse-Darmstadt.   Spain.
Mecklenburg-Schwerin.   Tuscany.
Mecklenburg-Strelitz.   Wurtemberg.
Naples.

The Powers which did accede to it were:—

Belgium . . . . .28th Dec., 1852.
Hanover . . . . .11th Dec., 1852.
Hesse-Cassel . . . . .16th Dec., 1852.
Naples. . . . . .28th Jan., 1853.
Netherlands . . . . .20th Dec., 1852.
Oldenburg . . . . .10th Dec., 1852.
Portugal   . . . . .19th Mar., 1853.
Sardinia . . . . 4th Dec., 1852.
Saxony . . . . 9th Dec., 1852.
Spain . . . . 6th Dec., 1852.
Tuscany . . . . 6th Dec., 1852.
Wurtemberg . . . . .28th Nov., 1852.

Oldenburg and Saxony, however, in their accessions, reserved certain rights contained in ancient Treaties.

The following States refused to accede to the Treaty until the views of the German Diet on the subject should have been made known:—

Baden . . . . 26th Jan., 1853.
Bavaria . . . . 20th Dec., 1852.
Hesse-Darmstadt . . . . . . 24th Jan., 1853.
Mecklenburg-Schwerin. . 10th Jan., 1853.
Mecklenburg-Strelitz . . 10th Jan., 1853.
Saxe-Weimar . . . . 31st Dec., 1852.

51

TREATY between Great Britain, Bavaria, France, Greece, and Russia, relative to the Succession to the Crown of Greece. Signed at London, 20th November, 1852. Ratifications exchanged at London, 1st February, 1853.

Reference to Convention of 7th May, 1832.
In the Name of the Most Holy and Indivisible Trinity.

HER Majesty the Queen of the United Kingdom of Great Britain and Ireland, the Prince President of the French Republic, and His Majesty the Emperor of All the Russias, being desirous to consolidate the order of Succession to the Throne of Greece, which is placed under their common Guarantee ; and acknowledging the necessity, for this purpose, of placing the stipulations of Article VIII of the Convention of the 7th May, 1832, in harmony with the condition established by Article XL of the Hellenic Constitution ; have resolved to conclude a Treaty to that effect, in conjunction with His Majesty the King of Bavaria, as a signing party to the Convention of 1832, and with His Hellenic Majesty as a party directly interested in a transaction intended to secure the future Tranquillity of Greece.

Their Majesties the King of Bavaria and the King of Greece having responded to that invitation, the High Contracting Parties have named as their Plenipotentiaries, that is to say:

Her Majesty the Queen of the United Kingdom of Great Britain and Ireland, the Right Honourable James Howard Earl of Malmesbury, Her Britannic Majesty's Principal Secretary of State for Foreign Affairs, &c. ;

His Majesty the King of Bavaria, the Sieur Augustus Baron de Cetto, his Chamberlain, Envoy Extraordinary and Minister Plenipotentiary of His Majesty the King of Bavaria to Her Britannic Majesty, &c. ;

The Prince President of the French Republic, the Sieur Alexander Colonna Count Walewski, Ambassador of the French Republic to Her Britannic Majesty, &c. ;

His Majesty the King of Greece, the Sieur Spyridion Tricoupi, a Senator of the Kingdom of Greece, Envoy Extraordinary and Minister Plenipotentiary of His Hellenic Majesty to Her Britannic Majesty, &c. ;

And His Majesty the Emperor of All the Russias, the Sieur Philip, Baron de Brunnow, his Privy Councillor, Envoy Extraordinary and Minister Plenipotentiary to Her Britannic Majesty, &c. ;

Who after having communicated to each other their Full Powers,

found in good and due form, have agreed upon and signed the following
Articles :

Religion of Successors to Crown of Greece.

ART. I. The Princes of the House of Bavaria entitled, under the
Convention of 1832 and under the Hellenic Constitution, to succeed
to the Crown of Greece in the event of King Otho dying without
direct and legitimate posterity, cannot ascend the Throne of Greece
unless they conform to Article XL of the Hellenic Constitution, which
is as follows :

" Every Successor to the Crown of Greece must profess the Religion
of the Orthodox Eastern Church."

Regency of Queen Amelia during Minority of Successor to the Throne.

ART. II. In conformity with the third Decree of the Hellenic Assembly,
Her Majesty Queen Amelia, during her widowhood, is of right entitled
to the Regency in the event of the Minority or of the absence of the
Successor to the Throne, according to the conditions of Article XL of
the Constitution.

Ratifications.

ART. III. The present Treaty shall be ratified, and the Ratifications
shall be exchanged at London in the period of 6 weeks, or sooner if
possible.

In witness whereof the respective Plenipotentiaries have signed the
same, and have affixed thereto the Seal of their Arms.

Done at London, the 20th day of November, in the year of Our
Lord, 1852.

> (L.S.) MALMESBURY.
> (L.S.) A. DE CETTO.
> (L.S.) A. WALEWSKI.
> (L.S.) S. TRICOUPI.
> (L.S.) BRUNNOW.

NOTE.—Previous to the conclusion of this Treaty, Conferences
were held in London, upon the subject of the Succession to the Throne
of Greece, between the Plenipotentiaries of Great Britain, France,
Russia, Bavaria, and Greece.

No.   LIST OF PROTOCOLS.

1. 21st October, 1852. *Great Britain, France, and Russia.*
        Annex Mem. by the British Plenipotentiary, the
                            Earl of Malmesbury.

2. 20th November, 1852. *Great Britain, France, Russia, Bavaria, and Greece.*

Annex A.   Mem. by the Bavarian Plenipotentiary, Baron de Cetto.

B.   Mem. by the Greek Plenipotentiary, M. Tricoupi.

52   TREATY OF CONSTANTINOPLE

TREATY between Great Britain, France, and Turkey, relative to Military Aid to be given to Turkey. Signed at Constantinople, 12th March, 1854. Ratifications exchanged in London, 25th April, 1854.

HER Majesty the Queen of the United Kingdom of Great Britain and Ireland, and His Majesty the Emperor of the French, having been requested by His Imperial Majesty the Sultan to assist him in repelling the Aggression which has been made by His Majesty the Emperor of All the Russias upon the territories of the Sublime Porte, an Aggression by which the Integrity of the Ottoman Empire and the Independence of the Throne of His Imperial Majesty the Sultan are menaced; and their said Majesties being fully persuaded that the existence of the Ottoman Empire in its present Limits is essential to the maintenance of the Balance of Power among the States of Europe, and having in consequence consented to afford to His Imperial Majesty the Sultan the assistance which he has requested for that purpose, it has appeared expedient to their said Majesties, and to His Imperial Majesty the Sultan, to conclude a Treaty in order to record their intentions in conformity with what has been stated above, and to regulate the manner in which their said Majesties shall afford assistance to His Imperial Majesty the Sultan. For this purpose their said Majesties and His Imperial Majesty the Sultan have named as their Plenipotentiaries, that is to say:

Her Majesty the Queen of the United Kingdom of Great Britain and Ireland, the Right Honourable Stratford, Viscount Stratford de Redcliffe, a Peer of the United Kingdom, a Member of Her Britannic Majesty's Privy Council, &c.;

His Majesty the Emperor of the French, the Count Baraguey d'Hilliers, General of Division, &c.;

And His Imperial Majesty the Sultan, Mustapha Reshid Pasha, his Minister for Foreign Affairs;

Who, after having communicated to each other their Full Powers, found in good and due form, have agreed upon the following Articles:

*Co-operation of Great Britain and France for the Defence of Turkey
against Russian Aggression.*

ART. I. Her Majesty the Queen of the United Kingdom of Great
Britain and Ireland, and His Majesty the Emperor of the French,
having already, at the request of His Imperial Majesty the Sultan,
ordered powerful divisions of their Naval Forces to proceed to Constantinople, and to afford to the Ottoman Territory and Flag such
Protection as the circumstances might admit of, their said Majesties
undertake by the present Treaty still further to co-operate with His
Imperial Majesty the Sultan for the defence of the Ottoman Territory
in Europe and in Asia against Russian Aggression, by employing for that
purpose such an amount of their Land Forces as may appear necessary to
attain the said object; which Land Forces their said Majesties will
immediately dispatch to such point or points of the Ottoman Territory
as shall be deemed expedient; and His Imperial Majesty the Sultan
agrees, that the British and French Land Forces thus sent for the
Defence of the Ottoman Territory shall meet with the same friendly
reception, and shall be treated with the same consideration as the
British and French Naval Forces, which have for some time past been
employed in the waters of Turkey.

*Proposals of Peace by Russia to be communicated to Contracting Parties.
Turkey not to conclude Peace without consent of her Allies.*

ART. II. The High Contracting Parties severally engage to communicate to each other, without loss of time, any proposition which
any one of them may receive on the part of the Emperor of Russia, either
directly or indirectly, with a view to the Cessation of Hostilities, to an
Armistice, or to Peace; and His Imperial Majesty the Sultan engages,
moreover, not to conclude any Armistice, nor to enter on any negotiation
for Peace, and not to conclude any Preliminary of Peace, nor any
Treaty of Peace, with the Emperor of Russia, without the knowledge
and consent of the High Contracting Parties.

*Evacuation of Ottoman Territory by British and French Troops on
conclusion of Peace.*

ART. III. As soon as the object of the present Treaty shall have been
attained by the conclusion of a Treaty of Peace, Her Majesty the Queen
of the United Kingdom of Great Britain and Ireland, and His Majesty
the Emperor of the French, will forthwith make arrangements for the
immediate Withdrawal of all their Military and Naval Forces which
shall have been employed to accomplish the object of the present Treaty;
and all the Fortresses or Positions in the Ottoman Territory which shall
have been temporarily occupied by the Military Forces of England and

France, shall be delivered up to the authorities of the Sublime Ottoman Porte in the space of 40 days, or sooner if possible, after the exchange of the Ratifications of the Treaty by which the present War shall be terminated.

Movements of Auxiliary Armies not to be controlled by Turkish Authorities.

ART. IV. It is understood that the Auxiliary Armies shall retain the power of taking such part as they may deem expedient in the operations directed against the common enemy, without the Ottoman Authorities, civil or military, having any pretension to exercise the slightest control over their movements; on the contrary, every aid and facility shall be afforded to them by those authorities, especially for their landing, their march, their quarters or encampment, their subsistence and that of their horses, and their communications, whether they act together or whether they act separately.

Commanders of Auxiliary Armies to maintain Discipline and respect for the Laws.

It is understood, on the other hand, that the Commanders of the said Armies undertake to maintain the strictest Discipline in their respective Troops, and shall cause them to respect the Laws and usages of the country.

Property to be respected.

As a matter of course, Property shall be everywhere respected.

Plan of Campaign to be settled by the 3 Commanders-in-Chief.

It is moreover understood, on either side, that the general Plan of Campaign shall be discussed and settled between the Commanders-in-Chief of the 3 Armies, and that if any considerable portion of the Allied troops should be acting in conjunction with the Ottoman troops, no operation shall be undertaken against the enemy without its having been previously concerted with the Commanders of the Allied Forces.

Demands on Turkey for Auxiliary Troops to be attended to.

Finally, attention shall be paid to any demand relative to the wants of the service which may be addressed by the Commanders-in-Chief of the Auxiliary Troops, either to the Ottoman Government through their respective Embassies, or, in case of urgency, to the local authorities, unless insuperable objections, to be clearly explained, should prevent compliance with such demands.

Ratifications.

ART. V. The present Treaty shall be ratified, and the Ratifications shall be exchanged at Constantinople in the space of 6 weeks, or sooner if possible, from the day of signature.

In witness whereof the respective Plenipotentiaries have signed the same, and have affixed thereto the Seal of their Arms.

Done in triplicate, for one and the same purpose, at Constantinople, the 12th day of March, 1854.

> (L.S.) STRATFORD DE REDCLIFFE.
> (L.S.) BARAGUEY D'HILLIERS.
> (L.S.) RESHID.

53

PROTOCOL of Conference between Great Britain, Austria, France, and Prussia, for the Maintenance of the Integrity of the Ottoman Empire. Vienna, 9th April, 1854.

Present: The Representatives of Austria, France, Great Britain, and Prussia.

(Extract.)

AT the request of the Plenipotentiaries of France and of Great Britain, the Conference met to hear the documents read which establish that the invitation addressed to the Cabinet of St. Petersburgh to evacuate the Moldo-Wallachian Provinces within a fixed time having remained unanswered, the state of War already declared between Russia and the Sublime Porte is in actual existence equally between Russia, on the one side, and France and Great Britain, on the other.

This change which has taken place in the attitude of two of the Powers represented at the Conference of Vienna, in consequence of a step taken directly by France and England, supported by Austria and Prussia as being founded in right, has been considered by the Representatives of Austria and Prussia as involving the necessity of a fresh Declaration of the Union of the 4 Powers upon the ground of the principles laid down in the Protocols of the 5th December, 1853, and the 13th January, 1854.

In consequence, the Undersigned have at this solemn moment declared that their Governments remain united in the double object of maintaining the Territorial Integrity of the Ottoman Empire, of which the fact of the Evacuation of the Danubian Principalities is and will remain one of the essential conditions; and of consolidating in an interest so much in conformity with the sentiments of the Sultan, and by every means compatible with his Independence and Sovereignty, the Civil and Religious Rights of the Christian subjects of the Porte.

The Territorial Integrity of the Ottoman Empire is and remains the *sine quâ non* condition of every transaction having for its object the re-establishment of Peace between the Belligerent Powers ; and the Governments represented by the Undersigned engage to endeavour in common to discover the Guarantees most likely to attach the existence of that Empire to the general equilibrium of Europe ; as they also declare themselves ready to deliberate and to come to an understanding as to the employment of the means calculated to accomplish the object of their agreement.

Whatever event may arise in consequence of this Agreement, founded solely upon the general interests of Europe, and of which the object can only be attained by the return of a firm and lasting Peace, the Governments represented by the Undersigned reciprocally engage not to enter into any Definitive Arrangement with the Imperial Court of Russia, or with any other Power, which would be at variance with the principles above enunciated, without previously deliberating thereon in common.

> BUOL-SCHAUENSTEIN.
> BOURQUENEY.
> WESTMORLAND.
> ARNIM.

54 CONVENTION OF LONDON

CONVENTION between Great Britain and France, relative to Military Aid to be given to Turkey. Signed at London, 10th April, 1854. Ratifications exchanged in London, 15th April, 1854.

THEIR Majesties the Queen of the United Kingdom of Great Britain and Ireland, and the Emperor of the French, having determined to afford their support to His Majesty the Sultan Abdul Medjid, Emperor of the Ottomans, in the War in which he is engaged against the Aggressions of Russia ; and being, moreover, compelled, notwithstanding their sincere and persevering efforts for the maintenance of Peace, to become themselves belligerent parties in a War which, without their active intervention, would have threatened the existing Balance of Power in Europe, and the interests of their own dominions ; have, in consequence, resolved to conclude a Convention in order to determine the object of their Alliance, as well as the means to be employed in common for fulfilling that object ; and have for that purpose named as their Plenipotentiaries :

Her Majesty the Queen of the United Kingdom of Great Britain and Ireland, the Right Honourable George William Frederick, Earl of Clarendon, Baron Hyde of Hindon, a Peer of the United Kingdom, a Member of Her Britannic Majesty's Most Honourable Privy Council, Her Britannic Majesty's Principal Secretary of State for Foreign Affairs, &c. ;

And His Majesty the Emperor of the French, the Sieur Alexander Colonna, Count Walewski, his Ambassador to Her Britannic Majesty, &c. :

Who, after having communicated to each other their Full Powers, found in good and due form, have agreed upon and signed the following Articles:

Measures for the re-establishment of Peace.

ART. I. The High Contracting Parties engage to do all that shall depend upon them for the purpose of bringing about the re-establishment of Peace between Russia and the Sublime Porte on solid and durable bases, and of preserving Europe from the recurrence of the lamentable complications which have now so unhappily disturbed the general Peace.

Naval and Military Assistance to Turkey.

ART. II. The Integrity of the Ottoman Empire being violated by the Occupation of the Provinces of Moldavia and of Wallachia, and by other movements of the Russian troops, their Majesties the Queen of Great Britain and Ireland and the Emperor of the French have concerted, and will concert together, as to the most proper means for liberating the Territory of the Sultan from Foreign Invasion, and for accomplishing the object specified in Article I. For this purpose they engage to maintain, according to the requirements of the War, to be judged of by common agreement, sufficient Naval and Military Forces to meet those requirements, the description, number, and destination whereof shall, if occasion should arise, be determined by subsequent Arrangements.

Contracting Parties not to enter into Arrangements with Russia without previous deliberation.

ART. III. Whatever events may arise from the execution of the Present Convention, the High Contracting Parties engage not to entertain any Overture or any Proposition having for its object the Cessation

of Hostilities, nor to enter into any Arrangement with the Imperial
Court of Russia, without having first deliberated thereupon in common.

Contracting Parties renounce the Acquisition of any Advantages.

ART. IV. The High Contracting Parties being animated with a desire
to maintain the Balance of Power in Europe, and having no interested
ends in view, renounce beforehand the Acquisition of any Advantage for
themselves from the events which may occur.

Admittance of European Powers into Alliance.

ART. V. Their Majesties the Queen of the United Kingdom of
Great Britain and Ireland and the Emperor of the French will readily
admit into their Alliance, in order to co-operate for the proposed object,
such of the other Powers of Europe as may be desirous of becoming
party to it.

Ratifications.

ART. VI. The present Convention shall be ratified, and the Ratifications shall be exchanged at London within 8 days.

In witness whereof the respective Plenipotentiaries have signed the
same, and have affixed thereto the Seal of their Arms.

Done at London, the 10th day of April, in the year of Our Lord,
1854.

(L.S.)   CLARENDON.
(L.S.)   A. WALEWSKI.

55

TREATY OF ALLIANCE, Offensive and Defensive, between Austria and Prussia. Signed and ratified at Berlin, 20th April, 1854.

HIS Majesty the Emperor of Austria and His Majesty the King of
Prussia, impressed with the deepest regret at the failure of the efforts
which they had made up to the present time to prevent the War between
Russia, on the one part, and Turkey, France, and Great Britain on
the other;

Faithful to the moral engagements which they contracted in signing
the Protocols of Vienna;

In presence of the ever-increasing developments made, on both sides,
by military measures, and the dangers arising therefrom to the Peace of
Europe;

Convinced of the high mission which, on the approach of a disastrous future, and in the interest of European well-being, is imposed on Germany, closely united to their respective States;

Have resolved to conclude, for so long as the War, which has just broken out between Russia, on the one part, and Turkey, Great Britain, and France, on the other, shall last, an Offensive and Defensive Alliance, and have appointed as their Plenipotentiaries to that effect, namely:

His Majesty the Emperor of Austria, Baron Henry de Hess, his Actual Intimate Councillor, &c.; and Count Frederick de Thun-Hohenstein, his Envoy Extraordinary and Minister Plenipotentiary to His Majesty the King of Prussia, &c.;

And His Majesty the King of Prussia, Baron Othon Theodor Manteuffel, his President of the Council of Ministers and his Minister for Foreign Affairs, &c.;

Who, after having exchanged their Full Powers, found to be in good and due form, have agreed upon the following Articles:

ARTS. I to VI.

Done at Berlin, 20th April, 1854.

(L.S.)   HENRY BON. DE HESS.
(L.S.)   F. THUN.
(L.S.)   BON. OTH. THEODOR MANTEUFFEL.

ADDITIONAL ARTICLE.

ACCORDING to the conditions of Article II of the Treaty concluded this day between His Imperial Majesty the Emperor of Austria and His Majesty the King of Prussia for the establishment of an Offensive and Defensive Alliance, a more intimate understanding with respect to the eventuality when an active advance of one of the High Contracting Parties may impose on the other the obligation of a mutual Protection of the Territory of both, was to form the subject of a Special Agreement to be considered as an integral part of the Treaty.

Their Majesties have not been able to divest themselves of the consideration that the indefinite continuance of the Occupation of the Territories on the Lower Danube, under the Sovereignty of the Ottoman Porte, by Imperial Russian troops, would endanger the political moral, and material interests of the whole German Confederation, as also of their own States, and the more so in proportion as Russia extends her warlike operations on Turkish Territory.

The Courts of Austria and Prussia are united in the desire to avoid every participation in the War which has broken out between Russia, on the one hand, and Turkey, France, and Great Britain, on the other, and at the same time to contribute to the restoration of general Peace. They more especially consider the Declarations lately made at Berlin by the Court of St. Petersburgh, to be an important element of pacification, the failure of the practical influence of which they would view with regret. According to these Declarations, Russia appears to regard the original motive for the Occupation of the Principalities as removed by the concessions now granted to the Christian subjects of the Porte, which offer the prospect of realisation. They therefore hope that the replies awaited from the Cabinet of Russia to the Prussian propositions, transmitted on the 8th, will offer to them the necessary Guarantee for an early withdrawal of the Russian troops. In the event that this hope should be illusory, the Plenipotentiaries named, on the part of His Majesty the Emperor of Austria, Freiherr Baron von Hess and Count Thun, and on the part of His Majesty the King of Prussia, Baron Manteuffel, have drawn up the following more detailed Agreement with respect to the eventuality alluded to in the above-mentioned Article II of the Treaty of Alliance of this day:

Aggression on Territories of one of the Contracting Parties to be repelled by Military Forces of the other.

SINGLE ARTICLE.—The Imperial Austrian Government will also on their side address a communication to the Imperial Russian Court with the object of obtaining from the Emperor of Russia the necessary orders that an immediate stop should be put to the further advance of his Armies upon the Turkish Territory, as also to request of His Imperial Majesty sufficient Guarantees for the prompt Evacuation of the Danubian Principalities; and the Prussian Government will again in the most emphatic manner, support these communications with reference to their proposals already sent to St. Petersburgh. Should the answer of the Russian Court to these steps of the Cabinets of Vienna and Berlin— contrary to expectation—not be of a nature to give them entire satisfaction upon the two points afore-mentioned, the measures to be taken by one of the Contracting Parties for their attainment, according to the terms of Article II of the Offensive and Defensive Alliance signed on this day, will be on the understanding that every hostile attack on the Territory of one of the Contracting Parties is to be repelled with all the Military Forces at the disposal of the other.

Cases in which Offensive Advance only shall be made.

But a mutual Offensive Advance is stipulated for only in the event of the incorporation of the Principalities, or in the event of an attack on or passage of the Balkan by Russia.

Ratifications.

The present Convention shall be submitted for the Ratification of the

High Sovereigns simultaneously with the above-mentioned Treaty.
Done at Berlin, the 20th April 1854.

(L.S.)   HESS.   (L.S.)   MANTEUFFEL.
(L.S.)   THUN.

56   CONVENTION OF BOYADJI-KEUY

CONVENTION between Austria and Turkey, relative to
the Austrian Occupation of the Danubian Principalities.
Signed at Boyadji-Keuy, 14th June, 1854. Ratifications
exchanged at Vienna, 30th June, 1854.

HIS Majesty the Emperor of Austria, fully recognising that the
existence of the Ottoman Empire within its present Limits is necessary
for the maintenance of the Balance of Power between the States of
Europe, and that, specifically, the Evacuation of the Danubian Principalities is one of the essential conditions of the Integrity of that Empire;
being, moreover, ready to join, with the means at his disposal, in the
measures proper to ensure the object of the Agreement established
between his Cabinet and the High Courts represented at the Conference
of Vienna.

His Imperial Majesty the Sultan having on his side accepted this offer
of Concert made in a friendly manner by His Majesty the Emperor of
Austria;

It has seemed proper to conclude a Convention, in order to regulate
the manner in which the Concert in question shall be carried into effect.

With this object His Imperial Majesty the Emperor of Austria and
His Imperial Majesty the Sultan have named as their Plenipotentiaries,
that is to say:

His Majesty the Emperor of Austria, M. le Baron Charles de Bruck,
his Internuncio and Minister Plenipotentiary at the Sublime Ottoman
Porte, &c.;

And His Imperial Majesty the Sultan, Mustapha Reshid Pasha, late
Grand Vizier, and at present his Minister for Foreign Affairs, &c.;

Who after having exchanged their Full Powers, found to be in good
and due form, have agreed upon the following Articles:

Means to be adopted for Evacuation of Danubian Principalities.

ART. I. His Majesty the Emperor of Austria engages to exhaust all the
means of negotiation and all other means to obtain the Evacuation of the
Danubian Principalities by the Foreign Army which occupies them, and

even to employ, in case they are required, the number of Troops necessary to attain this end.

Command of Austrian Army.

ART. II. It will appertain in this case exclusively to the Imperial Commander-in-Chief to direct the operations of his Army. He will, however, always take care to inform the Commander-in-Chief of the Ottoman Army of his operations in proper time.

Administration of Danubian Principalities.

ART. III. His Majesty the Emperor of Austria undertakes by common Agreement with the Ottoman Government to re-establish in the Principalities, as far as possible, the legal state of things such as it results from the Privileges secured by the Sublime Porte in regard to the Administration of those Countries. The local authorities thus reconstituted shall not, however, extend their action so far as to attempt to exercise control over the Imperial Army.

Sovereign Rights and Integrity of Ottoman Empire.

ART. IV. The Imperial Court of Austria further engages not to enter into any plan of accommodation with the Imperial Court of Russia which has not for its Basis the Sovereign Rights of His Majesty the Sultan, as well as the Integrity of his Empire.

Withdrawal of Austrian Troops from Principalities on conclusion of Peace with Russia.

ART. V. As soon as the object of the present Convention shall have been obtained by the conclusion of a Treaty of Peace between the Sublime Porte and the Court of Russia, His Majesty the Emperor of Austria will immediately make arrangements for withdrawing his Forces with the least possible delay from the Territory of the Principalities. The details respecting the retreat of the Austrian Troops shall form the object of a special understanding with the Sublime Porte.

Assistance to Austrian Troops from Ottoman Authorities.

ART. VI. The Austrian Government expects that the Authorities of the Countries temporarily occupied by the Imperial Troops will afford them every assistance and facility, as well for their march, their lodging or encampment, as for their subsistence and that of their horses, and for their communications. The Austrian Government likewise expects that every demand relating to the requirements of the service shall be complied with, which shall be addressed by the Austrian Commanders, either to the Ottoman Government through the Imperial Internunciate at Constantinople, or directly to the Local Authorities, unless more weighty reasons render the execution of them impossible.

Maintenance of Order by Commanders of Austrian Army.

It is understood that the Commanders of the Imperial Army will provide for the maintenance of the strictest discipline among their Troops, and will respect, and cause to be respected, the Properties as well as the Laws, the Religion, and the Customs of the Principalities.

Ratifications.

ART. VII. The present Convention shall be ratified, and the Ratifications shall be exchanged at Vienna in the space of 4 weeks, or earlier if possible, dating from the day of its signature.

In faith of which the respective Plenipotentiaries have signed it and set their Seals to it.

Done in duplicate, for one and the same effect, at Boyadji-Keuy, the 14th June, 1854.

(L.S.) V. BRUCK.   (L.S.) RESHID.

57 TREATY OF VIENNA

TREATY OF ALLIANCE between Great Britain, Austria, and France. Signed at Vienna, 2nd December, 1854.

Peace of Europe.

HER Majesty the Queen of the United Kingdom of Great Britain and Ireland, His Majesty the Emperor of Austria, and His Majesty the Emperor of the French, being animated with the desire of terminating the present War at the earliest possible moment, by the re-establishment of General Peace on solid bases, affording to the whole of Europe every Guarantee against the return of the complications which have so unhappily disturbed its repose; being convinced that nothing would be more conducive to that result than the complete Union of their efforts until the common object which they have in view shall be entirely attained; and acknowledging, in consequence, the necessity of coming to an immediate understanding with regard to their respective positions, and to arrangements for the future; have resolved to conclude a Treaty of Alliance, and have for that purpose named as their Plenipotentiaries:

Her Majesty the Queen of the United Kingdom of Great Britain and Ireland, the Right Honourable John Fane, Earl of Westmorland, Envoy Extraordinary and Minister Plenipotentiary to His Imperial and Royal Apostolic Majesty, &c.;

His Majesty the Emperor of Austria, the Sieur Charles, Count de Buol-Schauenstein, his Chamberlain and Privy Councillor, Minister for Foreign Affairs and of the Imperial House, &c.;

His Majesty the Emperor of the French, the Sieur Francis Adolphus, Baron de Bourqueney, his Envoy Extraordinary and Minister Plenipotentiary to His Imperial and Royal Apostolic Majesty, &c.;

Who, after having communicated to each other their Full Powers, found in good and due form, have agreed upon and signed the following Articles:

High Contracting Parties not to make Arrangements with Russia, without previous Deliberation in common.

ART. I. The High Contracting Parties refer to the Declarations contained in the Protocols of the 9th of April and 23rd of May of the present year, and in the Notes exchanged on the 8th of August last; and as they reserved to themselves the right of proposing, according to circumstances, such Conditions as they might judge necessary for the general interests of Europe, they engage mutually and reciprocally not to enter into any Arrangement with the Imperial Court of Russia without having first deliberated thereupon in common.

Occupation of Principalities of Moldavia and Wallachia by Austrian Troops during the War.

ART. II. His Majesty the Emperor of Austria having, in virtue of the Treaty concluded on the 14th of June last with the Sublime Porte, caused the Principalities of Moldavia and Wallachia to be occupied by his troops, he engages to defend the Frontier of the said Principalities against any return of the Russian Forces; the Austrian troops shall for this purpose occupy the positions necessary for Guaranteeing those Principalities against any attack. Her Majesty the Queen of the United Kingdom of Great Britain and Ireland, and His Majesty the Emperor of the French, having likewise concluded with the Sublime Porte on the 12th of March, a Treaty which authorises them to direct their forces upon every part of the Ottoman Empire, the above-mentioned Occupation shall not interfere with the free movement of the Anglo-French or Ottoman troops upon these same Territories against the Military Forces or the Territory of Russia. There shall be formed at Vienna between the Plenipotentiaries of Austria, France, and Great Britain, a Commission to which Turkey shall be invited to send a Plenipotentiary, and which shall be charged with examining and regulating every question relating either to the exceptional and provisional state in which the said Principalities are now placed, or to the free passage of the different armies across their Territory.

Offensive and Defensive Alliance in case of Hostilities between Austria and Russia.

ART. III. In case hostilities should break out between Austria and Russia, Her Majesty the Queen of the United Kingdom of Great Brjtain and Ireland, His Majesty the Emperor of Austria, and His Majesty the Emperor of the French, mutually promise to each other their Offensive and Defensive Alliance in the present War, and will for that purpose employ, according to the requirements of the War, Military and Naval Forces, the number, description, and destination whereof shall, if occassion should arise, be determined by subsequent arrangements.

High Contracting Parties not to entertain Overtures of Peace without previous Consultation.

ART. IV. In the case contemplated by the preceding Article, the High Contracting Parties reciprocally engage not to entertain any Overture or Proposition on the part of the Imperial Court of Russia, having for its object the Cessation of Hostilities, without having come to an understanding thereupon between themselves.

Deliberations in case of Non-conclusion of General Peace.

ART. V. In case the re-establishment of General Peace, upon the bases indicated in Article I, should not be assured in the course of the present year, Her Majesty the Queen of the United Kingdom of Great Britain and Ireland, His Majesty the Emperor of Austria, and His Majesty the Emperor of the French, will deliberate without delay upon effectual means for obtaining the object of their Alliance.

Invitation to Prussia to accede to Convention.

ART. VI. Great Britain, Austria, and France will jointly communicate the present Treaty to the Court of Prussia, and will with satisfaction receive its Accession thereto, in case it should promise its co-operation for the accomplishment of the common object.

Ratifications.

ART. VII. The present Treaty shall be ratified, and the Ratifications shall be exchanged at Vienna in the space of a fortnight.

In witness whereof the respective Plenipotentiaries have signed the same, and have affixed thereto the Seal of their Arms.

Done at Vienna, the 2nd of December, in the year of Our Lord, 1854.

(L.S.)   WESTMORLAND.

(L.S.)   BUOL-SCHAUENSTEIN.

(L.S.)   BOURQUENEY.

58

MILITARY CONVENTION between Great Britain, France, and Sardinia. Signed at Turin, 26th January, 1855. Ratifications exchanged at Turin, 4th March, 1855.

Reference to Treaty of 10th April, 1854.

His Majesty the King of Sardinia having acceded to the Treaty of Alliance concluded and signed at London on the 10th of April, 1854, between their Majesties the Queen of the United Kingdom of Great Britain and Ireland, and the Emperor of the French, and having engaged to concert, when necessary, with their said Majesties for the purpose of proceeding, conformably to Article II of the Treaty of the 10th of April, to the conclusion of the arrangements of detail which shall regulate the employment of his Land and Sea Forces, and determine the conditions and mode of their Co-operation with those of Great Britain and of France; their Majesties the Queen of the United Kingdom of Great Britain and Ireland, the Emperor of the French, and the King of Sardinia, have in consequence resolved to conclude a Military Convention destined to regulate the conditions and the mode of the Co-operation of the Sardinian troops with those of Great Britain and of France, and have named for that purpose as their Plenipotentiaries:

Her Majesty the Queen of the United Kingdom of Great Britain and Ireland, James Hudson, Esquire, her Envoy Extraordinary and Minister Plenipotentiary to His Majesty the King of Sardinia, &c.;

His Majesty the Emperor of the French, the Duke de Guiche, his Envoy Extraordinary and Minister Plenipotentiary to His Majesty the King of Sardinia, &c.;

And His Majesty the King of Sardinia, the Count Camille de Cavour, President of the Council of Ministers, and his Minister for Foreign Affairs, &c.;

Who, after having communicated to each other their Full Powers, found in good and due form, have agreed upon and signed the following Articles:

ARTS. I to VII.

Done at Turin, the 26th of January, in the year of Our Lord, 1855.

(L.S.) JAMES HUDSON.

(L.S.) GUICHE.

(L.S.) CAVOUR.

59

CONVENTION between Great Britain and Turkey, for the Employment of a body of Turkish Troops in the British Service. Signed at Constantinople, 3rd February, 1855. Ratifications exchanged at Constantinople, 12th March, 1855.

HER Majesty the Queen of the United Kingdom of Great Britain and Ireland, with a view to the more effectual prosecution of the War in which Her Majesty, the Emperor of the French, and His Imperial Majesty the Sultan are engaged, having proposed to His Imperial Majesty the Sultan to take into the British Service for a time, and in all respects provide for, such a proportion of Turkish troops as might be agreed upon between Her Majesty and the Sultan; and His Imperial Majesty the Sultan having signified his concurrence in that proposal of his Ally; their said Majesties have seen fit to conclude a Convention for the purpose of determining the conditions on which such Turkish troops shall be employed, and have named as their Plenipotentiaries, that is to say:

Her Majesty the Queen of the United Kingdom of Great Britain and Ireland, the Right Honourable Stratford, Viscount Stratford de Redcliffe, her Ambassador Extraordinary and Plenipotentiary to the Ottoman Porte, &c.;

And His Imperial Majesty the Sultan, Mustapha Rechid Pacha, his Grand Vizier; and Mehemed Ali Pacha, his Minister for Foreign Affairs;

Who, after having communicated to each other their respective Full Powers, found in good and due form, have agreed upon and concluded the following Articles:

1. Engagement of 20,000 Turkish Regular Troops (Rediffs) into Service of *Great Britain*, to be employed as deemed advisable.

2. Command of *Turkish* Troops. Rank to be conferred in *Turkish* Service on *British* Officers. *Turkish* Troops to be subject to Discipline and Regulations of *British* Service.

3. Arming, equipment, pay, clothing, and maintenance of *Turkish* Troops. Pay to correspond with Pay in Sultan's Service.

4. Non-interference with *Turkish* Officers and Men in Religious Observances.

5. Date at which *Turkish* Troops are to be considered in *British* Service.

6. On conclusion of Peace, Officers and Men to be placed at disposal of *Turkish* Government.

7. Rations and Punishments to be in accordance with system pursued in *Turkish* Army.

8. *Turkish* Troops on entering *British* Service, to enter it prepared to take the Field.

9. Ratifications.

Done in duplicate for one and the same purpose at Constantinople, the 3rd day of February, 1855.

(L.S.) STRATFORD DE REDCLIFFE.
(L.S.) RECHID.
(L.S.) AALI.

60   TREATY OF STOCKHOLM

TREATY between Great Britain, France, and Sweden and Norway. Signed at Stockholm, 21st November, 1855. Ratifications exchanged at Stockholm, 21st December, 1855.

Balance of Power in Europe.

HER Majesty the Queen of the United Kingdom of Great Britain and Ireland, His Majesty the Emperor of the French, and His Majesty the King of Sweden and Norway, being anxious to avert any complication which might disturb the existing Balance of Power in Europe, have resolved to come to an understanding with a view to secure the integrity of the United Kingdoms of Sweden and Norway, and have named as their Plenipotentiaries to conclude a Treaty for that purpose, that is to say:

Her Majesty the Queen of the United Kingdom of Great Britain and Ireland, Arthur Charles Magenis, Esquire, her Envoy Extraordinary and Minister Plenipotentiary to His Majesty the King of Sweden and Norway;

His Majesty the Emperor of the French, the Sieur Charles Victor Lobstein, his Envoy Extraordinary and Minister Plenipotentiary to His Majesty the King of Sweden and Norway, &c.;

And His Majesty the King of Sweden and Norway, the Sieur Gustavus Nicholas Algernon Adolphus Baron de Stierneld, his Minister of State and for Foreign Affairs, &c., &c., &c.;

Who, after having communicated to each other their respective Full Powers, found in good and due form, have agreed as follows:

Sweden not to make any Territorial Cessions or confer any Rights of Pasturage, &c., to Russia, in Sweden and Norway.

ART. I. His Majesty the King of Sweden and Norway engages not to cede to nor exchange with Russia, nor to permit her to occupy, any part of the Territories belonging to the Crowns of Sweden and Norway. His Majesty the King of Sweden and Norway engages, further, not to cede to Russia any Right of Pasturage, of Fishery, or of any other nature whatsoever, either on the said Territories or upon the Coasts of Sweden and Norway, and to resist any pretension which may be put forward by Russia with a view to establish the existence of any of the Rights aforesaid.

Co-operation of Great Britain and France to resist Pretensions or Aggressions of Russia.

ART. II. In case Russia should make to His Majesty the King of Sweden and Norway any Proposal or Demand having for its object to obtain either the Cession or the Exchange of any part whatsoever of the Territories belonging to the Crowns of Sweden and Norway, or the power of occupying certain points of the said Territories, or the Cession of Rights of Fishery, of Pasturage, or of any other Right upon the said Territories and upon the Coasts of Sweden and Norway, His Majesty the King of Sweden and Norway engages forthwith to communicate such Proposal or Demand to Her Britannic Majesty and His Majesty the Emperor of the French; and their said Majesties, on their part, engage to furnish to His Majesty the King of Sweden and Norway sufficient Naval and Military Forces to Co-operate with the Naval and Military Forces of His said Majesty, for the purpose of resisting the Pretensions or Aggressions of Russia. The description, number, and destination of such forces shall, if occasion should arise, be determined by common agreement between the 3 Powers.

Ratifications.

ART. III. The present Treaty shall be ratified, and the Ratifications shall be exchanged at Stockholm as soon as possible.

In witness whereof the respective Plenipotentiaries have signed the same, and have affixed thereto the Seal of their Arms.

Done at Stockholm, the 21st of November, in the year of Our Lord, 1855.

(L.S.) ARTHUR C. MAGENIS.

(L.S.) VOR. LOBSTEIN.

(L.S.) STIERNELD.

61   TREATY OF PARIS

GENERAL TREATY of Peace between Great Britain, Austria, France, Prussia, Russia, Sardinia, and Turkey. Signed at Paris, 30th March, 1856. Ratifications exchanged at Paris, 27th April, 1856.

Integrity and Independence of Ottoman Empire.

In the Name of Almighty God.

THEIR Majesties the Queen of the United Kingdom of Great Britain and Ireland, the Emperor of the French, the Emperor of All the Russias, the King of Sardinia, and the Emperor of the Ottomans, animated by the desire of putting an end to the calamities of War, and wishing to prevent the return of the complications which occasioned it, resolved to come to an understanding with His Majesty the Emperor of Austria as to the bases on which Peace might be re-established and consolidated, by securing, through effectual and reciprocal guarantees, the Independence and Integrity of the Ottoman Empire.

For this purpose their said Majesties named as their Plenipotentiaries, that is to say:

Her Majesty the Queen of the United Kingdom of Great Britain and Ireland, the Right Honourable George William Frederick, Earl of Clarendon, Baron Hyde of Hindon, a Peer of the United Kingdom, a Member of Her Britannic Majesty's Most Honourable Privy Council, Her Majesty's Principal Secretary of State for Foreign Affairs, &c., and the Right Honourable Henry Richard Charles Baron Cowley, a Peer of the United Kingdom, a Member of Her Majesty's Most Honourable Privy Council, Her Majesty's Ambassador Extraordinary and Minister Plenipotentiary to His Majesty the Emperor of the French, &c.;

His Majesty the Emperor of Austria, the Sieur Charles Ferdinant Count of Buol-Schauenstein, his Chamberlain and actual Privy Councillor, his Minister of the House and of Foreign Affairs, President of the Conference of Ministers, &c.; and the Sieur Joseph Alexander Baron de Hübner, his actual Privy Councillor, and his Envoy Extraordinary and Minister Plenipotentiary to the Court of France, &c.;

His Majesty the Emperor of the French, the Sieur Alexander Count Colonna Walewski, a Senator of the Empire, his Minister and Secretary of State for Foreign Affairs, &c.; and the Sieur Francis Adolphus Baron de Bourqueney, his Envoy Extraordinary and Minister Plenipotentiary to His Imperial and Royal Apostolic Majesty, &c.;

His Majesty the Emperor of All the Russias, the Sieur Alexis Count

Orloff, his Aide-de-Camp General and General of Cavalry, Commander of the Head-quarters of His Majesty, a Member of the Council of the Empire and of the Committee of Ministers, &c.; and the Sieur Philip, Baron de Brunnow, his Privy Councillor, his Envoy Extraordinary and Minister Plenipotentiary to the Germanic Confederation, and to the Grand Duke of Hesse, &c.;

His Majesty the King of Sardinia, the Sieur Camille Benso, Count of Cavour, President of the Council of Ministers, and his Minister Secretary of State for the Finance, &c.; and the Sieur Salvator Marquis de Villa-Marina, his Envoy Extraordinary and Minister Plenipotentiary to the Court of France, &c.;

And His Majesty the Emperor of the Ottomans, Mouhammed Emin Ali Pasha, Grand Vizier of the Ottoman Empire, &c.; and Mehemmed Djemil Bey, his Ambassador Extraordinary and Plenipotentiary to His Majesty the Emperor of the French, accredited in the same character to His Majesty the King of Sardinia, &c.;

Which Plenipotentiaries assembled in Congress at Paris.

An understanding having been happily established between them, their Majesties the Queen of the United Kingdom of Great Britain and Ireland, the Emperor of Austria, the Emperor of the French, the Emperor of All the Russias, the King of Sardinia, and the Emperor of the Ottomans, considering that in the interest of Europe, His Majesty the King of Prussia, a signing party to the Convention of the 13th of July, 1841, should be invited to participate in the new arrangements to be adopted, and appreciating the value that the concurrence of His said Majesty would add to a work of general pacification, invited him to send Plenipotentiaries to the Congress.

In consequence, His Majesty the King of Prussia named as his Plenipotentiaries, that is to say:

The Sieur Otho Theodore Baron de Manteuffel, President of his Council, and his Minister for Foreign Affairs, &c.; and the Sieur Maximilian Frederick Charles Francis, Count of Hatzfeldt Wildenburg-Schoenstein, his actual Privy Councillor, his Envoy and Minister Plenipotentiary to the Court of France, &c.;

The Plenipotentiaries, after having exchanged their Full Powers, found in good and due form, have agreed upon the following Articles:

Peace and Friendship.

ART. I. From the day of the exchange of the Ratifications of the present Treaty there shall be Peace and Friendship between Her Majesty the Queen of the United Kingdom of Great Britain and Ireland, His Majesty the Emperor of the French, His Majesty the King of Sardinia, His Imperial Majesty the Sultan, on the one part, and His

Majesty the Emperor of All the Russias, on the other part; as well as between their heirs and successors, their respective dominions and subjects, in perpetuity.

Evacuation of Territories.

ART. II. Peace being happily re-established between their said Majesties, the Territories conquered or occupied by their armies during the War shall be reciprocally evacuated.

Special arrangements shall regulate the mode of the Evacuation, which shall be as prompt as possible.

Restoration of Kars, &c., to Turkey.

ART. III. His Majesty the Emperor of All the Russias engages to restore to His Majesty the Sultan the Town and Citadel of Kars, as well as the other parts of the Ottoman Territory of which the Russian troops are in possession.

Restoration of Sebastopol, Balaklava, Kamiesch, Eupatoria, Kertch, Jenikale, Kinburn, &c., to Russia.

ART. IV. Their Majesties the Queen of the United Kingdom of Great Britain and Ireland, the Emperor of the French, the King of Sardinia, and the Sultan, engage to restore to His Majesty the Emperor of All the Russias, the Towns and Ports of Sebastopol, Balaklava, Kamiesch, Eupatoria, Kertch, Jenikale, Kinburn, as well as all other Territories occupied by the Allied Troops.

Amnesty.

ART. V. Their Majesties the Queen of the United Kingdom of Great Britain and Ireland, the Emperor of the French, the Emperor of All the Russias, the King of Sardinia, and the Sultan, grant a full and entire Amnesty to those of their subjects who may have been compromised by any participation whatsoever in the events of the War in favour of the cause of the enemy.

It is expressly understood that such Amnesty shall extend to the subjects of each of the Belligerent Parties who may have continued, during the War, to be employed in the service of one of the other Belligerents.

Prisoners of War.

ART. VI. Prisoners of War shall be immediately given up on either side.

Admission of the Sublime Porte into the European System.
Guarantee of Independence of Ottoman Empire.
ART. VII. Her Majesty the Queen of the United Kingdom of Great Britain and Ireland, His Majesty the Emperor of Austria, His Majesty the Emperor of the French, His Majesty the King of Prussia, His Majesty the Emperor of All the Russias, and His Majesty the King of Sardinia, declare the Sublime Porte admitted to participate in the advantages of the Public Law and System (*Concert*) of Europe. Their Majesties engage, each on his part, to respect the Independence and the Territorial Integrity of the Ottoman Empire; Guarantee in common the strict observance of that engagement; and will, in consequence, consider any act tending to its violation as a question of general interest.

Mediation in event of Misunderstanding between the Sublime Porte and one
or more of the Contracting Powers.
ART. VIII. If there should arise between the Sublime Porte and one or more of the other Signing Powers, any misunderstanding which might endanger the maintenance of their relations, the Sublime Porte, and each of such Powers, before having recourse to the use of force, shall afford the other Contracting Parties the opportunity of preventing such an extremity by means of their Mediation.

Amelioration of Condition of Christian Population of Ottoman Empire.
ART. IX. His Imperial Majesty the Sultan having, in his constant solicitude for the welfare of his subjects, issued a Firman, which while ameliorating their condition without distinction of Religion or of Race, records his generous intentions towards the Christian population of his Empire, and wishing to give a further proof of his sentiments in that respect, has resolved to communicate to the Contracting Parties the said Firman, emanating spontaneously from his Sovereign will.

Non-interference of Allies in Internal Affairs of Ottoman Empire.
The Contracting Powers recognise the high value of this communication. It is clearly understood that it cannot, in any case, give to the said Powers the right to interfere, either collectively or separately, in the relations of His Majesty the Sultan with his subjects, nor in the Internal Administration of his Empire.

Closing of Straits of Bosphorus and Dardanelles.
ART. X. The Convention of 13th of July, 1841, which maintains the ancient rule of the Ottoman Empire relative to the Closing of the Straits of the Bosphorus and of Dardenelles, has been revised by common consent.

The Act concluded for that purpose, and in conformity with that principle, between the High Contracting Parties, is and remains annexed to the present Treaty, and shall have the same force and validity as if it formed an integral part thereof.

Neutralisation of the Black Sea.

ART. XI. The Black Sea is Neutralised; its Waters and its Ports, thrown open to the Mercantile Marine of every Nation, are formally and in perpetuity interdicted to the Flag of War, either of the Powers possessing its Coasts, or of any other Power, with the exceptions mentioned in Articles XIV and XIX of the present Treaty.

Commercial Regulations in the Black Sea.

ART. XII. Free from any impediment, the Commerce in the Ports and Waters of the Black Sea shall be subject only to Regulations of Health, Customs, and Police, framed in a spirit favourable to the development of Commercial transactions.

Appointment of Foreign Consuls in Ports of Black Sea.

In order to afford to the Commercial and Maritime interests of every Nation the security which is desired, Russia and the Sublime Porte will admit Consuls into their Ports situated upon the Coast of the Black Sea, in conformity with the principles of International Law.

Military-Maritime Arsenals not to be Established or Maintained on Coasts of Black Sea.

ART. XIII. The Black Sea being Neutralised according to the terms of Article XI, the maintenance or establishment upon its Coast of Military-Maritime Arsenals becomes alike unnecessary and purposeless; in consequence, His Majesty the Emperor of All the Russias, and His Imperial Majesty the Sultan, engage not to establish or to maintain upon that Coast any Military-Maritime Arsenal.

Russian and Ottoman Naval Force in Black Sea.

ART. XIV. Their Majesties the Emperor of All the Russias and the Sultan having concluded a Convention for the purpose of settling the Force and the Number of Light Vessels, necessary for the service of their Coasts, which they reserve to themselves to maintain in the Black Sea, that Convention is annexed to the present Treaty, and shall have the same force and validity as if it formed an integral part thereof. It cannot be either annulled or modified without the assent of the Powers signing the present Treaty.

Free Navigation of the Danube.

ART. XV. The Act of the Congress of Vienna, having established the principles intended to regulate the Navigation of Rivers which separate or traverse different States, the Contracting Powers stipulate among themselves that those principles shall in future be equally applied to the Danube and its Mouths. They declare that its arrangement henceforth forms a part of the Public Law of Europe, and take it under their Guarantee.

Duties and Regulations of Police and Quarantine in the Danube.

The Navigation of the Danube cannot be subjected to any impediment or charge not expressly provided for by the Stipulations contained in the following Articles: in consequence, there shall not be levied any Toll founded solely upon the fact of the Navigation of the River, nor any Duty upon the Goods which may be on board of Vessels. The Regulations of Police and of Quarantine to be established for the safety of the States separated or traversed by that River, shall be so framed as to facilitate, as much as possible, the passage of Vessels. With the exception of such Regulations, no obstacle whatever shall be opposed to Free Navigation.

Appointment of Danube European Commission.

ART. XVI. With a view to carry out the arrangements of the preceding Article, a Commission, in which Great Britain, Austria, France, Prussia, Russia, Sardinia, and Turkey, shall each be represented by one delegate, shall be charged to designate and to cause to be executed the Works necessary below Isatcha, to clear the Mouths of the Danube, as well as the neighbouring parts of the Sea, from the sands and other impediments which obstruct them, in order to put that part of the River and the said parts of the Sea in the best possible state for Navigation.

Duties to be levied in the Danube.

In order to cover the Expenses of such Works, as well as of the establishments intended to secure and to facilitate the Navigation at the Mouths of the Danube, fixed Duties, of a suitable rate, settled by the Commission by a majority of votes, may be levied, on the express condition that, in this respect as in every other, the Flags of all Nations shall be treated on the footing of perfect equality.

Appointment of Danube River Commission.

ART. XVII. A Commission shall be established, and shall be composed of delegates of Austria, Bavaria, the Sublime Porte, and Wurtemberg (one for each of those Powers), to whom shall be added Commissioners from the Three Danubian Principalities, whose nomination shall have been approved by the Porte. This Commission, which shall be permanent: 1. Shall prepare Regulations of Navigation and River Police; 2. Shall remove the impediments, of whatever nature they may be, which still prevent the application to the Danube of the Arrangements of the Treaty of Vienna; 3. Shall order and cause to be executed the necessary Works throughout the whole course of the River; and 4. Shall, after the dissolution of the European Commission, see to maintaining the Mouths of the Danube and the neighbouring parts of the Sea in a navigable state.

Period of Dissolution of European Commission.

ART. XVIII. It is understood that the European Commission shall have completed its task, and that the River Commission shall have finished the Works described in the preceding Article, under Nos. 1 and 2, within the period of two years. The signing Powers assembled in Conference having been informed of that fact, shall, after having placed it on record, pronounce the Dissolution of the European Commission, and from that time the permanent River Commission shall enjoy the same powers as those with which the European Commission shall have until then been invested.

Right of Contracting Powers to establish Two Light Vessels at the Mouths of the Danube.

ART. XIX. In order to insure the execution of the Regulations which shall have been established by common agreement, in conformity with the principles above declared, each of the Contracting Powers shall have the right to station, at all times, Two Light Vessels at the Mouths of the Danube.

Rectification of Frontier of Bessarabia.

ART. XX. In exchange for the Towns, Ports, and Territories enumerated in Article IV of the present Treaty, and in order more fully to secure the Freedom of the Navigation of the Danube, His Majesty the Emperor of All the Russias consents to the rectification of his Frontier in Bessarabia.

The new Frontier shall begin from the Black Sea, one kilometre to the east of the Lake Bourna Sola, shall run perpendicularly to the Akerman Road, shall follow that road to the Val de Trajan, pass to the south of Bolgrad, ascend the course of the River Yalpuck to the Height of Saratsika, and terminate at Katamori on the Pruth. Above that point the old Frontier between the Two Empires shall not undergo any modification.

Delegates to trace New Frontier.

Delegates of the Contracting Powers shall fix, in its details, the Line of the new Frontier.

Russian Cessions in Bessarabia to be annexed to Moldavia.

ART. XXI. The Territory ceded by Russia shall be Annexed to the Principality of Moldavia, under the Suzerainty of the Sublime Porte.

Rights and Privileges of Inhabitants of ceded Territory.

The Inhabitants of that Territory shall enjoy the Rights and Privileges secured to the Principalities; and during the space of 3 years, they shall be permitted to transfer their domicile elsewhere, disposing freely of their Property.

Guarantee of Privileges and Immunities of Wallachia and Moldavia.

ART. XXII. The Principalities of Wallachia and Moldavia shall continue to enjoy under the Suzerainty of the Porte, and under the Guarantee of the Contracting Powers, the Privileges and Immunities of which they are in possession. No exclusive Protection shall be exercised over them by any of the guaranteeing Powers.

Non-interference in Internal Affairs.

There shall be no separate right of interference in their Internal Affairs.

Independent and National Administration, &c., of Principalities.

ART. XXIII. The Sublime Porte engages to preserve to the said Principalities an Independent and National Administration, as well as full liberty of Worship, of Legislation, of Commerce, and of Navigation.

Principalities.   Appointment of Commission for Revision of Laws and Statutes.

The Laws and Statutes at present in force shall be revised. In order to establish a complete agreement in regard to such revision, a Special Commission, as to the composition of which the High Contracting Powers will come to an understanding among themselves, shall assemble, without delay, at Bucharest, together with a Commissioner of the Sublime Porte.

Duties of Commission.

The business of this Commission shall be to investigate the present state of the Principalities, and to propose bases for their future organization.

Convocation of Divans ad hoc *for the Organization of Principalities.*
ART. XXIV. His Majesty the Sultan promises to convoke immediately in each of the two Provinces a Divan *ad hoc*, composed in such a manner as to represent most closely the interests of all classes of society. These Divans shall be called upon to express the wishes of the people in regard to the definitive organization of the Principalities.

Congress to issue Instructions.
An Instruction from the Congress shall regulate the relations between the Commission and these Divans.

Principalities. Result of Labours of Divans to be sent to Conferences.
ART. XXV. Taking into consideration the opinion expressed by the two Divans, the Commission shall transmit, without delay, to the present seat of the Conferences, the result of its own labours.

Principalities. Convention to record Final Agreement with Suzerain Power.
The Final Agreement with the Suzerain Power shall be recorded in a Convention to be concluded at Paris between the High Contracting Parties; and a Hatti-sheriff, in conformity with the stipulations of the Convention, shall constitute definitively the organization of those Provinces, placed thenceforward under the Collective Guarantee of all the signing Powers.

National Armed Force in Principalities.
ART. XXVI. It is agreed that there shall be in the Principalities a National Armed Force, organized with the view to maintain the security of the interior, and to ensure that of the Frontiers. No impediment shall be opposed to the extraordinary measures of defence which, by agreement with the Sublime Porte, they may be called upon to take in order to repel any external aggression.

Maintenance of Internal Tranquillity in Principalities.
ART. XXVII. If the Internal Tranquillity of the Principalities should be menaced or compromised, the Sublime Porte shall come to an understanding with the other Contracting Powers in regard to the measures to be taken for maintaining or re-establishing legal order.

Non-intervention by force of Arms in Principalities.
No armed Intervention can take place without previous agreement between those Powers.

Rights and Immunities of Servia guaranteed by Contracting Powers.

ART. XXVIII. The Principality of Servia shall continue to hold of the Sublime Porte, in conformity with the Imperial Hats which fix and determine its Rights and Immunities, placed henceforward under the Collective Guarantee of the Contracting Powers.

Servia.   Independent and National Administration.

In consequence, the said Principality shall preserve its Independent and National Administration, as well as full Liberty of Worship, of Legislation, of Commerce, and of Navigation.

Right of Garrison of Sublime Porte maintained.   Non-Intervention by force of Arms in Servia.

ART. XXIX. The right of garrison of the Sublime Porte, as stipulated by anterior regulations, is maintained. No Armed Intervention can take place in Servia without previous agreement between the High Contracting Powers.

Maintenance of Integrity of Russian and Ottoman Possessions in Asia.

ART. XXX. His Majesty the Emperor of All the Russias and His Majesty the Sultan maintain in its Integrity the state of their possessions in Asia, such as it legally existed before the rupture.

Line of Frontier to be verified.

In order to prevent all local dispute the Line of Frontier shall be verified, and, if necessary, rectified, without any prejudice as regards Territory being sustained by either Party.

Appointment of Frontier Commission.

For this purpose a Mixed Commission, composed of two Russian Commissioners, two Ottoman Commissioners, one English Commissioner, and one French Commissioner, shall be sent to the spot immediately after the re-establishment of diplomatic relations between the Court of Russia and the Sublime Porte. Its labours shall be completed within the period of 8 months after the exchange of the Ratifications of the present Treaty.

Evacuation of Territories by Allied Troops.

ART. XXXI. The Territories occupied during the War by the troops of their Majesties the Queen of the United Kingdom of Great Britain and Ireland, the Emperor of Austria, the Emperor of the French, and the King of Sardinia, according to the terms of the Conventions signed at Constantinople on the 12th of March, 1854, between Great Britain,

France, and the Sublime Porte; on the 14th of June of the same year, between Austria and the Sublime Porte; and on the 15th of March, 1855, between Sardinia and the Sublime Porte; shall be evacuated as soon as possible after the exchange of the Ratifications of the present Treaty. The periods and the means of execution shall form the object of an arrangement between the Sublime Porte and the Powers whose troops occupied its Territory.

Maintenance of Treaties of Commerce. Treatment of Most Favoured Nation.

ART. XXXII. Until the Treaties or Conventions which existed before the War between the Belligerent Powers have been either renewed or replaced by new Acts, Commerce of importation or of exportation shall take place reciprocally on the footing of the regulations in force before the War; and in all other matters their subjects shall be respectively treated upon the footing of the Most Favoured Nation.

Åland Islands.

ART. XXXIII. The Convention concluded this day between their Majesties the Queen of the United Kingdom of Great Britain and Ireland, the Emperor of the French, on the one part, and His Majesty the Emperor of All the Russias on the other part, respecting the Åland Islands, is and remains annexed to the present Treaty, and shall have the same force and validity as if it formed a part thereof.

Ratifications.

ART. XXXIV. The present Treaty shall be ratified, and the Ratifications shall be exchanged at Paris in the space of 4 weeks, or sooner if possible.

In witness whereof the respective Plenipotentiaries have signed the same, and have affixed thereto the Seal of their Arms.

Done at Paris, the 30th day of the month of March, in the year 1856.

         (L.S.)   CLARENDON.
         (L.S.)   COWLEY.
         (L.S.)   BUOL-SCHAUENSTEIN.
         (L.S.)   HUBNER.
         (L.S.)   A. WALEWSKI.
         (L.S.)   BOURQUENEY.
         (L.S.)   MANTEUFFEL.
         (L.S.)   C. M. D'HATZFELDT.
         (L.S.)   ORLOFF.
         (L.S.)   BRUNNOW.
         (L.S.)   C. CAVOUR.

(L.S.)   DE VILLAMARINA.
(L.S.)   AALI.
(L.S.)   MEHEMMED DJEMIL.

ADDITIONAL AND TRANSITORY ARTICLE.   PARIS, 30TH MARCH, 1856.

Stipulations relative to the Straits of Dardanelles and Bosphorus to take effect after Evacuation of Territories by Sea and Land.

The Stipulations of the Convention respecting the Straits, signed this day, shall not be applicable to the Vessels of War employed by the Belligerent Powers for the evacuation, by Sea, of the Territories occupied by their Armies; but the said Stipulations shall resume their entire effect as soon as the Evacuation shall be terminated.

Done at Paris, the 30th day of the month of March, in the year 1856.

(L.S.)   CLARENDON.
(L.S.)   COWLEY.
(L.S.)   BUOL-SCHAUENSTEIN.
(L.S.)   HUBNER.
(L.S.)   A. WALEWSKI.
(L.S.)   BOURQUENEY.
(L.S.)   MANTEUFFEL.
(L.S.)   C. M. D'HATZFELDT.
(L.S.)   ORLOFF.
(L.S.)   BRUNNOW.
(L.S.)   C. CAVOUR.
(L.S.)   DE VILLAMARINA.
(L.S.)   AALI.
(L.S.)   MEHEMMED DJEMIL.

6 2

CONVENTION between Great Britain, Austria, France, Prussia, Russia, and Sardinia, on the one part, and the Sultan, on the other part, respecting the Straits of the Dardanelles and of the Bosphorus. Signed at Paris, 30th March, 1856. Ratifications exchanged at Paris, 27th April, 1856.

[This Convention was annexed to the General Treaty of Peace of the same date, Article X]

In the Name of Almighty God.

Reference to Treaty of 13th July, 1841.

THEIR Majesties the Queen of the United Kingdom of Great Britain and Ireland, the Emperor of Austria, the Emperor of the French, the King of Prussia, the Emperor of All the Russias, signing Parties to the Convention of the 13th day of July, 1841, and His Majesty the King of Sardinia; wishing to record in common their unanimous determination to conform to the ancient rule of the Ottoman Empire, according to which the Straits of the Dardanelles and of the Bosphorus are Closed to Foreign Ships of War, so long as the Porte is at Peace;

Their said Majesties, on the one part, and His Majesty, the Sultan, on the other, have resolved to renew the Convention concluded at London on the 13th day of July, 1841, with the exception of some modifications of detail which do not affect the principle upon which it rests;

In consequence their said Majesties have named for that purpose as their Plenipotentiaries, that is to say:

Her Majesty the Queen of the United Kingdom of Great Britain and Ireland, the Right Honourable George William Frederick Earl of Clarendon, Baron Hyde of Hindon, Her Majesty's Principal Secretary of State for Foreign Affairs, &c.; and the Right Honourable Henry Richard Charles Baron Cowley, Her Majesty's Ambassador Extraordinary and Plenipotentiary to His Majesty the Emperor of the French, &c.;

His Majesty the Emperor of Austria, the Sieur Charles Ferdinand Count of Buol-Schauenstein, his Minister of the House and of Foreign Affairs, President of the Conference of Ministers, &c.; and the Sieur Joseph Alexander Baron de Hübner, his Envoy Extraordinary and Minister Plenipotentiary to the Court of France, &c;

His Majesty the Emperor of the French, the Sieur Alexander Count Colonna Walewski, his Minister and Secretary of State for Foreign Affairs, &c.; and the Sieur Francis Adolphus Baron de Bourqueney, his Envoy Extraordinary and Minister Plenipotentiary to His Imperial and Royal Apostolic Majesty, &c.;

His Majesty the King of Prussia, the Sieur Otho Theodore Baron de Manteuffel, President of his Council, and his Minister for Foreign Affairs, &c.; and the Sieur Maximilian Frederick Charles Francis Count of Hatzfeldt Wildenburg-Schoenstein, his Envoy Extraordinary and Minister Plenipotentiary to the Court of France, &c.;

His Majesty the Emperor of All the Russias, the Sieur Alexis Count Orloff, a Member of the Council of the Empire and of the Committee of Ministers, &c.; and the Sieur Philip Baron de Brunnow, his Privy

Councillor, his Envoy Extraordinary and Minister Plenipotentiary to the Germanic Confederation and to the Grand Duke of Hesse, &c.;

His Majesty the King of Sardinia, the Sieur Camille Benso, Count of Cavour, President of the Council of Ministers, and his Minister Secretary of State for the Finances, &c.; and the Sieur Salvator Marquis de Villamarina, his Envoy Extraordinary and Minister Plenipotentiary to the Court of France, &c.;

And His Majesty the Emperor of the Ottomans, Mouhammed Emin Aali Pasha, Grand Vizier of the Ottoman Empire, &c.; and Mehemmed Djemil Bey, his Ambassador Extraordinary and Plenipotentiary to His Majesty the Emperor of the French, accredited in the same character to His Majesty the King of Sardinia, &c.;

Who, after having exchanged their Full Powers, found in good and due form, have agreed upon the following Articles:—

Prohibition to Foreign Ships of War to enter Bosphorus and Dardanelles.

ART. I. His Majesty the Sultan, on the one part, declares that he is firmly resolved to mantain for the future the principle invariably established as the ancient rule of his Empire, and in virtue of which it has, at all times, been prohibited for the Ships of War of Foreign Powers to enter the Straits of the Dardanelles and of the Bosphorus; and that, so long as the Porte is at Peace, His Majesty will admit no Foreign Ship of War into the said Straits.

Agreement of 6 Powers to respect this Prohibition.

And Their Majesties the Queen of the United Kingdom of Great Britain and Ireland, the Emperor of Austria, the Emperor of the French, the King of Prussia, the Emperor of All the Russias, and the King of Sardinia, on the other part, engage to respect this determination of the Sultan, and to conform themselves to the principle above declared.

Admission, under Firman, of Light Vessels in Service of Foreign Missions.

ART. II. The Sultan reserves to himself, as in past times, to deliver Firmans of Passage for Light Vessels under Flag of War, which shall be employed, as is usual in the service of the Missions of Foreign Powers.

Light Vessels, under Flag of War, Stationed at Mouths of the Danube.

ART. III. The same exception applies to the Light Vessels under Flag of War, which each of the Contracting Powers is authorised to station at the Mouths of the Danube in order to secure the execution of the Regulations relative to the liberty of that River, and the number of which is not to exceed two for each Power.

Ratifications.

ART. IV. The present Convention, annexed to the General Treaty signed at Paris this day, shall be ratified, and the Ratifications shall be exchanged in the space of 4 weeks, or sooner if possible.

In witness whereof the respective Plenipotentiaries have signed the same, and have affixed thereto the Seal of their Arms.

Done at Paris, the 30th day of the month of March, in the year 1856.

(L.S.) CLARENDON.
(L.S.) COWLEY.
(L.S.) BUOL-SCHAUENSTEIN.
(L.S.) HUBNER.
(L.S.) A. WALEWSKI.
(L.S.) BOURQUENEY.
(L.S.) MANTEUFFEL.
(L.S.) C. M. D'HATZFELDT.
(L.S.) ORLOFF.
(L.S.) BRUNNOW.
(L.S.) C. CAVOUR.
(L.S.) DE VILLAMARINA.
(L.S.) AALI.
(L.S.) WEHEMMED DJEMIL.

63

CONVENTION between Russia and Turkey, limiting their Naval Force in the Black Sea. Signed at Paris, 30th March, 1856. Ratifications exchanged at Paris, 27th April, 1856.

This Convention was annexed to the General Treaty of Peace of the same date, Article XIV.

In the Name of Almighty God.

His Majesty the Emperor of All the Russias, and His Imperial Majesty the Sultan, taking into consideration the principle of the Neutralisation of the Black Sea established by the Preliminaries contained in the Protocol No. 1, signed at Paris on the 25th of February of the present year, and wishing, in consequence, to regulate by common agreement the number and the force of the Light Vessels which they have reserved to themselves to maintain in the Black Sea for the service of their coasts, have resolved to sign, with that view, a special Convention, and have named for that purpose:

His Majesty the Emperor of All the Russias, the Sieur Alexis Count Orloff, his Aide-de-Camp General and General of Cavalry, &c.; and the

Sieur Philip Baron de Brunnow, his Envoy Extraordinary and Minister Plenipotentiary to the Germanic Confederation, &c.;

And His Majesty the Emperor of the Ottomans, Mouhammed Emin Ali Pasha, Grand Vizier of the Ottoman Empire, &c.; and Mehemmed Djemil Bey, his Ambassador Extraordinary and Plenipotentiary to His Majesty the Emperor of the French, accredited in the same character to His Majesty the King of Sardinia, &c.;

Who, after having exchanged their Full Powers, found in good and due form, have agreed upon the following Articles:—

Vessels of War to be maintained in Black Sea.

ART. I. The High Contracting Parties mutually engage not to have in the Black Sea any other Vessels of War than those of which the number, the force, and the dimensions are hereinafter stipulated.

Number, Force, and Dimensions of Vessels of War to be maintained in Black Sea.

ART. II. The High Contracting Parties reserve to themselves each to maintain in that Sea 6 steam-vessels of 50 metres in length at the line of flotation, of a tonnage of 800 tons at the maximum, and 4 light steam or sailing vessels of a tonnage which shall not exceed 200 tons each.

Ratifications.

ART. III. The present Convention, annexed to the General Treaty signed at Paris this day, shall be ratified, and the Ratifications shall be exchanged in the space of 4 weeks, or sooner, if possible.

In witness whereof the respective Plenipotentaries have signed the same and have affixed thereto the Seal of their Arms.

Done at Paris, the 30th day of March, 1856.

        (L.S.)   ORLOFF.
        (L.S.)   BRUNNOW.
        (L.S.)   AALI.
        (L.S.)   MEHEMMED DJEMIL.

64

CONVENTION between Great Britain, France, and Russia, respecting the Åland Islands. Signed at Paris, 30th March, 1856. Ratifications exchanged at Paris, 27th April, 1856.

This Convention was annexed to the General Treaty of Peace of the same date. See Article XXXIII.

In the Name of Almighty God.

HER Majesty the Queen of the United Kingdom of Great Britain and

Ireland, His Majesty the Emperor of the French, and His Majesty the Emperor of All the Russias, wishing to extend to the Baltic Sea the harmony so happily re-established between them in the East, and thereby to consolidate the benefits of the General Peace, have resolved to conclude a Convention, and have named for that purpose:

Her Majesty the Queen of the United Kingdom of Great Britain and Ireland, the Right Honourable George William Frederick Earl of Clarendon, Her Majesty's Principal Secretary of State for Foreign Affairs, &c.; and the Right Honourable Henry Richard Charles Baron Cowley, Her Majesty's Ambassador Extraordinary and Plenipotentiary to His Majesty the Emperor of the French, &c.;

His Majesty the Emperor of the French, the Sieur Alexander Count Colonna Walewski, his Minister and Secretary of State for Foreign Affairs, &c.; and the Sieur Francis Adolphus Baron de Bourqueney, his Envoy Extraordinary and Minister Plenipotentiary to His Imperial and Royal Apostolic Majesty, &c;

And His Majesty the Emperor of All the Russias, the Sieur Alexis Count Orloff, his Aide-de-Camp General and General of Cavalry, &c.; and the Sieur Philip Baron de Brunnow, his Envoy Extraordinary and Minister Plenipotentiary to the Germanic Confederation, &c.;

Who, after having exchanged their Full Powers, found in good and due form, have agreed upon the following Articles:

Åland Islands not to be Fortified, or Military or Naval Establishments to be maintained.

ART. I. His Majesty the Emperor of All the Russias, in order to respond to the desire which has been expressed to him by Their Majesties the Queen of the United Kingdom of Great Britain and Ireland, and the Emperor of the French, declares that the Åland Islands shall not be fortified, and that no Military or Naval Establishment shall be maintained or created there.

Ratifications.

ART. II. The present Convention, annexed to the General Treaty signed at Paris this day, shall be ratified, and the Ratifications shall be exchanged in the space of 4 weeks, or sooner, if possible.

In witness whereof, the respective Plenipotentiaries have signed the same, and have affixed thereto the Seal of their Arms.

Done at Paris, the 30th day of March, 1856.

(L.S.)	CLARENDON.
(L.S.)	COWLEY.
(L.S.)	A. WALEWSKI.
(L.S.)	BOURQUENEY.
(L.S.)	ORLOFF.
(L.S.)	BRUNNOW.

65

PROTOCOL OF CONFERENCE between Great Britain, Austria, France, Prussia, Russia, Sardinia, and Turkey, suggesting the reference of Disputes between Foreign Powers to the Mediation of a Third Power, previous to Hostilities. Paris, 14th April, 1856.

Present: The Plenipotentiaries of Austria, France, Great Britain, Prussia, Russia, Sardinia, and Turkey.

Mediation previous to Hostilities.

(Extract.)

THE Earl of Clarendon having demanded permission to lay before the Congress a proposition which it appears to him ought to be favourably received, states that the calamities of War are still too present to every mind not to make it desirable to seek out every expedient calculated to prevent their return; that a stipulation had been inserted in Article VIII of the Treaty of Peace, recommending that in case of Difference between the Porte and one or more of the other signing Powers, recourse should be had to the Mediation of a friendly State before resorting to force.

The first Plenipotentiary of Great Britain conceives that this happy innovation might receive a more general application, and thus become a barrier against conflicts which frequently only break forth because it is not always possible to enter into explanation and to come to an understanding.

He proposes, therefore, to agree upon a resolution calculated to afford to the Maintenance of Peace that chance of duration hereafter, without prejudice, however, to the Independence of Governments.

Count Walewski declares himself authorised to support the idea expressed by the first Plenipotentiary of Great Britain: he gives the assurance that the Plenipotentiaries of France are wholly disposed to concur in the insertion in the Protocol of a wish which, being fully in accordance with the tendencies of our epoch, would not in any way fetter the free action of Governments.

Count Buol would not hesitate to concur in the opinion of the Pleni-potentiaries of Great Britain and of France, if the resolution of the Congress is to have the form indicated by Count Walewski, but he could not take, in the name of his Court, an absolute engagement calculated to limit the Independence of the Austrian Cabinet.

The Earl of Clarendon replies that each Power is and will be the sole judge of the requirements of its honour and of its interests: that it is by no means his intention to restrict the authority of the Governments, but only to afford them the opportunity of not having recourse to Arms whenever Differences may be adjusted by other means.

Baron Manteuffel gives the assurance that the King, his august Master, completely shares the ideas set forth by the Earl of Clarendon; that he therefore considers himself authorised to adhere to them, and to give them the utmost development which they admit of.

Count Orloff, while admitting the wisdom of the proposal made to the Congress, considers that he must refer to his Court respecting it, before he expresses the opinion of the Plenipotentiaries of Russia.

Count Cavour, before he gives his opinion, wishes to know whether, in the intention of the author of the proposition, the wish to be expressed by the Congress would extend to Military Interventions directed against de facto Governments, and quotes, as an instance, the Intervention of Austria in the Kingdom of Naples in 1821.

Lord Clarendon replies that the wish of the Congress should allow of the most general application; he observes that if the Good Offices of another Power had induced the Government of Greece to respect the Laws of Neutrality, France and England would very probably have abstained from occupying the Piræus with their troops. He refers to the efforts made by the Cabinet of Great Britain in 1823, in order to prevent the Armed Intervention which took place at that time in Spain.

Count Walewski adds, that there is no question of stipulating for a right or of taking an engagement; that the wish expressed by the Congress cannot in any case oppose limits to the liberty of judgment of which no Power can divest itself in questions affecting its dignity; that there is therefore no inconvenience in attaching a general character to the idea entertained by the Earl of Clarendon, and giving to it the most extended application.

Count Buol says that Count Cavour, in speaking in another sitting of the occupation of the Legations by Austrian Troops, forgot that other Foreign Troops have been invited into the Roman States. To-day, while speaking of the Occupation by Austria of the Kingdom of Naples in 1821, he forgets that that occupation was the result of an understanding between the 5 Great Powers assembled at the Congress of Laybach. In both cases he attributes to Austria the merit of an initiative and of a spontaneous action, which the Austrian Plenipotentiaries are far from claiming for her.

The Intervention, adverted to by the Plenipotentiary of Sardinia, took place, he adds, in consequence of the discussions of the Congress of Laybach; it therefore comes within the scope of the ideas expressed by Lord Clarendon. Similar cases might perhaps recur, and Count Buol does not allow that an Intervention carried into effect in consequence of an agreement come to between the 5 Great Powers, can become the object of remonstrances of a State of the second order.

Count Buol approves the proposition in the shape that Lord Clarendon has presented it, as having a humane object; but he could not assent to it if it were wished to give to it too great an extension, or to deduce from it consequences favourable to *de facto* Governments, and to doctrines which he cannot admit.

He desires besides that the Conference, at the moment of terminating its labours, should not find itself compelled to discuss irritating questions, calculated to disturb the perfect harmony which has not ceased to prevail among the Plenipotentiaries.

Count Cavour declares that he is fully satisfied with the explanations which he has elicited, and he accedes to the proposition submitted to the Congress.

Whereupon the Plenipotentiaries do not hesitate to express, in the name of their Governments, the wish that States between which any serious misunderstanding may arise, should, before appealing to Arms, have recourse, as far as circumstances might allow, to the Good Offices of a friendly Power.

The Plenipotentiaries hope that the Governments not represented at the Congress will unite in the sentiment which has inspired the wish recorded in the present Protocol.

(The Signatures follow.)

66

TREATY between Great Britain, Austria, and France, guaranteeing the Independence and Integrity of the Ottoman Empire. Signed at Paris, 15th April, 1856. Ratifications exchanged at Paris, 29th April, 1856.

Reference to Treaty of 30th March, 1856.

HER Majesty the Queen of the United Kingdom of Great Britain and Ireland, His Majesty the Emperor of Austria, and His Majesty the Emperor of the French, wishing to settle between themselves the combined action which any infraction of the stipulations of the Peace of Paris would involve on their part, have named for that purpose as their Plenipotentiaries, that is to say:

Her Majesty the Queen of the United Kingdom of Great Britain and Ireland, the Right Honourable George William Frederick Earl of Clarendon, Her Majesty's Principal Secretary of State for Foreign Affairs, &c.; and the Right Honourable Henry Richard Charles Baron Cowley, Her Majesty's Ambassador Extraordinary and Plenipotentiary to His Majesty the Emperor of the French, &c.;

His Majesty the Emperor of Austria, the Sieur Charles Ferdinand Count de Buol-Schauenstein, President of the Conference of Ministers, &c.; and the Sieur Joseph Alexander Baron de Hübner, Envoy Extraordinary and Minister Plenipotentiary to the Court of France, &c.;

And His Majesty the Emperor of the French, the Sieur Alexander Count Colonna Walewski, his Minister and Secretary of State for Foreign Affairs, &c.; and the Sieur Francis Adolphus Baron de Bourqueney, his Envoy Extraordinary and Minister Plenipotentiary to His Imperial and Royal Apostolic Majesty, &c.;

Who, after having exchanged their Full Powers, found in good and due form, have agreed upon the following Articles:

Guarantee of Independence and Integrity of the Ottoman Empire.
ART. I. The High Contracting Parties Guarantee, jointly and severally, the Independence and the Integrity of the Ottoman Empire, recorded in the Treaty concluded at Paris on the 30th of March, 1856.

Any Infraction of Treaty of 30th March, 1856, to be considered as a
casus belli.
ART. II. Any infraction of the stipulations of the said Treaty will be considered by the Powers signing the present Treaty as a *casus belli*. They will come to an understanding with the Sublime Porte as to the measures which have become necessary, and will without delay determine among themselves as to the employment of their Military and Naval Forces.

Ratifications.
ART. III. The present Treaty shall be ratified, and the Ratifications, shall be exchanged in a fortnight, or sooner if possible.

In witness whereof the respective Plenipotentaries have signed the same, and have affixed thereto the Seal of their Arms.

Done at Paris, the 15th day of the month of April, in the year 1856.

> (L.S.)   CLARENDON.
> (L.S.)   COWLEY.
> (L.S.)   BUOL-SCHAUENSTEIN.
> (L.S.)   HUBNER.
> (L.S.)   A. WALEWSKI.
> (L.S.)   BOURQUENEY.

6 7

DEFINITIVE ACT between the Commissioners of Great Britain, Austria, France, Russia, and Turkey, relative to the Bessarabian Frontier. Signed at Kichineff, 30th March/ 11th April, 1857.

Reference to Treaty of 30th March, 1856.

IN virtue of Article XX of the Treaty of Peace concluded at Paris the 18th/30th March, 1856, and for the purpose of fixing in detail the tracing of the new Frontier between the Empire of Russia and the Empire of Turkey in Bessarabia, their Majesties the Emperor of Austria, the Emperor of the French, the Queen of the United Kingdom of Great Britain and Ireland, the Emperor of All the Russias, and the Emperor of the Ottomans, have appointed as their Commissioners, namely:

His Majesty the Emperor of Austria, the Sieur Antoine Kalik, Colonel of the Imperial and Royal Staff, &c.;

His Majesty the Emperor of the French, the Sieur Pierre Marc Besson, Lieutenant-Colonel of the Imperial Staff, &c.;

Her Majesty the Queen of the United Kingdom of Great Britain and Ireland, the Sieur Edward Stanton, Lieutenant-Colonel of Engineers, &c.;

His Majesty the Emperor of All the Russias, the Sieur Michel Fanton de Verrayon, Major-General of the Imperial Staff, &c.; and the Sieur Alexander Baron de Stakelberg, Colonel of the Imperial Staff, &c;

His Majesty the Emperor of the Ottomans, Mouhliss Pasca, Prince Gregoire Stourdza, General of Division, &c.;

Who, after having exchanged their Full Powers, found to be in good and due form, have formed themselves into a Boundary Commission, 20th May/1st June, 1856.

The said Commissioners of the 5 Powers, after having determined upon the Territory, and in all its details on the new Frontier, in conformity, in so far as the disposition of the localities admit of it, with the directions of Article XX of the above-mentioned Treaty, and the stipulations of the Protocol of 6th January, 1857, declare the tracing of that Frontier to be established under the following principles and conditions:

Line of Demarcation.

ART. I. The Line of Demarcation which shall henceforth separate in Bessarabia, from the Black Sea, as far as the Pruth, the States of His Majesty the Emperor of All the Russias from those of His Majesty the Emperor of the Ottomans is marked on the Ground:

1. In the dry parts by a series of earthen truncated cones, each surmounted by a stone, numbered, and united to each other by a ditch:

2. In those parts where the Line follows the course of the waters, it shall be marked by the Thalweg.

Maps of Frontier.

ART. II. The said Line of Demarcation is drawn on a Topographical and Special Map, on the scale of 1/210000, and it is described in all its details in a specification.

A General Map has also been drawn up on a scale of 1/21000 of all the ceded Territory. The latter Map is accompanied by a Statistical Table, communicated by the Local Authorities, and containing a condition of the Towns, Boroughs, and Villages, &c., with an account of the amount of land and population.

ART. III. *Detailed Demarcation of Frontier.*

ART. IV. *Dimensions of Truncated Cones and Ditch.*

ART. V. *Repairs of Boundary Marks.*

ART. VI. *Right of Inhabitants of the two Banks to Watercourses forming the Frontier.*

ART. VII. *Five Copies of Topographical Map and Specification, as well as the General Map of the Ceded Territory and Statistical Table, to be signed by the Commissioners, one to be for each of the Powers.*

Ratifications.

ART. VIII. The present Definitive Boundary Act, in eight Articles, has been signed by all the Commissioners, in virtue of their Full Powers.

That Act shall be immediately submitted to the Ratification of the Governments of Austria, France, Great Britain, Russia, and Turkey, by their respective Commissioners.

Done at Kichineff, 30th March/11th April, 1857.
    (L.S.) KALIK.
    (L.S.) BESSON.
    (L.S.) ED. STANTON.
    (L.S.) M. FANTON DE VERRAYON.
    (L.S.) BARON A. DE STAKELBERG.
    (L.S.) MOUHLISS PRINCE G. STOURDZA.

68

TREATY between Great Britain, Austria, France, Prussia, Russia, Sardinia, and Turkey, relative to the Frontier in Bessarabia, the Isle of Serpents, and the Delta of the Danube. Signed at Paris, 19th June, 1857. Ratifications exchanged at Paris, 31st December, 1857.

Reference to Treaty of 30th March, 1856.

THEIR Majesties the Queen of the United Kingdom of Great Britain and Ireland, the Emperor of Austria, the Emperor of the French, the King of Prussia, the Emperor of All the Russias, the King of Sardinia, and the Emperor of the Ottomans, considering that the Boundary Commission charged with the execution of Article XX of the Treaty of Paris, of the 30th March, 1856, has terminated its labours, and desiring to act in conformity with the arrangements of the Protocol of the 6th of January last, by recording in a Treaty the Modifications made by common consent in that Article, as well as the Resolutions adopted with regard to the Isle of Serpents and the Delta of the Danube, and contained in the same Protocol, have named as their Plenipotentiaries for that purpose, that is to say:

Her Majesty the Queen of the United Kingdom of Great Britain and Ireland, the Right Honourable Henry Richard Charles, Earl Cowley, Her Majesty's Ambassador Extraordinary and Plenipotentiary to His Majesty the Emperor of the French, &c.;

His Majesty the Emperor of Austria, M. Joseph Alexander Baron de Hübner, and his Ambassador to His Majesty the Emperor of the French, &c.;

His Majesty the Emperor of the French, M. Alexandre Count Colonna Walewski, his Minister and Secretary of State for Foreign Affairs, &c.;

His Majesty the King of Prussia, M. Maximilian Frederick Charles Francis Count of Hatzfeldt-Wildenburg-Schoenstein, his Envoy Extraordinary and Minister Plenipotentiary to His Majesty the Emperor of the French, &c.;

His Majesty the Emperor of All the Russias, the Count Paul Kisseleff, his Ambassador Extraordinary and Plenipotentiary to His Majesty the Emperor of the French, &c.;

His Majesty the King of Sardinia, M. Salvator Marquis de Villa-marina, his Envoy Extraordinary and Minister Plenipotentiary to His Majesty the Emperor of the French, &c.;

And His Majesty the Emperor of the Ottomans, Mehemmed Djemil Bey, his Ambassador Extraordinary and Plenipotentiary to His Majesty the Emperor of the French, &c.;

Who, after having communicated to each other their respective Full Powers, found in good and due form, have agreed upon the following Articles:

Frontier of Russia and Turkey in Bessarabia.

ART. I. The Line of Frontier of Russia and of Turkey in Bessarabia is, and remains determined in conformity with the Topographic Map prepared by the Boundary Commissioners at Kitchenew on the 30th of March, 1857; which Map is annexed to the present Treaty, after having been initialled.

Islands of Mouths of the Danube to be under Sovereignty of Sultan of Turkey.

ART. II. The Contracting Powers agree that the Islands included between the different branches of the Danube at its mouth, and forming the Delta of that river, as shown by the Plan annexed to the Protocol of the 6th of January, shall, instead of being annexed to the Principality of Moldavia, as implied in the stipulations of Article XXI of the Treaty of Paris, be replaced under the immediate Sovereignty of the Sublime Porte, of which they formerly held.

Turkish Sovereignty over Island of Serpents.

ART. III. The Treaty of the 30th March, 1856, having, like the Treaties previously concluded between Russia and Turkey, been silent with regard to the Isle of Serpents, and the High Contracting Parties having agreed that it was proper to consider that Island as a dependency of the Delta of the Danube, its destination is fixed according to the arrangements of the preceding Article.

Maintenance by Turkey of Lighthouse on Island of Serpents.

ART. IV. In the general interest of maritime commerce, the Sublime Porte engages to maintain on the Isle of Serpents a Lighthouse destined to afford security to the navigation of vessels proceeding to the Danube and to the port of Odessa. The River Commission established by Article

XVII of the Treaty of the 30th of March, 1856, for the purpose of maintaining the mouths of that river and the neighbouring parts of the sea in a navigable state, will see to the regular performance of the service of such Lighthouse.

Ratifications.

ART. V. The present Treaty shall be ratified, and the Ratifications shall be exchanged in 4 weeks, or sooner if possible.

In witness whereof the respective Plenipotentiaries have signed the same, and have affixed thereto the Seal of their Arms.

Done at Paris, the 19th day of June, in the year of Our Lord, 1857.

(L.S.)	COWLEY.
(L.S.)	HUBNER.
(L.S.)	A. WALEWSKI.
(L.S.)	C. M. D'HATZFELDT.
(L.S.)	CTE. DE KISSELEFF.
(L.S.)	DE VILLAMARINA.
(L.S.)	MEHEMMED DJEMIL.

69

FINAL ACT of the Mixed Commission of Great Britain, Russia, and Turkey, on the Turco-Russian Boundary in Asia. Signed at Constantinople, 5th December, 1857.

Reference to Treaty of 30th March, 1856.

ART. XXX of the Treaty signed and concluded at Paris, 30th March, 1856, between Austria, France, Great Britain, Prussia, Russia, Sardinia, and the Ottoman Porte, having declared that His Majesty the Emperor of All the Russias, and His Majesty the Emperor of the Ottomans, shall retain in their integrity their possessions in Asia, such as they existed before the War, and that, in order to prevent all local mis-understanding, the Line of Frontier shall be verified, and if necessary rectified in such manner as that no Territorial loss shall be sustained by one or other of the two Parties, and that a Mixed Commission composed of two Russian Commissioners, two Turkish Commissioners, one French Commissioner, and one British Commissioner, shall be sent for that purpose on the spot immediately after the re-establishment of Diplomatic Relations between the Courts of Russia and the Sublime Porte.

His Majesty the Emperor of the French has appointed as his Com-missioner M. Edmond Pélissier, Consul-General, &c.;

Her Majesty the Queen of the United Kingdom of Great Britain and Ireland, has appointed as her Commissioner Mr. J. L. A. Simmons, Lieutenant-Colonel of Engineers, &c.;

His Majesty the Emperor of All the Russias has appointed as his Commissioners, M. Tchirikoff, Major-General, &c., and M. Michel Invanine, Colonel, &c.;

His Majesty the Emperor of the Ottomans has appointed as his Commissioners, Hussein Pacha, General of Brigade, &c., and Osman Bey, Colonel of the Staff, &c.:

Who, having communicated to each other their Full Powers, found to be in good and due form, having examined the Territory, heard witnesses and read the Documents produced on either side on all questions in litigation, decide as follows:

ART. I. *Detailed Description of Asiatic Frontiers.*

Map of Frontier.

ART. II. The whole of the Frontier has been marked by a dotted line, tinted red on the Map, signed by all the Members of the Mixed Commission, and annexed as forming part thereof to the present Final Act of the Labours of the said Commission.

Date of Execution of Final Act.

ART. III. The Arrangements concluded by the present Act must receive their full and entire execution by the 1st December, 1858.

Ratifications.

ART. IV. The present Act shall be ratified, and the Ratifications thereof shall be exchanged within two months, and sooner if possible.

Done at Constantinople, in quadruplicate, the 5th December, 1857.

> PELISSIER.
> J. L. A. SIMMONS.
> TCHIRIKOFF.
> IVANINE.
> HUSSEIN.
> OSMAN.

70　TREATY OF TIENTSIN

TREATY OF PEACE, FRIENDSHIP, and COMMERCE, between Great Britain and China. Signed at Tientsin, 26th June, 1858. Ratifications exchanged at Peking, 24th October, 1860.

HER Majesty the Queen of the United Kingdom of Great Britain

and Ireland, and His Majesty the Emperor of China, being desirous to put an end to the existing misunderstanding between the two countries, and to place their relations on a more satisfactory footing in future, have resolved to proceed to a revision and improvement of the Treaties existing between them; and, for that purpose, have named as their Plenipotentiaries, that is to say:—

Her Majesty the Queen of Great Britain and Ireland, the Right Honourable the Earl of Elgin and Kincardine, &c.;

And His Majesty the Emperor of China, the High Commissioners Kweiliang, a Senior Chief Secretary of State, &c.; and Hwashana, one of His Imperial Majesty's Expositors of the Classics, &c.;

Who, after having communicated to each other their respective full powers, and found them to be in good and due form, have agreed upon and concluded the following Articles:—

Confirmation of Treaty of 29th August, 1842.

ART. I. The Treaty of Peace and Amity between the two nations, signed at Nanking on the 29th day of August, in the year 1842, is hereby renewed and confirmed.

Abrogation of Trade Regulations of July, 1843, and of Supplementary Treaty of October, 1843.

The Supplementary Treaty and General Regulations of Trade having been amended and improved, and the substance of their provisions having been incorporated in this Treaty, the said Supplementary Treaty and General Regulations of Trade are hereby abrogated.

Appointment of Ambassadors, &c.

ART. II. For the better preservation of harmony in future, Her Majesty the Queen of Great Britain and His Majesty the Emperor of China mutually agree that, in accordance with the universal practice of great and friendly nations, Her Majesty the Queen may, if she see fit, appoint Ambassadors, Ministers, or other Diplomatic Agents to the Court of Peking; and His Majesty the Emperor of China may, in like manner, if he see fit, appoint Ambassadors, Ministers, or other Diplomatic Agents to the Court of St. James'.

Residence of British Representative at Peking.

ART. III. His Majesty the Emperor of China hereby agrees, that the Ambassador, Minister, or other Diplomatic Agent, so appointed by Her

Majesty the Queen of Great Britain, may reside, with his family and establishment, permanently at the capital, or may visit it occasionally, at the option of the British Government.

Ceremonial, &c.

He shall not be called upon to perform any ceremony derogatory to him as representing the Sovereign of an independent nation, on a footing of equality with that of China. On the other hand, he shall use the same forms of ceremony and respect to His Majesty the Emperor as are employed by the Ambassadors, Ministers, or Diplomatic Agents of Her Majesty towards the Sovereigns of independent and equal European nations.

Right of British Government to hire Houses, &c., at Peking.

It is further agreed, that Her Majesty's Government may acquire at Peking a site for building, or may hire houses for the accommodation of Her Majesty's mission, and that the Chinese Government will assist it in so doing.

Right of British Representative to choose his own Servants, &c.

Her Majesty's Representative shall be at liberty, to choose his own servants and attendants, who shall not be subjected to any kind of molestation whatever.

Non-Molestation of British Representative or his Suite.

Any person guilty of disrespect or violence to Her Majesty's Representative, or to any member of his family or establishment, in deed or word, shall be severely punished.

Rights and Privileges of British Representative.

Art. IV. It is further agreed, that no obstacle or difficulty shall be made to the free movements of Her Majesty's Representative, and that he, and the persons of his suite, may come and go, and travel at their pleasure. He shall, moreover, have full liberty to send and receive his correspondence, to and from any point on the sea-coast that he may select; and his letters and effects shall be held sacred and inviolable. He may employ, for their transmission, special couriers, who shall meet with the same protection and facilities for travelling as the persons employed in carrying despatches for the Imperial Government; and, generally, he shall enjoy the same privileges as are accorded to officers of the same rank by the usage and consent of Western nations.

Expenses of Mission to be borne by British Governemnt.

All expenses attending the Diplomatic Mission of Great Britain in China shall be borne by the British Government.

Transaction of Business between British Representative and Chinese Government.

ART. V. His Majesty the Emperor of China agrees to nominate one of the Secretaries of State, or a President of one of the Boards, as the high officer with whom the Ambassador, Minister, or other Diplomatic Agent of Her Majesty the Queen, shall transact business, either personally, or in writing, on a footing of perfect equality.

Privileges of Chinese, Ambassadors, &c., in Great Britain.

ART. VI. Her Majesty the Queen of Great Britain agrees that the privileges hereby secured shall be enjoyed in her dominions by the Ambassadors, Ministers, or Diplomatic Agents of the Emperor of China, accredited to the Court of Her Majesty.

Appointment of Consuls. Their Rights and Privileges.

ART. VII. Her Majesty the Queen may appoint one or more Consuls in the dominions of the Emperor of China; and such Consul or Consuls shall be at liberty to reside in any of the open ports or cities of China as Her Majesty the Queen may consider most expedient for the interests of British commerce. They shall be treated with due respect by the Chinese authorities, and enjoy the same privileges and immunities as the Consular officers of the most favoured nation.

Consuls and Vice-Consuls in charge shall rank with Intendents of Circuits; Vice-Consuls, Acting Vice-Consuls, and Interpreters, with Prefects. They shall have access to the official residences of these officers, and communicate with them, either personally or in writing, on a footing of equality, as the interests of the public service may require.

Religious Toleration.

ART. VIII. The Christian religion, as professed by Protestants or Roman Catholics, incalculates the practice of virtue, and teaches man to do as he would be done by. Persons teaching or professing it, therefore, shall alike be entitled to the protection of the Chinese authorities, nor shall any such, peaceably pursuing their calling, and not offending against the law, be persecuted or interfered with.

Passports.

ART. IX. British subjects are hereby authorized to travel, for their pleasure or for purposes of trade, to all parts of the interior, under passports which will be issued by their Consuls, and countersigned by the local authorities. These passports, if demanded, must be produced for examination in the localities passed through. If the passport be not irregular, the bearer will be allowed to proceed, and no opposition shall be offered to his hiring persons or hiring vessels for the carriage of his baggage or merchandise. If he be without a passport, or if he commit any offence against the law, he shall be handed over to the nearest Consul for punishment, but he must not be subjected to any ill-usage in excess of necessary restraint. No passport need be applied for by persons going on excursions from the ports open to trade to a distance not exceeding 100 *li*, and for a period not exceeding 5 days.

The provisions of this Article do not apply to crews of ships, for the due restraint of whom regulations will be drawn up by the Consul and the local authorities.

To Nanking, and other cities disturbed by persons in arms against the Government, no pass shall be given, until they shall have been recaptured.

Trade on the River Yang-tsze. Port of Chinkiang to be opened to Trade.

ART. X. British merchant ships shall have authority to trade upon the Great River (Yang-tsze). The Upper and Lower Valley of the river being, however, disturbed by outlaws, no port shall be for the present open to trade, with the exception of Chinkiang, which shall be opened in a year from the date of the signing of this Treaty.

Other Ports on the Yang-tsze to be opened.

So soon as peace shall have been restored, British vessels shall also be admitted to trade at such ports as far as Hankow, not exceeding 3 in number, as the British Minister, after consultation with the Chinese Secretary of State, may determine shall be ports of entry and discharge.

Ports of Newchwang, Chefoo, Taiwan (Formosa), Swatow, and Kiungchow (Hainan) opened to Trade.

ART. XI. In addition to the cities and towns of Canton, Amoy, Foochow, Ningpo, and Shanghai, opened by the Treaty of Nanking, it is agreed that British subjects may frequent the cities and ports of

Newchwang, Tangchow (Chefoo), Taiwan (Formosa), Chao-Chow (Swatow) and Kiungchow (Hainan).

They are permitted to carry on trade with whomsoever they please, and to proceed to and fro at pleasure with their vessels and merchandise.

Rent of Houses, Churches, Hospitals, Cemeteries, &c.

They shall enjoy the same privileges, advantages, and immunities, at the said towns and ports, as they enjoy at the ports already opened to trade, including the right of residence, of buying or renting houses, of leasing land therein, and of building churches, hospitals, and cemeteries.

Rent of Houses, Churches, Hospitals, Burial-Grounds, &c.

ART. XII. British subjects whether at the ports or at other places, desiring to build or open houses, warehouses, churches, hospitals, or burial-grounds, shall make their agreement for the land or buildings they require, at the rates prevailing among the people, equitably, and without exactions on either side.

Employment of Chinese by British Subjects.

ART. XIII. The Chinese Government will place no restrictions whatever upon the employment, by British subjects, of Chinese subjects in any lawful capacity.

Hire of Boats by British Subjects. No Monopoly. Smuggling.

ART. XIV. British subjects may hire whatever boats they please for the transport of goods or passengers, and the sum to be paid for such boats shall be settled between the parties themselves, without the interference of the Chinese Government. The number of these boats shall not be limited, nor shall a monopoly in respect either of the boats, or of the porters or coolies engaged in carrying the goods, be granted to any parties. If any smuggling takes place in them, the offenders will, of course, be punished according to law.

Jurisdiction of British Authorities in Questions affecting British Subjects.

ART. XV. All questions in regard to rights, whether of property or person, arising between British subjects, shall be subject to the jurisdiction of the British authorities.

*Administration of Justice. British Consular Jurisdiction in case of
Crimes committed by British Subjects.*

ART. XVI. Chinese subjects who may be guilty of any criminal act
towards British subjects shall be arrested and punished by the Chinese
authorities, according to the laws of China.

British subjects who may commit any crime in China shall be tried
and punished by the Consul, or other public functionary authorized
thereto, according to the laws of Great Britain.

Justice shall be equitably and impartially administered on both sides.

*Disputes between British Subjects and Chinese. Consular
Intervention.*

ART. XVII. A British subject having reason to complain of a Chinese,
must proceed to the Consulate, and state his grievance. The Consul will
inquire into the merits of the case, and do his utmost to arrange it
amicably. In like manner, if a Chinese have reason to complain of a
British subject, the Consul shall no less listen to his complaint, and
endeavour to settle it in a friendly manner. If disputes take place of such
a nature that the Consul cannot arrange them amicably, then he shall
request the assistance of the Chinese authorities, that they may together
examine into the merits of the case, and decide it equitably.

Protection of British Persons and Property.

ART. XVIII. The Chinese authorities shall at all times afford the fullest
protection to the persons and property of British subjects, whenever
these shall have been subjected to insult or violence. In all cases of
incendiarism or robbery, the local authorities shall at once take the
necessary steps for the recovery of the stolen property, the suppression
of disorder, and the arrest of the guilty parties, whom they will punish
according to law.

Pirates.

ART. XIX. If any British merchant vessel, while within Chinese waters,
be plundered by robbers or Pirates, it shall be the duty of the Chinese
authorities to use every endeavour to capture and punish the said robbers
or Pirates, and to recover the stolen property, that it may be handed
over to the Consul for restoration to the owner.

Wrecks, &c.

ART. XX. If any British vessel be at any time wrecked or stranded on the coast of China, or be compelled to take refuge in any port within the dominions of the Emperor of China, the Chinese authorities, on being apprised of the fact, shall immediately adopt measures for its relief and security; the persons on board shall receive friendly treatment, and shall be furnished, if necessary, with the means of conveyance to the nearest Consular station.

Surrender of Fugitive Criminals between China and Hong Kong.
ART. XXI. If criminals, subjects of China, shall take refuge in Hong Kong, or on board the British ships there, they shall upon due requisition by the Chinese authorities, be searched for, and, on proof of their guilt, be delivered up.

In like manner, if Chinese offenders take refuge in the houses or on board the vessels of British subjects at the open ports, they shall not be harboured or concealed, but shall be delivered up, on due requisition by the Chinese authorities, addressed to the British Consul.

British and Chinese fraudulent Debtors.
ART. XXII. Should any Chinese subject fail to discharge debts incurred to a British subject, or should he fraudulently abscond, the Chinese authorities will do their utmost to effect his arrest, and enforce recovery of the debts. The British authorities will likewise do their utmost to bring to justice any British subject fraudulently absconding or failing to discharge debts incurred by him to a Chinese subject.

Debts incurred by Chinese at Hong Kong.
ART. XXIII. Should natives of China who may repair to Hong Kong to trade incur debts there, the recovery of such debts must be arranged for by the English Courts of Justice on the spot; but should the Chinese debtor abscond, and be known to have property, real or personal, within the Chinese territory, it shall be the duty of the Chinese authorities, on application by, and in concert with, the British Consul, to do their utmost to see justice done between the parties.

Most-favoured-nation Treatment in respect to Imports and Exports.
ART. XXIV. It is agreed that British subjects shall pay, on all merchandise imported or exported by them, the duties prescribed by the Tariff, but in no case shall they be called upon to pay other or higher duties than are required of the subjects of any other foreign nation.

Payment of Import and Export Duties.

ART. XXV. Import duties shall be considered payable on the landing of the goods, and duties of export on the shipment of the same.

Revision of Tariff.

ART. XXVI. Whereas the Tariff fixed by Article X of the Treaty of Nanking, and which was estimated so as to impose on imports and exports a duty at about the rate of 5 per cent. *ad valorem*, has been found, by reason of the fall in value of various articles of merchandise, therein enumerated, to impose a duty upon these, considerably in excess of the rate originally assumed as above to be a fair rate, it is agreed that the said Tariff shall be revised, and that as soon as the Treaty shall have been signed, application shall be made to the Emperor of China to depute a high officer of the Board of Revenue to meet, at Shanghai, officers to be deputed on behalf of the British Government, to consider its revision together, so that the Tariff, as revised, may come into operation immediately after the ratification of this Treaty.

Duration and Revision of Treaty and Tariff.

ART. XXVII. It is agreed that either of the High Contracting Parties to this Treaty may demand a further revision of the Tariff, and of the Commercial Articles of this Treaty, at the end of 10 years; but if no demand be made on either side within 6 months after the end of the first 10 years, then the Tariff shall remain in force for 10 years more, reckoned from the end of the preceding 10 years; and so it shall be, at the end of each successive period of 10 years.

Transit Dues.

ART. XXVIII. Whereas it was agreed in Article X of the Treaty of Nanking, that British imports, having paid the Tariff duties, should be conveyed into the interior free of all further charges, except a transit duty, the amount whereof was not to exceed a certain percentage on tariff value; and whereas no accurate information having been furnished of the amount of such duty, British merchants have constantly complained that charges are suddenly and arbitrarily imposed by the provincial authorities as transit duties upon produce on its way to the foreign market, and on imports on their way into the interior, to the detriment of trade; it is agreed that within 4 months from the signing of this Treaty, at all ports now open to British trade, and within a similar period to all ports that may hereafter be opened, the authority appointed to superintend the collection of duties shall be obliged, upon application of the Consul, to declare the amount of duties leviable on produce between the place of production and the port of shipment, and upon imports between the Consular port in question and the inland markets named by the Consul; and that a notification thereof shall be published in English and Chinese for general information.

But it shall be at the option of any British subject, desiring to convey produce purchased inland to a port, or to convey imports from a port to an inland market, to clear his goods of all transit duties, by payment of a single charge. The amount of this charge shall be leviable on exports at the first barrier they may have to pass, or, on imports, at the port at which they are landed; and on payment thereof, a certificate shall be issued, which shall exempt the goods from all further inland charges whatsoever.

It is further agreed that the amount of this charge shall be calculated, as nearly as possible, at the rate of two and a half per cent. *ad valorem*, and that it shall be fixed for each article at the Conference to be held at Shanghai for the revision of the Tariff.

It is distinctly understood, that the payment of transit dues, by commutation or otherwise, shall in no way affect the Tariff duties on imports or exports, which will continue to be levied separately and in full.

Tonnage Dues.
ART. XXIX. British merchant-vessels, of more than 150 tons burden, shall be charged tonnage dues at the rate of 4 mace per ton; if of 150 tons and under, they shall be charged at the rate of one mace per ton.

Special Certificate to Vessels clearing from one Chinese Port to another Chinese Port and for Hong Kong.
Any vessel clearing from any of the open ports of China for any other of the open ports, or for Hong Kong, shall be entitled, on application of the master, to a special certificate from the Customs, on exhibition of which she shall be exempted from all further payment of tonnage dues in any open port of China, for a period of 4 months, to be reckoned from the date of her port clearance.

Tonnage Dues.   Exemption from Payment in certain cases.
ART. XXX. The master of any British merchant-vessel may, within 48 hours after the arrival of his vessel, but not later, decide to depart without

breaking bulk, in which case he will not be subject to pay tonnage dues. But tonnage dues shall be held due after the expiration of the said 48 hours. No other fees or charges upon entry or departure shall be levied.

Exemption of certain British Boats from Tonnage Dues.

ART. XXXI. No tonnage dues shall be payable on boats employed by British subjects in the conveyance of passengers, baggage, letters, articles of provisions, or other articles not subject to duty, between any of the open ports. All cargo boats, however, conveying merchandise subject to duty shall pay tonnage dues once in 6 months at the rate of 4 mace per register ton.

Buoys, Beacons, Lighthouses, &c.

ART. XXXII. The Consuls and Superintendents of Customs shall consult together regarding the erection of beacons or lighthouses, and the distribution of buoys and light-ships, as occasion may demand.

Payment of Duties in Sycee or Foreign Money.

ART. XXXIII. Duties shall be paid to the bankers, authorized by the Chinese Government to receive the same in its behalf, either in sycee or in foreign money, according to the assay made at Canton on the 13th of July, 1843.

Standard Weights and Measures to be deposited at each Consulate.

ART. XXXIV. Sets of standard weights and measures, prepared according to the standard issued to the Canton Custom-House by the Board of Revenue, shall be delivered by the Superintendent of Customs to the Consul at each port, to secure uniformity and prevent confusion.

Pilots.

ART. XXXV. Any British merchant-vessel arriving at one of the open ports, shall be at liberty to engage the services of a Pilot to take her into port. In like manner, after she has discharged all legal dues and duties, and is ready to take her departure, she shall be allowed to select a Pilot to conduct her out of port.

Custom-House Guards.

ART. XXXVI. Whenever a British merchant-vessel shall arrive off one of the open ports, the Superintendent of Customs shall depute one or more Customs officers to guard the ship. They shall either live in a boat of their own, or stay on board the ship, as may best suit their convenience. Their food and expenses shall be supplied them from the Custom-House, and they shall not be entitled to any fees whatever from the master or consignee. Should they violate this regulation, they shall be punished proportionately to the amount exacted.

Liability of Vessels entering Port.

ART. XXXVII. Within 24 hours after arrival, the ship's papers, bills of lading, &c., shall be lodged in the hands of the Consul, who will, within a further period of 24 hours, report to the Superintendent of Customs, the name of the ship, her register tonnage, and the nature of her cargo. If, owing to neglect on the part of the master, the above rule is not complied with within 48 hours after the ship's arrival, he shall be liable to a fine of 50 taels for every day's delay; the total amount of penalty, however, shall not exceed 200 taels.

Ships' Manifests and Bills of Lading.

The master will be responsible for the correctness of the manifest, which shall contain a full and true account of the particulars of the cargo on board. For presenting a false manifest, he will subject himself to a fine of 500 taels; but he will be allowed to correct, within 24 hours after delivery of it to the Customs officers, any mistake he may discover in his manifest, without incurring this penalty.

Permit to open Hatches and discharge Goods.

ART. XXXVIII. After receiving from the Consul the report in due form, the Superintendent of Customs shall grant the vessel a permit to open hatches. If the master shall open hatches and begin to discharge any goods without such permission, he shall be fined 500 taels, and the goods discharged shall be confiscated wholly.

Permits to Land and Ship Cargoes.

ART. XXXIX. Any British merchant who has cargo to land or ship, must apply to the Superintendent of Customs for a special permit. Cargo landed or shipped without such permit will be liable to confiscation.

Trans-shipments.

ART. XL. No trans-shipments from one vessel to another can be made without special permission, under pain of confiscation of the goods so trans-shipped.

Port-clearances.

ART. XLI. When all dues and duties shall have been paid, the Superintendent of Customs shall give a port-clearance, and the Consul shall then return the ship's papers, so that she may depart on her voyage.

Mode of levying ad valorem Duties.

ART. XLII. With respect to articles subject, according to the Tariff, to an *ad valorem* duty, if the British merchant cannot agree with the Chinese officer in fixing a value, then each party shall call two or three merchants to look at the goods, and the highest price at which any of these merchants would be willing to purchase them, shall be assumed as the value of the goods.

Mode of levying Duties on Goods.

ART. XLIII. Duties shall be charged upon the net weight of each article, making a deduction for the tare, weight of congee, &c. To fix the tare on any article such as tea, if the British merchant cannot agree with the Custom-House officer, then each party shall choose so many chests out of every 100, which being first weighed in gross, shall afterwards be tared, and the average tare upon these chests shall be assumed as the tare upon the whole; and upon this principle shall the tare be fixed upon all other goods in packages. If there should be any other points in dispute which cannot be settled, the British merchant may appeal to his Consul, who will communicate the particulars of the case to the Superintendent of Customs, that it may be equitably arranged. But the appeal must be made within 24 hours, or it will not be attended to. While such points are still unsettled, the Superintendent of Customs shall postpone the insertion of the same in his books.

Reduction of Duty on Damaged Goods.

ART. XLIV. Upon all damaged goods a fair reduction of duty shall be allowed, proportionate to their deterioration. If any disputes arise, they shall be settled in the manner pointed out in the clause of this Treaty having reference to articles which pay duty *ad valorum*.

Re-exportation of Duty-paid Goods.

ART. XLV. British merchants who may have imported merchandise into any of the open ports and paid the duty thereon, if they desire to re-export the same, shall be entitled to make application to the Super-intendent of Customs, who, in order to prevent fraud on the revenue, shall cause examination to be made by suitable officers, to see that the duties paid on such goods, as entered in the Custom-House books, cor-respond with the representation made, and that the goods remain with their original marks unchanged. He shall then make a memorandum on the port-clearance of the goods and of the amount of duties paid, and deliver the same to the merchant; and shall also certify the facts to the officers of Customs of the other ports. All which being done, on the arrival in port of the vessel in which the goods are laden, everything being found on examination there to correspond, she shall be permitted to break bulk, and land the said goods, without being subject to the payment of any additional duty thereon. But if, on such examination, the Superintendent of Customs shall detect any fraud on the revenue in the case, then the goods shall be subject to confiscation by the Chinese Government.

Drawback Certificates.

British merchants desiring to re-export duty-paid imports to a foreign country, shall be entitled, on complying with the same con-ditions as in the case of re-exportation to another port in China, to a drawback certificate, which shall be a valid tender to the Customs in payment of import or export duties.

Foreign Grain.

Foreign grain brought into any port of China in a British ship, if no part thereof has been landed, may be re-exported without hindrance.

Preventions against Fraud and Smuggling.

Art. XLVI. The Chinese authorities at each port shall adopt the means they may judge most proper to prevent the revenue suffering from Fraud or Smuggling.

British Vessels trading with Ports not opened by Treaty liable to Confiscation.

Art. XLVII. British merchant vessels are not entitled to resort to other than the ports of trade declared open by this Treaty. They are not unlawfully to enter other ports in China, or to carry on clandestine trade along the coasts thereof. Any vessel violating this provision, shall, with her cargo, be subject to confiscation by the Chinese Government.

Goods on British Vessels found concerned in Smuggling liable to Confiscation.

ART. XLVIII. If any British merchant vessel be concerned in Smuggling, the goods, whatever their value or nature, shall be subject to confiscation by the Chinese authorities, and the ship may be prohibited from trading further, and sent away as soon as her accounts shall have been adjusted and paid.

Penalties and Confiscations to belong to Chinese Government.

ART. XLIX. All penalties enforced, or confiscations made, under this Treaty, shall belong and be appropriated to the public service of the Government of China.

Language to be employed in Official Communications.

ART. L. All official communications, addressed by the Diplomatic and Consular Agents of Her Majesty the Queen to the Chinese authorities, shall, henceforth, be written in English. They will for the present be accompanied by a Chinese version, but it is understood that, in the event of there being any difference of meaning between the English and Chinese text, the English Government will hold the sense as expressed in the English text to be the correct sense. This provision is to apply to the Treaty now negotiated, the Chinese text of which has been carefully corrected by the English original.

The Chinese character " I " 虜 (barbarian) not to be applied to the British Government or to British Subjects.

ART. LI. It is agreed, that henceforth the character " I " 虜 (barbarian) shall not be applied to the Government or subjects of Her Britannic Majesty in any Chinese official document issued by the Chinese authorities in the capital or in the provinces.

Facilities to be granted to British Ships of War. Piracy, &c.

ART. LII. British ships of war coming for no hostile purpose, or being engaged in the pursuit of Pirates, shall be at liberty to visit all ports within the dominions of the Emperor of China, and shall receive every facility for the purchase of provisions, procuring water, and, if occasion require, for the making of repairs. The Commanders of such ships shall hold intercourse with the Chinese authorities on terms of equality and courtesy.

Measures to be taken for Suppression of Piracy.
ART. LIII. In consideration of the injury sustained by native and foreign commerce from the prevalence of Piracy in the seas of China, the High Contracting Parties agree to concert measures for its suppression.

Confirmation of previous Treaties. Most-favoured-nation Treatment conferred on British Subjects.
ART. LIV. The British Government and its subjects are hereby confirmed in all privileges, immunities, and advantages conferred on them by previous Treaties: and it is hereby expressly stipulated that the British Government and its subjects will be allowed free and equal participation in all privileges, immunities, and advantages that may have been, or may be hereafter, granted by His Majesty the Emperor of China to the Government or subjects of any other nation.

ART. LV.
A separate Article to be agreed upon, providing for the Indemnity to be paid for Losses, &c., of British Subjects at Canton.

Ratifications.
ART. LVI. The ratifications of this Treaty, under the hand of Her Majesty the Queen of Great Britain and Ireland, and His Majesty the Emperor of China, respectively, shall be exchanged at Peking, within a year from this day of signature.

In token whereof, the respective Plenipotentiaries have signed and sealed this Treaty.

Done at Tientsin, this 26th day of June, in the year of our Lord, 1858; corresponding with the Chinese date, the 16th day, 5th moon, of the 8th year of Hien Fung.

(L.S.)   ELGIN AND KINCARDINE.
Signature of 1st Chinese Plenipotentiary.
           Signature of 2nd Chinese Plenipotentiary.
      Seal of the Chinese Plenipotentiaries.

71

CONVENTION between Great Britain, Austria, France, Prussia, Russia, Sardinia, and Turkey, respecting the United Principalities of Moldavia and Wallachia. Signed at Paris, 19th August, 1858. Ratifications exchanged at Paris, 2nd October, 1858.

Reference to Treaty of 30th March, 1856.

THEIR Majesties the Queen of the United Kingdom of Great Britain and Ireland, the Emperor of Austria, the Emperor of the French, the King of Prussia, the Emperor of All the Russias, the King of Sardinia, and the Emperor of the Ottomans, wishing, in conformity with the stipulations of the Treaty concluded at Paris on the 30th March, 1856, to record in a Convention their Final Agreement in regard to the Definitive Organization of the Principalities of Moldavia and Wallachia, have named as their Plenipotentiaries for the purpose of negotiating and signing the said Convention, that is to say:

Her Majesty the Queen of the United Kingdom of Great Britain and Ireland, the Right Honourable Henry Richard Charles, Earl Cowley, Viscount Dangan, Baron Cowley, a Peer of the United Kingdom, a Member of Her Britannic Majesty's Privy Council, Her said Majesty's Ambassador Extraordinary and Plenipotentiary to His Majesty the Emperor of the French, &c.;

His Majesty the Emperor of Austria, M. Joseph Alexander Baron de Hübner, his actual Privy Councillor, and his Ambassador Extraordinary and Plenipotentiary to His Majesty the Emperor of the French, &c.;

His Majesty the Emperor of the French, M. Alexandre Count Colonna Walewski, a Senator of the Empire, his Minister and Secretary of State for Foreign Affairs, &c.;

His Majesty the King of Prussia, M. Maximilian Frederick Charles Francis Count of Hatzfeldt-Wildenburg-Schoenstein, his actual Privy Councillor, and his Envoy Extraordinary and Minister Plenipotentiary to His Majesty the Emperor of the French, &c.;

His Majesty the Emperor of All the Russias, the Count Paul Kisseleff, Knight of the Orders of Russia, his Aide-de-Camp General, a General of Infantry, a Member of the Council of the Empire, his Ambassador Extraordinary and Plenipotentiary to His Majesty the Emperor of the French, &c.;

His Majesty the King of Sardinia, M. Salvator Marquis de Villa-marina, his Envoy Extraordinary and Minister Plenipotentiary to His Majesty the Emperor of the French, &c.;

His Majesty the Emperor of the Ottomans, Mohammed Fuad Pasha, Muchir and Vizier of the Empire, his Minister for Foreign Affairs, &c.;

Who have met in Conference at Paris, furnished with Full Powers which have been found in good and due form, and have agreed upon the following arrangements:

Suzerainty of Sultan over United Principalities of Moldavia and Wallachia.

ART. I. The Principalities of Moldavia and Wallachia, constituted henceforward under the denomination of *United Principalities of Moldavia and Wallachia*, are placed under the Suzerainty of His Majesty the Sultan.

Guarantee by Contracting Powers of Privileges and Immunities of Principalities.

ART. II. In virtue of the Capitulations issued by the Sultans Bajazet I, Mahomet II, Selim I, and Soliman II, which constitute their self-government, settling their relations with the Sublime Porte, and which are recorded in various Hatti-Sheriffs, specially that of 1834; conformably also to Articles XXII and XXIII of the Treaty concluded at Paris on the 30th March, 1856, the Principalities shall continue to enjoy, under the Collective Guarantee of the Contracting Powers, the Privileges and Immunities of which they are in possession.

Free Administration.

Consequently, the Principalities shall carry on their own administration freely and exempt from any interference of the Sublime Porte, within the limits stipulated by the agreement of the Guaranteeing Powers with the Suzerain Court.

Public Powers confided in each Principality to a Hospodar and an Elective Assembly.

ART. III. The Public Powers shall be confided, in each Principality, to a Hospodar and an Elective Assembly, acting, in the cases provided for in the present Convention, with the concurrence of a Central Commission, common to both Principalities.

Executive Power.

ART. IV. The Executive Power shall be exercised by the Hospodar.

Legislative Power.

ART. V. The Legislative Power shall be exercised collectively by the Hospodar, the Assembly, and the Central Commission.

Laws to be prepared by Hospodar and voted by Assembly.

ART. VI. The Laws which specially concern each Principality shall be prepared by the Hospodar, and voted by the Assembly.

Laws relating to both Principalities to be voted by the Assembly.

The Laws which concern both Principalities in common shall be prepared by the Central Commission, and voted by the Assemblies, to which they shall be submitted by the Hospodars.

Judicial Power.

ART. VII. The Judicial Power, exercised in the name of the Hospodar, shall be confided to Magistrates appointed by him; but no person shall be withdrawn from his natural judges.

A Law shall determine the conditions of admission and promotion in the Magistracy, adopting for its basis the progressive application of the principle of irremovableness.

Annual Tribute.

ART. VIII. The Principalities shall pay to the Suzerain Court an Annual Tribute, the amount of which is fixed at the sum of 1,500,000 piastres for Moldavia, and at the sum of 2,500,000 piastres for Wallachia.

Investiture of Hospodars by Sultan.

Investiture shall be, as heretofore, conferred upon the Hospodars by His Majesty the Sultan.

Measures of Defence.

The Suzerain Court shall arrange with the Principalities the Measures for the Defence of their Territory, in case of external aggression, and it will be for that Court to initiate, by an understanding with the Guaranteeing Powers, the measures necessary for the re-establishment of order, in case it should be compromised.

Application of Treaties to Principalities.

As hitherto, the International Treaties which shall be concluded by the Suzerain Court with Foreign Powers, shall be applicable to the Principalities in all that shall not prejudice their immunities.

Violation of Immunities to be represented by Hospodars to the Suzerain and to Guaranteeing Powers.

ART. IX. In the event of a violation of the Immunities of the Principalities, the Hospodars shall address a representation to the Suzerain Power, and if their representation be not attended to, they may communicate it through their agents to the Representatives of the Guaranteeing Powers at Constantinople.

Hospodars to be represented at Suzerain Court.

The Hospodars shall be represented at the Suzerain Court by agents (*Capou-Kiaya*), who shall be native-born Moldavians or Wallachians, not holding of any foreign jurisdiction, and accepted by the Porte.

Election of Hospodar for Life.

ART. X. The Hospodar shall be elected for life by the Assembly.

Administration by Council of Ministers during Vacancy.

ART. XI. In case of a Vacancy, and until the installation of the new Hospodar, the Administration shall devolve on the Council of Ministers, which shall enter thereupon as of full right.

Functions to be purely Administrative.

Its Functions, which are purely Administrative, shall be limited to the transaction of business, without its being competent for them to dismiss Functionaries, unless for an offence judicially proved.

In that case it shall only supply their places provisionally.

Election of new Hospodar.

ART. XII. When the Vacancy shall occur, if the Assembly is in session, it must proceed within 8 days to the Election of the Hospodar.

If it be not in session, it shall be immediately convoked, and assembled within 10 days. In case it should be dissolved, new Elections shall take place within 15 days, and the new Assembly shall also meet within 10 days. Within 8 days after its meeting, it shall be bound to have proceeded to the Election of the Hospodar.

The presence of three-fourths of the number of members inscribed shall be necessary in order to proceed to the Election.

In case the Election shall not have taken place within the 8 days, on the 9th day, at noon, the Assembly shall proceed to the Election, whatever number of members be present.

Investiture shall be applied for as heretofore; it shall be given in a month at farthest.

Persons eligible to Hospodariate.

ART. XIII. Every person shall be eligible to the Hospodarate, who being 35 years of age, and son of a native-born Moldavian or Wallachian father, can prove himself possessed of an income of 3,000 ducats derived from real property, provided he has fulfilled public functions for the space of 10 years, or has been a member of the Assemblies.

Government of Hospodar.

ART. VIX. The Hospodar governs with the concurrence of Ministers appointed by himself. He sanctions and promulgates the Laws; he may refuse his sanction. He has the right of pardon, and that of commuting punishments in criminal matters, without the power of otherwise interposing in the administration of justice.

Laws submitted to Assembly by Hospodar.

He prepares the Laws which specially concern the Principality, and specifically the Budgets, and submits them to the deliberations of the Assembly.

Appointments made by Hospodar.

He appoints to all posts in the Public Administration, and makes the regulations necessary for the execution of the Laws.

Civil List of Hospodar.

The Civil List of each Hospodar shall be voted by the Assembly, once for all, at the time of his accession.

Acts of Hospodar to be countersigned by Ministers.

ART. XV. Every Act emanating from the Hospodar must be countersigned by the competent Ministers.

Responsibility of Ministers.

The Ministers shall be responsible for violation of the Laws, and particularly for any waste of Public Money.

Trial of Ministers.

They shall be triable by the High Court of Justice and Cassation.

Institution of Prosecutions.

Prosecutions may be instituted by the Hospodar or by the Assembly.

Majority of two-thirds necessary for Trial of Ministers.

The prosecution of the Ministers cannot be ordered but by a majority of two-thirds of the members present.

Duration of Elective Assembly.

ART. XVI. The Elective Assembly in each Principality shall be elected for 7 years, conformably to the electoral arrangements annexed to the present Convention.

Convocation of Assembly.
ART. XVII. The Assembly shall be convoked by the Hospodar, and shall meet every year on the first Sunday in December.

Duration of ordinary Session.
The duration of each ordinary session shall be 3 months.

Convocation and Dissolution of Assembly by Hospodar.
The Hospodar may, if there be occasion, prolong the session. He may convoke the Assembly extraordinarily, or dissolve it. In this last case, he is bound to convoke a new Assembly, which shall meet within 3 months.

Bishops to form part of Assembly.
ART. XVIII. The Metropolitan and the Diocesan Bishops shall, as of full right, form part of the Assembly.

Presidency of Assembly.
The Presidency of the Assembly shall belong to the Metropolitan. The Vice-Presidents and Secretaries shall be elected by the Assembly.

Admission of Public to Sittings of Assembly.
ART. XIX. The President fixes the conditions on which the Public shall be admitted to the Sittings, save as to exceptional cases which may be provided for by internal regulations.

Minutes of Sittings.
There shall be prepared, under the direction of the President, a brief Minute of each Sitting, which shall be published in the Official Gazette.

Assembly to discuss and vote Laws.
ART. XX. The Assembly shall discuss and vote the Drafts of Laws which shall be presented to it by the Hospodar. It may amend them, subject to the reservation stipulated by Article XXXVI with regard to Laws of general interest.

Right of Ministers to attend Assemblies and discuss Laws.
ART. XXI. If the Ministers are not Members of the Assemblies, they shall nevertheless have the right to attend there, and may take part in the discussion of Laws, without, however the power of voting.

Budget to be voted by Assembly.

ART. XXII. The Budget of Income and that of Expenditure, prepared annually for each Principality, under the direction of the respective Hospodars, and submitted to the Assembly, which may amend the same, shall not be definitive until after having been voted by it.

Provision for Public Services in case Budget is not voted.

If the Budget be not voted in sufficient time, the Executive Power shall provide for the Public Services, according to the Budget of the previous year.

Revenues to be included in Budget.

ART. XXIII. The different revenues arising, up to the present time, from special sources, and which the Government appropriates on various authorities, shall be included in the general Budget of Income.

Definitive Statement of Accounts.

ART. XXIV. The Definitive Statement of Accounts shall be presented to the Assembly in two years, at latest, from the close of each financial period.

Assembly to assent to Taxes.

ART. XXV. No Tax can be established or collected unless assented to by the Assembly.

Publication of Laws.

ART. XXVI. The Laws of Finance, as well as all Laws of common or special interst, and Regulations of Public Administration, shall be published in the Official Gazette.

Composition of Central Commission.

ART. XXVII. The Central Commission shall sit at Fockshani.

It shall be composed of 16 members, 8 Moldavians and 8 Wallachians. 4 shall be chosen by each Hospodar from among the members of the Assembly, or persons who have filled high offices in the country, and 4 by each Assembly from its own body.

Central Commission may take part in Election of Hospodars.

ART. XXVIII. The members of the Central Commission retain the right to take part in the election of Hospodars in the Assembly to which they belong.

Permanency of Central Commission.

ART. XXIX. The Central Commission is permanent. It may, however, when its business permits, adjourn for a period which shall in no case exceed 4 months.

Limit to Duration of Functions.

The Duration of the Functions of its Members, for each Principality, whether appointed by the Hospodar or chosen by the Assemblies, shall be limited to the duration of the Legislature.

Retiring Members to continue until Election of New ones.

The Functions of the retiring Members shall, however, not cease until the installation of the New Members.

Central Commission to be renewed on Opening of New Assemblies.

In case the term of both Assemblies should expire at the same time, the Central Commission shall be wholly renewed for both Principalities on the opening of the New Assemblies.

In case of the Dissolution of one of the Assemblies, the renewal shall take place only in regard to those Members of the Central Commission who belong to the Principality whose Assembly is re-elected.

Re-election of Retiring Members.

The retiring Members may be re-chosen.

Remuneration of Members of Central Commission.

ART. XXX. The Functions of a Member of the Central Commission shall be remunerated.

Presidency of Central Commission.

ART. XXXI. The Central Commission shall appoint its President.

In case the Votes should be equally divided between two candidates, a decision shall be taken by lot.

The Functions of the President shall cease with his appointment as Member of the Central Commission; they may be renewed.

In case of an equal division of Votes in the deliberations, the President shall have a Casting Vote.

The Central Commission shall provide for its own internal regulation. Its expenses of every kind shall be borne, in moieties, by the two Principalities.

New Organisation of Principalities under Protection of Central Commission.

ART. XXXII. The arrangements constituting the New Organisation of the Principalities are placed under the protection of the Central Commission.

Commission to point out Abuses and suggest Ameliorations.

The Commission may point out to the Hospodars the Abuses which it may deem urgent to reform, and may suggest to them the Ameliorations which it may be expedient to introduce in the different branches of the Administration.

Hospodars may submit Drafts of Laws to Central Commission.

ART. XXXIII. The Hospodars may send before the Central Commission all the propositions which it may appear to them expedient to convert into Drafts of Laws common to the two Principalities.

Central Commission to prepare Laws concerning both Principalities.

The Central Commission shall prepare the Laws which concern both Principalities in common, and shall submit those Laws, through the Hospodars, to the deliberation of the Assemblies.

Laws considered of General Interest to both Principalities.

ART. XXXIV. All those Laws are considered of general interest which have for their object Unity of Legislation, the establishment, maintenance, or improvement of the Union of Customs, Posts, and Telegraphs, the fixing of the Monetary Standard, and the different matters of Public Utility common to the two Principalities.

Central Commission to reduce the Laws to a Code.

ART. XXXV. The Central Commission, as soon as constituted, shall especially occupy itself in reducing the existing Laws to a Code, placing them in harmony with the Act which constitutes the new organisation.

Revision of Organic Regulations, Civil, Criminal, and Commercial Codes and Code of Procedure.

It shall revise the Organic Regulations, as well as the Civil, Criminal, and Commercial Codes, and the Code of Procedure, in such wise that, saving Laws of purely local interest, there shall thenceforward exist but one and the same system of legislation, which shall rule in both Principalities, after having been voted by the respective Assemblies, and sanctioned and promulgated by each Hospodar.

Amendments by Assemblies to Drafts of Laws of Central Commission.

ART. XXXVI. If the Assemblies introduce Amendments in the Drafts of Laws of general interest, the amended Draft shall be returned to the Central Commission, which shall consider and settle a definitive Draft, which the Assemblies can then only wholly adopt or wholly reject.

Central Commission to adopt Amendments voted by both Assemblies.

The Central Commission shall be bound to adopt the Amendments which shall have been concurrently voted by both Assemblies.

Laws not to be sanctioned by Hospodar without approval of Central Commission.

ART. XXXVII. The Laws which specially concern each of the Principalities shall not be sanctioned by the Hospodar, until after they have been communicated by him to the Central Commission, whose duty it will be to judge whether they are compatible with the arrangements which constitute the new organisation.

Appointment of High Court of Justice and Cassation for both Assemblies. Members irremovable.

ART. XXXVIII. There shall be instituted a High Court of Justice and Cassation common to both Principalities. It shall sit at Fockshani. Its constitution shall be provided for by a Law.

Its members shall be irremovable.

Orders of Courts and Decisions of Tribunals in Principalities to be brought before the Court in Cassation.

ART. XXXIX. The orders issued by the Courts, and the decisions pronounced by the Tribunals, in both Principalities, shall be brought exclusively before this Court in Cassation.

Rights of Revision and Jurisdiction of Court of Cassation.

ART. XL. It shall exercise a right of Revision and Control over the Courts of Appeal and the Tribunals.

It shall have the right of exclusive Jurisdiction over its own members in penal matters.

Rights as a High Court of Justice in Proceedings against Ministers.

ART XLI. As a High Court of Justice, it shall have cognisance of Proceedings which may have been instituted against the Ministers by the Hospodar or by the Assembly, and shall decide without appeal.

Identic Organisation of Regular Militias. Increase of Militia to be sanctioned by Suzerain Court.

ART. XLII. The regular Militias at present existing in the two Principalities shall receive an identic organisation, in order that they may, when necessary, unite and form a single Army.

The arrangements for this purpose shall be made by a common Law.

There shall, moreover, be an annual inspection of the Militia of the two Principalities by Inspector-General, named every year by each Hospodar alternately. Those Inspectors shall be charged to see to the entire execution of the arrangements designed to ensure to the Militia all the characters of two corps of one and the same Army.

The number of regular Militia, as fixed by the organic regulations, cannot be augmented by more than one-third, without previous understanding with the Suzerain Court.

Assembling of Militias.

ART. XLIII. The Militias shall be assembled whenever the safety of the interior or of the Frontiers may be threatened. The assembling may be demanded by either Hospodar, but it cannot take place unless by their common agreement, and notice thereof shall be given to the Suzerain Court.

On the proposition of the Inspectors, the Hospodars may also assemble the Militias, wholly or partly, in camp for manœuvring, or for the purpose of being reviewed.

Commander-in-Chief of Militias to be appointed alternately by each Hospodar.

ART. XLIV. The Commander-in-Chief shall be appointed alternately by each Hospodar, when there shall be occasion to assemble the Militias. He must be a Moldavian or Wallachian by birth. He may be susperseded by the Hospodar who appointed him. In each case the new Commander-in-Chief shall be appointed by the other Hospodar.

Colours of the two Militias.

ART. XLV. The two Militias shall retain their actual Colours but those Colours shall in future bear a blue pennon, conformable to the Drawing annexed to the present Convention.

Moldavians and Wallachians equal in the eye of the Law.

ART. XLVI. All Moldavians and Wallachians shall be equal in the eye of the Law, and with regard to taxation, and shall be equally admissible to public employments, in both Principalities.

Guarantee of Individual Liberty.

Their individual liberty shall be guaranteed. No one can be detained, arrested, or prosecuted, but in conformity with the Law.

Deprivation of Property.

No one can be deprived of his property unless legally, for causes of public interest, and on payment of indemnification.

Equality of Political Rights of Christians.　Extension to other Religions.

Moldavians and Wallachians of all Christian confessions shall equally enjoy Political Rights. The enjoyment of those Rights may be extended to other Religions by legislative arrangements.

Abolition of Privileges and Monopolies.

All Privileges, Exemptions, or Monopolies, which are yet enjoyed by certain classes, shall be abolished; and there shall, without delay, be undertaken a revision of the Law which regulates the relations of the owners of the soil with the cultivators, with a view to improve the condition of the peasants.

Development of Municipal Institutions.

The Municipal Institutions, as well in town as in country, shall receive all the developments which the stipulations of the present Convention will admit of.

Actual Legislation to remain in force until Revision of Laws.

ART. XLVII. Until such time as the Revision contemplated by Article XXXV shall have been accomplished, the legislation actually in force in the Principalities is maintained in regard to those arrangements which are not at variance with the stipulations of the present Convention.

Hatti-Sheriff to promulgate Convention.

ART. XLVIII. In order to fulfil Article XXV of the Treaty of the 30th of March, 1856, a Hatti-Sheriff, in exact accordance with the stipulations of the present Convention, shall promulgate the preceding arrangements, within the space of 15 days at latest, after the exchange of the Ratifications.

Administration to be made over by Caimacams to a Commission.

ART. XLIX. At the time of the publication of the said Hatti-Sheriff, the Administration shall be made over by the present Caimacams, in each Principality, to a Commission *ad interim* (*Caimacamie*), constituted in conformity with the arrangements of the organic regulation.

Composition of Commissions.

Those Commissions shall, consequently, be composed of the President of the Princely Divan, the Grand Logothete, and the Minister of the Interior, who were in office under the last Hospodars before the installation of the provisional Administrations in 1856.

Commissions to prepare Electoral Lists. Election of Hospodar.

The said Commissions shall immediately proceed with the preparation of the Electoral Lists, which shall be completed and published within the period of 5 weeks. The Elections shall take place 3 weeks after the publication of the Lists. On the tenth day following, the Deputies shall assemble, in each Principality, in order to proceed to the Election of the Hospodars within the periods hereinbefore prescribed.

Ratifications.

ART. L. The present Convention shall be ratified, and the Ratifications shall be exchanged at Paris in 5 weeks, or sooner if possible.

In witness whereof the respective Plenipotentiaries have signed the same, and have affixed thereto the Seal of their Arms.

Done at Paris, the 19th of August, 1858.

           (L.S.)   COWLEY.
           (L.S.)   HUBNER.
           (L.S.)   A. WALEWSKI.
           (L.S.)   C. M. D'HATZFELDT.
           (L.S.)   CTE. DE KISSELEFF.
           (L.S.)   DE VILLAMARINA.
           (L.S.)   FUAD.

Annex 1 (*in conformity with Article XLV*).
(*The Flag.*)

Annex 2.—Electoral Stipulations.
Composition of Elective Assembly. Metropolitan and Diocesan
Bishops. Members of Right.

ART. I. The Elective Assembly is composed, in each Principality, of members elected by districts and by towns. The Metropolitan and the Diocesan Bishops are Members thereof as of full right.

Electors either Primary or Direct.

ART. II. The Electors are either Primary or Direct.

Qualification as a Primary Elector.

ART. III. Any person is a Primary Elector who can prove himself possessed of an income of 100 ducats at least, derived from real property.

Qualification as a Direct Elector.

ART. IV. Any person is a Direct Elector:

In the districts, who can prove himself possessed of an income of 1,000 ducats at least, derived from real property.

In the towns, who can prove himself possessed of a capital in real, industrial, or commercial property, of 6,000 ducats at least, belonging to him absolutely or by marriage.

Age of Elector.   Must be a Subject by Birth or Naturalisation.

ART. V. No person can be an Elector unless he has completed his 25th year, and is a Moldavian or Wallachian by Birth or Naturalisation.

Persons Disqualified as Electors.

ART. VI. The following persons cannot be Electors:—

1. Individuals who hold of a foreign jurisdiction.
2. Those who are under an interdict.
3. Bankrupts not rehabilitated.
4. Those who shall have been condemned to corporal and degrading punishments, or to degrading punishments only.

Publication of Annual Electoral Lists.

ART. VII. The Electoral Lists are prepared annually in each district, under the direction of the Administration. They shall be published and exhibited on the first Sunday of January, wherever necessary.

Claims of Electors.

Claims shall be made before the Administration during the 3 weeks subsequent to the publication of the Lists. The Claimants may have recourse to the tribunal of the district, which shall decide immediately and without appeal.

Right of Elector to claim Insertion or Removal of Individuals in Lists.

ART. VIII. Any Elector may claim the Insertion or the Removal of any Individual omitted or unduly inserted in the List on which he is himself inscribed.

All persons in Colleges eligible.

ART. IX. Any person is eligible, without distinction, in all the Colleges, who being a Moldavian or Wallachian by birth or naturalisation, shall have completed his 30th year, and can prove himself possessed of an income of 400 ducats at least.

Primary Electors to elect one Deputy for each District.

ART. X. The Primary Electors, in the Districts, name in each respective arrondissement (under Administration) 3 Electors, who, assembling at the chief place of the District, shall elect One Deputy for each District.

Direct Electors to elect Two Deputies.

ART. XI. The Direct Electors, in the Districts, shall elect Two Deputies for each District.

Number of Deputies in Towns.

ART. XII. In the Town, the Direct Electors shall elect:—
At Bucharest and Jassy, 3 Deputies.
At Craïova, Ploïesti, Ibraïla, Galatz, and Ismaïl, Two Deputies.
In the other towns, chief places of districts, One Deputy.

Electors of each Class to assemble separately.

ART. XIII. The Electors of each Class shall assemble separately, in special Colleges, in order to proceed to their respective operations.

Convocation of Electoral Colleges.

ART. XIV. The Electoral Colleges shall be convoked by the Executive Power 3 weeks at least before the day fixed for the Election.

Voting for Deputies to be Secret.

ART. XV. The Voting for the election of Deputies is Secret.

Election by Majority of Votes.

ART. XVI. The Election is decided by the Majority of Votes recorded.
If no one of the candidates shall have obtained the majority, recourse shall be had to a second voting, and the candidate who shall obtain the greatest number of votes shall be elected.

Elections to be verified by the Assembly.

Art. XVII. The Electoral Operations are verified by the Assembly, which alone is the judge of their validity.

Deputies Elected in more than One District.

Art. XVIII. Any Deputy elected in more than One electoral District shall declare his option to the President of the Assembly within 10 days after the declaration of the Validity of the Election.

If he should not declare his option within that time, the matter shall be decided by lot.

Vacancies.

Art. XIX. In case of a Vacancy by option, death, resignation, or otherwise, the Electoral College which is to supply the vacancy, shall assemble within 3 months.

Freedom of Members of Assembly from Arrest or Prosecution during Session.

Art. XX. No Member of the Assembly can, during the session, be arrested or prosecuted in penal matters, except when taken in the fact, until after the Assembly shall have authorised the prosecution.

Punishment for Fraudulent Declarations, &c.

Art. XXI. Any person who shall have got himself inscribed upon the Electoral Lists, by means of Fraudulent Declarations, or by concealing any of the defined incapacities, or who shall have claimed and obtained inscription on more than one list, or who shall have voted, although not inscribed, or deprived of the electoral right, shall be punished by a fine of 100 ducats at least, or 1,000 ducats at most, or by an imprisonment of 8 days at least, or 3 months at most.

Criminal Prosecutions by Electors in case of Non-prosecution by Government.

Art. XXII. In default of action on the part of the Government Functionaries, 10 Electors assembled shall have the right to institute a Criminal Prosecution: 1. Against any individual who, during the electoral operations, shall have withdrawn, added to, or tampered with the bulletins. 2. Against any person who shall have disturbed the electoral operations, and interfered with the freedom of election, by fraudulent manoeuvres, violence, or menaces.

Articles to be annexed to Convention.

Art. XXIII. As the electoral stipulations composing the preceding 22 Articles are to be annexed to the Convention of this date, the 19th August, in conformity with Article XVI of the said Convention, the respective Plenipotentiaries have also signed the present Act, which contains the same, and have sealed it with their Arms.

Paris, the 19th August, 1858.

(L.S.) COWLEY.
(L.S.) HUBNER.
(L.S.) A. WALEWSKI.
(L.S.) C. M. D'HATZFELDT.
(L.S.) CTE. DE KISSELEFF.
(L.S.) DE VILLAMARINA.
(L.S.) FUAD.

72 PRELIMINARY TREATY OF VILLA FRANCA

PRELIMINARY TREATY of Peace between Austria and France. Signed at Villafranca, 11th July, 1859.

BETWEEN His Majesty the Emperor of Austria and His Majesty the Emperor of the French, it has been agreed as follows:—

Creation of Italian Confederation under Presidency of the Holy Father.
The two Sovereigns favour the creation of an Italian Confederation. This Confederation shall be under the honorary Presidency of the Holy Father.

Cession of Lombardy, except Fortresses of Mantua and Peschiera, to France.
The Emperor of Austria cedes to the Emperor of the French his rights over Lombardy, with the exception of the Fortresses of Mantua and Peschiera, so that the Frontier of the Austrian Possessions shall start from the extremity of the rayon of the Fortress of Peschiera, and extend in a straight line along the Mincio as far as Legrazia, thence to Szarzarola, and Lugano on the Po, whence the existing Frontiers continue to form the Boundaries of Austria.

Ceded Territory to be presented to Kind of Sardinia.
The Emperor of the French shall present the ceded Territory to the King of Sardinia.

Venetia to form part of Italian Confederation, subject to Crown of Austria.
Venetia shall form part of the Italian Confederation, remaining, however, subject to the Crown of the Emperor of Austria.

Restoration of Grand Duke of Tuscany and Duke of Modena.
Amnesty.

The Grand Duke of Tuscany and the Duke of Modena return to their States, granting a General Amnesty.

Reforms in States of the Church.

The two Emperors shall request the Holy Father to introduce in his States some indispensable reforms.

Full and complete Amnesty by France and Austria.

Full and complete Amnesty is granted on both sides to persons compromised on the occasion of the recent events in the territories of the belligerents.

Done at Villafranca, 11th July, 1859.

FRANCIS JOSEPH.

73

TREATY OF PEACE between Austria and France. Signed at Zurich, 10th November, 1859. Ratifications exchanged at Zurich, 21st November, 1859.

In the Name of the Most Holy and Indivisible Trinity.

HIS Majesty the Emperor of Austria, and His Majesty the Emperor of the French, desirous of putting an end to the calamities of War, and of preventing the recurrence of the complications which gave rise to it, by assisting to place on solid and durable bases the internal and external Independence of Italy, have resolved to convert into a Definitive Treaty of Peace the Preliminaries signed by their hand at Villafranca.

With this view their Imperial Majesties have named as their Plenipotentiaries, that is to say:

His Majesty the Emperor of Austria, the Sieur Alois Count Karolyi of Nagy Karoly, his Chamberlain and Minister Plenipotentiary, &c., &c.; and the Sieur Otho Baron de Meysenbug, his Minister Plenipotentiary and Aulic Councillor, &c.;

And His Majesty the Emperor of the French, the Sieur François Adolphe Baron de Bourqueney, Senator of the Empire, &c.; and the Sieur Gaston Robert Morin Marquis de Banneville, Officer of the Imperial Order of the Legion of Honour, &c., &c.;

Who, having met in Conference at Zurich, and after having exchanged their Full Powers, found in good and due form, have agreed upon the following Articles:

Peace and Friendship.

ART. I. There shall be in future Peace and Friendship between His Majesty the Emperor of Austria and His Majesty the Emperor of the French, as also between their heirs and successors, their respective States and subjects, for ever.

Restoration of Prisoners of War.

ART. II. The Prisoners of War shall be immediately given up on either side.

Restoration of Austrian Vessels not condemned as Prizes of War.

ART. III. To diminish the evils of War, and by an exceptional departure from the law generally observed, the captured Austrian Vessels which have not yet been condemned as Prizes shall be restored.

Vessels and Cargoes to be restored on Payment of all Expenses. No Indemnity to be claimed for Prizes Sunk or Destroyed.

The Vessels and Cargoes shall be restored in the state in which they were at the time of their capture, after payment of all expenses, and of all charges which may have been incurred on account of the convoy, and keeping of the said Prizes, as well as of any legal proceedings connected with them, and the usual allowance to the captors; and lastly, no Indemnity will be claimable on account of Prizes sunk or destroyed any more than for the capture of merchandize belonging to the enemy, even though it may not yet have been subjected to a decision of the Prize Court.

Decisions of Prize Courts to be held good.

It is well understood, on the other hand, that the Decisions pronounced by the Prize Court hold good in favour of those to whom the Prizes have been adjudged.

Cession of Lombardy to France, except Fortresses of Peschiera and Mantua.

ART. IV. His Majesty the Emperor of Austria renounces, for himself and all his descendants and successors, in favour of His Majesty the Emperor of the French, his Rights and Titles to Lombardy, with the exception of the Fortresses of Peschiera and Mantua, and of the Territories determined by the new delimitation, which remain in the possession of His Imperial and Royal Apostolic Majesty.

Line of Frontier.

The line of Frontier, starting from the southern limit of the Tyrol, on the Lac de Garda, will pass along the middle of the Lake, as high as Bardolino and Manerba, from whence it will rejoin in a striaght line, the point where the circle of defence of the Fortress of Peschiera intersects the Lac de Garda.

This circle will be determined by a circumference of which the radius, reckoned from the centre of the Fortress, is fixed at 3,500 mètres, plus the distance from the said centre to the glacis of the most advanced fort. From the point where the circumference thus designated intersects the Mincio, the Frontier will follow the thalweg of the River as far Le Grazie, will extend from Le Grazie in a straight line to Scorzarolo, will follow the thalweg of the Po to Luzzara, from which point there is no change in the present Limits as they existed before the War.

Military Commission to trace Line of Frontier.

A Military Commission, appointed by the Governments interested, will be charged with the duty of tracing the Line on the ground with the least possible delay.

Territories ceded to be handed over to King of Sardinia.

ART. V. His Majesty the Emperor of the French declares his intention of handing over to His Majesty the King of Sardinia the Territories ceded by the preceding Article.

Evacuation of Territories by Belligerents.

ART. VI. The Territories still occupied in virtue of the Armistice of the 8th July last, shall be reciprocally evacuated by the Belligerent Powers, the troops of which will retire immediately beyond the frontier line stipulated in Article IV.

Lombardy to pay part of Monte Lombardo Veneto-Debt.

ART. VII. The new Governemnt of Lombardy will undertake three-fifths of the debt of the Monte Lombardo-Veneto.

Part of National Loan to be paid by Lombardy.

It will equally be charged with a portion of the National Loan of 1854, fixed between the High Contracting Powers at 40,000,000 florins ("*Conventions-münz*").

Mode of Payment.

The manner of the payment of these 40,000,000 florins will be determined by an Additional Article.

Appointment of Commission for payment of Monte Lombardo-Veneto Debt.

ART. VIII. An International Commission shall be immediately appointed to wind up the affairs of the Monte Lombardo-Veneto; the creditor and debtor balance to be drawn on the principle of three-fifths to the new Government, and two-fifths to Austria.

Division of Assets of the Sinking Fund of the Monte. Division of Lands or Mortgages.

Of the assets of the Sinking Fund of the Monte and its deposits, consisting of public securities, the new Government will receive three-fifths and Austria two-fifths; and as to that part of the assets which consist of Lands or Mortgages, the Commission will effect the partition with reference to the situation of the real property in question, so as to allot the property, as far as possible, to that one of the two Governments upon whose Territory it may be situated.

Proportion to be paid by either Party.

As to the different categories of debts inscribed in the Monte Lombardo-Veneto, and to the capital placed at interest in the deposit bank of the sinking fund, the new Government undertakes three-fifths and Austria two-fifths, either for the payment of interest, or the reimbursement of the capital, in conformity with the regulations hitherto in force. The credits of Austrian subjects will, by preference, form part of the quota of Austria, who will transmit to the new Government of Lombardy specified lists of these papers, in three months' time from the exchange of Ratifications, or sooner, if possible.

Rights and Obligations of Lombardy relative to Austrian Contracts.

ART. IX. The new Government of Lombardy succeeds to the Rights and Obligations resulting from Contracts regularly stipulated by the Austrian Administration for objects of public interest, especially concerning the ceded Territory.

Reimbursements to be made by Austrian and Lombardo Governments.

ART. X. The Austrian Government is charged with the Reimbursement of all sums paid by Lombardo subjects, communal districts, public establishments, and religious societies, into the Austrian public banks, in the shape of caution-money, deposits, or consignments. In the same manner Austrian subjects, communal districts, public establishments, and religious societies, who have paid money into the Lombard Banks in the shape of caution-money, deposits, or consignments, will be punctually reimbursed by the new Government.

Recognition and Confirmation by Lombardy of Austrian Railway Concessions.

ART. XI. The new Government of Lombardy recognises and confirms the Concessions granted to the Railroads by the Austrian Government on the ceded Territory, to the full extent of all their arrangements and duration, and particularly the Concessions resulting from the Contracts passed under date of 14th March, 1856, 8th April, 1857, and 23rd September, 1858.

Austrian right of Devolution transferred to Lombardy.

From the time of the exchange of the Ratifications of this Treaty, the new Government is bound by all the agreements and obligations resulting to the Austrian Government from the above-mentioned Concessions, in regard to the lines of Railway situated on the ceded Territory; consequently the right of Devolution which belonged to the Austrian Government in respect to these Railroads, is transferred to the new Government of Lombardy.

Payments still due by Concessionaries to be paid in full to Austria.

The Payments which are still to be made on the sum due to the State by the Concessionaries in virtue of the Contract of 14th March, 1856, as an equivalent for the expense of construction of the said Railroads, will be paid in full into the Austrian Exchequer.

Austria to pay Credits of Building Contractors and Tradesmen, &c. International Service of Railways to be regulated by New Convention.

The Credits of the Building Contractors and Tradesmen, as well as the compensation-money for appropriation of land, which appertain to the time when the Railways in question were administered on account of the State, and which have not yet been paid, will be paid by the Austrian Government, and, in so far as they may be due from them in virtue of the Act of Concession, by the grantees of the Austrian Government. A special Convention will make arrangements, as soon as possible, for the International Service of the Railways between the respective Countries.

Lombard Subjects free to retire with their Moveables to Austria, and to keep their Immoveable Property in Lombardy.

ART. XII. Lombard subjects domiciled on the Territory ceded by the present Treaty will have, for the space of a year, from the date of the day on which the Ratifications are exchanged, and conditionally on a previous Declaration before the competent authorities, full and entire power to export their Moveables, free of duty, and to retire with their families into the States of His Imperial and Royal Apostolic Majesty, in which case their quality of Austrian subjects will be retained by them. They will be at liberty to keep their Immoveable Property situated on the Lombard Territory.

Same Liberty to Lombards living in Austria.

The same power is granted reciprocally to natives of the ceded Territory of Lombardy living in the States of His Majesty the Emperor of Austria.

Lombard Subjects to be free from Molestation.

The Lombards who profit by these arrangements cannot be, on account of their choice, disturbed on either side, in their person or their properties situated in the respective States.

Time within which Lombards are to make their choice.

The delay of one year is extended to two years, for the subjects, natives of the ceded Territory of Lombardy, who at the time of the exchange of the Ratifications of this Treaty are not within the Territory of the Austrian Monarchy. Their Declaration may be received by the nearest Austrian Mission, or by the superior authority of any Province of the Monarchy.

Lombard subjects in Austrian Army to return to their Homes.

ART. XIII. The Lombard subjects in the Austrian army, excepting those who are natives of the part of the Lombard Territory reserved to His Majesty the Emperor of Austria by this Treaty, will be immediately discharged from military service, and sent back to their homes.

Lombards free to remain in Austrian Service.

It is understood that those amongst them who declare their wish to remain in the service of His Imperial and Royal Apostolic Majesty will not be disturbed on this account, either in person or in property.

Civil Servants free to remain in Austrian Service.

The same guarantees are assured to the Civil employés, natives of Lombardy, who manifest the intention of keeping the offices they occupy in the Austrian Service.

Civil and Military Pensions to be paid by Lombardy.

ART. XIV. The Pensions, both Civil and Military, regularly paid, and which were paid out of the public funds of Lombardy, remain due to those entitled to them, and, if need be, to their widows and children, and will be paid in future by the new Government of Lombardy.

Former Civil and Military Pensions to be paid by Lombardy.

This stipulation is extended to the Pensioners, both Civil and Military, as well as to their widows and children, without distinction of origin, who keep their domicile in the ceded Territory, and whose salaries, paid up to 1814 by the former Kingdom of Italy, then became payable by the Austrian Treasury.

Archives, &c., belonging to non-ceded part of Lombardy and Venetia to be handed over to Austria.

ART. XV. The Archives containing the Titles to Property, and Documents regarding the administration of justice, applying either to the part of Lombardy of which the possession is reserved to His Majesty the Emperor of Austria by this Treaty, or by the Venetian Provinces, will be handed over to the Commissioners of His Imperial and Royal Apostolic Majesty as soon as possible.

Archives belonging to ceded Territory to be handed over to Lombardy.

Reciprocally, any Titles of Property, and Documents connected with the administration of justice applying to the ceded Territory, which may be in the Archives of the Emperor of Austria, will be handed over to the Commissioners of the new Government of Lombardy.

Documents to be reciprocally communicated.

The High Contracting Parties engage to consult each other, at the request of the superior administrative authorities, respecting all the Documents and informations relative to the affairs which concern both Lombardy and Venetia.

Religious Societies free to Dispose of their Moveable and Immoveable Property.

ART. XVI. The Religious Societies established in Lombardy will be at liberty to dispose of their Moveable and Immoveable Property, in case the new legislation, under which they pass, does not authorise the keeping up of their establishments.

Transfer of Lombardy by France to Sardinia.

ART. XVII. His Majesty the Emperor of the French reserves to himself the power of Transferring to His Majesty the King of Sardinia, in the form usual to international transactions, the rights and obligations resulting from Articles VII, VIII, IX, X, XI, XII, XIII, XIV, XV, XVI of this Treaty.

Austria and France to encourage establishment of a Confederation among Italian States.

ART. XVIII. His Majesty the Emperor of Austria and His Majesty the Emperor of the French engage to make every effort to encourage the creation of a Confederation amongst the Italian States, to be placed under the honorary presidency of the Holy Father, and the object of which will be to uphold the Independence and Inviolability of the Confederated States, to assure the development of their moral and material Interests, and to guarantee the Internal and External Safety of Italy by the existence of a Federal Army.

Venetia, subject to Austria, to form one of the States of the Confederation.

Venetia, which remains subject to the Crown of His Imperial and Royal Apostolic Majesty, will form one of the States of this Confederation, and will participate in the obligations, as in the rights, resulting from the Federal Pact, the clauses of which will be determined by an Assembly composed of the representatives of all the Italian States.

Reservation of Rights of Grand Duke of Tuscany, and Dukes of Modena and Parma.

ART. XIX. As the Territorial Delimitations of the Independent States of Italy, who took no part in the late War, can be changed only with the sanction of the Powers who presided at their formation and recognised their existence, the Rights of the Grand Duke of Tuscany, of the Duke of Modena, and of the Duke of Parma, are expressly reserved for the consideration of the High Contracting Parties.

Austria and France to recommend Reforms in States of the Church.

ART. XX. Desirous of seeing the tranquillity of the States of the Church and the power of the Holy Father assured; convinced that such object could not be more efficaciously attained than by the adoption of a system suited to the wants of the populations and conformable to the generous intentions already manifested by the Sovereign Pontiff, His Majesty the Emperor of the French and His Majesty the Emperor of Austria will unite their efforts to obtain from His Holiness that the necessity of introducing into the administration of his States the Reforms admitted as indispensable shall be taken into serious consideration by his Government.

Non-molestation, in Person or Property, of Individuals implicated in recent events.

ART. XXI. With a view to contribute by every effort to quiet the public mind, the High Contracting Parties declare and promise that in their respective Territories, and in the Lands restored or ceded, no Individual compromised by the recent events in the Peninsula, no matter what his rank or position in society, shall be prosecuted, annoyed, or troubled, in Person or Property, on account of his conduct or political opinions.

Ratifications.

ART. XXII. The present Treaty shall be ratified, and the Ratifications exchanged within a fortnight, or earlier if possible. In faith of which the respective Plenipotentiaries have signed it, and have affixed their Seals thereunto.

Done at Zurich, on the 10th day of the month of November, of the year of Grace, 1859.

> (L.S.) KAROLYI.
> (L.S.) MEYSENBUG.
> (L.S.) BOURQUENEY.
> (L.S.) BANNEVILLE.

ADDITIONAL ARTICLE.

Payments to be made by France to Austria, and repayment to be guaranteed by new Government of Lombardy.

THE Government of His Majesty the Emperor of the French engages itself towards the Government of His Imperial and Royal Apostolic Majesty to make, on account if the new Government of Lombardy, which will Guarantee its repayment, to pay to it 40,000,000 florins (*Conventions-münz*), stipulated by Article VII of the present Treaty. in the manner and at the periods hereinafter determined:—

8,000,000 of florins shall be paid cash, by a bill payable at Paris, without interest, on the expiration of the third month, dating from the day on which the present Treaty was signed. and which will be handed to the Plenipotentiaries of His Imperial and Royal Apostolic Majesty when the exchange of Ratifications takes place.

The payment of the remaining 32,000,000 florins shall take place at Vienna, cash, in 10 successive instalments, to be made every two months, by bills on Paris, at the rate of 3,200,000 florins (*Conventions-münz*) each. The first of these payments will be made two months after the payment of the bill of 8,000,000 florins above stipulated. For that date, as for the other following, the interest will be reckoned at 5 per cent., dating from the first day of the month which will follow the exchange of the Ratifications of the present Treaty.

The present Additional Article shall have the same force and value as if inserted *verbatim* in the Treaty of this day.

It shall be ratified in one single act, and the Ratifications exchanged at the same time.

In faith of which the respective Plenipotentiaries have signed the present Additional Article, and affixed their Seals thereunto.

Done at Zurich, on the 10th day of the month of November, of the year of Grace, 1859.

$$\begin{array}{ll} \text{(L.S.)} & \text{KAROLYI.} \\ \text{(L.S.)} & \text{MEYSENBUG.} \\ \text{(L.S.)} & \text{BOURQUENEY.} \\ \text{(L.S.)} & \text{BANNEVILLE.} \end{array}$$

74

TREATY OF PEACE between Austria, France, and Sardinia. Signed at Zurich, 10th November, 1859.

In the name of the Most Holy and Indivisible Trinity.

His Majesty the Emperor of Austria, His Majesty the Emperor of the French, and His Majesty the King of Sardinia, wishing to complete the conditions of Peace, the Preliminaries of which, arranged at Villafranca, have been converted into a Treaty signed this day between His Majesty the Emperor of Austria and His Majesty the Emperor of the French, wishing further to lay down in a common Act the Territorial Cessions as they have been stipulated in the above-mentioned Treaty, as well as in the Treaty concluded this same day between His Majesty the Emperor of the French and His Majesty the King of Sardinia, have named for this purpose as their Plenipotentiaries, that is to say:

His Majesty the Emperor of Austria, the Sieur Alois Count Karolyi of Nagy Karoly, Chamberlain and Minister Plenipotentiary, &c.; and the Sieur Otho Baron de Meysenbug, his Minister Plenipotentiary and Aulic Councillor, &c.;

His Majesty the Emperor of the French, the Sieur François Adolphe Baron de Bourqueney, Senator of the Empire, &c.; and the Sieur Gaston Robert Morin Marquis de Banneville, Officer of the Imperial Order of the Legion of Honour, &c.;

His Majesty the King of Sardinia, the Sieur François Louis Chevalier des Ambrois de Nevache, Vice-President of his Council of State, Senator and Vice-President of the Senate of the Kingdom, &c.; and the Sieur Alexandre Chevalier Jocteau, his Minister to the Swiss Confederation, &c.;

Who, after having exchanged their Full Powers, found in good and due form, have agreed upon the following Articles:

Peace and Friendship.

ART. I. There shall be from the date of the day of the exchange of the Ratifications of the present Treaty, Peace and Amity between His Majesty the Emperor of Austria and His Majesty the King of Sardinia, their heirs and successors, their respective States and subjects, in perpetuity.

Restoration of Prisoners of War.

ART. II. The Austrian and Sardinian Prisoners of War shall be immediately returned on either part.

Boundary between Italian Provinces of Austria and Sardinia.

ART. III. In pursuance of the Territorial Cessions stipulated in the Treaties concluded this day between His Majesty the Emperor of Austria and His Majesty the Emperor of the French, on one side, and His Majesty the Emperor of the French and His Majesty the King of Sardinia on the other, the Delimitation between the Italian Provinces of Austria and Sardinia shall in future be as follows:

Line of Frontier.

The Frontier, starting from the Southern Boundary of the Tyrol, on the Lake de Garda, will follow the middle of the Lake as far as the height of Bardolino and Manerba, whence it will meet, in a straight line, the point where the circle of defence of the Fortress of Peschiera intersects the Lake of Garda.

It will follow the circumference of this circle, the radius of which, reckoned from the centre of the Fortress is fixed at 3,500 mètres, plus the distance from the said centre to the glacis of the most advanced Fort. From the point of intersection of the circumference thus designated with the Mincio, the Frontier will follow the thalweg of the river as far as Le Grazie; will stretch from Le Grazie, in a straight line, to Scorzarolo; will follow the thalweg of the Po as far as Luzzara, beyond which point no change is made in the Boundaries such as they existed before the War.

Military Commission to trace Line of Frontier.

A Military Commission, appointed by the High Contracting Parties, will be charged with the duty of tracing the Boundary with the least possible delay.

Evacuation of Territories by Austrian and Sardinian Troops.

ART. IV. The Territories still occupied in virtue of the Armistice of the 8th of July last shall be reciprocally evacuated by the Austrian and Sardinian Troops, who shall immediately retire beyond the Frontiers determined by the preceding Article.

Sardinia to pay part of Monte Lombardo-Veneto Debt.

ART. V. The Government of His Majesty the King of Sardinia shall take upon itself three-fifths of the Debt of the Monte Lombardo-Veneto.

Part of National Loan to be paid by Sardinia.

It shall equally undertake a portion of the National Loan of 1854, fixed between the High Contracting Parties at 40,000,000 florins, "*monnaie de Convention.*"

Payments to be made by France to Austria.

ART. VI. With regard to the 40,000,000 florins stipulated in the preceding Article, the Government of His Majesty the Emperor of the French renews the engagement which it has entered into with the Government of His Majesty the Emperor of Austria, to effect the Payment of it according to the manner determined in the Additional Article to the Treaty signed this day between the two High Contracting Powers.

Reimbursements to be made to France by Sardinia.

On the other hand, the Government of His Majesty the King of Sardinia puts again on record the engagement which it has contracted by the Treaty likewise signed to-day between Sardinia and France, to reimburse this sum to the Government of His Majesty the Emperor of the French, according to the manner stipulated in Article III of the said Treaty.

Appointment of Commission for payment of Monte Lombardo-Veneto Debt. Division of Debts and Credits, and of Lands or Mortgages.

ART. VII. A Commission, composed of Delegates of the High Contracting Parties, will be immediately formed, in order to proceed to the liquididation of the Monte Lombardo-Venetian Debt. The Division of the Debts and Credits of this establishment will be effected on the basis of three-fifths for Sardinia, and two-fifths for Austria. Of the Assets of the Sinking Fund of the Monte and its Deposits, consisting of public securities, Sardinia will receive three-fifths, and Austria two-fifths; and as to that part of the Assets which consists of Lands or Mortgages, the Commission will effect the partition with reference to the situation of the Property in question, to allot such Property, as far as possible, to that one of the two Governments upon whose Territory it may be situated.

Proportion to be paid by either Party.

As to the different categories of Debts inscribed up to 4th June, 1859, in the Monte Lombardo-Veneto, and to the capital placed at interest in the deposit bank of the Sinking Fund, Sardinia undertakes three-fifths, and Austria two-fifths, either for the payment of the interest, or the reimbursement of the capital, in accordance with the regulations hitherto in force. The Credits of Austrian subjects shall come by preference into the quota of Austria, who shall, within 3 months after the exchange of Ratifications, or sooner if possible, transmit to the Sardinian Government specific lists of these Credits.

Rights and Obligations of Sardinia relative to Austrian Contracts.

ART. VIII. The Government of His Sardinian Majesty succeeds to the Rights and Obligations resulting from the Contracts regularly stipulated by the Austrian Administration in respect of all matters of public interests specially concerning the Territories ceded.

Reimbursements to be made by Austrian and Sardinian Governments.

ART. IX. The Austrian Government will remain charged with the reimbursement of all Sums deposited by Lombard subjects, by the communes, by public establishments and religious corporations, in the Austrian public Banks, by way of caution-money, deposits, or consignments. In like manner the Austrian subjects, communes, public establishments, and religious corporations who have deposited sums of money as caution-money, deposits, or consignments in the Banks of Lombardy, will be punctually reimbursed by the Sardinian Government.

Recognition and Confirmation by Sardinia of Austrian Railway Concessions.

ART. X. The Government of His Majesty the King of Sardinia acknowledges and confirms the concessions of Railways granted by the Austrian Government upon the Territory ceded in all their clauses, and during the whole duration of the concessions, and in particular the concessions made by Contracts dated 14th March, 1856, 8th April, 1857, and 23rd September, 1858.

Railways. Austrian Right of Devolution transferred to Sardinia.

From the day of the date of the exchange of the Ratifications of the present Treaty, the Sardinian Government is invested with all the rights and subjected to all the obligations appertaining to the Austrian Government in respect of the said concessions in all that relates to the railway lines situate on the Territory ceded. In consequence, the right of Devolution which belonged to the Austrian Government in regard to these Railways is transferred to the Sardinian Government.

Railways. Payments still due by Concessionaries to be paid in full to Austria.

The Payments which remain to be made on the sum due to the State by the grantees by virtue of the Contract of 14th March, 1856, by way of equivalent for the expenses of making the said Railways, will be paid in their entirety to the Austrian Treasury.

Railways. Austria to Pay Credits of Building Contractors and Tradesmen, &c.

The credits of the Building Contractors and Tradesmen, and also the compensation money for land taken, so far as they may appertain respectively to the time when the Railways in question were administered for the account of the State, and which have not hitherto been paid, will be borne by the Austrian Government, and, in so far as they may be due from them by virtue of the concession, by the grantees in the name of the Austrian Government.

International Service of Railways to be regulated by new Convention.

A special Convention will regulate, with as little delay as possible, the international service of the Railways between Sardinia and Austria.

Austria not to have any Right of Control or Surveillance over Railways in Territories ceded.

ART. XI. It is understood that the recovery of the Credits under paragraphs 12, 13, 14, 15, and 16 of the Contract of 14th March, 1856, shall not confer upon Austria any right of Control or Surveillance in the construction and working of the Railways in the Territories ceded. The Sardinian Government undertakes, for its part, to furnish the Austrian Government with all the information which it may require on this head.

Lombard Subjects free to retire with their Moveables to Austria, and to keep their Immoveable Property in Lombardy.

ART. XII. The Lombard Subjects domiciled on the ceded Territory shall enjoy for the space of one year, commencing with the day of the exchange of the Ratifications, and conditionally on a previous Declaration before the competent authorities, full and entire permission to export their Moveables, free of duty, and to withdraw with their families into the States of His Imperial and Royal Apostolic Majesty, in which case their quality of Austrian Subjects shall be retained by them. They shall be free to preserve their Immoveable property, situated on the Territory of Lombardy.

Same Liberty to Lombards living in Austria.

The same permission is accorded reciprocally to Individuals, Natives of the ceded Territory of Lombardy, established in the States of His Majesty the Emperor of Austria.

Lombard Subjects not to be molested on account of their choice.

The Lombards who shall profit by the present arrangements shall not be, on account of their choice, disturbed on one side or on the other, in their persons or in their properties situated in the respective States.

Time within which Lombards are to make their choice.

The delay of one year is extended to two years, for the Subjects, Natives of the ceded Territory of Lombardy, who, at the time of the exchange of the Ratifications of the present Treaty, shall be beyond the Territory of the Austrian Monarchy. Their Declaration may be received by the nearest Austrian Mission, or by the superior authorities of any province of the Monarchy.

Lombard Subjects in Austrian Army to return to their Homes.

ART. XIII. The Lombard subjects forming part of the Austrian Army, with the exception of those who are natives of the part of the Lombard Territory retained by His Majesty the Emperor of Austria, shall be immediately set free from Military Service and sent back to their homes.

Lombards free to remain in Austrian Service.

It is understood that those who declare their wish to remain in the service of His Imperial and Royal Apostolic Majesty shall not be disturbed on that account, either in their persons or in their properties.

Civil Servants free to remain in Austrian Service.

The same guarantees are given to persons in Civil Employments, natives of Lombardy, who shall manifest their intention of retaining the offices which they hold in the service of Austria.

Civil and Military Pensions to be paid by Sardinia.

ART. XIV. Pensions, Civil as well as Military, regularly paid, and which were charged on the public revenue of Lombardy, remain in the possession of those who are entitled to them, and when there is occasion, to their widows and their children, and shall be paid in future by the Government of His Sardinian Majesty.

Former Civil and Military Pensioners to be paid by Sardinia.

This stipulation extends to the holders of Pensions, Civil as well as

Military, as well as to their widows and children, without distinction of origin, who shall retain their domicile in the ceded Territory, and whose claims, paid up to 1814 by the *ci-devant* Kingdom of Italy, then fell to the charge of the Austrian Treasury.

Archives, &c., belonging to non-ceded part of Lombardy, and Venetia to be handed over to Austria.

ART. XV. The Archives containing the Titles of Property, and Documents connected with administration and civil justice, whether they relate to the part of Lombardy whose possession is reserved to His Majesty the Emperor of Austria, or to the Venetian Provinces, shall be handed over to the Commissioners of His Imperial and Royal Apostolic Majesty as soon as possible.

Archives belonging to Ceded Territory to be made over to Sardinia.

Reciprocally the Titles of Property, and Documents connected with administration and civil justice, concerning the ceded Territory, which may be found in the Archives of the Emperor of Austria, shall be handed over to the Commissioners of His Majesty the King of Sardinia.

The Governments of Sardinia and Austria bind themselves to communicate reciprocally on the demand of the higher administrative authorities, all the documents and information relative to matters concerning at once Lombardy and Venetia.

Religious Corporations free to dispose of their Moveable and Immoveable Property.

ART. XVI. The Religious Corporations established in Lombardy, whose existence the Sardinian laws would not authorise, shall be free to dispose of their Property, both Moveable and Immoveable.

Renewal of Treaties and Conventions. Treaties to be revised.

ART. XVII. All the Treaties and Conventions concluded between His Majesty the King of Sardinia and His Majesty the Emperor of Austria which were in force before the 1st April, 1859, are confirmed in as far as they are not modified by the present Treaty. At the same time the two High Contracting Parties bind themselves to submit, within the term of a year, these Treaties and Conventions to a general revision, in order to introduce into them by common agreement, such modifications as shall be considered in accordance with the interests of the two countries.

Treaties, &c., to extend to ceded Territory.

In the meanwhile these Treaties and Conventions are extended to the Territory recently acquired by His Majesty the King of Sardinia.

Free Navigation of Lake of Garda. Free Navigation of the Po.

ART. XVIII. The Navigation of the Lake of Garda is free, except as regards the special regulations of the Ports and the Water Police. The liberty of Navigation of the Po and its affluents is maintained in accordance with the Treaties.

Convention for the Prevention of Smuggling to be concluded between Austria and Sardinia.

A Convention designed to regulate the measures necessary to prevent and repress smuggling in these waters will be concluded between Sardinia and Austria, in the term of one year, to date from the exchange of the Ratifications of the present Treaty. In the meanwhile the arrangements stipulated in the Convention of the 22nd November, 1851, for the repression of smuggling on the Lake Maggiore, the Po, and the Ticino, shall be applied to the navigation; and during the same interval no innovation shall be made in the regulations and the rights of navigation in force with regard to the Po and its affluents.

Special Act to regulate Bridges, &c., on the Mincio where it forms the Frontier.

ART. XIX. The Sardinian Government and the Austrian Government bind themselves to regulate, by a special Act, all that relates to the ownership of, and the maintenance of the bridges and passages on the Mincio, where it forms the Frontier, and to such new buildings as may be made in that respect, the expenses which may result from them, and the taking of the Tolls.

Austria and Sardinia to enter into Arrangements relative to the Bed and Damming up of the Mincio.

ART. XX. Where the Valley of the Mincio shall henceforth mark the Frontier between Sardinia and Austria, the buildings intended for the rectification of the Bed and the Damming up of that River, or which shall be of a nature to alter its current, shall be made by common agreement between the two adjoining States. An ulterior arrangement will regulate this matter.

Facilities on the Banks of the Ticino.

ART. XXI. The inhabitants of the adjoining districts shall enjoy reciprocally the Facilities which were formerly assured to the dwellers on the Banks of the Ticino.

Non-molestation in Person or Property of Individuals implicated in late Events.

ART. XXII. In order to contribute, with all their efforts, to the pacification of men's minds, His Majesty the King of Sardinia and His Majesty the Emperor of Austria declare and promise that, in their respective Territories, and in the Countries restored or ceded, no Individual compromised on the occasion of the late events in the Peninsula, of whatever class or condition he may be, shall be prosecuted, disturbed, or troubled in his person or in his property, on account of his political conduct and opinions.

Ratifications.

ART. XXIII. The present Treaty shall be ratified, and its Ratifications exchanged at Zurich in the space of 15 days, or sooner if possible.

In faith of which the respective Plenipotentiaries have signed and sealed it.

Done at Zurich, on the 10th day of the month of November, in the year of Grace, 1859.

(L.S.)　KAROLYI.
(L.S.)　MEYSENBUG.
(L.S.)　BOURQUENEY.
(L.S.)　BANNEVILLE.
(L.S.)　DES AMBROIS.
(L.S.)　JOCTEAU.

In March, 1859, Proposals were made by Russia for the assembling of a European Congress to settle the Affairs of Italy. The British Government expressed its willingness to join such a Meeting, although preferring a Conference, provided a fixed basis was previously agreed upon; and the following 4 points were mentioned for discussion (19th March, 1859):—

1. Evacuation.
2. Reform.
3. Security of Sardinia against Austrian attack.
4. Substitution of a plan for the internal security of the small States, in place of the Treaties with Austria of 1847.

It was understood that the Territorial Arrangements of Europe, as fixed by the Treaty of 1815, should not be interfered with

A 5th Point was subsequently proposed by Austria (31st March, 1859), namely, that an agreement should be come to with regard to a simultaneous Disarmament by the Great Powers.

Insuperable difficulties presented themselves, and the Congress was not held.

75

TREATY OF ALLIANCE between France and Sardinia. Signed at Zurich, 10th November, 1859. Ratifications exchanged at Zurich, 21st November, 1859.

In the Name of the Most Holy and Indivisible Trinity.

HIS Majesty the Emperor of the French, and His Majesty the King of Sardinia, wishing to strengthen their Alliance, and to regulate by a definitive understanding the consequences of their participation in the last War, have determined to sanction by Treaty the Preliminary Arrangements of Villafranca, relative to the cession of Lombardy, they have named for this purpose as their Plenipotentiaries, that is to say:

His Majesty the Emperor of the French, the Sieur François Adolphe Baron de Bourqueney, Senator of the Empire, &c.; and the Sieur Gaston Robert Morin Marquis de Banneville, Officer of the Imperial Order of the Legion of Honour, &c.;

His Majesty the King of Sardinia, the Sieur François Louis Chevalier des Ambrois de Nevache, Vice-President of his Council of State, Senator and Vice-President of the Senate of the Kingdom, &c.; and the Sieur Alexandre Chevalier Jocteau, his Minister to the Swiss Confederation, &c.;

Who, after having exchanged their Full Powers, found in good and due form, have agreed upon the following Articles:

Transfer of Lombardy by France to Sardinia.

ART. I. By a Treaty of this day's date, His Majesty the Emperor of Austria having renounced, for himself and all his heirs and successors, in favour of His Majesty the Emperor of the French, to his Rights and Titles over Lombardy, His Majesty the Emperor of the French transfers to His Majesty the King of Sardinia the Rights and Titles accruing to him by Article IV of the above-mentioned Treaty, as follows:

Cession of Lombardy to France, except Fortresses of Peschiera and Mantua.

"His Majesty the Emperor of Austria renounces, for himself and all his descendents and successors, in favour of His Majesty the Emperor of the French, his Rights and Titles to Lombardy, with the exception of the Fortresses of Peschiera and Mantua, and of the Territories determined by the new Delimitation, which remain in the possession of His Imperial and Royal Apostolic Majesty.

Line of Frontier.

"The Line of Frontier, starting from the southern limit of the Tyrol, on the Lac de Garda, will pass along the middle of the Lake, as high as Bardolino and Manerba, from whence it will rejoin, in a straight line, the point where the circle of defence of the Fortress of Peschiera intersects the Lac de Garda.

"This circle will be determined by a circumference, of which the radius, reckoned from the centre of the fortress, is fixed at 3,500 mètres, plus the distance from the said centre to the glacis of the most advanced fort. From the point where the circumference thus designated intersects the Mincio, the Frontier will follow the thalweg of the River as far as Le Grazie, will extend from Le Grazie in a straight line to Scorzarolo, will follow the thalweg of the Po to Luzzara, from which point there is no change in the present Limits as they existed before the War.

Military Commission to trace Line of Frontier.

"A Military Commission, appointed by the Governments interested, will be charged with the duty of tracing the line on the ground with the least possible delay."

Acceptance by Sardinia of Cession of Lombardy.

ART. II. His Majesty the King of Sardinia, on taking possession of the Territories ceded to him by His Majesty the Emperor of the French, accepts the charges and conditions attached to that cession as they are laid down in Articles VII, VIII, IX, X, XI, XII, XIII, XIV, XV, and XVI of the Treaty of this day's date, between His Majesty the Emperor of the French and His Majesty the Emperor of Austria, as follows:

Lombardy to pay part of Monte Lombardo-Veneto Debt.

a. The new Government of Lombardy will undertake three-fifths of the debt of the Monte Lombardo-Veneto.

Part of National Loan to be paid by Lombardy.

It will equally be charged with a portion of the National Loan of 1854, fixed between the High Contracting Powers at 40,000,000 florins (*Conventions-münz.*)

Appointment of Commission for Payment of Monte Lombardo-Veneto Debt.

b. An International Commission shall be immediately appointed to wind up the affairs of the Monte Lombardo-Veneto; the creditor and debtor balance to be drawn on the principle of three-fifths to the new Government and two-fifths to Austria.

Division of Assets of Sinking Fund of the Monte. Division of Lands or Mortgages.

Of the assets of the sinking fund of the Monte and its deposits, consisting of public securities, the new Government will receive three-fifths and Austria two-fifths; and as to that part of the assets which consists of lands or mortgages, the Commission will effect the partition with reference to the situation of the real property in question, so as to allot the property, as far as possible, to that one of the two Governments upon whose territory it may be situated.

Proportion to be paid by either Party.

As to the different categories of debts inscribed in the Monte Lombardo-Veneto, and to the capital placed at interest in the Deposit Bank of the Sinking Fund, the new Government undertakes three-fifths and Austria two-fifths, either for the payment of interest or the reimbursement of the capital, in conformity with the regulations hitherto in force. The credits of Austrian subjects will, by preference, form part of the quota of Austria, who will transmit to the new Government of Lombardy specified lists of these papers, in 3 months' time from the exchange of Ratifications, or sooner, if possible.

Rights and Obligations of Lombardy relative to Austrian Contracts.

c. The new Government of Lombardy succeeds to the Rights and Obligations resulting from Contracts regularly stipulated by the Austrian Administration for objects of public interest, especially concerning the ceded Territory.

Reimbursements to be made by Austrian and Lombardo Governments.

d. The Austrian Government is charged with the reimbursement of all sums paid by Lombard subjects, communal districts, public establishments, and religious societies, into the Austrian public banks in the shape of caution money, deposits, or consignments. In the same manner Austrian subjects, communal districts, public establishments, and religious corporations, who have deposited sums of money as caution money, deposits, or consignments, in the banks of Lombardy, will be punctually reimbursed by the Sardinian Government.

Recognition and Confirmation by Sardinia of Austrian Railway Concessions.

e. The Government of His Majesty the King of Sardinia acknowledges and confirms the Concessions of Railways granted by the Austrian Government upon the Territory ceded, in all their clauses, and during the whole duration of the concessions, and in particular the concessions made by Contracts dated March 14, 1856, April 8, 1857, and September 23, 1858.

Austrian Right of Devolution transferred to Sardinia.

From the day of the date of the exchange of the Ratifications of the present Treaty, the Sardinian Government is invested with all the Rights and subjected to all the Obligations appertaining to the Austrian Government in respect of the said concessions in all that relates to the Railway lines situate on the Territory ceded. Consequently, the right of devolution which belonged to the Austrian Government in regard to these Railways is transferred to the Sardinian Government.

Payments still due by Concessionaries to be paid in full to Austria.

The payments which remain to be made on the sum due to the State by the grantees by virtue of the Contract of 14th March, 1856, by way of equivalent for the expenses of making the said Railways, will be paid in their entirety to the Austrian Treasury.

Austria to pay Credits of Building Contractors and Tradesmen, &c.

The credits of the Building Contractors and Tradesmen, and also the compensation money for land taken, so far as they may appertain respectively to the time when the Railways in question were administered for the account of the State, and which have not hitherto been paid, will be borne by the Austrian Government, and, in so far as they may be due from them by virtue of the concession, by the grantees in the name of the Austrian Government.

International Service of Railways to be regulated by Special Convention.

A special Convention will regulate, with as little delay as possible, the international service of the Railways between Sardinia and Austria.

Recovery of Credits.

It is understood that the recovery of the Credits under Paragraphs 12, 13, 14, 15, and 16 of the Contract of 14th March, 1856, shall not confer upon Austria any right of control or surveillance in the construction and working of the Railways in the Territories ceded. The Sardinian Government undertakes, for its part, to furnish the Austrian Government with all the information which it may require on this head.

Lombard Subjects free to retire with their Moveables to Austria, and to keep their Immoveable Property in Lombardy.

f. The Lombard subjects domiciled on the ceded Territory shall enjoy for the space of one year, commencing with the day of the exchange of the Ratifications, and conditionally on a previous Declaration before the competent authorities, full and entire permission to export their Moveables, free of duty, and to withdraw with their families into the

States of His Imperial and Royal Apostolic Majesty, in which case their quality of Austrian subjects shall be retained by them. They shall be free to preserve their Immoveable Property, situated on the Territory of Lombardy.

Same Liberty to Lombards living in Austria.

The same permission is accorded reciprocally to individuals, natives of the ceded Territory of Lombardy, established in the States of His Majesty the Emperor of Austria.

Lombard Subjects to be free from Molestation.

The Lombards who shall profit by the present arrangements shall not be, on account of their choice, disturbed on one side or on the other, in their persons or in their properties situated in the respective States.

Time within which Lombards are to make their Choice.

The delay of one year is extended to two years for the Subjects, natives of the ceded Territory of Lombardy, who, at the time of the exchange of the Ratifications of the present Treaty, shall be beyond the Territory of the Austrian Monarchy. Their Declaration may be received by the nearest Austrian Mission, or by the superior authorities of any province of the Monarchy.

Lombard Subjects in Austrian Army to return to their Homes.

g. The Lombard subjects forming part of the Austrian army, with the exception of those who are natives of the part of the Lombard Territory retained by His Majesty the Emperor of Austria, shall be immediately set free from military service and sent back to their homes.

Lombards free to remain in Austrian Service.

It is understood that those who shall declare their wish to remain in the service of His Imperial and Royal Apostolic Majesty shall not be disturbed on that account, either in their persons or in their properties.

Civil Servants free to remain in Austrian Service.

The same guarantees are given to persons in civil employments, natives of Lombardy, who shall manifest their intention of retaining the offices which they hold in the service of Austria.

Civil and Military Pensions to be paid by Sardinia.

h. Pensions, Civil as well as Military, regularly paid, and which were charged on the public revenue of Lombardy, remain in the possession of those who are entitled to them, and when there is occasion, to their widows and their children, and shall be paid in future by the Government of His Sardinian Majesty.

Former Civil and Military Pensions to be paid by Sardinia.

This stipulation extends to the holders of Pensions, Civil as well as Military, as well as to their widows and children, without distinction of origin, who shall retain their domicile in the ceded Territory, and whose claims, paid up to 1814 by the *ci-devant* Kingdom of Italy, then fell to the charge of the Austrian treasury.

Archives, &c., belonging to non-ceded part of Lombardy, and Venetia to be handed over to Austria.

i. The Archives containing the titles of property, and documents connected with administration and civil justice, whether they relate to the part of Lombardy whose possession is reserved to His Majesty the Emperor of Austria, or to the Venetian Provinces, shall be handed over to the Commissioners of His Imperial and Royal Apostolic Majesty as soon as possible.

Archives belonging to ceded Territory to be handed over to Sardinia.

Reciprocally the titles of property, and documents connected with administration and civil justice, concerning the ceded Territory, which may be found in the Archives of the Emperor of Austria, shall be handed over to the Commissioners of His Majesty the King of Sardinia.

Documents to be reciprocally Communicated.

The Governments of Sardinia and Austria bind themselves to communicate reciprocally, on the demand of the higher administrative authorities, all the Documents and information relative to matters concerning at once Lombardy and Venetia.

Religious Societies free to dispose of their Moveable and Immoveable Property.

j. The Religious Corporations established in Lombardy, whose existence the Sardinian laws would not authorise, shall be free to dispose of their Property, both Moveable and Immoveable.

Reimbursement to France by Sardinia of Payments to be made to Austria.

ART. III. By the Additional Article to the Treaty, concluded under this day's date between His Majesty the Emperor of the French, and His Majesty the Emperor of Austria, the French Government having engaged itself towards the Austrian Government to make, on account of the new Government of Lombardy the payment of the 40,000,000 florins (*Conventions-münz*) stipulated by Article VII of the above-mentioned Treaty, His Majesty the King of Sardinia, in accordance with the stipulations accepted by him in the preceding Article, engages to reimburse that amount to France in the following manner:

The Sardinian Government shall make over to that of His Majesty the Emperor of the French Sardinian 5 per cent. Stock to Bearer, to the amount of 100,000,000 francs. The French Government accepts at the current exchange of the Paris Bourse of the 29th October, 1859. The Interest on this Stock shall begin in favour of France on the day of the delivery of the Title Deeds, which shall take place one month after the exchange of the Ratification of the present Treaty.

Reimbursement of 60,000,000 Francs by Sardinia to France.

ART. IV. In order to lessen the charges which France undertook during the last War, the Government of His Majesty the King of Sardinia engages to reimburse to the Government of His Majesty the Emperor of the French the sum of 60,000,000 francs, for the payment of which 3,000,000 5 per Cent. Stock shall be inscribed on the Great Book of the Public Debt of Sardinia. The Vouchers shall be made to the French Government which accepts them at par. The Interest of that Stock shall begin, to the benefit of France, from the day of the delivery of the Vouchers, which shall take place one month after the exchange of the Ratifications.

Ratifications.

ART. V. The present Treaty shall be ratified, and the Ratifications thereof shall be exchanged at Zurich within 15 days, or sooner if possible.

In testimony whereof, the respective Plenipotentiaries have signed it, and have affixed thereto the Seal of their Arms.

Done at Zurich on the 10th day of the month of November, of the year of Grace, 1859.

(L.S.) BOURQUENEY.

(L.S.) BANNEVILLE.

(L.S.) DES AMBROIS.

(L.S.) JOCTEAU.

The Final Page of Notes, Drawn up in the Handwriting of Count Nigra, on the Results of the Meeting on July 20th, 1858, Between the Emperor Napoleon III and Count Cavour of Piedmont at Plombières. (This summarised accurately the treaty agreed to, which led to the events resulting in the Franco-Austrian War and the Treaties of Zurich.)

ART. I. Defensive and offensive alliance.

ART. II. For the purpose of cementing the alliance, marriage.

ART. III. In the event that war should break out in Italy between Sardinia and Austria, whether it be declared by Sardinia for grave and just causes, or whether it be declared by Austria, His Majesty the Emperor of the French engages to come to the aid of His Majesty the King of Sardinia by putting at his disposition an army corps and a fleet, in a manner that will be determined by a special convention.

ART. IV. Considered to be adequate causes for a declaration of war against Austria would be the occupation by Austrian troops of any part of Italian territory apart from that subjected to occupation by the Vienna treaties of 1815, Austrian violation of existing treaties, and other things of a similar kind.

ART. V. The French army corps mentioned above would be placed under the command of His Majesty the King of Sardinia.
Sardinian fleet joined to that of France and placed under the command of a French Admiral.

ART. VI. Once the war is under way, the High Contracting Parties engage to prosecute it until Austrian troops have left Italian soil.

ART. VII. The country conquered in Upper Italy and along the Po valley, including Venice, the Duchies, and the Legations, will be annexed to the Kingdom of Sardinia, which will assume the title of Kingdom of Upper Italy.

ART. VIII. Once the Kingdom of Upper Italy is constituted, the population of Savoy will be called upon to vote by universal suffrage on the annexation of that Duchy to France or to Upper Italy.

ART. IX. No separate treaties.

Equal treatment for the respective plenipotentiaries at the peace conferences.

(Il Carteggio Cavour-Nigra, I, 101-2)

7 6

DECLARATION between the Plenipotentiaries of Austria and France, declaring the Italian Provinces of Austria, which are to form part of the Italian Confederation. Zurich, 10th November, 1859.

Present: The Plenipotentiaries of Austria and France.

WITH the view of allowing no doubt to exist on the meaning of the engagement taken by His Imperial and Royal Majesty to favour, by common consent with His Majesty the Emperor of the French, the creation of an Italian Confederation, the Austrian Plenipotentiaries declare that it is well understood that the Italian Provinces of His Imperial and Royal Majesty which shall have to form part of the Italian Confederation, are composed of the Venetian Kingdom, within its actual Limits, and the part of Lombardy reserved to the Imperial Crown by the Treaty of Peace of 10th November, 1859, and that no Property or Territory possessed by His Imperial Majesty beyond the said Countries, can be claimed for the Confederation in question.

The French Plenipotentiaries made a note of this Declaration.

In faith of which the Plenipotentiaries have signed the present Protocol.

Done at Zurich, 10th November, 1859.

BOURQUENEY.	KAROLYI.
BANNEVILLE.	MEYSENBUG.

7 7   TREATY OF TURIN

TREATY between France and Sardinia, for the Annexation of Savoy and Nice to France. Signed at Turin, 24th March, 1860. Ratifications exchanged at Turin, 30th March, 1860.

(Translation as laid before Parliament.)

HIS Majesty the Emperor of the French having explained the considerations which, in consequence of the changes which have arisen in the Territorial relations between France and Sardinia, caused him to desire the Annexation of Savoy and the Arrondissement of Nice (*Circondario di Nizza*) to France, and His Majesty the King of Sardinia having shown himself disposed to acquiesce in it, their said Majesties have decided to conclude a Treaty for that purpose, and have named as their Plenipotentiaries:

His Majesty the Emperor of the French, Baron de Talleyrand-Périgord, &c.; and M. Vincent Benedetti, &c.; and His Majesty the King of Sardinia, His Excellency Count Camille Benso de Cavour, &c.; and His Excellency the Chevalier Charles Louis Farini, &c.;

Who, after having exchanged their Full Powers found to be in good and due form, have agreed upon the following Articles:

Union of Savoy and Nice to France.

ART. I. His Majesty the King of Sardinia consents to the Annexation of Savoy and the Arrondissement of Nice (*Circondario di Nizza*) to France, and renounces for himself, and all his Descendants and Successors, in favour of His Majesty the Emperor of the French, his Rights and Titles over the said Territories. It is understood between their Majesties that this Annexation shall be effected without any constraint of the wishes of the Populations, and that the Governments of the Emperor of the French and of the King of Sardinia will concert as soon as possible upon the best means of appreciating and verifying the manifestations of those wishes.

Conditions of Transfer to France of Neutralised Portions of Savoy. Reference to Vienna Congress Treaty.

ART. II. It is equally understood that His Majesty the King of Sardinia cannot transfer the Neutralised Parts of Savoy, except on the conditions upon which he himself possesses them, and that it will appertain to His Majesty the Emperor of the French to come to an understanding on this subject, both with the Powers represented at the Congress of Vienna, and with the Swiss Confederation, and to give them the Guarantees required by the Stipulations referred to in this Article.

Appointment of Mixed Boundary Commission.

ART. III. A Mixed Commission shall determine, in a spirit of equity, the Frontiers of the two States, taking into account the configuration of the Mountains and the requirements of defence.

Contributions of Savoy and Nice towards the Public Debt of Sardinia.

ART. IV. One or more Mixed Commissions shall be charged to examine and resolve as soon as possible the various incidental questions to which the Annexation will give rise, such as the settlement of the share to be contributed by Savoy and the Arrondissement of Nice (*Circondario di Nizza*) towards the Public Debt of Sardinia, and the execution of the obligations resulting from Contracts entered into with the Sardinian Government, which Government, however, reserves the right of itself terminating the labours undertaken for boring the Tunnel of the Alps (Mont Cenis).

Rights of Civil Servants and Soldiers of Savoy and Nice.

ART. V. The French Government will secure to the Civil and Military Functionaries belonging by birth to the Province of Savoy and to the Arrondissement of Nice (*Circondario di Nizza*), and who shall become French Subjects, the Rights due to them on account of the services rendered by them to the Sardinian Government; they shall especially enjoy the advantages resulting from the permanency of the Magisterial Appointments, and the guarantees ensured to the Army.

Nationality of Subjects of Savoy and Nice.

ART. VI. Sardinian Subjects natives of Savoy and the Arrondissement of Nice, at present domiciled in those Provinces, who shall desire to preserve their Sardinian Nationality, shall enjoy, during the space of one year from the date of the exchange of the Ratifications, and provided that they make a previous Declaration before the competent authority, the right of transporting their domicile into Italy, and of fixing it there; in which case, the character of Sardinian Citizen shall be continued to them.

Preservation of Immoveable Property in ceded Territories.

They shall be free to retain their Immoveable Property situated in the Territory annexed to France.

Execution of Treaty by Sardinia.

ART. VII. As concerns Sardinia, the present Treaty shall be in force as soon as the necessary Legislative Sanction shall have been given by Parliament.

Ratifications.

ART. VIII. The present Treaty shall be ratified, and the Ratifications of it shall be exchanged at Turin within 10 days, or sooner if possible.

In faith of which the respective Plenipotentiaries have signed it, and have affixed to it their Armorial Seals.

Done in Duplicate, at Turin, the 24th day of the month of March, of the year of Grace, 1860.

(L.S.) TALLEYRAND.	(L.S.) CAVOUR.
(L.S.) BENEDETTI.	(L.S.) FARINI.

78 CONVENTION OF PEKING

CONVENTION of Peace and Friendship between Great Britain and China. Signed at Peking, 24th October, 1860. Ratifications exchanged, 24th October, 1860.

HER Majesty the Queen of Great Britain and Ireland, and His

Imperial Majesty the Emperor of China, being alike desirous to bring to an end the misunderstanding at present existing between their respective Governments, and to secure their relations against further interruption, have for this purpose appointed Plenipotentiaries, that is to say:—

Her Majesty the Queen of Great Britain and Ireland, the Earl of Elgin and Kincardine;

And His Imperial Majesty the Emperor of China, His Imperial Highness the Prince of Kung;

Who, having met and communicated to each other their full powers, and finding these to be in proper form, have agreed upon the following Convention, in 9 Articles:—

Apology of Emperor for obstruction offered by garrison of Taku to passage of British Representative with Ratifications of Treaty of 26th June, 1858.

ART. I. A breach of friendly relations having been occasioned by the act of the garrison of Taku, which obstructed Her Britannic Majesty's Representative when on his way to Peking for the purpose of exchanging the Ratifications of the Treaty of Peace concluded at Tientsin in the month of June, 1858, His Imperial Majesty the Emperor of China expresses his deep regret at the misunderstanding so occasioned.

Right of British Representative to reside at Peking. Arrangement of October, 1858, cancelled.

ART II. It is further expressly declared, that the arrangement entered into at Shanghai in the month of October, 1858, between Her Britannic Majesty's Ambassador, the Earl of Elgin and Kincardine, and His Imperial Majesty's Commissioners, Kweiliang and Hwashana, regarding the residence of Her Britannic Majesty's Representative in China, is hereby cancelled; and that, in accordance with Article III of the Treaty of 1858, Her Britannic Majesty's Representative will henceforward reside permanently or occasionally at Peking as Her Majesty shall be pleased to decide.

Separate Article of Treaty of 26th June, 1858, annulled. Indemnity of 8,000,000 Taels, to be paid by instalments: 2,000,000 to British merchants for their losses at Canton, and 6,000,000 for War Expenses.

ART. III. It is agreed that the Separate Article of the Treaty of 1858 is hereby annulled; and that, in lieu of the amount of indemnity therein specified, His Imperial Majesty the Emperor of China shall pay the sum of 8,000,000 taels, in the following proportions or instalments, namely:— At Tientsin, on or before the 30th day of November, the sum of 500,000 taels; at Canton, and on or before the 1st day of December, 1860, 333,333 taels, less the sum which shall have been advanced by the Canton authorities towards the completion of the British Factory site at Shamien; and the remainder at the ports open to foreign trade, in quarterly payments, which shall consist of one-fifth of the gross revenue from Customs there collected. The first of the said payments being due on the 31st day of December, 1863, for the quarter terminating on that day.

It is further agreed that these moneys shall be paid into the hands of an officer whom Her Britannic Majesty's Representative shall specially appoint to receive them, and that the accuracy of the amounts shall, before payment, be duly ascertained by British and Chinese officers appointed to discharge this duty.

In order to prevent future discussion, it is moreover declared that, of the 8,000,000 taels herein guaranteed, 2,000,000 will be appropriated to the indemnification of the British mercantile community at Canton, for losses sustained by them, and the remaining 6,000,000 to the liquidation of war expenses.

Port of Tientsin opened to Trade.

ART. IV. It is agreed that on the day on which this Convention is signed, His Imperial Majesty the Emperor of China shall open the port of Tientsin to trade, and that it shall be thereafter competent to British subjects to reside and trade there under the same conditions as at any other port of China by Treaty open to trade.

Chinese Coolie Emigration.

ART. V. As soon as the ratifications of the Treaty of 1858 shall have been exchanged, His Imperial Majesty the Emperor of China will by Decree, command the high authorities of every province to proclaim throughout their jurisdictions, that Chinese choosing to take service in the British Colonies or other parts beyond sea, are at perfect liberty to enter into engagements with British subjects for that purpose, and to ship themselves and their families on board any British vessel at any of the open ports of China; also that the high authorities aforesaid shall, in concert with Her Britannic Majesty's Representative in China, frame such regulations for the protection of Chinese, emigrating as above, as the circumstances of the different open ports may demand.

Hong Kong. Cession to Great Britain of that portion of Township of Kowloon which was leased to Mr. Harry Parkes. Lease cancelled. Liquidation of Chinese Claims.

ART. VI. With a view to the maintenance of law and order in and about the harbour of Hong Kong, His Imperial Majesty the Emperor of China agrees to cede to Her Majesty the Queen of Great Britain and Ireland, and to Her heirs and successors, to have and to hold, as a dependency of Her Britannic Majesty's colony of Hong Kong, that portion of the township of Kowloon, in the Province of Kwang-tung, of which a lease was granted in perpetuity to Harry Smith Parkes, Esquire, Companion of the Bath, a member of the Allied Commission at Canton, on behalf of Her Britannic Majesty's Government by Lan Tsung Kwang, Governor-General of the Two Kwang.

It is further declared that the lease in question is hereby cancelled; that the claims of any Chinese to any property on the said portion of Kowloon shall be duly investigated by a Mixed Commission of British and Chinese officers; and that compensation shall be awarded by the British Government to any Chinese whose claims shall be by the said Commission established, should his removal be deemed necessary by the British Government.

Confirmation of Treaty of 26th June, 1858, with modifications.

ART. VII. It is agreed that the provisions of the Treaty of 1858, except in so far as these are modified by the present Convention, shall without delay come into operation as soon as the ratifications of the Treaty aforesaid shall have been exchanged.

No Separate Ratification of present Convention required.

It is further agreed that no separate ratification of the present Convention shall be necessary, but that it shall take effect from the date of its signature, and be equally binding with the Treaty above mentioned on the High Contracting Parties.

Treaty of 26th June, 1858, and present Convention to be published by Chinese Government.

ART. VIII. It is agreed that as soon as the ratifications of the Treaty of the year 1858 shall have been exchanged, His Imperial Majesty the Emperor of China shall, by Decree, command the high authorities in the capital and in the provinces to print and publish the aforesaid Treaty and the present Convention for general information.

Conditional Evacuation of Chusan and other places in China occupied by British Troops.

Art. IX. It is agreed that, as soon as this Convention shall have been signed, the ratifications of the Treaty of the year 1858 shall have been exchanged, and an Imperial decree respecting the publication of the said Convention and Treaty shall have been promulgated, as provided for by Article VIII of this Convention, Chusan shall be evacuated by Her Britannic Majesty's troops there stationed, and Her Britannic Majesty's force now before Peking shall commence its march towards the city of Tientsin, the forts of Taku, the north coast of Shang-tung, and the city of Canton, at each or all of which places it shall be at the option of Her Majesty the Queen of Great Britain and Ireland to retain a force until the indemnity of 8,000,000 taels, guaranteed in Article III, shall have been paid.

Done at Peking, in the Court of the Board of Ceremonies, on the 24th day of October, in the year of our Lord 1860.

(L.S.)　ELGIN AND KINCARDINE.

79

CONVENTION between Great Britain, Austria, France, Prussia, Russia, and Turkey, prolonging the European Occupation of Syria. Signed at Paris, 19th March, 1861. Ratifications exchanged at Paris, 18th May, 1861.

Reference to Convention of 5th September, 1860.

THEIR Majesties the Queen of the United Kingdom of Great Britain and Ireland, the Emperor of Austria, the Emperor of the French, the King of Prussia, the Emperor of All the Russias, and the Emperor of the Ottomans, having, after the exchange of explanations between their respective Governments, agreed to modify, by common consent, the Convention concluded between them on the 5th of September last, have for that purpose named as their Plenipotentiaries, that is to say:

Her Majesty the Queen of the United Kingdom of Great Britain and Ireland, the Right Honourable Henry Richard Charles Earl Cowley, her Ambassador Extraordinary and Plenipotentiary to His Majesty the Emperor of the French, &c;

His Majesty the Emperor of Austria, M. Richard Prince of Metternich-Winneburg, his Ambassador Extraordinary to His Majesty the Emperor of the French, &c.;

His Majesty the Emperor of the French, M. Edward Anthony

Thouvenel, his Minister and Secretary of State for the Department of Foreign Affairs, &c.;

His Majesty the King of Prussia, M. Albert Alexander Count de Pourtaèls, his Envoy Extraordinary and Minister Plenipotentiary to His Majesty the Emperor of the French, &c.;

His Majesty the Emperor of All the Russias, M. Paul Count de Kisséleff, his Ambassador Extraordinary and Plenipotentiary to His Majesty the Emperor of the French, &c.;

And His Majesty the Emperor of the Ottomans, Ahmed Vefyk Effendi, his Ambassador Extraordinary to His Majesty the Emperor of the French, &c.;

Who, after having communicated to each other their Full Powers, found in good and due form, have agreed upon the following Articles:

Prolongation of the Occupation of Syria.

ART. I. The duration of the European Occupation in Syria shall be prolonged until the 5th of June of the present year, at which date it is understood between the High Contracting Parties that it shall have reached its term, and that the Evacuation shall have been effected.

Stipulations of Convention of 5th September, 1860, to continue in Force.

ART. II. The stipulations contained in the second Article of the Convention of the 5th September, 1860, in so far as they have not yet been executed, or as they are not modified by the present Convention, shall continue in force during the period which will elapse between the date of the signature of the present Act and the 5th of June of the present year.

Ratifications.

ART. III. The present Convention shall be ratified, and the Ratifications shall be exchanged at Paris in 5 weeks, or sooner if possible.

In witness whereof the respective Plenipotentiaries have signed the same, and have affixed thereto the Seal of their Arms.

Done at Paris, the 19th of March, 1861.

(L.S.) COWLEY.

(L.S.) METTERNICH.

(L.S.) THOUVENEL.

(L.S.) A. POURTALES.

(L.S.) KISSELEFF.

(L.S.) AHMED VEFYK.

8 0

TREATY between Great Britain, France, and Russia, on the one part, and Denmark, on the other part, relative to the Accession of Prince William of Denmark to the Throne of Greece. Signed at London, 13th July, 1863. Ratifications exchanged at London, 3rd August, 1863.

Reference to Guarantee of Great Britain, France, and Russia.
In the Name of the Most Holy and Indivisible Trinity.

THEIR Majesties the Queen of the United Kingdom of Great Britain and Ireland, the Emperor of the French, and the Emperor of All the Russias, being anxious to smooth the difficulties which have occurred in the Kingdom of Greece, placed under their common Guarantee, have judged it necessary to come to an understanding with regard to the arrangements to be taken in order to give effect to the wish of the Greek Nation, which calls the Prince William of Denmark to the Hellenic Throne.

His Majesty the King of Denmark, on his part, responding to the invitation of their said Majesties, has consented to afford them his co-operation with a view to that result, conformable to the interests of the general Peace.

In consequence, their Majesties the Queen of the United Kingdom of Great Britain and Ireland, the Emperor of the French, and the Emperor of All the Russias, on the one part, and His Majesty the King of Denmark on the other, have resolved to conclude a Treaty, and have for that purpose named as their Plenipotentiaries, that is to say:

Her Majesty the Queen of the United Kingdom of Great Britain and Ireland, the Right Honourable John Earl Russell, her Principal Secretary of State for Foreign Affairs, &c.;

His Majesty the Emperor of the French, the Sieur John Baptist Louis Baron Gros, Ambassador Extraordinary and Plenipotentiary to Her Britannic Majesty, &c.;

His Majesty the Emperor of All the Russias, the Sieur Philip Baron de Brunnow, his actual Privy Councillor, Ambassador Extraordinary and Plenipotentiary to Her Britannic Majesty, &c.;

And His Majesty the King of Denmark, the Sieur Torben de Bille, his Chamberlain, his Envoy Extraordinary and Minister Plenipotentiary to Her Britannic Majesty, &c.;

Who, after having exchanged their Full Powers, found in good and due form, have agreed upon and signed the following Articles:

Acceptance of Hereditary Sovereignty of Greece by King of Denmark for Prince William of Denmark.

ART. I. His Majesty the King of Denmark, in accordance with the Prince Christian of Denmark, acting in the character of guardian of his second son the Prince Christian William Ferdinand Adolphus George, accepts for that Prince, a minor, the hereditary Sovereignty of Greece, which is offered to him by the Senate and the National Assembly of Greece in the name of the Hellenic Nation.

Title of King of the Greeks.

ART. II. The Prince William of Denmark shall bear the title of George I, King of the Greeks (*Roi des Grecs*).

Greece to form a Monarchical, Independent, and Constitutional State.

ART. III. Greece, under the Sovereignty of Prince William of Denmark, and the Guarantee of the 3 Courts, forms a Monarchical, Independent and Constitutional State.

Limits of Greek Territory. Annexation of Ionian Islands to Greece.

ART. IV. The Limits of the Greek Territory, determined by the arrangement concluded at Constantinople between the 3 Courts and the Ottoman Porte, on the 21st July, 1832, shall receive an extension by the Union of the Ionian Islands with the Hellenic Kingdom when such Union, proposed by the Government of Her Britannic Majesty, shall have been found to be in accordance with the wishes of the Ionian Parliament, and shall have obtained the assent of the Courts of Austria, France, Prussia, and Russia.

Union of Ionian Islands to be under Guarantee of Protecting Powers.

ART. V. The Ionian Islands, when their Union with the Kingdom of Greece shall have been effected, shall be comprised in the Guarantee stipulated by Article III of the present Treaty.

Crowns of Greece and Denmark never to be united.

ART. VI. In no case shall the Crown of Greece and the Crown of Denmark be united on the same head.

Religion of King of Greece.

ART. VII. In conformity with the principle of the Hellenic Constitution recognised by the Treaty signed at London, on the 20th November, 1852, and proclaimed by the Decree of the National Assembly of Greece, of the 30th March, 1863, the legitimate successors of King George I must profess the tenets of the Orthodox Church of the East.

Majority of King of Greece.

ART. VIII. The Majority of Prince William of Denmark, fixed by the law of the Royal Family at 18 years complete, that is to say, on the 24th December, 1863, shall be considered as attained before that date, if a Decree of the National Assembly should recognise the necessity thereof.

Appropriation by Ionian Islands to Civil List of King of the Greeks.

ART. IX. At the moment when the Union of the Ionian Islands with the Hellenic Kingdom shall take place, according to the terms of Article IV of the present Treaty, Her Britannic Majesty will recommend to the Government of the United States of the Ionian Islands to appropriate annually a sum of £10,000 sterling to augment the Civil List of His Majesty George I, King of the Greeks (*Roi des Grecs*).

Personal Dotation to King of the Greeks by Protecting Powers.

ART. X. Each of the 3 Courts will give up in favour of Prince William of Denmark £4,000 a year out of the sums which the Greek Treasury has engaged to pay annually to each of them, in pursuance of the arrangement concluded at Athens by the Greek Government, with the concurrence of the Chambers, in the month of June, 1860.

It is expressly understood that these three sums, forming a total of £12,000 sterling annually, shall be destined to constitute a personal Dotation of His Majesty the King, in addition to the Civil List fixed by the Law of the State.

Financial Engagements of Greece to be maintained. Greek Loan.

ART. XI. The Accession of Prince William to the Hellenic Throne shall not involve any change in the Financial Engagements which Greece has contracted by Article XII of the Convention signed at London, on the 7th May, 1832, towards the Powers Guarantees of the Loan.

It is equally understood that the Powers will, in concert, watch over the execution of the engagement taken by the Hellenic Government in the month of June, 1860, upon the representation of the 3 Courts.

Recognition of Prince William of Denmark by Foreign Powers.

ART. XII. The 3 Courts shall, from this moment, use their influence in order to procure the recognition of Prince William of Denmark in the character of King of the Greeks (*Roi des Grecs*), by all the Sovereigns and States with whom they have relations.

Arrival of King George I in Greece.

ART. XIII. His Majesty the King of Denmark reserves to himself to take the measures which may be most proper for facilitating the arrival of King George I in his dominions as soon as possible.

Support to Greek Government.

ART. XIV. The 3 Courts will bring the present Treaty to the knowledge of the Greek Government, and will afford to that Government all the support in their power, while awaiting the speedy arrival of His Majesty the King.

Ratifications.

ART. XV. The present Treaty shall be ratified, and the Ratifications shall be exchanged at London in 6 weeks, or sooner, if possible.

In witness whereof the respective Plenipotentiaries have signed the same, and have affixed thereto the Seal of their Arms.

Done at London, the 13th day of July, in the year of Our Lord, 1863.

(L.S.) RUSSELL.	(L.S.) BILLE.
(L.S.) BON. GROS.	
(L.S.) BRUNNOW.	

81

ADDITIONAL ACT to the Convention of 19th August, 1858, concluded between the Porte and Prince Couza, respecting the United Principality of Moldavia and Wallachia. Constantinople, 20th June, 1864.

Reference to Convention of 19th August, 1858.

THE Convention concluded in Paris on the 19th August, 1858, between the Suzerain Court and the Guaranteeing Powers is and remains the Fundamental Law of the United Principalities.

Although the United Principalities may in future modify or change the Laws which govern their internal administration, together with the legal concourse of all the Powers already established, and without any intervention whatsoever, it is nevertheless to be well understood that this faculty cannot extend to the ties which unite the Principalities to the Ottoman Empire, nor to the Treaties in force between the Sublime Porte and the other Powers, which are and remain equally binding for the said Principalities.

The events, however, which have succeeded one another since the conclusion of the Convention of Paris having made it necessary for some of the provisions of that Convention to be modified, the Sublime Porte has just come to an understanding with His Highness the Prince of the United Principalities, and to an Agreement with their Excellencies the Representatives of the Powers who signed the Treaty of Paris, upon the present Additional Act to the said Convention, resolved and agreed upon as follows:

Public Powers.

ART. I. The Public Powers are confided to the Prince, the Senate, and an Elective Assembly.

Legislative Power.

ART. II. The Legislative Power shall be exercised collectively by the Prince, the Senate, and the Elective Assembly.

Promulgation of Laws.

ART. III. The Prince can originate Laws. He prepares them with the aid of the Council of State, and submits them both to the Elective Assembly and to the Senate to be discussed and voted for.

No Law can be submitted to the Prince's approval unless it has previously been discussed and voted by the Elective Assembly and by the Senate. The Prince grants or refuses his sanction to it. Each Law requires the sanction of the 3 Powers.

Should the Government be obliged to take urgent measures requiring the aid of both the Elective Assembly and of the Senate at the time when those Assemblies are not sitting, the Ministry shall be bound to submit to them at their next Convocation the motives and the results of such measures.

Election of Deputies.

ART. IV. The Deputies to the Elective Assembly are elected according to the principles proclaimed in the annexed document, and which must form the basis of the new Electoral Law.

President of Elective Assembly named by the Prince.
Vice-Presidents, &c., by the Assembly.

The President of the Elective Assembly is named each year by the Prince. He is chosen from among the Members of the Assembly. The Vice-Presidents, the Secretaries, and the Treasurers are named by the Assembly.

Projects of Law voted by Assembly.

ART. V. The Elective Assembly Discusses upon and Votes for the Projects of Law. The Drafts presented by the Prince are defended in the Assembly by the Ministers, or by the Members of the Council of State, who will be named by the Prince for that purpose.

Budget to be voted by Assembly, and approved by Senate.

ART. VI. The Budget of the Receipts and of the Expenditure, which is yearly prepared by the Executive Power and submitted to the Assembly, who may amend it, shall only become definitive after being voted for by that Assembly and after such vote has been approved by the Senate. Should the Budget not be voted for in time, the Executive Power shall provide for the public service in the manner voted for in the last Budget.

Composition of Senate.

ART. VII. The Senate shall be composed of the Archbishops of the country, of the Bishops of the diocese, of the First President of the Court of Appeal, of the Senior General on the active list, and of 64 Members besides, 32 of whom shall be chosen and named by the Prince from among those who have exercised the highest functions in the country, or who can prove to be possessed of an annual income of 800 ducats. As to the other 32 Members, they shall be elected from among the Members of the General Councils of each District, and shall be selected by the Prince on the presentation to him of 3 candidates.

The Members of the Senate enjoy the inviolability guaranteed to the Deputies.

Renewal of Members of Senate.

ART. VIII. The 64 Members of the Senate selected in conformity with the provisions of the preceding Article, shall be half renewed every 3 years.

Re-election of Outgoing Members.

The Outgoing Members may be Re-elected; their functions will only cease upon the installation of the new Members.

Duration of Sessions of Senate.

ART. IX. The duration of the Sessions of the Senate, their Prolongation, and the Convocation of that body, are subject to the rules prescribed in Article XVII of the Convention of 1858, on the subject of the Elective Assembly.

Payment of Members of the Senate.

ART. X. The Members of the Senate shall be paid throughout the length of the Session.

President and Vice-Presidents of Assembly.

ART. XI. The Archbishop Primate is by right President of the

Senate. One of the Vice-Presidents, chosen from among the Senators, is named by the Prince; the other and the Committee are elected by the Assembly.

In the event of an equal division, the President has a casting vote.

Sittings of Senate to be Public.

The Sittings of the Senate are Public, unless the contrary be requested by one-third of the Members present.

Right of Ministers to sit in Senate.

The Ministers, even if they do not form part of the Senate, have a right to assist at, and to take part in the deliberations there; they shall be heard every time they wish to speak.

Constitutional Provisions to be under safeguard of Senate.

ART. XII. The Constitutional Provisions of the new organisation of the Principalities are placed under the safeguard of the Senate.

Mixed Commission to report to the Prince on Labours of the Session.

At the end of each Session the Senate and the Elective Assembly shall each name a Committee, the Members of which shall be chosen from among them. The two Committees shall join in a Mixed Commission, to report to the Prince on the labours of the previous Session, and to suggest to him such improvements as are deemed necessary in the various branches of the administration.

The suggestions may be recommended by the Prince to the Council of State to be converted into Projects of Law.

Projects of Law and parts of Budget to be voted by the Senate.

ART. XIII. Every Project of Law voted by the Elective Assembly, a part of the Budget of the Revenue and of the Expenditure is laid before the Senate to be discussed and voted for by the body.

Voting of Projects of Law.

ART. XIV. The Senate approves of the Project of Law such as it has been voted by the Assembly, or amends it, or rejects it altogether.

If the Project of Law is adopted without Amendment by the Senate, it is submitted to the Prince for approval.

If the Project of Law is Amended by the Senate, it is returned to the Elective Assembly.

If the Assembly approves the Amendments made by the Senate, the Project is submitted to the Prince for approval.

If, on the other hand, the Elective Assembly rejects the Amendments made by the Senate, the Project is sent back to the Council of State to be re-considered.

The Government can then lay before the Chambers in the course of the Session, or in the ensuing one, the Project revised by the Council of State.

If the Senate rejects altogether the Project voted by the Elective Assembly, that Project is referred to the Council of State to be re-considered.

Such a Project can be laid before the Elective Assembly in the ensuing Session only.

Right of Senate to receive Petitions.

ART. XV. The Senate has the right of receiving Petitions. These Petitions shall be examined by a Commission *ad hoc*. The Senate may, if they think fit, on the report of the Commission, forward them to the Members of the Government.

Internal Regulations of Assembly and Senate.

ART. XVI. The Internal Regulations of the Elective Assembly, and of the Senate, are prepared by the Government.

Oath of Fidelity by Public Functionaries.

ART. XVII. All the Public Functionaries are, without exception, obliged, on their entering office, to swear submission to the Constitution, to the Laws of the Country, and fidelity to the Prince.

Act and Electoral Law to become Law on sanction by Suzerain Court.

ART. XVIII. The Present Act, and the Electoral Law framed in conformity with the principles declared in the above-named Annex, shall become Law on the day when they are sanctioned by the Suzerain Court.

The new Elective Assembly and the Senate shall be constituted and convoked in the terms mentioned by Article XVII of the Convention of 1858.

Prince to form Council of State.

ART. XIX. The Prince shall form a Council of State composed of persons most competent by their merit and by their experience.

Duties of Council of State.

This Council can of itself wield no power, but its purpose shall be to study and to frame the Drafts of Law which the Prince shall refer to it. The Members shall be admitted to both Assemblies as Delegates of the

Prince, to explain and to defend the Project of Law which he lays before them.

Confirmation of Convention of 19th August, 1858, except in so far as is not modified by this Act.

ART. XX. All the Provisions of the Convention of Paris which are not modified by the present Act are confirmed afresh, and shall remain in full and entire force.

Principles intended to serve as a Basis for the Construction of a new Electoral Law.

[On the 14th May, 1864, Prince Couza issued a Decree on the subject of Elections, which was deemed contrary to the engagements established by the Convention of 19th August, 1858, and led to a remonstrance on the part of the Porte, and subsequently to a Meeting of a Conference at Constantinople of the Representatives of the Treaty Powers. On the 20th June, 1864, the above Additional Act was signed, modifying the Convention, or " Organic Statute " of 19th August, 1858.

Further Conferences were held at Paris between March and June, 1866.]

82

TREATY OF PEACE between Austria, Prussia, and Denmark. Signed at Vienna, 30th October, 1864.

Reference to Preliminaries of Peace of 1st August, 1864.

In the Name of the Most Holy and Indivisible Trinity.

His Majesty the King of Prussia, His Majesty the Emperor of Austria, and His Majesty the King of Denmark, have resolved to convert the Preliminaries signed on the 1st of August last into a Definitive Treaty of Peace.

To that effect, their Majesties have appointed as their Plenipotentiaries, namely:

His Majesty the King of Prussia, the Sieur Charles, Baron de Werther, Envoy Extraordinary and Minister Plenipotentiary to the Court of Austria, &c.; and

The Sieur Armand Louis de Balan, Member of the Council of State, Envoy Extraordinary and Minister Plenipotentiary, &c.;

His Majesty the Emperor of Austria, the Sieur Jean Bernard, Comte de Rechberg-Rothenlöwen, Chamberlain and Intimate Councillor, &c.; and

The Sieur Adolphe Marie, Baron de Brenner-Felsach, Envoy Extraordinary and Minister Plenipotentiary, &c.;

His Majesty the King of Denmark, the Sieur George Joaquim de Quaade, Chamberlain and Minister without Portfolio, &c.; and

The Sieur Henrik Auguste Theodore de Kauffmann, Chamberlain and Colonel of the Staff, &c.;

Who have assembled at Vienna, and after having exchanged their Full Powers, found to be in good and due form, have agreed upon the following Articles:

Perpetual Peace and Friendship.

ART. I. There shall be for the future Perpetual Peace and Friendship between their Majesties the King of Prussia, and the Emperor of Austria, and His Majesty the King of Denmark, as well as between their Heirs and Successors, their States, and their respective Subjects.

Renewal of Treaties.

ART. II. All Treaties and Conventions concluded before the War between the High Contracting Parties are re-established in their vigour, in so far as they are not abrogated or modified by the tenor of the present Treaty.

Renunciation by Denmark of Rights over Duchies of Schleswig, Holstein, and Lauenburg.

ART. III. His Majesty the King of Denmark renounces all his Rights over the Duchies of Schleswig, Holstein, and Lauenburg in favour of their Majesties the King of Prussia and the Emperor of Austria, engaging to recognise the dispositions which their said Majesties shall make with reference to those Duchies.

Cession of Islands and Territories of Schleswig.

ART. IV. The Cession of the Duchy of Schleswig includes all the Islands belonging to that Duchy, as well as the Territory situated on *terra firma*.

Cession of Jutland Territories enclosed in the Schleswig Territory.

In order to simplify the Delimitation, and to put an end to the inconveniences arising out of the position of the Jutland Territories enclosed in the Territory of Schleswig, His Majesty the King of Denmark cedes to their Majesties the King of Prussia and the Emperor of Austria the Jutland Possessions to the south of the southern Line of

Frontier of the District of Ribe, such as the Jutland Territory of Mœgeltondern, the Island of Amrom, the Jutland parts of the Islands of Fœhr, Sylt, and Rœmœ, &c.

Parts of Schleswig and Jutland to belong to Denmark.

In exchange, their Majesties the King of Prussia and the Emperor of Austria agree to an equivalent part of Schleswig, and including, besides the Island of Aerœ, Territories contiguous to the above-mentioned district of Ribe, with the remainder of Jutland, and to correct the Line of Frontier between Jutland and Schleswig, on the side of Kolding, being detached from the Duchy of Schleswig, and incorporated into the Kingdom of Denmark.

Boundary between Denmark and Schleswig.

Art. V. The new Frontier between the Kingdom of Denmark and the Duchy of Schleswig shall start from the middle of the mouth of the Bay of Hejlsminde on the little Belt, and after crossing that Bay, shall follow the southern Frontier of the Parishes of Hejls, Vejstrup, and Taps, the latter as far as the Stream to the south of Gejlbjerg and Bränore, thence following that Stream from its mouth in the Fovs-Aa, along the southern Frontier of the Parishes of Odis and Vandrup, and the western Frontier of the latter, as far as Königs-Au (Konge-Aa) to the north of Holte. From that point the Thalweg of the Königs-Au (Konge-Aa) shall form the Frontier as far as the Eastern Limit of the Parish of Hjortlund. Starting from that point, it shall follow the same Limit, and its continuation as far as the projecting angle to the north of the Village of Obekjär, and then the Eastern Frontier of that Village as far as the Gjels-Aa. From thence the Eastern Frontier of the Parish of Seem and the Southern Limits of the Parishes of Seem, Ribe, and Vester-Vedsted shall form the new Frontier, which, in the North Sea, shall pass at equal distances between the Islands of Manœ and Rœmœ.

Rights of New Sovereign Power.

In consequence of this new Delimitation, all Titles and Mixed Rights are declared to be extinct, secular as well as spiritual, which have heretofore existed within the enclosures, in the Islands, and in the Mixed Parishes. The new Sovereign Power, therefore, in each of the Territories separated by new Frontiers, shall enjoy in that respect its full Rights.

(Arts. VI to XXI. Contain comparatively inessential matter.)

Evacuation of Jutland.

Art. XXII. The Evacuation of Jutland by the Allied Troops shall be effected within the shortest possible delay, at latest within 3 weeks after the exchange of the Ratifications of the present Treaty.

Ratifications.

ART. XXIII. The present Treaty shall be ratified, and the Ratifications thereof shall be exchanged at Vienna within 3 weeks, or sooner if possible.

In testimony whereof the respective Plenipotentiaries have signed it, and have affixed thereto the Seal of their Arms.

Done at Vienna, the 30th day of October, in the year of Our Lord, 1864.

(L.S.)	QUAADE.	(L.S.)	WERTHER.
(L.S.)	KAUFFMANN.	(L.S.)	BALAN.
		(L.S.)	RECHBERG.
		(L.S.)	BRENNER.

ANNEX.   PROTOCOL *relative to the Evacuation of Jutland by the Allied Troops.*

[A Protocol, dated 1st April, 1865, was signed between Austria and Prussia, relative to the Indemnities, &c., to the Duke of Augustenburg.]

83   CONVENTION OF GASTEIN

CONVENTION between Austria and Prussia, respecting the Elbe Duchies of Schleswig, Holstein, and Lauenburg. Signed at Gastein, 14th August, 1865.

Reference to Treaty of 30th October, 1864.

THEIR Majesties the Emperor of Austria and the King of Prussia have become convinced that the Co-Sovereignty which has hitherto existed in the Territories ceded by Denmark in the Treaty of Peace of 30th October, 1864, leads to untoward results, which at the same time endanger both the good understanding between their Governments and the Interests of the Duchies. Their Majesties have therefore resolved for the future not to exercise in common the Rights which have accrued to them by Article III of the above-mentioned Treaty, but to divide the exercise thereof geographically until a further agreement may be made.

For this purpose His Majesty the Emperor of Austria, &c., has appointed as his Plenipotentiary, Count von Blome; the King of Prussia, &c., has appointed as his Plenipotentiary, M. von Bismarck-Schönhausen; who, after having communicated to each other their respective Full Powers, which were found in good and due form, have agreed upon the following Articles:

Austria to administer the Duchy of Holstein, and Prussia the Duchy of Schleswig.

ART. I. The exercise of the Rights acquired in common by the High Contracting Parties, in virtue of Article III of the Vienna Treaty of Peace of 30th October, 1864, shall, without prejudice to the continuance of those rights of both Powers to the whole of both Duchies, pass to His Majesty the Emperor of Austria as regards the Duchy of Holstein, and to His Majesty the King of Prussia as regards the Duchy of Schleswig.

Proposal to be made to Diet to establish a German Fleet in Harbour of Kiel.

ART. II. The High Contracting Parties will propose to the Diet the establishment of a German Fleet, and will fix upon the Harbour of Kiel as a Federal Harbour for the said Fleet.

Harbour of Kiel to be under command, &c., of Prussia.

Until the resolutions of the Diet with respect to this proposal have been carried into effect, the Ships of War of both Powers shall use this Harbour, and the Command and the Police Duties within it shall be exercised by Prussia. Prussia is entitled both to establish the necessary Fortifications opposite Friedrichsort for the protection of the entrance, and also to fit up along the Holstein bank of the inlet the Naval Establishments that are requisite in a Military Port. These Fortifications and Establishments remain likewise under Prussian command, and the Prussian marines and troops required for their Garrison and Protection may be quartered in Kiel and the neighbourhood.

Proposal to be made that Rendsburg be a German Federal Fortress.

ART. III. The High Contracting Parties will propose in Frankfort the elevation of Rendsburg into a German Federal Fortress.

Garrison of Fort of Rendsburg.

Until the Diet shall have issued the regulations respecting Garrisoning the said Fortress, the Garrison shall consist of Imperial Austrian and Royal Prussian troops under a command annually alternating on the 1st July.

Prussia to retain two Military Roads in Holstein.

ART. IV. Whilst the division agreed upon in Article I of the present Convention continues, the Royal Prussian Government shall retain two Military Roads through Holstein; the one from Lubeck to Kiel, the other from Hamburg to Rendsburg.

Regulations as to Military Roads.

All details as to the Military Stations, and as to the transport and subsistence of the Troops, shall be regulated as soon as possible in a Special Convention. Until this has been done, the Regulations in force as to the Prussian Military Roads through Hanover shall be observed.

Telegraph Communication with Kiel and Rendsburg.

ART. V. The Royal Prussian Government retains the disposal of one Telegraphic wire for communication with Kiel and Rendsburg, and retains also the right to send Prussian mail-vans, with its own officials on both lines through the Duchy of Holstein.

Railway from Lubeck through Kiel to Schleswig.

Inasmuch as the construction of a direct Railway from Lubeck through Kiel to the Schleswig Frontier is not yet assured, the concession thereof shall be granted on the request of Prussia, for the Territory of Holstein under the customary conditions; but no claim shall be made by Prussia for Rights of Sovereignty with regard to the line.

Entrance of Duchies into the Zollverein.

ART. VI. The High Contracting Parties entertain in common the intention that the Duchies shall enter the Zollverein. Until they shall enter the Zollverein, or until some further agreement shall be made, the system of Duties hitherto in force in both Duchies, and the equal division of the Revenues, shall continue to exist. If it should appear desirable to the Royal Prussian Government, even during the existence of the division agreed upon in Article I of the present Convention, to open negotiations respecting the entry of the Duchies into the Zollverein, His Majesty the Emperor of Austria is prepared to empower a Representative of the Duchy of Holstein to take part in such negotiations.

Canal between the North Sea and the Baltic, through Holstein.

ART. VII. Prussia is entitled to make the Canal that is to be cut between the North Sea and the Baltic, through the Territory of Holstein, according to the result of the professional investigations undertaken by the Prussian Government.

Rights of Prussia over Construction, &c., of Canal.

In so far as this shall be the case, Prussia shall have the right to determine the direction and the dimensions of the Canal; to acquire possession of the Land necessary for carrying out the work by means of expropriation, with an indemnification to the amount of the value; to conduct the construction of the Canal; to superintend the inspection and conservation of the Canal; and to give her assent to all regulations respecting the said Canal.

Dues to be Levied for the use of the Canal.

With the exception of the Navigation Dues, which are to be levied for the use of the Canal, and which are to be regulated by Prussia, and to be the same for the Ships of all Nations, no Transit Tolls or Dues upon Ship and Cargo are to be levied at any part of the Canal.

Financial Obligations.   Lauenburg released from Contribution towards Expenses of the War.

ART. VIII. Nothing is changed by the present Convention in the Stipulations of the Vienna Treaty of Peace of 30th October, 1864, relative to the Financial Obligations to be undertaken by the Duchies both as regards Denmark and as regards Austria and Prussia; but the Duchy of Lauenburg is to be released from every obligation of contributing towards the expenses of the War.

Division of Obligations between Holstein and Schleswig.

The division of these Obligations between the Duchies of Holstein and of Schleswig will be based upon the proportion of population.

Cession by Austria to Prussia of Right over Lauenburg. Indemnity to Austria for Lauenburg.

ART. IX. His Majesty the Emperor of Austria cedes to His Majesty the King of Prussia the Rights acquired in the aforementioned Vienna Treaty of Peace with respect to the Duchy of Lauenburg; and in return the Royal Prussian Government binds itself to pay to the Austrian Government the sum of 2,500,000 Danish rix-dollars, payable at Berlin in Prussian silver, 4 weeks after confirmation of the present Convention by their Majesties the Emperor of Austria and the King of Prussia.

Division of Co-Sovereignty over Holstein and Schleswig.

ART. X. The carrying into effect of the foregoing division of the Co-Sovereignty, which has been agreed upon, shall begin as soon as possible after the approval of this Convention by their Majesties the Emperor of

Austria and the King of Prussia, and shall be accomplished at the latest by the 15th September.

Cessation of Joint Command.

The joint Command-in-Chief, hitherto existing, shall be dissolved on the complete Evacuation of Holstein by the Prussian troops and of Schleswig by the Austrian troops, by the 15th September, at the latest.

Exchange of Declarations.

ART. XI. The present Convention shall be approved by their Majesties the Emperor of Austria and the King of Prussia by exchanging written Declarations at their next meeting.[1]

In witness whereof both the Plenipotentiaries named at the beginning have on this day set their signatures and seals to this Convention in duplicate copy.

Done at Gastein, 14th August, 1865.

(L.S.) G. BLOME.
(L.S.) Von BISMARCK.

84 PRELIMINARY TREATY OF NIKOLSBURG

PRELIMINARY TREATY OF PEACE between Austria and Prussia. Signed at Nikolsburg, 26th July, 1866.

THEIR Majesties the Emperor of Austria and the King of Prussia, animated with the desire of restoring the benefits of Peace to their Countries, have for that purpose, and in order to settle the Preliminaries of Peace, appointed Plenipotentiaries, that is to say:

His Majesty the Emperor of Austria, the Count Aloisius Karolyi, and the Baron Adolphus von Brenner-Felsach;

And His Majesty the King of Prussia, Otho, Count von Bismarck-Schönhausen, his President of the Council and Minister for Foreign Affairs;

Who, after exchanging their Full Powers, which were found in good and due form, have agreed upon the following fundamental points as the basis of the Peace to be concluded without delay

Austrian Territory to remain intact, with the exception of the Lombardo-Venetian Kingdom. Withdrawal of Prussian Troops.

ART. I. With the Exception of the Lombardo-Venetian Kingdom,

[1]Approved at Salzburg, 20th August, 1865.

the Territory of the Austrian Monarchy remains intact. His Majesty the King of Prussia engages to withdraw his Troops from the Austrian Territories occupied by them as soon as the Peace shall be concluded, under reservation of the arrangements to be made upon the definite conclusion of the Peace for guaranteeing the payment of the War Indemnity.

Dissolution of the Germanic Confederation. Formation of North German Confederation and a South German Union.

ART. II. His Majesty the Emperor of Austria recognises the Dissolution of the Germanic Confederation as it has existed hitherto, and consents to a new organisation of Germany without the participation of the Empire of Austria. His Majesty likewise promises to recognise the closer Union which will be founded by His Majesty the King of Prussia, to the north of the line of the Main, and he declares that he consents to the German States south of that line entering into a Union, the national relations of which, with the North German Confederation are to be the subject of an ulterior agreement between the two Parties.

Schleswig and Holstein to be transferred to Prussia except Northern part to be retroceded to Denmark on certain Conditions.

ART. III. His Majesty the Emperor of Austria transfers to His Majesty the King of Prussia all the Rights which the Treaty of Vienna of 30th October, 1864, recognised as belonging to him over the Duchies of Schleswig and Holstein, with this reservation, that the people of the Northern Districts of Schleswig shall be again united to Denmark if they express a desire to be so by a vote freely given.

Austria to pay War Expenses of Prussia.

ART. IV. His Majesty the Emperor of Austria undertakes to pay His Majesty the King of Prussia the sum of 40,000,000 thalers to cover a part of the Expenses which Prussia has been put to by the War. But from this sum may be deducted the amount of the Indemnity for the costs of War which His Majesty the Emperor of Austria still has the right of exacting from the Duchies of Schleswig and Holstein, by virtue of Article XII of the Treaty of Peace of 30th October, 1864, before cited, say 15,000,000 thalers, with 5,000,000 in addition, as the equivalent of the cost of providing for the Prussian army, maintained by the Austrian Countries occupied by that army until the time of the conclusion of the Peace.

Territorial State of the Kingdom of Saxony.

ART. V. In conformity with the wish expressed by His Majesty the

Emperor of Austria, His Majesty the King of Prussia declares his willingness to let the Territorial State of the Kingdom of Saxony continue in its present extent, when the modifications are made which are to take place in Germany; reserving to himself, however, to regulate in detail, by a special Peace with His Majesty the King of Saxony, the questions as to Saxony's part in the expenses of the War, as well as the future position of the Kingdom of Saxony in the North German Confederation.

Austria to recognise New Organisation of North Germany.

On the other hand, His Majesty the Emperor of Austria promises to recognise the New Organisation which the King of Prussia will establish in the North of Germany, including the Territorial modifications consequent thereon.

Preliminaries of Peace and Armistice to be recognised by King of Italy.

ART. VI. His Majesty the King of Prussia undertakes to prevail upon His Majesty the King of Italy, his Ally, to give his approval to the Preliminaries of Peace and to the Armistice based on those Preliminaries, so soon as the Venetian Kingdom shall have been put at the disposal of His Majesty the King of Italy by a Declaration of His Majesty the Emperor of the French.

Ratifications.

ART. VII. The Ratifications of the present Convention shall be exchanged at Nikolsburg in the space of two days at the latest.

Peace to be concluded on Basis of Preliminary Treaty.

ART. VIII. Immediately after the Ratification of the present Convention shall have been effected and exchanged, their Majesties the Emperor of Austria and the King of Prussia will appoint Plenipotentiaries, who will meet at a place to be hereafter named, to conclude the Peace upon the Basis of the present Preliminary Treaty, and to agree upon the details of the conditions.

Armistice to be concluded between Austria and Saxony and Prussia.

ART. IX. For that purpose the Contracting States, after having decided upon these Preliminaries, will conclude an Armistice for the Austrian and Saxon armies on the one part, and for the Prussian army on the other part, of which the detailed conditions, from the military point of view, are to be immediately determined. That Armistice shall date from the 2nd of August, the day to which the present Suspension of Arms shall be prolonged.

Conclusion of Armistice with other States.

The Armistice shall, at the same time, be concluded with Bavaria, and General the Baron von Manteuffel will be instructed to conclude with the Kingdom of Wurtemberg and the Grand Duchies of Baden and Hesse-Darmstadt, as soon as those States shall propose it, an Armistice beginning on the 2nd August, and founded on the state of military possession at the time.

In faith whereof the respective Plenipotentiaries have signed the present Convention, and to it have affixed the Seals of their Arms.

Done at Nikolsburg, 26th July, 1866.

(L.S.) KOROLYI.
(L.S.) BRENNER.

Accessories.

Baden..	13th August, 1866
Bavaria	17th August, 1866
Hesse-Darmstadt	22nd August, 1866
Saxe-Meiningen	8th October, 1866
Saxony	21st October, 1866
Wurtemberg ..	13th August, 1866

[A Convention of Armistice was concluded between Austria and Prussia at Vienna on the 26th July, 1866; and another Convention between the Austrian and Italian Military Commissioners on the 12th August, 1866.]

85   TREATY OF PRAGUE

TREATY OF PEACE between Austria and Prussia. Signed at Prague, 23rd August, 1866. Ratifications exchanged at Prague, 30th August, 1866.

Reference to Preliminaries of Peace of 26th July, 1866.

In the name o the Most Holy and Indivisible Trinity.

HIS Majesty the Emperor of Austria and His Majesty the King of Prussia, animated with the desire of restoring to their countries the benefits of Peace, have determined to convert the Preliminaries signed at Nikolsburg, on the 26th July, 1866, into a Definitive Treaty of Peace, and for that purpose their Majesties have appointed as their Plenipotentiaries, that is to say:

His Majesty the Emperor of Austria, the Baron Adolphus Maria von

Brenner-Felsach, his actual Privy Councillor and Chamberlain, Envoy Extraordinary and Minister Plenipotentiary, &c.; and

His Majesty the King of Prussia, the Baron Charles von Werther, his Chamberlain, actual Privy Councillor and Plenipotentiary, &c.;

Who met together in Conference at Prague, and after exchanging their Full Powers, which were found in good and proper form, agreed upon the following Articles:

Peace and Friendship.

ART. I. There shall be Peace and Friendship between His Majesty the Emperor of Austria and His Majesty the King of Prussia, and between their heirs and successors, as well as between their respective States and subjects, henceforth and for ever.

Accession of Austria to Declaration of French Ambassador of 29th July, 1866, respecting Cession of Venice to Italy. Union of the Lombardo-Venetian Kingdom with that of Italy. Debts.

ART. II. For the purpose of carrying out Article VI of the Preliminaries of Peace concluded at Nikolsburg on the 26th July, 1866, and as His Majesty the Emperor of the French officially declared through his accredited Ambassador to His Majesty the King of Prussia, on the 29th July, 1886, " qu'en ce qui concerne le Gouvernement de l'Empereur, la Vénétie est acquise a l'Italie pour lui être remise à la Paix,"—His Majesty the Emperor of Austria also accedes on his part to that Declaration and gives his consent to the Union of the Lombardo-Venetian Kingdom with the Kingdom of Italy, without any other burdensome condition than the liquidation of those Debts which, being charged on the Territories ceded, are to be recognised in accordance with the precedent of the Treaty of Zurich.

Prisoners of War.

ART. III. The Prisoners of War shall be set at liberty immediately on both sides.

Dissolution of the Germanic Confederation. Assent of Austria to her exclusion from New Organisation of Germany, and to the formation of a North German Confederation.

ART. IV. His Majesty the Emperor of Austria acknowledges the dissolution of the Germanic Confederation as hitherto constituted, and gives his consent to a new organisation of Germany without the participation of the Imperial Austrian State. His Majesty likewise promises to recognise the more restricted Federal relations which His Majesty the

King of Prussia will establish to the north of the line of the Main; and he declares his concurrence in the formation of an Association of the German States situated to the south of that line, whose national connection with the North German Confederation is reserved for further arrangement between the parties, and which will have an independent international existence.

Transfer by Austria to Prussia of all rights over Duchies of Holstein and Schleswig, acquired by Treaty of 30th October, 1864, on condition of Populations of Northern Districts of Schleswig being ceded to Denmark, if, by free vote, they should express a wish to be united to Denmark.

ART. V. His Majesty the Emperor of Austria transfers to His Majesty the King of Prussia all the rights which he acquired by the Vienna Treaty of Peace of 30th October, 1864, over the Duchies of Holstein and Schleswig, with the condition that the populations of the Northern Districts of Schleswig shall be ceded to Denmark if, by a free vote, they express a wish to be united to Denmark.

Existing Territorial condition of Saxony to remain as before. Special Treaty to be concluded between Prussia and Saxony respecting expenses of the War, and future position of Saxony in North German Confederation.

ART. VI. At the desire of His Majesty the Emperor of Austria, His Majesty the King of Prussia declares his willingness to let the present Territorial condition of the Kingdom of Saxony remain to the same extent as before, in the alterations which are about to be made in Germany; but he reserves to himself the right of arranging the contribution of Saxony to the expenses of the War, and the future position of the Kingdom of Saxony in the North German Confederation, by a special Treaty to be concluded with His Majesty the King of Saxony.

On the other hand, His Majesty the Emperor of Austria promises to recognise the new arrangements that will be made by His Majesty the King of Prussia in North Germany, including the Territorial alterations.

Appointment of Commission to determine as to disposal of late Federal Property.

ART. VII. For the purpose of making arrangements respecting the late Federal Property, a Commission will meet at Frankfort-on-the-Main within 6 weeks at farthest from the Ratification of this Treaty, to which Commission all claims and demands on the German Confederation are to be sent in, and they will be liquidated within 6 months. Austria and Prussia will send Representatives to that Commission, and all the other late Federal Governments are at liberty to do the same.

Disposal of Imperial Property in Federal Fortresses.

ART. VIII. Austria has the right of removing or otherwise disposing of the Imperial Property in the Federal Fortresses, and the part of the movable Federal Property belonging to Austria, according to specification; the same is the case with all the movable effects of the Confederation.

Pensions to Officials and others.

ART. IX. The Pensions to which the regular Officials, Servants, and Pensioners of the Confederation are entitled, or which have already been granted, will be secured to them *pro rata* of the register.

Pensions to Officers, &c., of former Schleswig-Holstein Army to be paid by Prussia.

The Royal Prussian Government, however, undertakes the Pensions and Allowances hitherto paid out of the Federal matriculation fund to the Officers of the former Schleswig-Holstein Army and their survivors.

Pensions granted by Austria in Holstein.

ART. X. The persons interested in the Pensions granted by the Imperial Royal Austrian Lieutenancy in Holstein will still be allowed to draw them.

Restoration by Austria of Danish State Bonds.

The sum of 449,500 thalers of Danish currency in 4 per cent. Danish State Bonds, which is still in the custody of the Imperial Royal Austrian Government, and which belongs to the Holstein Treasury, will be restored to it immediately after the Ratification of the present Treaty.

Non-molestation for Political conduct during the War.

No one belonging to the Duchies of Holstein and Schleswig, and no subject of their Majesties the Emperor of Austria and the King of Prussia will be prosecuted, molested, or obstructed in his person or property on account of his Political conduct during the late events and the War.

War Indemnity to be paid by Austria to Prussia.

ART. XI. His Majesty the Emperor of Austria undertakes to pay to His Majesty the King of Prussia the sum of 40,000,000 Prussian thalers, to cover part of the expenses which Prussia has been put to by the War. From that sum is however to be deducted the amount of the War expenses which His Majesty the Emperor of Austria has still to demand from the Duchies of Schleswig and Holstein, according to Article XII of the aforesaid Treaty of Vienna of the 30th October, 1864, to the extent of 15,000,000 Prussian thalers, as well as a further sum of 5,000,000, as an equivalent for the free maintenance which the Prussian Army is to have in those parts of the Austrian Territories which it occupies, until the conclusion of Peace; so that there only remain 20,000,000 to be paid in ready money.

One-half of that sum is to be settled when the Ratification of the present Treaty takes place, the second half 3 weeks later at Oppeln in cash.

Prussian Evacuation of Austrian Territories.

ART. XII. The Evacuation of the Austrian Territories held by the Royal Prussian troops shall be completed within 3 weeks after the exchange of the Ratifications of the Treaty of Peace. From the day of the exchange of the Ratifications the Prussian General Governments will confine their functions to the purely military sphere of operations.

The special stipulations according to which the Evacuation is to take place are settled in a separate Protocol which forms an Appendix to the present Treaty.

Renewal of Treaties. Proposed Abrogation of Monetary Convention of 24th January, 1857.

ART. XIII. All the Treaties and Conventions concluded between the High Contracting Parties before the War are hereby again brought into force, in so far as they by their nature, must not lose their effect by the dissolution of the relations of the Germanic Confederation. The General Cartel Convention between the German Federal States, of the 10th February, 1831, together with the supplementary stipulations belonging thereto, will especially retain its validity between Austria and Prussia. The Imperial Royal Austrian Government declares, however, that the Monetary Treaty concluded the 24th January, 1857, loses its most essential value for Austria by the dissolution of the German Federal relations, and the Royal Prussian Government declares its willingness to enter into negotiations with Austria and the other participators in that Treaty for the abrogation thereof.

Zollverein Treaty of 11th April, 1865, to be revised.

In like manner, the High Contracting Parties reserve to themselves to enter into a negotiation as soon as possible for the Revision of the Commercial and Customs Treaty of the 11th April, 1865, for the further facilitation of their reciprocal traffic. Meanwhile the said Treaty shall again come into force, on the condition that each of the High Contracting Parties reserves the right of putting an end to its operation after 6 months' notice.

Ratifications.

ART. XIV. The Ratifications of the present Treaty shall be exchanged at Prague within the space of 8 days, or sooner if possible.

In witness whereof the respective Plenipotentiaries have signed the present Treaty, and have affixed to it the Seals of their Arms.

Done at Prague, on the 23rd day of the month of August, in the year of Grace, 1866.

(L.S.) BRENNER.   (L.S.) WERTHER.

APPENDIX

PROTOCOL *respecting the delivery of the Prisoners of War, and the Evacuation of Austrian Territory by Prussian Troops.*

FOR the execution of Articles III and XII of the Treaty of Peace concluded this day, the High Contracting Parties have agreed upon the following stipulations:

1. On the 3rd day after the Ratification of the Treaty all the Royal Prussian Prisoners of War, and from the same day the Imperial Royal Austrian Prisoners of War, will be delivered up at Austrian Oderberg (railway station) in echelons of about 1,000 men each, which are to follow on the successive days (not more than 6 echelons within 24 hours).

2. The Royal Prussian Prisoners of War who are in the Bohemian Fortresses and in Olmütz, are to be delivered, so soon as the account of the Ratification of this Treaty reaches those Fortresses, to the nearest division of the Royal Prussian troops.

3. Commissioners from both Armies will be stationed at Austrian Oderberg, to attend to the delivery, so far as it takes place at Oderberg, and to arrange jointly for the railway transport to the south.

On the Imperial Royal Austrian side a detachment of troops of about 200 men will be stationed at Austrian Oderberg for the reception and care of the Prisoners.

4. Prisoners of War who are too unwell to be removed are to remain in the Hospitals on both sides with the regular treatment and maintenance of the native troops, until they can be delivered up at Oderberg.

5. The expenses arising from the attendance upon the sick Prisoners of War left behind will be liquidated and defrayed on both sides, from the third day after the Ratification, at the regular rates for hospital attendance in both armies.

6. For the accomplishment of the Evacuation of the Imperial Royal Austrian territories which is to be effected within 3 weeks after the Ratification of this Treaty, the tract south of the line of Napagedl, Brünn, Iglau, Tabor (exclusive of those places), will be evacuated on the Royal Prussian side on the 7th day, and all the country lying south of

the Pilsen-Prague-Littau railway line, and beyond a straight line from Littau to the mouth of the Oppa in the Oder, on the 15th day after the Ratification.

For all possible acceleration of this Evacuation the time between the signing and the Ratification of this Treaty will be employed on the Royal Prussian side in preparatory measures.

7. The Imperial Royal Austrian troops during the time of evacuation, will, in re-occupying the country, keep themselves at a distance of 3 miles from the rear of the Royal Prussian columns. The times of re-treating on each line of march are therefore left to the arrangement of the Commanders on both sides.

8. On the Imperial Austrian side the use of the railway line leading by Pilsen to the Kingdom of Bavaria, will be allowed for the Royal Prussian military transports for the purpose of evacuating Bohemia.

9. During the time of evacuation the Royal Prussian army will retain the unrestricted control over the railway lines within the ranges which it occupies, for sending back troops and war materials, under application of the Convention dated Brünn, the 1st August, 1866, and definitively concluded on the 17th August. It is settled as a rule that even during the evacuation there shall be a train in each direction for public traffic every day on all the railways; only unforeseen interruptions of the military transports can justify any departure from this rule for the particular day.

10. From the day following the Ratification the Royal Prussian Government undertakes all the expenses of maintenance for the Royal Prussian troops, which however are to have free quarters without maintenance in the territories which they occupy. The local authorities are bound to provide the relays required by the Royal Prussian troops, for which the troops are to pay immediately in ready money according to the Imperial Royal Austrian Tariff for relays now in force. That tariff is in the possession of the national and local authorities.

11. The sick of the Royal Prussian army who cannot be removed are to remain in the military hospitals or local infirmaries, under the superintendence and treatment, so far as necessary, of the Royal Prussian military physicians. The Imperial Royal Austrian Government promises to make arrangements for the most careful treatment of those left behind, and for complying as far as possible with the necessary requisitions of the physicians for the treatment of the sick.

12. Before the evacuation the Royal Prussian Commanders will send in to the Imperial Royal Lieutenancies of Bohemia, Moravia, and Silesia, through the Royal Prussian General Governments at Prague and Brünn, a list of the sick who are to be left behind, with a statement of the place where they lie.

13. For the delivery of the Hospitals at Brünn, Prague, Pardubitz, and Königinhoff, Commissioners of the respective Armies will meet at the places named, on the day of the evacuation of those towns, to complete the delivery and draw up a Protocol.

14. The expenses of attending on the sick will be paid by the Royal Prussian Government immediately after liquidation, according to the established regulations for the Imperial Royal Austrian troops.

Prague, 23rd August, 1866.

WERTHER.
BRENNER.

[Oldenburg formally withdrew from the Germanic Confederation on the 20th June, 1866, and renounced its Rights over the Duchies of Holstein and Schleswig in favour of Prussia on the 27th September, 1866.]

86   TREATY OF VIENNA

TREATY OF PEACE between Austria and Italy. Signed at Vienna, 3rd October, 1866. Ratifications exchanged at Vienna, 12th October, 1866.

Reference to Treaties of Zurich of 10th November, 1859.
In the name of the Most Holy and Indivisible Trinity.

His Majesty the King of Italy and His Majesty the Emperor of Austria having resolved to establish between their respective States a sincere and lasting Peace, His Majesty the Emperor of Austria having ceded to His Majesty the Emperor of the French the Lombardo-Venetian Kingdom, His Majesty the Emperor of the French on his part having declared himself ready to recognise the Union of the said Lombardo-Venetian Kingdom to the States of His Majesty the King of Italy, with the reservation of the consent of the Populations being duly consulted; His Majesty the King of Italy and His Majesty the Emperor of Austria have appointed as their Plenipotentiaries, namely:

His Majesty the King of Italy, the Sieur Louis Frederic Count Menabrea, Senator of the Kingdom, Lieutenant-General, &c.;

His Majesty the Emperor of Austria, the Sieur Felix Count Wimpffen, his actual Chamberlain, Envoy and Minister Plenipotentiary, on an Extraordinary Mission, &c.;

Who, after having exchanged their respective Full Powers, found to be in good and due form, have agreed upon the following Articles:

Peace and Friendship.

ART. I. There shall be from the date of the exchange of the
Ratifications of the present Treaty, Peace and Friendship between
His Majesty the King of Italy and His Majesty the Emperor of Austria,
their heirs and successors, their States and their respective subjects in
perpetuity.

Delivery of Prisoners of War.

ART. II. The Italian and Austrian Prisoners of War shall be immediately delivered up on both sides.

Union of Lombardo-Venetian Kingdom to Italy.

ART. III. His Majesty the Emperor of Austria agrees to the Union
of the Lombardo-Venetian Kingdom to the Kingdom of Italy.

Frontier of Ceded Territory.

ART. IV. The Frontier of the Ceded Territory is determined by
the actual administrative confines of the Lombardo-Venetian Kingdom.

Appointment of a Military Commission.

A Military Commission appointed by the two Contracting Powers
shall be entrusted with the execution of the tracing on the spot within
the shortest possible delay.

Evacuation of Ceded Territory.

ART. V. The evacuation of the Ceded Territory determined by
the preceding Article, shall begin immediately after the signature
of Peace, and shall be terminated in the shortest possible delay, in
conformity with the arrangements agreed upon between the Special
Commissioners appointed to that effect.

*Amounts to be paid by Italy on account of the Monte Lombardo-
Veneto Debt, and for War Material.*

ART. VI. The Italian Government will take upon itself:

1st. The portion of the Monte Lombardo-Veneto which devolved
upon Austria in virtue of the Convention concluded at Milan in 1860
for the execution of Article VII of the Treaty of Zurich;

2ndly. The Debts added to the Monte Lombardo-Veneto since the
4th of June, 1859, up to the day of the conclusion of the present Treaty;

3rdly. A sum of 35,000,000 florins, Austrian currency, in cash, for the
portion of the Loan of 1854, allotted to Venetia, and for the price of the
non-transportable War Material. The manner of paying that sum of
35,000,000 florins, Austrian currency, in cash, shall, in conformity

with the precedent of the Treaty of Zurich, be determined in an Additional Article.

Appointment of a Commission for the Payment of Monte Lombardo-Veneto Debt.

ART. VII. A Commission, composed of Italian, Austrian, and French Delegates, shall proceed to the liquidation of the different classes mentioned in the two first paragraphs of the preceding Article, taking into account the Sinking Fund already paid, and the Property, Assets, of every kind, constituting the Sinking Fund. That Commission shall proceed with the Definitive Regulation of the Accounts between the Contracting Parties, and shall fix the time and method to be employed for the liquidation of the Monte Lombardo-Veneto.

Rights and Obligations of Italy relative to Austrian Contract.

ART. VIII. The Government of His Majesty the King of Italy succeeds to the Rights and Obligations resulting from Contracts regularly stipulated by the Austrian Administration for objects of public interest, especially concerning the ceded Territory.

Reimbursements to be made by Austrian and Italian Governments.

ART. IX. The Austrian Government is charged with the Reimbursement of all sums paid by subjects of the ceded Territory, communal districts, public establishments, and religious societies into the Austrian public Banks in the shape of caution-money, deposits, or consignments. In the same manner, Austrian subjects, communes, public establishments, and religious societies, who have paid money into the Banks of the ceded Territories in the shape of caution-money, deposits, or consignments, will be punctually reimbursed by the Italian Government.

Recognition and Confirmation by Italy of Austrian Railway Concessions.

ART. X. The Government of His Majesty the King of Italy recognises and confirms the concessions granted to the Railroads by the Austrian Government in the ceded Territory, to the full extent of all their arrangements and duration, and particularly the concessions resulting from the Contracts passed under date of 14th March, 1856, 8th April, 1857, and 23rd September, 1858.

Recognition of Austrian Railway Conventions by Italy.

The Italian Government also recognises and confirms the stipulations of the Convention of 20th November, 1861, between the Administration of the South Lombardo-Venetian and Central Italian Railway Company, as well as the Convention of the 27th February, 1866, between the Imperial Minister of Finances and Commerce and the South Austrian Society.

Austrian Right of Devolution transferred to Italian Government.

From the time of the exchange of the Ratifications of this Treaty, the Italian Government is bound by all the Rights and Obligations resulting to the Austrian Government by the above-mentioned Convention, in regard to the Lines of Railway situated on the ceded Territory; consequently the right of Devolution which belonged to the Austrian Government.

Payments still due by Concessionaries to be paid in full to Austria.

The Payments which are still to be made of the sum due to the State by the Concessionaries in virtue of the Contract of 14th March, 1856, as an equivalent for the expense of construction of the said Railroads, shall be paid in full into the Austrian Exchequer.

Austria to pay Credits of Building Contractors and Tradesmen, &c.

The Credits of the building Contractors and Tradesmen, as well as the Indemnities for appropriation of land, which appertain to the time when the Railways in question were administered on account of the State, and which have not yet been paid, will be paid by the Austrian Government, and, in so far as they may be due from them in virtue of the Act of Concession by the grantees of the Austrian Government.

Austria to have no control over Railways in ceded Territory.

ART. XI. It is understood that the recovery of the debts, resulting from Paragraphs 12, 13, 14, 15, and 16 of the Contract of the 14th March, 1856, will give Austria no right of control or superintendence over the construction and working of Railways in the ceded Territory. The Italian Government engages on its part to communicate all the information which may be asked for on the subject by the Austrian Government.

Convention to be entered into with South Austrian Railway Company.

ART. XII. In order to extend to the Venetian Railways the Stipulations of Article XV of the Convention of the 27th February, 1866, the High Contracting Parties engage to enter as soon as possible, in concert with the South Austrian Railway Company, into a Convention for the administrative and economical separation of the Venetian and Austrian Railways.

Division of Payment of Railway Guarantee.

In virtue of the Convention of the 27th February, 1866, the guarantee that the State has to pay to the South Austrian Railway Company shall be calculated on the basis of the net produce of the whole of the Venetian and Austrian Lines forming the networks of the South Austrian Railways actually conceded to the Company. It is understood that the Italian Government will take upon itself a proportionate part of that Guarantee corresponding to the Lines in the ceded Territory, and that the basis of the net produce of the Austrian and Venetian Lines conceded to the said Company shall still form the basis for the evaluation of that Guarantee.

Increase of Railway Communications.

Art. XIII. The Italian and Austrian Governments, desirous of extending the relations between the two States, engage to facilitate Railway Communications and to favour the establishment of new Lines to unite the Italian and Austrian networks. The Government of His Imperial Royal Apostolic Majesty promises besides to hasten as much as possible the conclusion of the Brenner Line destined to unite the Valley of the Adige with that of the Inn.

Inhabitants or Natives of ceded Territory free to retire with their Moveables to Austria, and to keep their Immovable Property in Lombardy.

Art. XIV. Inhabitants or natives of the Territory ceded by the present Treaty will have, for the space of a year, from the day of the date on which the Ratifications are exchanged, and conditionally on a previous declaration before the competent authorities, full and entire power to export their Moveables, free of duty, and to retire with their families into the States of His Imperial and Royal Apostolic Majesty, in which case their quality of Austrian subjects will be retained by them. They will be at liberty to keep their immoveable property situated on the ceded Territory.

Same liberty to Lombards living in Austria.

The same power is granted reciprocally to natives of the ceded Territory of Lombardy living in the States of His Majesty the Emperor of Austria.

Lombard Subjects to be free from Molestation.

The Lombards who profit by these arrangements cannot be, on account of their choice, disturbed on either side, in their person or their properties situated in the respective States.

Time within which Lombards are to make their choice.

The delay of one year is extended to two years, for the subjects, natives of the ceded Territory of Lombardy, who at the time of the exchange of the Ratifications of this Treaty are not within the Territory of the Austrian Monarchy. Their Declaration may be received by the nearest Austrian Mission, or by the superior authority of any province of the Monarchy.

Lombardo-Venetian Subjects in Austrian Army to return to their Homes.

ART. XV. The Lombardo-Venetian subjects in the Austrian army, will be immediately discharged from military service and sent back to their homes.

Lombards free to remain in Austrian Service.

It is understood that those amongst them who declare their wish to remain in the service of His Imperial and Royal Apostolic Majesty shall be free to do so, and will not be disturbed on this account, either in person or in property.

Civil Servants free to remain in Austrian Service.

The same guarantees are assured to the Civil Employés, natives of the Lombardo-Venetian Kingdom, who manifest their intention of keeping the offices they occupy in the Austrian Service.

Civil Servants free to choose between the Austrian and Italian Service.

Civil Servants born in the Lombardo-Venetian Kingdom shall have the choice, either of remaining in the Austrian Service, or entering the Italian Administration, in which case the Government of His Majesty the King of Italy engages, either to place them in positions analogous to those which they occupied, or allot them Pensions, the amount of which shall be fixed according to the Laws and Regulations in force in Austria. It is understood that the said Civil Servants shall act under the disciplinary Laws and Regulations of the Italian Administration.

Italian Officers in Austrian Army free to remain or enter Italian Army.

ART. XVI. Officers of Italian origin, who are actually in the Austrian Service, shall have the choice, either of remaining in the Service of His Imperial and Royal Apostolic Majesty or of entering the Army of His Majesty the King of Italy, with the Rank they hold in the Austrian Army, provided they make the request within 6 months after the Ratification of the present Treaty.

Civil and Military Pensions.

ART. XVII. The Pensions, both Civil and Military, regularly paid, and which were paid out of the public funds of the Lombardo-Venetian Kingdom, remain due to those entitled to them, and, if need be, to their widows and children, and will be paid in future by the Government of His Italian Majesty.

This stipulation is extended to the Pensioners, both Civil and Military, as well as to their widows and children, without distinction of origin, who keep their domicile in the ceded Territory, and whose salaries, paid up to 1814 by the then Government of the Lombardo-Venetian Provinces, then became payable by the Austrian Treasury.

Archives of Republic of Venice.

ART. XVIII. The Archives of the ceded Territories containing the titles to property, and documents regarding the administration of justice, as well as the Political and Historical Documents of the old Republic of Venice, will be handed over to the Commissioners who shall be appointed thereto, to whose care shall be delivered the objects of Art and Science specially belonging to the ceded Territory.

Austrian Archives in ceded Territory to be made over to Austria.

Reciprocally, the titles to property, and documents connected with the administration and civil justice applying to the Austrian Territories, which may be in the Archives of the ceded Territory, will be handed over to the Commissioners of His Imperial and Royal Apostolic Majesty.

The Governments of Italy and Austria engage to consult each other, at the request of the superior administrative authorities, respecting all the documents and information relative to the affairs which concern both the ceded Territory and the adjoining country.

Permission to make Copies of Documents.

They also engage to allow authentic Copies to be taken of Historical and Political Documents which may interest the Territories remaining respectively in the possession of the other Contracting Power, and which, in the interest of science, cannot be taken from the Archives to which they belong.

Customs Facilities.

ART. XIX. The High Contracting Powers engage reciprocally to grant the greatest possible Customs Facilities to the bordering Inhabitants of the two Countries for the improvement of their property and the exercise of their trade.

Renewal of Treaties and Conventions.

ART. XX. The Treaties and Conventions which have been confirmed by Article XVII of the Treaty of Peace signed at Zurich, on the 10th November, 1859, shall be temporarily renewed for one year, and shall extend to all the Territories of the Kingdom of Italy. In the case where those Treaties and Conventions shall not be denounced 3 months before the expiration of a year dating from the exchange of the Ratifications, they shall remain in force, and so on, from year to year.

ART. XXI. The two High Contracting Powers reserve to themselves to enter, as soon as possible, into negotiations on the widest bases reciprocally to facilitate business between the two Countries.

Renewal of Treaty of Commerce of 18th October, 1851.

Until then, and for the term fixed in the preceding Article, the Treaty of Commerce and Navigation of the 18th October, 1851, shall remain in force and shall apply to the whole Territory of the Kingdom of Italy.

Restoration of Personal and Real Estates to Princes and Princesses of the House of Austria.

ART. XXII. The Princes and Princesses of the House of Austria, as well as the Princesses who have entered into the Imperial Family by marriage, shall, on proving their Titles, recover their Private Property in full and entire possession, as well Personal as Real, which they shall be allowed to enjoy and to dispose of without being molested in any manner in the enjoyment of their Rights.

Reservation of the Rights of the State and of Individuals.

Nevertheless, all the Rights of the State and of Individuals are reserved to be prosecuted by legal means.

Armistice to Individuals implicated in Political Events.

ART. XXIII. With a view to contribute by every effort to quiet the public mind, the King of Italy and His Majesty the Emperor of Austria declare and promise that in their respective Territories there shall be a full and entire armistice for all individuals compromised on account of Political Events in the Peninsula up to the present time; consequently no individual, no matter what may be his rank or position in society, shall be prosecuted, annoyed, or troubled, in person or property, or in the exercise of his rights, on account of his conduct or political opinions.

Ratifications.

ART. XXIV. The present Treaty shall be ratified, and the Ratifications exchanged at Vienna within a fortnight, or earlier if possible.

In faith of which, the respective Plenipotentiaries have signed it, and have affixed their Seals thereunto.

Done at Vienna, on the 3rd day of the month of October, of the year of Grace, 1866.

(L.S.)   MENABREA.

(L.S.)   WIMPFFEN.

ADDITIONAL ARTICLE.

Periods of Payments to be made by Italy on the Monte-Lombardo Debt, and for War Material.

The Government of His Majesty the King of Italy engages itself towards the Government of His Imperial and Royal Apostolic Majesty to pay 35,000,000 florins, Austrian value, equivalent to 87,500,000 francs, stipulated by Article VI of the present Treaty, in the manner and at the periods hereinafter determined:

7,000,000 florins shall be paid in cash by 7 Bills or Treasury Bonds to the order of the Austrian Government, payable at Paris, at the residence of the first Bankers, or of an Establishment of the first order, without interest, on the expiration of the 3rd month, dating from the day of the signature of the present Treaty, and which will be handed to the Plenipotentiary of His Imperial Royal and Apostolic Majesty at the time of the exchange of Ratifications.

The payment of the remaining 28,000,000 florins shall take place in Vienna cash, in 10 Bills or Treasury Bonds to the order of the Austrian Government, payable at Paris, at the rate of 2,800,000 florins (Austrian value) each. These 10 Bills or Treasury Bonds shall likewise be handed to the Plenipotentiary of His Imperial and Royal Apostolic Majesty on the exchange of the Ratifications. The first of these Bills, or Treasury Bonds, will be made two months after the payment of the Bills or Treasury Bonds of 7,000,000 florins above stipulated. For that date, as for the others following, becoming due on every succeeding two months, the interest will be reckoned at 5 per cent., dating from the first day of the month which will follow the exchange of the Ratifications of the present Treaty.

The payment of the Interest shall take place at Paris at the expiration of each Bill or Treasury Bond.

The present Additional Article shall have the same force and value as if inserted word for word in the Treaty of this day.

Vienna, 3rd October, 1866.

(L.S.)   MENABREA.

(L.S.)   WIMPFFEN.

Conventions between Austria and France were signed on the 24th August and 1st October, 1866, regulating the details for the Cession of Venice to France; and a Procès-Verbal delivering Venice over to the Italian Government was signed by the French Commissioner on the 19th October, 1866.

On the 9th October, 1866, a Procès-Verbal delivering Peschiera over to the Municipality of that Place was signed by the French Commissioner; and on the 11th of the same month a Procès-Verbal was signed delivering Mantua over to the Municipality of that Town.

87

CONVENTION BETWEEN THE USA AND RUSSIA
Ceding Alaska. Concluded 30th March, 1867. Ratifications exchanged 20th June, 1867.

The United States of America and His Majesty the Emperor of all the Russias, being desirous of strengthening, if possible, the good understanding which exists between them, have, for that purpose, appointed as their Plenipotentiaries: the President of the United States, William H. Seward, Secretary of State; and His Majesty the Emperor of all the Russias, the Privy Counsellor Edward de Stoeckl, his Envoy Extraordinary and Minister Plenipotentiary to the United States.

And the said Plenipotentiaries, having exchanged their full powers, which were found to be in due form, have agreed upon and signed the following articles:

ART. I. His Majesty the Emperor of all the Russias agrees to cede to the United States, by this convention, immediately upon the exchange of the ratifications thereof, all the territory and dominion now possessed by his said Majesty on the continent of America and in the adjacent islands, the same being contained within the geographical limits herein set forth, to wit: The eastern limit is the line of demarcation between the Russian and the British possessions in North America, as established by the convention between Russia and Great Britain, of February 28-16, 1825, and described in Articles III and IV of said convention, in the following terms:

"Commencing from the southernmost point of the island called Prince of Wales Island, which point lies in the parallel of 54 degrees 40 minutes north latitude, and between the 131st and 133^{d} degree of west longitude (meridian of Greenwich), the said line shall ascend to the north along the channel called Portland channel, as far as the point of the continent where it strikes the 56th degree of north latitude; from this last mentioned point, the line of demarcation shall follow the summit of the mountains situated parallel to the coast as far as the point of intersection of the 141st degree of west longitude, (of the same meridian;) and finally, from the said point of intersection, the said meridian line of the 141st degree, in its prolongation as far as the Frozen ocean.

" IV. With reference to the line of demarcation laid down in the preceding article, it is understood—

" 1st That the island called Prince of Wales Island shall belong wholly to Russia," (now, by this cession, to the United States.)

" 2d. That whenever the summit of the mountains which extend in a direction parallel to the coast from the 56th degree of north latitude to the point of intersection of the 141st degree of west longitude shall prove to be at the distance of more than ten marine leagues from the ocean, the limit between the British possessions and the line of coast which is to belong to Russia as above mentioned (that is to say, the limit to the possessions ceded by this convention) shall be formed by a line parallel to the winding of the coast, and which shall never exceed the distance of ten marine leagues therefrom."

The western limit within which the territories and dominion conveyed, are contained, passes through a point in Behring's straits on the parallel of sixty-five degrees thirty minutes north latitude, at its intersection by the meridian which passes midway between the islands of Krusenstern, or Ignalook, and the island of Ratmanoff, or Noonarbook, and proceeds due north, without limitation, into the same Frozen Ocean. The same western limit, beginning at the same initial point, proceeds thence in a course nearly southwest, through Behring's straits and Behring's sea, so as to pass midway between the northwest point of the island of St. Lawrence and the southeast point of Cape Choukotski, to the meridian of one hundred and seventy-two west longitude; thence, from the intersection of that meridian, in a south-westerly direction, so as to pass midway between the island of Attou and the Copper island of the Kormandorski couplet or group, in the North Pacific ocean, to the meridian of one hundred and ninety-three degrees west longitude, so as to include in the territory conveyed the whole of the Aleutian islands east of that meridian.

ART. II. In the cession of territory and dominion made by the preceding article, are included the right of property in all public lots and squares, vacant lands, and all public buildings, fortifications, barracks, and other edifices which are not private individual property. It is, however, understood and agreed, that the churches which have been built in the ceded territory by the Russian government, shall remain the property of such members of the Greek Oriental Church resident in the territory, as may choose to worship therein. Any Government archives, papers, and documents relative to the territory and dominion aforesaid, which may now be existing there, will be left in the possession of the agent of the United States; but an authenticated copy of such of them as may be required, will be, at all times, given by the United States to the Russian government, or to such Russian officers or subjects as they may apply for.

Art. III. The inhabitants of the ceded territory, according to their choice, reserving their natural allegiance, may return to Russia within three years; but if they should prefer to remain in the ceded territory, they, with the exception of uncivilized native tribes, shall be admitted to the enjoyment of all the rights, advantages and immunities of citizens of the United States, and shall be maintained and protected in the free enjoyment of their liberty, property and religion. The uncivilized tribes will be subject to such laws and regulations as the United States, may from time to time, adopt in regard to aboriginal tribes of that country.

Art. IV. His Majesty the Emperor of all the Russias shall appoint, with convenient despatch, an agent or agents for the purpose of formally delivering to a similar agent or agents appointed on behalf of the United States, the territory, dominion, property, dependencies and appurtenances which are ceded as above, and for doing any other act which may be necessary in regard thereto. But the cession, with the right of immediate possession, is nevertheless to be deemed complete and absolute on the exchange of ratifications, without waiting for such formal delivery.

Art. V. Immediately after the exchange of the ratifications of this convention, any fortifications or military posts which may be in the ceded territory, shall be delivered to the agent of the United States, and any Russian troops which may be in the Territory shall be withdrawn as soon as may be reasonably and conveniently practicable.

Art. VI. In consideration of the cession aforesaid, the United States agree to pay at the Treasury in Washington, within ten months after the exchange of the ratifications of this convention, to the diplomatic representative or other agent of His Majesty the Emperor of all the Russias, duly authorized to receive the same, seven million two hundred thousand dollars in gold. The cession of territory and dominion herein made is hearby declared to be free and unincumbered by any reservations, privileges, franchises, grants, or possessions, by any associated companies, whether corporate or incorporate, Russian or any other, or by any parties, except merely private individual property-holders; and the cession hereby made, conveys all the rights, franchises, and privileges now belonging to Russia in the said territory or dominion, and appurtenances thereto.

ART. VII. When this convention shall have been duly ratified by the President of the United States, by and with the advice and consent of the Senate, on the one part, and on the other by His Majesty the Emperor of all the Russias, the ratifications shall be exchanged at Washington within three months from the date hereof, or sooner, if possible.

In faith whereof, the respective plenipotentiaries have signed this convention, and thereto affixed the seals of their arms.

Done at Washington, the thirtieth day of March in the year of our Lord one thousand eight hundred and sixty-seven.

EDOUARD DE STOECKL,
WILLIAM H. SEWARD.

88

TREATY between Great Britain, Austria, Belgium, France, Italy, the Netherlands, Prussia, and Russia, relative to the Grand Duchy of Luxemburg and the Duchy of Limburg. Signed at London, 11th May, 1867. Ratifications exchanged at London, 31st May, 1867.

In the Name of the Most Holy and Indivisible Trinity.

HIS Majesty the King of the Netherlands, Grand Duke of Luxemburg, taking into consideration the change produced in the situation of the Grand Duchy in consequence of the dissolution of the ties by which it was attached to the late Germanic Confederation, has invited Their Majesties the Queen of the United Kingdom of Great Britain and Ireland, the Emperor of Austria, the King of the Belgians, the Emperor of the French, the King of Prussia, and the Emperor of All the Russias, to assemble their Representatives in Conference at London, in order to come to an understanding, with the Plenipotentiaries of His Majesty the King Grand Duke, as to the new arrangements to be made in the general interest of Peace.

And Their said Majesties, after having accepted that invitation, have resolved, by common consent, to respond to the desire manifested by His Majesty the King of Italy to take part in a deliberation destined to offer a new pledge of security for the maintenance of the general tranquillity.

In consequence, Their Majesties, in concert with His Majesty the King of Italy, wishing to conclude a Treaty with a view to that object, have named as their Plenipotentiaries, that is to say:—

Her Majesty the Queen of the United Kingdom of Great Britain

and Ireland, the Right Honourable Edward Stanley, commonly called Lord Stanley, a Member of Her Britannic Majesty's Most Honourable Privy Council, a Member of Parliament, her Principal Secretary of State for Foreign Affairs;

His Majesty the Emperor of Austria, King of Hungary and Bohemia, the Sieur Rudolph Count Apponyi, Chamberlain and Privy Councillor of His Imperial Royal and Apostolic Majesty, his Ambassador Extraordinary to Her Britannic Majesty, &c.;

His Majesty the King of the Belgians, the Sieur Sylvain Van de Weyer, Minister of State, his Envoy Extraordinary and Minister Plenipotentiary to Her Britannic Majesty, &c.;

His Majesty the Emperor of the French, the Sieur Godfrey Bernard Henry Alphonse, Prince de la Tour d'Auvergne Lauraguais, his Ambassador Extraordinary and Plenipotentiary to Her Britannic Majesty, &c.;

His Majesty the King of Italy, the Sieur Emmanuel Taparelli de Lagnasco, Marquis d'Azeglio, his Envoy Extraordinary and Minister Plenipotentiary to Her Britannic Majesty, &c.;

His Majesty the King of the Netherlands, Grand Duke of Luxemburg, the Sieur Adolphus Baron Bentinck, his Chamberlain and Minister of State, his Envoy Extraordinary and Minister Plenipotentiary to Her Britannic Majesty, &c.; the Baron Victor de Tornaco, Minister of State, President of the Government of the Grand Duchy, his Honorary Chamberlain, &c.; and the Sieur Emanuel Servais, Vice-President of the Council of State and of the Superior Court of Justice, formerly Member of the Government, &c.;

His Majesty the King of Prussia, the Sieur Albert Count de Bernstorff-Stintenburg, his Minister of State and Chamberlain, his Ambassador Extraordinary and Plenipotentiary to Her Britannic Majesty, &c.;

And His Majesty the Emperor of All the Russias, the Sieur Philip Baron de Brunnow, his Actual Privy Councillor, Ambassador Extraordinary and Plenipotentiary to Her Britannic Majesty, &c.;

Who, after having exchanged their Full Powers, found in good and due form, have agreed upon the following Articles:—

Maintenance of Rights of the House of Orange-Nassau.

ART. I. His Majesty the King of the Netherlands, Grand Duke of Luxemburg, maintains the ties which attach the said Grand Duchy to the House of Orange-Nassau, in virtue of the Treaties which placed that State under the Sovereignty of the King Grand Duke, his descendants and successors.

The Rights which the Agnates of the House of Nassau possess with regard to the Succession of the Grand Duchy, in virtue of the same Treaties, are maintained.

The High Contracting Parties accept the present Declaration, and place it upon record.

Grand Duchy to form a Perpetual Neutral State under Guarantee of Contracting Parties.

ART. II. The Grand Duchy of Luxemburg, within the Limits determined by the Act annexed to the Treaties of the 19th April, 1839, under the Guarantee of the Courts of Great Britain, Austria, France, Prussia, and Russia, shall henceforth form a perpetually Neutral State.

It shall be bound to observe the same Neutrality towards all other States.

The High Contracting Parties engage to respect the principle of Neutrality stipulated by the present Article.

That principle is and remains placed under the sanction of the collective Guarantee of the Powers signing Parties to the present Treaty, with the exception of Belgium, which is itself a Neutral State.

Luxemburg to cease to be a Fortified City. Troops to be maintained by the King Grand Duke.

ART. III. The Grand Duchy of Luxemburg being Neutralised, according to the terms of the preceding Article, the maintenance or establishment of Fortresses upon its Territory becomes without necessity as well as without object.

In consequence, it is agreed by common consent that the City of Luxemburg, considered in time past, in a military point of view, as a Federal Fortress, shall cease to be a fortified city.

His Majesty the King Grand Duke reserves to himself to maintain in that city the number of troops necessary to provide in it for the maintenance of good order.

Evacuation of Fortress of Luxemburg by Prussian Troops.

ART. IV. In conformity with the stipulations contained in Articles II and III, His Majesty the King of Prussia declares that his troops actually in garrison in the Fortress of Luxemburg shall receive orders to proceed to the Evacuation of that place immediately after the exchange of the Ratifications of the present Treaty. The withdrawal of the artillery, munitions, and every object which forms part of the equipment of the said Fortress shall commence simultaneously. During that operation there shall remain in it no more than the number of troops necessary to provide for the safety of the material of war, and to effect the dispatch thereof, which shall be completed within the shortest time possible.

Demolition of Fortress of Luxemburg by the Netherlands.

ART. V. His Majesty the King Grand Duke, in virtue of the rights of Sovereignty which he exercises over the City and Fortress of Luxemburg, engages, on his part, to take the necessary measures for converting the said Fortress into an open city by means of a demolition which His Majesty shall deem sufficient to fulfil the intentions of the High Contracting Parties expressed in Article III of the present Treaty. The works requisite for that purpose shall be commenced immediately after the withdrawal of the garrison. They shall be carried out with all the attention required for the interests of the inhabitants of the city.

Fortifications not to be restored.

His Majesty the King Grand Duke promises, moreover, that the Fortifications of the city of Luxemburg shall not be restored in future, and that no Military Establishment shall be there maintained or created.

Duchy of Limburg to form an integral part of the Kingdom of the Netherlands.

ART. VI. The Powers signing Parties to the present Treaty recognise that the Dissolution of the Germanic Confederation having equally produced the Dissolution of the ties which united the Duchy of Limburg, collectively with the Grand Duchy of Luxemburg, to the said Confederation, it results therefrom that the relations, of which mention is made in Articles III, IV, and V of the Treaty of the 19th April, 1839, between the Grand Duchy and certain Territories belonging to the Duchy of Limburg, have ceased to exist, the said Territories continuing to form an integral part of the Kingdom of the Netherlands.

Ratifications.

ART. VII. The present Treaty shall be ratified, and the Ratifications shall be exchanged at London within the space of 4 weeks, or sooner if possible.

In witness whereof the respective Plenipotentiaries have signed the same, and have affixed thereto the Seals of their Arms.

Done at London, the 11th day of May, in the year of Our Lord, 1867.

(L.S.)	STANLEY.
(L.S.)	APPONYI.
(L.S.)	VAN DE WEYER.
(L.S.)	LA TOUR D'AUVERGNE.
(L.S.)	D'AZEGLIO.
(L.S.)	BENTINCK.
(L.S.)	TORNACO.
(L.S.)	E. SERVAIS.
(L.S.)	BERNSTORFF.
(L.S.)	BRUNNOW.

89   DECLARATION OF PARIS

DECLARATION of the Allied Powers (Great Britain, Austria, France, Italy, Prussia, Russia, and Turkey), relative to the Obligations of Greece towards Turkey, and the restoration of Friendly Relations between those States. Paris, 20th January, 1869.

THE Plenipotentiaries of Austria-Hungary, France, Great Britain, Italy, Prussia and Russia affix their Signatures to the document, which is finally settled in the following terms:

DECLARATION

" Justly pre-occupied with the dangers which may arise from the rupture of Relations between Turkey and Greece, the Powers, signataries of the Treaty of 1856, have come to an understanding to settle the dispute which has arisen between the two States, and for this purpose have authorised their Representatives at the Court of His Majesty the Emperor of the French to meet in Conference.

" After an attentive study of the documents exchanged between the two Governments, the Plenipotentiaries have agreed in regretting that, yielding to impulses with regard to which she may have been led astray by her patriotism, Greece should have given occasion for the grievances specified by the Ottoman Porte in the Ultimatum transmitted on the 11th December, 1868, to the Foreign Minister of His Majesty the King of the Hellenes. It is indeed unquestionable that the principles of International Law oblige Greece, like all other Nations, not to allow that Bands should be recruited on her territory, or that Vessels should be armed in her ports to attack a neighbouring State.

" Persuaded, moreover, that the Cabinet of Athens could not mis-understand the thought which suggests this view to the 3 Courts, protectors of Greece, and to all the other Powers, signataries of the Treaty of 1856, the Conference declares that the Hellenic Government is bound to observe in its Relations with Turkey the rules of conduct common to all Governments, and thus to satisfy claims put forward by the Sublime Porte in respect to the past, by re-assuring her at the same time with regard to the future.

" Greece ought, therefore, in future, to abstain from favouring or tolerating:

" The formation on her Territory of any Band recruited with a view to an aggression against Turkey.

" The Equipment in her Ports of Armed Vessels intended to succour, under any form whatever, any attempt at Insurrection in the possessions of His Majesty the Sultan.

" With regard to the demands of the Porte relative to the repatriation of Cretans emigrated to Hellenic Territory, the Conference takes note of the Declarations made by the Cabinet of Athens, and is convinced that it will, as far as depends upon it, be ready to facilitate the departure of the Candiot families who may wish to return to their country.

" As to the private losses sustained by Ottoman subjects, the Hellenic Government, in no way contesting the right of Turkey to endeavour to obtain by legal means the compensation which may be due, and Turkey accepting on her side the jurisdiction of the Greek Tribunals, the Pleni-potentiaries do not think that they ought to enter upon an examination of the facts, and are of opinion that the Cabinet of Athens ought to neglect no legal means to enable justice to be done in due course.

" The Conference cannot doubt that, in presence of the unanimous expression of the opinion of the Plenipotentiaries on the questions sub-mitted to their examination, the Hellenic Government will hasten to conform its acts to the principles which have just been stated, and that the grievances as set forth in the ultimatum of the Porte will by the very fact be definitively removed.

" This Declaration shall be made known without delay to the Cabinet of Athens, and the Plenipotentiaries are convinced that the Sublime Porte will forego carrying out the measures announced as intended to follow upon the rupture of diplomatic relations, if, in a communication notified to the Conference, the Hellenic Government defers to the opinion expressed by it.

" The Plenipotentiaries appealing, then, to the same sentiments of conciliation and peace which animate the Courts whose Representatives they are, express the hope that the two Governments will not hesitate to renew their Relations, and thus to efface, in the common interest of their subjects, every trace of the disagreement which led to the assembling of the Conference."

The Turkish Plenipotentiary says that he will sign the Protocol in which the Declaration is to appear, but will abstain from signing the Document itself which is to be presented to the Cabinet of Athens. In acting thus, in conformity with the instructions which he has received, he yields to a feeling of reserve and moderation, which appears to him to coincide with the views of the Conference.

The Marquis de Lavalette announces that he proposes to transmit the Declaration to the Greek Minister of Foreign Affairs, by the Messenger who will leave Paris on Friday the 22nd January.

The French Plenipotentiary calls attention to an anxiety felt by the Ottoman Government, and which the Turkish Ambassador has mentioned to him.

Disposed to conform to the wish expressed in the Declaration, that diplomatic relations should not any longer remain interrupted between the two countries, the Porte is in doubt what steps should be taken for the renewal of relations, and thinks it necessary that the Hellenic Government should take the initiative in this respect. The French Plenipotentiary is of opinion that it would be advantageous to arrange this difficulty in order to remove beforehand everything which might delay the reconciliation which it has been their object to bring about.

As soon as Greece adheres to the Declaration, Turkey having on her side, and on this condition renounced carrying out the threatening measures indicated in the ultimatum, it might be decided that the relations of the two Cabinets should be thereby re-established.

The Conference comes to a resolution in this sense.

It is agreed at the same time that the letter addressed to the Greek Minister for Foreign Affairs, transmitting the Declaration signed to-day shall contain a statement of the wish unanimously expressed on this subject by the Plenipotentiaries.

The French Plenipotentiary asks that the terms of this despatch may be immediately settled. He reads the draft prepared by him, in conformity with the ideas exchanged at the preceding sitting. The draft is adopted after being completed in accordance with the decision just taken.

On the proposition of the Russian Plenipotentiary it is agreed that this document shall be annexed to the Protocol.

The Marquis de Lavalette observes that his intention being to send off the day after to-morrow the communication which he is charged to address to the Cabinet of Athens, it is of pressing importance to notify the different Courts; and the Plenipotentiaries of Austria-Hungary, Great Britain, Italy, Prussia, and Russia, undertake to inform their Governments, in order that the Legations in Greece may be instructed to give their support to the proceeding of the President of the Conference.

Done at Paris, the 20th January, 1869.

[Here follow the Signatures.]

Greece gave its adhesion to this Declaration on the 6th February, 1869.

90   DECLARATION OF WASHINGTON

DECLARATION MADE BY GREAT BRITAIN AND THE USA approving and adopting the maps prepared by the joint commission of the northwest boundary for survey-ing and marking the boundaries between the British possess-ions and the United States along the 49th parallel of north latitude, under the first article of the Treaty of 15th June, 1846. Signed at Washington, 24th February, 1870.

The undersigned Hamilton Fish, Secretary of State of the United States, and Edward Thornton, Esquire, Her Britannic Majesty's Envoy Extraordinary and Minister Plenipotentiary to the United States, duly authorized by their respective Governments, having met together:

The set of maps, seven in number, which have been prepared by the Commissioners appointed by the two Powers to survey and mark out the Boundary between their respective Territories under the first article of the Treaty concluded between them at Washington on the 15th of June, 1846, having been produced;

And it appearing that they do correctly indicate the said Boundary from the point where the Boundary laid down in Treaties and Con-ventions prior to June 15th, 1846, terminates Westward on the 49th Parallel of North Latitude to the Eastern shore of the Gulf of Georgia, which Boundary has been defined by the Commissioners by marks upon the ground;

The undersigned, without prejudice to the rights of their respective Governments as to the settlement and the determination of the re-mainder of the said Boundary, hereby declare that the said maps certified and authenticated under the signatures of Archibald Campbell, Esquire, the Commissioner of the United States, and of Colonel John Summer-field Hawkins, Her Britannic Majesty's Commissioner, and of which duplicate copies similarly certified and authenticated are in the possession of the Government of Her Britannic Majesty have been duly examined and considered, and, as well as the marks by which the Boundary to the Eastern shore of the Gulf of Georgia has been defined upon the ground, are approved, agreed to, and adopted by both Governments.

In witness whereof the respective Plenipotentiaries have signed the same and have affixed thereto their respective seals.

Done at Washington the twenty-fourth day of February, in the year of our Lord, one thousand eight hundred and seventy.

HAMILTON FISH

EDWD. THORNTON

91

TREATY between Great Britain and Prussia, relative to the Independence and Neutrality of Belgium. Signed at London, 9th August, 1870. Ratifications exchanged at London, 26th August, 1870.

Reference to Treaties of 19th April, 1839.

HER Majesty the Queen of the United Kingdom of Great Britain and Ireland, and His Majesty the King of Prussia, being desirous at the present time of recording in a solemn Act their fixed determination to maintain the Independence and Neutrality of Belgium, as provided in Article VII of the Treaty signed at London on the 19th April, 1839, between Belgium and the Netherlands, which Article was declared by the Quintuple Treaty of 1839 to be considered as having the same force and value as if textually inserted in the said Quintuple Treaty, their said Majesties have determined to conclude between themselves a separate Treaty, which, without impairing or invalidating the conditions of the said Quintuple Treaty, shall be subsidiary and accessory to it; and they have accordingly named as their Plenipotentiaries for that purpose, that is to say:

Her Majesty the Queen of the United Kingdom of Great Britain and Ireland, the Right Honourable Granville George Earl Granville, Lord Leveson, Her Britannic Majesty's Principal Secretary of State for Foreign Affairs, &c.;

And His Majesty the King of Prussia, his Excellency the Minister of State, Albert Count of Bernstorff-Stintenburg, Ambassador Extraordinary and Plenipotentiary to Her Britannic Majesty from His said Majesty for the North German Confederation, &c.;

Who, after having communicated to each other their respective Full Powers, found in good and due form, have agreed upon and concluded the following Articles:

Co-operation of Great Britain with Prussia in case of violation of Neutrality of Belgium by France.

ART I. His Majesty the King of Prussia having declared that notwithstanding the Hostilities in which the North German Confederation is engaged with France, it is his fixed determination to respect the Neutrality of Belgium, so long as the same shall be respected by France, Her Majesty the Queen of the United Kingdom of Great Britain and Ireland on her part declares that, if during the said Hostilities the Armies of France should violate that Neutrality, she will be prepared to co-operate with His Prussian Majesty for the defence of the same in such manner as may be mutually agreed upon, employing for that purpose her Naval and Military Forces to insure its observance, and to maintain, in conjunction with His Prussian Majesty, then and thereafter, the Independence and Neutrality of Belgium.

Great Britain not engaged to take part in War between North German Confederation and France, except as regards Violation of Belgian Neutrality.

It is clearly understood that Her Majesty the Queen of the United Kingdom of Great Britain and Ireland does not engage herself by this Treaty to take part in any of the general operations of the War now carried on between the North German Confederation and France, beyond the Limits of Belgium, as defined in the Treaty between Belgium and the Netherlands of 19th April, 1839.

Co-operation of Prussia with Great Britain in case of Violation of Neutrality of Belgium by France.

ART II. His Majesty the King of Prussia agrees on his part, in the event provided for in the foregoing Article, to co-operate with Her Majesty the Queen of the United Kingdom of Great Britain and Ireland, employing his Naval and Military Forces for the purpose aforesaid; and, the case arising, to concert with Her Majesty the measures which shall be taken, separately or in common, to secure the Neutrality and Independence of Belgium.

Treaty to be binding until conclusion of a Treaty of Peace between France and Prussia.

ART III. This Treaty shall be binding on the High Contracting Parties during the continuance of the present War between the North German Confederation and France, and for 12 months after the Ratification of any Treaty of Peace concluded between those Parties; and on the expiration of that time the Independence and Neutrality of Belgium will, so far as the High Contracting Parties are respectively concerned, continue to rest as heretofore on Article I of the Quintuple Treaty of the 19th April, 1839.

Ratifications.

ART. IV. The present Treaty shall be ratified, and the Ratifications shall be exchanged at London as soon as possible.

In witness whereof the respective Plenipotentiaries have signed the same, and have affixed thereto the Seal of their Arms.

Done at London, the 9th day of August, in the year of Our Lord, 1870.

(L.S.) GRANVILLE.
(L.S.) BERNSTORFF.

9 2

TREATY between Great Britain and France, relative to the Independence and Neutrality of Belgium. Signed at London, 11th August, 1870. Ratifications exchanged at London, 26th August, 1870.

Reference to Treaties of 19th April, 1839.

HER Majesty the Queen of the United Kingdom of Great Britain and Ireland, and His Majesty the Emperor of the French, being desirous at the present time of recording in a solemn Act their fixed determination to maintain the Independence and Neutrality of Belgium, as provided by Article VII of the Treaty signed at London on the 19th April, 1839, between Belgium and the Netherlands, which Article was declared by the Quintuple Treaty of 1839 to be considered as having the same force and value as if textually inserted in the said Quintuple Treaty, their said Majesties have determined to conclude between themselves a Separate Treaty, which, without impairing or invalidating the conditions of the said Quintuple Treaty, shall be subsidiary and accessory to it; and they have accordingly named as their Plenipotentiaries for that purpose, that is to say:

Her Majesty the Queen of the United Kingdom of Great Britain and Ireland, the Right Honourable Granville George Earl Granville, Lord Leveson, Her Britannic Majesty's Principal Secretary of State for Foreign Affairs, &c.;

And His Majesty the Emperor of the French, his Excellency the Marquis de La Valette, his Ambassador to Her Britannic Majesty, &c.;

Who, after having communicated to each other their respective Full Powers, found in good and due form, have agreed upon and concluded the following Articles:

Co-operation of Great Britain with France in case of Violation of Neutrality of Belgium by Prussia.

ART. I. His Majesty the Emperor of the French having declared that, notwithstanding the Hostilities in which France is now engaged with the North German Confederation and its Allies, it is his fixed determination to respect the Neutrality of Belgium, so long as the same shall be respected by the North German Confederation and its Allies, Her Majesty the Queen of the United Kingdom of Great Britain and Ireland on her part declares that, if during the said Hostilities the Armies of the North German Confederation and its Allies should violate that Neutrality, she will be prepared to co-operate with His Imperial Majesty for the defence of the same in such manner as may be mutually agreed upon, employing for that purpose her Naval and Military Forces to insure its observance, and to maintain, in conjunction with His Imperial Majesty, then and thereafter, the Independence and Neutrality of Belgium.

Great Britain not engaged to take part in War between France and North German Confederation, except as regards Violation of Belgian Neutrality.

It is clearly understood that Her Majesty the Queen of the United Kingdom of Great Britain and Ireland does not engage herself by this Treaty to take part in any of the general operations of the War now carried on between France and the North German Confederation and its Allies, beyond the Limits of Belgium as defined in the Treaty between Belgium and the Netherlands of 19th April, 1839.

Co-operation of France with Great Britain in case of Violation of Neutrality of Belgium by Prussia.

ART. II. His Majesty the Emperor of the French agrees on his part, in the event provided for in the foregoing Article, to co-operate with Her Majesty the Queen of the United Kingdom of Great Britain and Ireland, employing his Naval and Military Forces for the purpose aforesaid; and, the case arising, to concert with Her Majesty the measures which shall be taken, separately or in common, to secure the Neutrality and Independence of Belgium.

Treaty to be Binding until conclusion of a Treaty of Peace between France and Prussia.

ART. III. This Treaty shall be binding on the High Contracting Parties during the continuance of the present War between France and the North German Confederation and its Allies, and for 12 months after the Ratification of any Treaty of Peace concluded between those Parties; and on the expiration of that time the Independence and Neutrality of Belgium will, so far as the High Contracting Parties are respectively concerned, continue to rest, as heretofore, on Article I of the Quintuple Treaty of the 19th April, 1839.

ART. IV. The present Treaty shall be ratified, and the Ratifications shall be exchanged at London as soon as possible.

In witness whereof the respective Plenipotentiaries have signed the same, and have affixed thereto the Seal of their Arms.

Done at London, the 11th of August, 1870.

(L.S.)   GRANVILLE.
(L.S.)   LA VALETTE.

The index to both volumes is at the end of Volume 2